P9-BYV-734

Ref

WITHDRAWN

ENCYCLOPEDIA OF

DRUGS, ALCOHOL & ADDICTIVE BEHAVIOR

EDITORIAL BOARD

ENCYCLOPEDIA OF
DRUGS, ALCOHOL & ADDICTIVE BEHAVIOR

THIRD EDITION

Volume 3

M–R

Pamela Korsmeyer and Henry R. Kranzler

EDITORS IN CHIEF

MACMILLAN REFERENCE USA
A part of Gale, Cengage Learning

Detroit • New York • San Francisco • New Haven, Conn • Waterville, Maine • London

Encyclopedia of Drugs, Alcohol, & Addictive Behavior, 3rd edition

Pamela Korsmeyer and Henry R. Kranzler, Editors in Chief

For product information and technology assistance, contact us at
Gale Customer Support, 1-800-877-4253.
For permission to use material from this text or product,
submit all requests online at **www.cengage.com/permissions.**
Further permissions questions can be emailed to
permissionrequest@cengage.com

Since this page cannot legibly accommodate all copyright notices, the acknowledgments constitute an extension of the copyright notice.

While every effort has been made to ensure the reliability of the information presented in this publication, Gale, a part of Cengage Learning, does not guarantee the accuracy of the data contained herein. Gale accepts no payment for listing; and inclusion in the publication of any organization, agency, institution, publication, service, or individual does not imply endorsement of the editors or publisher. Errors brought to the attention of the publisher and verified to the satisfaction of the publisher will be corrected in future editions.

Library of Congress Cataloging-in-Publication Data

Encyclopedia of drugs, alcohol & addictive behavior / Pamela Korsmeyer and Henry R. Kranzler. -- 3rd ed.
 p. cm.
 Includes bibliographical references and index.
 ISBN 978-0-02-866064-6 (set) -- ISBN 978-0-02-866065-3 (vol. 1) -- ISBN 978-0-02-866066-0 (vol. 2) -- ISBN 978-0-02-866067-7 (vol. 3) -- ISBN 978-0-02-866068-4 (vol. 4)
 1. Drug abuse--Encyclopedias. 2. Substance abuse--Encyclopedias. 3. Alcoholism--Encyclopedias. 4. Drinking of alcoholic beverages--Encyclopedias. I. Korsmeyer, Pamela, 1945- II. Kranzler, Henry R., 1950-

HV5804.E53 2009
362.2903--dc22   2008012719

Gale
27500 Drake Rd.
Farmington Hills, MI 48331-3535

ISBN-13: 978-0-02-866064-6 (set)   ISBN-10: 0-02-866064-1 (set)
ISBN-13: 978-0-02-866065-3 (vol. 1)   ISBN-10: 0-02-866065-X (vol. 1)
ISBN-13: 978-0-02-866066-0 (vol. 2)   ISBN-10: 0-02-866066-8 (vol. 2)
ISBN-13: 978-0-02-866067-7 (vol. 3)   ISBN-10: 0-02-866067-6 (vol. 3)
ISBN-13: 978-0-02-866068-4 (vol. 4)   ISBN-10: 0-02-866068-4 (vol. 4)

This title is also available as an e-book.
ISBN-13: 978-0-02-866114-8; ISBN-10: 0-02-866114-1
Contact your Gale sales representative for ordering information.

Printed in the United States of America
1 2 3 4 5 6 7 12 11 10 09 08

CONTENTS

MANDATORY SENTENCING.

Mandatory sentencing laws provide that people convicted of particular crimes receive particular sentences. Examples include laws specifying that people convicted of selling heroin or cocaine within 1,000 yards of a school receive at least a three-year prison term or that people convicted of selling more than four ounces of heroin or cocaine receive at least a five-year prison term. The latter are referred to as mandatory minimum sentences. Some mandatory sentencing laws require life sentences. A Michigan law, for example, which the U.S. Supreme Court upheld against a claim that mandatory life sentences constitute "cruel and unusual punishment" in violation of the Eighth Amendment to the U.S. Constitution, required life sentences without possibility of parole for people convicted of possessing more than 650 grams of cocaine (*Harmelin v. Michigan*, 49 Cr.L. 2350 [6/27/91]). An Alabama law required life sentences for people who, having previously been twice convicted of felonies, are convicted of a third felony. Laws like Alabama's are sometimes called *habitual offender* or *predicate felony* laws.

ENACTMENT OF MANDATORY SENTENCING LAWS

An unprecedented number of mandatory sentencing laws were enacted during the 1970s and 1980s. Most involve drugs, firearms, or both. New York, under Governor Nelson Rockefeller, was the first state to enact mandatory sentences. Known as the Rockefeller drug laws, these acts imposed mandatory 15-year and life sentences for certain drug offenses. These harsh laws set off a chain reaction. Between 1978 and 1981, forty-nine states enacted mandatory sentencing laws. Every state and the federal government enacted mandatory sentencing laws during the 1980s. In 2007, over one hundred separate mandatory minimum penalty provisions were contained in federal criminal statutes.

Apart from specific offenses that carry mandatory sentences, state and federal sentencing guidelines mandated that judges impose minimum sentences based on the crime committed, aggravating factors, and the criminal history of the defendant. These guidelines increased punishment for criminal offenses and limited judicial discretion in sentencing by identifying the punishment required upon conviction for a particular offense. Many of these statutes eliminated or greatly restricted parole for prison inmates. Congress passed the Sentencing Reform Act of 1984 (SRA), which eliminated parole for federal prisoners and reduced the amount of time off granted for good behavior. The SRA also established the U.S. Sentencing Guidelines Commission and directed it to create a new sentencing system. In 1987, the commission's guidelines became effective.

The popularity of sentencing guidelines in the United States marked a rejection of indeterminate sentencing. Under indeterminate sentencing, judges set maximum lengths of prison sentences, and sometime minimums, but parole boards decide when a prisoner will be released. In contrast, the Federal Sentencing Guidelines shift the focus in sentencing from the offender to the offense. The guidelines categorize offenses and identify the sentence required upon conviction. Judges are allowed to increase or decrease sentences, which are called *departures*, only if they have good reasons and cite these reasons into the trial record. *Upward departures* are easy to achieve, as judges are allowed to consider all relevant conduct. This conduct can include the circumstances surrounding the crime, offenses that were committed at the same time as the charged offense but were not charged, prior convictions, and acts for which the defendant was previously tried but acquitted. Federal judges have a more difficult time decreasing a sentence. A *downward departure* is acceptable if the defendant accepts responsibility for the crime or committed the crime to avoid a more serious offense. Prosecutors often successfully challenge decreases in sentences on appeal.

Mandatory sentencing laws have long been controversial. The American Law Institute, an association of lawyers, judges, and law professors that created the Model Penal Code, a model law on which the criminal laws of nearly half the states are patterned, opposes enactment of mandatory sentencing laws. So does the American Bar Association. Many U.S. federal judges favored repeal of federal laws calling for mandatory sentences in drug cases.

Despite this opposition, it took a U.S. Supreme Court decision rather than an act of Congress to reduce the absolutism of the federal guidelines. In 2005 the Court ruled that the guidelines violated the Sixth Amendment because any fact that increases the penalty for a crime beyond the prescribed statutory maximum must be submitted to a jury and proved beyond a reasonable doubt. The sentencing guidelines violated this principle because judges could increase sentences by applying aggravating factors that the jury never considered. Having made the guidelines advisory, the Court also ruled that the guidelines must still be consulted by judges to help them fashion valid sentences. If a sentence is challenged on appeal, the federal courts must determine if the sentence was reasonable. This decision has set in motion challenges to state sentencing guidelines.

OBJECTIONS TO MANDATORY SENTENCING LAWS

Opponents of mandatory sentencing laws oppose them for a variety of reasons. Many judges and lawyers believe that mandatory sentencing laws are arbitrary and sometimes require judges to impose sentences that are unduly harsh. They think that justice requires that sentences be individualized to fit the circumstances of the offender and of the crime. They also think that sentences should vary depending on considerations such as whether the offender was a ringleader or a follower; whether the offender played a major role or a minor one; whether he or she was motivated by greed or poverty; whether a seller of drugs was an addict raising money to support a drug habit or a professional drug dealer; and whether the quantity involved was large or small. A law requiring that anyone convicted of selling more than a small amount of heroin receive a five-year prison sentence ignores all such distinctions.

Opponents also complain that mandatory sentencing laws adversely affect court operations. Because prosecuting attorneys decide what charges to file in each case, mandatory sentencing laws shift power from the judge to the prosecutor. Most crimes are not covered by mandatory sentencing laws. Typically, for example, trafficking in drugs is subject to mandatory penalties, but possession of drugs is not. Since nearly every drug trafficker also possesses drugs, prosecutors can decide which charge to file; a trafficking charge ties the judge's hands; a possession charge gives the judge discretion.

Another objection is that mandatory penalties remove much of the defendant's incentive to plead guilty and thus increase the frequency of trials and lengthen the time required to resolve cases. In most courts, 85 to 95 percent of convictions result from guilty pleas. Many result from plea bargains, in which the prosecutor agrees either to dismiss some charges or to approve a particular sentence if the defendant pleads guilty. If mandatory penalties remove incentives from plea bargains, then trials, backlogs, and delays increase. Yet another objection is that mandatory sentencing laws sometimes result in deceptive practices on the part of judges. To avoid imposing sentences that they believe are too severe, judges sometimes ignore the mandatory sentence law and impose some other sentence or acquit defendants of crimes that bear mandatory penalties.

In the context of drug laws, the controversy over disparate mandatory minimum sentences for dealers of crack and powder cocaine raged from the late 1980s until 2007. Under a 1986 federal law, one gram of crack is equivalent to 100 grams of powder cocaine. The U.S. Sentencing Guideline Commission adopted this ratio when it revised its guidelines that year. However, in 1988 Congress amended the law to establish mandatory minimum sentences for cocaine dealing. Thus, selling five grams of crack cocaine is punishable by a mandatory minimum sentence of five years. To receive the same sentence for trafficking in powder cocaine, a defendant would have to sell 500 grams. This resulted in longer prison sentences for small-time crack dealers than for cocaine wholesalers. The federal law and similar state laws have been challenged as violations of equal protection, as African Americans have been charged with more crack cocaine offenses than whites. Similarly, whites have been charged with selling powder cocaine more often than African Americans.

These legal arguments met with little success. By the mid-1990s, the U.S. Sentencing Guideline Commission sought to reduce the disparity in sentencing. Finally, in 2007 the commission modified the guidelines, reducing the sentence range for first-time offenders possessing five grams or more of crack cocaine to 51 to 63 months. The old range was 63 to 78 months. The new range for first-time offenders possessing at least 50 grams is 97 to 121 months in prison, decreasing from 121 to 151 months. A commission analysis estimated that changing the crack guidelines would reduce the size of the federal prison population by 3,800 in fifteen years. The commission also asked Congress to repeal the mandatory prison term for simple possession and increase the amount of crack cocaine required to trigger five-year and ten-year mandatory minimum prison terms. The commission contended this was a way to focus on major drug traffickers.

ARGUMENTS FOR MANDATORY SENTENCING LAWS

Supporters of mandatory sentences are not troubled by the harshness of the laws or the fact that they shift power from the judge to the prosecutor. One of the goals of such laws is to assure that the mandated sentence will be imposed whether the judge agrees with the sentence or not. Supporters are troubled by deceptive efforts of judges (and sometimes of prosecutors) to avoid applying them. They argue that judges are wrong to try to circumvent mandatory sentences, that if legislatures pass laws, judges should enforce them whether or not they agree with them. Finally, supporters say they regret that mandatory sentencing

affects guilty pleas, trial rates, and court delays, but they regard those problems as a price worth paying.

Proponents of mandatory sentencing laws make four arguments. First, they argue that the laws allow legislators to assure citizens their concerns are being taken seriously. Second, they assert that harsh mandatory sentencing laws deter offenders from committing crimes. Third, they claim that certain crimes are so serious that people who commit them should be severely punished and that legislators should insist judges impose severe penalties in such cases. Fourth, they contend that mandatory sentencing laws are a device for assuring that offenders who commit the same crime will receive the same penalty.

RESEARCH ON MANDATORY SENTENCING LAWS

Evaluations of mandatory sentencing laws offer greater support to their opponents than to their supporters. Studies on the deterrent effect of mandatory sentencing laws conclude either that passage of such laws has no deterrent effect or that they have a modest deterrent effect that soon disappears. Research on how mandatory sentencing laws affect court operations shows that such laws do shift power from judges to prosecutors, do sometimes result in lower guilty plea rates and higher trial rates, often cause case processing delays, and frequently result in imposition of sentences that the judges and lawyers involved believe are harsher than the defendant deserves. All of these conclusions were reached by the evaluators of the Rockefeller Drug Laws in New York State in the mid-1970s, yet the laws remain on the books despite widespread criticism.

The conclusions of earlier research were confirmed by the most ambitious and sophisticated study of mandatory penalties ever completed: a report on mandatory penalties in the U.S. federal courts by the U.S. Sentencing Commission. That study concluded that people convicted of crimes subject to mandatory penalties were two and one-half times more likely to be convicted after trials (30% of convictions) than are other federal defendants (12.5%). The study found that "mandatory minimums transfer sentencing power from the court to the prosecutor," that "honesty and truth in sentencing" are compromised by prosecutors' and judges' efforts to work around mandatory sentences, and that "lack of uniform application [of mandatories] creates unwarranted disparity in sentencing."

Thus, on the major empirical issues about which opponents and supporters of mandatory penalties disagree, the great weight of the evidence supports opponents' views. Empirical evidence, however, cannot refute supporters' normative claims that mandatory penalties should be enacted to assure citizens that their concerns about crime are taken seriously or that certain crimes deserve severe punishment and that mandatory sentencing laws should be enacted to increase the likelihood that such punishments will be imposed. Opponents of mandatory penalties do not necessarily disagree that lawmakers should try to respond to citizens' concerns or that some crimes deserve harsh penalties; they do believe that mandatory penalties are an ineffective way to achieve those goals. In addition, the costs of long small-term incarceration continue to take large bites out of state revenues as correctional agencies struggle to house the steady flow of prisoners convicted of drug crimes.

See also **Civil Commitment; Drug Laws, Prosecution of; Legal Regulation of Drugs and Alcohol; Treatment Accountability for Safer Communities (TASC).**

BIBLIOGRAPHY

American Law Institute. (1962). *Model penal code (proposed official draft)*. Philadelphia: The Institute.

Gray, Madison. (2007, August 17). Mandatory sentencing: stalled reform. *Time*. Available from http://www.time.com/.

U.S. Sentencing Commission. (2007). Cocaine and federal sentencing policy. Washington, DC: U.S. Government Printing Office.

MICHAEL TONRY
REVISED BY FREDERICK K. TONRY (2009)

MARIJUANA (CANNABIS). *Marijuana* is the most common name used in the United States for the *Cannabis sativa* plant, which is one variety of the cannabis or hemp plant family. *Cannabis* is the more appropriate scientific term and the more common term used throughout the

Figure 1. Marijuana. ILLUSTRATION BY GGS INFORMATION SERVICES. GALE, CENGAGE LEARNING

world to refer to the various psychoactive products derived from the *Cannabis sativa* plant that are used by humans to alter their state of mind. Slang terms for marijuana and other psychoactive products derived from *Cannabis sativa* change over time but some stable and more current terms include: weed, pot, herb, grass, reefer, Mary Jane, dagga, bhang, Aunt Mary, skunk, boom, gangster, kif, ganja, hashish, and hash oil. Cannabis remains in the early twenty-first century the most widely used illicit substance in the United States and in most other developed countries that regulate marijuana. Between the late 1960s and 2008, marijuana use has generated continued controversy regarding its addictive potential, health consequences, potential for medical use, and legal status.

THE CANNABIS PLANT
Cannabis sativa grows easily throughout the tropics, subtropics, and temperate regions. It can also grow in colder climates with a shortened growing season. As of 2008 it was grown in most states across the United States. Once established, the plant can reseed and spread. Marijuana comes from the dried flowering tops (buds or heads), leaves, and stems of the harvested plant. The primary mind-altering ingredient in cannabis is delta-9-tetrahydrocannabinol (THC). The THC concentration (strength of the marijuana) partially depends

upon growing conditions and the genetics of the plant. Generally, THC concentration is greatest in the buds, then the leaves, and finally the stems and seeds. Sophisticated growing techniques and breeding of alternative genetic strains have resulted in producing more potent marijuana, with potencies of that confiscated in the first decade of the twenty-first century by legal authorities in the United States and of other samples tested in the Netherlands ranging from approximately 2 percent to more than 20 percent.

Hashish or *hash* is another way that Cannabis sativa is prepared for use. Hash consists of dried cannabis resin and compressed flowers. Its THC concentration is usually 2 to 8 percent, but can get as high as 10 to 15 percent. Extracting THC from hash or marijuana using filtering and purification processes produces hash oil, and its concentration of THC can range from 20 to 60 percent.

USING CANNABIS

The most popular way to use cannabis and hash is by smoking (inhaling) it in pipes or rolling it in cigarette papers (joints, reefers, doobies, spliffs). Water pipes or bongs (a type of pipe) are also used because they cool the smoke and there is not as much marijuana lost through smoke that escapes when a standard pipe is used. Another method for smoking that has become common is rolling cannabis into an emptied cigar casing. This product is usually called a *blunt*, and has become popular because it looks like a legal substance, it can be re-lit easily, and some people report enjoying the effect of the mixture of marijuana and tobacco. Note that the term *spliff* also can be used to refer to a cigarette that is a mixture of marijuana and tobacco. Hash is also typically smoked in some form of a pipe, and hash oil is usually used by adding a few drops to a cigarette or to the mixture in a pipe. Also, the oil can be heated by itself and the vapors inhaled. Marijuana or hash can also be taken orally (eaten), and usually eating has involved cooking or baking it in foods (e.g., brownies). When eaten, the onset of the effects is delayed by about an hour because the drug needs to be absorbed through the stomach, but the effects can last several hours longer.

HISTORY

The use of cannabis as a medicine dates back to the third millennium BCE in China, and to the second and first millennia BCE in India and ancient Assyria. This drug's history offers a collage of medicinal, agricultural, industrial, religious, cultural, and political tales, each of which can be traced back over many centuries. In his 1980 book, *Marihuana: The First Twelve Thousand Years*, Ernest Abel notes:

> Armies and navies have used it to make war, men and women to make love. Hunters and fishermen have snared the most ferocious creatures, from the tiger to the shark, in its herculean weave. Fashion designers have dressed the most elegant women in its supple knit. Hangmen have snapped the necks of thieves and murderers with its fiber. Obstetricians have eased the pain of childbirth with its leaves. Farmers have crushed its seeds and used the oil within to light their lamps. Mourners have thrown its seeds into blazing fires and have had their sorrow transformed into blissful ecstasy by the fumes that filled the air.

In the United States, approximately 30 cannabis preparations, including Chlorodyne, a concoction of morphine and cannabis, were marketed in the 1930s. Superior medications eventually became available, and the drug was removed from the *U.S. Pharmacopoeia and National Formulary* in 1941.

Periodically, commissions of inquiry, for example, the 1925 Panama Canal Zone Committee and the 1944 Mayor's Committee on Marihuana (The LaGuardia Committee), were formed to assess the degree of risk posed to public health by recreational cannabis use. A movement grew to prohibit cannabis possession, and by 1937, when the federal Marijuana Tax Act was passed, all states had banned the drug. The Vietnam antiwar movement saw a substantial increase in the drug's popularity, particularly among young adults in the United States. In reaction to the long prison terms being imposed for possession, the National Commission on Marihuana and Drug Abuse recommended in 1972 that cannabis possession be decriminalized. In that decade a number of states replaced prison terms with either civil penalties or misdemeanor fines. While cannabis remained classified under federal law as having high risk and no accepted medical use, the last decades of the twentieth century saw a number of states enacting laws designed to protect patients from prosecution if a physician recommended use of cannabis. In 1999 the Institute on Medicine released a comprehensive report on the status of marijuana as a recreational drug and its potential for use as a medicine.

CHEMISTRY / PHARMACOLOGY

Cannabis sativa contains over 400 chemical substances. The compounds responsible for most direct effects are called cannabinoids, and over 66 such cannabinoids have been identified. The three most abundant are cannabidiol, tetrahydrocannabinol (THC), and cannabinol. Delta-9-THC is the compound that causes the most notable effects of cannabis. Cannabidiol and cannabinol do not appear to have strong psychoactive properties, but it is thought that they may modify the effects of THC. The proportions of these cannabinoids can vary among strains and can be modified by breeding, resulting in cannabis with different effects and varying potencies.

The effects of THC result from its ability to activate receptors on the surface of specific cells in the brain and body. In the late 1980s it was discovered that humans and animals have an endogenous cannabinoid system, indicating that THC interacts with a naturally occurring system in the body. Two specific types of cannabinoid receptors have been identified (the CB1 and CB2 receptors). CB1 receptors are located primarily on nerve cells in the brain and spinal cord, as well as in some tissues outside the brain. CB2 receptors are located mostly on cells of the immune system and do not appear to be present in the brain. An endogenous cannabinoid, anandamide, has also been identified. The role of the cannabinoid system has only begun to be explored. The effects of cannabinoids known from animal and human experiments include appetite modulation, pain relief, impairment of memory and the control of movements, and reductions in body temperature and in the activity of the gut. Research on cannabinoid pharmacology continues to grow rapidly in the early twenty-first century, and promises to facilitate the understanding of the role of endogenous cannabinoids and the effects of cannabis.

DIRECT EFFECTS AND PSYCHOPHARMACOLOGY

Approximately 30 percent of the THC is delivered into the blood stream when cannabis is smoked. A lower proportion of THC is absorbed after taking cannabis by mouth because THC is metabolized in the liver, but its metabolite is also psychoactive and thus likely prolongs its effects. THC is distributed widely throughout the body via the bloodstream and is stored primarily in fatty tissues. The effects of smoking marijuana are felt within minutes, with maximal effects typically experienced thirty to ninety minutes after smoking. The effects of eating marijuana are usually not felt for about thirty to sixty minutes, and they peak 120 to 240 minutes after ingestion. The direct effects of smoked marijuana may persist for approximately four to six hours; effects following oral consumption may last six to eight hours. The slow release of THC from fatty tissues produces low levels of THC metabolites for many days but no significant effects appear to be caused by such release. Nonetheless, storage and slow release from fatty tissues result in THC being detectable in urine for long periods of time (up to a month) following its ingestion.

When THC enters the brain, it activates the release of dopamine, a neurotransmitter, which is important because dopamine release is associated with the rewarding properties of most drugs and thus may contribute to repeated use and perhaps addiction. Marijuana's actions include a wide range of fairly diverse effects. Indeed, it is difficult to classify marijuana into other common drug categories. In most classification systems, marijuana is either placed in its own category or included with the hallucinogens.

Although wide variation in the effects of marijuana is observed based on an individual's previous experience with the drug, the dose smoked or consumed, and the current smoking environment, the early effects are usually more stimulating in nature: feeling high or a mild euphoria; increased silliness, laughter, and talkativeness; having altered perceptual experiences that include a distorted sense of time and more intense experiences of hearing music, seeing colors, watching movies or television, and eating. Some of the effects might not be pleasant. The most commonly reported unpleasant effects are anxiety, panic reactions, fear of going crazy, and depression. At very high doses, the experience may seem more intense, and one may even feel a sense of depersonalization or experience delusions (beliefs not based in reality) or hallucinations (seeing or hearing things that are not there). These more extreme unpleasant psychological effects are usually felt by infrequent users who are less familiar with the effects of marijuana or by people who have eaten or smoked more marijuana than they are used to. Also, using marijuana with a higher THC concentration or that is laced with other substances can cause such effects. These experiences are typically short-lived and stop when the high obtained from marijuana ends.

Subsequent effects of use are more relaxing, and individuals may become more introspective, with thought or concentration requiring more effort, and memory and psychomotor tasks becoming more difficult. Common physiological effects include increased pulse rate, reddening of the eyes, dry mouth, thirst and hunger, and drowsiness.

With repeated and regular use, tolerance to many of marijuana's effects can develop, which means the user may take more marijuana to achieve an effect or feel less effect when using the same amount of marijuana. Different degrees of tolerance develop for different effects of marijuana. For example, tolerance to the increase in heart rate can develop rapidly. Whether substantial tolerance develops to feeling euphoric is debated.

A withdrawal syndrome can occur in many persons who have been using marijuana heavily for a substantial period of time. The symptoms of this withdrawal syndrome appear somewhat similar to that described with tobacco smokers. The most common symptoms reported are: irritability/anger, restlessness, nervousness, sleep difficulties, vivid dreams, and nausea, craving, and depressed mood. These symptoms typically appear within two to four days after stopping regular use and may last two to three weeks.

EPIDEMIOLOGY

Cannabis remains the most widely used illicit substance in most developed countries that regulate its use, and its rate of use is also increasing in developing countries. In the United States, it is estimated that 98 million people (39 percent) have used the drug; 15 million (6 percent) are currently using it (i.e., at least once in the past month); and 3.1 million are using cannabis daily. Cannabis use is most prevalent among adolescents and young adults aged sixteen to twenty-five. Approximately 34 percent of high school seniors and 28 percent of sophomores have used marijuana at least once, and daily use approximates 6 percent and 4 percent among seniors and sophomores, respectively. Although illegal in the United States, marijuana is readily accessible; approximately 40 percent of eighth graders, 73 percent of tenth graders, and 86 percent of twelfth graders report that they know where to get marijuana.

As with other drugs of abuse, cannabis is used more often by males than females. Cannabis is used across all regions of the United States with minimal variance, although some states have significantly higher rates of use than others. Prevalence of use across major ethnic and racial groups is similar, though there is some indication of slightly higher rates among African Americans, American Indians, and those who claim membership in two or more races.

ADVERSE HEALTH, COGNITIVE, AND BEHAVIORAL CONSEQUENCES

Much remains unknown about cannabis. Moreover, proving that the drug's use causes specific adverse effects, rather than their simply co-occurring with those effects or perhaps being an attempt at self-medication to ameliorate those effects, is an ongoing challenge in cannabis research with humans. Alternative explanations can and should be considered viable until well-controlled research necessitates their being ruled out. This caveat notwithstanding, the findings to date warrant mention of the following potential adverse consequences.

Personal Development. The possibility that cannabis use contributes to disturbances in normal adolescent development is of considerable concern. Frequent cannabis use by adolescents is correlated with such negative psychosocial outcomes as poorer academic performance, truancy, and dropping out of school. Teens who initiate use earlier are at higher risk of developing dependence. There are mixed findings concerning the suggestion that cannabis may interfere with normal adolescent brain development.

Cognitive Function. Although the findings are mixed, some studies indicate that heavy and long-term cannabis use impairs memory and executive functioning, with these consequences persisting after cannabis use has ceased. Moreover, there is evidence that the onset of use before age sixteen or seventeen respectively predicts poorer performance in tasks requiring focused attention and lower verbal IQ in adulthood.

Affective and Psychotic Disorders. Brief psychotic episodes that mimic schizophreniform disorders can occur following cannabis consumption and are generally short-lived. Such episodes are more likely following heavy consumption. In those who are susceptible to schizophrenia, cannabis use increases the likelihood of an acute episode, an earlier relapse, more frequent hospitalization, and poorer psychosocial functioning. There is also evidence that heavy cannabis use can be a contributing factor in the development of psychotic illness in those without such a predisposition, although conclusions concerning this relationship remain contentious.

There appears to be a small but significant risk of major depression occurring in young adults who are current cannabis users. Early onset and frequent use may increase the risk of both anxiety and depression in young adulthood.

Respiratory System. Heavy cannabis smokers have a greater risk of chronic cough, chronic sputum production, wheezing, and episodes of acute bronchitis than nonsmokers. Additionally, cannabis smokers are at an increased risk of such infectious diseases as pneumonia. Bronchial biopsies give evidence of precancerous pathological changes suggestive of an elevated risk of respiratory tract cancers. One New Zealand population-based case control study in adults fifty-five years of age and younger found that the risk of lung cancer increased 8 percent for each year of cannabis smoking. In contrast, a large case control survey in California found no association between cannabis use and these types of cancer.

Cardiovascular System. For individuals with cardiovascular disease, increased stress on the heart due to the effects of cannabis on the circulatory system may increase the risk of chest pain, heart attack, or stroke.

Driving. Due to cognitive and psychomotor impairments when high, drivers who have consumed cannabis are at a modestly increased risk of accidents.

Fetal Development. Subtle disturbances of brain development may result in cognitive impairment in the offspring of women who use cannabis during pregnancy. The impairment may not appear until preschool or school age.

DEPENDENCE (ADDICTION)

Although the concept of dependence or addiction in relation to cannabis has been questioned by some, diagnostic, epidemiological, laboratory, and clinical studies clearly indicate the existence, importance, and potential for harm of cannabis addiction. As with other substances, including alcohol and tobacco, a subset of individuals who try to continue to use cannabis eventually develops what is labeled as dependence or addiction. It is estimated that 9 percent of those who have used marijuana at least once meet the diagnostic criteria for cannabis dependence, which compares to approximately 15 percent for cocaine, 24 percent for heroin, and 32 percent for tobacco cigarettes. More frequent marijuana use results in greater risk for developing dependence, and in heavier users the proportion meeting dependence criteria may be as high as 50 percent. Between 1992 and 2002, the prevalence of marijuana use disorders among adults increased despite a stabilization of overall rates of marijuana use, and both the rates of use and prevalence of disorders increased among adolescents. It appears that the risk of developing cannabis dependence is elevated (one in six or seven) for users who first use the drug at a young age. Compared with adults, adolescent cannabis users qualify for a diagnosis of dependence with a lower frequency and quantity of cannabis consumption. Cannabis dependence as reported by those seeking treatment because of marijuana-related problems appears highly similar to other substance dependence disorders, although it is usually less severe than most others.

TREATMENT

Treatment admissions in the United States for primary cannabis abuse more than doubled between 1993 and 2003, and similar trends have been observed in such other countries as Australia. There is increased recognition that cannabis is a drug that can lead to addiction and significant negative consequences in a subset of those who use it. This awareness has led to the development of cannabis-specific interventions and treatment materials paralleling those used with other substance use disorders. These advances have increased the acceptability of seeking and providing treatment for cannabis dependence, and consequently the number of individuals seeking help has increased. Types of treatments shown to be effective include: motivational enhancement therapy, cognitive-behavioral treatments, contingency management, and various behavioral family-based treatments (for adolescents). However, as with treatment for other substance use disorders, many individuals do not respond well to these interventions; hence, there is a continued need to develop more effective treatment options.

Optimistic expectations for continued enhancements to treatment approaches appear warranted given that behavioral treatments continue to demonstrate incremental gains in efficacy as innovative interventions are evaluated. Furthermore, rapid advances in understanding the neurobiology of cannabis and the cannabinoid system provide further hope for increasingly effective treatment options (e.g., medications).

MEDICAL USE

Cannabis may have beneficial effects for a number of medical conditions. Oral THC has been approved by the U.S. Food and Drug Administration for use as an appetite- and food-intake stimulant in patients with AIDS wasting syndrome and as an antinausea and antiemetic agent in cancer patients receiving chemotherapy. In 1999 the Institute of Medicine and the National Institutes of Health acknowledged the importance of initiating additional scientific study of the risks and benefits of cannabis use and, in particular, the use of smoked cannabis for specific medical conditions. The interest in the benefits of smoked cannabis in contrast to oral THC arises primarily from differences in the pharmacokinetics of these two routes of administration. Through the oral route, THC absorption is slow and variable; and as a result, clinical effects have a slower onset and longer duration than smoked cannabis. In addition, smoked cannabis delivers both delta-9-THC and other compounds (e.g., delta-8-THC and cannabidiol), which may have direct or interactive effects of therapeutic interest. As of 2008, research comparing the efficacy of oral THC and smoked cannabis for various medical conditions was needed.

By 2008 the medicinal effects of cannabis were being studied regarding a number of other conditions, including as pain relief (analgesia), for the treatment of neuromuscular symptoms (tremors, spasms, or loss of coordination associated with multiple sclerosis or other neurological disorders such as spinal cord injury), and for glaucoma (a disorder of the eye associated with increased intraocular pressure). Case studies and laboratory research suggest that cannabis can positively affect these conditions. Unfortunately, research on these conditions and those for which oral THC has been approved had yet to advance to allow (a) a clear determination of the positive and negative effects of smoked cannabis on each condition; (b) comparisons of oral THC with smoked cannabis; and (c) a comparison of smoked cannabis with other types of medications or medical treatments.

As of 2008, much more data on the effectiveness of smoked cannabis and oral THC for various medical conditions were expected to become available because a number of funding sources had initiated focused efforts to stimulate research in this area. Of additional importance, there was much optimism that additional advancements in research on the newly discovered cannabinoids and the cannabinoid system would result in the development of effective alternative medications that could accentuate the positive effects of cannabis but not produce the other potentially problematic effects of THC and smoke such as sedation, memory problems, intoxication, carcinogens, and respiratory irritation.

LEGAL STATUS

As of 2008, THC was a Schedule I drug (i.e., one that has a high potential for abuse, has no currently accepted medical indication, and for which there is a lack of accepted safety when used under medical supervision). Under the U.S. Controlled Substances Act, a first conviction for cannabis possession can result in a term of imprisonment of not more than one year, a minimum fine of $1,000, or both. A first conviction for trafficking in cannabis (1 to 49 plants) can result in up to five years of imprisonment and a fine of up to $250,000. However, there has been a long history of controversy concerning the drug's legal status. Signatories to the 1961 United Nations Single Convention on Narcotic Drugs agreed to "[a]dopt such measures as may be necessary to prevent the misuse of, and illicit traffic in the leaves of the cannabis plant." Despite the subsequent enactment of prohibition legislation to comply with the Convention, in the latter half of the twentieth century cannabis became the most widely used illicit drug in the Western world.

In the United States in 1972, the National Commission on Marihuana and Drug Abuse recommended that cannabis possession be decriminalized. The Commission members reasoned that overly severe penalties risked undermining the credibility of government in educating the public about potential drug-related harms, and the rationale for decriminalization (i.e., removing criminal penalties for possession while retaining them for selling) was to avoid that consequence while continuing to discourage cannabis use. The Netherlands in 1976, seeking to distinguish among drugs according to risk level, classified cannabis as a *soft drug*. Possession, cultivation, and sale of small amounts, while remaining illegal, would not be prosecuted. Subsequently, other countries, most notably Canada, Australia, New Zealand, Switzerland, Germany, Spain, Austria, Belgium, Luxembourg, Portugal, Italy, and some U.S. jurisdictions, reduced emphasis on a criminalization approach to cannabis use prevention.

Some people in the United States have argued for full legalization, that is, permitting over-the-counter sale of all drugs. An alternative model that has been suggested is a regulatory system in which cannabis sale is authorized in state-licensed establishments. Proponents of retaining criminal sanctions argue that cannabis use can be harmful and that restrictive laws have effectively kept levels of cannabis use lower than they would be if the drug were to be legalized. Policy reform advocates argue that using criminal penalties to protect users from harming themselves is an unwarranted infringement of individual liberty and that criminalizing cannabis possession has failed to prevent its use.

See also **Adolescents and Drug Use; Cannabis Sativa; Controls: Scheduled Drugs/Drug Schedules, U.S; Driving, Alcohol, and Drugs; Monitoring the Future.**

BIBLIOGRAPHY

Abel, E. L. (1980). *Marihuana: The first twelve thousand years.* New York: Plenum.

Budney, A. J., Moore, B. A., & Vandrey, R. (2008). Health consequences of marijuana use. In J. Brick (Ed.), *Handbook of medical consequences of alcohol and drug abuse* (2nd ed., pp. 251–282). New York: Haworth Press.

Budney, A. J., Roffman, R., Stephens, R. S., & Walker, D. (2007). Marijuana dependence and its treatment. *Addiction Science & Clinical Practice, 4*(1), 4–15.

Hall, W., & Pacula, R. L. (2003). *Cannabis use and dependence: Public health and public policy.* Cambridge, UK: Cambridge University Press.

Roffman, R. A., & Stephens, R. S. (Eds.) (2006). *Cannabis dependence: Its nature, consequences, and treatment.* Cambridge, UK: Cambridge University Press.

ALAN J. BUDNEY
ROGER A. ROFFMAN

MDMA. MDMA (3,4-methylenedioxymethamphetamine) is popularly known as Ecstasy, XTC, and Adam. It is a ring-substituted derivative of the parent compound amphetamine and family member, methamphetamine. The addition of the methylenedioxy ring to the methamphetamine backbone confers its selectivity for binding to serotonin transporters over dopamine transporters. It is also structurally related to the hallucinogen mescaline. Consequently, the pharmacological effects of MDMA are a combination of the effects of the amphetamines and mescaline. These compounds are structurally related to the phenethylamine-type neurotransmitters dopamine, norepinepherine, and epinephrine. Many analogs of these compounds have been synthesized and are sometimes found on the street—the so-called designer drugs.

MDMA was first synthesized in 1912 by Merck; however, the first toxicology studies of the drug were not performed until the 1950s. It was first reported to be psychoactive in humans in 1978. During the 1980s MDMA began to be used in psychotherapy and was reported to increase patients' self-esteem and help facilitate communication with the therapist. Even with these positive effects, in 1985 the U.S. Drug Enforcement Agency classified MDMA as a Schedule I drug due to its high abuse potential, lack of clinical application, and the emerging evidence that it induced serotonergic nerve terminal degeneration in experimental animals. Despite these claims, and since the mid-1980s, MDMA has become a popular club drug, taken at rave parties because of its mild stimulant properties and the sense of euphoria, increased self-esteem, and heightened awareness it induces. Normally taken in tablet form, the average recreational dose of Ecstasy is one to two tablets each containing 60–120 milligrams of MDMA, or a dose of 0.75-4 milligrams/kilograms in a 70-kilogram individual.

Along with the positive subjective effects of MDMA, users have reported adverse physiological effects such as nausea, jaw clenching and teeth grinding, increased muscle tension, blurred vision, and panic attacks. It also causes amphetamine-like stimulation of the autonomic nervous system, producing increases in blood pressure, heart rate, and body temperature. While the drug does not typically result in a hangover, users have reported

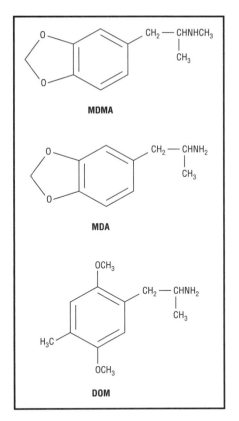

Figure 1. Phenethylamine hallucinogens. ILLUSTRATION BY GGS INFORMATION SERVICES. GALE, CENGAGE LEARNING

experiencing midweek blues as well as headaches, insomnia, fatigue, drowsiness, sore jaw muscles, and loss of balance, any of which may last for several days after ingestion. In extreme cases MDMA is lethal due to the pathological consequences of severe hyperthermia (elevated body temperature) as well as liver and cardiovascular toxicity.

Following ingestion, MDMA increases the release of the neurotransmitters serotonin and dopamine by interacting with nerve terminal transporters to cause the outflow of the neurotransmitters and the blockage of their reuptake. These interactions of MDMA with brain serotonergic and dopaminergic systems are likely responsible for its physical, psychological, and behavioral effects.

By the early 1990s increasing evidence indicated that MDMA could damage neurons in the brain. In laboratory animal experiments, MDMA was shown to produce long-lasting reductions in serotonin content in many regions of the brain. More advanced techniques have shown that MDMA causes a destruction of neuronal axon terminals while leaving the cell body intact. Single doses of the drug have been shown to deplete serotonin for several weeks and in some cases serotonin neuron terminals remain decreased for as long as one year after drug administration. In these experiments the extent of serotonin terminal loss appears to depend on the dose and the number of times the drug is administered. The exact mechanisms of MDMA-induced neurotoxicity are unknown at present but studies point to several contributing factors including excessive dopamine and serotonin release, the ability of MDMA to produce hyperthermia, the generation of harmful reactive oxygen species (very small molecules that are highly reactive and thereby damage tissue with which they come in contact), and the formation of neurotoxic breakdown products.

Controversy concerning whether findings from studies in laboratory animals can be applied to human MDMA users have been addressed by several groups. The concept of interspecies scaling suggests that neurotoxic doses of the drug in rodents correspond to recreational doses in humans, if one takes into account the differences in circulation time, organ blood flow and surface area, and liver metabolic enzymes between rodents and humans. Furthermore, increasing evidence suggests that brain function can be altered in humans exposed to the drug. Since the 1990s, considerable research has suggested the presence of cognitive and behavioral deficits associated with long-term MDMA use. Several studies have shown impairments in learning and memory as well as the development of depression and heightened anxiety after heavy MDMA use, all of which appear to correlate with decreases in the number of serotonin transporter sites in the brain as visualized with brain imaging techniques. Based on the implication of serotonergic systems in the control of cognition, sleep, food intake, sexual behavior, anxiety, mood, and the neuroendocrine system, loss of serotonin terminals after MDMA use can have major physical, psychological, and behavioral consequences in humans.

See also **Complications: Mental Disorders; Dopamine; Methamphetamine; Serotonin.**

BIBLIOGRAPHY

Green, A. R., Mechan, A. O., Elliot, J. M., O'Shea, E., & Colado, M. I. (2003). The pharmacology and clinical pharmacology of 3,4-methylenedioxymethamphetamine

(MDMA, "Ecstasy"). *Pharmacological Reviews, 55*(3), 463–508.

Gudelsky, G. A., & Yamamoto, B. K. (2003). Neuropharmacology and neurotoxicity of 3,4-methylenedioxymethamphetamine. *Methods in Molecular Medicine, 79*, 55–73.

Quinton, M. S., & Yamamoto, B. K. (2006). Causes and consequences of methamphetamine and MDMA toxicity. *AAPS Journal, 8*(2), E337–E347.

Ricaurte, G., Bryan, G., Strauss, L., Seiden, L., & Schuster, C. (1985). Hallucinogenic amphetamine selectively destroys brain serotonin nerve terminals. *Science, 229*, 986–998.

DANIEL X. FREEDMAN
R. N. PECHNICK
REVISED BY BETHANN N. JOHNSON (2009)
BRYAN K. YAMAMOTO (2009)

MEDIA. Drugs, drug abuse, addiction, and drug traffic have been attractive topics for journalists since about 1900 and nearly as long for screenwriters. As subjects, they incorporate a number of reliable story elements: personal tales of temptation, sin, and redemption (or damnation); the sacrifice of innocents; and lurking (but often unrecognized) dangers. Historically, mainstream media presentations of drug problems (abuse, addiction, and trafficking) have varied along several lines: the drugs in question, the actual incidence of the problems, which demographic groups are using the drugs or seem most at risk; and the overall political climate, which went through several cycles of relative tolerance and intolerance during the twentieth century.

HISTORY OF MEDIA INTERPRETATION AND EMPHASIS

Although media treatments of drug problems have varied over time, they also have been fairly consistent in their use of common themes and language. From the 1920s to the early 2000s, media accounts often described drugs as powerful, seductive, irresistible, and instantly addicting; drug use or abuse was repeatedly termed an *epidemic*, a *scourge*, a *plague*, or a *crisis*. They routinely presented drugs as a direct cause of crime, violence, theft, and other deviant behavior, or as the cause of economic, social, and moral failure. Other common themes included the physical damage caused by drugs, including users' deaths and effects on users' offspring; the association of drugs with various social *outgroups* or minority groups; and drugs as a hidden peril that threatens respectable citizens, professionals, and children.

Prior to 1905, very few articles on drug addiction appeared in the popular press. Americans were much more concerned about alcohol than about other intoxicants between 1820 and 1920. Most of the people writing about drugs such as opium, morphine, and cocaine were physicians and social workers and sometimes missionaries to China. Addict memoirs made occasional appearances as well. These accounts varied in their assessments of the nature and prevalence of addiction.

Popular articles on drug problems increased from 1906 to 1914, and focused on three related drug problems: Opium traffic in China and the Philippines and struggles to establish international controls; domestic efforts to control patent medicines and get dangerous or adulterated products off the market; and increasing cocaine use between about 1907 and 1912. Together, these problems helped justify the passage of the first federal narcotic-control law in 1914. For several years after the passage of the 1914 Harrison Narcotic Act, popular articles were actually quite sympathetic toward the pitiful addicts whose supplies were now curtailed. Some local governments experimented until the early 1920s with heroin maintenance clinics to deal with the problem, and journalists chronicled the efforts of addiction specialists to develop a cure for the victims of addiction. By the mid-1920s, however, antidrug reformers were describing the U.S. *narcotics problem* in apocalyptic terms that later became so familiar. Once regarded as merely unfortunate, drug use was increasingly described as the root of all social evil. By the end of the decade sympathetic accounts of addiction had largely disappeared. The change in rhetoric stemmed partly from genuine increases in addiction and the advent of a new drug (cocaine), but it also had much to do with increasing lower-class recreational drug use and declining middle-class therapeutic use, the success of the alcohol prohibition movement, and the social and cultural effects of the World War I (e.g., xenophobia, fears of Communism, and rejection of traditional culture).

IMPACT OF REFORMERS

The changing media presentations of drug problems after 1920 owe much to the efforts of antidrug activists such as Richmond P. Hobson (1870–1937). A Spanish-American War hero, former congressman, and well-regarded temperance crusader, Hobson became involved in the campaign against the *dope traffic* in 1920, writing articles and giving talks about the threat of narcotic addiction. He went on to establish several antinarcotic organizations: the International Narcotic Education Association in 1923, the World Conference on Narcotic Education in 1926, and the World Narcotic Defense Organization in 1927. These groups worked hard to raise public awareness, using many of the tactics that had worked so well for the Anti-Saloon League and Woman's Christian Temperance Union against alcohol: enlisting the aid of prominent citizens (e.g., physicians, attorneys, judges, and legislators) and civic organizations, holding national and international conferences, agitating for stricter controls, and sponsoring Narcotic Education Week during the last week in February beginning in 1927. They sent out (by Hobson's account) millions of pamphlets and article reprints, gave interviews, contributed articles to magazines and newspapers, and contacted teachers and school superintendents. Hobson and other reformers such as Sara Graham Mulhall made regular appearances in the *New York Times* and magazines and often gave speeches to women's clubs and other civic groups in New York City. Mulhall published a well-received book (*Opium, the Demon Flower*) in 1926, which was based on her experiences as deputy commissioner of the New York State Narcotic Board. Hobson and his associates were also able to reach a wide audience through the new medium of radio. In all of these forums, the reformers gave wildly exaggerated estimates of the number of drug users, sensational accounts of drug-induced depravity, and gruesome details of the physiological damage drugs caused.

Newspaper Sensationalism and William Randolph Hearst.
Hobson and company had an important ally in publisher William Randolph Hearst (1863–1951), and longtime Hearst writer Winifred Black, who wrote under the name Annie Laurie. Black, one of the pioneers of the *sob sister* style of journalism, had been writing exposés for Hearst papers since 1889. It is not clear whether Hearst cared about drug reform before 1920, but he had long used his papers and magazines to promote any cause with a potential for sensation and increased circulation. By 1923, Hearst's media

empire was huge, including 22 daily papers (with a total circulation of 3 million), 15 Sunday papers (total circulation of 3.5 million) and 9 magazines (total circulation of 2.7 million). An estimated one of every four American families read a Hearst publication, so any Hearst crusade was guaranteed a large audience. Hearst exerted considerable editorial control over his publications, and, typically, they all ran the same major stories.

Hearst's newspaper crusade against the narcotics threat opened in October 1921, with Annie Laurie's front page *San Francisco Examiner* story, "Drug Evil Invades Cities, Towns, as Ruthless Rings Coolly Recruit Victims." In a month-long series, Laurie detailed the growing menace of efficient, well-organized, cunning drug trafficking rings, whose agents invaded American towns and cities, seducing teenagers and young adults into lives of cocaine and heroin addiction, crime, and squalid degradation. Hearst and his editors wrote frequent editorials (often accompanied by evocative cartoons) likening the *dope problem* to the bubonic plague, urging government to "get after the rats" that spread it. Similar editorials and feature articles continued throughout the decade in Hearst papers (*San Francisco Examiner*, October 21, 1921, p. 24). By 1930, antidrug activists had developed a journalistic template for talking about drug problems that was used with only minor modifications throughout the twentieth and into the twenty-first century.

Federal Bureau of Narcotics and Harry J. Anslinger.
Traffic in opiates and cocaine seemed to be coming under control by the late 1920s, and reformers targeted another menacing drug, marijuana, which had escaped regulation under the 1914 Harrison Act and subsequent amendments. In early 1928, the Hearst papers ran a series on the new peril posed by marijuana, which supposedly brought on murderously insane rages in its users. For reformers, and for Harry J. Anslinger (1892–1975), first chief of the Federal Bureau of Narcotics, marijuana was *the* demon drug of the late 1920s and 1930s. Anslinger's position made him the authority of record regarding drugs. He was in great demand for interviews, speeches, and radio addresses on this topic, and co-authored an article titled "Marihuana: Assassin of Youth" for *American Magazine* in July of 1937. His stories of marihuana-induced atrocities and depravity strongly echoed

earlier accounts in Hearst's papers: young men and women with no history of antisocial behavior would, once under the influence of cannabis, ax-murder their families, casually kill strangers and policemen, rob, rape, kidnap, and torture. He also popularized the idea that marijuana use was an inevitable stepping stone to heroin use. The 1936 film *Reefer Madness*, while low-budget and not widely distributed at the time, incorporated many of the themes present in media accounts. Marijuana was outlawed by the 1937 Marijuana Tax Act. Charged with controlling the drug traffic on a very limited budget, Anslinger deftly used the media to present drugs and their users as negatively as possible.

POST-1940S RESURGENCE OF MEDIA ATTENTION

Although stories about drug problems were typically sensational, they were not especially numerous during the 1930s, when Americans were preoccupied with the economic depression and recovery. The topics of drugs and addiction disappeared from the media almost completely during the 1940s; World War II and its aftermath, coupled with federal drug-control efforts disrupted the drug trade for much of that time, and many journalists assumed the drug issue was finished. By late 1950, however, newspapers and magazines were once more running alarming stories about a resurgence of heroin use among teenagers in New York and other major cities, often in conjunction with reports of juvenile delinquency. Initial stories focused on poor minority youths, but journalists soon reported that the problem had left the slums and invaded middle-class schools and neighborhoods. The media accounts were similar in many respects to those in the pre-war years, but several new elements appeared as well. First, there was Anslinger's assertion that Communist China, dumping tons of opium on the world market to raise cash, was behind the phenomenon. Second, many of the articles included statements from addiction researchers at the federal narcotics hospital in Lexington, Kentucky, which introduced the idea that addiction was a chronic relapsing disease suffered by those with an addictive personality. Although the wave of concern over teenaged heroin addicts led to the most stringent narcotics laws yet (the 1951 Boggs Act, which included mandatory minimum sentences for narcotics possession, and the 1956 Narcotics Control Act, which allowed the death penalty for those selling to minors), there was a clear trend toward more sympathetic portrayals of addicts in the media; addict memoirs appeared more frequently, showing users as basically good people who were victimized by their own bad judgment, bad companions, and predatory dealers, and more articles discussed addiction treatment (though facilities were quite scarce at the time).

"Pep Pills" and "Peace Pills": Amphetamine and Meprobamate.

The 1950s also brought the first media accounts of several other psychoactive drugs, notably amphetamine and meprobamate. Amphetamine, a stimulant drug developed before World War II, was prescribed as an antidepressant or as a weight-loss aid. Articles about its medical use expressed little concern about abuse or addiction and indeed emphasized its usefulness. Popular literature about non-medical use of the drug was quite different. From the early 1950s, increasing numbers of highway accidents were attributed to truckers' overuse of these *pep pills*, and by 1955 a federal campaign was underway to stop illicit sales to truck drivers. Illicit amphetamines also were featured in articles about thrill-seeking teenagers, who committed various sorts of mayhem while high on *bennies*. In 1957, another media furor resulted from news that recent great athletic feats had been made possible because many of the nation's athletes were "gobbling pep pills (*Time*, June 17, 1957, p. 56)."

Meprobamate (Miltown, Equanil), the first minor tranquilizer, was the subject of hundreds of articles after its introduction in 1954. Many accounts praised its effectiveness, safety, and lack of addictive potential, embracing it as the perfect remedy for keyed-up, tension-ridden, nervous Americans; some even predicted that such drugs might prevent mental illness. The tranquilizers seemed so innocuous during their first decade that some writers dubbed them *peace pills*, *happiness pills*, and *emotional aspirin*. Cartoonists also found tranquilizers to be useful humorous elements, a trend that would continue well into the 1970s. By 1960, when the first benzodiazepine tranquilizer, Librium, appeared, media accounts were more varied. The phenomenal number of prescriptions written (an estimated 8.8 million for Librium alone in 1961, according to the *National Prescription Audit*) prompted worries that tranquilizers were being used as a panacea.

And other writers feared that tranquilizers would completely eliminate "normal healthy anxiety" and divest life of the struggles that properly define humanity (*Reader's Digest*, January, 1957). Pharmaceutical manufacturers, lauded as heroes in the post-penicillin era of drug discovery, were increasingly viewed with suspicion, as profits from tranquilizer sales ballooned.

Concern about psychoactive prescription drugs continued to grow during the 1960s and 1970s, as their use—and, many argued, overuse—expanded. Journalists increasingly blamed the pharmaceutical industry for over-promoting tranquilizers to physicians, and physicians for prescribing the drugs for every complaint. But they primarily blamed middle-class Americans themselves, for expecting to have pills to relieve all of life's ailments and pressing their doctors to furnish them. Media images of other drugs, such as amphetamines and barbiturates (widely prescribed as sleeping aids) became much darker; stories of harrowing side effects (up to and including death) increased, and one widely quoted senator, Thomas Dodd, asserted that the country was in the midst of a "nice-drug epidemic." There was a growing media interest in middle-class addiction, and in the idea of a drug abuse epidemic to which everyone was vulnerable.

Prescription Drugs in the Media. Media coverage of prescription drug problems during the 1970s showed two striking and connected trends: they increasingly focused on women and drugs, and they increasingly portrayed drug users as victims rather than self-indulgent seekers of fast relief. In these accounts, the users were not criminals or thrill seekers, but average Americans, often housewives, being overmedicated by physicians who sought to render them less troublesome and perhaps more conforming to middle-class norms. Many women's magazines ran stories on the dangers of tranquilizer and amphetamine use, focusing on their addictive potential and the large numbers of prescriptions written. At first these emphasized education and better communication between women and their physicians, but by the late 1970s, physicians were under increasing fire for not giving patients enough information, for being dependent on pharmaceutical *detail men* for drug information, and for prescribing instead of listening to their patients. The worst examples of such

negligence included the *diet doctors* such as Max Jacobsen (Dr. Feelgood), who had supplied countless politicians and celebrities with the injectable amphetamine they needed to maintain hectic lifestyles, with sometimes tragic results, and the psychiatrist in Barbara Gordon's 1979 memoir, *I'm Dancing as Fast as I Can*, who responded to all of her complaints by prescribing stronger tranquilizers.

Former First Lady Betty Ford provided part of the impetus for this change of focus. In 1978, Mrs. Ford publicly confessed her long-term—and largely invisible—dependence on alcohol, tranquilizers, and other drugs, and encouraged other victims to recognize their addictions and get treatment. A 1975 study conducted by the National Institute of Drug Abuse (NIDA) indicated that women accounted for the majority of *nice drug* prescriptions, lending support to the idea of a hidden drug problem propagated by greedy drug manufacturers and negligent physicians. From this point on, middle-class, non-counterculture addictions were treated sympathetically in popular accounts; for some celebrities, addiction and recovery even became a badge of honor and spawned a new genre of addict memoirs. As their authors did not always limit their substance use to prescribed drugs and alcohol, these memoirs often included tales of various illicit drugs as well.

Late 1960s Counter-Culture "Drug Problems." Mainstream media coverage of counter-culture and recreational drug use during the 1960s and 1970s reflected the varied and often confusing nature of the drug problems that developed during those years. Heroin use increased to worrisome levels during the 1960s, especially among inner-city residents and soldiers returning from Vietnam. Both amphetamines and barbiturates crossed over into illicit markets and, like heroin, were associated with crime and juvenile delinquency. These and relatively unfamiliar drugs such as LSD, peyote, and cocaine also began appearing on college campuses, as did marijuana, embraced as paths to enlightenment or just liberation from societal norms. Especially after the 1967 Summer of Love in San Francisco's Haight Ashbury district, media coverage of drug use increased sharply. Many of these articles emphasized the dangers involved in drug use: the day-to-day degradation of heroin use and addiction; the bad LSD trips that caused users to commit suicide; or the amphetamine diet pill habit that turned users into emaciated, wild-eyed, violently psychotic *speed freaks*. They also emphasized with alarm the magnitude of the abuse problem, the villainy of drug dealers, and, usually, the extreme addictiveness of the drug, as had journalists in earlier eras.

However, the articles from about 1965 to 1980 were marked by an unusual level of tolerance. Public perceptions of addicts as dangerous deviants had waned by the early 1960s, to be replaced (if briefly) by a more compassionate attitude. In 1962, the Supreme Court ruled that addiction is a disease, not a crime; the following year, a presidential commission recommended that penalties for narcotics offenses be reduced, and funding for addiction treatment increased. This action was in keeping with the overall approach taken toward social problems during the Kennedy and Johnson administrations. So, even as they recounted the horrors of drug addiction to readers, writers also discussed addiction as a disease that could be amenable to treatment. In 1971, President Richard Nixon, declaring that drugs were "public enemy number one," further legitimized this approach by vastly increasing funding for treatment (including methadone maintenance) and education as part of his antidrug initiative (Massing 1998, p. 112). Likewise, popular accounts stressed the importance of education and parent-child communication in combating the various drug epidemics. In the process, they often confused and conflated the various abused drugs and their different pharmacological effects and abuse patterns, probably misinforming as they tried to educate.

Marijuana in the Late 1970s. Marijuana received a lot of coverage during this era, largely because the experiences of millions of young users seemed to disprove all the *Reefer Madness* horror stories of earlier decades. Debates went on for many years, with opponents, often from the drug-control establishment, maintaining that it had dangerous potential for habituation and was a stepping stone to more serious drug use, and proponents arguing that the drug was benign and should be decriminalized. By 1977, President Carter and some of his drug policy advisors had cautiously considered proposals for decriminalization. This period of tolerance was short-lived; by the late 1970s and early 1980s public sentiment was turning against marijuana and drug use in general, led by an influential parent movement. These grassroots antidrug activists soon enlisted policy advisors and First Lady Nancy Reagan in their campaign for a drug-free nation. The ensuing "Just Say No" and *zero-tolerance* approach to drug use would be fed during the next several decades by alarm not over marijuana, but over cocaine.

LATE TWENTIETH CENTURY DRUG CRISES

Media coverage of drug abuse was dominated by cocaine during the 1980s. Expensive and comparatively scarce during the 1970s, cocaine was not considered a high-risk drug even by many treatment experts. Its scarcity and association with wealthy celebrity parties (plus its pleasant stimulant effects, no doubt) glamorized it and increased demand. By the early 1980s supplies had increased, prices had dropped, and *Time* magazine proclaimed that it was the "All-American drug," the first choice of trendy, upwardly mobile middle-class citizens (July 6, 1981). As use increased, however, so did the number of problems.

In late 1985, stories began appearing about a dangerous new drug, a new smokeable form of cocaine called *crack*. Crack use was increasing rapidly in inner cities, contributing to crime and straining treatment facilities. In June 1986, athletes Len Bias and Don Rogers died of cocaine overdoses, and cocaine was immediately transformed from *glitzy party drug* to *killer* in media accounts. For the next decade it seemed that little else mattered; cocaine, crack, and other illicit drugs rapidly went to the top of editorial and political agendas. During the last half of 1986, approximately one thousand stories on crack cocaine appeared in national newspapers and magazines. *Time* and *Newsweek* each devoted five cover stories to the *drug crisis*. In the month of July 1986, major television networks ran 74 evening news pieces on drugs, and in September the CBS news special *48 Hours on Crack Street* earned the highest newsshow Nielsen ratings in five years (Reeves & Campbell, 1994). Newspapers, magazines, and television programs carried a steady stream of horror stories about the burgeoning crack trade in the inner cities, often accompanied by gang-style violence and killing; about the addicts' rapid descent into a hellish world of crime, prostitution, and crack houses; about the destruction of families and entire neighborhoods by the crack trade; about the violent behavior caused by the drugs; about the sinister South American drug cartels that kept the traffic going.

Politicians quickly joined the hue and cry and initiated new legislation to "get tough on drugs" (*Newsweek*, August 18, 1986, p. 16). The drug-war budget was greatly increased, and various crime bills and drug control measures imposed mandatory minimum sentences and longer jail terms overall for drug-related offenses. Treatment experts declared that crack was instantaneously addicting, and the confessions of addicts seemed to support this view. The crack problem was widely touted as the most horrible threat the nation had ever faced. More dramatic writers compared U.S. drug use to the bubonic plague of medieval times. *Newsweek*, for example, noted that an entire generation of American youth was "increasingly at risk to the nightmare of addiction," because a "flood tide of cocaine," ("the most glamorous, seductive, destructive, dangerous drug on the supersaturated national black market,") was reaching consumers of all ages in this country (March 11, 1986, p. 58). Within a few years, *crack babies* born to addicted mothers joined the list of victims in media accounts.

Other drugs, such as MDMA (Ecstasy), also captured a fair amount of media attention during the 1990s, but they never eclipsed cocaine as top stories. For a few years after the terrorist attacks of September 11, 2001, not surprisingly, drug abuse and the war on drugs, like many other topics, were largely sidelined except as they related to the war on terror. Subsequently, cocaine and crack lost their media ranking as "America's Most Dangerous Drugs" to methamphetamine, a substance similar in its effects and its abuse patterns. Likewise, media stories about *meth* were similar to earlier accounts of crack cocaine in their tone and emphasis. Addiction science made great progress in the 1970s, exploring the brain chemistry and genetic components of addiction and holding out the hope of better treatment if not cures. Such advances were enthusiastically reported in the media, though they were sometimes used only to buttress the more traditional horror stories. As public enthusiasm for wars on drugs waned, media accounts and policy discussions seemed to enter another cycle of relative tolerance or at least of greater openness to fresh approaches to a perennial problem.

DRUGS IN FILM AND TELEVISION

Like newspaper and magazine accounts, film and television renderings of drug use, addicts, and antidrug enforcers have often reflected cultural climates of tolerance or intolerance. Between 1934 and about 1965, a period of relative intolerance, Hollywood producers and screenwriters were constrained by the Hays Code. Also known as the Production Code, it prohibited the depiction of illegal drug use, along with many other elements that might lower the moral standards of movie audiences. Earlier films did sometimes incorporate drugs as tragic or comic devices, and various non-Hollywood tabloid-type films after the mid-30s dramatized the horrors of addiction, often for educational purposes. Produced before the Hays Code was widely enforced, Charlie Chaplin's 1936 *Modern Times*, in which the hero accidentally pours cocaine on his food with hilarious results, was probably the last film to feature any sort of drug humor until the 1970s. Otto Preminger's *The Man with the Golden Arm* (1955) was released without the Motion Picture Association's approval. The film's depiction of a reformed heroin addict struggling to stay clean was controversial but garnered several Academy Award nominations. Hays Code restrictions were gradually eased during the next decade, allowing drugs, sex, crime, and other risky topics to be featured in movies.

Films during the 1960s and 1970s depicted drug use much more frequently, though addiction *per se* was rarely the main focus (1971's *The Panic in Needle Park* is one exception). More often, the seedy underworld of drug trafficking provided primary or secondary story lines (e.g., 1971's *The French Connection*). In many films, as in newspapers and magazines of these decades, drug use—especially heroin or amphetamine—ended in tragedy. Marijuana use, in keeping with the times, was depicted as part of the youth-culture backdrop, as was cocaine. Though depictions of heroin use might be grim, marijuana and cocaine intoxication furnished comic elements in many films. When the cocaine and crack crisis developed during the 1980s, films mirrored the grim new reality in stories such as *Scarface* (1983) and *Clean and Sober* (1988). Later films featured more graphic descriptions of drug use and addict life (e.g., *Trainspotting* and *Pulp Fiction*.) As in the print media, there was also a trend away from moralizing about drugs, instead looking with a critical eye at the world created by current policies (e.g., 2000's *Traffic* and television dramas such as *The Wire*).

See also **Epidemics of Drug Abuse in the United States; Internet: Impact on Drug and Alcohol Use; Movies; Music; Parent Movement, The; Zero Tolerance.**

BIBLIOGRAPHY

Massing, M. (1998). *The fix.* New York: Simon & Schuster.

Reeves, J. L. & Campbell, R. (1994). *Cracked coverage: Television news, the anti-cocaine crusade, and the Reagan legacy.* Durham: Duke University Press.

Reinarman, C., & Levine, H. G. (1997). The crack attack: Politics and media in the crack scare. In C. Reinarman & H. G. Levine (Eds.), *Crack in America: Demon Drugs and Social Justice* (pp. 18–51). Berkeley: University of California Press.

Speaker, S. L. (1997). From happiness pills to national nightmare: Changing cultural assessments of minor tranquilizers in America, 1955–1980. *Journal of the History of Medicine and Allied Sciences, 52,* 338–376.

Speaker, S. L. (2002). Creating a monster: Newspapers, magazines, and the framing of America's drug problem. *Molecular Interventions, 2,* 201–204.

SUSAN L. SPEAKER

MEMORY, EFFECTS OF DRUGS ON.

Research investigating the effects on memory of alcohol (ethanol) and drugs of abuse is disproportionately small in relation to the widespread use of these substances worldwide. The available evidence clearly indicates that ethanol and abused drugs significantly affect memory processes. Much of the knowledge of the effects of such commonly used substances on memory is based on experiments using laboratory animals. In typical experiments, the animals are trained in a learning task and given a memory retention test after a delay of one day or longer. In experiments on commonly used learning tasks, the animals are trained to acquire responses that provide escape from, or avoidance of, aversive (unpleasant) stimulation. Appetitive motivation (food or water reward) is used to train animals in mazes and other types of spatial learning.

When investigating acute (single treatment) influences on learning and memory, drugs can be administered before the training, shortly after the training, or before the memory test. When drugs are administered before training, it is difficult to differentiate effects on memory from influences on sensory, motivational, and motor processes. When administered within a few minutes after training, but not after a delay of several hours, drugs of many classes can enhance or impair memory. Such findings are interpreted as indicating that the drugs can modulate memory-consolidation processes after a training session. The drug effects are typically dose-dependent. For example, drugs that enhance memory when administered in low doses may impair memory when administered in higher doses. Experiments examining the effects of a drug administered prior to memory testing are difficult to interpret, as drugs can alter many processes affecting behavior other than memory. For the same reasons, the alterations in memory performance that are produced by the chronic (long-term) administration of drugs are also difficult to interpret.

ALCOHOL (ETHANOL)

In rats and mice, an acute one-time dose of alcohol prior to learning usually impairs memory of the training. The effect is heightened by the drug clonazepam, a benzodiazepine receptor agonist; it is lessened by bicuculline and picrotoxin, drugs that block receptors for the inhibitory neurotransmitter GABA (GABA-A receptors). Such findings suggest that ethanol-induced amnesia is mediated by the benzodiazepine/GABA-A receptor complex. These findings are consistent with extensive evidence that benzodiazepines (see section below) induce amnesia in humans as well as in laboratory animals. Memory impairment induced by a large dose of alcohol is also lessened by physostigmine, the acetylcholinesterase inhibitor, suggesting that ethanol influences on memory involve cholinergic mechanisms (i.e., those involving the neurotransmitter acetylcholine).

Chronic administration of a high dose of ethanol to rats or mice over time induces memory impairment, accompanied by a decreased function of specific brain regions, including the hippocampus and neocortex. The syndrome can be reversed by an implant, into either brain structure, of fetal brain tissue that has high numbers of cholinergic cells or by giving oxotremorine, the cholinergic muscarinic agonist (i.e., an agent that simulates the actions of acetylcholine), prior to memory testing. Such findings suggest that the memory impairment resulting from chronic ethanol ingestion is associated with a deficit of brain cholinergic function.

Acute or chronic ethanol ingestion in humans also produces memory problems. Large amounts of ethanol taken over a short period (hours or days) may cause a severe amnesia—a *blackout* for events occurring during and/or shortly before the period of intoxication. Some alcoholic blackouts may be partially state dependent—that is, during a later intoxication, individuals may sometimes remember experiences that occurred during a previous blackout. This phenomenon was illustrated in Charles Chaplin's 1931 film *City Lights*, in which the hard-drinking millionaire remembered Charlie only when under the influence of alcohol. Some drinking patterns may have a more harmful effect on brain function than others. Research has shown that college students who binge drink (i.e., episodically drink heavily) perform more poorly on cognitive tests, most notably measures of working memory, than non-binge drinkers who consume the same amount of alcohol, but do so more moderately but more frequently. Working memory refers to the process of storing and manipulating information and involves frontal lobe brain systems. The mechanism for this is not known, but binge drinking may have effects similar to those of repeated episodes of alcohol withdrawal, which is associated with cognitive impairment in alcoholics undergoing recovery. Moreover, the effects of binge drinking on brain function seem to be greater among women.

Studies of alcohol-related brain dysfunction have quantified what has been known for hundreds of years, namely that chronic alcohol use can have a harmful effect on human memory. The most severe forms of alcohol-related memory loss are Korsakoff's syndrome and alcohol dementia. Korsakoff's syndrome is due to Vitamin B_1 (thiamine) deficiency, resulting from poor food intake during sustained periods of alcohol consumption and reduced absorption of the vitamin due to the adverse gastrointestinal effects of heavy drinking. Korsakoff's syndrome is characterized by profound memory loss and impaired executive functioning, but relatively normal IQ scores. Alcoholics who meet the usual *DSM-IV* criteria for dementia, including profound amnesia without preserved intelligence, are often given the diagnosis of alcohol dementia, although some consider alcohol dementia to be the result of multiple causes. Improvements in such patients are seen if they abstain from alcohol. However, most memory deficits are permanent.

It is not known whether the deficits seen in early alcohol dementia and in Korsakoff's syndrome are accompanied by alterations in GABAergic or cholinergic functioning. The changes seen in late alcoholic dementia, like those of Alzheimer's disease, involve multiple focal (in particular regions) brain lesions, primarily in the temporal lobe but also in other brain regions, and involve deficits in glutaminergic, GABAergic, and cholinergic systems.

Large-scale studies of non-demented alcoholics in treatment have shown that, during the intermediate abstinence period, which begins after detoxification and extends through the first two months of abstinence, as many as half of recovering alcoholics have measurable brain abnormalities and cognitive deficits, including memory loss. Significant recovery with continued abstinence is typical. However, there is considerable variability among patient populations depending on the age, health, and presence of comorbid psychopathology.

BENZODIAZEPINES

Benzodiazepines are used clinically in the treatment of anxiety and the induction of sleep. These drugs have also been widely abused. It has been known for several decades that benzodiazepines, including diazepam (Valium), triazolam (Halcion), and chlordiazepoxide (Librium) impair the creation of new memories in humans. Studies using laboratory animals indicate that benzodiazepines impair memory when administered before training, but they generally do not impair memory when administered after training. The lack of post-training effects may be due, at least in part, to the fact that benzodiazepines are absorbed slowly and are slow to reach peak concentrations in the brain following peripheral injections.

Benzodiazepines act by modulating GABA-A neurotransmitter receptors on the benzodiazepine/GABA receptor complex. Their effects on memory appear to be mediated primarily by the brain structures designated as the amygdaloid complex and hippocampus. When administered acutely (one-time dose), either into the system or directly into specific brain regions, including the amygdaloid complex and the hippocampus, immediately following training, retention is enhanced by flumazenil, the benzodiazepine-receptor antagonist, and by the GABA-A-receptor antagonists (blockers) bicuculline and picrotoxin. Findings indicating that the amnesia induced by peripherally administered benzodiazepines is blocked by GABAergic antagonists administered directly into the amygdaloid complex, as well as by lesions of the amygdaloid complex, provide additional evidence that this brain region is involved in benzodiazepine effects on memory. Although benzodiazepine-like substances are found in the brain, it is not yet known whether they are synthesized in brain cells or derived from food. Evidence that training releases these naturally occurring substances in the brain suggests that they may play a role in modulating memory-storage processes.

MARIJUANA

In laboratory animals, both acute and chronic administration of marijuana extracts or of their active agents, the tetrahydrocannabinols (THC), have been reported to impair the acquisition and retention of a wide variety of tasks. It is not known whether these effects are due to influences on memory or simply to the sedative effects of the drug. There is also evidence that chronic exposure to the chemicals found in marijuana produces permanent working memory impairment in adolescent but not adult rats, suggesting an interaction with brain development.

Evidence suggests that acute and chronic use of marijuana affects human memory beyond the period of intoxication. Memory deficits have been detected for up to seven days after heavy marijuana use but were reversed with sustained abstinence. Years of long-term marijuana abuse appear to produce memory loss during abstinent periods. Although the mechanism is not well understood, some evidence shows that THC affects neuronal functioning in the prefrontal cortex and hippocampus, two regions critical for normal memory.

OPIATES AND OPIOID PEPTIDES

The opiate drugs morphine and heroin, administered after training, impair retention in laboratory animals. Opiate-receptor antagonists, including naloxone and naltrexone, enhance memory and block the memory impairment produced by opiates. Endogenous opioid peptides (brain peptides that mimic the effects of morphine, heroin, and other opiates) also affect memory. The opioid beta-endorphin is released in the brain when animals are exposed to novel training situations. Post-training injections of beta-endorphin cause memory impairment as do injections into several brain regions, including the amygdaloid complex and medial septum. Opiate antagonists administered into these brain regions enhance memory. Under some conditions, beta-endorphin administered (or released by the individual) prior to memory testing may lessen the memory impairment induced by a post-training injection of the peptide.

Despite the widespread and long-standing use of opiate drugs by humans, there have been no systematic studies on the effect of morphine, heroin, or other opiates on human memory. Chronic opiate users do show memory deficits, but these may result from general deterioration rather than from any specific effect of the opiates. Acute administration of opiates (as in pre-anesthetic medication, for example) may induce a temporary amnesia. The failure of patients to remember experiences immediately prior to surgery may be due, at least in part, to an effect on memory of the opiates used for pain suppression. The effect of opiate antagonists for the treatment of dementias has been studied, but with limited success.

AMPHETAMINE

In laboratory animals, chronic administration of amphetamine prior to training impairs performance in many types of learning tasks. Such effects are typically obtained in experiments using high doses of amphetamine and complex learning tasks. In contrast, extensive evidence from studies using a variety of training tasks indicates that acute post-training injections of amphetamine produce enhancement of memory depending on the size of the dose. Retention is also enhanced by direct administration of amphetamine into several brain regions. Amphetamine acts by releasing and blocking the reuptake of the catecholamines epinephrine, norepinephrine, and dopamine from cells. Amphetamine effects on memory appear to result primarily from influences on brain dopaminergic systems as well as through the release of peripheral catecholamines.

Amphetamine users often report that their "learning capacity" is enhanced by single doses of the substance. Because there are few systematic and well-controlled studies of the effects of amphetamine on memory in humans, however, it is not known whether such reports reflect subjective changes in perception and mood or actual effects on memory. Chronic amphetamine use is usually accompanied by a deterioration of memory function, an effect that subsides with cessation of use.

COCAINE

Despite the extensive use and abuse of cocaine, little is known about cocaine effects on memory. Results of studies using rats and mice indicate that acute post-training administration induces dose-dependent effects comparable to those of amphetamine: Memory is enhanced by low doses and impaired by higher doses. The brain processes affecting cocaine influences on memory have not been extensively investigated. The effects appear to be mediated by influences on noradrenergic and dopaminergic systems. Also, as with amphetamine, cocaine users report that memory is enhanced by one-time doses, but impaired by chronic use. Systematic, well-controlled studies of the effects of cocaine on human memory are lacking.

The effects on memory and intellectual functioning of other drugs—such as phencyclidine (PCP), barbiturates, nicotine, and inhalants—are considered in connection with these agents and in separate articles.

See also **Abuse Liability of Drugs: Testing in Humans; Agonist; Alcohol: Chemistry and Pharmacology; Amphetamine; Analgesic; Antagonist; Anxiety; Barbiturates; Benzodiazepines; Brain Structures and Drugs; Cannabinoids; Catecholamines; Chlordiazepoxide; Cocaine; Complications: Cognition; Coping and Drug Use; Drug Interaction and the Brain; Endorphins; Gamma-Aminobutyric Acid (GABA); Heroin; Inhalants; Morphine; Naloxone; Naltrexone; Neurotransmitters; Nicotine; Opiates/ Opioids; Phencyclidine (PCP); Productivity: Effects of Alcohol on; Research, Animal Model: An Overview; Research: Measuring Effects of Drugs on Behavior; Risk Factors for Substance Use, Abuse, and Dependence: Learning; Synapse, Brain; Wikler's Conditioning Theory of Drug Addiction.**

BIBLIOGRAPHY

Hardy, J., & Allsop, D. (1991). Amyloid deposition as the central event in the etiology of Alzheimer's Disease. *Trends in Pharmacological Sciences, 12,* 383–388.

Izquierdo, I., & Medina, J. H. (Eds.). (1993). *Naturally occurring benzodiazepines: Structure, distribution and function.* London: Ellis and Horwood.

Kaplan, R. F. (2004). Neuropsychology of alcoholism: Effects of premorbid and comorbid disorders (pp. 461–486). In H. R. Kranzler & J. A. Tinsley (Eds.), *Dual diagnosis and treatment: Substance abuse and comorbid disorders.* (2nd ed.). New York: Marcel Dekker.

McGaugh, J. L. (1989). Dissociating learning and performance: Drug and hormone enhancement of memory storage. *Brain Research Bulletin, 23,* 339–345.

McGaugh, J. L. (1989). Involvement of hormonal and neuromodulatory systems in the regulation of memory storage. *Annual Review of Neuroscience, 12,* 255–287.

McGaugh, J. L., Introini-Collison, I. B., & Castellano, C. (1993). Involvement of opioid peptides in learning and memory. In A. Herz, H. Akil, & E. J. Simon (Eds.), *Handbook of experimental pharmacology: Opioids, part II.* Heidelberg: Springer-Verlag.

O'Shea, M., Singh, M. E., McGregor, I. S., & Mallet, P. E. (2004). Chronic cannabinoid exposure produces lasting memory impairment and increased anxiety in adolescent but not adult rats. *Journal of Psychopharmacology, 18,* 502–508.

Pope, Jr., H. G., Gruber, A. J., Hudson, J. I., Huestis, M. A., Yurgelun-Todd, D., McLean Hospital, et al. (2001). Neuropsychological performance in long-term cannabis users. *Archives of General Psychiatry, 58,* 909–913.

Solowij N., Stephens, R. S., Roffman, R. A., Babor, T., Kadden, R., Miller, M., et al. (2002). Cognitive functioning of long-term heavy cannabis users seeking treatment. *Journal of the American Medical Association, 287,* 1123–1131.

Weingartner, H., & Parker, E. S. (Eds.). (1984). *Memory consolidation.* Hillsdale, NJ: Lawrence Erlbaum.

IVAN IZQUIERDO
REVISED BY JAMES L. MCGAUGH (2001)
RICHARD KAPLAN (2009)

MEPERIDINE. Meperidine is a totally synthetic opioid analgesic (painkiller) with a structure quite distinct from that of morphine, a natural opiate. Unlike morphine's rigid fused ring structures, the structure of meperidine is flexible; it is a

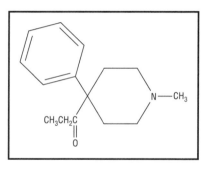

Figure 1. Chemical structure of meperidine. ILLUSTRATION BY GGS INFORMATION SERVICES. GALE, CENGAGE LEARNING

phenylpiperidine and bends so that the key portions of the molecule can assume positions similar to those of morphine. A number of other compounds with similar structures are widely used in medicine, including loperamide (used primarily for treating diarrhea) and the extraordinarily potent analgesic agents fentanyl, sufentanil, lofentanil, and alfentanil (for treating pain).

Meperidine is a compound with strong analgesic effects similar to morphine's, although greater amounts are needed to produce the same level of analgesia. It is one of the more commonly prescribed opioid analgesics and is better known under one of its brand names, Demerol. Given by injection, 100 milligrams of meperidine equals 10 milligrams of morphine. Meperidine can be administered orally as well as by injection; but its potency it not as great following oral administration, so the dose must be increased proportionally. Like morphine, continued use of meperidine is associated with decreased analgesia—tolerance—as well as physical dependence. As with the other opioids, addiction (defined as a drug-seeking behavior) is not commonly observed with this drug when used for medicinal purposes, but meperidine is highly valued on the street and is widely abused, particularly in its injectable forms.

Medically, meperidine is a significant problem in patients with kidney conditions, in which drug-removal from the body is impaired. Metabolized to normeperidine, a closely related compound, it is eliminated by the kidneys. In patients with kidney problems, this metabolite can accumulate to high levels that can cloud mental processes and even produce convulsions. Since elderly patients often have impaired kidney function, special care must be taken when using meperidine with them.

See also **Addiction: Concepts and Definitions; Opioid Complications and Withdrawal.**

BIBLIOGRAPHY

Kenakin, T. (2003). *A pharmacology primer: Theory, application and methods.* New York: Academic Press.

Reisine, T., & Pasternak, G. (1996). Opioid analgesics and antagonists. In J. G. Hardman et al. (Eds.), *The Pharmacological Basis of Therapeutics*, 9th ed. New York: McGraw-Hill Medical. (2005, 11th ed.)

Seifert, C. F., & Kennedy, S. (2004). Meperidine is alive and well in the new millennium: Evaluation of meperidine usage patterns and frequency of adverse drug reactions. *Pharmacotherapy, 24,* 6, 776–783. New York: Oxford University Press USA.

GAVRIL W. PASTERNAK

MEPROBAMATE. Meprobamate is a sedative-hypnotic drug that is now typically used to treat muscle spasms. Meprobamate is prescribed and sold as Deprol, Equagesic, Equanil, Meprospan, and Miltown. Because of its abuse potential, it is included in Schedule IV of the Controlled Substances Act. It was first introduced into clinical medicine in 1955 for the treatment of anxiety. At the time it was thought to have specific antianxiety effects and to be quite different from other sedative-hypnotics. Also introduced at about the same time were chlorpromazine (Thorazine), which had remarkable antipsychotic effects, and reserpine, which had tranquilizing as well as blood pressure-lowering effects. These three agents were considered the harbingers of the new era of psychopharmacology and helped popularize the new term *tranquilizer.*

Within a year or two after its introduction, meprobamate had become one of the most widely prescribed drugs in the United States. It was not long, however, before its distinction from other sedative-hypnotic agents was reassessed; and within a decade it was recognized that meprobamate shared many of the properties of such other central nervous system depressants, as the barbiturates. By the early 1960s, its use for the treatment of anxiety was eclipsed by the benzodiazepines. Although it is prescribed as a muscle relaxant, the only use currently

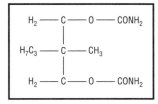

Figure 1. Chemical structure of meprobamate. ILLUSTRATION BY GGS INFORMATION SERVICES. GALE, CENGAGE LEARNING

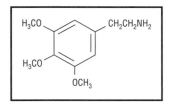

Figure 1. Chemical structure of mescaline. ILLUSTRATION BY GGS INFORMATION SERVICES. GALE, CENGAGE LEARNING

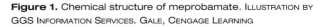

approved in the United States by the Food and Drug Administration is as a sedative-hypnotic.

Meprobamate has a number of side effects, including tremor, nausea, depression, and various allergic reactions. Continued use of high doses can result in tolerance and physical dependence. Convulsions and other signs of withdrawal are reported upon termination of high-dose treatment or inappropriate use.

See also **Anxiety; Barbiturates; Sedative-Hypnotic.**

BIBLIOGRAPHY

Hobbs, W. R., Rall, T. W., & Verdoorn, T. A. (1996) Hypnotics and sedatives; ethanol. In J. G. Hardman et al. (Eds.), *The Pharmacological Basis of Therapeutics*, 9th ed. New York: McGraw-Hill Medical. (2005, 11th ed.)

Schatzberg, A. F., Cole, J. O., & DeBattista, C. (2007). *Manual of clinical psychopharmacology*, 6th ed. Washington, D.C.: American Psychiatric Publishing.

SCOTT E. LUKAS

of mescaline are very similar to those produced by lysergic acid diethylamide (LSD); however, it is approximately 100 to 1,000 times less potent than LSD, although the effects of mescaline last from 10 to 12 hours.

See also **Psilocybin; Religion and Drug Use.**

BIBLIOGRAPHY

Efron, D. H., Holmstedt, B., & Kline, N.S., Eds. (1979). *Ethnopharmacologic search for psychoactive drugs.* New York: Raven Press.

Hanson, G. R., Venturelli, P. J., & Fleckenstein, A. E. (2005). Hallucinogens (Psychedelics). In *Drugs and Society*. Sudbury, MA: Jones & Bartlett Publishers.

Lewis, W. H. (2005). Hallucinogens. In *Medical botany: Plants affecting human health*. Hoboken, NJ: John Wiley & Sons.

DANIEL X. FREEDMAN
R. N. PECHNICK

MESCALINE. Mescaline is a naturally occurring hallucinogen, one of the oldest psychedelic substances known. It was first obtained from the peyote cactus (*Lophophra williamsii* or *Anhalonium lewinii*), which grows in the southwestern United States and northern Mexico. Peyote buttons, the dried tops of the peyote cactus, were originally used by pre-Columbian Native Americans in those regions as an antispasmodic as well as for highly structured religious rituals; the button was eaten or was steeped to make a drink. It continues to be used in ritual by the Native American Church.

Mescaline is a member of the phenethylamine-type family of hallucinogens, which includes DOM, MDA, and MDMA. The overall behavioral effects

METHADONE MAINTENANCE PROGRAMS. The history of methadone treatment offers a striking example of the benefits and limits of research findings on public attitudes and policies regarding methadone maintenance treatment. To understand methadone maintenance treatment, it is necessary to appreciate the profound stigma attached to both patients and treatment providers. This establishes the context for understanding how a modality with the most extensive research base in the addiction treatment field can still engender passionate dispute.

Methadone maintenance was developed as a treatment modality in the mid-1960s by Vincent Dole and Marie Nyswander in response to prevailing concerns about epidemic levels of heroin addiction and related health problems, mortality (especially among young people 15 to 35 years old), and high relapse rates. Methadone was synthesized in Germany during World War II as a synthetic analgesic, and after the war it was studied at the U.S. Public Health Service Hospital in Lexington, Kentucky. The drug was approved by the U.S. Food & Drug Administration in August 1947 for use in the treatment of pain. Its initial use in the treatment of addiction was to ease withdrawal in individuals being treated for heroin addiction; it was subsequently determined to be well suited to long-term maintenance treatment.

As a treatment tool, methadone provides a safe and effective way to eliminate drug craving, withdrawal, and drug-seeking behavior, thus freeing patients to lead productive lives. In conjunction with educational, medical, and counseling services, it has been thoroughly documented as enabling patients to discontinue or reduce illicit drug use and associated criminal activity, improve physical and mental well-being, become responsible family members, further their education, obtain and maintain stable employment, and resume or establish a productive lifestyle. Yet despite over four decades of research confirming its value, methadone maintenance treatment remains a source of contention among treatment providers, the public, and particularly among officials and policymakers. As an example of this modality's value, a 2002 Cochrane Review concluded that this form of treatment is superior in terms of patient retention and reduction of heroin use to nonpharmacological therapies for opioid dependence (Mattick et al., 2002). Unlike controversies based on a difference of opinion between informed parties, debate about methadone usually involves several common misunderstandings about the drug and its uses.

COMMON MISUNDERSTANDINGS

Much of the uneasiness about methadone stems from the idea that it is "just substituting one addictive drug for another." Indeed, this is technically correct—methadone treatment is drug-replacement therapy in which a long-acting, orally administered preparation is substituted for a short-acting opioid that is used intravenously. The long-acting (24 to 36 hours) effect of preventing withdrawal allows most patients to receive a dose and function in a stable manner, without the four-hour cycles of euphoria and withdrawal that characterize heroin use. The objection that methadone is "addictive" reflects the recognition that the medication produces dependence.

However, addiction treatment professionals increasingly distinguish between physical dependence and addiction, the latter being characterized by behavior that is compulsive and out of control, that persists despite adverse consequences, and where the relationship with the substance is more salient to the addict than anything else. On the other hand patients with chronic pain will develop physical dependence on a drug, though their overall functioning is improved. Appropriate prescribing of benzodiazepines for patients with anxiety disorders is another example of a dependence-producing drug used beneficially for thousands of patients. Although physical dependence is a factor to be considered, the use of methadone provides a neurochemical platform of stability, allowing the patients to reorient their lives so that their relationship with opioids is no longer the central organizing factor of their lives.

Another point of discord is the belief that "methadone keeps you high," a notion that reflects a misunderstanding of the effects of a properly adjusted dose. Once stabilized, most patients experience little or no subjective effects. Indeed, heroin addicts will readily state that they seek methadone to avoid becoming sick (prevent withdrawal effects), not to get high. When the patient's dose is being stabilized, he or she may experience some subjective effects, but the wide therapeutic window allows for the dose to be adjusted to avoid craving (due to an inadequate dose) and somnolence (due to an excessive dose). Dose adjustment may take some weeks and may be disrupted by a variety of medical and lifestyle factors, but once it is achieved the patient should function normally.

There is also ample scientific evidence that the long-term administration of methadone results in no physical or psychological impairment of any kind that can be perceived by the patient, observed by a physician, or detected by a scientist. More specifically, there is no impairment of balance, coordination, mental abilities, eye-hand coordination, depth perception, or psychomotor functioning, unless the patient is using other impairing drugs or medications (Lenné et al., 2003).

A third point of resistance—the objection to long-term, or even life-long, maintenance—is better addressed following the presentation of some basic information about opioid addiction and the nature of treatment.

HOW DOES METHADONE TREATMENT WORK?

Most addiction specialists agree that addictive disorders are complex phenomena involving the interaction of biologic, psychosocial, and environmental variables, all of which need to be considered to make treatment effective. Dole and Nyswander, who pioneered the use of methadone, held the view that there was something unique about opioid addiction that made it difficult for patients to remain drug-free. Although originally intended as a long-term treatment for a metabolic defect, many initially hoped that methadone could be used to transition heroin addicts to a drug-free lifestyle and then be discontinued. Research in the subsequent decades indicates that less than 20 percent of patients will be able to discontinue methadone and remain drug-free. As his thinking evolved, Dole postulated in 1988 that a receptor system dysfunction resulting from chronic use leads to permanent alterations that medical science does not currently know how to reverse. New brain imaging technology holds the promise of better understanding and, eventually, improved intervention, but in the interim it appears that methadone is corrective but not curative for the severely addicted person. Two important questions for future research are whether a preexisting condition enhances the vulnerability of some patients to addiction, and what the differences are among opioid addicts who respond to short- or intermediate-term treatment versus those who need indefinite maintenance therapy due to permanent brain dysregulation.

Studies indicate that methadone is a benign drug that exhibits stability of receptor occupation and thus permits interacting systems to function normally. One example of this is the normalization of hormone cycles and the return of regular menstrual cycles in women. This distinguishes it from heroin, a short-acting narcotic that produces rapid

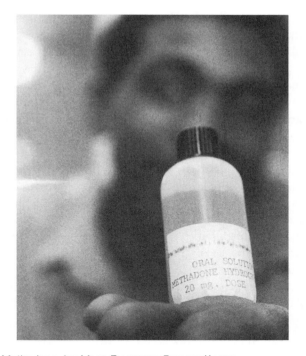

Methadone. Ian Miles–Flashpoint Pictures/Alamy.

changes and makes a stable state of adaptation impossible. Although tolerance develops to most effects of methadone, it is fortunate that even long-term use (30 years or more) does not produce tolerance to the reduced craving effect or to the narcotic withdrawal prevention effect.

The desired response to methadone depends on the maintenance of a stable blood level at all times. Appropriate doses usually keep the patient in the therapeutic range of 150 to 600 nanograms per milliliter (ng/mL) in the blood, which produces the stable state so important for rehabilitation. What is referred to as a "rush" or "high" is the result of rapidly changing blood (and brain) levels. Thus, once therapeutic levels are achieved and maintained, the patient experiences little subjective effect.

Unfortunately, negative attitudes toward methadone have historically played a significant role in dosing practices. In particular dose ceilings were imposed by state or local regulations without regard to medical criteria. Such policies placed a value on giving as little of the drug as possible (versus the therapeutic level needed to accomplish the goal), influenced in part by the unsubstantiated belief that lower doses would make it easier to discontinue methadone. It was common to have dose ceilings of 40 milligrams per day. It is now well established that this is inadequate to maintain the necessary plasma concentrations to be effective—the effective range is between 60 and 120 milligrams per day for most patients, with some needing less than 60 milligrams and others considerably more than 120 milligrams. Higher doses are strikingly well correlated with reductions in illicit drug use and improved retention in treatment (Ward et al., 1998). Subsequent to studies that documented the prevalence of insufficient dose levels in methadone programs in the United States (D'Aunno and Vaughan, 1992), there has been a vigorous effort to educate treatment staff, including program physicians, about proper methadone dosing through publications from the American Society for Addiction Medicine and accreditation guidelines promulgated by the Center for Substance Abuse Treatment in 1999 (and revised in 2007).

Initial hopes that methadone could be used to transition patients to a medication-free lifestyle have proven unrealistic. Studies indicate that although short-term abstinence is common, there are high rates of relapse to opioid use after methadone treatment is discontinued (Magura and Rosenblum, 2001). Moreover, research indicates that indefinite methadone treatment is more cost-effective than a 180-day detoxification protocol (Masson et al., 2004). Clinicians who have worked with this population over the long term believe that although lifestyle changes are essential to successfully discontinuing methadone, such changes in conjunction with high motivation will still be insufficient for most patients, and that neurobiological factors remain a deciding factor. Increasingly, opioid addiction, as with other forms of addiction, are being viewed as chronic medical diseases for which medication-assisted treatment is not curative but rather provides the patients with tools they can use for a healthier life (McLellan et al., 2000). It is to be hoped that this changing conceptualization of addiction will lead patients on methadone to feel less pressure—from family, employers, health and social service providers, fellowship support group members, and themselves—to discontinue methadone treatment prematurely.

METHADONE AND OTHER DRUGS

Methadone patients may engage in alcohol, cocaine, and other drug use prevalent in their communities, even to the level of addiction. It is important to remember that methadone is opioid-specific and does not in itself increase or prevent other kinds of drug use. It does, however, offer the enormous advantage of making the patient accessible to other kinds of intervention. Rules governing take-home medication are intended to reduce the diversion of methadone onto the illicit market. At a minimum, they mandate that the patient initially come to the clinic six days per week, with decreasing clinic visits for dosing achieved over time. Thus, the patient can be exposed to educational presentations and materials, and to counseling interventions as indicated by an individualized treatment plan, which is required as part of the treatment effort.

Cocaine, methamphetamine, and benzodiazepine abuse have received particular attention, because continuing abuse of or addiction to these drugs predict poorer retention in (and response to) methadone treatment. Research and training efforts have been brought to bear on this problem, but the lack of effective addiction medications for these substances, in addition to resistance by residential treatment providers to admit methadone treatment patients who might need that in-patient, more structured (as compared to out-patient) level of care for their addiction to other drugs, present barriers to potentially effective interventions.

Alcohol use also remains a problem, particularly because many patients define their difficulty in terms of illicit drug use and are resistant to the notion of giving up drinking. Given the high prevalence of hepatitis C infection in patients in methadone treatment, attention to patients' use of alcohol, which is toxic to the liver, is both a medical and an abuse-addiction problem. Accreditation guidelines and best practices documents—such as Treatment Improvement Protocol (TIP) Series 43, devised by the Center for Substance Abuse Treatment (CSAT)—draw attention to methods of dealing with these other substance use problems. Finally, nicotine dependence is highly prevalent among patients in methadone treatment, and programs are starting to develop interventions to address this problem.

TREATING OPIOID-ADDICTED PREGNANT WOMEN

Methadone maintenance has been viewed as an effective treatment for opioid addiction in pregnant women since the early 1970s. In addition to the benefits of psychosocial interventions provided by the program, methadone maintenance treatment prevents erratic maternal opioid drug levels, thus protecting the fetus from repeated episodes of withdrawal. Programs either provide prenatal care onsite or monitor the patient to see that prenatal care is obtained elsewhere, thus reducing the incidence of obstetrical and fetal complications, reducing *in utero* growth retardation, and improving neonatal outcomes (Finnegan, 1991; Burns et al., 2006). Exposure to HIV infection through ongoing needle use is also reduced. Programs typically provide interventions focusing on nutrition, parenting skills, exercise, and other health-related topics.

Methadone-maintained mothers produce offspring more similar to drug-free controls, in contrast to the poorer health status of offspring born to women using street drugs. Methadone substantially reduces the highs and lows in maternal serum opioid levels that typically occur with the repeated use of heroin and other short-acting opioids, thereby reducing the harm to the fetus caused by repeated intoxication and withdrawal (Kaltenbach et al., 1998). Although expectant mothers can be stabilized on methadone, body changes specific to pregnancy frequently cause them to develop increasing signs and symptoms of withdrawal as the pregnancy progresses, and they may need dose increases to maintain a therapeutic plasma level and remain comfortable. Splitting the dose so that it can be ingested twice daily often produces better results, as this both reduces fetal stress and increases the comfort of the pregnant woman (CSAT, 2005).

There is inconsistent evidence to support the commonly held belief that the severity of the neonatal abstinence syndrome (central nervous system irritability, gastrointestinal dysfunction, and respiratory distress in the infant generally appearing in the newborn within the first 72 hours after birth) is proportional to the methadone dose, but many programs urge the expectant mothers to reduce their dose so the "baby won't be born addicted." In fact, the management of the neonatal abstinence syndrome is relatively straightforward—fetal discomfort can usually be eliminated within hours, and withdrawal can be accomplished within 14 to 28 days. No lasting impairment from these experiences has been demonstrated. Breast-feeding is encouraged for newly delivered mothers on methadone, regardless of their dose level, unless otherwise medically contraindicated (American Academy of Pediatrics, 2001).

ADDRESSING PSYCHOLOGICAL ISSUES

Extensive research over a long period of time has clarified the importance of the psychosocial component of methadone treatment. The stigma against heroin addicts in general, and methadone patients in particular, has created a treatment climate in which both patients and treatment providers may become demoralized about the value of these interventions. Often isolated from the mainstream, providers may not be able to obtain access to resources for patients on methadone. For example, methadone patients are often excluded from housing support (including recovery housing), mental health treatment, and vocational training programs. Nonetheless, evidence is growing that minimal intervention using methadone reduces illicit drug use (and hence needle sharing), while enhanced treatment accomplishes a great deal more (McLellan et al., 1993 and 1998).

In 1997 a National Institutes of Health (NIH) consensus panel recognized the importance of attention to medical, psychiatric, and socioeconomic issues, as well as drug counseling, in optimizing the effectiveness of methadone treatment. Psychosocial counseling focuses on managing the patient's personal problems, particularly those specific to drug use, physical health, interpersonal relationships, family interactions, and vocational and educational goals. The counselor also performs the role of the case manager and is a liaison between physicians and medical institutions, courts, and social services. Counselors help the patient to develop coping strategies for current problems, perform initial screening for medication and other program services, and attend to issues concerning program rules, privileges, and policies. The federal and state regulations and accreditation guidelines governing methadone treatment are more complex, detailed, and restrictive than others in medicine or psychology, and maintaining a therapeutic alliance while meeting these obligations is a daunting task for clinical staff.

A recent large scale epidemiologic study found that among the respondents with a twelve month substance use disorder about 20 percent had a co-occurring mood disorder with depression being predominant and about 18 percent had a co-occurring anxiety disorder (Grant et al., 2004) and depression is particularly common among the opioid-dependent population. Treatment outcome is improved by adding supplemental psychotherapy with professionally trained staff for patients with substantial co-occurring psychiatric symptoms (Woody, 2003). It is important that such staff be well integrated into the treatment team. Psychiatric medication may also be given concurrently with methadone, and the use of antidepressants is increasingly common for methadone patients. Possible pharmacokinetic interaction effects are manageable with consistent monitoring and good staff teamwork. Psychotic conditions are less common, but clinics are likely to have some experience with highly disturbed individuals, and they should therefore be able to recognize and manage these patients appropriately. The patients benefit from the structure of frequent clinic attendance.

Twelve-step programs actively promote abstinence from all potentially addictive drugs, and this has been a barrier to the participation of methadone patients in these programs. Coupled with this are negative attitudes toward methadone and its users. The founders of Alcoholics Anonymous (AA) viewed medication interventions such as methadone as being compatible with twelve-step program participation (Zweben, 1991), but AA meeting participants may not always be open to participation by methadone patients. This climate has begun to change, however, and methadone patients are increasingly attending twelve-step meetings. Methadone maintenance programs are developing their own special meetings onsite, which in turn encourage patients' utilization of twelve-step meetings in the larger community.

HIV/AIDS AND HEPATITIS C

A positive reexamination of methadone treatment has been greatly stimulated by the documentation of its role in reducing the spread of HIV. Seroprevalence is much lower among those who have been on long-term maintenance, particularly those who entered treatment prior to the onset of the rapid spread of HIV in the local population (Batki, 1988). Research suggests that drug-use risk reduction is more likely to be achieved by those patients, both those uninfected and those infected with HIV, who remain in methadone treatment. Further, patients who drop out and return, as well as those who continue to inject while in treatment, may also benefit in this respect (Thiede et al., 2000). Clinic attendance makes large numbers of intravenous drug users accessible to efforts at prevention and education, screening, testing, and

counseling. Because methadone patients have a continuing forum to discuss their life issues, counselors may be able to facilitate behavior change in relation to safer sex practices and other high-risk behaviors. Further gains accrue as the patient progresses in treatment, as an abstinent person is in a better position to exercise good judgment than an intoxicated one. Efforts are therefore being made to integrate HIV/AIDS-related activities as fully as possible into methadone treatment programs.

The hepatitis C virus (HCV) has emerged as a problem of major significance, with many clinics reporting a prevalence of up to 80 percent. Among those with HIV, co-infection with HCV is high. Inasmuch as 50 to 80 percent of new injectors become infected with HCV within 6 to 12 months, methadone maintenance will not reduce its spread as effectively as has occurred with HIV. However, it does provide a structured system in which the patient can be medically monitored, informed of emerging treatments, and educated about health practices to reduce the burden on the liver while more promising treatments are being developed. There are many complications to the provision of integrated care to these patients (Sylvestre et al., 2004).

WHAT THE FUTURE HOLDS

Methadone maintenance has demonstrated its effectiveness in reducing illicit drug use and facilitating the transition to a productive lifestyle. In the mid-to-late 1990s, two major scientific bodies, the NIH and the Institute of Medicine (IOM) reviewed the evidence on methadone maintenance and concluded that it was an effective modality whose usefulness was greatly reduced by stigma and overregulation (National Consensus Development Panel on Effective Medical Treatment of Opiate Addiction, 1998; Rettig & Yarmolinsky, 1995). Partially in response to these two reviews, federal oversight in the United States shifted in 2001 from the Food and Drug Administration (FDA) to the Center for Substance Abuse Treatment (CSAT). That shift, accompanied by changing regulations requiring accreditation for opioid treatment programs (42 CFR Part 8), has made the service delivery system more flexible and responsive to patients' needs. Additionally, CSAT's TIP 43 provides practitioners with guidelines for best practices in methadone treatment. The release of TIP 43 was accompanied by a widespread dissemination effort designed to increase the adoption of these practices among Opiate Treatment Programs (OTPs).

Research, including long-term follow-up studies, indicates that stabilized and socially responsible methadone patients can be safely given a month's worth of take-home medication by physicians in an office-based practice (Novick & Joseph, 1991; Novick et al., 1994). CSAT's regulations, based on that research, permit clinics to give patients up to one month's supply of medication. Take-home privileges are awarded in a step-wise fashion, with the requirements for frequency of clinic attendance decreasing over time based on the patient's progress in recovery and demonstrated responsibility in handling take-home medication.

Buprenorphine, a partial opioid agonist, has been developed and made available to opioid addicts, both in methadone clinic practice as well as from qualified physicians in office-based practice. This medication can be used for both detoxification and maintenance of opioid dependent individuals, and research seems to indicate treatment outcomes similar to methadone (Mattick et al., 2003). It is hoped that this additional medication and new treatment setting will broaden the options and possibilities for effective intervention. Federally sponsored training efforts have improved the quality of care and will continue to be essential in disseminating current information and providing opportunities for skill development. Slowly, patients have emerged as visible examples of success, and these patients are serving as positive role models for others and coming together to act as advocates for this modality. Mobile dispensing services have also been implemented. Thus, barriers to participation in residential treatment are beginning to be removed. It is hoped that these developments will engender future gains and allow methadone maintenance to gain the acceptance it so greatly deserves.

See also **Addiction: Concepts and Definitions; Hepatitis C Infection; Heroin; Injecting Drug Users and HIV; Opiates/Opioids; Opioid Complications and Withdrawal; Opioid Dependence: Course of the Disorder Over Time; Pregnancy and Drug Dependence; Rhetoric of Addiction; Treatment, Behavioral Approaches to: Twelve-Step and Disease Model Approaches; Treatment, Pharmacological Approaches to: Buprenorphine; Treatment, Pharmacological Approaches to: Methadone; U.S. Government Agencies: Center for Substance Abuse Treatment (CSAT); U.S. Government Agencies: Substance Abuse and Mental Health Services Administration (SAMHSA).**

BIBLIOGRAPHY

American Academy of Pediatrics, Committee on Drugs. (2001). "Transfer of drugs and other chemicals into human milk." *Pediatrics 108(3)*, 776 –789.

Ball, J. C., & Ross, A. (1991). *The effectiveness of methadone maintenance: Patients, programs, services, and outcomes.* New York: Springer-Verlag.

Batki, S. (1988). Treatment of intravenous drug users with AIDS: the role of methadone maintenance. *Journal of Psychoactive Drugs, 20(2),* 213–216.

Burns, L., Mattick, R. P., Lim, K., & Wallace, C. (2006). "Methadone in pregnancy: treatment retention and neonatal outcomes." *Addiction, 102(2),* 264–270.

Center for Substance Abuse Treatment. (2005). *Medication-assisted treatment for opioid addiction in opioid treatment programs, treatment improvement protocol (TIP) Series 43.* Rockville, MD: Substance Abuse and Mental Health Services Administration.

Center for Substance Abuse Treatment. (2007). *Guidelines for the accreditation of opioid treatment programs.* Rockville, MD: Substance Abuse and Mental Health Services Administration.

D'Aunno, T., & Vaughn, T. E. (1992). Variations in methadone treatment practices result from a national study. *Journal of the American Medical Association, 267(2),* 253–258.

Dole, V. (1988). Implication of methadone maintenance for theories of narcotic addiction. *Journal of the American Medical Association, 260(20),* 3025–3029.

Finnegan, L. (1991). Treatment issues for opioid-dependent women during the perinatal period. *Journal of Psychoactive Drugs, 23(2),* 191–201.

Grant, B. F., Stinson, F. S., Dawson, D. A., Chou, S. P., Dufour, M. C., Compton, W., et al. (2004). Prevalence and co-occurrence of substance use disorders and independent mood and anxiety disorders: Results from the national epidemiological survey on alcohol and related conditions. *Archives of General Psychiatry (61),* 807–816.

Kaltenbach, K., Berghella, V., & Finnegan, L. (1998). Opioid dependence during pregnancy. *Obstetrics and Gynecology Clinic of North America, 25,* 139–151.

Lenné, M. G., Dietze, P., Rumbold, G. R., Redman, J. R., & Triggs, T. J. (2003). The effects of the opioid pharmacotherapies methadone, LAAM and buprenorphine, alone and in combination with alcohol, on simulated driving. *Drug and Alcohol Dependence, 72(3),* 271–278.

Magura, S., & Rosenblum, A. (2001). Leaving methadone treatment: Lessons learned, lessons forgotten, lessons ignored. *Mount Sinai Journal of Medicine 68(1),* 62–74.

Masson, C. L., Barnett, P. G., Sees, K. L., Delucchi, K. L., Rose, A., Wong, W., & Hall, S. M. (2004). Cost and cost-effectiveness of standard methadone maintenance treatment compared to enriched 180-day methadone detoxification. *Addiction, 99(6)*, 718–726.

Mattick, R. P., Breen C., Kimber J., & Davoli, M. (2002). Methadone maintenance therapy versus no opioid replacement therapy for opioid dependence. *Cochrane Database of Systematic Reviews, (4)*.

Mattick, R. P., Kimber, J., Breen, C., & Davoli, M. (2003). Buprenorphine maintenance versus placebo or methadone maintenance for opioid dependence. *Cochrane Database of Systematic Reviews (2)*.

McLellan, A. T., Arndt, I. O., Metzger, D. S., Woody, G. E., & O'Brien, C. P. (1993). The effects of psychosocial services in substance abuse treatment. *Journal of the American Medical Association, 269(15)*, 1953–1996.

McLellan, A. T., Hagan, T. A., Levine, M., Gould, F., Meyers, K., Bencivengo, M., et. al. (1998). Supplemental social services improve outcomes in public addiction treatment. *Addiction, 93(10)*, 1489–1499.

McLellan, A. T., Lewis, D. C., O'Brien, C. P., & Kleber, H. D. (2000). Drug dependence, a chronic medical illness. *Journal of the American Medical Association, 284(13)*,1689–1695.

National Consensus Development Panel on Effective Medical Treatment of Opiate Addiction. (1998). Effective medical treatment of opiate addiction. *Journal of the American Medical Association, 280(22)*, 1936–1943.

Novick, D. M., & Joseph, H. (1991). Medical maintenance: The treatment of chronic opiate dependence in general medical practice. *Journal of Substance Abuse Treatment, 8(4)*, 233–239.

Novick, D. M., Salsitz, E. A., Kalin, M. F., Keefe, J. B., Miller, E. L., & Richman, B. L. (1994). Outcomes of treatment of socially rehabilitated methadone maintenance patients in physician's offices (medical maintenance): Follow-up at three and a half to nine and a fourth years. *Journal of General Internal Medicine, 9(3)*, 127–130.

Payte, J. T., Zweben, J. E., & Martin, J. (2003). Opioid maintenance treatment. In A. W. Graham, T. K. Schultz, M. F. Mayo-Smith, R. K. Ries, & B. B. Wilford (Eds.), *Principles of Addiction Medicine* (751–766). Chevy Chase, MD: American Society of Addiction Medicine.

Regier, D. A., Farmer, M. E., Rae, D. S., Locke, B. Z., Keith, S. J., Judd, L. L., & Goodwin, F. K. (1990). Comorbidity of mental disorders with alcohol and other drug abuse. *Journal of the American Medical Association, 264(19)*, 2511–2518.

Rettig, R. A., & Yarmolinsky, A. (Eds.). (1995). *Federal regulation of methadone treatment*. Washington, DC: National Academy Press.

Sylvestre, D. L., Loftis, J. M., Hauser P., Genser S., Cesari, H., Borek, N., et al. (2004) Co-occurring Hepatitis C, substance use, and psychiatric illness: Treatment issues and developing integrated models of care. *Journal of Urban Health 81(4)*, 719–734.

Thiede, H., Hagan, H., & Murrill, C. S. (2000). Methadone treatment and HIV and hepatitis B and C risk reduction among injectors in the Seattle area. *Journal of Urban Health 77(3)*, 331–345.

Ward, J., Mattick, R. P., & Hall, W. (Eds.). (1998). *Methadone maintenance treatment and other opioid replacement therapies*. Amsterdam: Harwood.

Woody, G. E. (2003). Research findings on psychotherapy of addictive disorders. *American Journal on Addictions, 12(Suppl. 2)*, S19–S26.

Zarkin, G. A., Dunlap, L. J., Hicks, K. A., & Mamo, D. (2005). Benefits and costs of methadone treatment: results from a lifetime simulation model. *Health Economics, 14(11)*, 1133–1150.

Zweben, J. E. (1991). Counseling issues in methadone maintenance treatment. *Journal of Psychoactive Drugs, 23(2)*, 177–190.

JOAN ELLEN ZWEBEN
J. THOMAS PAYTE
REVISED BY T. RON JACKSON (2009)

METHAMPHETAMINE. Methamphetamine, also known as meth, speed, or crank, is an illegal psychostimulant that is abused by more than 35 million individuals worldwide; in contrast, 15 million people in the world abuse cocaine. The structure of methamphetamine is similar to that of amphetamine. Speed is abused because of its powerful stimulant properties that cause the user to experience a longer "high" than the one experienced by people who take cocaine. The drug can be taken in multiple ways, including through oral, intravenous, and smoking routes. Because it is so inexpensive to produce and to buy, users can readily gain access to it. It is eliminated more slowly from the body, and its actions can last 10 times longer than those of cocaine; this allows more time between "hits" and longer binge episodes.

Meth abuse has reached severe epidemic proportions in western, midwestern, and southern U.S. cities. Surveys have shown that about 5.2 percent of the adult U.S. population has used meth at least once, and about 6 percent of high school students have tried it. Meth-related emergency room admissions increased from 10 to 52 per 100,000 admissions between 1992 and 2002. In the past, meth abusers were mostly truck drivers and motorcycle gang members, but more college students and young professionals are now using the drug. The greatest increase in meth use has been among men who have sex with men, because the drug is reported to boost sexual performance. Therefore, there is now a greater occurrence of meth addiction in homosexual and bisexual men than in the general population. These numbers are of concern because meth use leads to participation in high-risk sexual activities, such as frequent changes of sexual partners and involvement in unprotected intercourse.

CLINICAL TOXICOLOGY

Although meth is used because of its euphorigenic effects, the abuse of this drug is associated with serious health consequences in humans. Meth users show acute clinical signs and symptoms that include agitation, anxiety, aggressive behaviors, paranoia, hypertension, hyperthermia, cerebral vasculitis, and psychosis that resemble either manic or schizophrenic symptoms. Physicians from Japan have published papers showing that these psychotic symptoms can be long-lasting. Ingestion of large doses of the drug can cause life-threatening hyperthermia above 41°C (105.8°F), cardiac arrythmias, heart attacks, cerebrovascular accidents or strokes due to hemorrhage or vasospasm, cerebral edema, seizures, renal and liver failure, as well as death.

PSYCHIATRIC PROBLEMS OF ABUSERS

Serious concerns have also arisen over the potential chronic consequences of meth abuse. For example, neuropsychological studies utilizing a battery of tests have shown significant deficits in attention, working memory, and executive functions in chronic meth addicts. Neuroimaging studies have shown extensive damage in the brains of meth abusers. Abusers have persistent decreases in the levels of dopamine (DA) transporters in several regions of their brain. These brain regions include the orbitofrontal cortex, dorsolateral prefrontal cortex, and the caudate-putamen,

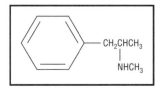

Figure 1. Chemical structure of methamphetamine. ILLUSTRATION BY GGS INFORMATION SERVICES. GALE, CENGAGE LEARNING

which are important in daily decision making. In addition, studies done on the brains of meth abusers who died of an overdose or of other causes exhibit a 50–60 percent decrease in DA levels in the caudate-putamen. DA is the substance that is abnormal in patients who suffer from Parkinson's disease.

The density of serotonin (5-HT) transporters (5-HTT) is also decreased in the brains of meth abusers. This could be related to depression, from which some meth abusers suffer. Structural magnetic resonance imaging (MRI) studies in meth abusers have shown that they lose brain matter in several regions that are important for maintaining attention or making decisions. Therefore, the cognitive impairments and psychiatric symptoms observed in meth users might be related to these toxic effects of the drug on the brain.

See also **Amphetamine Epidemics, International; Designer Drugs; Epidemics of Drug Abuse in the United States.**

BIBLIOGRAPHY

Cadet, J. L., Krasnova, I. N., Jayanthi, S., & Lyles, J. (2007). Neurotoxicity of substituted amphetamines: Molecular and cellular mechanisms. *Neurotoxicity Research, 3*(4), 183–202.

Darke, S., Kaye, S., McKetin, R., & Duflou, J. (2008). Major physical and psychological harms of methamphetamine use. *Drug and Alcohol Review, 27*, 253–262.

Owen, F. (2007). *No speed limit: The highs and lows of meth.* New York: St. Martin's Press.

JEAN LUD CADET

METHANOL. Methanol (methyl alcohol, CH_3OH) is the simplest of the alcohols. It is the natural by-product of wood distillation—an older method of producing drinking alcohol (ethanol). Chemically synthesized methanol is a common industrial solvent found in paint remover, cleansing agents, and antifreeze. It is used to denature the ethanol found in some of these solutions and thereby render them unfit for drinking.

Methanol ingestion is usually accidental, but some alcoholics resort to the desperate measure of consuming methanol when they cannot obtain beverage ethanol. Persons working in poorly ventilated areas can suffer ill effects from inhaling methanol-containing products, and ingestion of methanol is considered a medical emergency. Methanol is metabolized to formaldehyde and formic acid by the same liver enzymes that break down ethanol (these are alcohol dehydrogenase and aldehyde dehydrogenase). The formaldehyde and formic acid are toxic metabolites responsible for the symptoms of methanol poisoning; these appear several hours or days after methanol ingestion. Blurred vision, leading to permanent bilateral blindness, is characteristic of methanol poisoning. The accumulation of formic acid results in severe metabolic acidosis, which can rapidly precipitate coma and death. Other symptoms of methanol toxicity include dizziness, headaches, cold clammy extremities, abdominal pain, vomiting, and severe back pain.

The treatment for methanol poisoning is sodium bicarbonate, given to reverse the acidosis. In more serious cases, dialysis may be required; in addition, ethanol is given intravenously because it competitively binds to alcohol dehydrogenase, thereby slowing the production of toxic metabolites and allowing unchanged methanol to be excreted in the urine.

See also **Alcohol: Chemistry and Pharmacology.**

BIBLIOGRAPHY

Karch, S. B. (2006). *Drug abuse handbook.* Boca Raton, FL: CRC Press.

Klaassen, C. D. (1996). Nonmetallic environmental toxicants: Air pollutants, solvents and vapours, and pesticides, 1673–1696. In Hardman, J.G., Limbird, L. E., Molinoff, P. B., Ruddon, R. W., Gilman, A. G. *The pharmacological basis of therapeutics*, 9th ed. New York: McGraw-Hill Medical. (2005, 11th ed.)

Olson, K. R. (2006). *Poisoning and drug overdose*, 5th ed. New York: McGraw-Hill Medical.

MYROSLAVA ROMACH
KAREN PARKER

METHAQUALONE. Methaqualone is a nonbarbiturate, short-acting sedative-hypnotic drug that has been used to treat insomnia. It was originally introduced in 1951 as a treatment for malaria. In the 1960s and 1970s, it became a popular drug of abuse among college students. Frequently called Quaaludes or "Ludes," the drug, like the short-acting barbiturates, produced euphoric effects; some users claimed it has aphrodisiac effects.

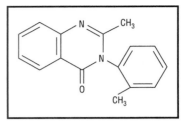

Figure 1. Chemical structure of methaqualone. ILLUSTRATION BY GGS INFORMATION SERVICES. GALE, CENGAGE LEARNING

It is usually taken in pill form, and depending on the dose, the effects last a few hours. The body eliminates about half of the ingested dose in about ten to forty hours, so that even forty-eight hours after ingestion, some drug may still be present. Prolonged use of methaqualone in high doses can lead to tolerance and physical dependence, and abrupt cessation of daily ingestion can result in withdrawal symptoms that are quite similar to those seen in barbiturate withdrawal. Fatal convulsions have resulted from sudden withdrawal. Fatal overdoses can occur when the drug is used alone, but especially when it is mixed with ethanol (alcohol) and/or barbiturates. Because it was so commonly abused in the United States, the drug was shifted to Schedule I of the Controlled Substances Act in the 1980s. Thus it can no longer be prescribed and its nonmedical use is subject to severe criminal penalties. Although methaqualone is rarely used illicitly in the United States, it is still available in other countries and is a drug of abuse in some.

See also **Addiction: Concepts and Definitions.**

BIBLIOGRAPHY

Hanson, G. R., Venturelli, P. J., & Fleckenstein, A. E. (2005). CNS depressants: Sedative-hypnotics. In *Drugs and Society*. Sudbury, MA: Jones & Bartlett Publishers.

Harvey, S. C. (1980). Hypnotics and sedatives. In A. G. Gilman et al. (Eds.), *Goodman and Gilman's the pharmacological basis of therapeutics*, 6th ed. New York: Macmillan. (2005, 11th ed. New York: McGraw-Hill Medical.

SCOTT E. LUKAS

METHEDRINE. Methedrine was the proprietary name given to methamphetamine hydrochloride by the pharmaceutical company Burroughs Wellcome.

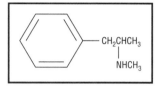

Figure 1. Chemical Structure of methedrine. ILLUSTRATION BY GGS INFORMATION SERVICES. GALE, CENGAGE LEARNING

It was sold in ampules and until 1963–1964 was readily available by prescription. Methedrine (or "meth") became one of the street names of methamphetamine during the 1960s and early 1970s, when high-dose methamphetamine ("speed") was a major drug of abuse. It was a particular problem in northern California where, after the manufacturer withdrew commercially made methedrine from the market in 1963, large quantities of black-market, illicitly synthesized methamphetamine became available for sale.

See also **Amphetamine Epidemics, International; Designer Drugs; Epidemics of Drug Abuse in the United States.**

BIBLIOGRAPHY

Toolaney, G. H. (2006). *New research on methamphetamine abuse.* New York: Nova Science Publishers.

Yudko, E., Hall, H. V., & McPherson, S. B. (2003). *Methamphetamine use: Clinical and forensic aspects.* Boca Raton, FL: CRC Press.

MARIAN W. FISCHMAN

METHYLPHENIDATE. Methylphenidate is a central nervous system stimulant, structurally related and with similar effects to amphetamine. It is used by prescription as Ritalin. It was initially marketed as a mood enhancer in the mid-1950s and described as having less abuse potential than amphetamine; however, within a few years a number of dramatic reports of its abuse and toxicity were published. Methylphenidate is commercially available (by prescription) in pill form, reaching peak effect in one to two hours. Like the amphetamines and other stimulant drugs, methylphenidate is a controlled substance, placed in Schedule II of the Controlled Substances Act to indicate that although it has medical utility, it also has substantial abuse liability.

In most people, methylphenidate increases general levels of activity, decreases food intake, produces positive subjective effects (an elevated mood), and can interfere with sleep. With continued use, tolerance can develop to these effects; users will often escalate their doses to achieve the desired effects of their initial doses of methylphenidate. Continued high-dose methylphenidate use can result in toxic consequences similar to those seen after amphetamine use—with anxiety, sleeplessness, and eventually a toxic paranoid psychosis. High-dose users often begin with oral methylphenidate use but switch to injecting the drug in order to maximize the effect and achieve the initial "rush" that is typical of intravenous drug abuse. Commercially manufactured methylphenidate pills (the only form available) contain talcum, an insoluble substance, which can cause toxic effects (such as abscesses) when the pills are dissolved in water and injected intravenously or under the skin.

Laboratory animals tested with methylphenidate show increases in locomotor activity after single doses; increased sensitivity to this effect after repeated doses; and the development of stereotyped repetitive behavior patterns after chronic dosing. In addition, these animals remain more responsive to methylphenidate even after the drug treatment has been discontinued. It has been suggested that the continuous repetition of behavior that characterizes the response to chronic methylphenidate treatment is a good model for the human stimulant psychosis. As in animals, humans who use high doses become increasingly sensitive to such stimulants as methylphenidate, with psychosis increasingly likely at lower doses after its initial appearance. There are, however, no data to support this hypothesis.

In addition to its action as an appetite suppressant, methylphenidate has been found to have other therapeutic utility. Like *d*-amphetamine, it has been used successfully in the treatment of attention-deficit hyperactivity disorder (ADHD), a syndrome that first becomes evident during childhood and is characterized by excessive activity and difficulty in maintaining attention. Because of its relatively short half-life, two or three doses of methylphenidate are required each day, although recently a slow-release form of the medication has become available, promising more stable blood levels with only a single daily dosing. Methylphenidate has been shown to alleviate or moderate many of the symptoms of this disorder, although it is not effective in all cases and its long-term efficacy is not well understood.

Side effects of treatment can include insomnia, loss of appetite, and weight loss, all effects of stimulant drugs in general. In addition, concern about the longer-lasting effects on learning and cognition in youngsters maintained on this drug for many years has made practitioners cautious and often unwilling to prescribe it. Recent research and practice, however, has supported methylphenidate as the stimulant of choice for treating this disorder. As with the amphetamines, methylphenidate is also effective in the treatment of narcolepsy, in which sudden attacks of sleep can occur unexpectedly.

See also **Amphetamine; Anxiety; Attention Deficit Hyperactivity Disorder.**

BIBLIOGRAPHY

Greenhill, L. L. (2000). *Ritalin: Theory and practice*, 2nd ed. New York: Mary Ann Liebert.

Grilly, D. M. (1989). *Drugs and human behavior.* Needham, MA: Allyn & Bacon. (2005, 5th ed.)

Iversen, L. (2008). *Speed, ecstasy, ritalin: The science of amphetamines.* New York: Oxford University Press USA.

Kalant, O. J. (1973). *The amphetamines: Toxicity and addiction*, 2nd ed. Springfield, IL: Charles C. Thomas.

MARIAN W. FISCHMAN

MEXICO. The following text will discuss different issues of the addictive substances in Mexico, with a special focus in psychoactive drugs: the evolution of the trends in their consumption; the changes in official perceptions of drugs; the organized crime dimension of the problem; some of the policies that the Mexican government has developed to confront the drug trafficking; and the general perspective of the bilateral relation of Mexico and the United States on the topic.

THE ILLICIT DRUG TRADE

A number of different plants that are used to produce psychoactive substances and drugs have long been a natural part of the Mexican landscape. In the fields of some states, including Oaxaca, Guerrero, Michoacán, Sinaloa, Durango, and Chihuahua, the marijuana plant (*Cannabis sativa*) grows naturally, while some states, such as Guerrero, Sinaloa, and Durango, have been fertile ground for the opium poppy (*Papaver somniferum*). Such other states as San Luis Potosí, Chihuahua, Oaxaca, and some others in the central region, are native soil for a variety of hallucinogenic plants, principally the peyote cactus (*Lophophora williamsii*), which contains the psychoactive substance mescaline.

In Sinaloa, for example, one of the emblematic states of modern drug production in Mexico, statistical data show that the opium poppy and marijuana plant were part of the local flora in 1886. In the nineteenth century, it was not illegal to grow, possess, use, or sell such plants; in addition they had a number of legal uses, including medical and industrial purposes.

In the early twentieth century, however, the Mexican government began to legislate the use of these plants and substances. Despite these early prohibitions, the plants continued to be harvested for illegal use. Since that time all these states have been affected by the increasing development of illegal organizations seeking to profit from the illicit drug business.

By 1926 there were several cultivated poppy fields in Sonora in northwestern Mexico. The opium produced there went to the Chinese community in Mexico and to the U.S. market. The smoking of opium was associated with Chinese communities, and it fostered racist attitudes and actions against the Chinese. There were even policies of segregation in some northern states, such as Sinaloa and Sonora, at this time.

The expansion of the illegal export of illicit substances strained U.S.-Mexico relations. By 1947 the U.S. Federal Bureau of Narcotics estimated that Mexican poppies covered 4,000 to 5,000 hectares (10,000 to 12,500 acres), yielding between 32 and 40 metric tons of opium, at least half of which was turned into morphine or heroin. Mexican brown heroin became an increasingly important staple in the U.S. market, where it served as a substitute for white heroin from the Middle East and Far East from the 1950s through the 1970s.

Beginning in the 1970s, Mexico also became an important bridge for South American drugs such as cocaine (methylbenzoyl ecgonine) and white heroin, a purer version of the brown heroin processed in Mexico. These drugs are generally smuggled into Mexican territory from Colombia and Peru. In addition, from the 1990s through the first decade of the twenty-first century, such synthetic drugs as methamphetamine were increasingly being produced in clandestine laboratories in Mexico.

THE CONSUMPTION OF ILLICIT AND LICIT ADDICTIVE SUBSTANCES

According to Astorga (2005, pp. 17–24), between 1888 and 1911 the importation of opium to Mexico ranged from 800 kilograms (about 1,600 pounds) to around 12 tons. Although the opium poppy was part of the flora of Mexico, the chemical process to turn it into drugs was developed and used mostly by pharmaceutical laboratories of more industrialized countries. The product usually came from Europe and the United States; and the use of opium derivates, for medical purposes, was legal and accepted. In the eighteenth century, curative properties were attributed to such substances as cocaine (which was diluted in wine) and marijuana (which was purported to heal asthma), and they were sold legally. Until the 1930s, it was not unusual for such substances to be considered curative, and they were advertised as such throughout the country.

There is no evidence of serious problems of addiction within the Mexican population during the eighteenth and nineteenth centuries, and even up to the second third of the twentieth century. This is partly because recreational drug use was not common, while medical usage generally encouraged a controlled pattern of consumption as recommended by healthcare practitioners and the pharmaceutical laboratories (Astorga 2005, p. 24). In fact, up until the last third of the twentieth century the recreational use of such drugs was not socially supported. Even in the areas where marijuana and amapola (poppies) were grown, there was an implicit cultural framework that allowed men to drink alcohol in large quantities as a way to show their manhood but discouraged the use of drugs because it was considered a sign of a weak spirit.

However, these patterns of consumption have changed to a certain degree, and the use of these drugs has increased consistently since the 1980s, especially in some urban zones. For example, between 1988 and 1998, the consumption of marijuana in males between thirty-five and sixty-five years of age increased from 3.6 percent to 9.8 percent. Among the same population, cocaine use grew from 0.4 percent to 2.1 percent. Heroin usage also grew from 0.01 percent to 0.3 percent, but its consumption is still considered marginal. A survey of Observatorio Epidemiológico de las Drogas (Epidemiologic Observatory of Drugs), published in 2001, revealed that only 1 percent of the population had used marijuana more than fifty times in their lives, while 0.3 percent had used cocaine in this quantity, and only 0.1 percent had consumed this much heroin.

Data from the 2002 *Encuesta Nacional de Adicciones* (National Survey of Addictions) revealed that 3,508,641 persons in Mexico had used illicit drugs at some point in their lives. Data from the Consejo Nacional de Población (National Council of Population) establishes that in 2002, the population of Mexico approximated 103 million people.

Of this universe of consumers, 1,182,345 had used drugs more than six times in their lives. The most commonly used drug was marijuana and the second was cocaine. The utilization of heroin was marginal, however. This preference in consumption was consistent between the early 1990s and 2002.

Information from 2001 established that drug consumption was highest in the city of Tijuana, where 6.7 percent of the population had used drugs at some point in their lives, followed by Ciudad Juárez (5 percent), Ciudad de Mexico (3.3 percent), Guadalajara (2.2 percent, which is the national average), Monterrey (1 percent), and Matamoros (0.9 percent).

The National Survey of Addictions (2002) reveals that licit addictive substances clearly have a wider use than illicit substances in Mexico, as they do elsewhere. In 2002, it was reported that more than 16,371,601 people in the country smoked tobacco, and 1,009,128 of them were considered to be dependent on it. At the same time 7,639,874 consumed cigarettes on a daily basis but did not show symptoms of dependency. Of the total population of smokers, 71.8 percent were older than 35 years of age; 25.7 percent were between 18 and

34 years old; and 2.5 percent were legally under age for smoking tobacco.

Alcohol has also been a frequently used substance in Mexican culture, and it has had a tradition of wider social acceptance than psychoactive substances and illicit drugs. In 2002 the number of people who had consumed alcohol at least once during their lifetime was 32,315,760. Of these, 4,914,166 reported that they drank from one to four times a week, while 947,099 declared that they consumed alcohol almost daily.

Official consumption surveys have been a useful tool in evaluating drug trends among the Mexican population. The methodology used is believed to be accurate and is generally compatible with international standards. However, one of the concerns that has arisen is the long delay in the disclosure of the data. The 2002 National Survey of Addictions was still the most recent source of information in 2008 because the 2004 survey had not yet been released. This delay presents obvious difficulties in evaluating consumption trends, making it extremely difficult to determine if the use of drugs is becoming a greater or lesser problem within the Mexican population.

DRUG CONTROL AND THE EVOLUTION OF THE PROBLEM

Mexico's international drug-control efforts began with the Shanghai Convention of 1909 and the Hague Opium Convention of 1911–1912. Drugs were proscribed through different legal measures during the first third of the twentieth century. In 1920 the Mexican government forbade the growing of marijuana and restricted the cultivation of poppies. In 1923 Mexico's president, Álvaro Obregón, prohibited the production of opium. By the early 1920s the Mexican press had begun to publish reports of isolated violent crimes committed by intoxicated people. The statistical data, however, do not support an assessment that drugs were causing higher levels of violence at this time. While this was a relatively violent period in Mexican history, the causes of this violence were mainly due to the aftereffects of the Mexican Civil War (1910–1920).

During this period, Mexican authorities agreed to cooperate with international efforts to reduce the supply of illicit psychoactive drugs, particularly measures aimed at poppy and marijuana cultivation. This was more a gesture of good will to international cooperation than a strong effort to solve an unperceived problem for the country. In 1934, President Lázaro Cárdenas del Río created the government's first centralized narcotics unit. Because drugs were considered a public health problem rather than a criminal problem, the unit was put under the direction of the secretary of health.

Mexico gradually moved toward a more restrictive policy against narcotics, including the use of law enforcement agencies, but it was not until the late 1990s that the effects of crime rings and violence related to drugs became a real concern. Despite official speeches by high-ranking public servants, the perspective of the Mexican government and the public was that Mexico merely served as a "bridge" for foreign drugs on their way to the big market in the north. The customary public discourse was to blame the demand for drugs in the United States for all the undesirable issues related to drugs in Mexico.

OPERATION CONDOR AND CORRUPTION

It was not until 1975 that the Mexican federal government developed a more concerted effort to eradicate the illicit cultivation of psychoactive plants. This effort, known as "Operation Condor," included the deployment of 10,000 troops in the rural areas of the most affected states (Sinaloa, Durango, and Chihuahua), as well as enforcement operations by the Dirección Federal de Seguridad (Federal Security Directorate, or DFS) in the cities. The origins of this effort can be traced to American public concern about drug shipments that were smuggled through the Mexican frontier. U.S. pressures had led to the virtual closure of the border in the San Ysidro area for three weeks in 1969, and the Mexican government eventually felt the need to take stronger actions.

The campaign produced some results in the short term, but it certainly did not eradicate the drug problem in Mexico. Unfortunately, the operation led to a dramatic increase in human rights abuses and to higher levels of corruption in the federal agencies, especially the DFS. Some of this agency's chief commanders became protectors of criminal groups, and some became drug traffickers themselves. The involvement of several DFS commanders in the protection of drug-trafficking operations was uncovered after Enrique Camarena, an agent of the U.S. Drug Enforcement Agency (DEA), was kidnapped, tortured, and murdered in 1985. The murder was plotted by Rafael Caro Quintero, a member of the ring of Miguel Angel Félix Gallardo, and owner of Rancho "El Búfalo," in Chihuahua, where in November 1984 a massive quantity of marijuana (between 5,000 and 10,000 tons) was discovered under the custody of DFS agents. Camarena's murder was assumed to be a retaliation for the seizure of El Búfalo. The high level of corruption within DFS was clear when Caro Quintero was arrested after Camarena's murder: he had an official identification as a DFS member, signed by his General Director, Antonio Zorrilla Pérez. The level of corruption became so untenable at this point that the DFS was dissolved.

The murder of Camarena focused public attention on the decreasing effectiveness of Mexican drug-control efforts and the pervasive corruption that had eroded Mexican security institutions. It was also a turning point in U.S.-Mexico relations. Drugs became a confrontational issue at uncharacteristically high levels of the two governments. Both the U.S. secretary of state and Mexico's foreign minister spoke of the murder (and the subsequent government response) as a paramount diplomatic issue. From this point forward, drug control would no longer be treated only as a law-enforcement issue. In response to continuing U.S. pressure, the Mexican government took a series of actions that resulted in the apprehension and incarceration of several drug traffickers. Nevertheless, trafficking and corruption increased, and tensions between the two governments remained high throughout the 1990s.

In the mid-1970s and early 1980s, the traffic in cocaine also increased in Mexico. The United States strengthened its patrols along the shores of Miami, which pushed the already dominant Colombian cartels to seek out different routes for their illegal product. This development then fostered contacts between Mexican and Colombian traffickers. Up until this time, the Mexican drug rings dealt only with marijuana and lower-quality heroin, but this new relationship with the Colombians allowed them to trade in cocaine, a drug that was more in demand and more profitable.

At the beginning of this alliance, the Colombian cartels used their Mexican partners merely to carry their product; but different local conditions, the presence of Mexican criminal networks that had already commercialized other drugs, and the often necessary passage through Mexican territory to reach the U.S. market led to a larger role for the Mexican cartels. In the first decade of the twenty-first century, U.S. authorities estimated that around 80 percent of the cocaine that reached American territory was coming through Mexico and being transported by Mexican criminal organizations.

The Mexican cartels further strengthened their power during the 1990s, and the corruption problems within the government agencies remained. Even higher Mexican officials were prosecuted for protecting criminal organizations, including Jesús Gutiérrez Rebollo, the director of the National Institute to Combat Drugs (INCD), who was arrested on corruption charges in 1997. He was condemned by Mexican courts for crimes against health (*delitos contra la salud*), organized crime (*delincuencia organizada*) and bribery (cohecho). He has been in a high security prison at Almoloya de Juárez, Estado de México since the year of his arrest.

Several authoritarian features of the Mexican political regime of this period, which was marked by decades of one-party rule, actually encouraged the drug business. There were high levels of impunity within the government and a gradual loss of control of the different security institutions, leading to a weak rule of law, poor accountability, and a strongly rooted belief in the private use of public resources. The administration of President Ernesto Zedillo (1994–2000) dealt a blow to the corrupt political structure that protected drug-trafficking operations, but it could not dismantle it completely. In 1997 the level of cooperation between Mexico and the United States was improved through the establishment of the United States-Mexico Bi-National Drug Strategy, which was an effort to create a more integrated effort to confront the drug problem.

A NEW PRESIDENT AND RENEWED HOPE

The 2000 election of Vicente Fox as president marked the end of seventy-one years of rule by the Institutional Revolutionary Party (PRI). Along with renewed hopes for a democratic revival, there were expectations of a dramatic change in the fight against drug trafficking and corruption. The Fox administration (2000–2006) was able to bring some important kingpins to justice but lacked an internal strategy to confront the criminal organizations, and did not continue its predecessors fight against high-level corruption. Several of these groups were thus able to maintain or even increase their operations. Ironically, as these criminal organizations grew stronger, they found they were no longer hemmed in by the corrupt schemes of the old regime. As in many corrupt systems, various mechanisms of control had been established by the police and other government agencies, and these had served to constrain the criminal enterprises to some extent. Corruption remained embedded in local institutions; neither did it completely disappear from the federal government.

The most powerful drug organizations in Mexico in 2006 were the Sinaloa Cartel, directed by Joaquín "el Chapo" Guzmán Loera; the Gulf Cartel, which was led by Osiel Cárdenas until he was extradited to the United States in 2007; the Juárez Cartel, of the Carrillo Fuentes family and whose former leader, Amado Carrillo-Fuentes, died in 1997; the Tijuana Cartel, also known as the Arellano-Felix Cartel; the Millenium Cartel, led by Armando and Luis Valencia; the Amezcua-Contreras organization; and the Díaz Parada Cartel, whose leader, Pedro Díaz Parada, was arrested in January of 2007.

The pervasive corruption in local public power matched the interest of unleashed criminal groups in escaping the constraints placed on them by the old mechanisms of control that Federal police exerted. Under the Fox administration, criminal organizations sought to expand their areas of influence and control strategic places from which to export drugs to the American market. They also increased their ability to sell drugs in Mexico itself. A weakened federal capacity to impose the rule of law (or even the old clandestine agreements), the lack of political will to fight corruption that protected the criminal organizations, and the ambitions of criminal organizations resulted in previously unseen levels of drug-related violence. There is no official account of the homicides linked to the struggles of the cartels during this period; but prestigious press publications, such as *Reforma Daily*, have estimated that more than 12,000 people were killed between 2000 and 2007.

In the last third of his administration, Vicente Fox developed a program called *México Seguro* (Operation Secure Mexico), which was designed to reduce this violence. It consisted principally of the federal forces patrolling the streets of some cities and the establishment of checkpoints along certain highways. The results were poor, however, even though Mexican eradication efforts had improved since the mid-1990s. President Felipe Calderón, who took office on December 1, 2006, has shown an especial interest in fighting Mexican drug-trafficking organizations, and his government has deployed military forces in the states that have been most affected by drug-related violence. His administration has also been open to wider international cooperation, especially with the United States. For example, some of the important drug kingpins that were in Mexican prisons were extradited to the United States at the beginning of Calderón's tenure. The government has also set up a support plan, called *Iniciativa Mérida*, which will distribute material resources from the U.S. government—US $1.5 billion distributed over three years—in order to reinforce Mexican capabilities against drug organizations. The violence continues, however, and it is not clear that the new strategy will be effective in controlling the drug problem. Many feel that the policy lacks a core component necessary for it to succeed. They feel that the lack of a strategy to fight the corruption, which has been the central factor eroding the nation's capacity to control violence and drugs, dooms the policy to failure.

See also **Bolivia; Colombia; Drug Interdiction; International Drug Supply Systems.**

BIBLIOGRAPHY

Astorga, L. (2005). *El Siglo de las Drogas: El narcotráfico, del Porfiriato al nuevo milenio.* Mexico City: Plaza y Janés.

Bureau of International Narcotics Matters, U.S. Department of State. (1991, 1992). *International narcotics control strategy report (INCSR).* Washington, DC: Author.

Consejo Nacional Contra las Adicciones. (2004). *Encuesta Nacional de Adicciones 2002 (ENA 2002).* Mexico City: Instituto Nacional de Estadística, Geografía e Informática (INEGI).

Courtwright, D. (2001) *Forces of habit: Drugs and the making of the modern world.* Cambridge, MA: Harvard University Press.

Craig, R. (1980). Operation Condor: Mexico's anti-drug campaign enters a new era. *Journal of Interamerican Studies and World Affairs, 22(3),* 346–347.

Craig, R. (1980). Operation Intercept: The international politics of pressure. *Review of Politics, 42*(4), 556–580.

Craig, R. (1987). *United States antidrug policy with Mexico: Consequences for American society and U.S.-Mexican relations.* Paper presented to the Bilateral Commission on the Future of United States-Mexican Relations, Queretaro, Mexico.

Flores, C. (2005). *El Estado en crisis: crimen organizado y política. Desafíos para la consolidación democrática.* Unpublished doctoral dissertation, Universidad Nacional Autónoma de México, Mexico City.

Observatorio Epidemiológico en Drogas (2001). *El fenómeno de las adicciones en México.* Mexico City: Secretaría de Salud, 17–25.

Partiva, V. (2002). *Situación demográfica actual.* Mexico City: Consejo Nacional de Población, 1–2.

Van Wert, J. M. (1982). *Government of Mexico herbicidal opium poppy eradication program: A summative evaluation.* Unpublished doctoral dissertation, University of Southern California, Los Angeles.

Van Wert, J. M. (1986). El control de los narcóticos en México: Una década de institucionalización y un asunto diplomático (Mexican narcotics control: A decade of institutionalization and a matter for diplomacy). In Gabriel Szekely (Ed.), *Mexico-Estados Unidos 1985.* Mexico City: Colegio de Mexico.

Walker, W. O., III. (1989). *Drug control in the Americas.* (Rev. ed.) Albuquerque: University of New Mexico Press.

White House Office of National Drug Control Policy. (2000). *National Drug Control Strategy: 2000 Annual Report.* Washington, DC: Author.

JAMES VAN WERT
REVISED BY CARLOS ANTONIO FLORES PÉREZ (2009)

MICHIGAN ALCOHOLISM SCREENING TEST (MAST).

The Michigan Alcoholism Screening Test (MAST) is a brief self-report questionnaire designed to detect alcoholism (Selzer 1971). The twenty-four items were designed to provide a consistent, quantifiable structured interview that could be rapidly administered by nonprofessional as well as professional personnel. Although it was once used widely in clinical and research settings, it has since been supplanted by such other screening tests as the Alcohol Use Disorders Identification

Test. The twenty-four scored items assess symptoms and consequences of alcohol abuse, such as guilt about drinking; blackouts; delirium tremens; loss of control; family, social, employment, and legal problems following drinking bouts; and help-seeking behaviors, such as attending Alcoholics Anonymous meetings or entering a hospital because of drinking. Symptoms included in the MAST are not explicitly linked to any standard diagnostic system, such as the criteria for alcohol dependence in *DSM-IV* or *ICD-10*. Rather, the items were derived from the author's clinical experience or borrowed from epidemiological surveys of alcoholism and problem drinking conducted in the 1960s.

To complete the MAST, individuals answer yes or no to each item. The items are weighted on a scale of 1 to 5, depending on the assumed severity of the symptom. For example, items concerning prior alcohol-related treatment experiences and help-seeking behaviors receive higher weights. The total MAST score (range: 0–53) is derived by adding the weighted scores from all items that are endorsed. Studies indicate that the long version of the MAST possesses good internal-consistency reliability, as indicated by Cronbach's alpha coefficients of .83 to .93 (Gibbs 1983). This result suggests that the scale measures a unitary disorder.

Selzer (1971) originally recommended adopting a cutting score of 5 or higher for a diagnosis of alcoholism with the MAST. However, since this cutting score produced a relatively high percentage of false positives (Gibbs 1983), Selzer, Vinokur, and van Rooijen (1975) suggested the following cut points: 0 to 4, absence of alcoholism; 5 to 6, possible alcoholism; 7 or more, probable alcoholism. Skinner (1982) recommended that scores of 7 to 24 be regarded as clear evidence of alcohol problems, and that scores of over 25 be considered evidence of substantial alcohol problems. Ross, Gavin, and Skinner (1990) compared scores on the MAST to diagnoses of alcoholism obtained from the National Institute of Mental Health Diagnostic Interview Schedule (NIMH-DIS) (Robins, et al. 1981). A score of 13 or greater yielded the highest overall classification accuracy.

Several shorter versions of the MAST have been developed, including the thirteen-item Short-MAST (SMAST) (Selzer, et al. 1975) and the ten-item Brief-MAST (Pokorny, et al. 1972). The validity of the MAST has been examined in a number of studies in which MAST scores, or scores from the shorter versions of the instrument, were compared to other measures of drinking status, including diagnostic interviews, physicians' diagnoses, and other self-report instruments. In reviewing twelve of these studies, Gibbs (1983) concluded that MAST diagnoses agreed with diagnoses of alcoholism reached through other assessment procedures in about 75 percent of cases. Where inconsistencies between results were found, the MAST tended to overdiagnose alcoholism. This finding probably reflects the fact that a cutting score of 5 or higher on the MAST was used in these studies. By adopting a cutting score of 13, Ross and colleagues (1990) were able to achieve a greater degree of agreement when comparing MAST scores to DIS-derived diagnoses.

As with any instrument that relies on the veracity of self-report information, the reliability and validity of the MAST are dependent on the willingness of the interviewee to answer the items truthfully. All the items possess high face validity, which means it is relatively easy to answer so as to appear non-alcoholic. The MAST may, therefore, not be a useful screening tool with individuals who are motivated to conceal their alcohol problems.

See also **Addiction Severity Index (ASI); Diagnosis of Substance Use Disorders: Diagnostic Criteria; Diagnostic and Statistical Manual (DSM); Minnesota Multiphasic Personality Inventory (MMPI); Models of Alcoholism and Drug Abuse.**

BIBLIOGRAPHY

Gibbs, L. E. (1983). Validity and reliability of the Michigan Alcoholism Screening Test: A review. *Drug and Alcohol Dependency, 12,* 279–285.

Pokorny, A. D., Miller, B. A., & Kaplan, H. B. (1972). The brief MAST: A shortened version of the Michigan Alcoholism Screening Test. *American Journal of Psychiatry, 129,* 118–121.

Robins, L. N., Helzer, J. E., Croughan, J., & Ratcliff, J. S. (1981). National Institute of Mental Health Diagnostic Interview Schedule: History, characteristics, and validity. *Archives of General Psychiatry, 38,* 381–389.

Ross, H. E., Gavin, D. R., & Skinner, H. A. (1990). Diagnostic validity of the MAST and the Alcohol Dependence Scale in the assessment of DSM-III alcohol disorders. *Journal of Studies on Alcohol, 51,* 506–513.

Selzer, M. L. (1971). The Michigan Alcoholism Screening Test: The quest for a new diagnostic instrument. *American Journal of Psychiatry, 127,* 1653–1658.

Selzer, M. L., Vinokur, A., & van Rooijen, L. (1975). A self-administered short version of the Michigan Alcoholism Screening Test (SMAST). *Journal of Studies on Alcohol, 43,* 117–126.

Skinner, H. A. (1982). *Guidelines for using the Michigan Alcoholism Screening Test.* Toronto: Addiction Research Foundation.

A. THOMAS MCLELLAN
REVISED BY THOMAS F. BABOR (2009)

MIDDLE EAST. Persia was one of the first regions to cultivate and consume wine. Jars found in the Zagros Mountains dating from 5400 to 5000 BCE. contain remnants of wine. Writings found at Persepolis highlight the extensive wine consumption at Persian banquets. The Greek philosopher Herodotus commented on the abundance of wine in Persia and its extensive use during feasts.

WINE

Within pre-Islamic Zoroastrianism, wine symbolized liquid gold and the fire of the sun. Drinking wine at dawn represented the joining together of the new moon and the sun. When the ruler (*sahibqiran*) drank wine, he brought the two together becoming the *master of conjunction*, the title of the Shah.

Islamic prohibitions against the use of alcohol never eradicated its use. Sufis and other sects such as Qalanders defied religious orthodoxy with their open consumption of alcohol. Persian poetry from the Islamic era, in fact, contains positive wine imagery celebrating Dionysian excess.

The Mongols, who dominated vast areas of the Middle East in the thirteenth century, both drank and were licentious. The Mongol taste for alcohol shifted from fermented mare's milk to stronger varieties when they conquered Persia. Brothels and taverns flourished under Mongol rule (1295–1304) within Persia. This culture of excessive alcohol consumption affected the early Ottoman sultans Bayazid I (1389–1402), as well as Timur Lang, the central Asian warlord, and Sultan Babur (1483–1530), founder of the Indian Mughals.

When the Christian territories of Georgia and Armenia both fell under Persian suzerainty, large numbers of enslaved males were forced into the elite Ghulam military caste. Nominally converting to Islam, they brought their wine-making skills into elite Safavid Persian society.

The Persian town of Shiraz became famous for its red and white wine brewed by Armenian and Jewish minorities. Shiraz wine was reserved specifically for the Shah. Iranian rulers generally only consumed Persian wine and abhorred the alcoholic gifts presented by Europeans. The poor did not consume alcohol because it was reserved for the elites. The decisive defeat at the battle of Chaldiran in 1514 by the Ottoman Turks was perceived to have been caused by inebriated commanders.

The Safavid rulers initiated periodic edicts banning alcohol for various reasons: for atonement, to display leadership strength, due to a pious vizier's influence, because of adverse economic conditions, due to the need to raise taxes from a minority, for scapegoating, or as a result of health advice provided by a physician. Essentially these edicts were attempts to set limits on public behavior, but they never affected choices within private spaces. Therefore, what happened in people's homes was left to the residents, and alcohol consumption was never eradicated. The royal cellars were locked, for example, but their contents were never destroyed.

With the development of distilled liquors in the West, the elite tastes in the Ottoman and Qajar dynasties changed to rum, vodka, and champagne. Concurrent with the increase in consumption of distilled liquors, there was a decline in religious observance in the latter part of the nineteenth century and a growing belief in Sufism. The general open disregard for religious observance and the adoption of English and French cultural tastes outraged the religious orthodoxy.

TOBACCO

The English began to use tobacco extensively around 1580. Persia and the Middle East were introduced to tobacco by Portuguese sailors around 1590. By 1620 the German traveler Heinrich von Poser noted the extensive use of tobacco in Qandahar. The English originally imported tobacco to the region, although its strong flavor and cost allowed the Indian variety with its milder taste and affordability to capture the market.

In the 1650s tobacco imports dwindled as the Persians cultivated the plant. By 1700 Persia was exporting tobacco to the Ottoman Empire and Russia. The main form of inhalation was performed via a water pipe and the Iranian varieties were grown specifically for this market. The use of tobacco grew among the poor, the military, and the social elite. People differentiated their social status by the tobacco ritual and the implements they used. The poor used the base of a coconut or a gourd and the rich had jewel-encrusted crystal pipes, known as *qalyan*.

OPIUM

Opium was used throughout ancient Middle Eastern civilizations. Sumerians, Assyrians, Babylonians, and Egyptians, all describe its use in their earliest recorded histories. Grown extensively in Asia Minor and in Mesopotamia, it was traded among the Greeks, Jews, Persians, and Carthaginians. Part of an international currency, opium was used for various ancient economies among people involved in trade, slavery, travel, and war.

The evidence for widespread opium use in the Middle East is derived from a number of historical sources. The Roman writer Prosper Alpinus stated Egyptian opium was consumed in the form of *cretic wine opium*, a wine flavored with spices. The Egyptian town Sicyon became known to the Greeks as Mekone, a Greek work for poppy, so named for its extensive opium cultivation. The *Ebers Papyrus*, dating from 1500 BCE, describes an Egyptian opium mixture used to put children to sleep and stop them from crying. Homer (ninth century BCE) mentions opium in his epics *Iliad* and *Odyssey* as being used by warriors. Nepenthes (from a Greek word meaning "grief or sorrow") fortified with opiates became the drink of forgetfulness, used by Greek warriors before battle to dull their fears. The Greek god of sleep Hypnos is depicted as pouring poppy juice over his eyelids to assist his descent into sleep. Opium-laced electuaries (from a Greek word meaning "to lick up", medicinal mixtures made with jam or honey) were also used within the ancient world to prolong and enhance sexual performance. In Jewish history bronze coins of John Hyrcanus, prince and high-priest of the race of the Maccabees (135–106 BCE), portray the poppy plant. Hebrews called it *ophion*; Arabs, *af-yun*; the Chinese, *o-fuyung*; and the Greeks, *opion*.

After the Islamic conquest of the ancient world, Arab physicians drew on this ancient knowledge.

Opium was used to cure diarrhea. Avicenna (CE 980–1037, Abū 'Alī al-Husayn ibn Sina) described opium as the most powerful of the soporifics in *The Canon of Medicine*. This classic text, which was translated into Latin in 1175, became the standard medical textbook until the seventeenth century. The noted Ottoman physician Serafeddin Sabuncuoglu used opium in the fourteenth century to treat headaches, migraines, and other ailments as noted in his *Surgical Atlas.*

Opium was apparently brought to China and other parts of the eastern world in the ninth century by Arab traders. In 1511, while he was in India, Duarte Barbosa described opium as an Indian product in his description of the Malabar Coast. In 1546, French naturalist Pierre Belon traveled through Asia Minor and Egypt and found its extensive use among Turkish people, who were impoverished by their addiction.

In Persia during the Safavid period (1501–1722), opium was used by all social classes. It was more easily obtained than alcohol and had less religious strictures placed upon its use. Although widespread among the intelligentsia it was also extensively used by the poor. Opium was cheap, suppressed the appetite, and alleviated misery. It was also used by soldiers to boost strength, administered as a medicine, and used by libertines to prolong sexual satisfaction.

Although subject to ban in the Qajar period (1794–1906), in 1796 the population ignored the ban. Opium, though ingested widely in the Persian Empire, was consumed within limits. Women and men used the drug as a panacea for the rigors of aging, to fortify the body and the spirit against the loss of physical strength.

In the 1880s there was a gradual switch from opium eating to opium smoking. Drug use became a paramount preoccupation. The change arose from the introduction of smokable forms of opium from China.

Iran's increasing use of opium was supported by internal production. As an example, in 1859, around 42,000 pounds of opium were grown. By 1926, the amount had increased to one million pounds. Initially Iranian merchants tried to export opium to China thereby undercutting the British trade. The British responded by imposing high tariffs, which made the trade expensive and led to adulteration of the drug to boost profits. Chinese dissatisfaction caused the trade to dwindle in the late nineteenth century. However, Iranian peasants switched from growing cereals to poppy cultivation, and new markets opened as Iranian opium became the major export crop. The effect on the home market was extensive. In 1910 opium smoking was banned, although the population could still consume it. In 1928 a taxation system was introduced to limit production and consumption.

In 1936 Iran was producing 1,350 tons of opium, one of the largest supplies in the world, earning the country 15 percent of its foreign exchange. Iran's drug using population was second only to China by 1949, with an estimated 1.3 million people addicted, one in nine of the population. Iran exported opium to the Allies and the Axis Powers during World War II. Iran's great families had become rich from the opium trade, including the Pahlevi family, the ruling dynasty that owned numerous opium fields. In 1943 following the Third Millspaugh mission, the United States took over the Iranian economy, which involved overseeing the opium production. Iranian opium was sent to Kachin soldiers in Burma by the United States.

Between 1951 and 1953 Prime Minister Mohammed Mossadegh (1882–1967) of Iran banned opium consumption and production. His government also nationalized oil firms, which resulted in Operation Ajax, a coup organized by the British and American Secret Services. During the ban the estimated number of addicts fell to 350,000. Production shifted to Turkey and Afghanistan, which produced opium and heroin for Iranians. The ban in Iran lasted nominally for 14 years, but U.S. antinarcotic sources noted the ban did not apply to the ruling family who returned to power with U.S. and British support. Iran bordered the U.S.S.R. and was a bulwark against Soviet expansion into the oilfields of the Middle East. Following the toppling of Mossadegh, heroin use continued to escalate.

The Iranian revolution of 1979 created a seismic shift in Middle Eastern politics, producing the first nonaligned Muslim state following the abdication of the shah. Smokable forms of heroin were introduced in the United Kingdom by Iranian refugees fleeing the revolution.

Any nominal limits placed upon the internal opium trade by the previous regime disintegrated. Ayatollah Khomeini (1902–1989), although denouncing drug dealers as traitors, concentrated on banning alcohol. Despite the Western perception that the regime had complete authoritarian control, drug use significantly increased with an estimated 2 million people addicted. With the explosion in drug use, Iranian drug cultivation expanded to meet the new demand. This meant the Afghan/Pakistan heroin production could no longer penetrate this particular market and had to find other trade routes.

OPIUM AND WAR IN THE MIDDLE EAST (AFGHANISTAN, LEBANON, AND IRAQ)

The war in Afghanistan against the Soviets from 1978 until 1989 allowed Afghan heroin to find a new supply route onto the streets of Berlin, Amsterdam, Milan, and London rather than into the streets of Tehran. It was through this burgeoning opium trade the *mujaheddin* (holy warriors) were able to finance their war of liberation and establish a Muslim state. The mujaheddin were assisted by Western security forces that financed Hekmatyar, an Afghani heroin warlord. The Afghani heroin trade expanded in response to the 1979 Soviet invasion, destabilizing the region.

The United States had maintained a constant presence in Lebanon following World War II. There, the U.S. provided support for the Christian Maronite community, who were involved extensively in the growth and distribution of Lebanese cannabis. In 1958 the CIA assisted the Christian Maronites in gaining political power by becoming involved in elections in Lebanon. Subsequently, there were questions regarding the legitimacy of the election results and the CIA's role in the political process.

During the Lebanese Civil War (1975–1990) Lebanon's Beqaa Valley became a major center of opium and cannabis production, which helped the militias purchase weapons. The Beqaa is situated 30 kilometers (19 miles) east of Beirut between Mount Lebanon to the west and the Anti-Lebanon mountain ranges to the east.

In the time of the Roman Empire, the Beqaa Valley was a major supplier of grain to the Levant. In the early twenty-first century, the area represents 40 percent of Lebanon's arable land. The valley produces hashish and cultivates opium poppies along with other produce. U.S. pressure on Syria, the occupying force, brought about the eradication of cannabis and opium poppies after the civil war ended. One unintended consequence of the U.S. eradication program was the switch by the Lebanese narcotics producers to importing morphine base from Afghanistan/Southeast Asia and coca base from South America. These narcotics were refined into heroin, cocaine, and crack in chemical laboratories in the Beqaa Valley and then exported.

The Hezbollah conflict with Israel in 2006 saw the reseeding of plants as governance in the area disintegrated. The UN also reneged on promises made to the farmers, who had been enticed to give up production in return for alternative crop subsidies, new electric power stations and irrigation projects. As of 2008, Hezbollah controls much of the Beqaa Valley. Officially Hezbollah is opposed to narcotics but cannot risk armed confrontation with the powerful Beqaa Valley clans.

The U.S.-led invasion of Iraq in 2003 entailed a shift to growing locally produced opium, sold by the various militia vying to fill the vacuum following the ousting of the Ba'ath Party. Heroin and opium use within Iraq expanded as a result of the fighting following the occupation. There has been an expansion of opium poppy cultivation and a marked increase in heroin use by Iraqi youth.

See also **Foreign Policy and Drugs, United States; International Drug Supply Systems.**

BIBLIOGRAPHY

Fisk, R. (2002). *Pity the nation: The abduction of Lebanon.* London: Nation Books.

Matthee, R. (2005). *The pursuit of pleasure: Drugs and stimulants in Iranian history, 1500–1900.* Princeton, NJ: Princeton University Press.

McCoy, A. W. (2003). *The politics of heroin: CIA complicity in the global drug trade.* New York: Lawrence Hill Books.

Strang, J., & Gossop, M. (Eds.). (1994). *Heroin addiction and drug policy: The British system* (Oxford Medical Publications). New York: Oxford University Press.

Valentine, D. (2006). *The strength of the wolf: The secret history of America's war on drugs.* London: Verso.

DEAN WHITTINGTON

MILITARY, DRUG AND ALCOHOL ABUSE IN THE UNITED STATES.

The United States military has been associated with substance use in various contexts from the inclusion of rum in daily rations prior to the 1830s (Musto, 2002), to free cigarettes being made available to troops during both world wars (Sloan, Smith, & Taylor, 2002; Tate, 1999) and to the use of narcotics during the Vietnam War (Robins, 1993). A better understanding of substance use in the military, however, must begin with a more general discussion of drug use in the civilian population.

DRUG AND ALCOHOL ABUSE IN THE UNITED STATES

In 2004 Sarah W. Tracy and Caroline Jean Acker averred that the use of consciousness-altering substances has a long history in the United States. Included in this history is the legal status of substances. For example, Griffith Edwards (2004) discussed the criminalization of drugs such as opiates and cocaine that began in the early 1900s with the Harrison Act and the prohibition of cannabis, which began in the 1930s with the Marijuana Tax Act, in his book *Matters of Substance, Drugs—and Why Everyone's a User*. In his 2004 book, *Altering American Consciousness: The History of Alcohol and Drug Use in the United States, 1800–2000*, Ron Roizen asserted that alcohol, briefly prohibited legally during the 1920s, was subject to a "relative tightening in drinking norms" (p. 69) during the 1980s that may have co-occurred with a reduction in use. Tobacco, although still legal, is the target of both scientific research as reviewed in a 2004 report of the surgeon general issued by the U.S. Department of Health and Human Services, and social movements against the substance as explored by Mark Wolfson in 2001.

Results of the 2006 National Survey on Drug Use and Health (NSDUH) illuminate differences in rates of use between illicit and licit substances. Illicit drug use, with marijuana being the most commonly used drug, was reported among the civilian population of the United States, aged 12 or older, at a rate of 8.3 percent in 2006. These statistics provided by the Substance Abuse and Mental Health Services Administration in 2007 also showed that the nonmedical use of prescription-type psychotherapeutic drugs exceeded that of

cocaine, hallucinogens, and methamphetamine. Inhalant use was at 1.8 percent. In contrast, 23 percent of persons aged 12 or older reported binge drinking, defined as five or more drinks on the same occasion at least one day in the preceding month. Additionally, 6.9 percent of persons over the age of 12 reported participation in heavy drinking, defined as binge drinking at least five days in the preceding month. The rate for adults aged 18 to 25 was higher at 15.6 percent. A quarter of the population reported current cigarette smoking.

DRUG AND ALCOHOL ABUSE IN THE MILITARY

In their 2007 article, Robert M. Bray and Laurel L. Hourani describe how the Department of Defense (DoD) has collected comprehensive data regarding substance use and other health behaviors among military personnel using the Worldwide Survey of Alcohol and Nonmedical Drug Use since 1980. According to a comparison in 1991 by Bray, Mary Ellen Marsden, and Michael R. Peterson of the 1985 DoD survey and the 1985 National Household Survey, which was standardized with regard to age, race, education, and sex, illicit drug use among military personnel was lower than drug use in the civilian population. In 2007 Bray and Hourani reported that the rate of illicit drug use started dropping after the initial DoD survey series in 1980 and began to level off in 1992. Between 1998 and 2002, rates of illicit drug use remained relatively unchanged. Bray and others (2006) showed that in 2005 the standardized rate of illicit drug use for military personnel was still lower than that of civilians. Illicit drug use among military personnel in 2005 was not comparable to previous years due to a change in the wording of questions.

For alcohol use, the picture is much different. In 1985 both male and female military personnel between the ages of 18 and 25 were more likely to report drinking any alcohol than were civilians, according to Bray et al. (1991). Military men between the ages of 18 and 55 reported more heavy drinking than civilian men. A study published in 2007 by Katy L. Benjamin, Nicole S. Bell, and Ilyssa E. Hollander comparing alcohol-related hospitalization rates from 1980 to 1995 found that although both groups demonstrated increases in rates that eventually resolved to earlier levels, the army increases began earlier, rose higher, and lasted longer. Army rates began to increase in 1984 and returned to earlier levels by 1991. The authors of this study hypothesized that this may have been due to a "substitution effect," the result of 1984 DoD mandatory drug-testing regulations. However, research published in 2007 by Bray and Hourani, using the DoD surveys, indicates that the heavy drinking rate among military personnel in 2005 was very similar to the rate in 1980. In a 1992 article Bray and colleagues noted that, although the reduction in alcohol use among military personnel during the 1980s was similar to the decrease among civilians, controlled analyses revealed that those in the military were still more likely to be heavy drinkers than civilians. Additionally, heavy alcohol use among military personnel increased between 1998 and 2005, according to Bray and Hourani's 2007 study using the 2005 DoD survey and the 2004 NSDUH. In 2006 Bray and his colleagues reported a standardized comparison of military personnel and civilians that again revealed a higher percentage of heavy drinkers in the military. When the samples were stratified by age group, the difference was only significant for personnel aged 18 to 25.

Tobacco trends reflect a decline since 1980 as demonstrated by Bray and Hourani in 2007, but are more similar to those of alcohol with respect to civilian comparisons. In the standardized comparison of military and civilian substance use in 1985 by Bray and others in 1991, military personnel were more likely to report any smoking or heavy smoking than civilians. Further, Bray and Hourani's 2007 analysis of the most recent DoD survey indicates that for the first time since 1980, between 1998 and 2002 there was an increase in smoking rates among military personnel from 29.9 percent to 33.8 percent. In 2005 cigarettes were used more often than alcohol, with 32.2 percent of service personnel reporting use in the previous 30 days. A standardized comparison between military and civilian populations by Bray and others in 2006 showed that although service members aged 26 to 55 reflect a similar rate of smoking, the rate for service members aged 18 to 25 was higher than that of civilians.

In 2000 Bray and Marsden stated that the demographic composition of the military had changed; potential reasons they described include the abolition of the draft and the resulting career-oriented workforce. Using DoD data collected between 1980 and 1995 standardized to the first year by demographic composition, they found that although cigarette use and illicit drug use have demonstrated declines, heavy drinking has remained more consistent. Bray and colleagues (2000) hypothesize that a possible reason for the reduction in the use of illicit drugs may be effective military policies. In contrast, the authors state that the declining trend for heavy alcohol use may be accounted for in part by demographic changes in the military.

Bray and colleagues (1991) have also argued that while the military policy of drug testing may have been a significant deterrent to drug use, other aspects of military life may be influential in higher smoking and drinking rates compared to civilians. In 2007 using DoD survey data, Bray and Hourani indicated that it was likely that at least one in six military personnel in 2005 was a heavy drinker. Explanations for the increase in cigarette and heavy alcohol use offered by Bray and colleagues (2007) included demanding recruitment goals, possibly reaching a population that already had these habits. The authors suggested that specific increases between 1998 and 2002 may have been due to increased stress related to preparations for Afghanistan operations in 2001 while the similarity or decrease of rates of these substances between 2002 and 2005 may be the result of reduced access during operations. In a previous study published in 1999, military personnel of both genders were more likely to report that their military duties were stressful compared to their personal lives, and Bray, John A. Fairbank, and Marsden further found that stress related to work or the military was associated with increased likelihood of substance use.

THE IMPACT OF DEPLOYMENT
The impact of deployment on substance use has also been examined. Using the Millennium Cohort study, a sample of active duty personnel and members of the reserves or guard that oversampled for those deployed between 1998 and 2000 to southwest Asia, Bosnia, or Kosovo, Riddle and others (2007) discovered that alcohol abuse was by far the most reported disorder in the study, which used the Primary Care Evaluation of Mental Disorders Patient Health Questionnaire (PHQ). The prevalence for alcohol abuse was 12.6 percent with the

next largest percentage being 3.2 for major depressive disorder. However, personnel recently deployed to southwest Asia, Bosnia, or Kosovo did not report higher rates of alcohol abuse than those who had been deployed earlier. In contrast, E. Belle Federman, Bray, and Larry A. Kroutil's 2000 article that described a study of active duty personnel, employing the DoD survey from 1995, showed that deployment in the last 30 days was associated with higher rates of heavy alcohol use among men and women. Bray and colleagues' 2006 report that used the 2005 DoD survey also listed heavy alcohol use, illicit drug use, and tobacco use among the outcomes reported by higher percentages of personnel deployed within the past three years compared to those who had not deployed. Specifically, those deployed to Iraq and Afghanistan reported higher rates of heavy alcohol use in the past 30 days and smoking in the past year than those who were not serving in any operations, while those deployed elsewhere reported higher rates of illicit drug use and smoking in the past year compared to those not serving in any operations. However, a slightly lower percentage of personnel reported starting or increasing alcohol use after being deployed than those who reported reducing or stopping alcohol use, with the exception of army personnel.

Potential reasons for the different results may include the composition of the samples: the Millennium Cohort included active duty and reserve/guard personnel whereas the DoD surveys included only active duty service members (Bray et al., 2006; Federman et al., 2000; Riddle et al., 2007). Measurement for each study was different as well. The Millennium Cohort study employed a list of five questions including items addressing whether a series of usual activities had been adversely affected by their drinking. The DoD surveys employed an algorithm based on the frequency and amount of use to create the categories of abstinence, non-heavy use, and heavy use.

Research on deployment and substance use is not limited to alcohol. For example, in a study of naval personnel during the first Persian Gulf War, published in 1996, that included only deployed service members, Lorraine B. Forgas, Mark E. Cohen, and Daniel M. Meyer demonstrated that 7 percent of personnel who smoked began smoking after being stationed in the Gulf. Federman and colleagues (2000) also found an association between deployment and higher rates of smoking among men. In the 1996 Persian Gulf study by Forgas and colleagues, it was found that although 6.2 percent of smoking naval personnel reported quitting or smoking less, slightly less than a third of smoking personnel reported that they smoked more after being stationed there. In contrast, Bray and colleagues (2006) found that a slightly higher percentage of personnel deployed in the previous year reported quitting or smoking less than those who began to smoke or smoke more, with the exception of army personnel.

The most frequent reasons reported by Forgas and colleagues in 1996 for changing smoking habits were stress and boredom. Bray and colleagues (2006) reported that in the 2005 DoD survey, deployment was the second most often reported stressor, behind that of being away from family. This finding is similar to that of Federman and colleagues in 2000 regarding reasons for an association between substance use and deployment. They concluded that stress and length of deployment provided a portion of the explanation for the association between deployment and increased substance use, but asserted that there were other important unmeasured factors that may have accounted for this. In their discussion, the authors suggest examining potential changes in norms and attitudes toward substance use during deployment.

DRUG AND ALCOHOL ABUSE AMONG MILITARY VETERANS

One of the most intensely studied groups of military personnel has been Vietnam veterans. Although narcotic use was widespread among service members during this conflict, Lee N. Robins, John E. Helzer, and Darlene H. Davis's 1975 study of military personnel returning from Vietnam in September 1971 reports that alcohol use and marijuana use were even more common. Christian Ritter, Richard R. Clayton, and Harwin L. Voss (1985) indicated that marijuana use during the Vietnam War may have been influenced by time of service. Veterans reporting use of marijuana during their time in the service were more likely to have served in 1970 or later. The authors hypothesized that this related in part to an increase in the availability of marijuana during and after 1970 in Vietnam. Availability has also been cited among the reasons for the use of narcotics during this conflict. In 1993 Robins asserted that the rate of use was in response to the high availability and low cost of narcotics and possibly the concurrent lack of availability of alcohol for soldiers under the age of 21.

This military engagement also provided insight into the potential protracted effects of substance use and military service. In a study published in 2004 Seth A. Eisen and others estimated a lifetime rate as high as 54.6 percent for alcohol abuse and/or dependence among a large sample of Vietnam War era veterans interviewed in 1992. However, the rate of alcohol abuse and/or dependence at some point during the twelve months preceding the interviews was much lower at 17.3 percent. With respect to narcotics, in 1975 Robins and colleagues indicated that only a small percentage of service members who were addicted in Vietnam were still addicted after they returned to the United States. Considering veterans more broadly, Todd H. Wagner, Katherine M. Harris, Belle Federman, Lanting Dai, Yesenia Luna, and Keith Humphreys (2007) used the National Household Survey of Drug Abuse (NHSDA) data from 2000 to 2003 and estimated higher rates of heavy drinking for veterans (7.5%) compared to nonveterans (6.5%). A study done by Jillian C. Shipherd, Jane Stafford, and Lynlee R. Tanner in 2005 that was restricted to Persian Gulf War veterans indicated higher rates of substance use problems during the six years following return from service in 1991, with 14–15 percent and 2–3 percent of the sample subscribing to alcohol and drug problems, respectively.

MENTAL HEALTH DIAGNOSES AND ALCOHOL AND DRUG USE

As noted by Denise B. Kandel, Fung-Yea Huang, and Mark Davies in 2001, substance dependence demonstrated associations with increased odds of a probable psychiatric disorder, such as depressive or anxiety syndromes using data from the 1994 to 1996 NHSDA. Substance abuse and affective disorders were among the conditions identified as having high non-combat related impact on the health of U.S. military members in John F. Brundage, Karen E. Johnson, Jeffrey L. Lange, and Mark V. Rubertone's 2006 analysis of 2002 data from the Defense Medical Surveillance System. Alcohol disorders were, by far, the most common mental disorders reported as a primary diagnosis

among all active-duty personnel from 1990 to 1999 in both hospitalizations and number of ambulatory visits, according to Charles W. Hoge and colleagues in 2002. Alcohol and substance abuse also have implications for other psychiatric outcomes. Using data from the Veterans Affairs National Registry for Depression collected between 1999 and 2004, Kara Zivin and colleagues reported in 2007 that any diagnosis of alcohol or substance abuse in the 12 months preceding study entry through the study period was associated with a higher rate of suicide among depressed patients. Paige C. Ouimette, Pamela J. Brown, and Lisa M. Najavits's review of the literature published in 1998 about the course and treatment of patients with substance use and post-traumatic stress disorder (PTSD) across multiple samples, including veterans in Veterans Affairs treatment centers, noted that substance abuse patients with PTSD may be more vulnerable to poorer post-treatment outcomes.

DEMOGRAPHIC PATTERNS IN DRUG AND ALCOHOL ABUSE

Over the period from 1980 to 1992, men in the military demonstrated a greater rate of heavy alcohol use than women, although rates of illicit drug use across gender were similar during much of that period according to Bray, Kroutil, and Marsden (1995). An analysis of data by Bray and colleagues from the DoD survey in 1995 published in 1999 demonstrated that while men and women were similar in rates of illicit drug use, men were slightly more likely to smoke and were more than three times as likely to be heavy drinkers. Bray and others reported (2006) that in 2005 the greatest distinction in rate of heavy drinking between civilians and military personnel appeared to be among males between the ages of 18 and 25 serving in the U.S. Army and Marine Corps in stratified analyses. The percentage of female military personnel and female civilians aged 18 to 25 who engaged in heavy drinking were similar except among women in the Marine Corps, who exhibited a higher rate than civilian women.

Although military duties were associated with stress in both genders, the reasons reported for stress that were associated with substance use varied by gender according to Bray and others in 1999. For example, one-third of the women reported they experienced high stress specifically related to being a woman in the military; experiencing high levels of this type of stress was associated with increased odds of illicit drug use in the past 12 months and cigarette use in the past month compared to experiencing low levels. Military men experiencing high stress at work were more likely to report heavy alcohol or cigarette use in the past month and illicit drug use in the past 12 months compared to men experiencing low stress at work.

OTHER ADDICTIONS NOT READILY DIAGNOSABLE

Some addictions that are not readily apparent have been examined among military personnel. Benjamin W. Lacy and Thomas F. Ditzler argued in 2007 that the use of inhalants can affect military readiness and impact service members' health but that inhalants have received less attention than other drugs as far as prevention, detection, and treatment. The authors hypothesized that the short-lasting effects and the ability to return to work without appearing intoxicated may be attractive to military personnel. In 2006 Bray and others reported the prevalence of active military service members reporting inhalant use in the past 12 months during 2005 was highest among Marines (3.4%) while the overall prevalence was 2.1 percent. Gambling has also been studied among military personnel. The prevalence of active military service members answering affirmatively to one of ten questions assessing gambling-related problems in 2002 was 6.3 percent, according to Bray et al. (2003). Only 1.2 percent answered affirmatively to five or more questions, an indication of probable pathological gambling. The 2003 published report of the 2002 data also described how in previous years, prevalence of three affirmative responses was reported, and this rate remained consistent at approximately 2 percent across 1992, 1998, and 2002.

TREATMENT AND PREVENTION STRATEGIES

In a discussion of the progress that has been made among military personnel in the U.S., in 1992 Bray and colleagues summarized DoD directives and sinstructions in the four major program areas that the military highlights: assessment, deterrence and detection, treatment and rehabilitation, and education and training. Methods of carrying out these directives include the Worldwide

Surveys, background checks, initial and random drug tests, the operation of a large drug and alcohol abuse treatment and rehabilitation program, and the provision of education and training. There is also treatment available for non-substance addictions. For example, in a 2004 article, Otto Kausch reported that one veterans' hospital has offered treatment for gambling since 1972. Treatment specifically for gambling offered overseas within the Substance Abuse Rehabilitation Program inside the navy has been described by Carrie H. Kennedy, Jeffrey H. Cook, Daniel R. Poole, Christopher L. Brunson and David E. Jones in 2005. However, it was also reported that service members seeking help for gambling express fear of discovery. Similarly, it has also been found that potential disciplinary action or concern for their military career may prevent personnel from seeking treatment for substance use (Bray et al., 1992).

In 1993 Robins argued that availability is the main explanation for the increased prevalence of narcotic use and addiction among the military population during the Vietnam War. This idea has also been discussed in reference to alcohol. In 1992 Bray and colleagues stated that a number of people in the military believe that policies such as setting hours and prices for alcohol sales and policing the availability of drugs have affected the accessibility of these substances. However, there may be room for further improvement. For example, in 1996 Forgas and colleagues conducted a study of naval personnel during the Persian Gulf War. They found that, although nearly a quarter of the sample stated that military efforts to influence them to quit their tobacco habits were successful, sailors paid much less for cigarettes than civilians and some also reported receiving free cigarettes from the United Service Organizations (USO) and tobacco companies.

CONCLUSION

The military has made great strides toward reducing the rate of illicit drug use. These same reductions have not been achieved in heavy drinking and tobacco use. In this, the armed forces face the same challenge as civilians: discouraging the use and abuse of licit drugs. In contrast, military personnel must resist using drugs and alcohol to cope with the unique challenges related to military life. In 2005 Bray and others (2006) reported that more than 25 percent of military personnel used alcohol or tobacco as coping mechanisms. It is clear that the United States military must expand its efforts to improve the reduction of substance use and abuse.

See also **Addiction: Concepts and Definitions; Alcohol: Psychological Consequences of Chronic Abuse; Cocaine; Coping and Drug Use; Depression; Drug Testing Methods and Clinical Interpretations of Test Results; Gambling; Marijuana (Cannabis); Risk Factors for Substance Use, Abuse, and Dependence: Stress; Suicide and Substance Abuse; Tobacco: Dependence; U.S. Government Agencies: Substance Abuse and Mental Health Services Administration (SAMHSA); Vietnam Era Study (VES), Washington University; Vietnam War: Drug Use in U.S. Military; Women and Substance Abuse.**

BIBLIOGRAPHY

Benjamin, K. L., Bell, N. S., & Hollander, I. E. (2007). A historical look at alcohol abuse trends in army and civilian populations, 1980–1995. *Military Medicine, 172*(9), 950–955.

Bray, R. M., Fairbank, J. A., & Marsden, M. E. (1999). Stress and substance use among military women and men. *American Journal of Drug and Alcohol Abuse, 25*(2), 239–256.

Bray, R. M., & Hourani, L. L. (2007). Substance use trends among active duty military personnel: Findings from the United States Department of Defense Health Related Behavior Surveys, 1980–2005. *Addiction, 102*, 1092–1101.

Bray, R. M., Hourani, L. L., Rae, K. L., Dever, J. A., Brown, J. M., Vincus, A. A., et al. (2003). *2002 Department of Defense Survey of Health Related Behaviors Among Military Personnel*. Final Report [prepared for the Assistant Secretary of Defense (Health Affairs) U.S. Department of Defense, Cooperative Agreement no. DAMD17-00-2-0057, RTI/7841/006-FR]. Research Triangle Park, NC: Research Triangle Institute. Available from http://www.tricare.mil/.

Bray, R. M., Hourani, L. L., Rae Olmstead, K. L., Witt, M., Brown, J. M., Pemberton, M. R., et al. (2006). *2005 Department of Defense Survey of Health Related Behaviors Among Military Personnel*. Final Report [prepared for the Assistant Secretary of Defense (Health Affairs) U.S. Department of Defense, Cooperative Agreement no. DAMD17-00-2-0057, RTI/7841/106-FR]. Research Triangle Park, NC: Research Triangle Institute. Available from http://www.ha.osd.mil/.

Bray, R. M., Kroutil, L. A., & Marsden, M. E. (1995). Trends in alcohol, illicit drug, and cigarette use among U. S. military personnel: 1980–1992. *Armed Forces & Society, 21*(2), 271–293.

Bray, R. M., & Marsden, M. E. (2000). Trends in substance use among U. S. military personnel: The impact of changing demographic composition. *Substance Use & Misuse, 35*(6–8), 949–969.

Bray, R. M., Marsden, M. E., Herbold, J. R., & Peterson, M. R. (1992). Progress toward eliminating drug and alcohol abuse among U.S.military personnel. *Armed Forces & Society, 18(4)*, 476–496.

Bray, R. M., Marsden, M. E., & Peterson, M. R. (1991). Standardized comparisons of the use of alcohol, drugs, and cigarettes among military personnel and civilians. *American Journal of Public Health, 81*(7), 865–869.

Brundage, J. F., Johnson, K. E., Lange, J. L., & Rubertone, M. V. (2006). Comparing the population health impacts of medical conditions using routinely collected health care utilization data: Nature and sources of variability. *Military Medicine, 171*(10), 936–942.

Edwards, G. (2004). *Matters of Substance: Drugs—and why everyone's a user*. New York, NY: Picador.

Eisen, S. A., Griffith, K. H., Xian, H., Scherrer, J. F., Fischer, I. D., Chantarujikapong, S., et al. (2004). Lifetime and 12-month prevalence of psychiatric disorders in 8,169 male Vietnam War era veterans. *Military Medicine, 169*(11), 896–902.

Federman, E. B., Bray, R. M., & Kroutil, L. A. (2000). Relationships between substance use and recent deployments among women and men in the military. *Military Psychology, 12*(3), 205–220.

Forgas, L. B., Cohen, M. E., & Meyer, D. M. (1996). Tobacco use habits of naval personnel during Desert Storm. *Military Medicine, 161*(3), 165–168.

Hoge, C. W., Lesikar, S. E., Guevara, R., Lange, J., Brundage, J. F., Engel, C. C., et al. (2002). Mental disorders among U. S. military personnel in the 1990's: Association with high levels of health care utilization and early military attrition. *American Journal of Psychiatry, 159*(9), 1576–1583.

Kandel, D. B., Huang, F., & Davies, M. (2001). Comorbidity between patterns of substance use dependence and psychiatric syndromes. *Drug and Alcohol Dependence, 64*, 233–241.

Kausch, O. (2004). Pathological gambling among elderly veterans. *Journal of Geriatric Psychiatry and Neurology, 17*, 13–19.

Kennedy, C. H., Cook, J. H., Poole, D. R., Brunson, C. L., & Jones, D. E. (2005). Review of the first year of an overseas military gambling treatment program. *Military Medicine, 170*(8), 683–687.

Lacy, B. W., & Ditzler, T. F. (2007). Inhalant abuse in the military: An unrecognized threat. *Military Medicine, 172*(4), 388–392.

Musto, D. (2002). Alcohol: Introduction. In D. Musto (Ed.), *Drugs in America: A documentary history*. New York: New York University Press.

Ouimette, P. C., Brown, P. J., & Najavits, L. M. (1998). Course and treatment of patients with both substance use and posttraumatic stress disorders. *Addictive Behaviors, 23*(6), 785–795.

Riddle, J. R., Smith, T. C., Smith, B., Corbeil, T. E., Engel, C. C., Wells, T. S., et al. (2007). Millennium cohort: The 2001–2003 baseline prevalence of mental disorders in the U. S. military. *Journal of Clinical Epidemiology, 60*, 192–201.

Ritter, C., Clayton, R. R., & Voss, H. L. (1985). Vietnam military service and marijuana use. *American Journal of Drug and Alcohol Abuse, 11*(1 & 2), 119–130.

Robins, L. N. (1993). Vietnam veterans' rapid recovery from heroin addiction: A fluke or normal expectation? *Addiction, 88*, 1041–1054.

Robins, L. N., Helzer, J. E., & Davis, D. H. (1975). Narcotic use in Southeast Asia and afterward. *Archives of General Psychiatry, 32*, 955–961.

Roizen, R. (2004). How does the nation's "alcohol problem" change from era to era?: Stalking the social logic of problem-definition transformations since repeal. In S. W. Tracy & C. J. Acker (Eds.), *Altering American consciousness: The history of alcohol and drug use in the United States, 1800–2000*. Boston: University of Massachusetts Press.

Shipherd, J. C., Stafford, J., & Tanner, L. R. (2005). Predicting alcohol and drug abuse in Persian Gulf War veterans: What role do PTSD symptoms play? *Addictive Behaviors, 30*, 595–599.

Sloan, F. A., Smith, V. K., & Taylor, D. H. (2002). Information, addiction, and 'bad choices': Lessons from a century of cigarettes. *Economic Letters, 77*, 147–155.

Substance Abuse and Mental Health Services Administration. (2007). *Results from the 2006 National Survey on Drug Use and Health: National Findings* (Office of Applied Studies, NSDUH series H-32, DHHS publication no. SMA 07-4293) Rockville, MD. Available from http://www.oas.samhsa.gov/.

Tate, C. (1999). *Cigarette wars: The triumph of the little white slaver*. New York, NY: Oxford University Press.

Tracy, S. W., & Acker, C. J. (2004). Introduction: Psychoactive drugs: An American way of life. In S. W. Tracy & C. J. Acker (Eds.), *Altering American consciousness: The history of alcohol and drug use in the United States, 1800–2000*. Boston: University of Massachusetts Press.

U.S. Department of Health and Human Services. (2004). *The health consequences of smoking: A report of the Surgeon General*. Atlanta, GA: U.S. Department of Health and Human Services, Centers for Disease Control and Prevention, National Center for Chronic Disease Prevention and Health Promotion, Office on Smoking and Health.

Wagner, T. H., Harris, K. M., Federman, B., Dai, L., Luna, Y., & Humpreys, K. (2007). Prevalence of substance use disorders among veterans and comparable nonveterans from the National Survey on Drug Use and Health. *Psychological Services, 4*(3), 149–157.

Wolfson, M. (2001). *The fight against big tobacco: The movement, the state, and the public's health*. Hawthorne, NY: Aldine De Gruyter.

Zivin, K., Kim, M., McCarthy, J. F., Austin, K. L., Hoggatt, K. J., Walters, H., et al. (2007). Suicide mortality among individuals receiving treatment for depression in the veterans affairs health systems: Associations with patient and treatment setting characteristics. *American Journal of Public Health, 97*(12), 2193–2198.

LARA M. DePADILLA

MINI INTERNATIONAL NEUROPSYCHIATRIC INTERVIEW (MINI).

Structured diagnostic interviews were first used to standardize the collection of diagnostic information in psychiatric epidemiology studies. They are used frequently in multicenter, research treatment studies to standardize diagnostic eligibility criteria across sites, often in different countries and languages. They are used to improve diagnostic precision and to track a patient's progress in non-research settings. Examples include the diagnostic assessment of individuals applying for disability benefits, of people in correctional/prison systems, of military personnel entering and exiting theaters of conflict, in mental health screening institutions, and by managed health-care organizations and health-care delivery systems. Unlike the usual clinical interview, structured diagnostic interviews allow comparison across clinical centers, reduce variability in diagnosis, and help to improve quality of care.

HISTORY AND EARLY LIMITATIONS OF STRUCTURED INTERVIEWS

The early structured interviews had many limitations. They were often long, cumbersome, and required considerable training and expertise. These interviews included the Present State Exam (PSE), Diagnostic Interview Schedule (DIS), the Schedule for Affective Disorders and Schizophrenia (SADS), the Composite International Diagnostic Interview (CIDI) or Schedule for Clinical Assessment in

Neuropsychiatry (SCAN), and the Structured Clinical Interview for *DSM-III-R* (SCID). These interviews often took forty-five minutes or longer to administer.

Shorter structured diagnostic interviews, taking five to fifteen minutes to administer, were designed for primary care settings. These included the Symptom Driven Diagnostic System (SDDS) and the Primary Care Evaluation of Mental Disorders (Prime MD), which collected information on six major Axis I disorders.

In the early 1990s, with the globalization of health-care research, researchers from academia, regulatory agencies, national institutes, and the pharmaceutical industry thought there was a need for a structured interview that would bridge the gap between the older, detailed, time-consuming, diagnostic interview and the ultra short screening tests designed for primary care.

MINI DEFINED AND DESCRIBED

The Mini International Neuropsychiatric Interview (MINI) is a structured psychiatric interview for adults, which takes approximately fifteen minutes to administer. It assesses fifteen major Axis I disorders and one Axis II disorder (see Table 1). Validation and reliability studies have been done comparing the MINI to the SCID-P for *DSM-III-R* and the CIDI. The results of the studies showed that the MINI has acceptable high validation and reliability scores but can be administered in a much shorter period of time than the above referenced instruments. The MINI is short, inexpensive, simple to use, clear, easy to administer and to navigate, highly sensitive (a high proportion of patients with a disorder are detected) and specific (it has the ability to screen out patients without disorders). The MINI is compatible with international diagnostic criteria, including the *International Classification of Diseases* (*ICD-10*) as well as the *Diagnostic and Statistical Manual of Mental Disorders,* fourth edition, (*DSM-IV*). It is also able to capture important subsyndromal variants and is useful in both clinical psychiatry and in research settings.

The MINI is divided into modules identified by letters, each corresponding to a diagnostic category. At the beginning of each diagnostic module (except for the psychotic disorders module),

Disorder	Time Frame
1 Major Depressive Episode	Current (2 weeks), Recurrent and Past
2 Suicidality	Current (Past Month)
3 Manic Episode	Current and Past
Hypomanic Episode	Current and Past
4 Panic Disorder	Current (Past Month)
5 Agoraphobia	Current
6 Social Phobia (Social Anxiety Disorder)	Current (Past Month)
7 Obsessive-Compulsive Disorder	Current (Past Month)
8 Posttraumatic Stress Disorder	Current (Past Month)
9 Alcohol Dependence	Past 12 Months
Alcohol Abuse	Past 12 Months
10 Drug Dependence	Past 12 Months
Drug Abuse	Past 12 Months
11 Psychotic Disorders	Lifetime and Current
Mood Disorder with Psychotic Features	Current
12 Anorexia Nervosa	Current (Past 3 Months)
13 Bulimia Nervosa	Current (Past 3 Months)
14 Anorexia Nervosa, Binge Eating/ Purging Type	Current
15 Generalized Anxiety Disorder	Current (Past 6 Months)
16 Antisocial Personality Disorder	Lifetime

Table 1. Disorder diagnoses available on the MINI 6.0.0
ILLUSTRATION BY GGS INFORMATION SERVICES. GALE, CENGAGE LEARNING

screening questions corresponding to the main criteria of the disorder are presented in a gray box. At the end of each module, diagnostic boxes permit the clinician to indicate whether diagnostic criteria are met.

The MINI was not intended to replace the psychiatrist or physician. Rather, like a laboratory test in medicine, it is designed to capture routine and repetitive information, maximizing the efficiency of the medical encounter and leaving specialists time for other critical tasks. The MINI was designed to be administered by psychiatrists, psychologists, physicians, or by trained nurses or health information technicians. The MINI is not suitable for administration by lay interviewers because it requires clinical skill and experience to implement properly. Another limitation of the MINI is that it only covers 16 of the most common Axis I disorders. Many Axis I disorders are not screened by the MINI.

While the MINI questions patients about the presence or absence of *DSM-IV* criteria for alcohol and drug abuse and dependence, it is entirely dependent on the veracity of the patient for accuracy. It should never be construed as an adequate substitute for laboratory screening (urine and blood levels) of alcohol and drugs (which, of course, have their limitations as well).

The developers of the MINI included many suggestions and improvements offered by colleagues around the world, which led to the MINI "Family" of rating scales and to ever more useful versions.

The MINI Plus has 26 modules and covers 62 disorders and subtypes. It assesses all the subtypes and timeframes as well as all the disorders that might be reasonably included in clinical research studies. Even though the MINI Plus covers many more disorders, the format is less complex and easier to navigate than that of the other longer interviews.

The MINI Screen is a short, one page (two sides) screening instrument that is designed to assess patients quickly and determine if there might be further need for structured evaluation. It uses only the screening questions from the full MINI.

The child/adolescent variant of the MINI, called the MINI-KID is a structured diagnostic instrument for psychiatric disorders in children and adolescents. The questions are based primarily on those of the MINI but are phrased in a language easy for children to understand. The MINI-KID includes eight additional modules for disorders frequently found in children and adolescents such as attention deficit hyperactivity disorder, tic disorders, and conduct disorder. The MINI-KID is shorter and easier to administer than the other structured interviews available as of 2008 for children and adolescents. A validation and reliability study completed in 2007 compared the MINI-KID with the Kiddie-SADS. The MINI-KID had acceptable validity and reliability scores and could be administered in one-third the time of the Kiddie-SADS.

AVAILABILITY

As of 2008, the MINI was available in over fifty different languages. It was also available in a computerized form (eMINI) that could be integrated with medical screening or triage of large samples of patients. The computerized version is faster to implement in practice than the paper version because all the calculations and algorithms are calculated automatically in the background for the user, it prints out a clean copy of the executed interview, and stores all data for future export and analysis. The MINI is designed to be used in a variety of situations, from clinical research to actual clinical practice when a diagnosis is in question,

from tracking patients over time to computerized monitoring of patients in quality improvement programs. The Web site maintained by Medical Outcomes Systems provides more information about the MINI and allows free downloading of the different MINIs.

As of 2008, professionals anticipated increasing use of structured diagnostic interviews in electronic form for large-scale population screening and early detection of suicide risk and mental health.

See also **Diagnostic and Statistical Manual (DSM); International Classification of Diseases (ICD).**

BIBLIOGRAPHY

Amorim, P., Lecrubier, Y., Weiller, E., Hergueta, T., & Sheehan, D. (1998). *DSM-III-R* psychotic disorders: Procedural validity of the Mini International Neuropsychiatric Interview (M.I.N.I.). Concordance and causes for discordance with the CIDI. *European Psychiatry, 13,* 26–34.

Broadhead, W. E., Leon, A. C., Weissman, M. M., Barret, J. E., Blacklow, R. S., Gilbert, T. T., et al. (1995). Development and validation of the SDDS-PC screen for multiple mental disorders in primary care. *Archives of Family Medicine, 4,* 211–219.

Kessler, L. G., McGonagle, K. A., Zhao, S., Nelson, C. B., Hughes, M., Eshlerman, S., et al. (1994). Lifetime and 12-month prevalence of *DSM-III-R* psychiatric disorders in the United States: Results from the National Comorbidity Survey. *Archives of General Psychiatry, 51,* 8–19.

Lecrubier, Y., Sheehan, D., Weiller, E., Amorim, P., Bonora, I., Sheehan, K., et al. (1997). The MINI International Neuropsychiatric Interview (M.I.N.I.): A short diagnostic structured interview: Reliability and validity according to the CIDI. *European Psychiatry, 12,* 224–231.

Medical Outcomes Systems, Inc. Available from https://www.medical-outcomes.com/.

Regier, D. A., Myers, J. K., Kramer, M., Robins, L. N., Blazer, D. G., Hough, R. L., et al. (1984). The NIMH Epidemiologic Catchment Area Program: Historical context, major objectives, and study population characteristics. *Archives of General Psychiatry, 41,* 934–941.

Sheehan, D. V., Lecrubier, Y., Harnett-Sheehan, K., Amorim, P., Janavs, J., Weiller, E., et al. (1998). The Mini International Neuropsychiatric Interview (M.I.N.I.): The development and validation of a structured diagnostic psychiatric interview. *Journal of Clinical Psychiatry, 59*(Suppl. 20), 22–33.

Sheehan, D. V., Lecrubier, Y., Harnett-Sheehan, K., Janavs, J., Weiller, E., Bonara, L. I., et al. (1997). Reliability and validity of the MINI International Neuropsychiatric

Interview (M.I.N.I.): According to the SCID-P. *European Psychiatry, 12,* 232–241.

Spitzer, R. L., Williams, J. B. W., Gibbon, M., & First, M. B. (1990). *Structured clinical interview for DSM-III-R.* Arlington, VA: American Psychiatric Press.

Spitzer, R. L., Williams, J. B. W., Kroenke, K., Linzer, M., DeGruy, F.V., III, Hahn, S. R., et al. (1993, September 21). *The PRIME-MD 1000 study: Validation of a new system for diagnosing mental disorders in primary care.* Paper presented at the Seventh Annual NIMH International Research Conference on Mental Health Problems in the General Health Section, McLean, VA.

World Health Organization Composite International Diagnostic Interview (CIDI). (1990). Version 1.0. Geneva, Switzerland: World Health Organization.

JURIS JANAVS

MINIMUM DRINKING AGE LAWS.

Before the twentieth century, there were few legal restrictions on the consumption of alcoholic beverages by youth. Early in the twentieth century, laws prohibiting alcohol sales to minors began to be implemented as part of a broader trend of increasing legal controls on adolescent behavior. The temperance movement worked to establish national prohibition in 1919 but when the Eighteenth Amendment was repealed in 1933, all states implemented legal minimum ages for alcohol purchase or consumption, with most states setting the age at twenty-one.

From the 1930s through the 1960s, the issue received little public attention. In 1970, the Twenty-Sixth Amendment to the U.S. Constitution lowered the voting age in federal elections from twenty-one to eighteen. By 1974, all fifty states had lowered their voting ages for state elections to eighteen. As part of this trend of lowering the age of majority, twenty-nine states lowered their minimum drinking ages between 1970 and 1975, most setting the age at eighteen or nineteen. In the mid-1970s, studies began to emerge that showed significant increases in the rate of young drivers' involvement in traffic crashes following the reductions in the legal drinking age. The trend toward lower drinking ages was reversed, with Maine being the first state to raise its legal drinking age from eighteen to twenty in October 1977. Several other states soon followed, and research studies completed by the early 1980s found significant declines in youth traffic-crash involvement after states raised their legal drinking age. With the support of organized efforts by such citizen-action groups as Remove Intoxicated Drivers and Mothers Against Drunk Driving, federal legislation was passed in 1984 that called for the withholding of a portion of federal highway-construction funds from any state that did not have a legal drinking age of twenty-one by October 1986. As a result, all the remaining states with a lower legal drinking age raised their minimum age to twenty-one by 1988. Thus, all states as of 2008 have a uniform legal drinking age of twenty-one, although details in regard to the purchase, possession, consumption, sales, and furnishing of alcohol to underage youth vary from state to state.

The legal drinking age became a major issue because of the serious consequences of young people's consumption of alcohol. Most teenagers drink; in addition, almost one-third become regularly intoxicated (Johnston et al., 2007). Such use is not without considerable expense. Car crashes are the leading cause of death for teenagers, and nearly one-fourth of youth in fatal traffic crashes have been drinking (National Highway Traffic Safety Administration, 2006).These intoxicated drivers are a danger to themselves and a considerable danger to others, as half the people who die in crashes involving an underage drinking driver are people other than the driver (U.S. Department of Transportation, 2004). Other leading causes of death and disability among youth, such as suicide, homicide, assault, drowning, and recreational injury involve alcohol in one-fourth to three-fourths of cases (Smith et al., 1999). Injuries are only part of the problem. Early use of alcohol appears to affect multiple dimensions of physical, social, and cognitive development. Alcohol increases the odds of having unprotected sex (i.e., failure to use a condom); multiple partners; pregnancy; and contracting sexually transmitted diseases, including the human immunodeficiency virus (HIV; Cook & Clark, 2005; Dunn et al., 2003; Guo et al., 2002; Stueve & O'Donnell, 2005). Further, nearly three-fourths of date-rape situations involve individuals who have been drinking (Mohler-Kuo et al., 2004). Early use of alcohol increases the odds one will move on to using other drugs, such as marijuana, cocaine, or heroin (Kandel, 2002) and increases the likelihood of later addiction and criminal and violent behavior (Brown et al., 2000; Ellickson et al., 2003; Monti et al., 2005; Warner & White, 2003).

Additionally, research has shown that exposure to alcohol in adolescence can have detrimental long-term effects on brain development and intellectual capabilities (Brown et al., 2000; Monti et al., 2005). Despite the many problems associated with young people's drinking, the most obvious one, and the one that received the most attention in debates on the legal drinking age, is traffic-crash involvement.

EFFECTS OF THE DRINKING AGE ON CAR CRASHES

The legal drinking age is one of the most extensively researched policies designed to reduce traffic crashes and other alcohol problems, with nearly 150 empirical evaluations published since the early 1970s. Sixty-one published studies have assessed effects of changes in the legal minimum drinking age on indicators of driving after drinking and traffic crashes, providing over one hundred estimates of effect. While results vary across studies and across states, the preponderance of evidence indicates an inverse relationship between the minimum legal drinking age and traffic crashes: When the legal age increased, crashes decreased.

Twelve studies have examined the effects of lowering the minimum drinking age (usually from age twenty-one to eighteen) and most (exceptions are Bellows, 1980; Naor & Nashold, 1975) reported increases in fatal and injury-producing traffic crashes likely to involve alcohol (e.g., single-vehicle crashes occurring at night) following a decrease in the legal drinking age. Across all outcomes studied, over half (52 percent) of observed effects were statistically significant, with increases in youth involvement in fatal traffic crashes ranging from 2 to 30 percent (Shults et al., 2001).

Forty studies of the effects on traffic crashes of raising the legal age for drinking were published between 1979 and 2007. Nearly all found reductions in the involvement of youth in traffic crashes following increases in the legal drinking age (exceptions are Chung, 1997; Davis & Reynolds, 1990; Hughes & Dodder, 1992; Jones et al., 1992; Vingilis & Smart, 1981). Across all outcomes studied, 57 percent of observed effects were statistically significant. Typically, raising the drinking age resulted

in a 6 to 30 percent reduction in traffic crashes likely to involve alcohol (Shults et al., 2001).

Scientists and professionals in the field agree that lowering the legal age for drinking increased car crashes among youth and that subsequently raising the legal age reversed the effect: It lowered car crashes among youth (National Research Council and Institute of Medicine, 2004). There is a large, fairly consistent body of scientific literature substantiating these relationships, with 98 percent of all analyses reporting statistically significant effects finding higher drinking ages associated with lower rates of traffic crashes (Wagenaar & Toomey, 2002). The National Highway Traffic Safety Administration estimates that the U.S. age-twenty-one policy has saved nearly 22,000 lives, averaging over one thousand lives per year, in reduced car crashes alone (Kindelberger, 2005).

EFFECTS OF THE DRINKING AGE ON OTHER PROBLEMS

Thirty-one studies have examined effects of changes in the legal drinking age on indicators of other health and social problems. Among these thirty-one studies, there are over sixty estimates of effects on social and health outcome measures, including violence, homicide, suicide, and unintentional injury, and results are less consistent than those for traffic crash outcomes. Of all analyses that reported statistically significant effects, approximately 75 percent found higher drinking ages associated with lower rates of problems. Over 70 percent of analyses found no statistically significant association between the legal drinking age and indicators of other health and social problems; some of the studies had low power to detect effects.

EFFECTS OF THE DRINKING AGE ON ALCOHOL USE

Twelve studies examined the effect of the legal drinking age on aggregate alcoholic-beverage sales. Effects were mixed: Some studies found that alcohol sales were significantly inversely related to the legal age whereas others did not find such a relationship. These studies are difficult to interpret, as alcohol sales to young drinkers could not be distinguished from sales to older drinkers.

The effects of the legal minimum drinking age on self-report measures of alcohol consumption among youth are more prolific and have produced conflicting results. Forty-two studies assessing effects of changes in the legal minimum drinking age on self-reported indicators of alcohol consumption were published between 1975 and 2007, providing over sixty empirical estimates of effect. Among these studies, half found an inverse relationship between the legal drinking age and alcohol consumption; that is, as the legal age was lowered, drinking increased, and as the legal age was raised, drinking decreased. A major limitation of many of these studies was their use of nonrandom samples of youth from particular high schools, colleges, and local communities rather than samples that were broadly representative of the youth in a state (Wagenaar & Toomey, 2002). Surveys of college students, which are usually limited to students in introductory social science courses, frequently report finding little effect of the legal drinking age on drinking patterns. In contrast, surveys of random samples of high school seniors and eighteen- to twenty-year-olds across many states, including those entering college and those in the workforce, report finding significant reductions in drinking that are associated with higher legal drinking ages (Maisto & Rachal, 1980; O'Malley & Wagenaar, 1991; Wagenaar & Toomey, 2002). It appears on the basis of the best-designed studies that raising the legal drinking age resulted in important reductions in young people's drinking. The age-twenty-one policy, however, by no means eliminates drinking by youth.

ENFORCEMENT OF THE MINIMUM DRINKING AGE

While there were slight declines in the 1990s and early 2000s, alcohol remains the drug of choice among youth in the United States. When questioned, 45 percent of high school seniors reported drinking in the last month, and 30 percent reported having had five or more drinks at a time at least once in the previous two weeks (Figures 1 and 2; data from Johnston et al., 2007). Among the many reasons for youth alcohol consumption, one important reason is that alcohol remains easily accessible. Published studies indicate that despite the minimum legal age of twenty-one, underage buyers are able to purchase alcohol in many communities without showing age identification in 47 to 97 percent of attempts (Forster et al., 1994;

Grube, 1997; Paschall et al., 2007; Preusser & Williams, 1992).

It is notable that effects discussed here have been achieved with only modest (at best) enforcement of this law. While studies of enforcement effects are few, results show that enforcement has reduced illegal sales to youth (Grube, 1997; Huckle et al., 2005; Lewis et al., 1996; Scribner & Cohen, 2001; Wagenaar et al., 2005; Wilner et al., 2000). One study by Wagenaar and associates (2005) indicated that enforcement of the legal drinking age produced an immediate 17 percent reduction in the likelihood of sales to minors, with effects decaying within three months. Thus, enforcement needs to be ongoing to prevent the illegal sales of alcohol to teens.

Strong evidence showing that raising the drinking age to twenty-one reduced deaths and injuries in car crashes was a major factor in the debate about the drinking age. Other arguments were also heard, such as those that asked if it is unconstitutional to discriminate solely on the basis of age. Federal courts have ruled that the drinking age is not discriminatory because: (1) drinking is not a fundamental right; (2) age is not an inherently suspect criterion for discrimination; and (3) the higher drinking age has a rational basis and is reasonably related to a legitimate goal of the state to reduce death and injury from traffic crashes (Wagenaar & Toomey, 2002). In a democracy, laws should have the support of the governed. Repeated polls from the 1980s to early 2000s have shown that the majority of those asked clearly support a legal drinking age of twenty-one. Even among youth under the age of twenty-one, polls have shown majority support for this minimum drinking age.

Some people wonder if it is logical to set the legal age of drinking at twenty-one when other rights and privileges of adulthood (e.g., voting, signing legally binding contracts, enlisting in the armed forces) begin at age eighteen. Others answer that it is because there are many different legal ages, varying from twelve to twenty-one, for voting, driving, sale and use of tobacco, legal consent to sexual intercourse, marriage, access to contraception without parental consent, compulsory school attendance, and so forth. Minimum ages are not set uniformly; they depend on the specific

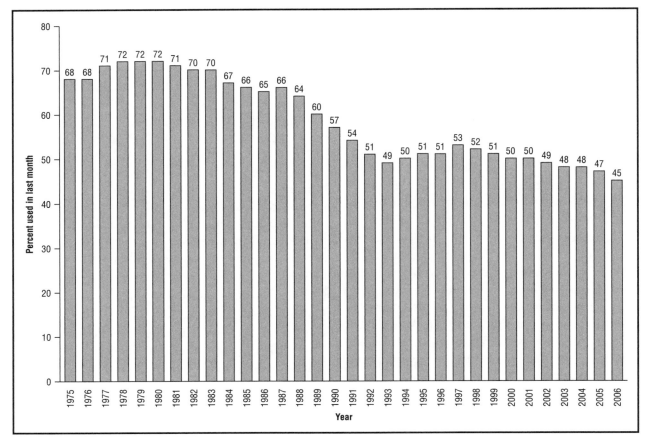

Figure 1. Percent of high school seniors reported drinking in the last month. (Source: Johnston, L. D., O'Malley, P. M., Bachman, J. G., & Schulenberg, J. E. (2007). *Monitoring the future: National results on adolescent drug use: Overview of key findings, 2006.* Bethesda, MD: National Institute on Drug Abuse. ILLUSTRATION BY GGS INFORMATION SERVICES. GALE, CENGAGE LEARNING

behavior involved, and they are determined by balancing the dangers and benefits of establishing the particular age.

Some have argued that a minimum drinking age of twenty-one will make matters worse when young people finally get legal access to alcohol. The idea here is that prohibiting teenagers from drinking causes a pent-up demand for alcohol as a forbidden fruit. At twenty-one, young adults will break loose and drink at significantly higher rates than they would have if they had been introduced to alcohol earlier. This theory is clearly not supported by research. For example, O'Malley and Wagenaar (1991) found just the opposite results in their nationwide study; that is, persons aged twenty-one to twenty-four drank at *lower* rates if they had to wait until twenty-one to have legal access to alcohol. A frequently heard related argument is that a minimum drinking age of twenty-

one may reduce car crashes among teenagers, but this will only be a temporary effect if it simply delays those problems until the teenagers reach age twenty-one. This argument also proves false. The minimum age of twenty-one significantly reduces car crashes among eighteen- to twenty-year-olds, and those injuries and deaths are permanently saved. There is furthermore no rebound effect at age twenty-one; in fact, the higher legal age appears to produce benefits that continue into a person's early twenties.

While the debate around the legal age for drinking appeared to be settled in the United States as of 2008, there are a few observers who are again voicing support for lowering the drinking age, arguing the U.S. has a continuing problem of teen drinking, and they posit that a lower drinking age might help. However, such a hypothesis ignores much of the scientific literature and the

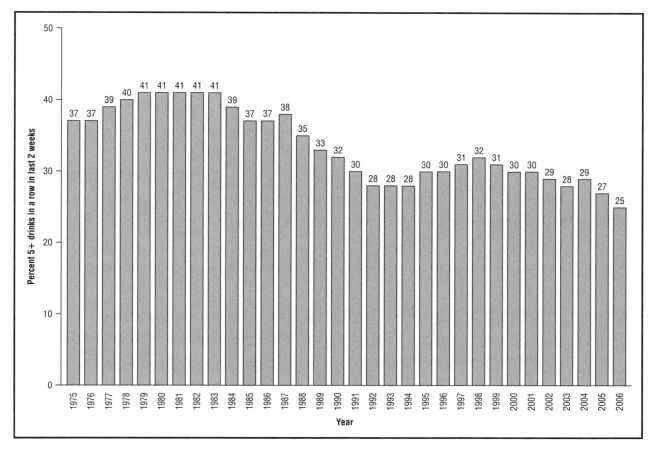

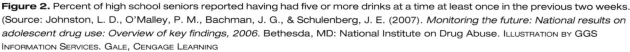

Figure 2. Percent of high school seniors reported having had five or more drinks at a time at least once in the previous two weeks. (Source: Johnston, L. D., O'Malley, P. M., Bachman, J. G., & Schulenberg, J. E. (2007). *Monitoring the future: National results on adolescent drug use: Overview of key findings, 2006.* Bethesda, MD: National Institute on Drug Abuse. ILLUSTRATION BY GGS INFORMATION SERVICES. GALE, CENGAGE LEARNING

direct experience obtained when states last experimented with the legal age in the 1970s and 1980s.

Professionals in the areas of public health and traffic safety, as well citizens, have realized the benefits of the age-twenty-one drinking law in the United States. Other countries are examining the experience in the United States, and are actively considering raising their legal age. The preponderance of evidence indicates that there is an inverse relationship between the minimum legal drinking age and two important outcomes: alcohol consumption and traffic crashes. Compared with a wide range of other programs and efforts to reduce drinking among teenagers, research shows increasing the legal age for purchase and consumption of alcohol to twenty-one has been the most successful prevention effort in decades. Considering the benefits that have been achieved with only modest enforcement, there

is great opportunity to even further reduce underage alcohol consumption, traffic crashes, and lives lost.

See also **Accidents and Injuries from Alcohol; Driving, Alcohol, and Drugs; Driving Under the Influence (DUI); Legal Regulation of Drugs and Alcohol; Prohibition of Alcohol; Social Costs of Alcohol and Drug Abuse; Temperance Movement.**

BIBLIOGRAPHY

Bellows, D. C. (1980). *The effects of lowering the drinking age in Nebraska: A quasi-experimental times-series analysis.* Unpublished doctoral dissertation, University of Nebraska, Lincoln.

Brown, S. A., Tapert, S. F., Granholm, E. & Delis, D. C. (2000). Neurocognitive functioning of adolescents: Effects of protracted alcohol use. *Alcoholism: Clinical and Experimental Research, 24*(2), 164–171.

Chung, H. B. (1997). Drunk driving and social control policies: Econometric analysis of policy effectiveness.

(Doctoral dissertation, University of Wisconsin-Madison, 1997) *Dissertation Abstracts International, 57,* 5291.

Cook, R. L., & Clark, D. (2005). Is there an association between alcohol consumption and sexually transmitted diseases? A systematic review. *Sexually Transmitted Diseases, 32,* 156–164.

Davis, J. E., & Reynolds, N. C. (1990). Alcohol use among college students: Responses to raising the purchase age. *College Health, 38,* 263–269.

Dunn, M. S., Bartee, R. T., & Perko, M. A. (2003). Self-reported alcohol use and sexual behaviors of adolescents. *Psychological Reports, 92*(1), 339–348.

Ellickson, P. L., Tucker, J. S., & Klein, D. J. (2003). Ten-year prospective study of public health problems associated with early drinking. *Pediatrics, 111*(5), 949–955.

Forster, J. L., McGovern, P. G., Wagenaar, A. C., Wolfson, M., Perry, C. L., & Anstine, P. S. (1994). The ability of young-people to purchase alcohol without age identification in northeastern Minnesota, USA. *Addiction, 89*(6), 699–705.

Grube, J. W. (1997). Preventing sales of alcohol to minors: Results from a community trial. *Addiction, 93*(Suppl. 2), S251–S260.

Guo, J., Chung, I. J., Hill, K. G., Hawkins, J. D., Catalano, R. F., & Abbott, R. D. (2002). Developmental relationships between adolescent substance use and risky sexual behavior in young adulthood. *Journal of Adolescent Health, 31*(4), 354–362.

Huckle, T., Conway, K., Casswell, S., & Pledger, M. (2005). Evaluation of a regional community action intervention in New Zealand to improve age checks for young people purchasing alcohol. *Health Promotion International, 20*(2), 147–155.

Hughes, S. P., & Dodder, R. A. (1992). Changing the legal minimum drinking age: Results of a longitudinal-study. *Journal of Studies on Alcohol, 53,* 568–575.

Johnston, L. D., O'Malley, P. M., Bachman, J. G., & Schulenberg, J. E. (2007). *Monitoring the Future: National results on adolescent drug use: Overview of key findings, 2006.* (NIH Publication No. 07–6202). Bethesda, MD: National Institute on Drug Abuse.

Jones, N. E., Pieper, C. F., & Robertson, L. S. (1992). The effect of legal drinking age on fatal injuries of adolescents and young adults. *American Journal of Public Health, 82,* 112–115.

Kandel, D. B., & Jessor, R. (2002). The gateway hypothesis revisited. In Denise B. Kandel (Ed.), *Stages and pathways of drug involvement: Examining the gateway hypothesis* (pp. 365–384). Cambridge, England: Cambridge University Press.

Kindelberger, J. (2005). *Traffic safety facts research note: Calculating lives saved due to minimum drinking age laws* (DOT Publication No. DOT HS 809 860). Washington, DC: National Center for Statistics and Analysis.

Lewis, R. K., Paine-Andrews, A. Fawcett, S. B., Francisco, V. T., Richter, K. P., Copple, B., et al. (1996). Evaluating the effects of a community coalition's efforts to reduce illegal sales of alcohol and tobacco products to minors. *Journal of Community Health, 21*(6), 429–436.

Maisto, S. A., & Rachal, V. (1980). Indications of the relationship among adolescent drinking practices, related behaviors, and drinking-age laws. In H. Wechsler (Ed.), *Minimum drinking-age laws* (pp. 155–176). Lexington, MA: D. C. Heath, Lexington Books.

Mohler-Kuo, M., Dowdall, G. W., Koss, M. P., & Wechsler, H. (2004). Correlates of rape while intoxicated in a national sample of college women. *Journal of Studies on Alcohol, 65,* 37–45.

Monti, P. M., Miranda, R., Nixon, K., Sher, K. J., Swartzwelder, H. S., Tapert, S. F., et al. (2005). Adolescence: Booze, brains, and behavior. *Alcoholism: Clinical and Experimental Research, 29*(2), 207–220.

Naor, E. M., & Nashold, R. D. (1975). Teenage driver fatalities following reduction in legal drinking age. *Journal of Safety Research, 7,* 74–79.

National Highway Traffic Safety Administration. (2006). *Traffic safety facts: 2005 data.* (DOT Publication No. DOT HS 810 630). Washington, DC: National Center for Statistics and Analysis.

National Research Council & Institute of Medicine. (2004). *Reducing underage drinking: A collective responsibility.* Washington, DC: National Academies Press.

O'Malley, P., & Wagenaar, A. C. (1991). Effects of minimum drinking age laws on alcohol use, related behaviors, and traffic crash involvement among American youth 1976–1987. *Journal of Studies on Alcohol, 52,* 478–491.

Paschall, M. J., Grube, J. W., Black, C., Flewelling, R. L., Ringwalt, C. L., & Biglan, A. (2007). Alcohol outlet characteristics and alcohol sales to youth: Results from alcohol purchase surveys in 45 Oregon communities. *Prevention Science, 8,* 153–159.

Preusser, D. F., & Williams, A. F. (1992). Sales of alcohol to underage purchasers in three New York counties and Washington, D.C. *Journal of Public Health Policy, 13*(3), 306–317.

Scribner, R., & Cohen, D. (2001). The effect of enforcement on merchant compliance with the minimum legal drinking age law. *Journal of Drug Issues, 31*(4), 857–866.

Shults, R. A., Elder, R. W., Sleet, D. A., Nichols, J. L., Alao, M. O., Carander-Kulis, V. G., et al. (2001). Reviews of evidence regarding interventions to reduce alcohol impaired driving. *American Journal of Preventive Medicine, 21*(Suppl. 4), 66–88.

Smith, G. S., Branas, C. C., & Miller, T. R. (1999). Fatal nontraffic injuries involving alcohol: A meta-analysis. *Annals of Emergency Medicine, 33*(6), 659–668.

Stueve, A., & O'Donnell, L. N. (2005). Early alcohol initiation and subsequent sexual and alcohol risk behaviors among urban youths. *American Journal of Public Health, 95*(5), 887–893.

U.S. Department of Transportation. (2004). *Fatality Analysis Reporting System*. Washington, DC: Author.

Vingilis, E., & Smart, R. G. (1981). Effects of raising the legal drinking age in Ontario. *British Journal of Addiction, 76*, 415–424.

Wagenaar, A. C., & Toomey, T. L. (2002). Effects of minimum drinking age laws: Review and analyses of the literature from 1960 to 2000. *Journal of Studies on Alcohol, Suppl. 14,* 206–225.

Wagenaar, A. C., Toomey, T. L., & Erickson, D. J. (2005). Preventing youth access to alcohol: Outcomes from a multi-community time-series trial. *Addiction, 100,* 335–345.

Warner, L. A., & White, H. R. (2003). Longitudinal effects of age at onset and first drinking situations on problem drinking. *Substance Use & Misuse, 38*(14), 1983–2016.

Wilner, P., Hart, K., Binmore, J., Cavendish, M., & Dunphy, E. (2000). Alcohol sales to underage adolescents: An unobtrusive observational field study and evaluation of a policy intervention. *Addiction, 95*(9), 1373–1388.

ALEXANDER C. WAGENAAR
REVISED BY AUTHOR (2009)
AMY L. TOBLER (2009)

MINNESOTA MULTIPHASIC PERSONALITY INVENTORY.

The MMPI was developed by Starke R. Hathaway and J. Charnley McKinley and first published in 1942 for the diagnosis of a variety of mental disorders and psychopathology. In its current form, the MMPI-2 (1989) is a self-report test containing 567 true/false items administered in 60–90 minutes and in a variety of formats: pen and pencil, computer, or audiocassettes (Butcher et al., 1989). As one of the most widely used personality assessment tools, the MMPI-2 is sometimes administered to individuals who abuse alcohol or drugs and to identify personality characteristics associated with the abuse.

The MMPI-2 has ten clinical scales that generate a profile identifying the patient's personality traits and disorders in relation to population norms. These norms were derived from normative samples consisting of adults aged 18–80 from diverse communities and regions across the United States. The clinical scales are: Hypochondriasis, Depression, Hysteria, Psychopathic Deviate, Masculinity-Femininity, Paranoia, Psychasthenia (a neurotic disorder with chief characteristics that include the presence of phobias, obsessions, and great anxiety), Schizophrenia, Hypomania, and Social Introversion. In addition, the MMPI-2 has several other scales, clinical subscales and newly developed supplementary scales, such as the Addiction Admissions Scale (AAS) and the Addiction Potential Scale (APS) to help validate and expand clinical diagnoses and enhance interpretation of the main clinical profile (Weed et al., 1992).

The MMPI-2 has three main applications to the evaluation, diagnosis, and study of substance-use disorders. First, it has been used to evaluate the effects of alcohol and drug abuse. Several studies (e.g., Babor et al., 1988) have shown that MMPI clinical scales measuring depression, paranoia, and other psychiatric symptoms tend to be higher than normal when alcoholics are drinking—but return to the normal range during periods of abstinence. Second, research on the MMPI has used cluster analysis to identify subtypes of alcoholics and drug users (e.g., Belding et al., 1998, Moss & Werner, 1992). For example, three types of alcoholics were identified based on their MMPI profiles: neurotic, psychotic, and psychopathic (Robyak et al., 1984). Third, the MMPI-2 has been used in the development of special scales for drug and alcohol abuse. The MacAndrew Alcoholism Scale (MAC) is used to measure impulsivity, pressure for action, and acting-out potential that may lead to alcoholism (Craig, 2005; MacAndrew, 1965). Similar to the MAC, the APS was designed to identify personality traits and factors that play a role in the addictions. The APS assesses the individual's acknowledgement or denial of substance abuse. The MMPI-2 can be used in research, but it is mostly used in clinical settings for intake assessments. The clinical profile generated by the MMPI-2 helps to determine and guide treatment plans.

See also **Addiction Severity Index (ASI); Diagnostic and Statistical Manual (DSM); Michigan Alcoholism Screening Test (MAST); Models of Alcoholism and Drug Abuse.**

BIBLIOGRAPHY

Babor, T. F., Dolinsky, Z., Rounsaville, B., & Jaffe, J. (1988). Unitary versus multidimensional models of alcoholism treatment outcome: An empirical study. *Journal of Studies on Alcohol, 49,* 167–177.

Belding, M. A., Iguchi, M. Y., Morral, A. R., & Husband, S. D. (1998). MMPI profiles of opiate addicts: Predicting response to treatment. *Journal of Personality Assessment, 70,* 324–339.

Butcher, J. N., Dahlstrom, W. G., Graham, J. R., Tellegen, A., & Kaemmer, B. (1989). MMPI-2: Manual for administration and scoring. Minneapolis: University of Minnesota Press.

Craig, R. J. (2005). Assessing contemporary substance abusers with the MMPI MacAndrews Alcoholism Scale: A review. Substance Use and Misuse, *40,* 427–450.

Moss, P. D., & Werner, P. D. (1992). An MMPI typology of cocaine abusers. *Journal of Personality Assessment, 58,* 269–276.

MacAndrew, C. (1965). The differentiation of male alcoholic outpatients from non-alcoholic psychiatric patients by means of the MMPI. *Quarterly Journal of Studies on Alcohol, 26,* 238–246.

Robyak J. E., Donham, C. W., Roy, R., & Ludenia, K. (1984). Differential patterns of alcohol abuse among normal, neurotic, psychotic, and characterological types. *Journal of Personality Assessment, 48,* 132–136.

Weed, N. C., Butcher, J. N., McKenna, T., & Ben-Porath, Y.S. (1992). New measures for assessing alcohol and drug abuse with the MMPI-2: The APS and AAS. *Journal of Personality Assessment, 58,* 389–404.

EFRAT AHARONOVICH

MODELS OF ALCOHOLISM AND DRUG ABUSE.

The development of conceptual models that define the essential characteristics of alcoholism and addiction has been an enduring preoccupation of drug and alcohol studies. The question of whether substance dependence is best conceptualized as a disease, a syndrome, a learned behavior, a bad habit, or a social process continues to produce discussion and dissent. Indeed, the debate concerns not only the nature of alcoholism addiction, but also the implications of different models. Does a disease model of addiction necessarily support medical treatment as the most effective intervention? Does it endorse abstinence as the only viable treatment goal? Does it undermine or enhance the stigma of addiction? Is a syndrome a disease by another name, or does it represent a challenge to the notion of a singular disease? Consensus is unlikely because of the different functions served by various models and the range of groups that have a stake in the issue. However, the articulation and refinement of conceptual frameworks is valuable in itself, and is characteristic of a vibrant research field. The adoption of different frameworks also has an impact on treatment and policy decisions, thereby affecting the experiences of those with drug and alcohol problems.

Rather than providing a comprehensive account of all current models of alcoholism and drug dependence in the following entry, it is important instead to focus on key approaches. It is possible to identify recurring (and recurringly contested) themes in definitions of alcohol and drug dependence: loss of control, craving, continued use despite harmful consequences, evidence of biological alteration such as withdrawal symptoms or tolerance, and individual vulnerability to dependence. The conceptualization of alcoholism as a disease is a central focus because it has been so prominent as "a governing image" of scientific and lay attempts to prevent and understand problem drinking and drug consumption (Room, 2001).

FROM SIN TO SICKNESS

Histories of addiction generally begin with the shift from pre-modern views of excessive drinking and drunkenness as willful and immoral conduct to the notion of alcoholism as a "disease of the will," (Valverde, 1998). According to Harry G. Levine's influential article (1978), "The Discovery of Addiction," the idea that habitual drunkenness represented a loss of control over drinking, occurred at the end of the eighteenth century, with the rise of the middle classes and the ideology of bourgeois individualism. Prior to this time people thought drunkards drank to excess because they chose to indulge in a pleasurable sin.

A key figure in the promotion of the new view of inebriety was the prominent American physician Benjamin Rush. Rush—who published his "Inquiry into the Effects of Ardent Spirits" in 1784—unified several ideas into a new paradigm to provide "the first clearly developed modern conception of alcohol addiction" (Levine, 1978, p. 151). The main tenets of this paradigm were that (a) chronic drunkenness represented a loss of control over drinking, (b) this condition was a disease with a tendency to progress, (c) "spirituous liquors" were the cause of the disease, and (d) abstinence was the only cure (Levine, 1978; White, 2000a). These ideas have remained prominent in understandings of addiction, especially the emphasis on compulsion as a feature that distinguishes the state of dependency from other forms of problem drinking.

As the nineteenth century progressed, physicians in both the United States and Britain used increasingly medicalized language to describe patients who exhibited recurring drunkenness. The terms used included "monomania of the will," "dipsomania," "habitual inebriation," and "the disease of inebriety" (White, 2004). The view that drunkenness was a medical problem that should concern doctors was supported by increased awareness of the detrimental physical effects of excessive alcohol intake. In 1849 Swedish physician Magnus Huss published a systematic study of the deleterious effects of alcohol on the body and concluded that these symptoms were "a disease group in themselves" (cited in White, 2000a, p. 49). Huss proposed the name *alcoholism* for this disease. As a disease, inebriety or alcoholism was seen as a treatable condition, and thus the doctors involved in the development of the medical paradigm also campaigned for specialist inebriate asylums (Valverde, 1998).

While the disease model developed in the nineteenth century is routinely contrasted with moral and religious views of the drunkard, the distinction between the two perspectives is not always clear-cut. The use of medical terminology does not preclude moral judgment, for example, that preachers often used words such as *disease* and *sickness* to describe morally reprehensible behavior without any commitment to a medical perspective (Ferentzy, 2001). Rush labeled chronic drunkenness a "disease induced by an act of vice" (Rush, 1943, p. 337).

In the early twentieth century the view of the addict as a patient deserving sympathy was overshadowed by an emphasis on the addict as a menace to society, reflected in and promoted by the increased criminalization of drug use (Musto, 1999). Disease metaphors were frequently used to demonize addicts and addiction during this period. In the early twenty-first century, the dominance of disease conceptions of addiction in the United States had not prevented the punitive measures and moralized rhetoric of the "war on drugs" (Keane, 2005).

THE MODERN DISEASE CONCEPT

In the mid-twentieth century a new version of the disease concept of alcoholism was developed that emphasized the role of individual vulnerability rather than the pernicious effects of alcohol (Mann et al., 2000). The idea of alcoholism as a disease was promoted and disseminated by scientists and other advocates through institutions such as the Yale Center of Alcohol Studies, the Research Council on Problems of Alcohol, and the National Committee for Education on Alcoholism (White, 2000b). Their advocacy of a scientific approach to the study of alcohol problems appealed to both "wet" and "dry" constituents in the post-Prohibition era (Roizen, 2004; Room, 1983). E. M. Jellinek, head of the Yale Center, was the most influential scientist in the field of alcohol studies, which developed from the alcoholism movement. His *Disease Concept of Alcoholism* (1960) is widely cited as the seminal text in the field, even if much of its detail has been forgotten.

Jellinek (1952) defined alcoholism expansively as any consumption of alcohol that causes damage to the individual or society. He saw it as a condition that progressed in severity through predictable stages of development, analogous to the natural history of a disease. But he classified only two out of five "species" of alcoholism as diseases, because they alone were based on a "physio-pathological process" involving adaptation of cell metabolism; acquisition of tolerance; and experience of withdrawal symptoms, craving and loss of control, or inability to abstain (Jellinek, 1960, p. 40). The World Health Organization (WHO) Committee on Addiction-Producing Drugs also emphasized physiological alteration as the basis of addiction when it set out two diagnostic categories in 1958, drug addiction and drug habituation, the former signifying the presence of both physical and psychological dependence, the latter "only" psychological (Room, 1998).

DEPENDENCE SYNDROME

In response to some of the shortcomings of Jellinek's one-dimensional and broad definition of alcoholism, British psychiatrists Griffith Edwards and Milton Gross proposed an alcohol dependence syndrome in 1976. Rather than a simple categorical definition, the dependence syndrome was a collection of seven elements that could differ in degree, thus allowing the syndrome to exist in a continuum of severity from mild to severe (Edwards & Gross, 1976, p. 1058). Crucially, the development of dependence resulted from both biological and learning processes. Edwards (1986) later identified the core elements of the syndrome as (a) impaired control over drinking behavior, and (b) withdrawal and its attendant behavior, including the subjective need for alcohol. Another influential aspect of the dependence syndrome model was the differentiation of dependence from heavy drinking and alcohol-related disabilities such as cirrhosis or marital breakdown.

The criteria for alcohol and substance dependence set out in WHO's *International Classification of Diseases* and the American Psychiatric Association's *Diagnostic and Statistical Manual* are largely based on Gross and Edwards's model. The most recent edition of the *International Classification of Diseases* (*ICD-10*) describes substance dependence syndrome as a "cluster of behavioral, cognitive and physiological phenomena that develop after repeated substance use" (World Health Organization, 1992, p. 321). Diagnosis is made if three of the following criteria are met: (a) a strong desire or sense of compulsion to take the substance, (b) impaired capacity to control its use, (c) a physiological withdrawal state, (d) evidence of tolerance, (e) preoccupation with substance use and decreased interest in other activities, and (f) persistent use despite clear evidence of harmful consequences (World Health Organization, 1993, p. 57).

The description in the American Psychiatric Association's most recent diagnostic manual (DSM-IV) is similar, defining substance dependence as "a maladaptive pattern of substance use, leading to clinically significant impairment or distress" (American Psychiatric Association, 1994, p. 181). For a positive diagnosis, three of the following criteria must occur: (a) tolerance (a need for increasing amounts of the drug to achieve the desired effect); (b) withdrawal; (c) taking the substance in larger amounts or over a longer period than intended; (d) a persistent desire for or unsuccessful efforts to control use; (e) a great deal of time spent obtaining, using, or recovering from use of the substance; (f) important social, occupational, or recreational activities given up or reduced because of substance use; and (g) continued use despite recognition that a physical or psychological problem is caused or exacerbated by the

substance. The DSM-IV description also states that tolerance, withdrawal, and compulsion are "usually" experienced while "craving," a strong subjective drive to take the substance, occurs in "most (if not all)" dependent individuals (American Psychiatric Association, 1994, p. 176). The differences between the British-based ICD-10 model of dependence and the American DSM-IV are significant, although subtle, reflecting differences in approach between American and British psychiatry. Room notes that British psychiatry has tended to take the view that social consequences do not belong in definitions of diseases or disorders (Room, 1998, p. 309).

Supporters of the dependence syndrome concept stress its flexibility; its inclusion of biological, psychological, and social factors' and its unwillingness to "assign a weight or special significance to any one factor or interaction" (Jaffe, 1992, p. 11). Indeed, as Room has pointed out, one of its most notable characteristics is that despite the sense of a unitary disorder conveyed by the term "substance dependence," no single affliction is described by this label (Room, 1998, p. 313). The diagnostic criteria are disjunctive, meaning that meeting any three qualifies as dependence; thus one sufferer could have no symptoms in common with another. There are many possible ways of being dependent on a substance, and there are a large number of substances one could be dependent on in all these various ways. Moreover, there is no single criterion shared by all who are diagnosed as dependent. However, unlike Edwards and Gross's provisional syndrome, the diagnostic approach of the ICD-10 and DSM-IV assumes that diseases are either present or absent, rather than existing in degrees of strength or manifestation.

Critics of the dependence syndrome have regarded it as both too similar to and too divergent from the disease concept. For many social scientists the dependence syndrome is simply the disease model repackaged, with all its major assumptions retained (Moore, 1992). In a wide-ranging critique, Stan Shaw (1979) argues that the dependence syndrome was not developed because of empirical or theoretical advances in the field, but in order to re-establish medical authority over addiction in the face of challenges from psychology and the social sciences.

Others in the field, especially those in the United States, regard the dependence syndrome as too vague about addiction as a primary and independent disease defined by specific and predictable symptoms. Norman S. Miller argues that the shift in terminology from drug addiction to substance dependence obscures the centrality of "loss of control" as the fundamental component (1995, p. 20). The use of the term *dependence* is also confusing, Miller suggests, because it can also refer solely to the physiological processes of adaptation. In this sense it is possible for someone to be dependent on a drug, after medical treatment for pain for example, but not to demonstrate the psychological and behavioral criteria of addiction (Miller, 1995, pp. 17, 21). For Miller it is clear that addiction is located in the drug-seeking behavior of the addict and, in particular, in the loss of control over his behavior. This emphasis on psychological and behavioral criteria, such as compulsion and craving, opens up the possibility for a range of non-substance based dependencies, such as sexual compulsion, food addiction, and exercise addiction (Jaffe, 1992). It also reinforces the status of psychiatry as the medical specialty best able to understand and treat addiction and alcoholism.

Biopsychosocial models are another example of expanded and updated understandings of addiction that retain a commitment to the disease concept. Advocates underscore the inclusivity and multidimensionality of biospsychosocial models, specifically their recognition of biological, behavioral, cognitive, psychosocial, and sociocultural elements in the etiology of addiction (Wallace, 1993). According to John Wallace, acceptance of what he calls the biopsychosocial disease model has the potential to end the "ideological skirmishes" over models of addiction (1993, p. 85). But although the model refers to social and cultural aspects of addiction, in practice these tend to be understood in a rather narrow way as individual risk factors and harmful consequences; for example, the role of peer groups in promoting drug use and the impact of drug use on relationships (see Landry, 1993).

NEUROLOGICAL AND LEARNING APPROACHES

With advances in neuroscience and imaging technologies, research on drug actions in the brain has become prominent in addiction science. Neurological accounts of addiction focus on the changes in "brain reward systems" that occur with the development of compulsive drug use, while accepting dominant medical models of dependence (for example, DSM-IV criteria). According to George F. Koob and colleagues, all drugs of abuse increase levels of the neurotransmitter dopamine in neural pathways that control pleasure (also known as the *mesolimbic system*) (Koob et al., 1999). It is hypothesized that as dependence develops, these pathways, which evolved to reinforce behaviors necessary to survival such as eating and sex, are "hijacked" by "artificial drug rewards" (Schultz, 2000; Nesse & Berridge, 1997). The brain adapts to the presence of a drug, and synapses and circuits are remodeled, increasing the reinforcing effects of the drug.

Neurological accounts of addiction have contributed to the increasing importance placed on positive reinforcement, or drug reward, in the production and maintenance of compulsive drug use. One of the most persistent debates in drug research is whether people continue to use drugs primarily to alleviate withdrawal and other negative states or primarily to experience positive rewarding effects (Jaffe, 1992). Neural models tend to focus on positive rather than negative reinforcement, specifically the brain rewards produced by psychoactive drugs (Wise, 1988). But the idea that physical dependence—defined by the presence of withdrawal symptoms—is the *sine qua non* of genuine addictive disease has remained influential. For example, Harold E. Doweiko's medical textbook published in 1993 uses "a demonstrated withdrawal syndrome" as the criterion to indicate whether a user "actually is addicted to a chemical" (Doweiko, 1993, p. 8). The use of physiological change as the criteria for addiction reflects a belief that a genuine disease is a fundamentally biological entity that affects the organic functioning of the body. It is noteworthy that a medical journal article by A. Thomas McLellan and colleagues based its conclusion that drug dependence was "a chronic medical illness" on its similarity to diabetes, asthma, and hypertension, rather than comparing it with psychiatric conditions (McLellan et al., 2000).

The implications of neurological accounts of addiction vary in relation to the disease status of addiction. On one hand, they highlight objective biological changes in brain anatomy and function as the basis of dependence. Alan Leshner, former head of the U.S. National Institute on Drug Abuse has argued that it is crucial to recognize addiction as a brain disease because there are observable differences between "the addicted brain" and "the non-addicted brain" (Leshner, 1996; 1999). According to Steven Hyman, the dopamine model of drug action suggests that addiction is a disease of learning and memory, based on the brain recording powerful but pathological associations between drug use and pleasure. The role of memory explains why addiction is a "recalcitrant, chronic and relapsing condition" (Hyman, 2005, p. 1414). On the other hand, the neurological processes involved in drug addiction are the same as those involved in other forms of learning and memory. This suggests that addiction is not necessarily a disease but rather a form of learned behavior like any other. The understanding of addiction as learned behavior is one that has a long history in behavioral psychology.

ADDICTION AS LEARNED BEHAVIOR

The learning model found in psychology offers an alternative to disease conceptions because it does not classify deviant or harmful behavior as different from "normal" behavior. It views addiction and alcoholism as learned behavioral disorders that have been acquired and maintained in the same way as other repetitive, habitual, and recurring patterns of conduct (Lindstrom, 1992). Rather than a qualitatively different state from normal drinking, alcoholism is an extreme on a continuum of drinking behavior. Treatment aims to teach alternatives to destructive and antisocial habits, assuming that the alcoholic's "loss of control" is an acquired pattern of consumption that can be changed, rather than a symptom of a disease. Experimental research, which demonstrated that alcoholics' drinking was influenced by expectancy (whether they believed a drink contained alcohol) as well as studies that suggested alcoholics could drink moderately without relapsing, supported this challenge to "loss of control" as the central feature of alcoholism (Marlatt, 1978; Sobell & Sobell, 1978; Fingarette, 1988). However, the evidence supporting controlled drinking as a viable treatment goal for alcoholics has been contested (Sobell & Sobell, 1995).

In his learning-based model, Jim Orford (2001) examines how a strong attachment to an "appetitive behavior" is acquired, resulting in "unmanageable and excessive consumption." His model emphasizes the opposing psychological, social, and moral forces that are at play in the development of excessive behavior (whether it be drinking or drug use, eating, sex, or gambling). These oppositional forces can be summarized as restraint versus inclination, incentives versus disincentives, and conformity versus deviance. Thus it is not simply attachment, but conflict over attachment, that defines addiction. According to Orford, addictive behavior actually consists of a person's reactions to having developed a costly appetite and his or her response to the negative reactions of others. In his view, giving up an addiction is a naturally occurring process that begins with a personal decision, a decision triggered by the increasing accumulation of costs and conflict produced by the excessive behavior.

ALCOHOLICS ANONYMOUS: DISEASE OF THE SELF

As well as scientific and clinical expertise, the everyday "techniques of sobriety" developed by Alcoholics Anonymous (AA) and other twelve-step fellowships have had a profound impact on public understandings of addiction (Valverde, 1998). AA played a large role in spreading the idea of alcoholism/addiction as a disease, and the twelve-step approach to recovery is incorporated into many drug and alcohol treatment programs (Kurtz, 2002). Its first step, which requires the alcoholic to admit his or her powerlessness over alcohol, is consistent with the medical concept of "loss of control." However, the AA notion of alcoholism as a disease is not medical in a technical or scientific sense. Although it defines alcoholism as a progressive and incurable disease, it stresses the spiritual nature of the alcoholic's disorder and the crucial role of moral growth in recovery (Kurtz, 2002; Keane, 2002). Not surprisingly, the AA notion of disease is dismissed by some researchers as a vague formulation "unsupported either by clinical evidence or research findings" (Johns, 1990, p. 13). However, this fails to recognize that twelve-step models of addiction and alcoholism aim to represent the experience of disorder and despair from the sufferer's perspective, rather than conform to standards of scientific rigor.

It is the connection made between a disordered body and a disordered self that gives the notion of addictive disease, popularized by AA, its explanatory and descriptive power. On one hand, it regards alcoholism (or addiction) as a bio-medical disease with specific predictable symptoms and a predictable natural course (Nowinski & Baker, 1992, p. xvii). But its symptoms, physical and behavioral, are nourished by a profound spiritual malaise. Self-pity, self-loathing, self-centeredness, and the absence of hope are viewed as the bedrock of the addict's existence but at the same time the addict is labeled as the victim of a physical disorder (Milhorn, 1994, pp. 32–42). The idea of a physiological anomaly that marks the addicted body is also used in a characteristically metaphorical manner to construct the addict as inherently and unchangeably different from "normal drinkers." Thus in AA the disease becomes the basis of a social identity that remains in place even if the alcoholic has achieved decades of sobriety.

MEDICAL DOMINANCE AND ITS CRITICS

Despite the success of self-help movements and the contributions of the psychological and social sciences, twenty-first-century alcohol and drug studies are marked by medical dominance. Alcohol and drug problems are seen as fundamentally biomedical issues, albeit issues with important psychological and social dimensions. In the United States biomedical research receives by far the greatest amount of the public funding in the alcohol field, and its dominance over areas like epidemiology and prevention is increasing (Midianik, 2006). Although the dependence syndrome model eschews the term *disease*, it is based on clinical observation of patients and sees the treatment of alcoholism and drug addiction as the responsibility of clinical medicine.

Social scientists have challenged medical perspectives on drug and alcohol use, pointing out the limitations of theories based on the small minority of drug users who seek treatment or medical care. Anthropologist David Moore argues that most drug use occurs in nonclinical populations and that it is unclear whether clinically defined dependence is applicable to community settings (1992, p. 462). He found that the notion of dependence as "a measurable psychobiological 'it'" made little explanatory sense when applied to the group of young amphetamine users he studied, whose drug use was best understood as part of the fluid and ongoing social action of their lives, and which increased and decreased in relation to cultural, social and economic

aspects (Moore, 1992, pp. 484–486). Another question raised by social researchers is the cross-cultural applicability of the models of addiction and alcoholism developed in the West and based on Western understandings of selfhood and identity (Room, 1985; Alasuutari, 1992; Room et al., 1996).

While social scientific research on addiction is often not directly engaged with treatment design, in 2008 Peter Adams proposed a social model of addiction with an explicit application to the provision of drug and alcohol services. According to Adams, dominant views of addiction, including both the medical, psychological, and biopsychosocial, operate within a "particle paradigm." That is, they focus on the person suffering from the disorder as a discrete individual. He argues that a shift to a social paradigm, which understands addiction as a social event and sees people in terms of the nature of their relationships with others, opens up new opportunities for effective intervention.

Adams replaces the model of "an addiction" with the concept of an addictive system, a multilayered network of relationships that includes the addictive relationship between a member of the system and a substance. Other members of the system include immediate intimates, friends, colleagues, and community residents. This network becomes fragmented and unbalanced as the addictive relationship grows in strength, thus one-on-one counseling will have limited success unless there is reconstruction of the person's connections with other people and activities.

As Adams points out, paradigms of addiction can have concrete consequences; for example, in most community addiction services, practitioners see clients in small offices that are not suitable for meeting more than two people at a time, because they assume that the individual is the focus of treatment (Adams, 2008, p. 244). The conceptualization of addiction and alcoholism as a disease promotes abstinence as a universal treatment goal, while the dependence syndrome model suggests that the appropriateness of controlled drinking as a goal depends on the severity of dependence. While the process of medicalization has cemented the role of professional expertise in addiction treatment, self-help movements that value lay knowledge produced through firsthand experience of the disease continue to flourish. In most U.S. treatment programs, professional medical and psychological services are combined with group therapies based on AA practice and ideals of fellowship (Yalisove, 1998). While it is useful to consider different models in their abstract conceptual form, in practice they are frequently combined in a pragmatic way, even when their assumptions may seem incompatible or contradictory.

See also **Addiction: Concepts and Definitions.**

BIBLIOGRAPHY

Adams, P. (2008). *Fragmented intimacy: Addiction in a social world.* New York: Springer.

Alasuutari, P. (1992). *Desire and craving: A cultural theory of alcoholism.* Albany: State University of New York Press.

American Psychiatric Association. (1994). *Diagnostic and statistical manual of mental disorders, DSM-IV.* Washington, DC: Author.

Doweiko, H. F. (1993). *Concepts of chemical dependency.* (2nd ed.). Pacific Grove, CA: Brooks/Cole Publishing.

Edwards, G. (1986). The alcohol dependence syndrome: A concept as stimulus to enquiry. *British Journal of Addiction, 81,* 171–183.

Edwards, G., & Gross, M. M. (1976). Alcohol dependence: Provisional description of a clinical syndrome. *British Medical Journal, 1,* 1058–1061.

Ferentzy, P. (2001). From sin to disease: Differences and similarities between past and current conceptions of chronic drunkenness. *Contemporary Drug Problems, 28,* 363–390.

Fingarette, H. (1988). *Heavy drinking: The myth of alcoholism as a disease.* Berkeley: University of California Press.

Hyman, S. (2005). Addiction: A disease of learning and memory. *American Journal of Psychiatry, 162(8),* 1414–1422. Available from http://ajp.psychiatry online.org/.

Jaffe, J. H. (1992). Current concepts of addiction. In C. P. O'Brien & J. H. Jaffe (Eds.), *Addictive states* (pp. 1–21). New York: Raven Press.

Jellinek, E. M. (1952). Phases of alcohol addiction. *Quarterly Journal of Studies on Alcohol, 13,* 637–684.

Jellinek, E. M. (1960). *The disease concept of alcoholism.* New Brunswick, NJ: Hillhouse Press.

Johns, A. (1990). What is dependence?. In H. Ghodse & D. Maxwell (Eds.), *Substance abuse and dependence: An introduction for the caring professions* (pp. 5–29). Hampshire, U.K. Macmillan Press.

Keane, H. (2002). *What's wrong with addiction?.* New York: New York University Press.

Keane, H. (2005). Addiction and the bioethics of compulsion and dependency. In M. Shildrick and R. Mykitiuk (Eds.), *Ethics of the body: Postconventional challenges* (pp. 91–112). Cambridge, MA: MIT Press.

Koob, G. F., Barak, C., Hyytia, P., Markou, A., Parsons, L. H., Roberts, A. J., et al. (1999). Neurobiology of drug addiction. In M. D. Glantz & C. R. Hartel (Eds.), *Drug abuse: Origins and interventions* (pp.161–190). Washington, DC: American Psychological Association.

Kurtz, E. (2002). Alcoholics Anonymous and the disease concept of alcoholism. *Alcoholism Treatment Quarterly, 20(3–4),* 5–39.

Landry, M. (1993). *Understanding drugs of abuse.* Washington DC: American Psychiatric Press.

Leshner, A. (1996). Understanding drug addiction: Implications for treatment. *Hospital Practice, 31(10),* 47–54, 57–59.

Leshner, A. (1999). Drugs of abuse and the brain, *Proceedings of the American Association of Physicians, 111(2),* 99–108.

Levine, H. G. (1978). The discovery of addiction: Changing conceptions of habitual drunkenness in America. *Journal of Studies on Alcohol, 39(1),* 143–174.

Lindstrom, L. (1992). *Managing alcoholism.* New York: Oxford University Press.

McLellan, A. T., Lewis, D. C., O'Brien, C. P., & Kleber, H. D. (2000). Drug dependence, a chronic medical illness: Implications for treatment, insurance and outcomes evaluation, *JAMA, 284(13),* 1689–1695.

Mann, K., Hermann, D., & Heinz, A. (2000). One hundred years of alcoholism: The twentieth century. *Alcohol and Alcoholism, 35(1),* 10–15.

Marlatt, G. A. (1978). Craving for alcohol, loss of control and relapse: A cognitive behavioral analysis. In P. Nathan, G. A. Marlatt, & T. Loberg (Eds.), *Alcoholism: New directions in behavioral research* (pp. 271–314). New York: Plenum Press.

Milhorn, H. T. (1994). *Drug and alcohol abuse: The authoritative guide for parents, teachers, and counselors.* New York: Plenum Press.

Midianik, L. (2006). *Biomedicalization of alcohol studies.* New Brunswick, NJ: Aldine.

Miller, N. S. (1995). *Addiction psychiatry: Current diagnosis and treatment.* New York: Wiley-Liss.

Moore, D. (1992). Deconstructing "dependence": An ethnographic critique of an influential concept. *Contemporary Drug Problems, 19(3),* 459–490.

Musto, D. (1999). *The American disease: Origins of narcotic control.* (3rd ed.). New York: Oxford University Press.

Nesse, R. & Berridge, K. (1997). Psychoactive drug use in evolutionary perspective. *Science, 278* (5335), 63–66. Available from http://www.sciencemag.org/.

Nowinski, J., & Baker, S. (1992). *The Twelve-Step facilitation handbook*. New York: Lexington Books.

Orford, J. (2001). *Excessive appetites: A psychological view of addictions*. (2nd ed.). Chichester, U.K.: John Wiley & Sons.

Pendery, M., Maltzman, I., & West, L. (1982). Controlled drinking by alcoholics? New findings and a re-evaluation of a major affirmative study. *Science, 217*, 169–175.

Roizen, R. (2004). How does the nation's "alcohol problem" change from era to era?: Stalking the social logic of problem-definition transformations since Repeal. In S. Tracy & C. Acker (Eds.). *Altering American consciousness: The history of alcohol and drug use in the United States 1800–2000* (pp. 61–87). Amherst: University of Massachusetts Press.

Room, R. (1983). Sociology and the disease concept of alcoholism. In R. G. Smart, R. J. Gibbins, Y. Israel, H. Kalant, R. E. Popham, & W. Schmidt. (Eds.), *Research advances in alcohol and drug problems*. (Vol. 7). (pp. 47–91). New York: Plenum Press.

Room, R. (1985). Dependence and society. *British Journal of Addiction, 80*, 133–139.

Room, R. (1998). Alcohol and drug disorders in the international classification of diseases: A shifting kaleidoscope. *Drug and Alcohol Review, 17*, 305–317.

Room, R. (2001). Governing images in public discourse about problematic drinking. In N. Heather, T. J. Peters, T. Stockwell (Eds.), *Handbook of alcohol dependence and alcohol-related problems* (pp. 33–45). Chichester, U.K.: John Wiley & Sons.

Room, R., Janca, A., Bennett, L. A., Schmidt, L., & Sartorius, N. (1996). WHO cross-cultural applicability research on diagnosis and assessment of substance use disorders. *Addiction, 91*(2), 199–220.

Rush, B. (1943). Inquiry into the effect of ardent spirits on the human mind and body. *Quarterly Journal of Studies on Alcohol, 4*, 321–341. (Original work published 1784).

Schultz, W. (2000). Multiple reward signals in the brain. *Nature Review Neuroscience, 1*, 199–207.

Shaw, S. (1979). A critique of the concept of the alcohol dependence syndrome. *British Journal of Addiction, 74*, 339–348.

Sobell, M. B., & Sobell, L. C. (1978). *Behavioral treatment of alcohol problems: Individual therapy and controlled drinking*. New York: Plenum Press.

Sobell, M. B., & Sobell, L. C. (1995). Controlled drinking after 25 years: How important was the great debate? *Addiction, 90*(9), 1149–1153

Valverde, M. (1998). *Diseases of the will: Alcohol and the dilemmas of freedom*. Cambridge: Cambridge University Press.

Wallace, J. (1993). Modern disease models of alcoholism and other chemical dependencies. *Drugs and Society, 8*(1), 69–87.

White, W. L. (2000a). Addiction as a disease: Birth of a concept. *Counselor, 1*(1), 46–51.

White, W. L. (2000b). The rebirth of the disease concept of alcoholism in the 20th century. *Counselor, 1*(2), 62–66.

White, W. L. (2004). The lessons of language: Historical perspectives on the rhetoric of addiction. In S. Tracy & C. Acker (Eds.), *Altering American consciousness: The history of alcohol and drug use in the United States 1800–2000* (pp. 33–60). Amherst: University of Massachusetts Press.

Wise, R. (1988). The neurobiology of craving: Implications for the understanding and treatment of addiction. *Journal of Abnormal Psychology, 97*, 118–132.

World Health Organisation (1992). *The ICD-10 classification of diseases and related health problems*. Geneva: Author.

World Health Organisation. (1993). *The ICD-10 classification of mental and behavioural disorders: Diagnostic criteria for research*. Geneva: Author.

Yalisove, D. (1998). The origins and evolution of the disease concept of treatment. *Journal of Studies on Alcohol, 59*(4), 469–476.

HELEN KEANE

MONEY LAUNDERING.

Obtaining the proceeds of crime has generally been but the first step for profit-motivated criminals. The use of those often has required a second step, whether it be to convert the money into form usable form for licit or illicit purposes, disguise its origins, avoid tax consequences, or make it possible to transport. As the quantity of money to be derived from illegal activity increases, the "laundering" of that money becomes more necessary with the internationalization of commerce, parallel markets, and increased technology. Money laundering has become more sophisticated as a consequence.

The International Financial Action Task Force, convened in 1989 by the G-8 Economic Summit, defines money laundering as "the process by which one conceals the existence, illegal source, or illegal use of the crime proceeds to make those proceeds appear legitimately derived." There are three steps to laundering funds: introducing the proceeds of criminal activity into the legitimate economy (commonly referred to as "placement"); engaging in financial transactions designed to limit the ability to trace the funds (commonly referred to as "layering"); and making the funds available for use (commonly referred to as "integration").

In fact, depending on the objectives of individual criminals as far as convenience and security are concerned, the laundering process can be effected with as few as one and as many as a dozen discrete steps. In its most familiar form, hundreds of thousands of dollars in drug proceeds are taken to a financial institution and exchanged for a cashier's check, which the trafficker can carry around (or out of the country) with much less suspicion than suitcases full of cash. A slightly more involved scenario entails taking the same cash to the same bank, where it is deposited into an account and then sent by wire transfer to a bank in a foreign country, probably a jurisdiction renowned for the relative secrecy it affords customers like the hypothetical drug dealer.

In even more elaborate schemes, the same funds are wire-transferred around a circuit of accounts in different countries bearing the names of legitimate businesses. After the transfer reaches its final destination abroad, the owner in the United States arranges a sham transaction to bring the funds back into this country, often as the proceeds of a purported loan. There are literally countless varieties of laundering schemes, limited only by the imaginations of criminals and a more widespread impatience with transferring one's funds too far away.

Traditionally money laundering was conducted by the same individuals who committed the underlying criminal activity. Today, the sophistication of the process has given rise to the professional money launderer. But as money laundering has become more invaluable for criminals and criminal networks, governments have increasingly come to see the process as a potential vulnerability in the business of crime and have increasingly sought to curtail and prosecute it.

The United States began its legislative efforts to crackdown on money laundering in 1970 by requiring the reporting of cash transactions as part of the Bank Secrecy Act. As now modified, $10,000 in cash deposited in a financial institution or paid to a business will trigger the reporting requirements by the recipient of the funds. And with the Money Laundering Control Act of 1986, codified as 18 USC 1956 and 1957, Congress made it a crime to move certain illegally obtained funds through the commercial or banking system. Enforcement of anti-money laundering legislation was not only accomplished through the traditional penalties of incarceration and fines but also enhanced with powerful forfeiture remedies. Finally, since 1988 federal legislation has required banks to report "suspicious transactions." Individual states have sought to control money laundering with their own statutory and regulatory schemes. Internationally, the Financial Action Task Force and Interpol have approved resolutions, protocols, and recommendations calling for nations to pass legislation that would make money laundering a crime; require reporting of suspicious transactions; permit forfeiture; and allow extradition in money laundering cases.

U.S. anti-laundering legislation is complex and often controversial but what is perhaps most remarkable is the fundamental change in enforcement policy it represents, wrought by the requirement that non-law enforcement entities be compelled to engage in the systematic reporting of potential illegal activity. As a result, compliance programs requiring the recipient of funds to know its customer's business and to establish baselines from which suspicious activities can be identified are now the norm. For better or for worse, money laundering has brought the private world of commerce into the public field of law enforcement.

BIBLIOGRAPHY

Kopp, P. (2004). *Political economy of illegal drugs.* London: Routledge.

Madinger, J. (2006). *Money laundering: A guide for criminal investigators,* 2nd ed. Boca Raton, FL: CRC Press.

RONALD GOLDSTOCK

MONITORING THE FUTURE. The use of illegal drugs by large numbers of young people in the United States became an issue of considerable concern during the late 1960s and early 1970s. At that time, there were few accurate data available to assess the extent of use on a national basis. In 1975, psychologists Lloyd Johnston and Jerald Bachman of the University of Michigan initiated *Monitoring the Future: An Ongoing Study of the Lifestyles and Values of Youth*, which was intended to address this lack of information.

One of the major purposes of the study was (and is) to develop an accurate picture of the nature and extent of drug use among young people. An accurate assessment of the amount and extent of illicit drug use in this group is a prerequisite for rational policy making. Reliable and valid data on prevalence are necessary to determine an appropriate allocation of resources and to prevent or correct misconceptions. Reliable and valid data on trends allow for early detection of emerging problems and make it possible to assess the impact of external events, including historical events and deliberate policy changes.

In addition, the study was designed to monitor factors that might help explain the observed changes in drug use—that is, it was intended to serve both an epidemiological function (to learn how many young people use drugs) and an etiological function (to study why young people use drugs). The factors measured included attitudes toward drugs; peer norms and behaviors in regard to drugs; beliefs about the dangers of drugs; perceived availability of drugs; religious attitudes; and various lifestyle factors. The monitoring of these factors has among other things provided the country with valuable information. A particular contribution has been to help address a central policymaking question in the nation's war on drugs: the relative importance of supply versus demand factors in bringing about some of the observed changes in drug use.

STUDY DESIGN

The core feature of the design is an annual survey of each new high school senior class, beginning with the class of 1975. Each year approximately sixteen thousand seniors are surveyed in approximately 135 public and private high schools that have been scientifically selected to provide an accurate, representative cross-section of high school seniors throughout the coterminous United States. Data are collected following standardized procedures via closed-ended questionnaires administered in classrooms by University of Michigan representatives and their assistants.

In 1991 the project was expanded to include nationally representative samples of students from the eighth and tenth grades as well as from the twelfth grade. Each year, approximately eighteen thousand eighth-graders and sixteen thousand tenth-graders are surveyed, using procedures similar to those used in the twelfth-grade surveys.

One limitation of the design is that it does not include in the target population the young men and women who drop out of high school before graduation, and who make up between 15 and 20 percent of each age group nationally, according to U.S. Census statistics. The omission of high school dropouts does introduce biases in the estimation of certain characteristics of the entire age group, but because the dropouts are a relatively small proportion of the entire group the bias due to their omission is small. Because relatively few adolescents drop out before the end of tenth grade, the bias is particularly small for the eighth- and tenth-graders. It should also be noted that because any bias resulting from exclusion of the dropouts usually remains constant from year to year, the exclusion of dropouts should introduce little or no bias in estimates of change or trends.

An issue that is relevant to the study of such sensitive behaviors as drug use is the extent to which respondents will answer honestly. Considerable inferential evidence suggests that the procedures used in this study produce largely valid data. This evidence includes the following points: Large proportions of respondents report using illegal substances; various drugs exhibit trends in different ways over time; there are very few missing data in response to questions on drug use, even though respondents are instructed not to answer questions they would prefer not to answer; the high correlations with such other behaviors as grades, delinquency, religious attitudes, and truancy indicate a high degree of construct validity; a high degree of consistency can be noted over time in individuals' reports (that is, the responses are reliable); and other factors that are discussed in detail elsewhere (see Johnston, O'Malley, Bachman & Schulenberg, 2007; O'Malley, Bachman & Johnston, 1983).

(Percent who used in last twelve months)

	1975	1980	1985	1990	1991	1992	1993	1994	1995	1996	1997	1998	1999	2000	2001	2002	2003	2004	2005	2006	2007
Any Illicit Drug[a]																					
8th Grade	—	—	—	—	11.3	12.9	15.1	18.5	21.4	23.6	22.1	21.0	20.5	19.5	19.5	17.7	16.1	15.2	15.5	14.8	13.2
10th Grade	—	—	—	—	21.4	20.4	24.7	30.0	33.3	37.5	38.5	35.0	35.9	36.4	37.2	34.8	32.0	31.1	29.8	28.7	28.1
12th Grade	45.0	53.1	46.3	32.5	29.4	27.1	31.0	35.8	39.0	40.2	42.4	41.4	42.1	40.9	41.4	41.0	39.3	38.8	38.4	36.5	35.9
Any Illicit Drug Other Than Marijuana																					
8th Grade	—	—	—	—	8.4	9.3	10.4	11.3	12.6	13.1	11.8	11.0	10.5	10.2‡	10.8	8.8	8.8	7.9	8.1	7.7	7.0
10th Grade	—	—	—	—	12.2	12.3	13.9	15.2	17.5	18.4	18.2	16.6	16.7	16.7‡	17.9	15.7	13.8	13.5	12.9	12.7	13.1
12th Grade	26.2	30.4	27.4	17.9	16.2	14.9	17.1	18.0	19.4	19.8	20.7	20.2	20.7	20.4‡	21.6	20.9	19.8	20.5	19.7	19.2	18.5
Marijuana/Hashish																					
8th Grade	—	—	—	—	6.2	7.2	9.2	13.0	15.8	18.3	17.7	16.9	16.5	15.6	15.4	14.6	12.8	11.8	12.2	11.7	10.3
10th Grade	—	—	—	—	16.5	15.2	19.2	25.2	28.7	33.6	34.8	31.1	32.1	32.2	32.7	30.3	28.2	27.5	26.6	25.2	24.6
12th Grade	40.0	48.8	40.6	27.0	23.9	21.9	26.0	30.7	34.7	35.8	38.5	37.5	37.8	36.5	37.0	36.2	34.9	34.3	33.6	31.5	31.7
Inhalants																					
8th Grade	—	—	—	—	9.0	9.5	11.0	11.7	12.8	12.2	11.8	11.1	10.3	9.4	9.1	7.7	8.7	9.6	9.5	9.1	8.3
10th Grade	—	—	—	—	7.1	7.5	8.4	9.1	9.6	9.5	8.7	8.0	7.2	7.3	6.6	5.8	5.4	5.9	6.0	6.5	6.6
12th Grade	—	4.6	5.7	6.9	6.6	6.2	7.0	7.7	8.0	7.6	6.7	6.2	5.6	5.9	4.5	4.5	3.9	4.2	5.0	4.5	3.7
LSD																					
8th Grade	—	—	—	—	1.7	2.1	2.3	2.4	3.2	3.5	3.2	2.8	2.4	2.4	2.2	1.5	1.3	1.1	1.2	0.9	1.1
10th Grade	—	—	—	—	3.7	4.0	4.2	5.2	6.5	6.9	6.7	5.9	6.0	5.1	4.1	2.6	1.7	1.6	1.5	1.7	1.9
12th Grade	7.2	6.5	4.4	5.4	5.2	5.6	6.8	6.9	8.4	8.8	8.4	7.6	8.1	6.6	6.6	3.5	1.9	2.2	1.8	1.7	2.1
MDMA (Ecstasy)																					
8th Grade	—	—	—	—	—	—	—	—	—	2.3	2.3	1.8	1.7	3.1	3.5	2.9	2.1	1.7	1.7	1.4	1.5
10th Grade	—	—	—	—	—	—	—	—	—	4.6	3.9	3.3	4.4	5.4	6.2	4.9	3.0	2.4	2.6	2.8	3.5
12th Grade	—	—	—	—	—	—	—	—	—	4.6	4.0	3.6	5.6	8.2	9.2	7.4	4.5	4.0	3.0	4.1	4.5
Cocaine																					
8th Grade	—	—	—	—	1.1	1.5	1.7	2.1	2.6	3.0	2.8	3.1	2.7	2.6	2.5	2.3	2.2	2.0	2.2	2.0	2.0
10th Grade	—	—	—	—	2.2	1.9	2.1	2.8	3.5	4.2	4.7	4.7	4.9	4.4	3.6	4.0	3.3	3.7	3.5	3.2	3.4
12th Grade	5.6	12.3	13.1	5.3	3.5	3.1	3.3	3.6	4.0	4.9	5.5	5.7	6.2	5.0	4.8	5.0	4.8	5.3	5.1	5.7	5.2
Crack Cocaine																					
8th Grade	—	—	—	—	0.7	0.9	1.0	1.3	1.6	1.8	1.7	2.1	1.8	1.8	1.7	1.6	1.6	1.3	1.4	1.3	1.3
10th Grade	—	—	—	—	0.9	0.9	1.1	1.4	1.8	2.1	2.2	2.5	2.4	2.2	1.8	2.3	1.6	1.7	1.7	1.3	1.3
2th Grade	—	—	—	1.9	1.5	1.5	1.5	1.9	2.1	2.1	2.4	2.5	2.7	2.2	2.1	2.3	2.2	2.3	1.9	2.1	1.9

Note: See Johnston, O'Malley, Bachman, & Schulenberg (2007) for more specific details about measures.
[a]Use of "any illicit drugs" includes any use of marijuana, hallucinogens, cocaine, or heroin, or any non-medical use of other opiates (12th only), amphetamines, barbiturates (12th only), or tranquilizers.
[b]In 1982, the question about amphetamine use was revised; the prevalence rate declined as a result.
[c]In 1993, the question about alcohol use was revised; the prevalence rate declined as a result.

Table 1. Trends in annual prevalence of use of various drugs among eighth, tenth, and twelfth graders. ILLUSTRATION BY GGS INFORMATION SERVICES. GALE, CENGAGE LEARNING

(Percent who used in last twelve months)

	1975	1980	1985	1990	1991	1992	1993	1994	1995	1996	1997	1998	1999	2000	2001	2002	2003	2004	2005	2006	2007
Heroin																					
8th Grade	—	—	—	—	0.7	0.7	0.7	1.2	1.4	1.6	1.3	1.3	1.4	1.1	1.0	0.9	0.9	1.0	0.8	0.8	0.8
10th Grade	—	—	—	—	0.5	0.6	0.7	0.9	1.1	1.2	1.4	1.4	1.4	1.4	0.9	1.1	0.7	0.9	0.9	0.9	0.8
12th Grade	1.0	0.5	0.6	0.5	0.4	0.6	0.5	0.6	1.1	1.0	1.2	1.0	1.1	1.5	0.9	1.0	0.8	0.9	0.8	0.8	0.9
Other Narcotics																					
8th Grade	—	—	—	—	—	—	—	—	—	—	—	—	—	—	—	—	—	—	—	—	—
10th Grade	—	—	—	—	—	—	—	—	—	—	—	—	—	—	—	—	—	—	—	—	—
12th Grade	5.7	6.3	5.9	4.5	3.5	3.3	3.6	3.8	4.7	5.4	6.2	6.3	6.7	7.0	6.7‡	9.4	9.3	9.5	9.0	9.0	9.2
Amphetamines[b]																					
8th Grade	—	—	—	—	6.2	6.5	7.2	7.9	8.7	9.1	8.1	7.2	6.9	6.5	6.7	5.5	5.5	4.9	4.9	4.7	4.2
10th Grade	—	—	—	—	8.2	8.2	9.6	10.2	11.9	12.4	12.1	10.7	10.4	11.1	11.7	10.7	9.0	8.5	7.8	7.9	8.0
12th Grade	16.2	20.8	15.8	9.1	8.2	7.1	8.4	9.4	9.3	9.5	10.2	10.1	10.2	10.5	10.9	11.1	9.9	10.0	8.6	8.1	7.5
Barbiturates																					
8th Grade	—	—	—	—	—	—	—	—	—	—	—	—	—	—	—	—	—	—	—	—	—
10th Grade	—	—	—	—	—	—	—	—	—	—	—	—	—	—	—	—	—	—	—	—	—
12th Grade	10.7	6.8	4.6	3.4	3.4	2.8	3.4	4.1	4.7	4.9	5.1	5.5	5.8	6.2	5.7	6.7	6.0	6.5	7.2	6.6	6.2
Tranquilizers																					
8th Grade	—	—	—	—	1.8	2.0	2.1	2.4	2.7	3.3	2.9	2.6	2.5	2.6‡	2.8	2.6	2.7	2.5	2.8	2.6	2.4
10th Grade	—	—	—	—	3.2	3.5	3.3	3.3	4.0	4.6	4.9	5.1	5.4	5.6‡	7.3	6.3	5.3	5.1	4.8	5.2	5.3
12th Grade	10.6	8.7	6.1	3.5	3.6	2.8	3.5	3.7	4.4	4.6	4.7	5.5	5.8	5.7‡	6.9	7.7	6.7	7.3	6.8	6.6	6.2
Alcohol[c]																					
Any use																					
8th Grade	—	—	—	—	54.0	53.7	48.5	46.8	45.3	46.5	45.5	43.7	43.5	43.1	41.9	38.7	37.2	36.7	33.9	33.6	31.8
10th Grade	—	—	—	—	72.3	70.2	66.4	63.9	63.5	65.0	65.2	62.7	63.7	65.3	63.5	60.0	59.3	58.2	56.7	55.8	56.3
12th Grade	84.8	87.9	85.6	80.6	77.7	76.8	74.4	73.0	73.7	72.5	74.8	74.3	73.8	73.2	73.3	71.5	70.1	70.6	68.6	66.5	66.4

Note: See Johnston, O'Malley, Bachman, & Schulenberg (2007) for more specific details about measures.

[a]Use of "any illicit drugs" includes any use of marijuana, hallucinogens, cocaine, or heroin, or any non-medical use of other opiates (12th only), amphetamines, barbiturates (12th only), or tranquilizers.

[b]In 1982, the question about amphetamine use was revised; the prevalence rate declined as a result.

[c]In 1993, the question about alcohol use was revised; the prevalence rate declined as a result.

Table 1 (continued). Trends in annual prevalence of use of various drugs among eighth, tenth, and twelfth graders. ILLUSTRATION BY GGS INFORMATION SERVICES. GALE, CENGAGE LEARNING

MAJOR FINDINGS

As a broad generalization, there were four periods of change in use of illicit drugs among twelfth-graders: (1) an increase between 1975 and about 1980; (2) more than a decade of decline from 1980 to the early 1990s; (3) an increase in the mid-1990s from 1991 or 1992 to about 1997; and (4) another decade of decline, from about 1997 to 2007. Some specific drugs followed differing patterns, but the overall pattern is as described. The early increase between 1975 and 1980 almost certainly continued a longer-term period of increase that began in the 1960s. The early increase and subsequent decline were not observed among eighth- and tenth-graders, because they had not been surveyed. The increase in the early and mid-1990s was observed; indeed, the eighth-graders were the first to show definite signs of an upturn. The subsequent decline from about 1997 to 2007 was also evident in eighth- and tenth-graders.

Illicit Drugs. Annual use of any illicit drug (that is, any use in the past twelve months) peaked among high school seniors in 1979, when more than half (54 percent) of all high school seniors reported having used at least one illicit drug. This peak occurred following a rise in the late 1970s—from 45 percent in 1975, when the first reliable national data were collected. By 1992, the proportion had fallen to 27 percent, half the peak rate.

The statistics for lifetime prevalence are also dramatic. In the peak year of 1981, 66 percent of the graduating class reported having used an illicit drug at some point in their lifetime. By 1992, that percentage was down by about one-third, to 41 percent.

Unfortunately, the numbers of young Americans involved in the use of illicit drugs increased substantially during the 1990s. After reaching a low of 27 percent in 1992, annual use among seniors was back up to 42 percent in 1997 (still well below the peak value of 54 percent); lifetime use was at 54 percent.

Increases were particularly sharp among the eighth- and tenth-graders. No data are available before 1991, so longer-term trends are not so clear. However, it is clear that there were significant increases in the 1990s. Among eighth-graders in 1991, 11 percent had used an illicit drug in the past twelve months; that figure increased to 22 percent by 1997 (and actually peaked in 1996 at 24

percent). Similarly, among tenth graders, annual use increased from 21 percent in 1991 to 39 percent in 1997.

In the fourth of the four phases of change, there were declines in use of illicit drugs in the decade between 1997 and 2007. Annual use in 2007 was at 13, 28, and 36 percent for eighth- tenth- and twelfth-graders, respectively. These figures are well below historic peaks, but still above the historic lows of 11, 20, and 27 percent, respectively.

Among the various illicit drugs, marijuana is the most prevalent. The use of marijuana, as indicated by its annual prevalence, peaked among high school seniors in 1979, when a majority (51 percent) reported that they had used it in the past twelve months. Usage steadily declined after that, reaching a low of 22 percent in 1992. The annual prevalence, thus cut by more than half, declined from one in two seniors in the class of 1979 to fewer than one in four seniors in the class of 1992. However, by 1997 the figure was back up to 39 percent, so that well over one in three seniors had used marijuana in the past twelve months. In 2007, the figure had declined to 32 percent, still well above the low of 22 percent.

A particularly striking trend in marijuana use occurred between 1975 and 1978, when the proportion of seniors who reported using marijuana on a daily or near-daily basis in the past thirty days increased from 6.0 percent to an unprecedented 10.7 percent. This figure subsequently came down by more than 80 percent and stood at 2.0 percent in 1992. By 1997 it was back to 5.8 percent, just about where it was in 1975; by 2007 it was down, but only slightly, to 5.1 percent.

Among eighth-graders, annual marijuana use almost tripled from 6.2 percent in 1991 to 18 percent in 1997. Among tenth-graders, annual marijuana use doubled between 1991 and 1997, from 17 percent to 35 percent. The figures for 2007 were 10 and 25 percent respectively, down considerably from the peak years, but still higher than the low points.

Never as common as marijuana, cocaine became the drug on which the most attention was focused during the mid-1980s, when the national concern about the drug epidemic was at its highest level. The concern with cocaine was well founded because this drug had not followed the general pattern of decline in the early to mid-1980s. As with marijuana, the use of cocaine had increased substantially between 1975 and 1979; annual prevalence doubled from 5.6 percent to 12.0 percent. Several years followed during which there was little change, with annual prevalence reaching a peak of 13 percent in both 1985 and 1986. A period of decline then ensued during which annual use declined to 3.1 percent in 1992; this was the lowest value recorded since reliable data had begun to be collected in 1975. Unlike marijuana, which peaked in 1996 or 1997, cocaine use increased throughout the 1990s, and by 1999 annual cocaine among seniors had again doubled, reaching 6.2 percent. By 2007, the figure was down slightly to 5.2 percent.

These data refer to the use of any form of cocaine, including crack cocaine. Crack cocaine first appeared in the early 1980s and became a significant factor among the illicit drugs in the mid-1980s. It was first assessed on a national basis in 1986, and its annual prevalence among high school seniors at that time was recorded at a disturbingly high 4.1 percent. That first reading turned out to be a peak level, and the use of crack cocaine declined thereafter, reaching 1.5 percent in 1992. Like powder cocaine, crack cocaine use increased through the 1990s in all three grades, then declined through 2007, when annual prevalence was between 1 and 2 percent in each grade.

Although inhalants are not actually illicit drugs, they are sometimes used illicitly for the purpose of "getting high." This particular behavior is generally more often seen among younger students rather than among high school seniors. In 2007, for example, 3.7 percent of twelfth-graders reported using inhalants to get high at least once in the past twelve months, compared to 6.6 percent of tenth-graders and 8.3 percent of eighth-graders.

Use of inhalants did not follow the four-phase pattern of change seen for illicit drugs in general. Among twelfth-graders, the longer-term trend in the use of inhalants was slightly upward from its lowest level of 3.0 percent in 1976 (when it was first assessed), to a peak level of 8.0 percent in 1995, before declining to 3.7 percent in 2007. Thus the use of this class of substance did not show the general decline from 1980 to 1992. All three grades showed some increase in the early 1990s, with peak levels in 1995, and overall, some

irregular decline since then. Hallucinogens are the other major class of illicit (or illicitly used) substances that did not evince declines in the late 1980s and the early 1990s. LSD (lysergic acid diethylamide) in particular is a very significant exception; its use hardly changed among high school seniors, remaining at an annual prevalence of about 5 percent from 1987 to 1991 after a period of some decline. Like marijuana however, there was an increase in the 1990s, reaching 8.8 percent in 1996, the highest level ever recorded. By 2007, use had declined substantially, to 2.1 percent. Very similar patterns of change were evident among eighth- and tenth-graders, albeit at lower levels.

Substances that generally showed declines during the period from the 1970s to the early 1990s include heroin, opiates other than heroin, amphetamines, sedative/barbiturates, and tranquilizers. All of these substances also showed an increase during the mid-1990s. The patterns diverged somewhat after about 1997; use of heroin, amphetamines, and tranquilizers declined, while the use of opiates other than heroin and sedative/barbiturates tended to hold level or increase. Indeed, the nonmedical use of prescription drugs emerged in the twenty-first century as a relatively larger part of the drug problem, in part because the use of street drugs had decreased. Two medications—Vicodin and OxyContin—were particularly susceptible to misuse, reaching annual prevalence rates of 9.6 and 5.2 percent, respectively, among twelfth graders in 2007.

In the late 1990s, some "club drugs" appeared on the drug scene. One in particular, MDMA (methylenedioxymethamphetamine, or "Ecstasy") showed substantial increases, reaching 9.2 percent annual prevalence among seniors in 2001. The corresponding figures for eighth- and tenth-graders were 3.5 percent and 6.2 percent. Use then dropped as sharply as it had increased for a few years before increasing again in 2006 and 2007; annual prevalence rates in 2007 were 1.5, 3.5, and 4.5 percent in grades eight, ten, and twelve.

Alcohol and Tobacco. The history of the use of the major licit drugs—alcohol and tobacco—is rather different from that of the use of most illicit drugs. One significant difference was the extent of the use of alcohol and tobacco. The daily use of cigarettes was far greater than the daily use of any other substance. In 1997, a quarter (25 percent) of high school seniors had smoked one or more cigarettes per day in the past thirty days. Even among eighth-graders, one in eleven was a daily cigarette smoker (9 percent). About one in twenty-five (3.9 percent) seniors drank alcohol daily or almost daily. All other drugs were used on a daily basis by 0.3 percent or less of seniors.

Alcohol is used pervasively throughout Western societies both as a food (beverage) and as an intoxicant. MTF asks students on how many occasions in the past two weeks they had five or more drinks in a row. The assumption is that anyone drinking that much would likely become intoxicated. The prevalence of this measure generally follows the four-phase pattern of change but at a more muted level, particularly in the 1991–2007 interval. The range from low point to high point in that interval was 25 to 32 percent among twelfth-graders, 21 to 26 percent among tenth-graders, and 10 to 16 percent among eighth-graders. During the 1980s, this measure of heavy drinking declined significantly among twelfth-graders, from a high of 41 percent to a low of 32 percent. Some, though not all, of the decline is likely attributable to raises in the minimum drinking age that occurred among many states as a result of federal legislation. Although heavy drinking has been declining very slightly in the new millennium, in 2007 this behavior was still at levels that most would consider unacceptably high —one in four twelfth-graders, one in five tenth-graders, and one in ten eighth-graders.

Cigarette smoking followed the recent pattern of a rise in the early 1990s, then a decline after about 1997. Unlike heavy drinking, the changes were substantial. Thirty-day prevalence ranged from the high point in 1996 or 1997 to the low point in 2007, from 37 to 22 percent for twelfth-graders, 30 to 14 percent for tenth-graders, and 21 to 7 percent for eighth-graders. Clearly, there was considerable progress made in reducing smoking, but equally clearly, there remained much room for additional progress.

DEMOGRAPHIC DIFFERENCES

Drug use among several demographic groups is monitored in the surveys, including gender, four-year college plans, parental education (an indicator of socioeconomic status), geographical region, population density, and racial or ethnic identification.

Gender. By senior year, male adolescents are more likely than female adolescents to use most illicit drugs, and the differences tend to be largest at the higher frequency levels. In 2007, for example, 6.8 percent of male high school seniors reported that they were using marijuana daily versus 3.2 percent of female seniors. For many specific substances, there is little gender difference in use among eighth- and tenth-graders. Indeed, eighth-grade females generally have slightly higher rates than males of annual use of inhalants, amphetamines, and tranquilizers.

There are gender differences in the prevalence of occasions of heavy drinking among high school seniors (31 percent for male adolescents versus 22 percent for female adolescents in 2007); thus, as with heavy use of illicit drugs, heavy use of alcohol is more likely among male adolescents than it is among female adolescents. This gender difference is considerably smaller than the one obtained in 1975, when the figures were 49 percent and 26 percent, respectively. The narrowing of the difference is primarily attributable to the greater decrease in heavy drinking among male adolescents than among female adolescents. The current differences are smaller among the younger students; among 2007 tenth graders, 23 percent of boys reported heavy drinking compared to 20 percent of girls; the corresponding figures for eighth-graders were 10 percent for each. Again, the narrowing of earlier differences reflects greater decreases among male adolescents.

In general, there is not much difference between male and female students in cigarette use.

College-Bound versus Non-College-Bound. Non-college-bound students are more likely than college-bound students to use any of the licit or illicit drugs. More frequent use of the drug tends to show greater differences. For example, in 2006 5.3 percent of non-college-bound eighth-graders reported smoking marijuana daily compared to less than 1 percent of the college-bound; corresponding figures for tenth- and twelfth-graders were 9 percent versus 2 percent, and 9 percent versus 4 percent, respectively. Striking differences show up between college-bound and non-college-bound students in cigarette smoking rates. For example, smoking a half pack or more a day was

(Percent who used daily in last thirty days)

	1975	1980	1985	1990	1991	1992	1993	1994	1995	1996	1997	1998	1999	2000	2001	2002	2003	2004	2005	2006	2007
Marijuana/Hashish any daily use																					
8th Grade	—	—	—	—	0.2	0.2	0.4	0.7	0.8	1.5	1.1	1.1	1.4	1.3	1.3	1.2	1.0	0.8	1.0	1.0	0.8
10th Grade	—	—	—	—	0.8	0.8	1.0	2.2	2.8	3.5	3.7	3.6	3.8	3.8	4.5	3.9	3.6	3.2	3.1	2.8	2.8
12th Grade	6.0	9.1	4.9	2.2	2.0	1.9	2.4	3.6	4.6	4.9	5.8	5.6	6.0	6.0	5.8	6.0	6.0	5.6	5.0	5.0	5.1
Alcohol[a] any daily use																					
8th Grade	—	—	—	—	0.5	0.6	0.9	1.0	0.7	1.0	0.8	0.9	1.0	0.8	0.9	0.7	0.8	0.6	0.5	0.5	0.6
10th Grade	—	—	—	—	1.3	1.2	1.7	1.7	1.7	1.6	1.7	1.9	1.9	1.8	1.9	1.8	1.5	1.3	1.3	1.4	1.4
12th Grade	5.7	6.0	5.0	3.7	3.6	3.4	3.0	2.9	3.5	3.7	3.9	3.9	3.4	2.9	3.6	3.5	3.2	2.8	3.1	3.0	3.1
5+ drinks in a row in last 2 weeks																					
8th Grade	—	—	—	—	12.9	13.4	13.5	14.5	14.5	15.6	14.5	13.7	15.2	14.1	13.2	12.4	11.9	11.4	10.5	10.9	10.3
10th Grade	—	—	—	—	22.9	21.1	23.0	23.6	24.0	24.8	25.1	24.3	25.6	26.2	24.9	22.4	22.2	22.0	21.0	21.9	21.9
12th Grade	36.8	41.2	36.7	32.2	29.8	27.9	27.5	28.2	29.8	30.2	31.3	31.5	30.8	30.0	29.7	28.6	27.9	29.2	27.1	25.4	25.9
Cigarettes any daily use																					
8th Grade	—	—	—	—	7.2	7.0	8.3	8.8	9.3	10.4	9.0	8.8	8.1	7.4	5.5	5.1	4.5	4.4	4.0	4.0	3.0
10th Grade	—	—	—	—	12.6	12.3	14.2	14.6	16.3	18.3	18.0	15.8	15.9	14.0	12.2	10.1	8.9	8.3	7.5	7.6	7.2
12th Grade	26.9	21.3	19.5	19.1	18.5	17.2	19.0	19.4	21.6	22.2	24.6	22.4	23.1	20.6	19.0	16.9	15.8	15.6	13.6	12.2	12.3
1/2 pack+/day																					
8th Grade	—	—	—	—	3.1	2.9	3.5	3.6	3.4	4.3	3.5	3.6	3.3	2.8	2.3	2.1	1.8	1.7	1.7	1.5	1.1
10th Grade	—	—	—	—	6.5	6.0	7.0	7.6	8.3	9.4	8.6	7.9	7.6	6.2	5.5	4.4	4.1	3.3	3.1	3.3	2.7
12th Grade	17.9	14.3	12.5	11.3	10.7	10.0	10.9	11.2	12.4	13.0	14.3	12.6	13.2	11.3	10.3	9.1	8.4	8.0	6.9	5.9	5.7

Note: See Johnston, O'Malley, Bachman, & Schulenberg (2007) for more specific details about measures.
[a] In 1993, the question about alcohol use was revised slightly.

Table 2. Trends in prevalence of daily use of marijuana, alcohol, and cigarettes among eighth, tenth, and twelfth graders. ILLUSTRATION BY GGS INFORMATION SERVICES. GALE, CENGAGE LEARNING

more than five times more prevalent among the non-college-bound 2006 eighth-graders than among the college-bound (5.8 percent versus 1.1 percent). Among seniors, half a pack or more smoking was more than three times as prevalent among the non-college-bound, 13 percent versus 4 percent. (The greater ratio in the younger students is likely due to the presence of the eventual dropouts in the eighth and tenth grades, because dropouts tend to have higher rates of smoking than nondropouts.) Non-college-bound students are also more likely than their college-bound counterparts to report having had five or more drinks in a row in the past two weeks (33 percent versus 21 percent among tenth graders, for example).

Parental Education. Among high school seniors there is (perhaps surprisingly) rather little association between parental education and use of illicit drugs. There is somewhat more of an association among the lower grades, particularly among eighth-graders, with the lowest level or lower two levels having somewhat higher use rates than the others.

Geographical Region. Overall, use of illicit drugs does not vary dramatically by region. Some differences emerge at times; for example, cocaine use was particularly high in the West in the early 1980s, and ecstasy use first emerged in the Northeast. However, use of specific illicit drugs usually spreads to all regions and differences become slight. Both the South and the West tend to exhibit slightly lower rates of alcohol use than the Northeast and the North Central states. For example, in 2007 the prevalence of heavy-drinking occasions (that is, five or more drinks in a row on at least one occasion in the past two weeks) among the seniors was 30 percent and 29 percent in the Northeast and North Central states, respectively, compared with 25 percent and 21 percent in the South and the West. Cigarette smoking tends to be lowest in the West.

Population Density. As of 2007, the differences in high school seniors' use of illicit drugs by population density were quite small. This lack of large differences reflects the fact that illicit drug use has spread widely throughout the nation. One substance that has shown some significant difference by population density over time is the use of cocaine. The substantial increase in cocaine use in the late 1970s and the continuing high levels of use until the mid-1980s were primarily an urban phenomenon. The annual prevalence rates for cocaine were nearly twice as high among high school seniors in the large standard metropolitan statistical areas as they were for seniors in the more sparsely populated areas. Unlike illicit drugs, cigarette use does vary somewhat by population density. For example, among tenth-graders, daily use in 2007 was at 10 percent in non-metropolitan areas, compared to 6 percent in the largest metropolitan areas and 7 percent in other metropolitan areas.

Racial or Ethnic Identification. It is difficult to make definitive statements about even the larger minority groups such as African Americans and Hispanics because of the relatively small numbers who participate in the surveys. Even Hispanics, who constitute a large segment of the population in many areas, often cannot be accurately represented because there are many important subgroups among the several Hispanic groups (e.g., Mexican, Puerto Rican, Cuban, and Latin American, among others). Nevertheless, certain findings appear to be reliable.

Among high school seniors, African American students report less use of virtually all substances than do white students. Generally, African American students in eighth and tenth grades also report less use of most substances, although marijuana is an exception in the eighth grade, where white students report less use.

By senior year, Hispanic students report higher rates of cocaine and crack cocaine than white or African American students. These differences are stronger among eighth- and tenth-graders. And particularly among eighth-graders, Hispanic students tend to show the highest rates of use for some substances, including marijuana, tranquilizers, and cigarettes. In other words, in eighth grade, before most dropping out of school occurs, Hispanic students are relatively high in use of substances, while white students tend to have higher rates by twelfth grade. Very likely, the higher rates of dropping out of school observed among Hispanic adolescents (U.S. Dept. of Education, 2007) accounts for the shift in differences.

Some of these differences could be due to differential reporting biases, but J. M. Wallace and J. G. Bachman (1993) argue that this is unlikely to be an important part of the explanation.

FOLLOW-UP SURVEYS AFTER HIGH SCHOOL
The core of the MTF study is the annual surveys of secondary school students as described above. However, there is another vitally important part of the study—follow-up surveys by mail of a sample of each high school graduating class. By following members of each class, the study is able to distinguish among three types of changes that can occur, specifically, age, period, and cohort (or birth group) effects. Knowledge that changes in, for example, alcohol use, are age-related (and not period- or cohort-related), is highly informative in revealing what kinds of variables might explain the age-related changes. All three types of changes have been found in varying degrees for the various substances (O'Malley, Bachman & Johnston, 1988; Johnston O'Malley, Bachman & Schulenberg, 2007). By following individuals through their post-high school lives, the study can also assess the impact of life-course changes that occur, particularly changes in social roles and social environments. Major transitions include higher education, moving out of the parental home, full-time employment, military service, getting married (and divorced), and becoming a parent. All these transitions have been explored by the project investigators, and results reported in various publications, including two books (Bachman et al., 1997; 2002). A further benefit of the follow-up surveys is that one important segment of the population—college students—is available for monitoring.

In addition to providing basic epidemiologic information on prevalences, trends, and demographic differences, the Monitoring the Future study also contributes information on the reasons for the trends and differences. The study's demonstration that attitudes and beliefs affect drug-use trends (especially in the case of marijuana and cocaine) is particularly important (Bachman, Johnston & O'Malley, 1990, 1998; Johnston, O'Malley, Bachman & Schulenberg, 2007). By virtue of its cohort-sequential design, the study has been able to distinguish among the several possible types of competing changes associated with trends in use; specifically, age, period, and cohort (or birth group) effects. A variety of changes in the post-

high school environments have been investigated. In addition, the study has been able to provide important data with which researchers could evaluate the effects of changes in the laws dealing with marijuana (Johnston O'Malley & Bachman, 1981) and alcohol (O'Malley & Wagenaar, 1991). All of these contributions have been vital in the continuing debates about policy regarding the use of licit and illicit drugs.

See also **Adolescents and Drug Use.**

BIBLIOGRAPHY

Bachman, J. G., Johnston, L. D., & O'Malley, P. M. (1990). Explaining the recent decline in cocaine use among young adults: Further evidence that perceived risks and disapproval lead to reduced drug use. *Journal of Health and Social Behavior, 31*, 173–184.

Bachman, J. G., Johnston, L. D., & O'Malley, P. M. (1998). Explaining the recent increases in students' marijuana use: The impacts of perceived risks and disapproval from 1976 through 1996. *American Journal of Public Health, 88*, 887–892.

Bachman, J. G., O'Malley, P. M., Schulenberg, J. E., Johnston, L. D., Bryant, A. L., & Merline, A. C. (2002). *The decline of substance use in young adulthood: Changes in social activities, roles, and beliefs.* Mahwah, NJ: Erlbaum.

Bachman, J. G., Wadsworth, K. N., O'Malley, P. M., Johnston, L. D., & Schulenberg, J. (1997). *Smoking, drinking, and drug use in young adulthood: The impacts of new freedoms and new responsibilities.* Mahwah, NJ: Erlbaum.

Johnston, L. D., O'Malley, P. M., & Bachman, J. G. (1981). *Marijuana decriminalization: The impact on youth, 1975–1980.* (Monitoring the Future Occasional Paper No. 13) Ann Arbor, MI: Institute for Social Research.

Johnston, L. D., O'Malley, P. M., Bachman, J. G., & Schulenberg, J. E. (2007). *Monitoring the Future national survey results on drug use, 1975–2006 Vol. I: Secondary school students* (NIH Publication No. 07-6205). Rockville, MD: National Institute on Drug Abuse.

Johnston, L. D., O'Malley, P. M., Bachman, J. G., & Schulenberg, J. E. (2007). *Monitoring the Future national survey results on drug use, 1975–2006 Vol. II: College Students & Adults, Ages 19–45* (NIH Publication No. 07-6206). Rockville, MD: National Institute on Drug Abuse.

Monitoring the Future. (2008). Available from http://www.monitoringthefuture.org.

O'Malley, P. M., Bachman, J. G., & Johnston, L. D. (1983). Reliability and consistency of self-reports of drug use. *International Journal of the Addictions, 18*, 805–824.

O'Malley, P. M., Bachman, J. G., & Johnston, L. D. (1988). Period, age, and cohort effects on substance use among young Americans: A decade of change,

1976–1986. *American Journal of Public Health, 78,* 1315–1321.

O'Malley, P. M., & Wagenaar, A. C. (1991). Effects of minimum drinking age laws on alcohol use, related behaviors, and traffic crash involvement among American youth: 1976–1987. *Journal of Studies on Alcohol, 52,* 478–491.

U.S. Department of Education, National Center for Educational Statistics. (2007). *The condition of education.* Washington, DC: U.S. Government Printing Office.

U.S. Department of Health and Human Services. National survey on drug use and health. Available from http://oas.samhsa.gov/.

Wallace, J. M., JR., & Bachman, J. G. (1993). Validity of self-reports in student-based studies on minority populations: Issues and concerns. In M. R. DeLaRosa & J. L. R. Adrados (Eds.), *Drug abuse among minority youth: Advances in research and methodology* (pp. 167–200). NIDA Research Monograph 130. (DHHS NIH Publication No. 93-3479) Rockville, MD: National Institute on Drug Abuse.

PATRICK M. O'MALLEY

MONOAMINE. A monoamine is an amine that has one organic substituent attached to the nitrogen atom (as RNH_2). Serotonin is such an amine, one that is functionally important in neurotransmission. Chemically, monoamines include the catecholamines (derived from tyrosine) and the indoleamines serotonin and melatonin (derived from the amino acid tryptophan). Acetylcholine also has only a single (but trimethylated) amine, while histamine (a diamine formed from histidine) stretches the condition only slightly. Neurotransmitters in this class share several properties—nanomolar concentrations/milligram protein; neurons (nerve cells) that contain thin, generally unmyelinated axons to many brain regions; and their receptors (except for the cholinergic nicotinic receptor and one of the ten or so subtypes of serotonin receptors) employ second-messenger coupled transduction. Monoamine neurotransmitters are often involved in the action of mind-altering drugs and have been well studied.

See also **Dopamine; Neurotransmitters.**

BIBLIOGRAPHY

Hanson, G. R., Venturelli, P. J., & Fleckenstein, A. E. (2005). *Drugs and Society.* Sudbury, MA: Jones & Bartlett Publishers.

Snyder, S. H. (1980). *Biological aspects of mental disorder.* New York: Oxford University Press.

Webster, R., Ed. (2001). *Neurotransmitters, drugs, and brain function.* Hoboken, NJ: Wiley.

FLOYD BLOOM

MOONSHINE. Moonshine (white lightning) is the colloquial term for illegally produced hard liquor—whiskey, rum, brandy, gin, and vodka. The term probably originated around 1785, when it was recorded in a British book on vulgar language—used to describe the white (clear) brandy that was smuggled to the coasts of Kent and Sussex in England. In the New World, moonshine was made in homemade stills, usually from corn, especially in rural areas in the southern United States—before, during, and after Prohibition—and continues to be made today. The ethanol (drinking alcohol) content is usually high, often approaching 80 percent (160 proof). First-run moonshine contains a number of impurities, some of which are toxic, so it is necessary to double- and triple-distill the liquor to purify it for drinking.

See also **Alcohol: History of Drinking (International); Alcohol: History of Drinking in the United States; Legal Regulation of Drugs and Alcohol; Still.**

BIBLIOGRAPHY

Bryce, J. H., and Stewart, G. G. (2004). *Distilled spirits: Tradition and innovation.* Nottingham, U.K.: Nottingham University Press.

Dabney, J. E. (1974). *Mountain spirits.* New York: Scribner's.

Ellison, B. B. (2003). *Illegal odyssey: 200 years of Kentucky moonshine.* Bloomington, IN: 1st Books Library.

S. E. LUKAS

MORNING GLORY SEEDS. The seeds of the morning glory, genus *Ipomoea* of the family Convolvulaceae, contain many lysergic acid derivatives, particularly lysergic acid amide. The hallucinogenic properties of some of these derivatives are not

Figure 1. Morning glory. ILLUSTRATION BY GGS INFORMATION SERVICES. GALE, CENGAGE LEARNING

known. The seeds can be ingested whole; they can be ground and used to prepare a tea; or the active compound can be extracted using solvents. The seeds have also been used as a source of precursors for the synthesis of lysergic acid diethylamide (LSD). Since the seeds contain lysergic acid derivatives, people ingesting morning glory seeds may feel "different"; however, the experience is not identical to an LSD-type "trip," even though the seeds are marketed on the street as an LSD equivalent.

Although morning glory seeds are easy to purchase legally, many varieties (those sold by reputable garden-supply distributors) have been treated with insecticides, fungicides, and other toxic chemicals—as well as with compounds that will induce vomiting if the seeds are eaten.

See also **Hallucinogenic Plants; Mescaline.**

BIBLIOGRAPHY

Efron, D. H., Holmstedt, B., & Kline, N.S., Eds. (1979). *Ethnopharmacologic search for psychoactive drugs.* New York: Raven Press.

Wills, S. (2005). *Drugs of Abuse.* London: Pharmaceutical Press.

DANIEL X. FREEDMAN
R. N. PECHNICK

MORPHINE. Morphine is a major component of opium, a product of the poppy plant (*Papaver somniferum* or *P. album*). Named after Morpheus, the Greek god of sleep, morphine is a potent analgesic (painkiller) that is widely used for moderate-to-severe pain. Morphine is one of approximately twenty alkaloids in opium. It was first purified in 1806; by the mid-1800s, pure morphine was widely used in medicine. At approximately the same time, the hypodermic needle and syringe were developed, which permitted the injection of the drug under the skin (subcutaneous [SC]), into muscles (intramuscular [IM]), or directly into the veins (intravenous [IV]). Together, these routes of administration are termed parenteral. Injections provide rapid relief from pain and can be used in patients who are unable to take medications by mouth. These advantages led to the widespread use of morphine injections during the American Civil War (1861–1865). At that time, the intense euphoria and addictive potential of these agents following injections was not fully appreciated, leading to the addiction of many soldiers. Indeed, morphine was legal and was sold over the counter or through mail order houses. Since that time, a major objective of pharmaceutical companies has been to develop a non-addictive analgesic with the potency of morphine.

PHYSICAL DEPENDENCE AND ADDICTION
The concepts of *physical dependence* and *addiction* were not clearly differentiated until the mid-twentieth century, and it is likely that most early addicts were attempting to prevent the onset of withdrawal symptoms. Physical dependence is a physiological response to continued dosing with the opiate. Addiction, by contrast, implies drug-seeking behaviors despite the negative consequences of taking the drug. In the early twenty-first century few patients become addicted to opiates despite the fact that with continued administration all will become physically dependent; this fact may reflect the improved understanding of the drugs plus the modern ability to take a patient off medications without precipitating withdrawal symptoms. Morphine produces a wide variety of actions, some desired and others not. The definition of a desired action and a side effect depends on the reason for using the drug. For example, such opiates as morphine can be used to treat diarrhea but their constipating actions are usually considered an undesirable side effect when they are used to treat pain. Clearly, the control of pain remains the most important use of morphine. Morphine and other opiates relieve pain without interfering with traditional sensations. Patients treated with morphine often report that the pain is still there but that it no longer hurts.

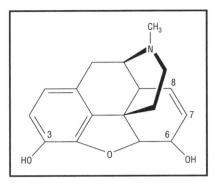

Figure 1. Chemical structure of morphine. ILLUSTRATION BY GGS INFORMATION SERVICES. GALE, CENGAGE LEARNING

RECEPTORS

Morphine works through mu opiate receptors located within the brain and the spinal cord and along sensory nerves in the periphery. Morphine has a number of other actions as well. Its ability to constrict the pupil is one of the most widely recognized signs of opiate use. In addition, morphine produces sedation, and at higher doses morphine will depress respiration. Very high doses of morphine stop breathing entirely, a common occurrence in overdoses and the primary cause of death due to overdose. Morphine also has a major influence on the gastrointestinal tract, which is the basis for its antidiarrheal effect. Here, morphine decreases the motility of the stomach and intestine through local actions on the organs themselves, as well as through control systems located within the brain and spinal cord. Other systems can be affected as well. Morphine produces vasodilation, in which the peripheral blood vessels are relaxed. This effect can lead to significant drops in blood pressure when a person shifts from a lying to a standing position as the blood is pooled in the legs. This ability to pool blood in relaxed blood vessels can be used clinically to treat such conditions as acute pulmonary edema, an accumulation of fluid within the lungs, which occurs in acute myocardial infarctions (heart attacks). Increasing the capacity of the vascular system by relaxing the blood vessels permits the reabsorption of the lung fluid. Finally, morphine and such similar drugs, as codeine are also effective agents in the control of coughing. All of the effects of morphine can be easily reversed by antagonists, of which naloxone is the most widely used. Given alone, it has virtually no actions; however, low doses of naloxone are able to block or reverse all the actions of morphine described above.

ADMINISTRATION

Morphine is given either by mouth or by injection. Oral administration is associated with significant metabolism of the drug by the liver, explaining its lower potency as compared to that attained by injections. From three to six times more morphine must be taken by mouth to produce the same effects as an injected dose. Thus higher doses are needed when giving the drug orally. Morphine injections can be given either intramuscularly, subcutaneously, or intravenously. Continuous infusions are also common but their use is restricted to physicians who are expert in the treatment of pain.

Morphine has a relatively short effect in the body, around two hours, and it is usually given to patients every four to six hours and is extensively metabolized. In the late 1980s, it was discovered that one of the metabolites (breakdown products) of morphine, morphine-6β-glucuronide, is very potent, far more potent than morphine itself. The importance of this compound following a single dose of morphine is probably not great; however, with chronic dosing, the levels of morphine-6β-glucuronide in the blood may actually exceed those of morphine, so this metabolite may be responsible for many of morphine's actions. Since this metabolite is removed from the body by the kidneys, special care must be taken when giving morphine to patients with kidney problems. One common problem associated with morphine is nausea. Nausea does not occur in all patients and often is seen with one opiate but not others. Thus a patient unable to tolerate morphine may be able to receive therapy with methadone.

With chronic use, morphine has a progressively smaller effect, a phenomenon termed *tolerance*. To maintain a constant action it is necessary to increase the dose. Along with tolerance, morphine also produces physical dependence. Physical dependence (physiological dependence; neuroadaptation) develops as the body attempts to compensate for many of morphine's actions. As long as a person continues to receive the drug, no symptoms are noted. Abrupt cessation of the drug or the administration of an antagonist, such as naloxone or the related compound naltrexone, produces a constellation of symptoms and signs termed the *withdrawal syndrome*. Early symptoms include restlessness, tearing from the eyes and a runny nose, yawning, and sweating. As the syndrome progresses, one sees dilated pupils, sneezing, elevations in heart rate and blood pressure, and gooseflesh (which is responsible for the term *cold turkey*). Cramping and abdominal pains are also common.

As mentioned above, physical dependence (or neuroadaptation) is a physiological response to repeated dosing with morphine and is seen in virtually all patients repeatedly given morphine or another opiate drug. Physical dependence, however, is distinguished from drug dependence or addiction, which is defined by drug-seeking behavior. While addiction is common among drug abusers, it is rare when morphine is used for appropriate medical conditions. The reasons for this difference were not clear as of 2008, and they remain a major issue in understanding and treating opiate addiction.

See also **Addiction: Concepts and Definitions; Diagnostic and Statistical Manual (DSM); Opiates/Opioids; Opioid Complications and Withdrawal.**

BIBLIOGRAPHY

Reisine, T., & Pasternak, G. (1996) Opioid analgesics and antagonists. In J. G. Hardman et al. (Eds.), *The pharmacological basis of therapeutics* (9th ed., pp. 521–555). New York: McGraw-Hill.

GAVRIL W. PASTERNAK

MOTHERS AGAINST DRUNK DRIVING (MADD).

Mothers Against Drunk Driving (MADD) is a national organization that works to reduce drunk driving and to help the victims of drunk driving accidents. Many of MADD's members are volunteers who have personally suffered from the results of drunk driving.

MADD was founded by Candy Lightner, whose 13-year-old daughter, Cari, was killed by a drunk driver on May 3, 1980. Lightner was outraged to learn that only two days before the accident that killed her daughter, the driver had been released from jail, where he had been held for another hit-and-run drunk driving crash. Although he had been arrested for drunk driving several times before, he was still driving with a valid California license. Candy Lightner decided to begin a campaign to keep drunk drivers off the road so that other mothers would not have to suffer the anguish she was experiencing. On September 5 (Cari's birthday), 1980, MADD was originated.

Since then, MADD has evolved into an organization with millions of members and hundreds of local chapters across the United States. Chapters have also been started in Canada, Great Britain, New Zealand, and Australia. Membership is not restricted to mothers of victims or to the victims themselves. Everyone who is concerned about the drunk driving issue is welcome to join. Funding for the organization comes from membership dues and contributions. MADD also applies for and receives grants from federal and state governments and private organizations. Paid staff members are employed to provide leadership on the state and national levels. MADD is involved in three major kinds of activity: (1) advocacy for stricter drunk driving laws and better enforcement, (2) promotion of public awareness and educational programs, and (3) assistance to victims.

THE LEGISLATIVE AGENDA

According to MADD, drunk driving is a violent crime. One of its rallying slogans is "Murder by Car Is Still Murder!" Over the years, MADD members have worked to generate public support for passage of stricter drunk driving legislation, punitive sanctions, and more consistent enforcement measures aimed at deterring drunk driving. In the 1980s, intense lobbying efforts were undertaken for the passage of laws making 21 the minimum legal age for drinking (now in force in all 50 states). The group believes that this measure has saved thousands of young lives that would have been lost in drunk driving crashes.

MADD has also lobbied for changes in judicial procedures that would make the system more responsive to victims of drunk driving. For example, in many states victims had been barred from the courtroom during the trial of their own drunk driving cases because their testimony (or even their presence) might prejudice the jury. Because of the efforts of MADD and other groups, victims' rights bills have now been passed in all states. These ensure that victims will be notified about court hearings and, in most states, allowed to testify about the impact of the crime on their lives. Other lobbying efforts have sought to close legal loopholes that drunk drivers were using to avoid punishment. For example, drivers might have refused to take a Breathalyzer or blood test for intoxication and were allowed to plead guilty to a lesser charge. In other cases, drivers were allowed to claim that despite their high blood alcohol content, their driving was not really impaired.

MADD has been instrumental in the passage of more than 1,000 tougher drunk driving laws that close these loopholes and institute other deterrent measures, such as mandatory jail sentences for drunk drivers. MADD also supports efforts to require offenders to undergo treatment for alcoholism and/or drug dependency, if this is deemed necessary.

PUBLIC AWARENESS AND EDUCATION

MADD is involved in various efforts to raise public awareness and concern about drunk driving. The National Candlelight Vigil of Remembrance and Hope is held in many locations each December, drawing victims together to give public testimony to the suffering that results from drunk driving. During the Red Ribbon: Tie One On for Safety campaign, which takes place between Thanksgiving and New Year's Day, MADD encourages citizens to attach a red ribbon to their car as a reminder to themselves and others to drive sober. MADD's well-known public awareness campaign of the past used the slogan, "Think... Don't Drink and Drive" in public-service announcements on radio and television and in print materials. A more recent campaign, "Keep It a Safe Summer (KISS)," emphasized the need for sobriety during recreational activities that involve driving, boating, and other activities that might pose a danger when under the influence of alcohol. MADD also provides curriculum materials for schools and each year sponsors a poster and essay contest for children on the subject of drunk driving.

ASSISTANCE TO VICTIMS

Programs that provide aid to victims of drunk driving crashes constitute the heart of MADD's mission. Support groups help victims share their pain with others who understand their feelings. MADD members send "We Care" cards to victims of recent crashes. Specially trained victim advocates offer a one-on-one personal relationship with victims, trying to respond to both their emotional and practical needs. Victims are briefed on their legal rights and on the judicial procedures relevant to their cases. They can call a toll-free number (1-800-GET MADD) for information and help in case of a crisis. MADD also offers death-notification training for police and specialized training for other community professionals, such as clergy and medical workers, who are called on to assist victims.

"20 × 2000"

Since the founding of MADD in 1980, the percentage of alcohol-related traffic fatalities has steadily decreased, from almost 60 percent to around 50 percent. In 1995, MADD established "20 × 2000," a program that sought to reduce that proportion by an additional 20 percent by the year 2000. Intensified efforts focused on more effective law enforcement, increased sanctions, and prevention programs that included education for youth and more responsible marketing and service practices in liquor establishments. The program coincided with federal laws tying state highway funding to passage of state legislation establishing zero tolerance laws aimed at drunk drivers. Because of its concerted efforts in changing the culture of how many Americans perceived drunk driving and its risks, MADD reached its "20 × 2000" goal three years early, when alcohol-related traffic fatalities fell to below 40 percent nationally by 1997.

See also **Blood Alcohol Concentration; Blood Alcohol Concentration, Measures of; Breathalyzer; Dramshop Liability Laws; Driving, Alcohol, and Drugs; Driving Under the Influence (DUI); Legal Regulation of Drugs and Alcohol; Minimum Drinking Age Laws; Psychomotor Effects of Alcohol and Drugs.**

BIBLIOGRAPHY

Bloch, S. A., & Ungerleider, S. (1988). Whither the drunk driving movement? The social and programmatic orientations of Mothers Against Drunk Driving. In F. B. Dickman (Ed.), *Alcohol and traffic safety.* New York: Pergamon.

Cerulo, K. A. (2006). *Never saw it coming: Cultural challenges to envisioning the worst.* Chicago: University of Chicago Press.

Lightner, C. (1987). Youth and the road toll. In P. C. Noordzij & R. Roszbach (Eds.), *Alcohol, drugs and traffic safety.* Amsterdam: Elsevier.

Mann, P. (1985). *Arrive alive.* New York: McGraw-Hill.

Mothers Against Drunk Driving home page: http://www.madd.org/.

Sadoff, M. (1990). *America gets MADD*. Irving, TX: Mothers Against Drunk Driving.

DIANNE SHUNTICH
REVISED BY MATTHEW MAY (2009)

MOVIES. The use and abuse of substances may be observed in movies from virtually any genre, location, and era. One of the earliest examples of drug use in film is the 1906 French movie *Les Rêves d'un Fumeur d'Opium* (The Opium Smoker's Dream). Substances may play a minor role in a movie, serving to enhance a particular storyline or character. Alternatively, they may play a central role, representing aspects of use and abuse at the individual, community, or societal level. Although the portrayal of substances in movies may have a particular entertainment value, it is important to recognize that they may also shape a viewer's belief system and stereotypes about persons who use and abuse substances.

Research guided by social learning theory shows that "learning is achieved through not only direct experience but also through observation" (Stout et al., 2004, p. 544; see also Bandura, 2002). This suggests that viewer perceptions of persons who use and abuse alcohol and drugs can be directly influenced by the portrayal of substances in films. In a review of more than 50 movies, Cape (2003) found that both positive and negative stereotyping surround the use and abuse of substances. The major stereotypes include the tragic hero, rebellious free spirit, demonized addict/homicidal maniac, and humorous/comedic user. In addition to shaping beliefs, films can provide a historical context, helping the viewer to understand the broader culture and beliefs about substances during a particular time. This entry highlights some of the different genres of movies that portray the use and abuse of substances, the types of characters exemplifying the stereotypes outlined by Cape (2003), and the interplay between different genres of movies and the historical context.

DRAMAS

Dramas provide fictional accounts of the lifestyle or culture associated with substance use, varying significantly in their realism. They offer the viewer a unique perspective into buying and selling substances, the social contexts in which they are used, and their biopsychosocial consequences, exhibiting significant heterogeneity in realism and accuracy. Some of the earliest movies were influenced by an era of severe moralistic reasoning. For example, Dorothy Davenport produced *Human Wreckage* (Davenport & Wray, 1923), which served as a drug-prevention film following the morphine-related death of her husband Wallace Reid. In this film, drug use was associated with moral deficiency in a propaganda-like manner. It provided definitions of moral behavior in the midst of numerous Hollywood scandals. Such events and the emphasis on morality guided the architecture of the Production Code of the Motion Picture Industry (better known as the Hays Code) of the 1930s. This was an attempt by the Motion Picture Association of America to explicitly define what was acceptable in movies, with the ultimate goal of advancing proper or moral behavior. From the Hays Code emerged films that contained substances as a central theme, with a clear purpose of propaganda.

At a time when very little knowledge about substances existed, these movies helped warn parents and youth about the jeopardy of one's morality when using illicit substances. For example, the films *Reefer Madness* (Hirliman & Gasnier, 1936) and *Assassin of Youth* (Brown & Clifton, 1937) showed well-adjusted individuals having extreme and sensational reactions when high on marijuana. These films suggested that typical responses include insanity, suicidal behavior, and violence, and connected marijuana use with premarital sex and listening to jazz music, two societal taboos of the time. Similar portrayals of other drugs can be found in films of the same period, such as *Cocaine Fiends* (Kent & O'Connor, 1935). In *The Lost Weekend* (Brackett & Wilder, 1945), the main character engages in a weekend of binge drinking. Subsequent to his intoxication, he becomes involved in criminal activity and serves time as a patient in a psychiatric ward.

The Man with the Golden Arm (Preminger & Preminger), released in the 1950s, also illustrated themes similar to those of the early propaganda films, highlighting the negative consequences of illicit drugs. This film opens with the release of the central character, Frankie Machine (played by Frank Sinatra), from prison, clean and sober from a heroin addiction. Upon returning home, he struggles in a social environment that challenges his sobriety, and he quickly succumbs to heroin use, illegal card dealing, and dodging the police. The insanity, violence, and deviant behavior of the characters in these films match the demonized addict/ homicidal maniac stereotype. These films often had subtle or explicit intentions to educate and instill fear associated with using substances. A viewer of the early twenty-first century might find the portrayal of the substances to be humorous, given available knowledge on the actual effects of the substances.

A shift from bombarding the viewer with the harmful effects of substances to a more tolerant view occurred in the 1960s and 1970s, during an era of counterculture, experimentation, and political unrest. A complete breakdown in social functioning due to substance use was no longer the norm. Such films featured the tragic hero stereotype, with the main characters retaining likable qualities despite their struggles and poor choices associated with substances. For example, *Easy Rider* (Fonda & Hopper, 1969) showed the main characters Captain America (played by Peter Fonda) and Billy (Dennis Hopper) traveling across the United States in search of freedom and financial gain by selling drugs. On their journey, Captain America and Billy fight locals who view the "hippie" drug salesmen as a detriment to their communities. The viewer is led to sympathize with the protagonists, rather than feeling disdain toward their drug dealing. The broader social and political context of such films, intertwined with the Vietnam War, made them appealing to a wide audience.

Another important social and political shift occurred in the 1970s and 1980s, with the end of the Vietnam War and a growing body of scientific evidence on drugs becoming available. Nancy Reagan championed the "Just Say No" campaign, and the Drug Abuse Resistance Education (DARE) program was implemented. Zero tolerance policies and harsh drug laws began to be enforced. This change in knowledge and beliefs gave rise to a much different portrayal of substances. It is not clear to what extent these policies shaped the portrayal of substances in the movies, especially with a greater emphasis on artistic and creative directorship. However, this period marked a return to portraying substances negatively with much realism. For example, *Ulee's Gold* (Gowan & Nunez, 1997) illustrates the troubling consequences that drug use can have on an addict as well as his family and friends. It bears noting that Peter Fonda starred in this film as well as *Easy Rider*, providing a stark contrast between two cultural moments. The audience becomes witness to a character's severe detoxification and to the dangerous people who are often associated with the drug scene. *Trainspotting* (Macdonald & Boyle, 1996) portrays the dark side of heroin dependence, including severe withdrawal symptoms, hallucinations, drug seeking behaviors, overdose, relapse, and troubled social relationships. *Go* (Freeman & Liman, 1999) depicts a group of young friends who use and sell Ecstasy at rave parties. These friends must confront the realities associated with drug dealing, including threats of violence and the need to engage in high-risk behaviors.

Besides showing the consequences of movies, it is important to note that many dramas also focus on issues related to recovery and treatment. As in the other films discussed, these films also reflect the current knowledge and beliefs at the time they were filmed. For example, the earlier *Days of Wine and Roses* (Manulis & Edwards, 1962) shows the struggles associated with recovering from an addiction. The film illustrates a married couple's personal, social, and professional struggles associated with their alcohol dependence. Alcohol is portrayed as being a major contributor to reckless and dangerous behavior when the intoxicated wife nearly kills herself and the couple's child after accidentally setting a fire in the family's apartment. The film closes with the husband achieving sobriety through the assistance of Alcoholics Anonymous and attempting to persuade his wife to join him in the journey to recovery. This was the only treatment option of the time. A more recent film, *28 Days* (Topping & Thomas, 2000), shows a woman, Gwen Cummings (played by Sandra Bullock), forced to make a choice between jail or 28 days in a rehabilitation center after she gets in a car accident while driving drunk. She fulfills her sentence at a rehabilitation center, with the treatment process involving the serenity prayer, a twelve-step program, and family therapy. Treatment and recovery films such as *28 Days* can have an impact on the way the viewer perceives people who seek help for their addiction. Hersey (2005) argues that this type of film may unrealistically portray individuals seeking treatment and the treatment process itself. The main characters tend to be white and upper-middle-class, and undergo treatment in expensive settings that are generally not reflective of typical treatment options, such as outpatient treatment.

COMEDIES

Although some films attempt to portray the negative consequences of substance abuse, many films take a different approach. That is, they glorify substance use and misuse using a comedic perspective. They tend to avoid showing the negative consequences of substance abuse or do so in a humorous way. Although the War on Drugs has had a lasting effect on the themes expressed in drug-related dramas, comedic films have more flexibility in their perspective and tone. Both the shift in societal perspective during the 1980s and current scientific data have illustrated the devastating physical consequences of narcotics such as cocaine, heroin, and opiates, making a comedy based on these substances unlikely. Comedic drug films tend to focus on the use of alcohol or marijuana, often distorting their true effects.

So-called stoner films center on the use of marijuana and typically have outlandish plots and humorous protagonists. Their titles often make explicit references to marijuana use, as evidenced by the films *Half Baked* (Simonds & Davis, 1998), *Dazed and Confused* (Daniel & Linklater, 1993), and *Up in Smoke* (Adler & Adler, 1978). *Half Baked*, like *Go*, features main characters involved in the drug-dealing business; unlike *Go*, however, the characters in *Half Baked* are never perceived to be in serious danger or trouble as a result of their involvement in this drug culture—despite a minor plot appearance from police and a greedy drug king. The hallucinations experienced by the characters in *Half Baked* are also quite different from those in more typical films with an antidrug message in that the *Half Baked* characters generally have fun and enjoy their humorous experiences while high.

Another common type of comedy portrays young characters eager to experiment with or use substances—partying. This genre of drug film typically involves using a large quantity of substances, especially alcohol, with kegs of beer and shots of hard liquor being commonplace. Parents are generally not main characters in these films as the majority of the film actually centers on the party and youth themselves. Much like stoner films, party films do not portray the negative consequences associated with substance use, or the consequences become a central point of the comedy. *National Lampoon's Animal House* (Reitman & Landis, 1978) is a classic party film. Such films frequently take place in a college, depicting the use of alcohol as a social lubricant and catalyst for many gags.

Comedic films often have characters that reflect the humorous/comedic user or rebellious free spirit stereotype. More times than not, the substance use or culture is the vehicle for humor. This is particularly evident when substances are a component of a party setting, as they tend to minimize any negative consequences associated with their use. A potential danger of this type of film, as suggested by social learning theory, is that the viewer misunderstands the actual consequences.

DOCUMENTARIES

Documentary or non-fiction movies are another means for portraying the use of alcohol and drugs. These movies allow the audience to view the experiences of an actual person or group of individuals rather than through a fictional account or storyline. For example, *Children Underground* (Belzberg & Belzberg, 2001) depicts the existence of impoverished Romanian youth who abuse inhalants and live in the subway system. The viewer learns about the consequences related to the youths' addiction to inhalants, including prostitution, stealing, begging, and other physical and mental health problems. The documentary *REHAB* (Okazaki & Okazaki, 2005) provides an insider's look into a 30-day rehabilitation facility for persons with various types of substance use disorders and histories. The people featured in this documentary share their struggles in recovery through anecdotes and day-to-day interactions during and after treatment. The documentary also highlights the challenges that individuals may face in their efforts to achieve and maintain sobriety.

Documentaries may lend themselves to a variety of stereotypes, depending on the viewpoint and story portrayed. In these examples, and many others, the tragic hero stereotype was exemplified. Although documentaries may attempt to depict true-life accounts of people or events, it is important to recognize that there is a fine line between an objective portrayal and propaganda. Beliefs about substances are arguably influenced by social, political, and moral values. Thus, documentaries may have an underlying motivation to advance a particular system of beliefs while maintaining a position of objectivity.

IN CONCLUSION

Tremendous diversity exists in the portrayal of alcohol and drug use in movies, including but not limited to the depiction of consequences, contexts surrounding use, and the extent to which use is sensationalized. The portrayal may be intended for purposes of entertainment. However, there are sometimes unintended consequences, such as advancing stereotypes about persons with substance use disorders and minimizing the actual risks of use, especially binge drinking. As alcohol and drugs are ubiquitous, particularly in American culture, the depiction of use and misuse can be expected to continue playing an important role in movies.

See also **Internet: Impact on Drug and Alcohol Use; Media; Music.**

BIBLIOGRAPHY

Adler, L. (Producer), & Adler, L. (Director). (1978). *Up in smoke* [Motion picture]. Hollywood, CA: Paramount Pictures.

Bandura, A. (2002). Social cognitive theory of mass communication. In J. Bryant & D. Zillmann (Eds.), *Media effects: Advances in theory and research* (pp. 61–90). Mahwah, NJ: Lawrence Erlbaum Associates.

Belzberg, E. (Producer), & Belzberg, E. (Director). (2001). *Children underground* [Motion picture]. Brooklyn, NY: Belzberg Films.

Brackett, C. (Producer), & Wilder, B. (Director). (1945). *The lost weekend* [Motion picture]. Hollywood, CA: Paramount Pictures.

Brown, C. A. (Producer), & Clifton, E. (Director). (1937). *Assassin of youth* [Motion picture]. Location unknown: BCM Roadshow Productions.

Cape, G. S. (2003). Addiction, stigma and movies. *Acta Psychiatrica Scandinavica, 107*(3), 163–169.

Daniel, S. (Producer), & Linklater, R. (Director). (1993). *Dazed and confused* [Motion picture]. Universal City, CA: Alphaville Films.

Davenport, D. (Producer), & Wray, J. G. (Director). (1923). *Human wreckage* [Motion picture]. Hollywood, CA: Film Booking Offices of America.

Fonda, P. (Producer), & Hopper D. (Director). (1969). *Easy rider* [Motion picture]. Culver City, CA: Columbia Pictures Corporation.

Freeman, M. (Producer), & Liman, D. (Director). (1999). *Go* [Motion picture]. Culver City, CA: Banner Entertainment.

Gowan, S. (Producer), & Nunez, V. (Director). (1997). *Ulee's gold* [Motion picture]. New York: Clinica Estetico.

Hersey, C. (2005). Script(ing) treatment: Representations of recovery from addiction in Hollywood film. *Contemporary Drug Problems, 32*(3), 467–493.

Hirliman, G. A. (Producer), & Gasnier, L. (Director). (1936). *Tell your children* (Also titled *Reefer madness*) [Motion picture]. Beverly Hills, CA: G&H Productions.

Kent, W. (Producer), & O'Connor, W. A. (Director). (1935). *The pace that kills* (Also titled *Cocaine fiends* and *Cocaine madness*) [Motion picture]. Location unknown: Willis Kent Productions.

Macdonald, A. (Producer), & Boyle, D (Director). (1996). *Trainspotting* [Motion picture]. Burbank, CA: Channel Four Films.

Manulis, M. (Producer), & Edwards, B. (Director). (1962). *Days of wine and roses* [Motion picture]. Beverly Hills, CA: Jalem Productions.

Okazaki, S. (Producer), & Okazaki, S. (Director). (2005). *REHAB* [Motion picture]. Santa Cruz, CA: Home Box Office.

Preminger, O. (Producer), & Preminger, O. (Director). (1955). *The man with the golden arm* [Motion picture]. Hollywood, CA: Otto Preminger Films.

Reitman, I. (Producer), & Landis, J. (Director). (1978). *National Lampoon's Animal house* [Motion picture]. Hollywood, CA: Universal Pictures.

Simonds, R. (Producer), & Davis, T. (Director). (1998). *Half baked* [Motion picture]. New York: Robert Simonds Productions.

Stout, P. A. (2004). Images of mental illness in the media: Identifying gaps in the research. *Schizophrenia Bulletin, 30*(3), 543.

Topping, J. (Producer), & Thomas, B. (Director). (2000). *28 Days* [Motion picture]. Culver City, CA: Columbia Pictures Corporation.

SAMANTHA BRANDFON
BRIAN PERRON

MPTP. MPTP is a neurotoxin that was accidentally produced during an illicit manufacturing process. To circumvent the laws regarding controlled drugs, a chemist attempted to synthesize a derivative of meperidine. By synthesizing a new derivative not specifically covered by the Controlled Substances Act and existing Drug Enforcement Agency laws and by synthesizing the drug and selling it within the same state, the chemist had hoped to profit while avoiding violation of the laws. This designer drug approach was being widely used to avoid prosecution for selling drugs of abuse—however, in this case a side product was also formed in this reaction, MPTP (1-methyl-4-phenyl-1,2,3,6-tetrahydropyridine). People who bought this mixture on the street quickly developed a neurological syndrome virtually indistinguishable from Parkinson's disease. Initially the cause of this problem remained unknown. With intense investigation, the blame was placed on the side product in the reaction, MPTP. MPTP had long been used as an intermediate in chemical synthesis and was commercially available. The ability of MPTP to provoke a Parkinson-like syndrome helped explain a report from years ago of a chemist working with this compound suddenly developing a disease resembling Parkinson's.

The Parkinson-like syndrome is very similar to the symptoms originally described in Parkinson's disease. The most notable aspects of the syndrome are the marked cog-wheel rigidity of the muscles, along with a generalized decrease in movement usually associated with problems initiating the movement. Patients often have difficulty with such fine motor skills as writing; and with walking, which usually becomes a series of small, shuffling steps termed a "festinating gait"; their greatest problem is starting and stopping. Diminished blinking coupled with a limited facial expression can be very prominent and is termed "masked facies." In Parkinson's disease, patients also have a pill-rolling tremor and a tendency to fall because of problems with blood pressure and the reflexes important to maintaining posture.

Pathologically, Parkinson's disease is noted for a degeneration of pigmented nuclei within the brain, including the substantia nigra. The loss of the dopaminergic neurons in the substantia nigra that project to the part of the brain called the striatum is responsible for the motor problems; while the degeneration of other areas of the brain, including the locus ceruleus, are presumably responsible for the autonomic problems. The cause of Parkinson's disease is still not known; treatment is symptomatic. Early studies demonstrated the ability of anticholinergic medications to help with many of the motor symptoms, especially the tremor. However, the drug of choice in the early 2000s is L-dopa, a precursor of dopamine. Unlike dopamine, which does not traverse the blood-brain barrier, L-dopa is readily transported into the brain where it is taken up into neurons and converted to dopamine—thereby helping to reduce symptoms caused by loss of dopamine-containing neurons. Replacement of the dopamine can markedly limit the severity of the motor symptoms; however, the duration of this benefit is often limited to only about five years, presumably due to the continued progression of the disease.

MPTP does not bind to opioid receptors and it has no opioid activity, although it is a side product in the synthesis of a meperidine analog. When ingested, it is taken up into neurons containing a catecholamine transporter, greatly limiting the neurons affected. Once in the cell, the drug is converted by the enzyme monoamine oxidase (type B) in a series of steps to another compound, MPP+, which is believed to be responsible for its toxic actions. The need for the transporter to take up the toxin into the cells partially explains its selective toxicity within the brain. There, this drug destroys the same groups of pigmented catecholinergic neurons affected in Parkinson's disease, including the substantia nigra and the locus ceruleus. The greater sensitivity of pigmented neurons to the toxin is still not completely understood. One hypothesis has been put forward: The color in the neurons is due to the pigment melanin, which actively binds the toxin. Therefore, it has been suggested that this binding results in the accumulation of very high levels of the drug, which persist in the neurons for long periods of time, enhancing its toxicity.

Clinically, MPTP produces a syndrome virtually identical to that seen in Parkinson's disease; but Parkinson's is a progressive degenerative disease, which, over the period of many years, gradually leads to a variety of difficulties with thought and memory. It is not thought that MPTP produces a

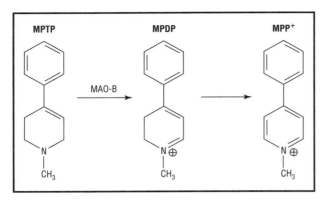

Figure 1. MPTP conversion to MPDP and MPP⁺. ILLUSTRATION BY GGS INFORMATION SERVICES. GALE, CENGAGE LEARNING

similar global, diffuse loss of function. The marked similarity, though, has led to the speculation that Parkinson's may be due to exposure to a toxin similar to MPTP. Since the toxicity of MPTP depends on its conversion by type B monoamine oxidase (MAO-B), it was suggested that inhibition of this enzyme may prove beneficial. Selegiline is a selective MAO-B inhibitor, and early clinical trials suggested that the progression of Parkinson patients taking this medication may be slower than in the control groups. In the 1990s Selegiline was approved by the FDA to treat Parkinson's disease. In 2006 it was approved to treat depression.

See also **Controlled Substances Act of 1970; Meperidine; Receptor, Drug.**

BIBLIOGRAPHY

Cedarbaum, J. M., Schleifer, L. S. (1990). Drugs for Parkinson's disease, spasticity, and acute muscle spasms. In A. G. Gilman et al. (Eds.), *Goodman and Gilman's the pharmacological basis of therapeutics*, 8th ed. New York: Pergamon. (2005, 11th ed. New York: McGraw-Hill Medical.)

Hanson, G. R., Venturelli, P. J., & Fleckenstein, A. E. (2005). *Drugs and Society.* Sudbury, MA: Jones & Bartlett Publishers.

Rosenbaum, R. B. (2006). *Understanding Parkinson's disease: A personal and professional view.* Westport, CT: Praeger Publishers.

GAVRIL W. PASTERNAK

MULTIDOCTORING.

Multidoctoring—also known as double-doctoring, doctor-shopping, or multisourcing—refers to the practice of utilizing more than one health-care provider or prescriber (e.g., a physician or mid-level practitioner, such as a nurse practitioner or physician assistant) as the source for medications or other medical services, without informing the individual practitioners of any medications already being prescribed. It typically refers more directly to obtaining scheduled drugs (or, more rarely, sexual performance enhancement medications) in quantities that would be difficult to obtain from one source. The medications involved are most commonly from the group considered to be "brain reward" or "euphoria producing" drugs. These drugs are considered to be potential drugs of abuse or addiction, and they generally have a value on the secondary, or "street," market. These medications produce an acute surge of dopamine from the midbrain (the ventral tegmental area [VTA] and nucleus accumbens) to the forebrain (the prefrontal cortex), which causes the brain-reward or euphoria effect. Since the mid-1990s, there has been a substantial increase in the abuse of controlled prescription drugs, as well as an attendant increase in concerns about the multisourcing of these drugs.

The classes of medications involved in multidoctoring include: (1) sedative hypnotics (benzodiazepines, barbiturates, and other sedative-like drugs), (2) the opioid and opiate analgesics, and (3) the psycho-stimulants. These drugs are typically covered under the Federal Controlled Substances Act and are scheduled in descending order of abuse potential as CII, CIII, CIV, or CV medications. A few non-scheduled drugs are also the focus of multisourcing activity, including carisoprodol (Soma), tramadol (Ultram), butalbital/acetaminophen (Fioricet), and (as mentioned above) the sexual performance enhancement or erectile dysfunction medications. Each of these medications has a street value that exceeds its pharmacy value, and this value is proportionally related to the amount of and rapidity of the euphoria-producing effect of each drug.

Individuals who engage in multidoctoring or multisourcing behavior may obtain the medications for their own use, or they may intend to resell the drugs on the street. People who seek controlled drugs for the purpose of abuse or resale are often very convincing in their appeals, and they can therefore often get physicians or mid-level practitioners to prescribe the drugs requested. To maintain their drug supply, addicted patients typically pressure the physician for more medication, pressure the physician or pharmacist for early refills, or seek additional sources of supply. Another hallmark of addiction is dishonesty, including dishonesty with the prescribing physician.

In Canada and the United States, legislation prohibits people from acquiring a narcotic prescription without informing the physician of other narcotics that have already been prescribed for them that month. Failure to do so can result in criminal charges. Physicians can record a patient's responses to questions about other prescribed narcotics, and about controlled drugs in general, as a means of discouraging multidoctoring. Several approaches are being developed to help combat multidoctoring through the use of pharmacy information databases. Since the early 1990s, insurers (including state Medicaid programs) have been performing drug utilization review (DUR) surveillance to attempt to identify those involved in multisourcing. In addition, regional and national pharmacy chain stores have developed computer prescription systems to help track prescription use patterns, and they can sometimes identify multisourcing. Several states, beginning with Kentucky in the mid-1990s, have implemented statewide controlled-drug databases, which are available on a password-protected basis to physicians. These databases can provide real-time reports of all scheduled-drug prescriptions filled at pharmacies in the state during the prior 12 months, as well as the number of different prescribers involved. Federal legislation has enabled the NASPER (National All Schedules Prescription Electronic Reporting Act) system to begin to further this initiative on a national level.

Physicians themselves may be involved at various levels in multidoctoring and the diversion of drugs to the street. Some physicians, known as "script doctors," willfully prescribe controlled substances to people seeking them. Others prescribe them as a result of being misled ("duped doctors"), while some are simply uninformed about the prevalence of multidoctoring and the substances involved ("dated doctors"). Educating the public about the risks of prescription medication abuse and increasing the skills of physicians, pharmacists, health-care organizations and state and federal regulators in recognizing patients engaged in multidoctoring will help to decrease the diversion and misuse of prescription drugs.

See also **Prescription Drug Abuse.**

BIBLIOGRAPHY

American Medical Association Council on Scientific Affairs. (1992). Drug abuse related to prescribing practices. *Journal of the American Medical Association, 247*(6), 864–866.

Goldman, B. (1987). Confronting the prescription drug addict: Doctors must learn to say no. *Canadian Medical Association Journal, 136*(8), 871–876.

Isaacson, J. H., Hopper, J. A., Alford, D. P., & Parran, T. (2005). Prescription drug use and abuse: Risk factors, red flags, and prevention strategies. *Postgraduate Medicine, 118*(1), 19–26.

Longo, L. P., Parran, T., Jr., Johnson, B., & Kinsey, W. (2000). Addiction: Part II. Identification and management of the drug-seeking patient. *American Family Physician, 61*, 2401–2408.

Miller, M. M., & Brown, R. T. (2007). Prescription drug monitoring programs. (Editorial). *American Family Physician, 75*, 810.

National Center on Addiction and Substance Abuse at Columbia University. (2005). *Under the counter: The diversion and abuse of controlled prescription drugs in the U.S.* New York: Author.

Parran, T., Jr. (1997). Prescription drug abuse: A question of balance. *Medical Clinics of North America, 81*(4), 967–978.

THEODORE PARRAN

MUSIC. "Opium? No! Cocaine? No! The Great American Brain Killer Is Dance Music!" Although printed in the Portland *Oregonian* in 1932, that quote neatly encapsulates the fears of mainstream society even today about the link between drugs and music: that outlaw musicians will lead our innocent children Pied Piper-like to their doom with their wild rhythms and coded songs glamorizing the use of drugs.

1930S THROUGH 1960S

Since the 1930s, all the main genres of popular music have been associated with certain drugs, although the nature of that relationship is often multilayered. For example, the use of heroin among the major jazz artists of the 1950s, such as Charlie Parker, Miles Davis, and Chet Baker, was both a product of a desire to set up barriers between the artist and the audience—to be detached and "cool"—and part of the coping mechanism black musicians used to deal with the daily miseries and humiliations of being black in 1950s America.

In the 1960s, the drugs-music dynamic was very different. Lysergic acid diethylamide (LSD) was an integral part of a zeitgeist looking for an alternative society through the expansion of consciousness. The effects of LSD directly influenced the sound of psychedelic music and the response of the audience. The three-minute dance song was replaced by the 20-minute meandering guitar exposition absorbed earnestly by young people sitting on the floor gently nodding.

ECSTASY AND THE RAVE

Different again was the use of the drug ecstasy in rave culture. For many, all-night dancing requires some form of stimulant drug simply to stay awake; so cocaine and amphetamines were used by '20s flappers, '50s rock 'n rollers, and '70s punks. Ecstasy (chemically related to amphetamine) was simply the latest manifestation of a decades-old phenomenon. The difference lay in the special effect of ecstasy: to engender a sense of empathy in the user toward other people. Because of this effect, it became known as the hug drug. Those who created the scene were attracted by the notion of having a good night out without all the unpleasantness and violence associated with alcohol consumption, although ecstasy itself was not without its dangers.

MUSICIANS AS WANDERERS

One could argue that musicians are simply reflecting back to their audience the common values they all share in any given youth culture. But mention names such as Jimi Hendrix, Janis Joplin, or Kurt Cobain and they are as likely to be remembered by the public for their involvement in the drug scene as for their contribution as professional musicians. So what is it about drugs and musicians?

Musicians have always been located in the outfield of society. In medieval England, the musician wandered rootless from town to town bringing news and gossip to people who would never travel more than five miles from home in their entire lives. The freedom of musicians to roam gave them an aura of mystery and romance. Flash forward to the rock tours of modern times, and you have musicians out on the road for months or even years

at a time. That mantle of freedom still hangs from their shoulders, and with it the sense that they can do what they like and move on. This translates itself to the stage where the rock star becomes a Dionysian figure, a blank slate onto which an audience can vicariously map all its desires and wishes and then go back to the office the next day unharmed. Unfortunately, there have been too many rock stars who believed their own mythology. Living the image offstage as well as on has claimed the lives of many musicians through drugs and alcohol.

THE DRIVE TO CREATE

The musician is also an artist and may well exhibit all the anxieties, insecurities, and frailties attending the drive to create. But unlike the writer or the painter, the musician has to operate in one of the toughest, most unforgiving of industries. The music business is a haven for the unscrupulous and downright crooked, where you are only as good as your last record and where all the egos and paranoia of the entertainment business conspire to wreck your ambition and extinguish your creative spark. Moreover, the musician has to be in the public eye, out on stage performing; many musicians are physically ill before a show.

Drug and alcohol abuse can be a form of self-medication to cope with the uncertainties and vicissitudes of the music business, but it can also be linked to another aspect of creativity known by some jazz musicians as the Charlie Parker death wish. This is the belief that because highly gifted musicians such as Parker, Miles Davis, Jimi Hendrix, and John Lennon used drugs, that is what one has to do to be a creative genius. The reality of course, is that these musicians were exceptional in spite of the drugs, not because of them.

However, it does raise the issue of the role of drugs in creativity. There is no question that at a certain level, moderate use of marijuana and alcohol will engender a feeling of relaxation that can facilitate the flow of ideas and also reduce inhibitions. For example improvising musicians may attempt to extend their playing during a live performance, whereas sobriety might have inhibited that stretch. But it can be limited by diminishing returns. One musician told this author that he felt alcohol helped him play the sounds he heard in his head, but it reached a point where he was drinking so much that his fingers just could not respond fast enough. It is hard to imagine that the iconic sounds of 1960s psychedelia could have been created without the influence of cannabis and LSD, yet heroin and cocaine have ruined untold numbers of recording sessions when not only musicians but also producers and engineers were too stoned or wired up to function.

LIVES OF FAME

In the late 1980s, Charlie Watts said of 25 years in the Rolling Stones, "It's been five years of playing and 20 years of hanging about." Drug and alcohol use can simply be a way to relieve the boredom of hours spent in airport lounges, hotel rooms, and studios. Then musicians have to be in top form for a two-hour show, pack in some leisure time, and sleep on demand to be ready to rush off to the next gig. On a long tour, it is easy to jump onto a chemical carousel of stimulants and sedatives and find it extremely difficult to jump off.

None of this is meant to be an excuse for musicians abusing drugs and alcohol, but simply to offer a brief overview as to the particular circumstances of the life of the professional musician, which can lead to dependency and, sadly, some tragic newspaper headlines. So substance misuse appears inextricably woven into the fabric of the music business, and therefore it is not surprising that musicians want to write about their drug and alcohol experiences as they write about a range of topics that affect their lives. But this has left the business mired in controversy as claims are made that musicians are encouraging the use of drugs among their young audiences and that they have a duty as role models to be more the model citizen than many of them can seem to manage.

DRUGS AND LYRICS

Since the early 1970s, academics have been conducting content analyses of song lyrics to identity reference to drugs and alcohol. These are invariably expressed in the drug slang of the day, which researchers often refer to as "code" as if to suggest a secret language known only to the musician and the audience. This dates to the 1930s, when jazz musicians under the threat of heavy prison sentences would sing about reefer and muggles (marijuana); kicking the gong around (opium

smoking), and wacky dust (cocaine). But as drug use spread more widely into the white, middle class student population in the 1960s, the intention of such content analysis was to highlight the supposed risk that young people would be influenced to try drugs through the coded language of their favorite performers.

For some, the fact that a rock band would sing about drugs at all was tantamount to glamorizing drugs, regardless of the nature of the song. A study by Brian Primack, Madeline Dalton, Mary Carroll, Aaron Agarwal, and Michael Fine, published in 2008, made much of the amount of time young people are exposed to music as opposed to health education in schools. And debate continues about whether the Beatles song "Lucy in the Sky with Diamonds" was really about LSD; even the Beatles have made contradictory comments on this point.

In general, songs fall into two categories: decidedly antidrug or neutral. Few songs actually declare that using drugs is exciting and fun—not least because they would never get airplay. The antidrug song can be found in all genres of music. Examples include "Needle of Death" (folk); "Dat Smell" (rock), "Cocaine" (blues), and "White Lines" (hip hop). Alcohol figures most prominently in country music, where much whiskey is consumed to drown out the many sorrows of the ordinary working man.

These songs are focused on the individual experience of the composer, but there have been a plethora of songs from black soul, hip-hop, and rap musicians commenting on the devastation that drugs, especially heroin and crack, have wrought within the black community. Songs about marijuana err more on the positive side, most prominently in reggae, where marijuana (ganja) is regarded by Rastafarians as a religious sacrament in much the same way that wine is used in Catholicism.

AN EFFECT ON TEENS?

The issue remains whether the exposure young people might have to songs about drugs and alcohol actually affects their own decisions about drug or alcohol use. Karl Witty from the U.K.-based National Collaborating Centre for Drug Prevention made an important point in a 2006 paper about celebrities and drug use: "The fundamental problem with existing media research in the context of celebrity influence is however the notion of causality. Research hints at causal links but fails to provide substantial evidence to endorse such insinuations, thus only providing largely hypothetical evidence."

Finally, there is the question of whether celebrity drug use sets a bad example for young people. Should popular music stars be role models? These musicians fill concert halls around the world, sell a significant number of recordings and much merchandise, and their posters adorn the walls of thousands of bedrooms. So surely they must influence the behavior of young people when they are known to be drug users? Well, there is not a shred of evidence to support what is, admittedly, a commonsense view. In fact when a group of British teenagers were asked by members of Parliament in March 2008 what they thought of such pop stars as Amy Winehouse and Pete Doherty, whose drug use is regularly featured in the British media, they said they simply felt sorry for them. Politicians in particular are wedded to the idea of using celebrities to warn against the dangers of drugs and are quick to condemn those who indulge. But they miss the point entirely. Young people might aspire to become singers or guitarists (or football players or film stars), but they do not aspire to become drug users, nor do they aspire to become role models for others.

The chances of actually becoming successful in the music business are extremely slim; those who make it (often barely out of their teens) can be suddenly catapulted into the public eye and are then expected to become role models. As for drug use among young people, the real decisions about whether to use drugs and alcohol are firmly rooted in their own personal, social, cultural, and economic environment—not in the antics of the rich and remote.

See also **Internet, Impact on Drug and Alcohol Use; Media; Movies.**

BIBLIOGRAPHY

Primack, B. A., Dalton, M. A., Carroll, M. V., Agarwal, A. A., & Fine, M. J. (2008). Content analysis of tobacco, alcohol, and other drugs in popular music. *Archives of Pediatrics and Adolescent Medicine, 162*(2), 169–175.

Shapiro, H. (2003). *Waiting for the man: The story of drugs and popular music.* London: Helter Skelter.

Witty, K. (2006). *The effects of drug use by celebrities upon young people's drug use and perception of use.* Liverpool: National Collaborating Centre for Drug Prevention. Available from http://www.drugprevention evidence.info/.

HARRY SHAPIRO

MYTHS ABOUT ADDICTION AND ITS TREATMENT.

The causes of addiction, its nature, the best ways to treat its symptoms, and the possibility of devising a full, permanent cure remain elusive. Why some people experiment with mood-altering substances, and why some of those people go on to become compulsive substance abusers to the detriment of their health, finances, personal relationships, ability to earn a living, and perhaps to their freedom, is not fully understood. Currently there are two general theories on the nature of addiction. Among addiction scientists, medical professionals, and treatment specialists, the most widely accepted theory of the nature of addiction is called the Disease model, which describes addiction as a "chronic relapsing brain disease." This description of addiction maintains that substance use alters the function of the brain in such a way that the addict becomes just as physically disordered, and just as incapable of managing the course of his or her illness, as a diabetic or a sufferer from heart disease, kidney failure, or schizophrenia.

The second theory or set of notions about addiction disorders is often called the Free Will model, which views the individual as an active agent in becoming addicted and in quitting use. This way of conceptualizing addiction emphasizes the fact that substance-dependent people can and do break their habits through their own volition, and that most people either decline to experiment with drugs in the first place or do so casually. Those who prefer this explanation of addiction point out that no amount of behavior change will free a diabetic or a cancer patient from his or her affliction, but that it is possible, though often difficult, for an alcoholic or a heroin addict to stop using alcohol or heroin, and thus be free of the physical symptoms that defined his or her status as an addict (sometimes assisted by drugs such as methadone, which relieve some of the physical discomfort of withdrawal). Once "detoxified," the

Common belief	Disease model response	Free will model response
1. After detoxification, given compliance with treatment and total abstinence from addictive substances, any changes in the pathways of the brain that had been caused by the abused substance disappear, and the brain returns to a more fully healthy state.	As a chronic, relapsing brain disease, substance dependence is an organic state in which neuro-transmitters in the brain have been altered by constant exposure to a psycho-active substance thereby severely limiting the addict's ability to make free choices. The brain usually returns to a better state of health than when the addiction was at its worst, but it takes a very long time to return completely to the health it enjoyed before the substance abuse began. For many addicts, part of the brain damage is permanent.	With the exception of brain damage caused by neuro-toxic substances such as methamphetamine and alcohol, substance dependence in and of itself does not "scar" the brain. Retained memories of drug-induced pleasure may be triggered in the context of mind set and environmental setting and result in the perception of craving, but the addict can resist acting upon it.

Substance dependence does have points in common with some diseases associated with behavior, HIV/AIDS, for example, in that something the sufferer did or did not do is usually the source of his or her condition. However, the substance-dependent person can, and often does, make life-changing decisions that free him or her from the condition – not a choice available to a sufferer of AIDS. |
2. Everyone has enough free will not to become an addict.	The choice to try an addictive substance for the first time may be voluntary. Surveys have shown that, as perceptions that drug use is dangerous increase in a population, drug use decreases. Yet freedom even in this choice may be weakened by such factors as peer pressure, a biological predisposition to addiction, (alcoholism, for example, tends to run in biological families), or a valid reason for taking it once (for example, as a pain killer prescribed by one's physician).	While some people seem predisposed to enjoy the sensations induced by psycho-active substances and therefore to seek to repeat the experience, others do not and are not inclined to continue using them. Even so, substance-dependent persons are not rendered completely passive by their addiction. No one would deny that it is very difficult to break addiction's grip but it is not impossible and maybe empowering.
3. Many substances are instantly addictive—one experiment will lead inexorably to a full-blown habit.	Addiction is a process. As the person slips from the first use to repeated use to misuse to full-fledged addiction and chemical dependence on the substance, freedom of choice diminishes and usually disappears. The term "disrupted self-control" has been used to describe this process by which the neural structures that underlie decision making are damaged by exposure to psycho-active substances.	Addiction is a process but there are many "exit ramps" along the way. Recovering addicts should not be encouraged to believe that they did not participate in any way in the process.
4. Addiction ends when detoxification removes all of the abused substance from the addict's body, and the pain following detoxification (the withdrawal syndrome) is gone.	Changes in the pathways of the brain, which had been caused by the abused substance, persist long after the last particle of the abused substance has left the body. The underlying addictive disorder (the cause, or set of causes, which made the person liable to become addicted in the first place) remain.	While the impact of the addiction experience on the psyche (and, less romantically, the brain) is profound, so is the impact of other experiences, both positive and negative. How long does it take to repair a "broken heart" after a love affair or the death of a loved one? Surely a long time, but the suffering lover will go on to love again, and the addict can strive to build, and succeed in building, a normal life.
5. A single, simple course of treatment ought to produce a permanent total cure in an addict. When a patient relapses (returns to addiction) after detoxification, then the detoxification of this patient must have failed as a treatment.	As a chronic disorder, addiction needs a lifelong treatment, like diabetes, asthma, arthritis, and high blood pressure, not just a one-time detoxification. One does not expect a single injection of insulin to cure a diabetic, or any single administration of medicine to relieve a patient forever of arthritis, asthma, or high blood pressure. Each treatment is successful if it improves the condition at the time; each needs to be repeated, often throughout the rest of the patient's life.	12-Step Programs such as Alcoholics Anonymous provide successful long-term support for many recovering addicts. Others find the strength necessary to minimize relapse in religion or in stable relationships with significant others. Still others may cycle in and out of treatment programs until they find their personal route to long-term sobriety. This may take as long as a decade but rarely is it longer than that. Meanwhile, while a substance-dependent person is in treatment, harm to self, family, friends, and society is reduced.
6. Once an addict is detoxified, as long as he or she does not take the abused substance (or a different abused substance) again, any medical, social, and occupational difficulties that had been associated with the addiction disappear.	Medical, social, and occupational consequences may last long after an addict has stopped taking any abused substance. Getting sober (detoxification) and remaining sober (compliance with the prescribed treatment) do not automatically repair the damage of a life of addiction. Active alcoholism, for example, may be gone, perhaps forever, but the destruction it may have caused often lasts indefinitely.	The task of rebuilding a responsible life after substance dependence is under control is difficult in the extreme, but it is not impossible. Hope for new relationships and a productive life for the ex-addict, as well as recognition that one is or has been substance-dependent, are essential to recovery.
7. Since most persons treated for addiction relapse sooner or later, treatment is by definition unsuccessful, and it makes no sense to try it.	Treatment is not unsuccessful because further treatments are needed. With addiction, as with diabetes, we must see treatment as an ongoing process, successful if at the time it reduces the severity of the disorder. It unfortunately does	Statistics on treatment success and failure are necessarily drawn from populations in treatment. A large percentage of substance dependent persons break their habits without treatment. This is particularly obvious in the case of tobacco but it is

[CONTINUED]

Table 1. Common beliefs about addiction and responses associated with general concepts about its nature. ILLUSTRATION BY GGS INFORMATION SERVICES. GALE, CENGAGE LEARNING

Common belief	Disease model response	Free will model response
	not have a permanent fix, like setting a broken bone or surgically removing all of a cancer. The goal is improvement, not cure.	also true for other substances.
8. There are no degrees of addiction. It is an all-or-none condition. A person is either a non-addict and never takes the tiniest amount of an abused substance or is a hopeless addict whose life centers on enjoying maximum amounts of the abused substance (or substances) all day every day for life.		

Agreement between the two Responses

At one extreme, there is an occasional addict who is satisfied with minimal intake and who functions well at home and on the job. At the other extreme is the addict who regularly takes such huge volumes of the abused substance as to lose consciousness. There is, indeed, a formal system for measuring the severity of a patient's addiction and the success of treatment at any given moment. It is called ASI (for ADDICTION SEVERITY INDEX). It considers such factors as whether the patient's substance abuse is decreasing, whether the patient is functioning better socially and enjoying better general health (rarely a complete return to the state before the first use of the abused substance), and to what degree, if any, the patient presents a danger to public health and safety (treatment of an alcoholic who continues to drink but has stopped driving after drinking as a result of psychotherapy would be a partial success).

| 9. Most substance-dependent persons engage in criminal activities, either to finance their habits or because their judgment is impaired by alcohol or other drugs. | | |

Agreement between the two Responses

The drug/crime relationship is difficult to quantify because:

- Most crimes result from a variety of factors (personal, situational, cultural, economic); even when drugs are a cause, they are likely to be only one factor among many.
- What is meant by "drug-related" varies from study to study; some studies interpret the mere presence of drugs as having causal relevance whereas other studies interpret the relationship more narrowly.
- Reports by offenders about their drug use may exaggerate or minimize the relevance of drugs; drug-use measures, such as urinalysis that identifies only very recent drug use, are limited.

The evidence indicates that drug users are more likely than nonusers to commit crimes, that arrestees frequently were under the influence of a drug at the time they committed their offense, and that drugs generate violence. Assessing the nature and extent of the influence of drugs on crime requires that reliable information about the offense and the offender be available and that definitions be consistent. In the face of problematic evidence, it is impossible to say quantitatively how much drugs influence the occurrence of crime

http://www.whitehousedrugpolicy.gov/publications/factsht/crime/index.html.

10. If treatment were possible, it would cost millions of dollars to treat a single patient. Treatment would cost more than putting a young person in prison for life. In terms of dollar value, treatment would cost even more than a single addict would be apt to steal in a lifetime.	One study in California showed that the benefits of treatment outweighed the cost of treatment at least four-to-one and as high as twelve-to-one, depending on the type of substance abused and the type of treatment employed. It is non-treatment that costs the United States billions of dollars a year.	Drug court "treatment" of addicts who are also criminal offenders is cost-effective and an excellent behavioral therapy that seeks to hold users accountable. Methadone treatment is inexpensive and reduces risk of HIV, incarceration, homelessness, and emergency room visits.
11. Even if methadone keeps an addict away from heroin, the methadone itself will leave the patient drugged and dangerous, so the patient might as well have stayed on heroin.	Methadone simply does not cause a drugged state, or even the appearances of a drugged state.	Methadone will not change the character of the recipient. A normal dose will mitigate withdrawal and suppress irritability thus reducing the possible harm to individuals and society. Criminal behavior will occur at a lower rate.
12. Even if methadone keeps an addict away from heroin and even if the methadone does not seem to leave the patient drugged and dopey, the patient could function successfully only at undemanding jobs such as raking leaves or checking out books in a library. Even this relatively fortunate patient would be, in effect, in a dangerous position in a job requiring quick reflexes or motor skills, a job such as driving a subway train or operating a forklift.		

Agreement between the two Responses

Patients on methadone can safely drive trains and run forklifts. Some people on methadone cannot do so. The difference between these two groups is not caused by the methadone but by pre-existing factors such as lack of education, physical or psychological problems. Methadone will not create or increase a danger even for these high-risk jobs, but neither will methadone remove a risk caused by a previously existing condition.

Table 1 (continued). Common beliefs about addiction and responses associated with general concepts about its nature.
ILLUSTRATION BY GGS INFORMATION SERVICES. GALE, CENGAGE LEARNING

addict can choose to begin the process of overcoming the social and personal consequences of a life of substance abuse.

The disease analogy does help to make addiction more comprehensible and less threatening to the general public. Many conditions that were once considered moral failings—sickle-cell anemia and other anemias, for example—are now understood as having a biological or neurological basis (Wailoo, 1999). Similarly, conditions that were considered the result of "bad habits" or effects of a pattern of immoral behaviors—including associating with the "wrong" kinds of people (e.g., polio or HIV/AIDs)—have typically taken a longer time to be recognized as diseases. The idea that dominant notions about disease transmission shape responses to its containment has been a major theme in the history of medicine. Polio so contradicted epidemiological models of disease transmission that lack of cleanliness was not recognized as an exacerbating factor until well into the twentieth century (Rogers, 1992). Addiction remains one of the last bastions of the belief that moral weakness or failures of will are responsible for the disease.

Nevertheless, advocates of the Free Will model would argue that addiction is, in the end, a problem of behavior. In this conception, relieving the addict of responsibility for his or her actions creates an unhealthy dependency on treatment providers and does not help the addict undertake the difficult but essential tasks of recognizing the consequences of substance use and rebuilding ties to mainstream society—of "getting a life," as the saying goes. Advocates of this point of view often maintain that efforts to mitigate the shame that a substance abuser may feel, far from encouraging him or her to seek treatment, exempt the addict from the social norms that human communities have developed to control "antisocial" behavior among their members.

Table 1 lists common beliefs about addiction, each followed by the responses associated with these two general concepts about its nature. Note that advocates of the two models are in agreement on some of their responses.

See also **Addiction: Concepts and Definitions.**

BIBLIOGRAPHY

Campbell, N. D. (2007). *Discovering addiction: The science and politics of substance abuse research*. Ann Arbor: University of Michigan Press.

Central Connecticut State University, Counseling and Wellness Center. (n.d.). *Myths and facts about addiction and treatment*. Available from http://www.ccsu.edu/.

Dalrymple, T. (Anthony Daniels). (2006, May 25). Poppycock. *Wall Street Journal.*

Deer, B. (1987). Terribly alive. *Times Educational Supplement (London)*, July 31.

DuPont, R. J. (1997). *The selfish brain: Learning from addiction*. Washington, DC: American Psychiatric Press.

Erickson, C. J. (2004, July 1). Field needs more street smarts about these drugs (Commentary). *Addiction Professional.*

Erickson, Carlton K. (2007). Myths of addiction. *Home Box Office (HBO): Understanding Addiction*. Available from http://www.hbo.com/.

Institute of Medicine, Committee to Identify Strategies to Raise the Profile of Substance Abuse and Alcoholism Research. (1997). *Dispelling the myths about addiction: Strategies to increase understanding and strengthen research*. Washington, DC: National Academy Press.

Interlandi, J. (2008, March 3). What addicts need. *Newsweek*. Available from http://www.newsweek.com/.

Lemonic, M. D. (2007, July 5). How we get addicted. *Time*. Available from http://www.time.com/.

National Institute on Alcohol Abuse and Alcoholism (NIAAA) Web site. Available from http://www.niaaa.nih.gov/.

National Institute on Drug Abuse Web site. Available from http://www.nida.nih.gov/.

National Institute of Mental Health Web site. Available from http://www.nimh.nih.gov/.

O'Brien , C. P., & McLellan, A. T. (1996). Myths about the treatment of addiction. *Lancet, 347*(8996), 237–240.

Office of National Drug Control Policy. (2000, March). Fact Sheet: Drug-related crime, March 2000. Available from http://www.whitehousedrugpolicy.gov/.

Pearson, G. (1987). *The new heroin users*. Oxford, UK: Blackwell.

Robert Wood Johnson Foundation, & Public Access Journalism. (1999). Top 10 addiction myths—and myth busters. *Silent treatment: Addiction in America*. Available from http://stories.silenttreatment.info/.

Rogers, N. (1992). *Dirt and disease: Polio before FDR*. New Brunswick, NJ: Rutgers University Press.

Roper, Charles N. Myths and facts about addiction and treatment. *Alcohol and Drug Abuse*. Available from http://www.alcoholanddrugabuse.com/.

Satel, S. (2007, July 10). The human factor. *The American: A Magazine of Ideas*, Available from http://www.american.com/.

Satel, S. (2007). In praise of stigma. In J. E. Henningfield, P. E. Santora, & W. K. Bickel (Eds.), *Addiction treatment: Science and policy for the twenty-first century.* Baltimore, MD: Johns Hopkins University Press.

Spickard, A., Jr., & Thompson, B. R. (2005). *Dying for a drink.* Nashville, TN: W Publishing Group. (See especially Chapter 15, Five myths of addiction.)

University of Texas at Austin, Addiction Science Research and Education Center. *Exploding drug myths.* Available from http://www.utexas.edu/.

Volkow, N., & Ting-Kai Li. (2005). The neuroscience of addiction. *Nature Neuroscience, 9,* 1429–1430.

Wailoo, K. (1999). *Drawing blood: Technology and disease identity in twentieth-century America.* Baltimore, MD: Johns Hopkins University Press.

Zimmer, L. E., & Morgan, J. P. (1997). *Marijuana myths, marijuana facts: A review of the scientific evidence.* New York: Lindesmith Center.

JAMES T. MCDONOUGH JR.
NANCY CAMPBELL
PAM KORSMEYER

N

NALOXONE. Naloxone is an opioid antogonist (i.e., a blocker of morphine-like agents) commonly used to reverse the actions of drugs such as morphine. In the early twenty-first century, it was the treatment of choice for reversing the life-threatening effects of opioid overdose. Structurally, naloxone is very closely related to oxymorphone, both compounds being derivatives of the opium alkaloid thebaine. Indeed, the structural differences between oxymorphone and naloxone are minimal; they are restricted to a simple substitution on the nitrogen atom. Oxymorphone has a methyl group whereas naloxone has an allyl substitution. This small substitution changes the pharmacology of the compound dramatically. Whereas oxymorphone is a potent analgesic with actions very similar to morphine, naloxone has no analgesic actions by itself and instead has the ability to antagonize, or reverse, virtually all the effects of morphine-like drugs. This ability to reverse opiate actions has proven valuable clinically. However, giving naloxone to opiate addicts will immediately precipitate withdrawal symptoms.

Naloxone is rapidly metabolized in the liver to inactive compounds, resulting in a relatively brief duration of action. When naloxone is used clinically to reverse the actions of morphine and other opiates, care must be taken to ensure that the drug being reversed does not last longer than the naloxone. Should that happen, a patient may be revived by naloxone only to relapse back into a coma or even die from the side effects of the initial opioid agonist. Despite its effectiveness following injection, naloxone is not very active when given orally; this, together with its short duration of action, prevents its widespread use as a treatment for opioid addiction.

See also **Naltrexone; Opioid Complications and Withdrawal; Treatment, Pharmacological Approaches to: Naltrexone.**

BIBLIOGRAPHY

Galea, S., et al. (2006). Provision of naloxone to injection drug users as an overdose prevention strategy: Early evidence from a pilot study in New York City. *Addictive Behaviors, 31,* 5, 907–912.

Howland, R. D., & Mycek, M. J. (2006). *Pharmacology,* 3rd ed. Philadelphia, PA: Lippincott, Williams & Wilkins.

Jaffe, J. H., & Martin, W. R. (1990). Opioid analgesics and antagonists. In A. G. Gilman et al. (Eds.), *Goodman and Gilman's the pharmacological basis of therapeutics,* 8th ed. New York: Pergamon. (2005, 11th ed. New York: McGraw-Hill Medical.)

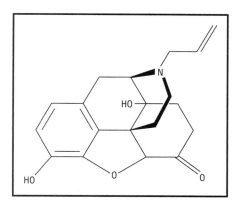

Figure 1. Chemical structure of naloxone. ILLUSTRATION BY GGS INFORMATION SERVICES. GALE, CENGAGE LEARNING

GAVRIL W. PASTERNAK

NALTREXONE.

Naltrexone is an opioid antagonist, which reverses or prevents the actions of morphinelike drugs. Its structure is very similar to that of another antagonist, naloxone, and to the potent analgesic (painkiller) oxymorphone.

Replacing the N-methyl group in these two drugs with a methylcyclopropyl group generates naltrexone, whereas substituting an allyl group produces naloxone. The replacement of the N-methyl group of oxymorphone dramatically alters the pharmacology of naloxone and naltrexone.

Naltrexone has no analgesic actions by itself. It has the ability to antagonize, or reverse, virtually all the effects of morphinelike drugs. When given regularly, it can prevent the actions of agents such as heroin, leading some to examine its potential in treating drug abuse. However, its use is limited, and it does not compare to alternative maintenance therapies with methadone or buprenorphine. Like naloxone, naltrexone will precipitate withdrawal in physically dependent people. Naltrexone is rapidly metabolized in the liver, but one of its metabolites is 6-naltrexol, which retains some activity and has a longer duration of action.

Clinically, the use of naltrexone remains limited. It has been used to treat opiate addiction by preventing the actions of heroin, and for the induction of rapid opioid detoxification. It has been approved by the U.S. Food and Drug Administration for the treatment of alcohol dependence following detoxification to reduce the likelihood of relapse. Most recently, a long-acting intramuscular formulation of naltrexone that can be given monthly has been approved and is available in the United States.

See also **Treatment: An Overview of Alcohol Abuse/ Dependence; Treatment, Pharmacological Approaches to: An Overview; Treatment, Pharmacological Approaches to: Naltrexone.**

BIBLIOGRAPHY

O'Brien, C. P. (2006). Drug addiction and drug abuse. In L. Brunton, J. Lazo, & K. Parker (Eds.), *The pharmacological basis of therapeutics* (11th ed., pp. 607–628). New York: McGraw-Hill.

Reisine, T., & Pasternak, G. (1996). Opioid analgesics and antagonists. In J. G. Hardman, et al. (Eds.), *The pharmacological basis of therapeutics* (9th ed., pp. 521–555). New York: McGraw-Hill.

GAVRIL W. PASTERNAK

NARCOTIC.

The term *narcotic* derives from the Greek *narkōtikos*, meaning benumbing. It was originally used (since the fourteenth century) to refer to drugs that produced a stupor associated with pain relief (analgesia)—primarily opium and its derivatives, the morphine-like strong analgesics, or the opium-like compounds (opioids). These drugs, in moderate doses, dull the senses, relieve pain, and induce profound sleep; but in large doses cause stupor coma, or convulsions.

During the nineteenth century, the term *narcotic* was widely used to include a number of agents that produced sleep. Toward the end of the nineteenth century, the term came to imply drugs that could lead to addiction, and so by the turn of the twentieth century, "narcotic" came to describe drugs as diverse as opioids and cocaine. During the twentieth century, the term became widely used in a legal context to refer to psychoactive drugs and drugs of abuse—those subject to restriction—as *addictive narcotics*, whether in fact the agents were physiologically addictive and narcotic or not. This imprecise usage has left the term nebulous, although it is still used extensively in the media and by the general population. The term is no longer used in scientific discourse to categorize drugs.

See also **Drug Types; Opiates/Opioids; World Health Organization Expert Committee on Drug Dependence.**

BIBLIOGRAPHY

Davenport-Hines, R. P. T. (2004). *The pursuit of oblivion: A global history of narcotics.* New York: W. W. Norton & Company.

International Narcotics Control Board (2007). *Narcotic drugs: Estimated world requirements for 2008.* New York: United Nations.

Jaffe, J. H., & Martin, W. R. (1990). Opioid analgesics and antagonists. In A. G. Gilman et al. (Eds.), *Goodman and Gilman's the pharmacological basis of therapeutics,* 8th ed. New York: Pergamon. (2005, 11th ed. New York: McGraw-Hill Medical.)

GAVRIL W. PASTERNAK

NARCOTIC ADDICT REHABILITATION ACT (NARA).

Public Law 89-793, the Narcotic Addict Rehabilitation Act (NARA), was passed by Congress in 1966. This legislation was designed to allow the use of the federal courts and criminal justice system to compel drug addicts to participate in treatment. Several developments provided the context for this legislation. In the early 1960s, the problem of narcotic drug use and addiction were perceived to be increasing. There was also a perception that treatment was not particularly effective and that the relapse rate was high. In response, California, in 1961, and New York, in 1962, passed legislation permitting the civil commitment of narcotic addicts; that is, they could be compelled to accept treatment even if they had committed no crime but could be shown to be using illicit narcotic drugs. In both of these states the legislatures also provided substantial funds to establish residential facilities where addicts could be treated initially as well as aftercare programs to provide supervision following their release from the residential facilities. Several other states, including Illinois, passed similar civil commitment legislation, but only New York and California launched massive programs to implement compulsory treatment and civil commitment.

In January 1963, the Presidential Advisory Commission on Narcotic and Drug Abuse appointed by President John F. Kennedy made a number of recommendations, including the enactment of a federal civil commitment statute that could provide an alternative to prison for confirmed narcotic or marijuana abusers convicted of federal crimes. The advisory commission also recommended increased assistance to states and municipalities to develop and strengthen their own treatment programs.

As passed by Congress, NARA had four titles, or main parts: Title I provided that eligible addicts charged with a federal offense could choose civil commitment or treatment instead of prosecution. After being examined by clinicians at a treatment center, an addict, if found suitable, could be committed to the custody of the surgeon general for thirty-six months of institutional treatment and aftercare. Title II provided for civil commitment after conviction. Title III stated that even if no federal crime had been committed, an addict or a related individual could petition the U.S. attorney in the district of residence and, if local facilities were unavailable, the U.S. District Court could commit the person to the custody of the surgeon general for treatment. Title IV provided for

funding to states and localities to establish or expand treatment for addicts.

Treatment under NARA began to be provided in 1967. The two U.S. Public Health Service Hospitals—in Lexington, Kentucky, and Fort Worth, Texas—which had been treating both addicted federal prisoners and voluntary patients, were redesignated "Clinical Research Centers" and became the sites for the institutional phase of treatment for addicts committed to the Surgeon General under NARA. Aftercare was provided by local programs supported by contracts with the NARA program administered by the Division of Narcotics within the National Institute of Mental Health (NIMH).

From 1967 through 1973, the two clinical centers admitted more than 10,000 NARA patients: 5 percent under Title I, 2 percent under Title II, and 93 percent under Title III. Women made up 15 percent of admissions. Race and ethnicity were noted for admissions between 1970 and 1973, during which time the designations and distribution were as follows: Anglo, 43 percent; black, 47 percent; Puerto Rican, 1 percent; Mexican American, 9 percent.

Many of the patients referred were found "not suitable for treatment" (38% at Fort Worth and 51% at Lexington), a designation that generally meant they were too disruptive or antagonistic. Some of this unsuitability was deliberate. Many of those under Title III, while not being charged with a federal crime, were under court pressure because of state or local crimes; as part of plea bargaining with local courts, they agreed to accept commitment under NARA Title III. They quickly learned that the centers would not require them to stay in residence, nor would NARA officials compel them to stay in aftercare. Once released from the centers as "not suitable," they would find ways to convey to the local courts how motivated for treatment they still were and how puzzled they were not to be offered treatment.

The general approach to treatment during the residential phase was based on therapeutic community principles, which delegate many responsibilities to former addicts and to patients participating in the program. The average duration of the residential phase of treatment was intended to be about six months, but of those admitted for examination, only about 35 percent were discharged to aftercare as having completed the residential phase. A number of studies have been conducted on the effectiveness of the NARA program, including aftercare. One study found that only 38 percent of the 35 percent that completed the residential phase remained in aftercare for the full six months after discharge from residential treatment. Reasons for attrition included death, disappearance, recommitment, conviction, and incarceration. One study by Gold and Chatham in 1971 found that 46 percent of addicts in aftercare had used an illegal drug during the month preceding the interview; about 50 percent were working. Another study found that 87 percent had used narcotics during the first six months after the residential phase; 65 percent had become readdicted.

While this rate of readdiction did not seem as bleak as that seen after the discharge of the early cohorts from Lexington, it was not seen as particularly successful, given the high cost of the six-month residential phase and the high attrition rates. Because of the attrition, the readdiction rate, while not inevitable, was occurring among only the better candidates. Another study by Mandell and Amsel (1973) compared the outcome of those treated compared to those found "not suitable" for treatment. The difference in outcome between the two groups was not significant.

While the legal authority for federal civil commitment remained in effect through the early twenty-first, the actual application of NARA fell into disuse in the mid-1970s as more federal prisons developed programs for Title II offenders and as more communities developed their own treatment programs. The use of treatment under civil commitment also declined because the involvement of courts and expensive legal procedures made it far more expensive than voluntary treatment. In 1971, the Fort Worth facility was closed and turned over to the Bureau of Prisons. The Lexington facility experienced the same fate in 1974.

See also **Civil Commitment; Coerced Treatment for Substance Offenders; New York State Civil Commitment Program.**

BIBLIOGRAPHY

Cohen, P. J. (2004). *Drugs, addiction, and the law: Policy, politics, and public health.* Durham, NC: Carolina Academic Press.

Gold, R., & Chatham, L. R. (1973). Characteristics of NARA patients in aftercare during June 1971. DHEW Publ. No. (HSM) 73-9054. Washington, D.C.: U.S. Government Printing Office.

Leukefeld, C. G., Tims, F. M., & Farabee, D. (2002). *Treatment of drug offenders: Policies and issues.* New York: Springer.

Lowinson, J. H. (2005). *Substance abuse: A comprehensive textbook.* Philadelphia, PA: Lippincott, Williams & Wilkins.

Maddux, J. F. (1978). History of the hospital treatment programs, 1935–1974. In W. R. Martin & H. Isbell (Eds.), *Drug addiction and the U.S. Public Health Service.* DHEW Publ. No. (ADM) 77–434. Washington, DC: U.S. Government Printing Office.

Mandell, W., & Amsel, Z. (1973). Status of addicts treated under the NARA program. Baltimore, MD: School of Hygiene and Public Health, The Johns Hopkins University.

JEROME H. JAFFE
JAMES F. MADDUX

NARCOTICS ANONYMOUS (NA).

Narcotics Anonymous (NA) was started in 1953 by Jimmy Kinnon and others who had been regularly attending Alcoholics Anonymous (AA) meetings in southern California. NA broadened the AA program of recovery from alcoholism to recovery from the entire range of psychoactive substances. Using the AA Twelve Steps and Twelve Traditions, Step One was altered to read: "We admitted that we were powerless over our addiction, that our lives had become unmanageable." The first NA World Conference was held in 1971, despite the fact that NA was largely confined to California, with small groups in other major U.S. cities. The late 1970s witnessed sudden rapid growth in NA so that by 1980 an estimated 20,000 people were attending regularly. A World Service Office was opened in 1977 and the first NA World Literature Conference was held in 1979. NA continued to grow steadily around the world so that by 2007 there were over 25,065 groups holding over 43,900 weekly meetings in 127 countries. NA is the second-largest (after AA) twelve-step organization in existence.

THE NA PROGRAM AND HOW IT WORKS

NA is a twelve-step program of recovery from drug addiction, modeled on AA. It is a nonprofit fellowship of women and men for whom drugs became a major problem. The only requirement for membership is a desire to stop using substances. Membership in NA is free; group expenses are covered by members' voluntary contributions.

Like AA, NA provides meetings in the community and institutions (hospitals, prisons) where members share their experience, strength, and hope. The NA program of recovery is based on the philosophy that addiction is a disease for which there is no cure. Recovery can and will take place if addicted individuals remain abstinent from substances and apply themselves to the program, including frequent and regular attendance at meetings, involvement with a home group (members who attend the same meeting on a regular basis to establish a recovery network and reliable routine), and regular commitment of service to that group (cleaning up, making coffee, etc.), the selection of an experienced NA member to be a sponsor on whom the member may call at any time for advice and guidance through the twelve steps, development of a relationship with a Higher Power based on a personal understanding of what that is, and a gradual but necessary understanding of the twelve steps of recovery. Service may involve taking a more formalized position at the group level, such as treasurer or secretary, or at NA area, regional, and world levels.

There are two basic kinds of meetings: open (anyone is welcome) and closed (limited to addicted individuals). Some meetings are common needs meetings, supporting a particular group based on gender, sexual identity, age, language, and so on (but any addicted person is welcome at any NA meeting). Meeting formats vary, but they often include reading NA literature and open voluntary sharing by people in attendance. Many NA members identify themselves in meetings by their first name only. This spirit of anonymity is based on placing "principles before personalities"; that is, no individual is superior to any other and recovery is not possible without the fellowship or its spiritual principles.

NA has several book-length pieces of fellowship-approved literature. *Narcotics Anonymous: Basic Text* is divided into two books: Book One discusses the basics of the NA program and the Twelve Steps and Traditions, and Book Two presents many personal stories. *It Works: How and Why* offers detailed discussion of the 12 Steps and Traditions. *The Step Working Guides* is a workbook with questions on each step. *Just for Today* is a book of daily meditations with quotations from other NA literature.

RESEARCH ON NA

NA is an important part of addiction treatment systems worldwide. Of the available empirical research on twelve step groups, most has been conducted on AA in the United States, with NA being the next most commonly studied organization. Research on people in substance abuse treatment has found that NA attendance after treatment is associated with less drug use up to five years later (Christo & Franey, 1995; Gossop, Stewart, & Marsden, 2007; Weiss et al., 2005). Weekly or more regular NA attendance is associated with favorable substance use outcomes; less than weekly attendance is no more effective than non-attendance (Best et al., 2001; Fiorentine & Hillhouse, 2000; Gossop et al., 2007). Regular NA attendance is more likely among people with more severe histories of drug use (Brown et al., 2001). In addition, a longer duration of NA attendance has been shown to facilitate both abstinence and long-term improvements in the psychological health (less anxiety; more self-esteem and self-efficacy) and social functioning of its members (Christo & Sutton, 1994; Humphreys et al., 2004; Toumbourou et al., 2002). Furthermore, NA members who engage in other group activities in addition to attending meetings, such as reading program literature, sponsoring new members, applying the twelve steps to daily life, are more likely to abstain from substances than are individuals who do not engage in these activities (Crape et al., 2002; Humphreys et al., 2004). These findings suggest that NA provides a useful supplement to addiction treatment, and regular contact with NA helps to maintain the benefits accrued initially from drug treatment programs (Vederhus & Kristensen, 2006).

See also **Addiction: Concepts and Definitions; Alcoholics Anonymous (AA); Models of Alcoholism and Drug Abuse; Treatment, Behavioral Approaches to: Minnesota Model; Treatment, Behavioral Approaches to: Self-Help and Anonymous Groups.**

BIBLIOGRAPHY

Barry, B. S., O'Grady, K. E., Farrell, E. V., Flechner, I. S., & Nurco, D. N. (2001). Factors associated with frequency of 12-step attendance by drug abuse clients. *American Journal of Drug and Alcohol Abuse, 27,* 147–160.

Best, D. W., Harris, J. C., Gossop, M., Manning, V. C., Man, L. H., Marshall, J., et al. (2001). Are the Twelve Steps more acceptable to drug users than to drinkers? *European Addiction Research, 7,* 69–77.

Christo, G., & Franey, C. (1995). Drug users' spiritual beliefs, locus of control and the disease concept in relation to Narcotics Anonymous attendance and six-month outcomes. *Drug and Alcohol Dependence, 38,* 51–56.

Christo, G., & Sutton, S. (1994). Anxiety and self-esteem as a function of abstinence time among recovering addicts attending Narcotics Anonymous. *British Journal of Clinical Psychology, 33,* 198–200.

Crape, B. L., Latkin, C. A., Laris, A. S., & Knowlton, A. R. (2002). The effects of sponsorship in 12-step treatment of injection drug users. *Drug and Alcohol Dependence, 65,* 291–301.

Fiorentine, R., & Hllhouse, M. P. (2000). Drug treatment and 12-step program participation: The addictive effects of integrated recovery activities. *Journal of Substance Abuse Treatment, 18,* 65–74.

Gossop, M., Stewart, D., & Marsden, J. (2007). Attendance at Narcotics Anonymous and Alcoholics Anonymous meetings, frequency of attendance, and substance use outcomes after residential treatment for drug dependence: A 5-year follow-up study. *Addiction, 103,* 119–125.

Humphreys, K., Wing, S., McCarty, D., Chappel, J., Gallant, L., Haberle, B., et al. (2004). Self-help organizations for alcohol and drug problems: Toward evidence-based practice and policy. *Journal of Substance Abuse Treatment, 26,* 151–158.

Toumbourou, J. W., Hamilton, M., U'ren, A., Stevens-Jones, P., & Storey, G., (2002). Narcotics Anonymous participation and changes in substance use and social support. *Journal of Substance Abuse Treatment, 23,* 61–66.

Vederhus, J.-K., & Kristensen, O. (2006). High effectiveness of self-help programs after drug addiction therapy. *BMC Psychiatry, 6,* 35–40.

Weiss, R. D., Griffin, M. L., Gallop, R. J., Najavits, L. M., Frank, A., Crits-Cristoph, P., et al. (2005). The effect of 12-step self-help group attendance and participation on drug use outcomes among cocaine-dependent patients. *Drug and Alcohol Dependence, 77,* 177–184.

Wells, B. (1987). Narcotics Anonymous (NA): The phenomenal growth of an important resource. *British Journal of Addiction, 82,* 581–582.

HARRISON M. TRICE
REVISED BY CHRISTINE TIMKO (2009)

NATIONAL COMMISSION ON MARIHUANA AND DRUG ABUSE.

In response to a substantial increase in drug-use patterns in American society during the 1960s and a swirling controversy about changing the marijuana laws to legalize the substance, in 1970 the U.S. Congress established the National Commission on Marihuana and Drug Abuse. The commission was directed to conduct a two-year study: the first on marijuana and the second on "the causes of drug abuse and their relative significance." The commission was composed of thirteen members, four appointed by the Congress (two each from the Senate and the House) and nine appointed by the president. The chair of the commission was Raymond P. Shafer, former governor of Pennsylvania, and the vice chair was Dana L. Farnsworth, M.D., the director of Student Health Services at Harvard University.

In March 1972, the commission issued its first report, *Marihuana: A Signal of Misunderstanding*, which recommended decriminalization of possession of marijuana for personal use. The commission's final report, *Drug Use in America: Problem in Perspective*, was issued in March 1973. The 500-page report was supplemented by 1,000 pages of appendices. In its report, the commission summarized its findings concerning the patterns of drug use in the United States, psychosocial and institutional influences on drug-using behavior, and the social impact of drug dependence and drug-induced behavior. The commission also proposed a framework for policymaking and made specific recommendations in the areas of legal regulation, prevention, treatment and rehabilitation, and research.

The most enduring impact of the commission's final report probably lies in its efforts to revise the vocabulary of the drug field. The commission insisted that alcohol be recognized as the major "drug" problem in the United States; it recommended that the term "drug abuse" be eschewed in favor of more descriptive terminology concerning drug-using behavior. For example, the commission developed a typology of drug-using behavior (experimental, recreational, situational, intensified, and compulsive use) and emphasized the need for different social responses for different patterns of use. In another important contribution, the commission fostered the development of information systems for monitoring changes in drug-using behavior in U.S. society, including national surveys of drug-using behavior among high-school students and in the general population.

The commission strongly endorsed the national treatment strategy, codified in the Drug Abuse Office and Treatment Act of 1972, which aimed to create a national network of treatment services and to establish appropriate incentives for people to seek these services voluntarily. In addition, the commission sought to reorient the rule of the criminal law in implementing a policy of discouraging drug use. In the short term, the commission concluded, the criminal sanction should be retained, but should be utilized primarily as leverage for entry into prevention and treatment programs. In regard to government organization, the commission recommended that the law-enforcement and public-health dimensions of national drug-abuse prevention policy be combined into a single agency.

See also **Anslinger, Harry Jacob, and U.S. Drug Policy; Legal Regulation of Drugs and Alcohol; U.S. Government.**

BIBLIOGRAPHY

Deitch, R. (2003). *Hemp: American history revisited*. New York: Algora Publishing.

Erlen, J., & Spillane, J. F., Eds. (2004). *Federal drug control: The evolution of policy and practice*. New York: Haworth Press.

National Commission on Marihuana and Drug Abuse. (1973). *Drug abuse in America: Problem in perspective*. Washington, D.C.: U.S. Government Printing Office.

National Commission On Marihuana And Drug Abuse. (1972). *Marihuana: A signal of misunderstanding*. Washington, D.C.: U.S. Government Printing Office.

RICHARD J. BONNIE

NATIONAL COMMISSION ON MARIHUANA AND DRUG ABUSE: RECOMMENDATIONS ON DECRIMINALIZATION.

Before 1960, use of marijuana in the United States was generally confined to drug-using subcultures in the inner cities or in rural areas. Sale and use of the drug were prohibited both by federal law and by the laws of every state. Because marijuana was classified in 1937 as a narcotic drug, along with cocaine and opiates, penalties were severe; simple possession for personal use was a felony in most states. During the 1960s, marijuana use suddenly became prevalent on college campuses for the first time among white middle-class youth of the baby-boom generation. Marijuana use also became associated, as a protest behavior, with dissenters (both adults and youth) against the war in Vietnam, and by the U.S. military serving in Vietnam, especially from 1963 to 1973. As use of the drug increased, so did the number of arrests and so did the surrounding controversy. Questions were raised about the actual effects of marijuana on the health and behavior of those who used it and about the wisdom of prevailing social policy.

In response to swirling controversy, many proposals were introduced in Congress for a commission to undertake an authoritative study of the marijuana issue. Eventually, in the Comprehensive Drug Abuse Prevention and Control Act of 1970 Congress established the National Commission on Marihuana and Drug Abuse to undertake a two-year study—the first year on marijuana and the second year on the causes of drug abuse in general.

The commission had thirteen members—four from Congress (two each from the House and the Senate) and nine appointed by the president. President Richard M. Nixon appointed Raymond P. Shafer, formerly governor of Pennsylvania, as chairman of the commission, and he appointed Dana L. Farnsworth, M.D., director of Student Health Services at Harvard University, to be vice-chairman. The executive director was Michael R. Sonnenreich, formerly the deputy chief counsel of the Bureau of Narcotics and Dangerous Drugs of the Justice Department.

The commission assimilated the available literature on marijuana use and its effects and also sponsored its own research, including a national survey of use patterns and public attitudes, and a study of enforcement of the marijuana laws in six jurisdictions. In March 1972, the commission issued its first report, *Marihuana: A Signal of Misunderstanding*.

PRINCIPAL FINDINGS
The commission estimated that although 24 million Americans had used marijuana at least once,

about 50 percent had simply experimented with the drug out of curiosity and given it up. Among the 50 percent who had continued to use marijuana, most used it only occasionally, once a week or less, for recreational purposes. A small percentage of the more frequent users (about 2% of the total ever-using population—or 4% of the continuing users) used the drug more than once daily. Marijuana use was clearly age-related: about half of the ever-users were 16 to 25 years of age, and 44 percent of those who were currently in college or graduate school had used marijuana at least once.

The commission concluded that there was "little proven danger of physical or psychological harm from the experimental or intermittent use" of marijuana. "The risk of harm," it continued, "lies instead in the heavy, long-term use of the drug, particularly of its more potent preparations." Even this risk was of uncertain dimensions, the commission noted, because the psychological consequences of long-term heavy use were unknown. In light of the fact that 90 percent of marijuana users used the drug only experimentally or intermittently, the commission judged that "its use at the present level does not constitute a major threat to public health." The commission also specifically found that marijuana did not induce physical dependence; did not lead, by virtue of its pharmacology, to use of other drugs; and did not cause criminal behavior.

POLICY RECOMMENDATIONS

The commission's principal policy recommendation was that possession of one ounce or less of marijuana for personal use be "decriminalized." At the same time, the commission rejected outright legalization of the drug and recommended perpetuation of prohibitions against cultivation and distribution for commercial purposes. The commission stipulated that social policy should aim to discourage use of the drug, but it emphasized that the costs of a criminal prohibition against possession far exceeded its benefits in suppressing use.

Although President Nixon disavowed the commission's principal recommendation on marijuana, it won widespread support. In 1973, the National Conference of Commissioners on Uniform State Laws promulgated amendments to the Uniform Controlled Substances Act that codified the commission's recommendation. Some form of

decriminalization was endorsed the same year by a variety of national organizations, including the American Bar Association and numerous state and local bar associations, the National Education Association, the Consumers' Union, the National Council of Churches, the American Public Health Association, and the governing board of the American Medical Association.

In 1973, Oregon became the first state to decriminalize possession of small amounts of marijuana. Within the next five years, ten additional states eliminated incarceration as a penalty for simple possession, usually substituting a $100.00 fine. Five of these states made possession a "civil offense"; in others, it remained a criminal offense although the law typically contained a provision for expunction of criminal records after a specified period of time. Decriminalization of marijuana use was endorsed by President Jimmy Carter in 1977.

Political and legislative support for decriminalization began to wane, however, even during the Carter Administration. The more permissive stance on marijuana use implicit in decriminalization efforts led to mounting public resistance. Some of the strongest opposition came from groups of parents who organized to lobby for more focus on prevention efforts. Although these parent groups were generally conservative politically, they gained a receptive ear in the Carter White House. Their arguments against decriminalization were bolstered by findings from the National High School Senior Survey showing that, starting in 1975, daily marijuana use had been increasing progressively among high school students. During the Reagan and Bush administrations the parents' movement and their concerns about marijuana use came to have a major influence on national drug policy. In the early 1990s, possession of the drug remained a criminal offense in most states, as well as under federal law.

See also **Anslinger, Harry Jacob, and U.S. Drug Policy; Legal Regulation of Drugs and Alcohol; Monitoring the Future; Prevention.**

BIBLIOGRAPHY

Bonnie, R. J. (1982). The meaning of "decriminalization": A review of the law. *Contemporary Drug Problems, 10,* 3, 277–289.

Bonnie, R. J., & Whitebread, C. H. (1974). *The marihuana conviction*. Charlottesville: University Press of Virginia.

Erlen, J., & Spillane, J. F., Eds. (2004). *Federal drug control: The evolution of policy and practice*. New York: Haworth Press.

Lowinson, J. H. (2005). *Substance abuse: A comprehensive textbook*. Philadelphia, PA: Lippincott, Williams & Wilkins.

Marlatt, G. A., Roffman, R., & Stephens, R. S., Eds. (2006). *Cannabis dependence: Its nature, consequences, and treatment*. Cambridge, U.K.: Cambridge University Press.

Musto, D. F. (1987). *The American disease*. New York: Oxford University Press. (1999, 3rd ed.)

National Commission on Marihuana and Drug Abuse. (1972). *Marihuana: A signal of misunderstanding*. Washington, D.C.: U.S. Government Printing Office.

RICHARD J. BONNIE

NATIONAL COUNCIL ON ALCOHOLISM AND DRUG DEPENDENCE (NCADD).

The National Council on Alcoholism and Drug Dependence (NCADD) is the oldest advocacy organization in the United States dedicated to addressing issues of alcohol and drug dependence. It is the country's major public advocate for the prevention and treatment of alcohol and other drug problems, and its explicit mission (reformulated in 2000) is to "fight the stigma and the disease of alcoholism and other drug addictions." Working through hundreds of local affiliate councils, state councils, and its national offices, NCADD sponsors prevention and education programs, information and referral services, scientific and clinical consensus development, public policy advocacy, and other related activities.

NCADD was established in 1944 as the National Committee for Education on Alcoholism. As the organization grew, its name and scope enlarged. It became the National Committee on Alcoholism in 1950, was renamed the National Council on Alcoholism in 1957, and assumed its present name in 1990.

NCADD was the idea of a single individual, Marty Mann; she was its director until her retirement in 1968 and its guiding spirit until her death in 1980. Mrs. Mann was the first woman to recover from alcoholism through the fellowship of Alcoholics Anonymous (AA). During the early years of her recovery, she became increasingly aware that the United States was uninformed about the disease of alcoholism. She concluded that the resulting stigma and prejudice kept alcoholics and their families from receiving the medical, social, and spiritual help they needed to recover. The structure and traditions of AA prevented it from becoming a public-health agency similar to those concerned with promoting prevention, treatment, and research for polio, tuberculosis, cancer, and heart disease. With the support of the Yale Center of Alcohol Studies, the council incorporated and established an office in the New York Academy of Medicine building in New York City. In 1950 it became independent of Yale. Ruth Fox, a psychiatrist who had helped found the council, became its first medical director in 1958. In 1969 she was succeeded by Frank A. Seixas, an internist.

During its early years, council activity consisted mainly of developing literature and presenting lectures to professional and lay groups on the concept of alcoholism as a disease and of organizing local affiliates to pursue this educational process in their own communities. By 1947 a survey of American adults showed that 36 percent believed alcoholism to be a disease, a remarkable increase from 6 percent who held this view in 1943. As interest in alcohol and drug problems expanded, the council developed and then published in 1972 the first set of medical criteria for the diagnosis of alcoholism. In 1976 it sponsored Operation Understanding, in which 52 men and women known for their contributions in the areas of government, medicine, industry, science, journalism, and the arts publicly revealed their histories of recovery from alcoholism.

During the 1980s, NCADD influenced the United States Postal Service to issue the first postal stamp dedicated to raising public awareness about alcoholism (1981). The organization changed its name and broadened its focus to include the disease of drug dependence and used national advocacy efforts to mandate that all bottles containing alcoholic beverages carry warning labels. NCADD lobbied for establishment of a minimum drinking age in America and established the national toll-free HOPE line to provide information and referrals related to alcohol and drug abuse. This was done in conjunction with the national network television screening of *The Betty Ford Story*. As of

2008, the HOPE line receives in excess of 30,000 calls per year.

In the 1990s the American Society of Addiction Medicine and NCADD collaborated on the creation of a comprehensive definition of alcoholism. Published in 1992 in the *Journal of the American Medical Association*, it is still utilized. During the 1990s, NCADD certified and trained affiliates, developed and implemented a family intervention network, and launched a widely acclaimed prevention program aimed at fostering conversations about alcohol use choices between parents and children. Meryl Streep narrated the companion video for this project, titled *What Should I Tell My Children About Drinking?* Updated versions of these materials continue to be in significant demand.

During the first decade of the twenty-first century, NCADD lauded Representative Jim Ranstad and Senator Paul Wellstone for sponsoring legislation aimed at preventing health care insurers from arbitrarily capping addiction treatment coverage. It held a series of Community Forums addressing issues of stigma and discrimination and successfully collaborated with several other advocacy organizations to prevent the mass marketing of a perfume called "Addiction" and to prohibit the NBC-TV from using national network television as a forum for advertising alcoholic beverages.

These and other activities have made NCADD an important force in the national development of service systems and health policy related to alcohol and other drug problems. NCADD helped establish the first industrial alcoholism programs, the first research society devoted to alcoholism, the first public education campaigns to promote the concept of alcoholism and other drug dependence as diseases, the movement to recognize the special needs of women with substance-related problems, and the national effort to understand and prevent fetal alcohol spectrum disorders (FASD) and FAS (Fetal Alcohol Syndrome).

NCADD is also a leader in the U.S. campaign against alcohol-related highway accidents and in promoting appropriate treatment services for substance-dependent pregnant and postpartum women and their children. Through its local affiliates, NCADD provides direct services, including education and prevention, in school and community settings, as well as information, intervention, and referral counseling, local alcohol- and drug-awareness campaigns, and other related activities.

See also **American Society of Addiction Medicine (ASAM); Association for Medical Education and Research in Substance Abuse (AMERSA); Models of Alcoholism and Drug Abuse; Parent Movement, The.**

BIBLIOGRAPHY

Anderson, P. (1990). Controlled drinking and a public health approach to alcohol. *Addiction, 90,* 1162–1164.

Burman, S. (1994). The disease concept of alcoholism: Its impact on women's treatment. *Journal of Substance Abuse Treatment, 11*(2), 121–126.

C. D. Smithers Foundation. (1979). *Pioneers we have known in the field of alcoholism.* Mill Neck, NY: C. D. Smithers Foundation.

Heather, N., & Robertson, I. (1997). *Problem drinking* (3rd ed.). New York: Oxford University Press.

Henderson, E. C. (2000). *Understanding addiction.* Jackson: University Press of Mississippi.

Jurd, S. M. (1992). Why alcoholism is a disease. *The Medical Journal of Australia, 156,* 215–217.

Kahler, C. W. (1995). Current challenges and an old debate. *Addiction, 90,* 1169–1171.

Lender, M. E., & Martin, J. K. (1987). *Drinking in America: A history.* New York: Free Press.

Meyer, R. E. (1996). The disease called addiction: Emerging evidence in a 200-year debate. *The Lancet, 347,* 162–166.

Morse, R. M., & Flavin, D. K. (1992). Joint Committee of the NCADD and the American Society of Addiction Medicine: The definition of alcoholism. *Journal of the American Medical Association, 268,* 1012–1014.

Murphy, W. *NCA's first forty years.* (1984). New York: National Council on Alcoholism and Drug Dependence.

National Council on Alcoholism, Criteria Committee. (1972). Criteria for the diagnosis of alcoholism. *Annals of Internal Medicine, 77,* 249–258.

National Council on Alcoholism and Drug Dependence. (2006). Available from http://www.ncadd.org/.

Seixas, F. A., Blume, S., Cloud, L. A., Lieber, C. S., & Simpson, R. K. (1976). Definition of alcoholism. *Annals of Internal Medicine, 85*(6), 764.

Straussner, L. L. A., & Brown, S. (2002). *The handbook of addiction treatment for women.* San Francisco: Jossey-Bass.

Tracy, S. W., & Acker, C .J. (Eds.). (2004). *Altering American consciousness: The history of alcohol and drug use in the United States, 1800–2000.* Amherst, MA: University of Massachusetts Press.

Van Wormer, K. (1995). *Alcoholism treatment: A social work perspective.* Chicago: Nelson-Hall.

Wallace, J. (1990). The new disease model of alcoholism. *The Western Journal of Medicine, 150*(5), 502–505.

Walters, G. D. (1999). *The addiction concept: Working hypothesis or self-fulfilling prophesy?* Boston: Allyn & Bacon.

Weisner, C. (1995). Controlled drinking issues in the 1990s: The public health model and specialty treatment. *Addiction, 90,* 1164–1166.

SHEILA B. BLUME
REVISED BY PAMELA V. MICHAELS (2009)

NATIONAL FORENSIC LABORATORY INFORMATION SYSTEM (NFLIS).

The Office of Diversion Control of the Drug Enforcement Administration (DEA) sponsors the National Forensic Laboratory Information System (NFLIS). NFLIS systematically collects and catalogs the results of drug analyses previously conducted by forensic laboratories at the regional, state, and local levels.

When drugs are seized by law enforcement agencies, whether they are illicit substances or legal prescription drugs (controlled or noncontrolled) being used in a manner other than that for which they were intended, they are catalogued and put through myriad analyses. By so doing, not only are the substances identified—giving important information as new illicit drugs are developed and trafficked—but the logging process affords an important means of tracking the movement of illicit substances into and out of the country, as well as the movement of drugs around the nation. It is also possible to track the movement of legally manufactured drugs into illegal markets.

NFLIS serves as both a storehouse and a clearinghouse for all local and statewide information and is able to track and record trends by regions and states or for the nation as a whole. The system is sufficiently sophisticated to identify new and existing substances by chemical composition and to ascertain quantity, purity, adulteration (cutting with other substances), and mixture with other drugs. The data and reports generated by NFLIS are used to inform drug scheduling efforts and to develop state and federal policy regarding illegal drug use as well as to provide support for drug enforcement operations.

NFLIS was created in 1997 and published its first annual report in 2000. By the end of 2007, NFLIS had become a nationwide, fully operational information management system, processing nearly 90 percent of the nation's more than 1.2 million drug analysis cases, with affiliated laboratories in 42 state systems; 92 local, municipal, or regional labs; and 1 territorial laboratory. In total, 274 labs submit data to NFLIS. Among the other databases sharing information with NFLIS is the DEA's System to Retrieve Information from Drug Evidence II (STRIDE II), which encompasses data from all of the analyses performed at DEA labs around the country. The overall goal of NFLIS is to incorporate the data from every local, regional, and state forensics laboratory in the United States as well as all federal laboratories.

In the first annual report (published in 2000), the ten most commonly seized/analyzed drugs nationwide were: cannabis (39.68%), cocaine (30.65%), methamphetamine (9.84%), heroin (7.54%), noncontrolled nonnarcotic drugs (0.99%), MDMA (0.73%), alprazolam (0.59%), hydrocodone (0.57%), diazepam (0.48%), and oxycodone (0.40%). The percentage of distribution of these drugs varied widely across regions of the country (South, Northeast, Midwest, and West).

By the midyear 2007 report, the most popular drugs had shifted positions a bit: cocaine (40.61%), cannabis/THC (27.99%), methamphetamine (6.39%), heroin (3.96%), hydrocodone (2.75%), alprazolam (2.83%), oxycodone (1.43%), noncontrolled nonnarcotics (1.04%), MDMA (1.45%), and methadone (0.62%).

See also **U.S. Government; U.S. Government Agencies.**

BIBLIOGRAPHY

Copies of NFLIS reports for all years can be found at: Office of Diversion Control. (2007). *National Forensic Laboratory Information System (NFLIS).* Available from http://www.deadiversion.usdoj. gov/.

Office of Diversion Control. (2007). *National Forensic Laboratory Information System: 2007 midyear report.* Washington, DC: U.S. Drug Enforcement Administration.

Strom, K. J., Wong, L., Fornnarino, L., Bethke, A., Ancheta, J., & Rachal, V. (2004). *NFLIS special report: Narcotic analgesics, 2001–2003.* Washington, DC: U.S. Drug Enforcement Administration.

Strom, K. J., Wong, L., Weimer, B., & Rachal, V. (2005). *NFLIS special report: Synthetic drugs, 2001–2004.* Washington, DC: U.S. Department of Justice.

Weimer, B. J., Peters, D., Sannerud, C., Eicheldinger, C., Ancheta, J., Strom, K., et al. (2007). *The National Forensic Laboratory Information System: 2006 annual report.* Washington, DC: U.S. Drug Enforcement Administration.

Weimer, B. J., Wong, L., Eicheldinger, C., Bethke, A., Ancheta, J., Strom, K., et al. (2005). *The National Forensic Laboratory Information System: 2005 midyear Report.* Washington, DC: U.S. Drug Enforcement Administration.

Weimer, B. J., Wong, L., Sannerud, C., Eicheldinger, C., Ancheta, J., Strom, K., et al. (2006). *The National Forensic Laboratory Information System: 2005 annual report.* Washington, DC: U.S. Drug Enforcement Administration.

Weimer, B. J., Wong, L., Sannerud, C., Eicheldinger, C., Ancheta, J., Strom, K., et al. (2006). *The National Forensic Laboratory Information System: 2006 midyear report.* Washington, DC: U.S. Drug Enforcement Administration.

PAMELA V. MICHAELS

NATIONAL SURVEY ON DRUG USE AND HEALTH (NSDUH).

The National Survey on Drug Use and Health (NSDUH), formerly called the National Household Survey on Drug Abuse, is the primary source of information in the U.S. federal government on the nature and extent of substance use and abuse in the United States. Conducted since 1971, the survey collects data by administering questionnaires to a representative sample of persons aged 12 or older at their places of residence. Data from the survey are used extensively by policymakers and researchers to measure the prevalence and correlates of licit and illicit substance use, to identify and monitor trends in substance use, and to analyze differences in substance use patterns by population subgroups.

HISTORY OF THE SURVEY

The survey traces its origin to studies conducted by the National Commission on Marihuana and Drug Abuse. The commission was created in 1970 to develop recommendations for legislation and administrative actions to address increasing public concerns about illicit drug abuse. The commission conducted two national surveys, in 1971 and 1972, to obtain data on the public's beliefs, attitudes, and use of marijuana and other drugs. When the Alcohol, Drug Abuse, and Mental Health Administration (ADAMHA) was created in 1974, with the National Institute on Drug Abuse (NIDA) as one component, NIDA continued conducting the survey to monitor the incidence and prevalence of drug use in the United States. The survey became known as the National Household Survey on Drug Abuse (NHSDA).

Since 1971, the survey has undergone a variety of changes in its sample design as data priorities have changed. During the 1970s and 1980s, it was a relatively small, periodic survey. Conducted every two or three years, the sample size grew gradually from about 3,000 respondents per survey in the early 1970s to 8,814 in 1988. In the late 1980s, the U.S. cocaine abuse problem became a major concern of the public and of politicians. Congress passed legislation that increased funding for substance abuse data collection and created the White House Office of National Drug Control Policy (ONDCP), which began producing annual national strategies that used NHSDA data extensively in setting goals and tracking the progress of drug abuse policies and programs. With the increase in funds and greater reliance on NHSDA data by policymakers and researchers, annual fielding of the survey began in 1990, and a significant expansion of the sample began in 1991. The basic national sample size throughout the 1990s was about 18,000 respondents per year.

The ADAMHA Reorganization Act of 1992 moved NIDA to the National Institutes of Health and created a new services-focused agency, the Substance Abuse and Mental Health Services Administration (SAMHSA). Under this reorganization, the Office of Applied Studies, SAMSHA, was given the responsibility for managing the NHSDA.

Throughout the survey's history, interest in particular subpopulations led to sample design changes and augmentations. Rural areas were oversampled in 1979 and 1994, and the survey oversampled blacks and Hispanics from 1985 through 1998. Supplemental samples of six metropolitan areas were included from 1990 through 1993, and supplemental samples in California and Arizona were added in 1997 and 1998.

Changes in the data collection methodology prior to 1999 were infrequent and relatively minor.

The survey used the same basic methodology from 1971 through 1998: a confidential, anonymous, face-to-face interview conducted in households and employing self-administration of sensitive substance use items. However, some small but important changes were made in the survey procedures that affected survey estimates of substance use prevalence. In 1982, questions on nonmedical use of psychotherapeutic drugs were converted from interviewer-administered to self-administered. Similarly, tobacco questions were shifted to self-administration in 1994. Machine editing procedures were incorporated into the NHSDA data processing for the first time in 1988. In 1994, following extensive research, the NHSDA questionnaire and editing procedures were modified to provide more reliable substance use prevalence estimates.

Methodological research demonstrated the benefits of audio-computer-assisted self-interviewing (ACASI) in collecting data on sensitive behaviors such as substance use in household surveys. Studies indicate that respondents are more willing to report sensitive behaviors with ACASI than with other modes of data collection. Based on this research, SAMHSA decided in 1995 to initiate development and testing of a computer-assisted interview (CAI), including ACASI, in the NHSDA.

At the same time that the new NHSDA CAI was being developed, a long-standing interest in state-level substance use prevalence data was culminating in legislation that resulted in the redesign of the NHSDA sample. With the passage in 1996 of voter initiatives legalizing marijuana use for medical purposes in California and Arizona, and the substantial role of federal block grant funds given to states for substance abuse prevention and treatment, Congress and the Clinton administration concluded it would be useful to have state-level estimates.

Thus, in 1999, a major redesign of the NHSDA was implemented involving both the sample design and the data collection method of the survey. The national design was changed to a much larger, state-based design with 67,500 respondents per year. The data collection method was changed from a paper-and-pencil interview (PAPI) method to CAI, primarily to improve the quality of NHSDA estimates. Then in 2002, in order to improve response rates and more accurately reflect

the focus of the survey, the name of the survey was changed to the National Survey on Drug Use and Health, and a remuneration of $30 for all survey respondents was initiated. These two changes, along with enhanced data collection quality control procedures introduced around the same time, affected survey respondents' reporting of substance use, causing a discontinuity in trend measurement between 2001 and 2002.

DESIGN OF NSDUH
Starting in 2002 and expected in 2008 to continue through 2009, the NSDUH was to maintain a consistent survey design, which facilitated trend comparisons and pooling of multiple years of data for in-depth analysis. Details of the design during this period are given below.

Target Population. The respondent universe is the civilian, noninstitutionalized population aged 12 years or older residing within the United States and the District of Columbia. Persons excluded from the universe include active-duty military personnel, persons with no fixed household address (e.g., homeless and/or transient persons not in shelters), and residents of institutional group quarters, such as jails and hospitals.

Sample Design. Eight states (California, Florida, Illinois, Michigan, New York, Ohio, Pennsylvania, and Texas) were designated as large sample states with samples of about 3,600 respondents. For the remaining 42 states and the District of Columbia, samples of about 900 persons were selected. Within each state, samples were equally allocated to three age groups: 12 to 17, 18 to 25, and 26 and older. States were first stratified into a total of 900 state sampling regions (SSR), with 48 regions in each large sample state and 12 regions in each small sample state. These regions were contiguous geographic areas designed to yield the same number of interviews on average (about 75 per year). Within sampled census tracts, adjacent census blocks were combined to form the second-stage sampling units or area segments. One segment was selected within each sampled census tract with probability proportional to population.

Each year, eight sample segments per SSR are fielded. These sampled segments are allocated equally into four separate samples, one for each

Drug	2002	2003	2004	2005	2006
Illicit drugs[1]	108,255[b]	110,205	110,057	112,085	111,774
Marijuana and Hashish	94,946[a]	96,611	96,772	97,545	97,825
Cocaine	33,910	34,891	34,153	33,673	35,298
Crack	8,402	7,949	7,840	7,928	8,554
Heroin	3,668	3,744	3,145[a]	3,534	3,785
Hallucinogens	34,314	34,363	34,333	33,728	35,281
LSD	24,516	24,424	23,398	22,433	23,346
PCP	7,418	7,107	6,762	6,603	6,618
Ecstasy	10,150[b]	10,904[b]	11,130[a]	11,495	12,262
Inhalants	22,870	22,995	22,798	22,745	22,879
Nonmedical Use of Psychotherapeutics[2]	46,558[b]	47,882[a]	48,013	48,709	49,842
Pain Relievers	29,611[b]	31,207[b]	31,768[a]	32,692	33,472
OxyContin®	1,924[b]	2,832[b]	3,072[b]	3,481[b]	4,098
Tranquilizers	19,267[b]	20,220	19,852[a]	21,041	21,303
Stimulants	21,072	20,798	19,982	19,080	20,118
Sedatives	9,960[a]	9,510	9,891[a]	8,982	8,822

*Low precision; no estimate reported.
[a]Difference between estimate and 2006 estimate is statistically significant at the 0.05 level.
[b]Difference between estimate and 2006 estimate is statistically significant at the 0.01 level.
[1]Illicit Drugs include marijuana/hashish, cocaine (including crack), heroin, hallucinogens, inhalants, or prescription-type psychotherapeutics used nonmedically. Illicit Drugs Other Than Marijuana include cocaine (including crack), heroin, hallucinogens, inhalants, or prescription-type psychotherapeutics used nonmedically.
[2]Nonmedical use of prescription-type psychotherapeutics includes the nonmedical use of pain relievers, tranquilzers, stimulants, or sedatives and does not include over-the-counter drugs.

SOURCE: SAMHSA, Office of Applied Studies, National Survey on Drug Use and Health, 2002, 2003, 2004, 2005, and 2006.

Table 1. Types of illicit drug use in lifetime among persons aged 12 or older: Numbers in thousands, 2002–2006. (Source: SAMHSA, Office of Applied Studies, National Survey on Drug Use and Health, 2002, 2003, 2004, 2005 and 2006.) ILLUSTRATION BY GGS INFORMATION SERVICES. GALE, CENGAGE LEARNING

three-month period (calendar quarter) during the year, so that the survey is essentially continuous in the field. In each of these area segments, a listing of all addresses is made, from which a sample of about 180,000 addresses is selected. Of the selected addresses, about 150,000 are determined to be eligible sample units. About 91 percent of these eligible units (which can be either households or units within group quarters) participate in the survey, completing a short automated screener on household composition. Based on this information, zero, one, or two sample persons are randomly selected to be interviewed in each unit. The weighted response rate for interviewing in 2006 was 74 percent.

Data Collection Methodology. The data collection method used in NSDUH involves in-person interviews with sample persons, incorporating procedures that increase respondents' cooperation and willingness to report honestly about their illicit drug use behavior. Confidentiality is stressed in all written and oral communications with potential respondents. Respondents' names are not collected with the data, and ACASI maximizes privacy and confidentiality.

Interviewers immediately attempt to conduct the NSDUH interview with each selected person in the household. The interviewer requests the selected respondent to identify a private area in the home as the location for the interview away from other household members. The interview takes about an hour. All respondents who complete a full interview receive a $30 cash payment as a token of appreciation for their time.

A key feature of the interview is a core/supplement structure. A core set of questions critical for basic trend measurement of prevalence estimates remains in the survey every year and comprises the first part of the interview. Supplemental questions, or modules, that can be revised, dropped, or added from year to year make up the remainder of the interview. The core consists of initial demographic items (which are interviewer-administered) and self-administered questions pertaining to the use of tobacco, alcohol, marijuana, cocaine, crack cocaine, heroin, hallucinogens, inhalants, pain relievers, tranquilizers, stimulants, and sedatives. Supplemental topics in the remaining self-administered sections include (but are not limited to) injection drug use, perceived risks of substance use, substance dependence or abuse, arrests, treatment for substance use problems, pregnancy and health care issues, and mental health issues.

Supplemental demographic questions (which are interviewer-administered and follow the ACASI questions) address such topics as immigration, current school enrollment, employment and workplace issues, health insurance coverage, and income. It should be noted that some of the supplemental portions of the interview have remained in the survey, relatively unchanged, every year (e.g., current health insurance coverage, income). Some questionnaire modules have been included in the survey for a single year in response to requests from other agencies such as the Centers for Disease Control (sexual behaviors module in 1996) and the National Highway Traffic Safety Administration (driving behaviors module in 1996).

ANALYSES OF NSDUH DATA

The following section discusses various issues related to the analysis of NSDUH data, including how the results are reported, access to the data files for research, quality of the data, and how NSDUH estimates compare with estimates from other surveys. Finally, a brief summary of some of the most important findings from NSDUH is included.

Reporting the Results. NSDUH results are made available by SAMHSA in a variety of forms. The first release of each year's national results typically occurs about eight months after data collection is completed. At that time, a comprehensive report of the national results is published, along with numerous detailed tabulations and technical information on the survey, and a press conference is held to announce the results. Subsequently, various other analytic reports focusing on specific issues of interest are produced by SAMHSA from the latest survey. Whereas some studies address trends over time, much of the analysis is done by combining multiple years of data, to increase the statistical power of comparisons between groups and the study of correlates. State-level estimates are published annually using a model-based estimation method (Hierarchical Bayes Estimation) that incorporates each state's sample data with external local area predictors and a national regression model. Two years of data are combined for these state estimates. SAMHSA also periodically produces sub-state estimates, based on at least three years of data.

Access to Data Files. Complete analytic data files are used by NSDUH project staff to produce SAMSHA reports and special analyses. These files have not been made available to analysts outside the project because of legal requirements to protect the confidentiality of survey respondents. However, project statisticians often provide special tabulations or analyses when requested, subject to the availability of resources to support this work. Public use data files are made available free of charge to researchers within 12 months of the completion of data collection. These files are created through a process of disclosure limitation that maximizes the utility of the data for various analyses, while eliminating the risk that the identities of respondents could be ascertained by persons accessing the files, which is done using a combination of techniques, including random removal of records, elimination of identifying variables (especially geographic location data), and recoding of some variables. As of the early twenty-first century, SAMHSA had initiated procedures to make the full analytic NSDUH data files available to researchers, following guidelines specified in the Confidential Information Protection and Statistical Efficiency Act of 2002 (CIPSEA).

Strengths and Limitations of the NSDUH. The major strengths of the NSDUH are its size, continuity, and representativeness. The survey has a sample large enough to allow detailed analysis of small subgroups (sociodemographic or geographic) and for rare characteristics. The comprehensive questionnaire provides a rich database for examining multiple factors associated with various substance use behaviors and problems, including substance use initiation, dependence and abuse, and treatment. The methodology employed in NSDUH has been extensively evaluated and found to be effective in eliciting valid data from respondents. Participation rates are excellent, with 91 percent of selected households participating and 74 percent of selected persons participating in 2006. The major limitations are the exclusion of certain high-risk subgroups (homeless not in shelters, incarcerated persons, and those in long-term health care facilities) and the reliance on self-report. NSDUH estimates for most illicit substances, especially heroin and cocaine, are generally considered to be conservative.

Comparisons with Other Surveys. NSDUH is one of several national and local surveys that assess substance use prevalence. Each survey may have its own purposes, definitions, and design. Nevertheless, policymakers and epidemiologists often compare and contrast the findings from these different data sources, which can sometimes lead to confusion and skepticism when findings differ. Research has established that surveys of substance use and other sensitive topics often produce inconsistent results because of different methods used. For example, reported levels of substance use increased significantly in NSDUH when the incentive payment and name change were introduced in 2002. School-based surveys collecting data in classrooms have consistently reported higher levels of substance use than surveys such as NSDUH that collect data from youths in households. Moreover, household surveys like NSDUH that collect data using self-administration (respondents answer questions privately) tend to obtain higher levels of substance use than surveys in which interviewers record the verbal responses of survey participants. Other factors that can account for differing results across surveys are definitions used, populations covered, and low response rates, which are a particular problem in telephone-based surveys.

FINDINGS FROM NSDUH

Regarding substance use prevalence, the 2006 NSDUH estimated that nearly half of the U.S. adults aged 18 or older (47.5%) had used illicit drugs in their lifetime, and 8.3 percent were current (past month) users. Among youths aged 12 to 17, more than one-fourth (27.6%) had ever used and 9.8 percent used currently. However, there are wide variations in use rates by age, with 3.1 percent of 12-year-olds and 17.1 percent of 17-year-olds using in the past year. Similarly, among adults, the past year rate was 22.2 percent among young adults 18 to 20, but only 6.0 percent among persons age 50 to 54 and below 1 percent for those aged 65 or older. Periodic changes in the survey methodology have limited the ability of NSDUH to track trends, but the survey has documented important trends such as the substantial increases in marijuana and other illicit drug use during the 1960s and

1970s, followed by significant declines during the 1980s. Reaching a low point in 1992, the rate of use among youths had nearly tripled by the end of the decade then declined slightly from 2002 to 2006. Trends among youth reported by NSDUH have been very similar to those seen in other youth surveys, including Monitoring the Future and the Youth Risk Behavior Survey.

Regarding other key findings, the depth of the NSDUH interview and wide population coverage facilitates investigation into many areas of interest to policymakers and researchers. The data have been critical in quantifying substance abuse treatment need, estimating that about 23.6 million Americans needed treatment for a substance use problem in 2006, while only 2.5 million (10.8%) had received specialty treatment. Only 4.5 percent of the 21.1 million persons needing but not receiving treatment actually reported that they perceived a need for treatment. NSDUH data have also been widely used in the study of underage drinking. The survey estimated that in 2006, 28.3 percent of youths aged 12 to 20 were current drinkers and that this rate had been unchanged since at least 2002.

See also **Drug Abuse Warning Network (DAWN); Monitoring the Future; U.S. Government Agencies; U.S. Government Agencies: National Institute on Drug Abuse (NIDA).**

BIBLIOGRAPHY

Gfroerer, J., Eyerman, J., & Chromy, J. (Eds.). (2002). Redesigning an ongoing national household survey: Methodological issues (DHHS Publication No. SMA 03-3768). Rockville, MD: Substance Abuse and Mental Health Services Administration, Office of Applied Studies. Available from http://www.oas.samhsa.gov/.

Kennet, J., & Gfroerer, J. (Eds.). (2005). *Evaluating and improving methods used in the National Survey on Drug Use and Health* (DHHS Publication No. SMA 05-4044, Methodology Series M-5). Rockville, MD: Substance Abuse and Mental Health Services Administration, Office of Applied Studies. Available from http://www.oas.samhsa.gov/.

Office of Applied Studies, Substance Abuse, and Mental Health Services Administration. (2007). *National Survey on Drug Use and Health: Methodological resource book*. Available from http://www.oas.samhsa.gov/.

Office of Applied Studies, Substance Abuse, and Mental Health Services Administration. (2007). *Results from the 2006 National Survey on Drug Use and Health: National findings* (DHHS Publication No. SMA 07-4293, NSDUH Series H-32). Rockville, MD: Substance Abuse and Mental Health Services Administration, Office of Applied Studies. Available from http://www.oas.samhsa.gov.

Office of Management and Budget (2007). *Implementation Guidance for Title V of the E-Government Act, Confidential Information Protection and Statistical Efficiency Act of 2002* (CIPSEA). Available from http://www.whitehouse.gov/.

Turner, C. F., Lessler, J. T., & Gfroerer, J. C. (Eds.). (1992). *Survey measurement of drug use: Methodological studies* (DHHS Publication No. ADM 92-1929). Rockville, MD: National Institute on Drug Abuse.

JOSEPH GFROERER

NEEDLE AND SYRINGE EXCHANGES AND HIV/AIDS.

AIDS (acquired immunodeficiency syndrome) was first observed in homosexual men and injecting drug users (IDUs) in 1981. The discovery of the human immunodeficiency virus (HIV) and the development of a test for the HIV antibody in 1984 and 1985 confirmed that AIDS could be transmitted through the micro-transfusions that occur when IDUs share needles and syringes. HIV antibody testing also indicated that large numbers of IDUs were already infected with HIV—approximately 50 percent in New York City (Des Jarlais & Friedman, 1988) and Edinburgh (Robertson et al., 1986; Skidmore, Robertson, & Savage, 1990) and over 30 percent in Amsterdam (Buning, van Brussel, & van Santen, 1988). Two types of innovative programs, community outreach and syringe exchange, were developed in order to reduce HIV transmission among IDUs.

Outreach programs (Coyle, Needle, & Normand, 1998) use trained health-care workers to provide AIDS education to IDUs in the community. The outreach workers are usually former drug users, although sometimes individuals with good knowledge of the community but without any personal history of drug use are employed, as are active drug users. These outreach programs are effective in educating IDUs about HIV and AIDS and in motivating change in their behaviors (NIH, 1997).

INITIAL SYRINGE-EXCHANGE PROGRAM DEVELOPMENT

The first syringe-exchange program was instituted in Amsterdam in 1984, out of concern about the Hepatitis B virus not HIV infection. A large

pharmacy in the city center changed its policy and stopped selling needles and syringes to drug injectors. The local health department then worked with the Amsterdam drug users' union (Junkie Bonden) to establish a program whereby drug users would turn in their used needles and syringes for new ones at no cost. Within a year HIV antibody testing started in Amsterdam, leading to the realization that a substantial percentage of local IDUs were already infected with HIV (Buning, 1991). The syringe-exchange program was then rapidly expanded.

Syringe-exchange programs were subsequently implemented in many locales in the late 1980s. In most industrialized countries, syringe exchange became part of the national AIDS prevention plan. The United States and Sweden were the two notable exceptions, but even in these nations syringe-exchange programs were often implemented at the local level. The first regular syringe-exchange programs commenced in the United States in 1988, and there were approximately 180 such programs as of 2006 (McKnight et al., 2007).

EFFECTIVENESS OF SYRINGE-EXCHANGE PROGRAMS

A large number of studies have evaluated syringe exchange, both in the United States and in other industrialized countries (NIH, 1997; Normand, Vlahov, & Moses, 1995; Committee on the Prevention of HIV Infection, 2006; Des Jarlais et al., 1996; Stimson, 1995; and Wodak & Cooney, 2006). All concluded that syringe-exchange programs are effective in reducing HIV transmission among IDUs, and that they are best implemented as part of a comprehensive HIV prevention program for drug users, including community outreach and drug abuse treatment.

Even the best syringe-exchange programs do not eliminate injection risk behavior (the sharing of needles, syringes, and other drug injection equipment) among IDUs. (There are no HIV prevention programs that eliminate risk behavior in any population at high risk for HIV.) Because of the continuation of some injecting risk behavior, syringe-exchange programs and HIV prevention programs, in general, are best begun when few persons infected with HIV exist within the local population. If syringe-exchange and community outreach programs begin when HIV infection rates are low (an HIV prevalence of 5% or less), it is possible to prevent HIV epidemics among IDUs (Des Jarlais et al., 1995).

Controlling an HIV epidemic that has already reached a high level of infection (an HIV prevalence of 20% or greater) is considerably more difficult. With large numbers of individuals capable of transmitting HIV and large numbers susceptible to becoming infected, even moderate rates of risk behavior can lead to unacceptably high rates of new infections. There is increasing evidence, however, that syringe-exchange and other HIV prevention programs for IDUs can halt high HIV prevalence epidemics among IDUs (Des Jarlais et al., 2005; Lindenberg et al., 2006).

Although syringe-exchange and community outreach programs generally may be highly effective in reducing HIV transmission among IDUs, not all individual programs have controlled HIV transmission in the local population of IDUs. Vancouver, Canada, experienced an outbreak of HIV transmission among IDUs despite having a syringe-exchange program. Multiple factors contributed to this outbreak, including a change from heroin to cocaine injecting, which requires many more syringes if safe injection is to be practiced, a strict limit (4) on the number of syringes that could be exchanged at each visit, and concentration of the homeless or multiply disadvantaged IDUs in a specific area of the city (Strathdee et al., 1997).

LACK OF UNDESIRABLE CONSEQUENCES

When syringe-exchange programs were first proposed, intense opposition existed in several countries—particularly the United States and Sweden. Fears were expressed that syringe exchanges would lead to increases in illicit drug injection and to greater numbers of syringes discarded in public places. None of these undesirable consequences has occurred. Because so many syringe-exchange programs assist drug users in entering drug abuse treatment, they have probably led to a reduction in the numbers of illicit drug users. And because the existence of a syringe-exchange program gives economic value to a used syringe (it can be exchanged for a new sterile syringe), exchanges have probably led to a net reduction in the number of used syringes discarded in public places (Committee on the Prevention of HIV Infection, 2006).

SYRINGE-EXCHANGE BEST PRACTICE: SECONDARY EXCHANGE

The core idea of syringe exchange is that a drug injector brings used needles and syringes to the exchange and is then given new sterile ones. A very important corollary to this basic concept is that drug users should be able to exchange syringes not only for their own personal use but also for their peers (what is known as *secondary exchange*). Secondary exchange's major benefit is providing syringe exchange to injectors who cannot or do not want to personally attend a program. Given that most programs have limited hours of operation and a limited number of sites, and that many drug users need to protect their confidentiality, secondary exchange is a critical aspect of HIV prevention for IDUs in many communities.

Programs can encourage secondary exchange in several ways. First, there should be no limit on the number of needles and syringes that can be exchanged in a single visit to the program. In many programs, it is not unusual for an individual to exchange hundreds of used needles and syringes in a single visit. Many programs now train selected participants to provide peer-delivered syringe-exchange services, including education and referral services in addition to sterile syringes.

SYRINGE-EXCHANGE BEST PRACTICE: MULTIPLE SERVICES

In addition to the core mission of providing access to sterile needles and syringes in order to reduce HIV transmission, the great majority of syringe-exchange programs provide a variety of other services. These services can be offered either on site at the exchange or through referral. In the United States, the vast majority of syringe-exchange programs (90% or more) provide condoms, alcohol pads for cleaning skin prior to injection, referrals to substance abuse treatment, education on Hepatitis A, B, and C prevention, education on safer injection and vein care, and HIV counseling and testing. Forty to 80 percent provide clothes, food, and hygiene items, HAV and HBV vaccination, and screening for sexually transmitted diseases (McKnight et al., 2007).

Although the continuing importance of reducing HIV transmission among IDUs cannot be overestimated, syringe-exchange programs have evolved into organizations that provide a wide variety of health and social services to a highly vulnerable population.

Given the modest budgets of most syringe-exchange programs, the generally excellent relationships between the programs and their participants, and the high cost of providing services to IDUs through the usual settings such as emergency rooms, the provision of multiple services via syringe-exchange programs is almost certain to be highly cost-effective.

LOW- AND MIDDLE-INCOME COUNTRIES

While syringe exchange may be considered a highly successful health-care innovation in high-income countries, the situation is much more problematic in low- and middle-income nations. According to one recent estimate (Aceijas et al., 2006), there are 13 million IDUs in the world, and over 10 million of them live in low- and middle-income countries. HIV continues to spread rapidly among IDUs in many parts of Eastern Europe and Asia (UNAIDS/WHO, 2007). In general, syringe exchange (and other programs to prevent HIV transmission among IDUs) have been implemented only at the pilot program level in low- and middle-income countries (Sharma, Burrows, & Bluthenthal, 2008).

Scaling up HIV prevention for IDUs in low- and middle-income nations presents a unique public health situation. The technology for controlling HIV transmission is readily available. The challenge is developing the political will and resources to implement programs for a highly stigmatized population.

HARM REDUCTION

The public health crisis of HIV transmission among IDUs and their sexual partners that led to the wide-scale adoption of syringe-exchange programs has also furthered policy development in the drug abuse field. HIV transmission among IDUs is a clear example of when an individual and social harm associated with illicit psychoactive drug use can be greatly reduced without having to solve the underlying very difficult problem of getting people to stop using drugs. As such, syringe exchange epitomizes what has become known as the *harm reduction* approach to the problems of psychoactive drug use (IHRA, 2008).

Harm reduction is based on two fundamental principles. First, drug users are seen as members of the community, having human rights and deserving to be treated with dignity and respect. Second, programs and public policy should be based on empirical evidence of what does and does not work rather than on symbolic value.

Given the nature of the human nervous system, it would not seem possible to create societies that do not include psychoactive drug use. At the same time, advances in scientific research on psychoactive drug use will create new opportunities to address the many problems associated with legal and illicit drug use. Harm reduction offers a perspective within which new scientific knowledge can be incorporated into public health (Des Jarlais, 1995).

See also **Alcohol and AIDS; Complications: Route of Administration; Injecting Drug Users and HIV; Substance Abuse and AIDS.**

BIBLIOGRAPHY

Aceijas, C., et al. (2006). Estimates of injecting drug users at the national and local level in developing and transitional countries, and gender and age distribution. *Sexually Transmitted Infections, 82*(Suppl. III), iii10–iii17.

Buning, E. C. (1991). Effects of Amsterdam needle and syringe exchange. *International Journal of the Addictions, 26*, 1303–1311.

Buning, E. C., van Brussel, G. H. A., & van Santen, G. (1988). Amsterdam's drug policy and its implications for controlling needle sharing. In R. J. Battjes & R. W. Pickens (Eds.), *Needle sharing among intravenous drug abusers: National and international drug perspectives*, Research Monograph 80 (pp. 59–74). Rockville, MD: National Institute on Drug Abuse.

Committee on the Prevention of HIV Infection Among Injecting Drug Users in High Risk Countries. (2006). *Preventing HIV infection among injecting drug users in high risk countries: An assessment of the evidence.* Washington, DC: Institute of Medicine.

Coyle, S., Needle, R., & Normand, J. (1998). Outreach-based HIV prevention for injecting drug users: A review of published outcome data. *Public Health Reports, 113*(Suppl. 1), 19–30.

Des Jarlais, D. C. (1995). Harm reduction—a framework for incorporating science into drug policy. *American Journal of Public Health, 85*(1), 10–12.

Des Jarlais, D. C., & Friedman, S. R. (1988). Intravenous cocaine, crack, and HIV infection. *Journal of the American Medical Association, 259*(13), 1945–1950.

Des Jarlais, D. C., et al. (1995). Maintaining low HIV seroprevalence in populations of injecting drug users. *Journal of the American Medical Association, 274*(15), 1226–1231.

Des Jarlais, D. C., et al. (1996). HIV incidence among injecting drug users in New York City syringe-exchange programmes. *Lancet, 348*, 987–991.

Des Jarlais, D. C., et al. (2005). HIV incidence among injection drug users in New York City, 1990 to 2002: Use of serologic test algorithm to assess expansion of HIV prevention services. *American Journal of Public Health, 95*(8), 1439–1444.

International Harm Reduction Association (IHRA). (2008). Key documents section of Web site. Available from http://www.ihra.net

Lindenberg, C., et al. (2006). Decline in HIV incidence and injecting, but not in sexual risk behaviour, seen in drug users in Amsterdam: A 19-year prospective cohort study. *AIDS, 20*(13), 1771–1775.

McKnight, C., et al. (2007). Syringe exchange programs—United States, 2005. *Morbidity and Mortality Weekly Report* (MMWR), *56*(44), 1164–1167.

National Institutes of Health (NIH). (1997). *Proceedings of the NIH Consensus Development Conference on Interventions to Prevent HIV Risk Behaviors.* Bethesda, MD: Author.

Normand, J., Vlahov, D., & Moses, L. E. (Eds.). (1995). *Preventing HIV transmission: The role of sterile needles and bleach.* Washington, DC: National Academy Press/National Research Council/ Institute of Medicine.

Robertson, J. R., et al. (1986). Epidemic of AIDS related virus (HTLV-III/LAV) infection among intravenous drug users. *British Medical Journal, 292*, 527–529.

Sharma, M., Burrows, D., & Bluthenthal, R. (2008). Improving coverage and scale-up of HIV prevention, treatment and care for injecting drug users: Moving the agenda forward. *International Journal of Drug Policy, 19*(Suppl. 1), 1–4.

Skidmore, C. A., Robertson, J. R., & Savage, G. (1990). Mortality and increasing drug use in Edinburgh: Implications for HIV epidemic. *Scottish Medical Journal, 35*(4), 100–102.

Stimson, G. (1995). AIDS and injecting drug use in the United Kingdom, 1987–1993: The policy response and the prevention of the epidemic. *Social Science and Medicine, 41*(5), 699–716.

Strathdee, S., et al. (1997). Needle exchange is not enough: Lessons from the Vancouver injection drug use study. *AIDS, 11*, F59–F65.

UNAIDS/WHO. (2007). *AIDS epidemic update: December 2006.* Joint United Nations Programme on HIV/AIDS.

Wodak, A., & Cooney, A. (2006). Do needle syringe programs reduce HIV infection among injecting drug users: A comprehensive review of the international evidence. *Substance Use and Misuse, 41*, 777–813.

Don C. Des Jarlais

NETHERLANDS. Drug use in the Netherlands occurs in the context of a specific culture of informal social control and a liberal and nonrestrictive national drug policy that has sustained itself for almost a half century. After the explosive global growth of drug use in the 1960s and 1970s, the Dutch government moved away from traditional prohibition policies and developed a national policy of "harm reduction." Since then, many countries have adopted the innovations in harm reduction developed in the Netherlands. In addition, since the late 1990s, the emphasis of the Dutch harm reduction policy has been modified and more focused on "risk reduction." Health protection and risk reduction among vulnerable populations in the society has become the national policy priority. These vulnerable populations include various categories of youth, ranging from ethnic minority neighborhood youth to homeless and detained youth and schoolchildren and adolescents. New techniques for screening and early intervention to protect health using multidisciplinary teams utilizing genetic and social risk profiles have also become an emerging instrument of national policy.

The harm reduction drug policy of the Netherlands has been built on two main principles—the separation of the markets of so-called soft drugs (e.g., cannabis) and hard drugs (e.g., heroin and cocaine), and the normalization of drug problems. The "separation of markets" principle is based on the idea that drugs can be classified pharmacologically according to their socially acceptable risks, and that drug markets should be controlled on the basis of this classification.

CANNABIS

In the Netherlands, cannabis has been considered a drug of acceptable risk. Tolerating the sale and use of cannabis in "coffee shops" (cafes in which cannabis can be bought and used but that do not serve alcohol) was seen as a way of controlling and normalizing this drug use in society. With the sale of cannabis tolerated in a socially visible and acceptable market (although formally illegal), it was felt that the informal social control of society would be increased. Local authorities could impose standardized regulations and enforcement techniques that could be compared to alcohol and tobacco control.

Dutch jurisprudence, through the "opportunity principle," was used to legitimate this approach, by which the local criminal justice authorities could choose not to enforce a given law if the social harm caused by this action was greater than the crime itself. The latest figures from 2005 show that there are coffee shops in 105 of the 467 cities in the Netherlands, with a total of 729 shops in the country. Most cities of under 50,000 population do not have coffee shops, and the relatively larger cities that do have coffee shops show a rate of 0.55 coffee shops per 10,000 habitants.

The official position on cannabis, however, is showing signs of change in light of the modifications to the original harm reduction policy, which was predicated on a model of informed individual decision making. This policy has been giving way instead to a policy of public health protection. A tendency toward stricter control measures can be observed, and any deviance from the regulations is enforced. The government clearly wants fewer coffee shops in the country, and none are wanted near schools or border crossings (where "drug tourism" creates problems related to all types of drugs). Specifically, under pressure from the government, more and more municipalities have imposed regulations that do not allow a coffee shop to be located within about 250 meters of a school. In order to reduce the problem of drug tourists, discussions are under way concerning how far a coffee shop can be from a national border. Coffee shops have also been experimentally placed outside city centers. Hallucinogenic mushrooms, which are sold in "smart shops" (a kind of specialty shop that sells fresh mushrooms, cognitive enhancers, and high energy preparations but does not allow the use of these substances on the premises), have also been gaining popularity with drug tourists. Because of this and other alleged problems, the government has been moving to close these smart shops and place hallucinogenic mushrooms under the Opium Law, the criminal statute for drugs in the Netherlands.

Cannabis trafficking has been, and remains, clearly illegal in the Netherlands. The so-called AHOJ-G policy for marketing cannabis has been sustained and expanded. This policy requires the coffee shops to: limit advertising (A); not sell hard drugs (cocaine or heroin) on the premises (H);

have no social nuisance (O, or "overlast, meaning offenses to the public order"); have no youths under 18 years of age on the premises (J); sell only small amounts (G), meaning 5 grams per transaction, with a maximum of 500 grams in stock. Additional local regulations are also in force, and serving and consuming alcohol is not allowed in coffee shops. There are also regulations regarding the locations where coffee shops can do business. Despite the existence of this extensive coffee shop system, an illegal cannabis market also exists, consisting of fixed sales points such as house dealers, under-the-counter sales in pubs and cafes, and mobile sales through cell phones and home delivery services. Law enforcement efforts are vigorous in suppressing these nontolerated markets and keeping cannabis distribution within the formal social control of the coffee shop system.

IMPACT OF DUTCH POLICIES ON INTERNATIONAL RELATIONS AND CONTROL

The drug policies of the Netherlands have been continuously criticized because of the perception that the country has become an international center of drug use and drug trafficking. This perception is changing, however, in light of new developments in law enforcement and the criminal justice system. Since the coffee shops were established, they have been a continuous source of tension between the Netherlands and its neighbors. The Schengen Accord, an agreement on border control among 9 European nations, went into effect in 1995 and made an official distinction between "inner" and "outer" borders, with the trafficking in drugs and the existence of coffee shops forbidden along these borders.

In the past, most of the pressure on the Netherlands was asserted at the national level from the European Union, and the Dutch government issued a "Cannabis Letter" in 2004 that acknowledged that the coffee shops were damaging the international relationships of the Netherlands. Earlier, Germany had argued forcibly that the Dutch coffee shops, as well as the "low threshold" methadone programs, undermined their prevention and treatment policies for reducing youth drug use. Along this same line, in 1999 the French president had threatened to close France's inner border in response to drug tourism, though his remarks had the unanticipated effect of increasing the number of young French drug tourists. These kind of international events surrounding the interpretation of the Schengen Accord resulted in a decision within the European Union to encourage the member states to articulate a policy on drug tourism as part of their actions against drug trafficking.

The international tensions still persist in the first decade of the twenty-first century, but they seem to be expressed more and more at the local level in the border areas. For example, it is estimated that each week 22,000 Belgian and French drug tourists buy cannabis from coffee shops in Bergen op Zoom and Roosendaal, two Dutch cities close to the Belgian border. Some Dutch communities have implemented a zero tolerance policy on coffee shops while others have initiated special restrictions. While the local Dutch communities have worked hard to develop an effective policy to restrict drug tourists, it is often the case that the neighboring communities have not created a complementary policy to improve the situation, being satisfied to merely criticize and complain. Working together across the borders to solve this problem is rare.

Three special criminal justice policy programs can be singled out as exemplary of the Dutch trend to more vigorously assert its compliance in drug policy as a member state in the European Union: (1) the combined effort to reduce the production and trafficking of Ecstasy; (2) the comprehensive plan to reduce cocaine smuggling through Schiphol Airport; and (3) the intensified enforcement of the cannabis cultivation laws, with an emphasis on organized crime. Despite these increasingly stringent initiatives, the government still receives substantial internal and external criticism that these national policies have not been effective. Yet, the prevalence of drug use in the Netherlands is not higher, and is in fact considerably lower, than in the United States and most other European countries. Citizen groups and mothers' groups operate in many Dutch cities, organizing against the problems caused by drug users and pressuring the government for tougher policies.

Given the shortcomings of the national policy (as pointed out by its critics), most indicators show that the policy of risk reduction reinforced by targeted law enforcement and criminal justice programs is succeeding, and that drug use in the Netherlands has stabilized. A 2005 national survey of the general population (between the ages of 15 and 64) found that the percentage of those who had used drugs in the preceding year had not increased substantially since 2001, with the lifetime prevalence of having tried various drugs at least once as follows: cannabis, 5.4 percent; cocaine, 0.6 percent; amphetamine, 0.3 percent; and Ecstasy, 1.2 percent. Surveys of the school population show similar stable patterns. However, indications from the nightlife scenes are not consistent. In Amsterdam the number of emergencies for GHB, a popular club drug, have increased. The *National Drug Monitor*, an annual report that compiles data from several sources, reports an increase and a large variation in the use of cocaine by young adults in the "club scene."

COCAINE AND HEROIN

For crack cocaine and opiates, there have been no new estimates since 2001 that would indicate a change in the rate of users of 3.1 per 1,000 in the population. The 2006 estimate of these "hard drug" users indicated there were 33,499 users, with a confidence interval of between 23,773 and 46,466. Most hard drug users consume heroin and cocaine daily. While injecting drug use has been decreasing—and with it the percentage of AIDS cases and Hepatitis C attributable to injecting drug use—the prevalence of HIV is relatively high in Amsterdam (26%) and Heerlen (22%), a small city in the south of the country. The population of hard drug users is also substantial in Rotterdam (10%) and Utrecht (10%). In addition, an increase in the prevalence of psychiatric and somatic co-occurring disorders is reported in this population. Studies have found that one-third of this population suffers from major depression and that 60 percent show conduct disorders.

The demand for treatment among users of heroin and methadone has declined over the past years, according to the *National Drug Monitor*. Innovative techniques such as cue exposure therapy to extinguish cravings are available for those addicts who do present for treatment. However, notable increases in treatment demand among other groups of users have been observed. Since the indicators of drug use seem to be stable, these increases in treatment demand are likely to be due to other factors, such as the changes in the national drug policy targeting indicated vulnerable groups and, to a lesser degree, increases in potency of drugs.

Although there was a strong growth in the number of primary cocaine users between 1994 and 2004 (from 2,500 to 10,000) this trend did not continue in 2005 and 2006. The number of amphetamine users reported by drug treatment programs is relatively limited (4% of all drugs clients in 2006) but has shown a clear upward trend since 2001. The most pronounced increase in treatment demand has been in the number of cannabis users, which rose from 1,951 in 1994 to 6,544 in 2006. The average THC concentration in Dutch home-grown marijuana peaked in 2004 (20%), leveled off in 2005 and 2006 (18%), and decreased in 2007 (16%). Considering this indicator alone, cannabis treatment demand can be expected to stabilize or decrease in the near future. In addition, vigorous prevention campaigns carried out among vulnerable populations will quite likely also contribute to a reversal in the demand for cannabis treatment. Treatment targeting vulnerable subpopulations of adolescents has adopted multidimensional family therapy approaches from the United States. (Indeed, almost every kind of drug treatment for any kind of drug problem is available in the Netherlands.)

The principle of the normalization of drug problems argues that much of the harm attributed to the use of hard drugs, such as heroin, is based on the negative definitions, stigmatization, and discrimination of society that is internalized by the hard drug users. The principle of normalization leads to multiple efforts to reintegrate the heroin user into the community and to fight against his or her stigmatization. However, this effort has been expanded not only to the negative labeling of the hard drug user by society, but also to addressing the large amount of public nuisance caused by this vulnerable population. The primary instrument to achieve these policy goals is an extensive system of methadone maintenance programs (a widely used pharmacotherapy for heroin users), which is enhanced by counseling and social service support. In addition, drug users are encouraged to organize self-help groups and mobilize for positive changes in their own subcultures.

In the mid-1990s the national government launched an ambitious experiment that prescribed heroin to an indicated group of chronic treatment-resistant heroin addicts who were not responding well to the methadone services and becoming an increasing source of public nuisance. The experiment was launched in the larger cities of the Netherlands and involved the establishment of specialized clinical facilities where heroin was prescribed. The clinically based prescription of heroin was carefully evaluated and monitored according to the highest standards of clinical management science. The results showed a resounding success, and in 2004 the Dutch government decided that the medical prescription of heroin should expand its treatment capacity from 300 to 1,000 slots. Following this expansion of treatment capacity, and after extensive deliberations, heroin became normalized through its official registration as a medicinal product indicated for chronic treatment-resistant heroin addicts. The prescription of drugs has also included medical marijuana, which is regulated by an office in the Ministry of Public Health and resembles the systems developing in several states in the United States.

LAW ENFORCEMENT INITIATIVES

Another national experiment targets the vulnerable subpopulation of hard drug users, the "prolific offenders" who especially contribute to the public nuisance problem. The experiment provides these individuals with a highly articulated form of compulsory treatment. The intervention aims at the prevention and reduction of crimes committed by drug users, since a considerable proportion of crime and recidivism in Dutch cities is attributable to this subpopulation. The experiment is consistent with the Dutch harm reduction axiom that a substantial reduction of the crime caused by this subpopulation's members could be reduced by providing a structured program of treatment and social services that addresses their addiction problems.

In 2001 the experiment known as the Court Ordered Treatment for Drug-Dependent Offenders (Strafrechtelijke Opvang Verslaafden, or SOV) was launched. The evaluation study of the SOV program found that it was more effective than regular imprisonment in terms of crime reduction, illicit drug use, and social participation. Drug users participating in SOV are engaged in a stepwise, phased reintegration program into society, with each phase lasting six to nine months. An initial closed phase (day-and-night in SOV) is followed by a second half-open phase (extramural during daytime, in SOV during the night). Re-entry into society occurs in a final open extramural phase. In 2006 the SOV was replaced by the broader Placement in an Institution for Repeat Offenders (Inrichting voor Stelselmatige or ISD) program, which does not limit participation to men without psychiatric problems and has became a regular program within prisons.

DRUG RESEARCH AND INTERNATIONAL COOPERATION

Research in the Netherlands continues to play a pivotal role in a constant process of modification of Dutch drug policy. The experimental and scientifically based foundation of Dutch drug policy provides a persistent counterforce to tendencies in the government and civil society for moralistic redefinitions of the country's drug problems. A number of universities, along with private and governmental institutions, conduct research in all areas of drug use, with funding provided by national and city governmental agencies and private foundations. This research contributes important publications to the international scientific and policymaking communities. The joint research program of the Netherlands Organization for Health Research and Development (ZonMw) and the U.S. National Institute on Drug Abuse (NIDA) evidences the prestige of Dutch drug research. Research teams from both countries contribute to joint projects that are prioritized in joint meetings. This program has established a unique and effective forum for identifying similarities and differences in national drug-policy priorities in a historical context of profound policy differences.

Examples of some of the current joint projects that encompass representatives from all regions of the two countries include: drug prevention in schoolchildren; drug interventions in the dance club scene in Rotterdam and San Francisco; implicit cognition and early intervention; prevention of substance abuse in ADHD children; a genetic approach to opioid receptors and addiction; and analysis of the brain development of adolescent marijuana users. Yet while this research program provides a good example of the international recognition of Dutch research on drugs, it also stands in contrast with the continuing tensions

and problems that Dutch drug policy, especially in the area of cannabis, has with the neighboring countries of Belgium, Germany, and France.

TOBACCO

Around 20,000 people die each year in the Netherlands as a direct consequence of the use of tobacco. Tobacco smoking in early adolescents has increased rapidly in the Netherlands. In 2005 the prevalence of tobacco use among 16 year olds was estimated at 52 percent for boys and 59 percent for girls. In 1998 a prevention platform for the selling of tobacco to youth was organized, and since 2003 the sale of tobacco to youth aged 16 or under has been prohibited. However, the effectiveness of these measures has been questioned because it has been reported that the sellers are not consistently asking for identification from those making purchases.

To increase the vigor of the public health efforts to reduce the risks, a ban on the use of tobacco in all cafes and restaurants was initiated on July 1, 2008. This measure is another example of the attempts by the Netherlands to be consistent with the norms of the European Union. Apart from changing the normal environment of Dutch public life, there has been much discussion about how this ban will affect the coffee shops. On one side is the opinion that this ban will lead to the closing of the shops, while the opposite viewpoint is that the ban is only for tobacco and does not apply to cannabis. Informal changes are already being observed in local coffee shop rules, such as only allowing pure cannabis to be smoked. Since the preferred method of smoking cannabis in the Netherlands has been in a "joint" containing a mixture of tobacco and cannabis, the tobacco ban is an example of the far-reaching affects of the tobacco ban on the formal and informal regulation of other substances.

ALCOHOL

there is widespread use of alcohol in the Netherlands, with the prevalence in the general population (individuals aged 12 years and older) put at 81 percent. While it is generally recognized that moderate use of alcohol has few health risks, alcohol abuse is seen as one of the top 10 health problems in the country. Between 2,000 and 3,000 people die each year of alcohol abuse. The awareness of the health risks of alcohol has been substantially increased through public discussion about the role of genetic vulnerability to alcohol problems and what the policy consequences of this new knowledge should be. In November 2007, the government issued its " Main Line Alcohol Policy Letter," in which the priority goal of the nation's alcohol policy was held to be the prevention of harmful alcohol use. The most important target group for this policy is youth. The new policy recommends vigorous measures that will prevent children and adolescents from using alcohol before the age of 16.

However, the existing data since 1984 show that there have only been slight fluctuations in the use of alcohol among the school population. Measurements show a slight decrease in lifetime prevalence, from 85 percent in 2003 to 79 percent in 2007. Nevertheless, research has led to recommendations that parents more actively attempt to delay the onset of alcohol use in their children.

The focus on the family has been combined with special attention to alcohol use at work, in the club scenes, and while driving. More attention is also being given to the control of the selling of alcohol to youth. For example, it is now required that identification be shown before purchasing alcohol and for entrance to clubs where alcohol is served. However, the consequences of these policy requirements are not yet known.

See also **Cannabis; Club Drugs; Coca/Cocaine, International; Coerced Treatment for Substance Offenders; European Union; France; Germany; Harm Reduction; Heroin; International Control Policies; Marijuana (Cannabis); Methadone Maintenance Programs; Needle and Syringe Exchanges and HIV/AIDS.**

BIBLIOGRAPHY

Barendrecht, C., van der Poel, A., & van de Mheen, D. (2006). The rise of the mobile phone in the hard drug scene of Rotterdam. *Journal of Psychoactive Drugs, 38*(1), 77–87.

Bieleman, B., & Kruize, A. (2008) *Alcoholverstrekking aan jongeren 2007: Naleving leeftijdsgrenzen 16 en 18 jaar uit de Drank- en Horecawet: Metingen 1999, 2001, 2003, 2005 en 2007* (Youth Alcohol Distribution Measures: 1999, 2001, 2003, 2005 and 2007). Groningen-Rotterdam: St. Intraval.

Bieleman, B., & Kruize, A. (2008). *Monitor tabaksverstrekking jongeren 2007: Naleving leeftijdsgrens 16 jaar: metingen 1999, 2001, 2003, 2005 en 2007*. (Monitor Youth Tobacco Distribution 2007 Measures: 1999, 2001, 2003, 2005 and 2007). Groningen-Rotterdam: St. Intraval.

Bieleman, B., & Naayer, H. (2006). *Coffeeshops in Nederland 2005: Aantallen coffeeshops en gemeentelijk beleid 1999–2005* (Coffee shops in the Netherlands 2005: Coffee shop numbers and city policy 1999–2005). Groningen: St. Intraval.

Bieleman, B., & Snippe, J. (2006). Coffeeshops en criminaliteit (Coffee shops and criminality). In *Coffeeshops en cannabis* (pp. 46–59). Groningen: St. Intraval.

Bieleman, B., Snippe, J., Biesma, S., & Kaplan, C. H. (1999). "Overlast": Erscheinungsformen, Erfahrungen der Burger und Massnahmen bei der Einfuhg neure Projekte fur Drogenabhangige ("Nuisance": Forms, citizen experience, and implementation of a new project for drug addicts). In B. Westerman, G. Bellmann, & C. Jellinek, (Eds.). *Heroinverschreibung: Wirkungen und nebenwirkungen* (*Heroin prescription: Effects and side effects*) (pp. 237–246). Cologne: Deutscher Studien Verlag.

Biesma, S., de Jong, A., & Bieleman, B. (2003). Drugs en drang (Drugs and force). *Tijdschrift over Samenleving en Criminaliteitspreventie (SEC), 17e jaargang*(5), 23–26.

Coumans, M., Knibbe, R. A., & van de Mheen, D. (2006). Street-level effects of local drug policy on marginalization and hardening: An ethnographic study among chronic drug users. *Journal of Psychoactive Drugs, 38*(2), 61–71.

de Kort, M. (1994). The Dutch cannabis debate, 1968–1976. *Journal of Drug Issues, 24*(3), 417–427.

Henquet, C. E. C., Kraabbendam, L., et al. (2005). A Prospective cohort study of cannabis use, psychosis liability and psychotic symptoms in young people. *British Medical Journal, 330*(7481), 11–15.

Knibbe, R. A., Joosten, J., et al. (2007). Culture as an explanation for substance-related problems: A cross-national study among French and Dutch adolescents. *Social Science & Medicine, 64*(3), 604–616.

Krabben, A., Pieters, T., & Snelders, S. (2008) *Chemie van verslaving: Over genen, hersenstofjes en sociale zwakte* (The chemistry of addiction: On genes, neurotransmitters, and social weakness). Houten: Prelum.

Laar, M. van, Cruts, G., et al. (2008). *The Netherlands Drug Situation 2007: Report to the EMCDDA by the Reitox National Focal Point*. Utrecht: The Trimbos Institute.

Leuw, E., & Marshall, I. H. (Eds.). (1994). *Between prohibition and legalization: The Dutch experiment in drug policy*. Amsterdam: Kugler.

Marissen, M. A., Franken, I. H., et al. (2007). Cue exposure therapy for the treatment of opiate addiction: Results of a randomized controlled trial. *Psychotherapy and Psychosomatics, 76*(2), 97–105.

Michel, L., Carrieri, M. P., & Wodak, A. (2008). Harm reduction and equity of access to care for French prisoners: A review. *Harm Reduction Journal, 5*(17), 1–11.

Monshouwer, K., Verdurmen, J., et al. (2008) *Jeugd en riskant gedrag 2007: Kerngegevens uit het peilstation-sonderzoek scholieren Roken, drinken, drugsgebruik en gokken onder scholieren vanaf tien jaar.* (Youth and Risk Behavior 2007: Core Data from a School Study of Smoking, Drinking, Drug Use, and Gambling). Utrecht: Trimbos-instituut.

Ostini, R., Bammer, G., Dance, P. R., & Goodin, R. E. (1993). The ethics of experimental heroin maintenance. *Journal of Medical Ethics, 19*, 175–182.

Rigter, H. (2006). What drug policies cost: Drug policy spending in the Netherlands in 2003. *Addiction, 101*(3), 323–329.

Snippe, J., Kruize, A., & Bieleman, B. (2004). XTC in de houdgreep (XTC [Ecstasy] on hold). *Tijdschrift over Samenleving en Criminaliteitspreventie (SEC), 18*(3), 5–7.

Toonen, M., Ribot, S., & Thissen, J. Y. (2006). Yield of illicit indoor cannabis cultivation in the Netherlands. *Journal of Forensic Science, 51*(5), 1050–1054.

Uitermark, J., & Cohen, P. (2005). A clash of policy approaches: The rise (and fall?) of Dutch harm reduction policies towards ecstasy consumption. *International Journal of Drug Policy, 16*(1), 65–72.

van den Brink, W., Hendriks, V., et al. (2003). Medical prescription of heroin to treatment resistant heroin addicts: Two randomised controlled trials. *Addiction, 100*(1), 89–95.

van Vliet, H. J. (1990). Separation of drug markets and the normalization of drug problems in The Netherlands: An Example for Other Nations? *Journal of Drug Issues, 20*(3), 463–471.

Wiers, R. W., Houben, K., & de Kraker, J. (2007). Implicit cocaine associations in active cocaine users and controls. *Addictive Behaviors, 32*(6), 1284–1289.

CHARLES KAPLAN
BERT BIELEMAN

NEUROLEPTIC.

Neuroleptic includes any of a group of drugs that are also called antipsychotics. Neuroleptics are used as medications in the treatment of acute psychoses of unknown origin, including mania and schizophrenia. The prototype neuroleptic drugs are chlorpromazine (Thorazine), haloperidol (Haldol), clozapine (Clozaril), lithium (Lithonate), and thioridazine (Mellaril). Some of the newer drugs include risperidone (Risperdal), quetiapine (Seroquel), and olanzapine (Zyprexa). The site of action for these drugs (receptor site) is the central nervous system where they produce antipsychotic effects.

These drugs are also used for antianxiety, although other agents are more effective and do not have the long-term side effects that neuroleptics do. Drug therapy alone is not entirely effective in treating psychoses, and it is used in combination with acute and long-term support and medical care. Some neuroleptics are also used in the treatment of nausea, vomiting, alcoholic hallucinosis, neuropsychiatric diseases marked by movement disorders (e.g., Huntington's disease and Gilles de la Tourette's syndrome), pruritus, and intractable hiccough.

See also **Schizophrenia.**

BIBLIOGRAPHY

Baldessarini, R. J. (1996). Drugs and the treatment of psychiatric disorders—mood disorders. In A. G. Gilman et al. (Eds.), *Goodman and Gilman's the pharmacological basis of therapeutics*, 9th ed. New York: McGraw-Hill Medical. (2005, 11th ed.)

Howland, R. D., & Mycek, M. J. (2006). *Pharmacology*, 3rd ed. Philadelphia, PA: Lippincott, Williams & Wilkins.

Ross-Flanigan, N. (1999). Antipsychotic drugs. In *Gale Encyclopedia of Medicine*, 1st ed. Farmington Hills, MI: Gale Group. (2006, 3rd ed.)

GEORGE R. UHL
VALINA DAWSON

NEURON.

The gross anatomy of the central nervous system—the brain and spinal cord—was studied in some detail during the seventeenth and eighteenth centuries, but not until the nineteenth century did scientists begin to appreciate that the central nervous system (CNS) was composed of many millions of separate cells, called neurons (also called nerve cells). This discovery had to await technical improvements in the microscope and the development of specialized stains that permitted scientists to observe the microscopic anatomy of the nervous system.

HISTORY

In the 1870s, the Italian anatomist Camillo Golgi developed such a special staining technique, and he and other scientists were then able to observe under the microscope the fine structures of the cells of the nervous system. Yet Golgi may not have fully appreciated that what seemed to be an extended network of nerve tissue were in reality millions of distinct neurons with fine fibrils touching each other. It was the Spanish scientist Santiago Ramón y Cajal who was credited with expounding the neuron theory. In 1906, Golgi and Ramón y Cajal shared the Nobel Prize in physiology/medicine for their discoveries on the nature of the nervous system.

Even after the concept of separate neurons was generally accepted, there was controversy for many years about how the separate neurons communicated with each other. At the end of the nineteenth century, many scientists believed they did so by means of electric impulses. Others believed there was a chemical messenger that allowed neurons to influence each other. Around 1920, acetylcholine was discovered, the first of many nerve messengers that would be discovered during the subsequent decades.

FUNCTION

The neuron is the basic functional cellular unit of nervous system operations; it is the principal investigational target of research into the actions of addictive drugs and alcohol. An essential feature of the cellular composition of the brain is the high density of extremely varied, heterogeneously shaped neuron groups (see Figure 1). To understand the specialized aspects of neurons and their function, therefore, requires a discussion of the general structural and functional features characteristic to all neurons and the degree to which unique variations form consistent subsets of neurons.

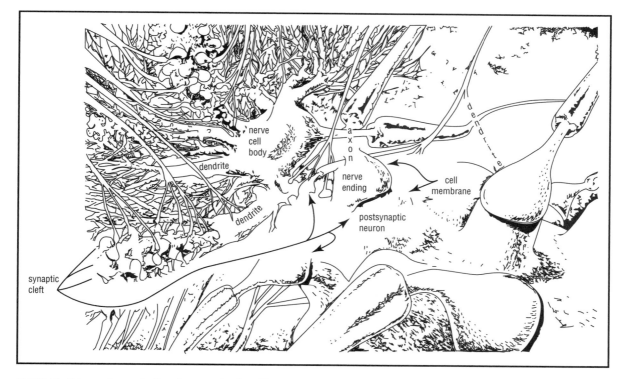

Figure 1. Neuronal complexity. The complexity of the neuronal network in the brain is demonstrated by this bundle of neurons, which form a vast and ramified structure with their cell bodies, outgrowths, and intercellular contact points. (Modified from Figure 1, in M.J. Kuhar's Introduction to Neurotransmitters and Neuroreceptors in *Quantitative Imaging*, edited by J.J. Frost and H.N. Wagner. Raven Press, New York, 1990.) ILLUSTRATION BY GGS INFORMATION SERVICES. GALE, CENGAGE LEARNING

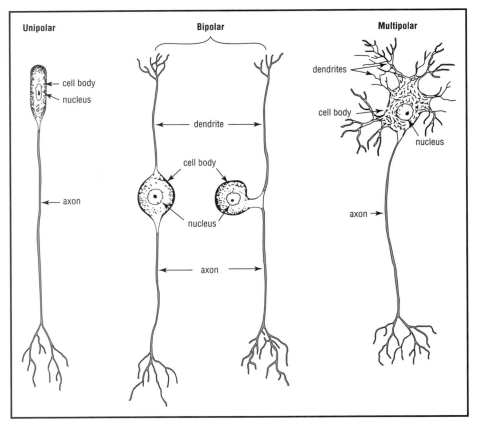

Figure 2. Three types of neurons. ILLUSTRATION BY GGS INFORMATION SERVICES. GALE, CENGAGE LEARNING

Neurons share many cellular properties that distinguish them significantly from other cell types in other tissues; those changes within the cell's regulatory processes of greatest interest to researchers of addictive drugs, however, depend on features that form distinctions within the class of cells called neurons. Furthermore, the assembly of individual neurons into functional systems, through highly precise circuitry employing highly specified forms of chemical interneuronal transmission, allows for the sensitivity of a brain to addictive drugs.

In some organs of the body—such as the liver, kidney, or muscle—each cell of the tissue is generally similar in shape and function. Within that tissue, all perform in highly redundant fashion to convert their incoming raw material into, respectively, nutrients, urine, or contractions, which establishes the function of the specific tissue. In the nervous system, the variously (heterogeneously) shaped neurons (see Figure 2), supported by an even larger class of similarly (homogeneously) shaped non-neuronal cells,

termed *neuroglia*, convert information from external or internal sources into information ultimately integrated into programs for the initiation and regulation of behavior.

This integrative conversion of sensory information into behavioral programs results from the rich interconnections between neurons, and it depends on the extremely differentiated features of neurons—their size and shape; their extended cell-surface cytoplasmic processes (dendrites and axons); and their resultant interconnections that establish the sources of their incoming (afferent) information and the targets of their outgoing (efferent) communication (see Figure 3).

COMMON FEATURES

As cells, neurons share some features in common with cells in all other organ systems (see Figure 4). They have a *plasma membrane* acting as an external cell wall to form a distinct boundary between the environment inside (intracellular) and outside

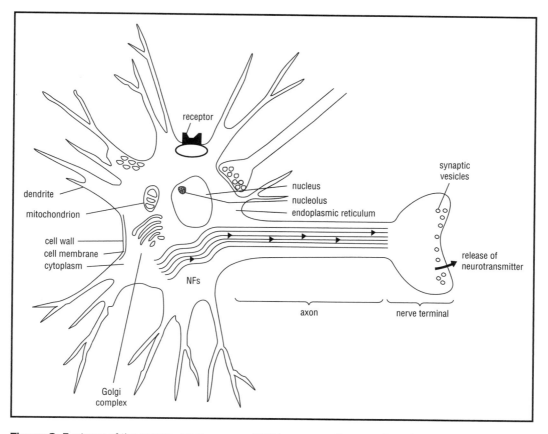

Figure 3. Features of the neuron. ILLUSTRATION BY GGS INFORMATION SERVICES. GALE, CENGAGE LEARNING

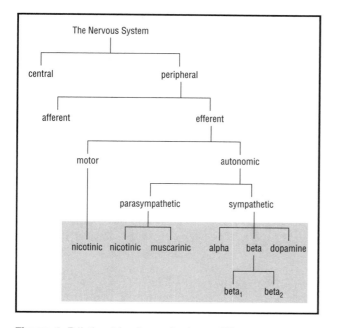

Figure 4. Relationship of receptor types. Efferent nerves in the peripheral nervous system. (Receptor subdivisions for alpha and dopaminergic receptors are not included.) ILLUSTRATION BY GGS INFORMATION SERVICES. GALE, CENGAGE LEARNING

(extracellular) the cells. The intracellular material enclosed by the plasma membrane is termed *cytoplasm*. Like all other cells (except red blood cells), neurons have numerous specialized intracellular organelles, which permit them to maintain their vitality while performing their specialized functions.

Thus, neurons have *mitochondria* (singular, mitochondrion), by which they convert sugar and oxygen into intracellular energy molecules, which then fuel other metabolic reactions. Neurons have abundant *microtubules*: thin intracellular tubular struts by which they form and maintain their often highly irregular cell structure. Neurons are also rich in a network of intracellular membranous channels, the *endoplasmic reticulum*, through which they distribute the energy molecules, membrane components, and other synthesized products required for functioning. Like other cells that must secrete some of their synthesized products for functioning, as neurons do with their neurotransmitters, some parts of the endoplasmic reticulum, such as the *smooth endoplasmic reticulum*, are specialized for the packaging of secretion products into storage particles, which in neurons are termed *synaptic vesicles*. At the center of the pool of cytoplasm, neurons possess a *nucleus*, which, as in other nucleated cells, contains the full array of the genetic information characteristic of the individual organism. From this nucleus, selected subsets of genetic information are expressed to provide for the general shared and the specific unshared features of the cell. The nucleus of the neuron cell is enclosed within a membranous envelope that, as in many other types of cells, exhibits multiple nuclear pores through which information can be conveyed to and from the nucleus.

UNIQUE FEATURES

The plasma membrane of neurons differs from that of non-neuronal cells in that it contains special proteins, termed *voltage-sensitive ion channels*. Such channels are conceptually small tubular proteins embedded in the membrane of the neuron, which, when activated under specific conditions, allow positively charged ions of sodium, potassium, and calcium to enter the neuron. The existence of such electrically sensitive channels permits the neuron to become electrically excitable. The expression and selective distribution (compartmentalization) of such electrically excitable channels along its efferent processes, the axons, permit neurons to conduct signals efficiently for long distances; this also accounts for the bioelectrical activity of the brain assessed by *electroencephalography (EEG)*. Similarly, the distribution of such electrically excitable ion channels along the receptive surfaces of the neurons (its dendrites and cell body [soma]) allows them to conduct and integrate signals from all over the extended shape of the neuron.

The smooth endoplasmic reticulum of the neuron is somewhat more elaborate and extensive than other cells that secrete their products; this specialized and extensive smooth endoplasmic system is termed the *Golgi complex* (or *Golgi apparatus*). Discovered accidentally, it was a useful marker for staining the nervous system to distinguish neurons from other cells of the brain when under inspection by microscope.

The nucleus of neurons is often highly elaborated, with multiple creases or infoldings, exhibiting complex configurations, within which are typically dense accumulations of cytoplasmic organelles, and almost always a very distinctive intranuclear clustering of genetic material, the *nucleolus*. Differentiated neurons—neurons whose developmental stage is past the step at which cell-type dedication has occurred—are unable to undergo cell division, in distinct contrast to comparably metabolically active cells in such complex tissues as liver, kidney, muscle, or skin. As a result, mature neurons can repair themselves, up to a point, but are unable to regenerate themselves or respond to their growth factors in a manner that would in other tissues lead to cell division and replacement.

The most distinctive cellular feature of neurons is the degree to which they express unique patterns of size and shape. In mammals, all neurons have highly irregular shapes; such shape variations are categorized in terms of the number of cell surface extensions, or neuronal processes, that the neuronal subset expresses, as in Figure 2.

Some neurons have only one cellular process extending from the surface of a round or nearly round cell body; this form of neuron, a *unipolar* neuron, is typical of invertebrate nervous systems. Typical unipolar neurons are the cells of the dorsal root ganglia, in which a single efferent axon conducts information toward or away from the cell body through a branched axon.

Most neurons of the central nervous system of mammals are multipolar. That is, in addition to the efferent axon, which may also have many subsets of secondary axons, called *collateral branches*, that stem from the main efferent process axon, elaborations may also be expressed from the cell body surface. The latter elaborations are termed *dendrites*, because their shape resembles the limbs of trees. Dendrites protrude from the cell body, and they, as well as the cell body, constitute the receptive surfaces of the target neuron onto which the afferent connections make their synaptic connections.

DISTINGUISHING NEURONS

Since neurons come in so many shapes and sizes, early investigators of the brain sought to make distinctions among them, based in part on their locations, their sizes and shapes, and the connections they could be shown to receive or emit. Every scientist who worked in the formative era of brain research sought to describe a unique subset of neurons that were forever after named for their initial describer or the unique property defined. Thus, we have *Betz neurons*, large layer V–VI neurons of the motor cortex, and *Purkinje neurons*, the major output neurons of the cerebellar cortex, as well as neurons named for their shapes and appearance—*pyramidal neurons* of the cerebral and hippocampal cortices, *mitral* and *tufted neurons* of the olfactory bulb, and *granule cell neurons* of the cerebellar, hippocampal, and olfactory cortices. The last mentioned have relatively compact cell bodies, densely packed together, giving the brain a granular appearance by optical microscopy.

Dendrites and axons exhibit highly distinctive morphological patterns. The surfaces of dendrites and axons can be distinctive in the shapes of their branches. This permits fine discrimination among neurons (stellar, or star-shaped, neurons; chandelier neurons; or mossy or climbing axon fibers). Some neurons exhibit dendrites whose surfaces are smooth (aspiny); others are highly elaborated (spiny), which may serve to enlarge the receptive surfaces and enhance the degree to which such neurons may integrate afferent information.

Similarly, the morphology and stability of the axons may also be highly variable. Some neurons direct their axons to highly constrained targets in a more or less direct route; others may be highly branched, with multiple collateral branches to integrate communications from one cell cluster to many divergent targets. To provide the essential support of anabolic and secretory materials within these highly elaborated cellular structures, neurons have evolved an efficient form of intracellular transport, an energy-dependent, microtubule-guided, centripetal and centrifugal process by which organelles are dispensed to and returned from the distal processes (as well as probable macromolecular signals sensed by pinocytotic-like [fluid uptake] incorporation of such signals by distal dendrites and axons). Such signals may serve as local growth-regulatory factors, allowing even the nondividing neurons to alter their shape and connections in response to activity and signals received from their afferent sources.

NEURONAL IDENTITY

An individual neuron may be referred to on the basis of its size (magnocellular, parvicellular). A layer or "nuclear" cluster of neurons may be referred to by shape (pyramidal, mitral), the morphology of its axon terminals (i.e., *basket cells*, whose axon terminals make basket-shaped terminations on their targets), and its position in a sensory or motor circuit. In the latter classification scheme, those neurons closest to the incoming sensory event or to the outgoing motor-control event are termed *primary sensory* or *motor* neurons, respectively, whereas neurons at more distal positions of circuitry from the primary incoming or outgoing event are termed *secondary, tertiary*, and so on, depending on their position in that hierarchy.

In addition to these morphological qualities, neurons may also be separately distinguished on the basis of the functional systems to which they are connected (visual, auditory, somatosensory, proprioceptive, attentional, reinforcing, etc.) and on the basis of the neurotransmitters they employ to communicate with the neurons to which they are connected (cholinergic, adrenergic, GABAergic, etc.). Each of those features provides for a multidimensional definition of virtually every neuron in the brain.

See also **Brain Structures and Drugs; Neurotransmission; Neurotransmitters; Receptor, Drug; Reward Pathways and Drugs.**

BIBLIOGRAPHY

Bear, M. F., Connors, B. W., & Paradiso, M. A. (2006). *Neuroscience: Exploring the brain.* Philadelphia, PA: Lippincott, Williams & Wilkins.

Corsi, P., Ed. (1991). *The enchanted loom: Chapters in the history of neuroscience.* New York: Oxford University Press.

Martin, R. A., Wallace, B. G., & Fuchs, J. G., Eds. (2001). *From neuron to brain: A cellular and molecular approach to the function of the nervous system,* 4th ed. Sunderland, MA: Sinauer Associates.

Nieuwenhuys, R., Voogd, J., & van Huijzen, C. (2007). *The human central nervous system,* 4th ed. New York: Springer.

FLOYD BLOOM

NEUROTRANSMISSION. Neurons (nerve cells) communicate chemically by releasing and responding to a wide range of chemical substances, referred to in the aggregate as neurotransmitters. The process of *neurotransmission* refers to this form of chemical communication between cells of the central and peripheral nervous system at the anatomically specialized point of transmission, the synapse (synaptic junctions). Thus, it is convenient to conceive of "the" neurotransmitter for a specific instance of synaptic connections between neurons in one brain location (the source neurons) and their synaptic partner cells (the target neurons) in another neuronal location. For example, the phrase "dopaminergic neurons of the nigro-accumbens circuit" refers to the dopamine-transmitting synaptic connections between the brain neurons of the substantia nigra and their targets in the nucleus Accumbens. Current concepts of neurotransmission, however, require a broader view; they would consider as neurotransmitters all the chemical substances that a given neuron employs to signal the other neurons to which it is anatomically connected (its synaptic targets) and through which that neuron may also be able to influence other neuronal and non-neuronal cells in the adjacent spatial environment of its circuitry (nonsynaptic targets).

In some cases—more frequent in invertebrate nervous systems, in more primitive vertebrates, and in the embryonic nervous system than in the adult mammalian nervous system—neurons may also communicate "electrically," by direct ionic coupling between connected cells, through specialized forms of intercellular junctions referred to as "gap junctions," or *electrotonic junctions.* Such electrotonic transmission sites are of relatively little direct concern to the actions of addictive drugs and alcohol. In contrast, it is the more pervasive process of chemical neurotransmission that underlies the main molecular and cellular mechanisms by which addictive drugs act—and through which the nervous system exposed to such drugs undergoes the adaptations that may lead to dependence, Habituation, withdrawal, and the more enduring changes that persist after withdrawal from the once-dependent state.

The critical characteristic of a substance designated as a neurotransmitter is the manner in which it is made and secreted. To qualify as a neurotransmitter, the release of the substance must be coupled to neuronal activity according to two rather stringent functional rules (see Figure 1).

1. The transmitter substance must be synthesized by the transmitting neuron. In most cases, the substance is made well in advance and stored in small organelles (synaptic vesicles) within the terminal axons of the source neuron, ready for eventual release when called upon.

2. The transmitter substance must be released by that neuron through a special form of activity-dependent, calcium ion (Ca^{2+})-selective, excitation-secretion coupling. Substances released through other nonactivity-coupled and non-Ca^{2+}-coupled mechanisms may be regarded as excretion (as with metabolic byproducts to be degraded), rather than secretion.

The synaptic junction is the site at which the axons of the source neuron physically make most intimate contact with the target neuron to form an anatomically specialized junction; concentrated there are the proteins that mediate the processes of transmitter release (from the presynaptic neuron) and response (by the postsynaptic neuron). Indirect evidence for some neurotransmitter systems has suggested to some scientists a general concept of *nonsynaptic* interneuronal communication, sometimes also referred to as *paracrine* or *volume-transmission* communication, in which the neurotransmitter released by a designated set of presynaptic terminals may diffuse to receptive neurons that are not in anatomic contact. The sets of chemical substances that neurons can secrete when they are active can also influence the non-neuronal cells, such as the cells of the vascular system (the glia) and the inflammatory-immune cells (the microglia).

The activity of neurons can also be modified by substances released from the non-neuronal cells of the central or peripheral nervous system, substances often termed *neuromodulators.* This same term, however, is frequently applied to the effects of neuron-produced transmitter substances whose mechanisms of action and whose time course of effect differ from those of the classic junctional neurotransmitter acetylcholine.

The current research on neurotransmitters and neuromodulators pertinent to drugs and alcohol is devoted to (1) understanding how exposure to addictive drugs may regulate the genes that control the synthesis, storage, release, and metabolism of known neurotransmitters; (2) identifying new substances that may be recognized as neurotransmitters, whose effects may be related to the effects of or reactions to addictive drugs and alcohol; (3) understanding the molecular events by which neurons and other cells

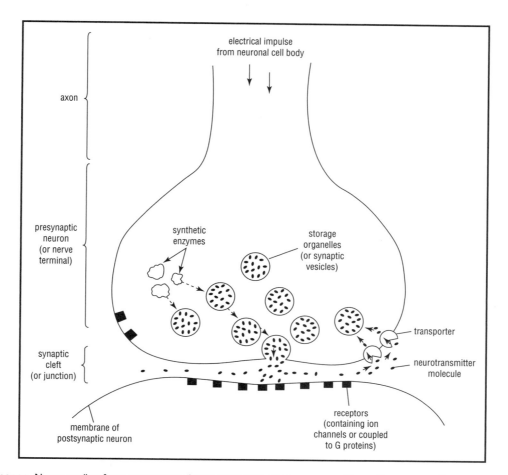

Figure 1. Synapse. Nerve ending from one neuron forms a junction, the synapse, with another neuron (the postsynaptic neuron). The synaptic junction is actually a small space, sometimes called the synaptic cleft. Neurotransmitter molecules are synthesized by enzymes in the nerve terminal, stored in vesicles, and released into the synaptic cleft when an electrical impulse invades the nerve terminal. The electrical impulse originates in the neuronal cell body and travels down the axon. The released neurotransmitter combines with receptors on postsynaptic neurons, which are then activated. To terminate neurotransmission, transporters remove the neurotransmitter back into the nerve terminal that released it. ILLUSTRATION BY GGS INFORMATION SERVICES. GALE, CENGAGE LEARNING

react to neurotransmitters in both short-term and long-term time frames (a process often termed *signal transduction*, which cells of the nervous system share with most other cells of the body) and how these processes may themselves be perturbed by the influence of addictive drugs and alcohol; and (4) understanding the operations of neuronal communication in an integrative context of the circuits that release and respond to specific transmitters, and the way in which these neuronal circuits participate in defined types of behavior, either normal or abnormal.

NEUROTRANSMITTER ORGANIZATION
There are three major chemical classes of neurotransmitters.

1. *Amino acid transmitters*: glutamate (GLU) and aspartate are recognized as the major excitatory transmitting signals; gamma aminobutyrate (GABA) and glycine are the major inhibitory transmitters. These transmitter substances occur in concentrations of one millionth part per milligram (μM/mg) protein. Since they are considered the most frequently employed transmitter substances, they have been linked to many aspects of the actions of addictive drugs.

2. *Aminergic transmitters*: acetylcholine, epinephrine (also called adrenaline), norepinephrine (also called noradrenaline), dopamine, serotonin, and histamine. The aminergic neurons constitute a minor population of neuronal

transmission sites, as reflected in the fact that their concentrations in the brain are roughly 1/1000th that of the amino acid transmitters or one billionth part per milligram (μM/mg protein). Because of their divergent anatomy (a few clusters of aminergic neurons may project onto literally millions of target neurons in many locations of the brain) and the ability of their synaptic signals to produce long-lasting effects, the aminergic neurons represent a very powerful subset of transmission conditions that is important to the effects of addictive drugs. Of particular relevance are the dopaminergic neurons—for their pertinence to the sites of reward for stimulants, opiates, and certain aspects of ethanol (alcohol) action—and the noradrenergic and serotonergic neurons—for their association with the phenomena of drug adaptation and tolerance.

3. *Neuropeptides*: of which there are dozens. Peptides are molecules containing a specific series of 2–50 amino acids, chemically arranged in a specialized "head-to-toe" chemical linkage known as a peptide bond. The order and number of the linked amino acids determine the linear structure of the peptide. In the nervous system, peptides, in general, occur in still lower concentrations than do the two prior classes of transmitter, namely at 10–100 trillionth part per milligram (pM/mg) protein. A revolutionary finding has emerged here in concepts of brain system interactions: It would now seem that neuropeptides are almost certainly never the sole signal to be secreted by a central neuron that contains such a signaling molecule, but rather accompany either an amino acid or an amine transmitter (at intrasynaptic terminal concentrations a thousand to a millionfold higher), such sites may even contain a second or third peptide as well.

Neuropeptides are of interest to the molecular and cellular mechanisms of addictive drug and alcohol action, because they may provide the postsynaptic receptors through which the drugs act (as in the case of the opiates and possibly the case for the natural benzodiazepines) or modify the effects of the presynaptic transmitters (as in the case of the peptide cholecystokinin that accompanies some forms of dopaminergic transmission, through which stimulants act and may modify responses to that amine if cosecreted).

Because of the ability to read the linear sequences of the amino acids, it has become clear that many of the neuropeptides share select small sequences and thus conceptually constitute "families" of peptides. For example, the opioid peptides all share one or more repeats of the amino-acid sequence tyrosine-glycine-glycine-phenylalanine; thus, each of the opioid-peptide genes leads to the expression of a different pre-prohormone by different sets of neurons of the central and peripheral nervous system. The existence of the shared amino-acid sequences implies that at some point in evolution, there may have been only one opioid-peptide signal, which was then duplicated and modified for use by the increasing number of neurons that came with the evolution of the mammalian brain. Such family relationships also exist for other peptide families (oxytocin/vasopressin; the tachykinin peptides; the secretin/glucagon-related peptides; the pancreatic polypeptide-related peptides), whose amino-acid sequences have shown great conservation over large domains of the evolutionary tree, attesting to the high signal quality of these molecules and the transductive mechanisms of their receptors. Other peptides, such as somatostatin and gonadotropin-releasing hormone, have no known family relationships as yet—but the discovery process here is probably not complete.

OTHER TRANSMITTER CANDIDATES

Other kinds of molecules may also be made within neurons to play auxiliary roles in intercellular transmission in the nervous system—from purines like adenosine triphosphate, lipids like arachidonic acid and prostaglandins, and steroids similar to those made and released by the adrenal cortex and the gonads. These substances may, in some cases, act as intracellular second messengers to underlie the effects of the aminergic and peptidergic transmitters (see below); they therefore have implicit relevance to the effects of the addictive drugs whether or not they may also serve as primary transmission signals.

Investigators have revealed that under some conditions active neurons may synthesize gaseous signals, such as nitric oxide and carbon monoxide, which can carry rapidly evanescent signals over short distances. The effects of these transmission-related substances will undoubtedly become of increasing importance to the explanations of the mechanisms of action or adaptation to the addictive drugs.

SIGNAL TRANSDUCTION ORGANIZATION

Aside from the chemistry of the neurotransmitter substances, further insight into their role in the actions of addictive drugs arises from the viewpoint of their synaptic physiology and their underlying mechanisms of signal transduction. When neurons respond to neurotransmitters, the ultimate changes in the excitability and metabolic activity of the responding neuron generally require changes into or out of the cell in the flow of ions (natural chemical elements of the extracellular fluid)—some with positive charge (sodium, potassium, and calcium) and others with negative charge (chloride).

As a general rule, it would appear that every neurotransmitter has more than one form of post-synaptic receptor through which its effects are mediated. Before the ability to characterize these receptors through molecular genetics, such receptor subtypes were identified on the basis of the comparative pharmacological potency of synthetic agonists or antagonists of the natural transmitter. With the advent of molecular cloning, however, an even finer subtyping would appear to be required, since many of the conclusions on receptor pharmacological patterns were based on analyses of tissue fractions that undoubtedly contained many molecular forms. A major effort in the future will be to link more explicitly the molecular and pharmacological characterization of neurotransmitter receptor subtypes and to determine which of them are most critical to the effects of, and adaptations to, addictive drugs.

Three major formats have been revealed for the transductive process.

1. *Directly regulated ion channels.* Here the ion channel to be opened is formed by the units of the receptor molecule itself, as recently established by direct cloning of several such receptorionophores. Such receptors are now known to be the motif of the nicotinic-cholinergic receptors of the neuromuscular junction and the central nervous system, as well as for the three types of glutamate receptor, the several isoforms of the GABAA receptor, the glycine receptor, and at least one form of a serotonin receptor.

Common features of these receptors are (a) they are composed of several (3–5) subunits, called monomers, that apparently may be combined in differing ratios (so-called multimeric recombinations) by various neurons to constitute the "holoreceptor"; (b) each monomer consists of four presumed transmembrane domains; and (c) discrete sections of the receptor monomer, either within the membrane or the cytoplasm, account for their voltage and chemical sensitivity, and for the ease and duration of openings in the ion channel.

2. *Indirectly regulated ion channel-receptors.* This form is based on the similarities between the visual pigment rhodopsin—the molecule used by photoreceptor neurons (rods, cones) to transduce light into signals to other neurons of the retina—and the beta-adrenergic receptor—one of the types of receptors regulated by the amine norepinephrine. This general form of transducing molecule was later found to be the form also used by the cholinergic muscarinic receptor, as well as by most serotonin and all known dopamine receptors, plus all the known peptide receptors.

The common features of this class are (a) the receptor is a single molecule, with seven transmembrane domains; (b) activation of these receptors by their signaling molecules leads to further interactions of the receptor with other large proteins, some of them enzymes, within or near the plane of the membrane; and (c) the eventual indirect regulation of the ion channel, either the opening or closing of the channel, is then mediated through small molecular intracellular second messengers, such as the calcium ion (Ca^{2+}) or the products of the associated enzymes, yielding intracellular second-messenger molecules, such as cyclic adenosine monophosphate (cAMP), or a lipid such as an inositol phosphate, diacyl-glycerol, or an arachadonic acid catabolite. The essential common second step of such transduction cascades is that the activated receptor interacts with a guanosine triphosphate (GTP)-binding protein (termed a *G-protein*) composed of three monomer subunits. The G-protein complex dissociates to activate the enzyme making the second messenger and, at the same time, hydrolyses the GTP and reassociates to end the cycle of signal generation. The second messenger consequences of this form of transduction, however, may be more enduring—activating one or more enzymes (protein kinases or phosphatases) that can add or remove phosphate groups on structural proteins or other enzymes, to activate or inactivate them. Such events can significantly shift the metabolic state of the responding cell and eventually regulate the expression of its specific genes. One such gene target is the immediate early genes of the nervous system, the protooncogenes, discovered some years ago because of the mutated forms used by oncogenic viruses, which induce cancer in non-neuronal cells.

3. *The receptor-enzyme.* This third major molecular motif of signal transduction has been elucidated recently; although it is already clear that this form does exist in the mammalian brain, it has been studied more in non-neuronal systems. This motif's characteristics are that the receptor for some peptides is itself the enzyme guanylate cyclase, which is directly activated by receptor-ligand binding, leads to an intracellular generation of cyclic guanosine monophosphate, and then to a cascade of events similar to that described for AMP.

SYNAPTIC INTERACTIONS

Most neurons receive synaptic input simultaneously from hundreds of other neurons, each of which employs its own mix of transmitters. The transductive processes underlying these individual events can influence the intensity and duration of the subsequent responses, thereby integrating incoming signals and providing the basis by which activity in assemblies of interconnected neurons results in behavioral output by the brain.

To gain insight into the basis by which the events of neurotransmission can lead to multi-neuronal programs of interaction, such as those required to initiate responding for an addictive drug, requires knowledge both of the anatomical substrate over which such programs of neuronal activity take place and of the effects of the neurotransmitters at each of the cellular elements of such an interactive ensemble of neurons.

See also **Addiction: Concepts and Definitions; Brain Structures and Drugs; Limbic System; Tolerance and Physical Dependence.**

BIBLIOGRAPHY

Barondes, S. H. (1993). *Molecules and mental illness.* New York: Scientific American Library. (New ed. [1999] New York: W.H. Freeman & Company.)

Bear, M. F., Connors, B. W., & Paradiso, M. A. (2006). *Neuroscience: Exploring the brain.* Philadelphia, PA: Lippincott, Williams & Wilkins.

Bloom, F. E. (1990). Neurohumoral transmission in the central nervous system. In A. G. Gilman et al. (Eds.), *Goodman and Gilman's the pharmacological basis of therapeutics,* 8th ed. New York: Pergamon. (2005, 11th ed. New York: McGraw-Hill Medical.)

Cooper, J. R., Bloom, F. E., & Roth, R. H. (1991). *The biochemical basis of neuropharmacology,* 6th ed. New York: Oxford University Press. (2002, 8th ed.)

Donnerer, J., & Lembeck, F. (2006). *The chemical languages of the nervous system.* Basel, Switzerland: Karger Publishers.

Korneman, S. G., & Barchas, J.D., Eds. (1993). *Biological basis of substance abuse.* New York: Oxford University Press.

Nieuwenhuys, R., Voogd, J., & van Huijzen, C. (2007). *The human central nervous system,* 4th ed. New York: Springer.

Watson, R. R., Ed. (1992). *Drugs of abuse and neurobiology.* Boca Raton, FL: CRC Press.

FLOYD BLOOM

NEUROTRANSMITTERS.

A neurotransmitter is any chemical substance (the first recognized was acetylcholine) that neurons (nerve cells) secrete to communicate with their target cells (glands, muscles, and other neurons). Neurotransmitters diffuse from their sites of release—from the presynaptic nerve terminal—across the synaptic cleft, to bind to receptors on the external surface of the postsynaptic cell. Activation of these receptors allows for the transmission of commands (excitation, inhibition, and other more complex forms of regulation) from the presynaptic neuron to the postsynaptic cell.

A neurotransmitter is released from a nerve ending, interacts with specific receptors, and is then either transported back into the presynaptic neuron or destroyed by metabolic enzymes in the synaptic cleft.

Chemically, neurotransmitters are amino acids, amines, or peptides. Peptide transmitters commonly coexist and may be cosecreted with amino acid or amine transmitters.

See also **Dopamine; Endorphins; Neurotransmission; Norepinephrine; Serotonin.**

BIBLIOGRAPHY

Barondes, S. H. (1993). *Molecules and mental illness.* New York: Scientific American Library. (New ed. [1999] New York: W.H. Freeman & Company.)

Bloom, F. E. (1990). Neurohumoral transmission in the central nervous system. In A. G. Gilman et al. (Eds.), *Goodman and Gilman's the pharmacological basis of therapeutics,* New York: Pergamon. (2005, 11th ed. New York: McGraw-Hill Medical.)

Cooper, J. R., Bloom, F. E., & Roth, R. H. (1991). *The biochemical basis of neuropharmacology,* 6th ed. New York: Oxford University Press. (2002, 8th ed.

Donnerer, J., & Lembeck, F. (2006). *The chemical languages of the nervous system.* Basel, Switzerland: Karger Publishers.

Korneman, S. G., & Barchas, J. D., Eds. (1993). *Biological basis of substance abuse.* New York: Oxford University Press.

Watson, R. R., Ed. (1992). *Drugs of abuse and neurobiology.* Boca Raton, FL: CRC Press.

FLOYD BLOOM

NEW YORK STATE CIVIL COMMITMENT PROGRAM.

The New York State Civil Commitment Program was the largest and most expensive drug treatment program of its kind during the 1960s and 1970s. Modeled after the California Civil Addict Program (CAP), it was established in the early 1960s in response to the dramatic rise of New York's heroin-addict population. The first reaction to the problem was expressed in the Metcalf-Volker Narcotic Addict Commitment Act of 1962, which sent arrested addicts to state mental-hygiene facilities for treatment. The total failure of this program prompted New York Governor Nelson Rockefeller to substantially modify and expand the program in 1966 by creating a Narcotic Addiction Control Commission (NACC). NACC was established to administer the New York State Civil Commitment Program, which involved a major statewide network of residential treatment centers.

Six different types of centers handled the following phases of treatment: examination and detention; detoxification, orientation, and screening; residential treatment and rehabilitation; temporary return; indefinite return; and halfway houses. Those who were eligible for treatment at a center included addicted individuals who had been arrested or convicted for a felony or misdemeanor, who had been involuntarily committed by their family or a friend, or who had volunteered to be treated. The treatment process consisted of a period of commitment within the institution, followed by community aftercare. Clients were under the control of the agency for an average of twenty-five months, of which ten months was spent in residence at the institution (Winick, 1988).

THE PROGRAM'S DEMISE

The program reached its peak in 1970 when twenty-four state facilities with 4,100 beds and a staff of over 5,000 provided services to 6,600 addicts. Followup studies of the program at this time were few, but they tended to indicate some positive outcomes (Winick, 1988). After 1970, the program began to lose public support and became a regular political target because of charges of cost overruns, allegations of staff brutality, and questionable administrative procedures (Winick, 1988). There was also a general change in philosophy that drew politicians away from supporting state-run institutions and toward recommending community-based treatment. In addition, political leaders began to move away from rehabilitation and toward harsh criminal sanctions for persons possessing or selling narcotics.

Governor Rockefeller announced in 1971 that he had lost confidence in the New York program and initiated a two-thirds cutback in budget and clients. The number of occupied beds steadily diminished because of these cuts and by 1979 the last two centers shut down (Winick, 1988). From 1966 to 1979, the program had cost approximately $1 billion. By the time the program was closed, each resident was costing an average of $29,000 per year, as compared with $8,500 for a resident in a therapeutic community and $14,500 for a prison inmate (Winick, 1988). In 1980, the state legislature repealed the civil commitment law.

WHY THE PROGRAM FAILED

Poor planning played a major part in the failure of the program (Winick, 1988). Due to political pressure, the first eight facilities opened in less than a year. Staffing was an immediate problem. The directors of the treatment facilities had inadequate administrative or clinical experience, since they were mostly political and civil service appointees (Inciardi, 1988). Facilities also were ill chosen and they too contributed to staffing deficiencies. NACC purchased underused prisons from the New York Department of Corrections and used them as treatment facilities. Many of the former prison guards were maintained as rehabilitation officers who performed both a counseling and custodial function. These officers were inadequately trained for their new positions, and they often disciplined program participants too harshly (Inciardi, 1988). The result was an environment that did not offer therapeutic benefits and was not conducive to behavioral change.

The screening of candidates for the program, moreover, was not consistent, and the criteria for completion of the program were ambiguous. The reentry and aftercare programs were equally ill equipped to handle the task at hand. The aftercare "officers" had no authority to arrest a client for violation of aftercare conditions, and their caseloads were too large to allow close supervision. As a consequence, a great number of parolees fled or stopped reporting (Winick, 1988).

Apart from programmatic failings, the civil commitment program began just as political leaders started to move away from rehabilitative models. Governor Rockefeller provides a telling example. By the early 1970s, when heroin addiction showed no signs of abating, Rockefeller decided that the criminal justice system should be directed more forcefully at drug users. In 1973, a group of statutes, popularly known as the Rockefeller laws, went into effect. These laws imposed mandatory prison sentences on those that possessed or sold drugs. These sentences, even for first-time offenders, were very long. Repeat offenders could receive life imprisonment. With the Civil Commitment Program unable to produce

reliable and cost-effective results, the impulse to incarcerate drug users proved almost irresistible.

See also **Civil Commitment; Coerced Treatment for Substance Offenders; Narcotic Addict Rehabilitation Act (NARA); Prisons and Jails; Rockefeller Drug Laws.**

BIBLIOGRAPHY

Cohen, P. J. (2004). *Drugs, addiction, and the law: Policy, politics, and public health.* Durham, NC: Carolina Academic Press.

Inciardi, J. A. (1988). Compulsory treatment in New York: A brief narrative history of misjudgment, mismanagement and misrepresentation. *Journal of Drug Issues, 18,* 4, 547–560.

Leukefeld, C.G., & Tims, F. M. (1988). Compulsory treatment: A review of findings. In: *Compulsory treatment of drug abuse: Research and clinical practice* NIDA Research Monograph 86. Rockville, MD: U.S. Department of Health and Human Services.

Lowinson, J. H. (2005). *Substance abuse: A comprehensive textbook.* Philadelphia, PA: Lippincott, Williams & Wilkins.

Tsimbinos, S. A. (1999). Is it time to change the Rockefeller drug laws? *St. John's Journal of Legal Commentary* 13, 613.

Winick, C. (1988). Some policy implications of the New York State Civil Commitment Program. *Journal of Drug Issues, 18,* 4, 561–574.

HARRY K. WEXLER
REVISED BY FREDERICK K. GRITTNER (2001)

NFLIS. *See* **National Forensic Laboratory Information System (NFLIS).**

NICOTINE. This is a psychoactive chemical substance found in tobacco products, including cigarettes, cigars, pipe tobacco, and smokeless tobacco such as chewing (spit) tobacco and oral and nasal snuff. The nicotine molecule is composed of a pyridine ring (a 6-membered nitrogen-containing ring) with a pyrrolidine ring (a 5-membered nitrogen-containing ring).

Nicotine can occur in two forms. The active form, called L-nicotine, is found in tobacco plants of the genus *Nicotiana*. These are chiefly South

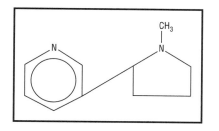

Figure 1. Chemical structure of nicotine. ILLUSTRATION BY GGS INFORMATION SERVICES. GALE, CENGAGE LEARNING

American plants of the nightshade family (*Solanaceae*)—annuals cultivated since pre-Columbian times for their leaves, especially *Nicotiana tabacum*. The inactive form, D-nicotine, is not present in tobacco leaves but is formed, to a small extent, in the combustion of tobacco during smoking. These two forms are stereoisomers, meaning that even though they are both nicotine, they have different three-dimensional structures. In pure form, nicotine is a colorless liquid, but it turns brown on exposure to air.

Nicotine is water-soluble and transfers from tobacco to cigarette smoke readily, because it vaporizes easily. Once it is in the body, conditions are ideal for rapid distribution to blood and tissues because nicotine is a weak base, and when un-ionized under alkaline conditions, such as those found in the blood stream, it crosses cell membranes easily.

The primary natural source of nicotine is the tobacco plant, but nicotine is also found in some amount in related plants. Small amounts are in foods of the nightshade family, such as tomatoes and eggplants. Consumption of nicotine has not been limited to the use of plants in which it naturally occurs. In 1828, the German scientists Posselt and Reiman isolated nicotine from tobacco leaves, and since then it has been added to other products. For example, it is widely used as an insecticide in such products as Black Leaf 40, which contains 40 percent nicotine sulfate.

EFFECTS OF NICOTINE

The first pharmacological studies of nicotine were initiated in 1843 by Orfila. Nicotine is an alkaloid that affects major organs, such as the heart and brain. It also affects the body at the cellular level.

Effects in the Body. The actions of nicotine in a human body are complex. They depend on the amount of nicotine given, the route of administration (e.g., by mouth or intravenously), the time over which the dose is given, and the individual's history of exposure to nicotine. In high doses, nicotine produces nausea, vomiting, convulsions, muscle paralysis, cessation of breathing, coma, and circulatory collapse. Such high doses are seen after accidental absorption of a nicotine-containing insecticide or an overdose of nicotine.

In lower doses, such as those used by people who consume tobacco products, the effects are very different. They include a speed up in heart rate and blood pressure; increased force of contraction of the heart; constriction of blood vessels in the skin, producing cool, pale skin; constriction of blood vessels in the heart; relaxation of skeletal muscles; increased body metabolic rate; and the release of hormones such as epinephrine (adrenaline), norepinephrine, and cortisol into the bloodstream. Nicotine's effects on the brain are very complex because nicotine works in part by enhancing the release of chemicals that transmit information from one neuron to another (neurotransmitters) by brain cells. For example, nicotine enhances the release of dopamine, which may produce pleasure; norepinephrine, which may suppress appetite; acetylcholine, which produces arousal; serotonin, which may reduce anxiety; and beta endorphin, which may reduce pain. The development of addiction to nicotine in tobacco users is attributed in part to many of the effects of nicotine that people find desirable.

Effects of Nicotine in Cells. Nicotine binds (attaches) to receptors on cell membranes that normally bind a neurotransmitter called acetylcholine. Acetylcholine, like other neurotransmitters, is a chemical released by nerve endings in the body that binds to certain receptors on cells and activates them. The activated cells communicate messages to other nerves or produce specific actions on body organs. Nicotine activates only certain of the receptors that bind acetylcholine. These receptors are now called nicotinic cholinergic receptors. Using the selective action of nicotine on cholinergic receptors, scientists are able to observe their activity separately from muscarinic cholinergic receptors, receptors activated by a chemical called muscarine.

Nicotinic cholinergic receptors are located at the ganglia in the autonomic nervous system, where there are specialized areas for communications between nerves, in the adrenal gland, at the neuro-muscular junctions, where nerves attach to and activate muscles, and in many parts of the brain.

The greatest number of nicotine cholinergic receptors in the brain are found in the hypothalamus, hippocampus, thalamus, midbrain, brain stem, and many parts of the cerebral cortex. Nicotine acts on sensory receptors, including those that mediate pain sensations. The effects of nicotine on these specific receptors have been an important tool in studying the effects of neurotransmitters on cell receptors and on the nervous system as a whole. In addition, these studies provide information about the widespread effects of nicotine introduced into the body during tobacco use.

DEVELOPMENT OF PHYSICAL DEPENDENCE ON NICOTINE

Nicotine is the chemical substance responsible for physical dependence on tobacco products. During the development of physical dependence on a drug such as nicotine, brain chemistry and function change. They return to normal in the presence of nicotine and come to depend on the drug for normal function.

The change that results in normal function in the presence of nicotine is called neuroadaptation or tolerance. When tolerance develops after a period of use of nicotine, or of any drug, the same dose produces less of an effect than previously. Tolerance develops to many of the effects of nicotine. It is well-known that people smoking their first cigarette often experience nausea and vomiting. However, after repeated exposure to cigarette smoke, these effects disappear. Their disappearance is the development of tolerance to the toxic effects of nicotine in the cigarette smoke. Tolerance also develops to the more desirable effects of nicotine such as pleasure and alertness.

The development of tolerance is associated with changes in the brain, such as an increased number of nicotinic cholinergic receptors found in the brains of smokers studied at autopsy. The changes in the brain correspond to a state in which the tolerant brain comes to depend on nicotine for

normal functioning. This state is called physical dependence.

Physical dependence also means that abstinence or withdrawal symptoms occur when a person who has taken a drug on a regular basis stops taking it. Physical dependence on nicotine has been clearly demonstrated. Thus a person who stops using tobacco after his or her body has adapted to the presence of nicotine will experience withdrawal symptoms in the form of irritability, restlessness, drowsiness, difficulty concentrating, impaired job performance, anxiety, hunger, weight gain, sleep disturbances, slow down in heart rate, and a strong urge for nicotine. In general, withdrawal symptoms are opposite to the effects produced by nicotine when a person who is not tolerant uses it. Thus a person will start using tobacco primarily to experience the desired effects of nicotine, but once the addiction develops, use of tobacco may be chiefly to prevent the emergence of unpleasant withdrawal symptoms. Use of a drug to prevent withdrawal is common in people who are addicted to a drug.

ABSORPTION OF NICOTINE FROM TOBACCO

Nicotine, which is absorbed into the body when tobacco products are used, can be absorbed by different routes and at different rates. Some products deliver nicotine in smoke that is inhaled. In tobacco smoke, nicotine is present in droplets that also contain water and tar. These droplets are carried by gases that include carbon monoxide, hydrogen cyanide, and nitrogen oxides. Such suspended droplets carried by gas are called an aerosol. When the aerosol is inhaled, the droplets are deposited in the small airways of the lungs, from which nicotine is absorbed into the blood stream. After absorption through the lungs, blood containing nicotine moves into the heart and then into the arterial circulation, including the brain. Nicotine reaches the brain within 10 to 15 seconds after a puff on a cigarette. This rapid delivery of nicotine to the brain produces more intensive effects than following slower delivery and provides the close temporal link between smoking and the development of addiction.

Nicotine is absorbed into the body in other ways. It can be absorbed in the mouth even if not inhaled in pipe or cigar smoke. In addition, not all tobacco products deliver nicotine through smoke. Chewing tobacco consists of shredded tobacco or plugs of tobacco that are enhanced with licorice and other flavorings. These products are periodically chewed, and the saliva generated is spat out, hence the term *spit tobacco*. Oral snuff is finely cut tobacco. A portion of oral snuff, called a pinch, is placed between the lip and the gum. Nicotine is absorbed from these forms of tobacco more slowly than from inhaled smoke, but the total amount absorbed is similar. Nasal snuff is finely powdered tobacco that is sniffed into the nose, where nicotine is rapidly absorbed.

DOSES OF NICOTINE TAKEN IN TOBACCO

The dose of nicotine absorbed from a cigarette is on average about 1 milligram (mg). The average user smokes about 25 cigarettes a day, an average nicotine intake of 20 to 30 mg daily. The average amount of nicotine absorbed from chewing tobacco or snuff per day is similar to that obtained from cigarettes. A person who smokes 25 cigarettes a day will absorb about 200 grams of nicotine in 20 years of smoking.

NICOTINE-CONTAINING MEDICATIONS

Nicotine is available as a medication, used to assist people in quitting smoking. These medications are meant to provide nicotine to smokers as a substitute for nicotine formerly consumed from tobacco use. Nicotine medications reduce withdrawal symptoms and increase the likelihood that the individual will quit tobacco use. Two forms of nicotine medication are currently available. Nicotine chewing gum (nicotine polacrilex, also known as Nicorette) consists of nicotine in a gum that slowly releases nicotine during chewing. Each gum is typically chewed for about 30 minutes. People chew up to 16 pieces per day when trying to quit smoking.

Nicotine patches are applied to the skin. They release nicotine slowly through the skin over 16 or 24 hours, depending on the patch used.

Both forms of nicotine-replacement medication deliver doses of nicotine equivalent to that taken in by the average tobacco user. Nicotine chewing gum delivers about 1 to 2 mg per piece. Nicotine patches deliver from 5 to 21 mg, depending on the patch and its strength.

ELIMINATION OF NICOTINE FROM THE BODY

Nicotine in the body is eliminated primarily by breakdown by the liver. The rate of breakdown is such that the level of nicotine in the blood falls about one-half after two hours. This rate is also known as a half-life of two hours. The primary breakdown product of nicotine is cotinine. Cotinine levels in the body are about 10 times higher than those of nicotine. The half-life of cotinine is 16 hours, and cotinine persists in the body for 4 days after a person stops smoking. Cotinine levels can be measured as an indicator of how much nicotine a person is taking in.

NICOTINE ADDICTION

Addiction to nicotine is well documented. The development and characteristics of nicotine addiction are described in detail in a report from the U.S. Surgeon General published in 1988. In this report, *The Health Consequences of Smoking: Nicotine Addiction*, the surgeon general presents criteria for nicotine addiction including the following:

1. Highly controlled or compulsive use. Smokers have great difficulty abstaining. Seventy percent of the 45 million smokers in the United States today report that they would like to quit and can not.

2. Psychoactive effects. Nicotine, as described earlier in this article, has pronounced effects on the brain.

3. Drug-reinforced behavior. Tobacco use is motivated by a desire for the effects of nicotine. People do not smoke cigarettes that do not contain nicotine. Very few people choose to smoke cigarettes that deliver very low doses of nicotine.

Other factors lead to the conclusion that nicotine is addictive:

1. It is used despite harmful effects. Most people know that smoking is harmful to their health and continue to smoke. Many people who have nicotine-related diseases are still unable to quit.

2. Relapse following abstinence. Most smokers can quit for a few days or even weeks (abstinence), but most of these smokers return to smoking within a month. Typically, it takes

four or five attempts before a smoker is successful at quitting permanently.

3. Recurrent drug cravings. Most smokers have an intense craving or urge to smoke when they have not smoked for some period of time.

4. Tolerance

5. Physical dependence

6. Pleasurable effects

The last three factors were described previously.

Smokers carefully regulate nicotine intake to maintain desired levels of nicotine in the body. Such careful regulation is further evidence that nicotine is addictive. Smokers keep the amount of nicotine obtained from cigarettes constant in two ways.

1. When people are given cigarettes that are labeled as low-yield (see tobacco history for detailed discussions of yields), they smoke more intensively to obtain the same dose of nicotine they were used to obtaining from the higher-yield cigarettes.

2. When they are forced to cut down on the number of cigarettes they smoke each day, they will take in more nicotine per cigarette. Thus when smoking is restricted, smokers tend to maintain the nicotine in their bodies at close to levels maintained during unrestricted nicotine intake.

BEHAVIORAL ASPECTS OF TOBACCO ADDICTION

People continue to smoke both because they enjoy the direct drug effects of nicotine and because use of nicotine becomes associated with other pleasures through learning—for instance, when the pleasurable effects of nicotine occur repeatedly in the presence of specific cues or events in the environment. Eventually, those cues and events become a signal to smoke. For example, people often smoke after meals, while drinking a cup of coffee or an alcoholic beverage, during a break from work, while talking on the phone, or while with friends who smoke. After smoking in these situations hundreds of times, the user may find that these situations themselves produce a powerful urge for a cigarette.

There are other learned pleasures that keep people smoking independent of the pharmacological effects of nicotine. Handling of smoking materials, and the taste, smell, or feel of tobacco smoke in the throat, all can become associated with the effects of nicotine and then become pleasurable in themselves. A person who tries to quit must learn to give up not only the pharmacological actions of nicotine but also the aspects of smoking that have become pleasurable through learning. Urges aroused after learning an association between aspects of the environment and the pleasures of smoking prompt relapses in many people who have already overcome withdrawal from nicotine and quit tobacco use.

Smokers report many other reasons for their habit. For example, many smokers, particularly women, smoke to maintain lower body weight. Others seem to use tobacco to control mood disturbances, such as depression or anxiety.

COMPARISON OF ADDICTION TO NICOTINE AND OTHER DRUGS

Nicotine addiction is similar to and as powerful as addiction to other drugs, such as heroin, alcohol, and cocaine. All these drugs have psychoactivity and produce pleasure. They increase the likelihood that people will spend time looking for them and engaging in rituals while taking them and that users will continue to take them in the face of risk to their well-being and health. The psychoactivity of nicotine is subtle and does not interfere with normal functioning in daily life. Thus nicotine's psychoactivity differs from that of heroin and cocaine, which produces more intense euphoria and may be disruptive to everyday functioning. Despite this difference, nicotine is addictive. A subtle psychoactive effect, especially when experienced with each puff of smoke, taken hundreds of times a day, exerts a powerful effect on behavior over time. The magnitude of effect becomes apparent when each puff of cigarette is considered as a dose of nicotine. A smoker who takes 8 puffs per cigarette and smokes 20 cigarettes per day is receiving up to 160 doses of nicotine per day. The dosing is equivalent to 58,400 doses a year, or 1,168,000 doses after 20 years of smoking.

When difficulty in quitting and relapse after attempting to quit are compared, it becomes apparent that nicotine is even more addictive than other drugs of abuse. Ninety percent of all people who smoke cigarettes are addicted and have difficulty quitting. In contrast, only about 10 percent of people who drink alcohol at all have difficulty controlling use and would be classified as addicted. The percentage of occasional versus addicted users of heroin and cocaine is not known, but when multidrug users are asked about which drug they would have most difficulty giving up, the choice is most commonly nicotine (that is, cigarettes). Relapse rates among adults after cessation of alcohol, heroin, and tobacco use are similar.

NICOTINE ADDICTION IN YOUTH

Ninety percent of all tobacco users begin smoking before the age of 20. The earlier in life one starts smoking, the more likely he or she is to become a regular smoker and the more cigarettes he or she will smoke as an adult. The development of addiction in youth involves a series of steps including

- a trying stage
- experimentation
- regular smoking
- nicotine addiction

The typical interval between trying and addiction is 2 to 3 years.

Initially, young people smoke for social and psychological reasons. The motivations include the influence of parents and friends who are smokers, and the positive images of smoking perpetuated in television and movies and in advertisements in magazines, at music and sports events, and on billboards. Personal factors also play a role. Some include poor school performance, low self-esteem, poor self-image, sensation seeking, rebelliousness, failure to take seriously the adverse effects of tobacco use, and depression or anxiety. While early stages of smoking usually consist of occasional sessions with friends, tolerance develops and withdrawal symptoms are experienced between cigarettes as smoking becomes more frequent. Many youths report withdrawal symptoms and difficulty quitting. They consider themselves addicted to tobacco.

TREATMENT OF NICOTINE ADDICTION

Treatment of nicotine addiction is discussed in the articles entitled *Treatment: Tobacco.* The approach may be summarized as follows. Initial therapy usually does not include drugs. Smokers are encouraged to pick a day and just stop (go cold turkey). Some smokers participate in formal behavioral therapies, such as those available in smoking-cessation clinics. Those who are unable to stop on their own or with behavior therapies are more likely to be highly addicted to nicotine and are candidates for pharmacological (drug) therapy. The main drug therapies for smoking are nicotine-containing medications such as chewing gum or transdermal (skin) patches.

See also **Addiction: Concepts and Definitions; Adolescents and Drug Use; Reward Pathways and Drugs; Tobacco: Smokeless; Tolerance and Physical Dependence; Withdrawal: Nicotine (Tobacco).**

BIBLIOGRAPHY

Benowitz, N. L. (1988). Pharmacologic aspects of cigarette smoking and nicotine addiction. *New England Journal of Medicine, 319*, 1318–1330.

George, T. P.. (2006). *Medication treatments for nicotine dependence.* Boca Raton, FL: CRC Press.

Maldonado, R.. (2003). *Molecular biology of drug addiction.* Totowa, NJ: Humana Press.

Naff, C. F.. (2007). *Nicotine and tobacco.* San Diego, CA: ReferencePoint Press.

Novartis Foundation. (2006). *Understanding nicotine and tobacco addiction.* Hoboken, NJ: Wiley.

U.S. Surgeon General. (1988). *The health consequences of smoking: Nicotine addiction.* Washington, D.C.: U.S. Government Printing Office.

NEAL L. BENOWITZ
ALICE B. FREDERICKS

NICOTINE DELIVERY SYSTEMS FOR SMOKING CESSATION.

The majority of people who smoke want to stop; however, many find this task difficult due to their dependence on nicotine. The most likely cause for relapse early in a quit attempt is the occurrence of tobacco or nicotine withdrawal symptoms such as urges to smoke (craving) and mood disturbances. Smokers intuitively know that the most effective way to relieve such symptoms is by smoking a cigarette (relapse), and so dependence is perpetuated.

Six different nicotine delivery systems are licensed for smoking cessation, usually referred to as nicotine replacement therapy (NRT). The rationale for using NRT is to provide a temporary supply of clean nicotine (i.e., without the disease-causing agents found in tobacco smoke) to help ease the severity of tobacco withdrawal symptoms. Tobacco withdrawal symptoms are generally worst in the first two to four weeks after stopping smoking, but smokers are advised to use NRT for at least eight to twelve weeks. Although NRT is not a magic bullet, it nearly doubles the likelihood of long-term abstinence, and no difference in efficacy is observed between products. Such an effect on abstinence is independent of the intensity of behavioral support provided.

NRT products typically provide less nicotine than the average smoker obtains from cigarettes, and nicotine plasma concentrations are usually half those achieved from smoking. These products also provide nicotine more slowly than cigarettes, with time to reach peak plasma concentration longer than that observed after cigarette smoking. These pharmacokinetic differences may partially explain why NRT does not reduce withdrawal symptoms as effectively as cigarettes.

Despite evidence for the effectiveness of NRT, some smokers are reluctant to use it. One such barrier is the incorrect belief that nicotine is the main component in tobacco smoke responsible for smoking-related disease. Other barriers include beliefs that NRT is ineffective or not required, having heard of other smokers who have successfully quit unaided. Some smokers have tried NRT in the past and found it unhelpful. Common reasons for this failure are unrealistic expectations of how NRT works, incorrect use, and discontinuing the use of the product too early in the recovery period.

PRODUCTS AVAILABLE AS OF 2008

Nicotine Chewing Gum. Nicotine chewing gum was the first NRT developed and licensed for smoking cessation. The nicotine within the gum resin is released when chewed and absorbed via the buccal mucosa (lining of the mouth). For optimal use, the gum is chewed until a hot peppery taste is experienced, and then the gum is placed in the side of the mouth to maximize buccal absorption of nicotine. This process, known as the chew-park-chew technique, is then repeated over some thirty minutes.

The gum is available in two strengths, containing two or four milligrams of nicotine. People who are highly dependent (e.g., smoke their first cigarette of the day within thirty minutes of waking) should use the higher strength formulation. Approximately half of the nicotine contained within the gum is absorbed.

Nicotine Transdermal Patch. The transdermal patch provides a simple and discreet method of delivering a continuous, controlled nicotine dose. Two types of patches are available (sixteen and twenty-four hour delivery systems) with equal efficacy, and no evidence favors either system. Smokers should generally start on the highest strength patches and use these for eight weeks. During the following four weeks lower dose patches are available for weaning, although weaning is not strictly required. High dose (e.g., 42mg/24 hour versus 21mg/24 hour standard dose) patch use shows a modest treatment benefit over standard dose. However, this treatment may be reserved for smokers with high severity of tobacco dependence. Skin irritation is the most common side effect, so users should be informed to rotate the site of application daily.

Nicotine Nasal Spray (NNS). Nicotine nasal spray delivers nicotine in a way that produces blood concentrations that most closely resemble those following smoking, with peak plasma concentration of nicotine reached in about five to ten minutes. Each dose (one spray in each nostril) provides one milligram of nicotine. Some studies have shown NNS to be particularly helpful in highly dependent smokers. Disadvantages of NNS are commonly reported adverse effects (burning sensation in the nose, runny nose, watering eyes, sneezing, and cough), which are often a barrier to further use. However, informing people of such effects and reassuring them that they will become tolerant to these effects in a short time may mitigate early discontinuation of treatment.

Nicotine Inhaler. The inhaler is a small plastic tube containing a replaceable nicotine cartridge. Nicotine vapour is released on puffing. Despite the product name nicotine is not inhaled into the lungs but absorbed through the lining of the mouth. With ideal use (puffing on the inhaler for twenty minutes) up to two milligrams of nicotine can be absorbed, thereby reaching the amount of nicotine supplied by one cigarette. As with nicotine gum, lozenge, and sublingual tablets, a peak plasma nicotine concentration is reached within twenty to thirty minutes. The inhaler may be beneficial to people who miss the behavioral and sensory aspects of smoking.

Sublingual Tablets (Microtabs). These small tablets, containing two milligrams of nicotine, are designed to be placed under the tongue where they dissolve slowly over twenty to thirty minutes. Approximately half of the nicotine contained in these tablets is absorbed. This product is suitable for all smokers and one or two tablets can be used on an hourly basis. Advantages of this product are that it is small and discrete and is a good option for those that cannot chew gum (e.g., people with dentures, or poor dentition, commonly found in older smokers).

Lozenges. The lozenges are available in high and low strengths, which differ in nicotine content depending on the manufacturer (e.g., Novartis: 2 mg and 1 mg; GlaxoSmithKline: 4 mg and 2 mg). Like the nicotine gum the higher strengths are recommended for highly dependent smokers. Lozenges are generally easy to use.

With all oral NRT products (gum, sublingual tablet, lozenge, inhaler), nicotine is absorbed across the lining of the mouth. It is, therefore, important to ensure correct usage of these products to maximise nicotine delivery. Incorrect use of oral products, for example, chewing gum too vigorously, usually results in more nicotine being swallowed. Doing so is not hazardous but reduces the efficacy of the product because swallowed nicotine is not systemically absorbed (due to high first pass liver metabolism from nicotine absorbed from the gut) and increases the likelihood of adverse effects such as local irritation of the throat and esophagus from nicotine often results in heartburn or hiccups. Also common to oral NRT products is an initial unpleasant, irritating taste, which may be a barrier to correct use. Users of such products should be warned of this effect and assured that tolerance to this taste develops after a short period

(usually a few days). While these products can be used on a regular (for example, hourly) basis, they may be used either more frequently and/or when urges to smoke are more intense.

COMBINING NRT PRODUCTS
NRT products can be safely combined and such use increases the odds of stopping smoking compared with using a single product. This advice contradicts some NRT product labelling that often states the contrary, that patients must use only one nicotine product at a time. Smokers should be informed of this contradiction when a clinician advocates combination therapy. A combination strategy usually combines a patch with a faster acting product for relief of breakthrough craving. The increase in effectiveness may be due to either higher nicotine levels or the additional sensory replacement achieved with the second product.

SAFETY OF NRT
Many smokers are concerned about the safety of using nicotine replacement products to quit smoking. Despite its addictive properties, nicotine has not been linked to the pathogenesis of respiratory disease, atherosclerosis, or carcinogenesis. Nicotine exposure increases heart rate and causes vasoconstriction of some blood vessels, which has led to concern when using NRT in patients with cardiovascular disease. However, controlled studies have demonstrated that, even in groups of smokers at high risk of cardiovascular disease, the use of NRT products does not increase the likelihood of acute coronary syndromes. NRT use in acutely ill patients has not been studied in detail; however, such treatment is a lesser hazard than continued smoking.

LONG-TERM USE
NRT is generally used for up to three months, although a small proportion of patients may need to continue to use it for longer. Of those who start NRT, 5 percent will generally continue to use it for up to a year. Patients who use NRT for longer are typically highly dependent smokers, so long-term NRT may be necessary to help them maintain long-term abstinence. Such long-term use has not been linked to any adverse outcomes.

Despite the strength of evidence supporting the use of NRT, it is not a panacea for smoking cessation. At most, the long-term abstinence rates are about 20 percent. This outcome leaves people to wonder what makes the cigarette a better delivery system than currently available NRT products. The speed of nicotine delivery and total nicotine dose may be part of the answer; however, even nicotine given intravenously (simulating the rapid absorption achieved from a cigarette) does not completely remove urges to smoke. Research suggests that other, non-nicotine, components of tobacco smoke may have a role to play in reinforcing properties of smoking. These components include sensory and behavioral cues (e.g., the sensory effects of smoke in the mouth and throat and the action of puffing on a cigarette) and other chemicals that may increase the effect of nicotine on the mesolimbic dopaminergic pathway (the main pathway in the brain assumed to be responsible for dependence on tobacco and other addictive drugs).

New nicotine delivery systems are in development. Some aim to provide greater and faster nicotine delivery (e.g., NicoNovum oral pouch and mouth spray), whereas others are trying to combine nicotine with the sensory and behavioral components of smoking (e.g., Ruyan e-cigarette). Such products are hoped to provide greater withdrawal relief than products available as of 2008 and help more smokers to stop permanently. In the meantime, use of available NRTs should be encouraged and if used correctly will assist many smokers to achieve their goal of long-term abstinence.

See also **Tobacco: Dependence; Tobacco: Medical Complications; Tobacco: Smoking Cessation and Weight Gain.**

BIBLIOGRAPHY

McEwen, A., Hajek, P., McRobbie, H., & West, R. (2006). *Manual of smoking cessation: A guide for counsellors and practitioners.* Oxford: Blackwell.

McRobbie, H., & Hajek, P. (2001). Nicotine replacement therapy in patients with cardiovascular disease: Guidelines for health professionals. *Addiction, 96*(11), 1547–1551.

National Institute of Clinical Excellence. (2002). *Guidance on the use of nicotine replacement therapy (NRT) and bupropion for smoking cessation.* London: National Institute of Clinical Excellence.

Rose, J. E., Behm, F. M., Westman, E. C., & Johnson, M. (2000). Dissociating nicotine and nonnicotine components of cigarette smoking. *Pharmacology, Biochemistry, and Behavior, 67*(1), 71–81.

Stead, L. F., Perera, R., Bullen, C., Mant, D., & Lancaster, T. (2008). Nicotine replacement therapy for smoking cessation. *Cochrane Database of Systematic Reviews* (1), CD000146.

HAYDEN MCROBBIE
SIMON THORNLEY

NIGERIA.

BACKGROUND

With 140 million inhabitants (United Nations Development Programme [UNDP], 2007) Nigeria is by far the most populous country in Africa, accounting for one out of five people in the continent. The population is projected to grow to 176 million by 2015 and more than 300 million by 2050. About half of all Nigerians are under twenty-five years of age and the urban population more than doubled in thirty years, growing from 23 percent in 1975 to 48 percent in 2005. This relative youthfulness of the population and the rapid rate of urbanization (largely due to rural-to-urban migration) have major implications for psychoactive substance abuse in the country.

The use of licit and illicit drugs for a variety of social and psychological reasons is very much a feature of life in contemporary Nigeria. Alcohol is consumed more often than other drugs (especially in the non-Muslim regions of the country) but other substances—tobacco products, cannabis, amphetamine-type stimulants, cocaine, heroin, prescription drugs, and inhalants—are increasingly being used, especially among young people in urban areas.

Though there has been a relatively long tradition of research on the production, supply, and use of addictive substances, a lot remains to be known about the level of use of these substances in the general population and the consequences of their use on individuals, communities, and the society at large.

ALCOHOL

Although illicit drugs have focused the attention of policymakers and the public today, concerns about the role of alcohol in health and social problems in

Nigeria predate the country's independence in 1960 and were raised by both colonial administrators and local chiefs (Pan, 1965). Much of what is known today about drinking habits is based on surveys in the non-Muslim populations of central and southern Nigeria. There is agreement from several studies that at least 50 percent of adult males in Nigeria consume alcohol, with some surveys showing higher consumption rates (Ibanga, 2005; Gureje et al., 2007; Obot, 2007).

Many western commercial beverages are available in the country but beer is the most popular drink. Traditional homemade beverages (especially palm wine, fermented drinks, and distilled products) may account for more than 50 percent of the drinking by some people, particularly among those in rural areas and the impoverished in urban settings.

An analysis performed by the World Health Organization (WHO) of alcohol per capita consumption (APC) places Nigeria at the high end, with an adult APC of ten liters in 2001, the second highest in Africa after Uganda (WHO, 2004). What this figure means is that although a high proportion of Nigerians (especially women) do not drink at all, the drinkers among them consume large amounts of alcohol when they drink. Indeed drinking in Nigeria (as in many developing countries) is characterized by a pattern of heavy episodic consumption that is common to both male and female drinkers.

This habit of drinking to intoxication results in injuries and an overall high burden of disease. Although no separate analysis has yet been conducted for Nigeria, the country belongs in the group of African countries with the highest levels of estimated detrimental effects attributable to alcohol (deaths and years of life lost) especially among men (Roerecke et al., 2008). Hospital admissions data indicate that harmful drinking also seems to have significant effects on the mental health of Nigerians and has been implicated in road traffic accidents and violence.

TOBACCO

There has been a longstanding local production of tobacco products, especially cigarettes and snuff, in Nigeria dating back to about 1912 when the Nigerian Tobacco Company (NTC) was established.

In 2000 the NTC merged with British American Tobacco (BAT) to form a company that today dominates a growing and unregulated cigarette market in Nigeria. The tobacco industry is supported by tens of thousands of local growers in the western and northern parts of the country and encouraged by favorable government policies.

Studies conducted in the 1970s and 1980s showed that more than 20 percent of adults were lifetime cigarette smokers (Obot, 1990). According to data compiled by WHO, 20 to 29 percent of boys and more than 10 percent of girls of high school age have smoked at least once. In a recent study by Oye Gureje et al. (2007) 17 percent of the adults (18 years and older) sampled randomly from across the country reported lifetime use of tobacco products and less than 4 percent were current users. Though findings from various studies are incomparable, what seems to be true is that a typical smoker in Nigeria smokes fewer cigarettes per year than a smoker in western countries, probably because of the cost involved.

Most Nigerian smokers are male but the use of snuff might be equally prevalent among adult males and females. Although there is little debate that tobacco use is associated with a wide array of health problems, few studies exist that link smoking with these problems in Nigeria. But there is bound to be more interest in smoking-related problems because of increased marketing and promotion activities by the tobacco industry.

CANNABIS

Among the illicit drugs used in Nigeria, cannabis has been around the longest, and public concerns about its abuse started soon after the country gained its independence. The use of the drug can be traced to the first generation of published papers on substance use (Asuni, 1964; Lambo, 1965). The plant, *Cannabis sativa*, was brought to the country by soldiers returning from the Second World War in North Africa and the Indian subcontinent (hence known locally as Indian hemp) in the 1940s (Asuni, 1964). Since then it has become highly domesticated, growing easily in the tropical and semitropical regions of the country and providing an avenue for illegal activities among many young people.

Cannabis has received overwhelming attention among illicit drugs partly because it has been around longer and also because of early studies linking its use to mental disorders. These studies showed that 8 to 20 percent of young people admitted into psychiatric hospitals had histories of cannabis use (e.g., Lambo, 1965). Later studies have confirmed the high prevalence of reported cannabis use among psychiatric inpatients and outpatients (Ohaeri & Odejide, 1993).

Studies among university students in the 1980s showed lifetime use of up to 8 percent, and 2 percent among secondary-school students. A recent general population survey of adults showed lifetime use of nearly 3 percent and less than 1 percent in the past year. Other studies in special populations, for example, school dropouts in urban areas, show much higher rates—as high as 10 percent in the past year and 8 percent in the past month (Obot et al., 2001). Like many other substances, including cocaine and heroin, cannabis seems to be a drug of choice of young people, especially those living in urban areas where access is much easier.

COCAINE, HEROIN, AND INJECTING DRUGS

It was not until the early 1980s that other illicit drugs began to make their mark in the country as commercial and consumer products. Although there had been anecdotal evidence of cocaine and heroin use during parties by "well placed Nigerians" and "expatriate workers" in the early 1980s (Ebie & Pela, 1981), it was not until the first arrest of a trafficker in 1982 that the two drugs became known by the Nigerian public (Obot, 2004). Since then and following what at times has been a significant role of Nigerians in the international drug trade (serving mostly as traffickers between producing and consuming countries), cocaine and heroin have entered into the national discourse on security issues, international relations, and criminal justice.

Like cannabis, information gathered from psychiatric hospital clients provided the warning signs that young Nigerians were not only involved in trafficking these drugs but also using them. In nontreatment samples almost all available studies show that approximately 1 percent of young people surveyed have used one or more of these drugs at least once, usually in their smokable forms or by inhalation (*chasing the dragon*).

Information regarding the use of drugs via injection is known today largely based on three studies funded by the World Health Organization and the United Nations Office on Drugs and Crime (UNODC) (Adelekan & Lawal, 2006). Twenty-one percent of more than 1,000 drug users interviewed had injected heroin, cocaine, or some other drug at least once, and 8 percent were current injectors. The studies did not show that drug injectors were more likely than non-injectors to be infected with HIV.

NONPRESCRIPTION USE OF SEDATIVES AND STIMULANTS

While there has been greater regulation of the manufacture, prescription, and sale of pharmaceutical products in recent years, limited availability and poor accessibility of professional health-care services have forced many to self-medicate with over-the-counter and prescription drugs, some of which have high abuse potentials. Many of the drugs used without prescription are tranquillo-sedatives (sleeping aids) and opioids or analgesics (to suppress pain). The abuse of pethidine (meperidine) by physicians and nurses was reported in the early 1980s and valium and codeine remain popular drugs of abuse.

In a recent general population survey of about 7,000 adults, 16 percent of males and 12 percent of the females interviewed reported lifetime nonprescription use of sedatives (Gureje et al., 2007). Unlike the use of other substances initiated in early adolescence, this study showed that prescription drug use started between twenty and forty years of age.

The use of drugs that stimulate the central nervous system is an old practice in Nigeria. One of the most culturally accepted addictive substances is the kola nut, the dried cotyledon of the local tree *Cola acuminata*, grown mostly in the south but chewed by adults across the country. The use of modern stimulants (known in different regions as *brain pills* or *sleepless pills*) was identified in the 1970s as a problem among young people who took dexamphetamines (Dexedrine) and Pro Plus (a preparation containing 50 milligrams of caffeine per tablet) as study aids (Oviasu, 1976). Other psychostimulants like pemoline, ACD (alleged to be a mixture of aspirin, codeine, and dexamphetamine), and native herbal preparations are also used by workers, long-haul drivers and students for increased energy and to stay awake (Ohaeri & Odejide, 1993). Like cannabis, stimulants were associated with mental illness among young users, especially males (Oviasu, 1976). A mental condition identified in Nigeria in 1960 and known as *brain fag syndrome* was suspected to be associated with the abuse of these drugs by students who sought relief from the mental fatigue that developed from studying for exams.

RESPONSE TO DRUG PROBLEMS

Laws against illicit drugs were enacted after Nigeria's independence, beginning with the Indian Hemp Decree of 1966 to the omnibus National Drug Law Enforcement Decree of 1989, and remain the basis of legislations. Stringent punishment for possession and use of cannabis, cocaine, and heroin has been at the center of these legislations (Obot, 1992). Nigeria is a signatory to all UN conventions on drug control and has also ratified the Framework Convention on Tobacco Control (FCTC), but it currently lacks a policy framework for controlling the sale of and harmful consumption of alcohol.

Demand for the treatment of drug and alcohol problems has been growing for many years but opportunities are still grossly limited. Although nonprofit organizations and religious groups are increasingly involved in the provision of services, most available treatment slots are still in psychiatric hospitals and only some of these have dedicated units.

Like other developing countries, Nigeria is struggling with many seemingly unyielding social problems and little attention is paid to substance use and dependence except for declarations of war against illicit drugs and sporadic activities on demand control—prevention of use and treatment of dependent individuals. However, like smoking, illicit drug use and harmful consumption of alcohol increases among Nigeria's growing population of young adults in urban settings. The country will have to come to terms with the health and social burden that substance abuse imposes on the society and seek effective ways to confront the problem.

See also **Africa; Foreign Policy and Drugs, United States; International Drug Supply Systems; Kenya; South Africa.**

BIBLIOGRAPHY

Adelekan, M. L., & Lawal, R. A. (2006). Drug use and HIV infection in Nigeria: A review of recent findings. *African Journal of Drug and Alcohol Studies, 5*(2), 117–128.

Asuni, T. (1964). Socio-psychiatric problems of cannabis in Nigeria. *Bulletin on Narcotics, 16*(2), 17–28.

Ebie, J. C., & Pela, O. A. (1981). Some sociocultural aspects of the problem of drug abuse in Nigeria. *Drug and Alcohol Dependence, 8*, 301–306.

Gureje, O., Degenhardt, L., Olley, B., Uwakwe, R., Udofia, O., Wakil, A., et al. (2007). A descriptive epidemiology of substance use and substance use disorders in Nigeria during the early 21st century. *Drug and Alcohol Dependence, 91*, 1–9.

Ibanga, A. K. J. (2005). The contexts of alcohol consumption in Nigeria. In I. S. Obot & R. Room (Eds.), *Alcohol, gender and drinking problems: Perspectives from low and middle income countries.* Geneva: World Health Organization.

Lambo, T. A. (1965). Medical and social problems of drug addiction in West Africa. *Bulletin on Narcotics, 17*(1), 3–13.

Obot, I. S. (1990). The use of tobacco products among Nigerian adults: A general population survey. *Drug and Alcohol Dependence, 26*(2), 203–208.

Obot, I. S. (1992). Ethical and legal issues in the control of drug abuse and drug trafficking: The Nigerian case. *Social Science and Medicine, 35*(4), 481–493.

Obot, I. S. (2004). Assessing Nigeria's drug control policy, 1994–2000. *The International Journal of Drug Policy, 15*, 17–26.

Obot, I. S. (2007). Nigeria: Alcohol and society today. *Addiction, 102*, 519–522.

Obot, I. S., Ibanga, A. K., Ojiji, O. O., & Wai, P. (2001). Drug and alcohol consumption by out-of-school Nigerian adolescents. *African Journal of Drug & Alcohol Studies, 1*(2), 98–109.

Ohaeri, J. U., & Odejide, A. O. (1993). Admissions for drug and alcohol-related problems in Nigerian psychiatric care facilities in one year. *Drug and Alcohol Dependence, 31*, 101–109.

Oviasu, V. O. (1976). Abuse of stimulant drugs in Nigeria: A review of 492 cases. *British Journal of Addiction, 71*, 51–63.

Pan, L. (1965). Alcohol in colonial Africa. Helsinki: Finnish Foundation for Alcohol Studies.

Roerecke, M., Obot, I. S., Patra, J., & Rehm, J. (2008). Volume of alcohol consumption, patterns of drinking and burden of disease in sub-Saharan Africa, 2002. *African Journal of Drug and Alcohol Studies, 7*(1) (in press).

United Nations Development Programme. (2007). *Human development report 2007/2008*. New York: UNDP.

World Health Organization. (2004). *Global status report on alcohol 2004*. Geneva: World Health Organization.

ISIDORE OBOT

NMDA (N-METHYL D-ASPARTIC ACID). *See* Receptor: NMDA (N-Methyl D-Aspartic Acid).

NORDIC COUNTRIES (DENMARK, FINLAND, ICELAND, NORWAY, AND SWEDEN). This article deals with alcohol, tobacco, and drugs in the Nordic countries situated at the northwest corner of Europe: Denmark, Finland, Iceland, Norway, and Sweden. Denmark is the southernmost of the Nordic countries; it has a land border with Germany in the south and is separated in the north from Norway by the Skagerrak strait and from Sweden by the Kattegat and Öresund straits. Since 2000 a bridge has also connected Denmark with Sweden. Norway lies farthest west on the Scandinavian Peninsula, separated mainly by mountains from Sweden that occupy the eastern side of the peninsula. Finland lies east of Sweden and has a land border with both Norway and Sweden in the north; in the west it is separated from Sweden by the Gulf of Bothnia. In the south the Gulf of Finland separates Finland from Estonia and in the east Finland has a nearly 1,300 kilometer land border with Russia. Iceland lies in the Atlantic Ocean about 1,000 kilometers west of Norway.

The history of Denmark goes back to the beginning of the Viking age, from approximately 800 to 1050. In 1397 the Kalmar Union brought together the thrones of Denmark, Norway, and Sweden under Queen Margrethe I of Denmark. Finland became a part of Sweden in the twelfth century. Sweden broke from the Kalmar Union in 1523 and developed into a powerful European nation. Norway remained in the union until 1814 when it was given to Sweden as a consequence of the Napoleonic wars. In 1809 Sweden lost Finland to Russia. Finland became independent in 1917. In 1905 Norway peacefully separated from Sweden.

Iceland, populated in the late ninth century, belonged to Denmark from 1262 to 1944 when it became independent.

The Nordic countries are quite homogenous with regard to population and language. Finland is an exception insofar as Finnish belongs to the Finno-Ugric language family, whereas the languages spoken in the other Nordic countries are considered Germanic. In all Nordic nations the principal church is Evangelical Lutheran, although many belong to the church only in name. As of 2008, a clear majority of the population lives in cities and towns, and about two-thirds of those employed work in the service sector. Less than 5 percent earn their livelihood from agriculture. In the Nordic countries, as in all industrialized European nations, this is the outcome of a pronounced migration of people from the countryside to towns and larger cities and from agriculture to industries and services. In 2006 the gross domestic product per capita was about 30,000 euros in the Nordic countries, with the exception of Norway where it was 42,000 euros. The Nordic nations are famous for their welfare state system. Welfare schemes are universal and they guarantee social and economic security and welfare services, which include health care, unemployment benefits, and education.

This entry will first give a brief historical overview of the appearance of alcoholic beverages, tobacco products, and other drugs in the Nordic countries. It will then examine the consumption and control of alcohol from about 1850, when home distilling was prohibited and the downward trend in alcohol consumption began. This is followed by an analysis of smoking and its control, from the late nineteenth through twentieth centuries, when mass-produced cigarettes became the most important way to smoke and consume tobacco. Illegal drugs are treated in a similar manner, starting with developments in the 1960s when recreational drug use began to spread to the Nordic countries. Differences in the regulation of alcoholic beverages, tobacco, and drugs will be addressed in the concluding section.

APPEARANCE OF ALCOHOLIC BEVERAGES, TOBACCO, AND DRUGS IN THE NORDIC COUNTRIES
During the Viking age, beer was the dominant alcoholic beverage in Nordic countries. At that

time beer was also an important beverage with meals and it was commonly consumed. The quality and alcohol content of Viking age beer were, however, lower than those of beer brewed in this century. Mead was also a popular alcoholic beverage, but it was later replaced by imported wine.

Wine is not produced in the Nordic countries, but the Vikings did become familiar with it during their journeys to the British Isles, Mediterranean countries, and Russia. As an imported product, wine was quite expensive and, therefore, its regular consumption did not spread among the common people. Like beer from the same period, the wine of the Middle Ages had low alcohol content, and transporting wine from central Europe to the Nordic countries only further worsened its quality. As a result, honey and spices were frequently added to wine to make it drinkable.

Beer continued to be the dominant alcoholic beverage in the Nordic countries until the eighteenth century. In the late seventeenth century distilled spirits first became known in the Nordic countries as a medicine. However, they quite rapidly transformed into a widely used intoxicant, soon replacing beer as the dominant alcoholic beverage. According to some estimates, the per capita consumption of distilled spirits in Sweden in the first half of the nineteenth century was about 40 liters or nearly 20 liters converted to 100 percent alcohol. At that time, the consumption of distilled spirits was also very high in other Nordic countries.

Smoked and smokeless tobacco became known in Europe in the late sixteenth century after Europeans had encountered and traded with Native Americans. The use of tobacco spread very quickly in Europe and reached the Nordic countries at the beginning of the seventeenth century. At that time, the most common tobacco products were chewing tobacco and powder tobacco for nasal inhalation. Moist snuff is another form of smokeless tobacco that became very popular in Sweden in the late eighteenth century when the habit of smoking was still uncommon, given the expense of producing cigars, cigarettes, and pipes. Smoking tobacco also needed a safe and ready source of fire. In the nineteenth century, however, pipe smoking became increasingly popular in the Nordic countries and paved the way for a great increase in smoking, one connected with the mass production of cigarettes and the development of safety matches later that same century.

Opium, morphine, and heroin arrived on the Nordic scene solely in the form of medicines at the end of the nineteenth century. Regarded as poisons and strong medications, they were soon placed under the control of pharmacies and the medical profession. In the Nordic countries the misuse of these medicines seems to have been limited to a few persons, primarily those who had easiest access to them, such as doctors and nurses. Morphine and heroin were used more extensively as cough medicines and painkillers in wartime. It was estimated in 1946, for instance, that during World War II some 100 to 200 former soldiers in Finland had become addicted to heroin. Otherwise, the framework for a control policy in this area may be said to have developed in international organizations such as the League of Nations and later the United Nations, in which international conventions aiming to control and criminalize the production, trade, and use of drugs for other than medical purposes were designed. When the Nordic countries became parties to these conventions, the abuse of drugs including cannabis was largely unknown in that part of the world.

USE AND CONTROL OF ALCOHOLIC BEVERAGES

In the eighteenth century the distilling of spirits was already controlled in the Nordic countries, not so much because of the adverse effects of drinking on public health or social order, but because distilling spirits competed with another important use of grain, namely to feed people and especially soldiers. At the beginning of the nineteenth century, restrictions on home distilling weakened, and along with the increase in drinking and peacetime after the Napoleonic wars, the consumption of distilled spirits came to be regarded more and more as a question of social order.

The mid-nineteenth century saw the birth of the temperance movement in the Nordic countries, with nationwide total prohibition as its ultimate goal. At that time, the Nordic countries also needed more and more tax revenue for several important purposes, such as building railways and other modern infrastructure. These two factors together resulted in the banning of home distilling in the Nordic countries in the mid-nineteenth century, with the purpose of moving the distilling of spirits into more controllable licensed distilleries.

In the second half of the nineteenth century the attempts to control the adverse social effects of drinking led to more stringent alcohol control measures. In Finland, for example, this meant that by World War I alcoholic beverages, with the exception of beer, were no longer available in the countryside. In towns, the Gothenburg system, designed to reduce private profit motives and to derive public revenues from the sale of alcoholic beverages as well as to control alcohol-related social problems, was spreading very quickly. The Gothenburg system had originated in the Swedish mining town of Falun in the 1850s. Starting in 1870, locally authorized liquor stores had also been established in Norway. As a direct result of these policy measures, distilled spirits and total alcohol consumption continued to decrease in all Nordic countries until World War I, which became a turning point in Nordic developments concerning alcohol.

In 1917 Denmark, because of the shortage of foodstuff, increased the tax on distilled spirits 12-fold and the tax on beer by 60 percent. This led to a dramatic decrease in spirits consumption, and in one year the share of beer in total alcohol consumption increased from 30 to 83 percent. At that time, wine's share of total Danish alcohol consumption was about 5 percent. The tax increase was followed by a decrease in alcohol-related problems and also the Danish temperance movement lost its rather strong foothold. Consequently, Denmark never established any prohibition acts or state alcohol monopolies, and public attitudes toward the drinking of alcoholic beverages focused, until the early twenty-first century, almost exclusively on the need for individual self-control and responsibility.

In Sweden in 1917, the Gothenburg system evolved into a system whereby local monopolies were granted exclusive rights to the sale of wine and distilled spirits. In addition, a monopoly on the production, import, and wholesale distribution of distilled spirits was established. After a referendum in 1922, in which the temperance movement lost, a unique system known as the Bratt system was introduced in Sweden. This system was based on

the use of a ration book that was forwarded to those citizens assumed to drink distilled spirits without causing social damage. Generally, ration books were issued only to men because married women were expected to share their husband's allocation. Unmarried women and young males had smaller monthly rations than adult men, whose share as a rule was set at 4 liters of distilled spirits per month. The minimum age for receiving a ration book was 25 years. The ration book permitted alcohol purchases in only one monopoly shop; all purchases were recorded in it and government authorities could also seize the book if they noted that circumstances warranted such. The Bratt system was eliminated in 1955 at the same time as a law came into effect permitting the sale of beer with greater alcohol content in Sweden.

Iceland introduced prohibition in 1915. In Finland and Norway, the shortage of food during World War I led to a nearly complete prohibition of alcoholic beverages. In Finland, a prohibition act was passed by a unanimous vote in parliament in 1907 but only became effective in 1919; it banned all beverages containing more than 2 percent ethyl alcohol by volume. Norway instituted a prohibition of distilled spirits and fortified wines after a nationwide referendum in 1919. The prohibition on fortified wines was revoked in 1923 and that on distilled spirits in 1927. In Finland, prohibition was repealed in 1932. In Iceland, prohibition lasted until 1922 with regard to wine and until 1935 with regard to distilled spirits; beer was prohibited until 1989.

After prohibition ended, Finland, Iceland, and Norway introduced an alcohol control system based on a comprehensive state alcohol monopoly, the restricted physical availability of alcoholic beverages, and high alcohol excise duties and prices. After the Bratt system, Sweden also adopted a similar kind of alcohol control system but with two separate monopolies: one for the off-premise retail sale of alcoholic beverages and one for their production, import, export, and wholesale distribution.

Nordic control systems have differed on how beer sales are controlled. In Norway, beer with greater alcohol content was sold in ordinary grocery stores until 1993, after which it has only been sold in the alcohol monopoly's outlets. In Finland, all beers were sold only in monopoly liquor stores until 1968, after which beer with a maximum alcohol content of 4.7 percent by volume has been sold in ordinary grocery stores. In Sweden, beer with a medium amount of alcohol was sold in groceries from 1965 to 1977, after which all beers over 3.5 percent alcohol by volume have been sold only in monopoly liquor stores.

During the period between World War I and II, Sweden experienced the highest alcohol consumption in the Nordic countries, about 3 liters per capita a year. In Finland, annual per capita alcohol consumption was just a little over 1 liter, the lowest figure among the Nordic countries at that time. Between the world wars, distilled spirits was still the most preferred alcoholic beverage category in the Nordic countries, with the exception of Denmark.

After World War II, alcohol consumption grew in the Nordic countries as in all Western industrialized nations until the mid-1970s. At that time, recorded annual alcohol consumption in Denmark reached 10 liters per capita. In Finland and Sweden, the corresponding figure was 6 liters, and in Norway and Iceland, about 4 liters. Besides economic growth, an increase in leisure time, migration, and other significant changes in living conditions as well as the increase in alcohol availability contributed to this growth. The number of retail outlets also increased, as did their hours of operation. Many regulations making the consumption of alcoholic beverages quite difficult in restaurants have been lifted and age limits for the purchase of alcoholic beverages have been lowered.

Since the mid-1970s recorded alcohol consumption in Denmark has decreased to 9 liters per capita a year. In Finland, it has increased to nearly 9 liters. If unrecorded alcohol use is added to the recorded statistics, total annual alcohol consumption in Denmark and Finland is approximately 10.5 liters, the same as in France and higher than in Italy. In 2006, annual recorded alcohol consumption was just over 5 liters in Iceland, Norway, and Sweden. When unrecorded alcohol consumption is added, total annual alcohol consumption in Sweden was 8 liters and in both Iceland and Norway about 6 liters per capita.

During the last three decades of the twentieth century the consumption of distilled spirits decreased and wine consumption increased in all Nordic countries. Beer consumption decreased in Denmark, stayed about the same in Sweden, and increased in Finland, Iceland, and Norway. These developments meant that as of 2008, the most preferred alcoholic beverage in all Nordic countries was beer, followed closely by wine in Denmark and Sweden.

Until the 1990s, changes in alcohol availability were mostly of domestic origin. After Finland and Sweden joined the European Union (EU) in 1995, and Iceland and Norway decided to participate in the European Economic Area agreement in 1994, mostly international developments molded the Nordic alcohol control system. In practice, this meant that the Nordic monopoly countries have lost their monopolies on the production, import, export, and wholesale distribution of alcoholic beverages.

European economic integration has also affected alcohol taxes as the creation of a single European market eliminated travelers' alcohol import quotas. This put pressure on the Nordic countries through border trade, as their neighboring EU countries had significantly lower alcohol excise duties and prices. Denmark, an EU member from 1973, decreased its taxes on beer and wine by 50 percent in the early 1990s, and in 2003 decreased its taxes on distilled spirits by 45 percent. After its neighbor Estonia became a member of the EU, Finland was forced to decrease its alcohol taxes by 33 percent on average. Likewise, Sweden and Norway felt the pressure to reduce their high alcohol taxes although they decreased them to a lesser extent than Denmark and Finland. As an island, Iceland has been able to maintain its excise duties on alcohol, which remain the highest in Europe.

Increased economic integration has led to further increases in alcohol consumption in the Nordic countries since the mid-1990s with the exception of older EU-member Denmark. Especially in Finland and Sweden, travelers' alcohol imports rose to a new high in the beginning of the twenty-first century. Furthermore, the possibilities for making private profits in the alcohol industry have increased and led to harsher competition in alcohol markets with increasing marketing and advertising of alcoholic beverages.

In the early twenty-first century alcoholic beverages are commonly used in the Nordic countries, with only 5 to 15 percent of the population reportedly abstaining from alcohol during the last 12 months. Among youngsters alcohol consumption is becoming more frequent from the age of 14 to 16, and at the age of 18 the rate of abstainers is almost the same as that among adults. No clear differences exist between the drinking habits of young adult males and those of females. Alcoholic beverages are most commonly used during leisure time involving recreational activities. In the Nordic countries, alcoholic beverages are not used regularly as beverages with meals, but it is quite common for those drinking to become intoxicated.

USE AND CONTROL OF TOBACCO

As long as tobacco use has existed in the Nordic countries, there have been constant debates about its influences and consequences, and both arguments of approval and disapproval have been voiced. For instance, in Sweden in the early twentieth century lively public debates ensued on both the negative health consequences of tobacco and on the moral character of young men in particular. Such concern, however, was confined to smaller societal circles until the 1950s.

Cigarette smoking became increasingly common and socially accepted during the twentieth century. One could say that smoking was the norm embedded in most social contexts. During wartime a ration of cigarettes was seen as every soldier's right and the tobacco industry boomed. Later, there were compartments for smokers in buses, trains, and airplanes and few restrictions on smoking in public places. At good dinners the host's offer of a cigarette was customary. Sporting activities and tobacco were seen as an acceptable combination, and up until the 1960s and 1970s cigarettes figured freely in advertisements, news clips, television programs, and movies. Smoking was seen, however, as an adult preoccupation, and thus in Norway, for instance, the municipalities could restrict selling tobacco to youngsters under the age of 15, and after 1935, the law forbade pupils and students to smoke in the nearby surroundings of their schools. In the 1970s in Finland, in contrast, ashtrays, which older pupils used during breaks, were often observed in schoolyards.

In the majority of the Nordic countries the generations born between 1910 and the end of the 1930s, especially men, were the most frequent smokers. At the end of the 1940s around 75 percent of all Finnish men in the 20 to 40 age group and in Norway 80 percent of all men 20 to 24 years old were smokers. Even if it was customary to smoke tobacco in pipes, cigarette smoking became the dominant mode during World War II. Interestingly enough, homemade cigarettes were the most frequently used form of tobacco in Norway in 1960. Also in Sweden, 50 percent of all men and 9 percent of all women were regular smokers in 1946, the smoking habit being, however, even more prevalent among younger age groups. Sweden was a clear exception to the smoking habit: In the 1840s moist snuff, called *snus*, became the most popular tobacco product among men, but in the period after World War II until 1970 the sales as well as the use of snus declined.

In the 1950s, and especially in the 1960s, medical evidence on the disastrous health effects of tobacco smoking, especially its relation to lung cancer, spread throughout the world. The effects on consumption were soon seen all over Europe, and smoking rates have declined in the decades since. In the early 1970s, 51 percent of adult Norwegian men smoked daily compared to 32 percent of women. In 2007 these figures were 21 and 23 percent, respectively. Similar statistics apply to the other Nordic countries: Between 2002 and 2005 the overall rates of daily smokers in the entire population averaged between 16 and 25 percent, rates that from a European perspective are at the lower end. The lowest percentage may be attributed to Sweden, given the persistent use of snus. In 2006 only 12 percent of Swedish men and 17 percent of women were daily smokers. The fact that more women than men are regular smokers is internationally unique. The use of snus has, on the other hand, increased during the last 15 years. As of 2008, Sweden is the only EU country in which trade with snus is allowed. Snus usage is a distinct male habit making up for the comparatively low levels of smoking among Swedish men. In the late 1980s 17 percent of Swedish men were regular snus users, increasing to 23 percent by 2005. The corresponding figures for women were 1 percent and 3 percent. The European Economic Area Agreement also allows for snus in Norway but the snus market there has remained small.

Measures to reduce smoking and the consumption of tobacco products in general have been taken up in all the Nordic countries since the 1960s, and they have with small variations followed the same path. On the whole, Denmark is the nation that seems the least restrictive and was also the last to introduce new restrictions. Thus, for instance, both Norway and Finland banned tobacco advertisements and sponsorship in the 1970s as well as the use of tobacco brand-names for other products in 1997. Health warnings on tobacco products were also instituted. In Denmark only, ads on radio and television, and youth-directed advertising, were not prohibited until the end of the 1980s, and it was not until 2001 that Denmark also forbade the use of cigarette names on other products. In the 1970s the Nordic countries also explicitly outlawed the sale of tobacco to young people, the age limit often being 16, as was mandated in Norway in 1975 and in Finland in 1977. In these nations, as well as in Sweden the age limit was raised to 18 in the mid-1990s, whereas Denmark introduced the age limit of 16 in 2004.

In the 1980s and 1990s, again on the basis of increasing evidence of the negative effects of so-called second-hand, or passive, smoking, the focus in tobacco control shifted to the protection of third parties. First in line were restrictions on smoking in public places, and in connection with that the protection of the workforce in workplaces in general and in restaurants in particular. As of 2008, all Nordic countries have either completely prohibited or severely restricted smoking in restaurants or cafés. In the early twenty-first century tobacco control developed within the EU system with directives and regulations in several key areas: public health policy, taxation, workplace environment, and agricultural policy.

USE OF OTHER DRUGS AND DRUG CONTROL

In contrast to drinking, drug use has never been regarded as a socially or culturally acceptable behavior in the Nordic countries. Ever since the early beginnings of recreational drug use in the 1960s it was recognized as a serious social problem. It thus has attracted much public interest and attention.

Drug use spread to the Nordic countries in the 1960s and 1970s in connection with the student and youth movements, "flower power," and alternative lifestyle ideologies. The fact that drug use was mostly confined to these cultural settings meant that it was mainly an urban phenomenon among upper- or middle-class youth as well as segments of the cultural elites. By the time the use of drugs spilled over from better-off young people to "not so well to do" youth, the assortment of available drugs, which originally included cannabis and psychedelic drugs such as LSD, also incorporated amphetamines and opiates. In addition to experimental or recreational drug use, which mostly consisted of pot smoking, more problematic consumption and abuse emerged.

In Denmark and Norway, the intravenous use of opiates dominated heavy drug use, whereas intravenous amphetamine use dominated problematic drug use in Sweden. Both experimental and problem use was much more prevalent in Denmark than in any other Nordic country, with Finland and Iceland recording the least use, and Norway and Sweden somewhere in between. However, during this same time period the vast majority of youth and adults in all Nordic countries had no personal experiences with illegal drugs.

The initial appearance of drugs in the Nordic countries was countered by reformulations of existing criminal laws and specific new national drug laws. A range of behaviors, especially those tied to selling or marketing drugs, were criminalized and harsh penalties mandated. Societal measures also included the establishment of youth clinics and therapeutic communities for young abusers, and the compulsory treatment of young, mostly underaged, users.

Until the 1980s drug policy was a kind of residual system: It had few features of its own but worked mostly on the basis of more general criminal, welfare, and health policies. Increasing international cooperation on drug policy emerged with the Western War on Drugs ideology, but Nordic drug policy also became more distinct in its own right, even if the responses to the drug problem differed somewhat between countries. One common feature was the emphasis on a balanced approach to contain the drug problem: prevention, treatment, and control. In Denmark, legislation made a distinction between soft drugs (mostly cannabis) and hard drugs, and Denmark also embraced early on an approach more oriented toward harm reduction. Sweden and to some degree Norway aimed at a drug-free society and pursued a rigorous policy toward achieving this goal.

In the 1990s new recreational lifestyles brought with them new drugs, such as Ecstasy and other party mixtures, and their use spread among youth in the Nordic countries. Compared to the 1960s, this second drug wave was more pervasive as it took place in a new media- and information-oriented society, with an emphasis on consumption, risk-taking behaviors, and individualism. The growth of drug use in the Nordic countries was also facilitated by easier access to and the lower costs of drugs, due partly to the new drugs arriving from Eastern Europe. The increase in drug use was most obvious in Nordic countries other than Denmark, but still by the mid-1990s only about 1 out of every 3 adults in Denmark, and 1 out of every 10 adults in other Nordic countries, had any experience with drugs.

The growth in the experimental use of drugs plateaued in the late 1990s, even reversing itself in the early twenty-first century. Data from the European School Survey Project on Alcohol and Other Drugs (ESPAD) on drug use among 15- and 16-year-olds show that in 2003 some 20 to 25 percent of Danish youth had used cannabis, whereas the corresponding figure in Iceland was approximately 15 percent and about 10 percent in each of the three remaining Nordic countries. The experimental use of drugs other than cannabis among 15- and 16-year-olds was much lower, between 1 and 4 percent.

Even if the trends in heavy drug use among the Nordic countries are difficult to discern, some characteristics stand out. The latest data indicate that the situation in Denmark is stable. In 2006 around 27,000 persons out of the Danish population of 5.4 million were estimated to be problematic drug users; of these, 7,000 used mainly cannabis. In Finland, whose total population is 5.3 million, the estimates are based on administrative statistics that revealed approximately 14,000 to 19,000 individuals used either amphetamines or opiates. In Norway, with 4.6 million inhabitants, the estimate of intravenous drug users is around 8,000 to 12,000, with most of them reporting opiates as their main drug. In Sweden, with 9 million inhabitants, the estimates on heavy drug

users in 2004 placed that number at approximately 26,000, or the same as in 1998. The above figures are crude estimates based on different kinds of data and methods and are not directly comparable. Clinical data show that in Denmark and Norway heroin is still the most frequently used drug among problem drug users, whereas in Sweden, which previously reported the widespread use of injected amphetamines, opiates are used almost as frequently as amphetamines. In Finland, as of 2008, nonprescribed buprenorphine was above amphetamine as the most popular drug among heavy drug abusers. Iceland has also reported some heavy use of amphetamines and prescription medicines containing opioids.

It is a well-known fact that drug use may have various adverse health effects and cause premature death. Infectious diseases are more widespread among problem drug users, and their death rate is significantly higher than in the general population. In the Nordic countries, the overall level of HIV infections and proportion of individuals infected by intravenous drug use have remained low. Finland experienced a minor epidemic when injecting drug use increased rapidly in the late 1990s and the proportion of such users in the HIV-infected population reached 60 percent. By the early twenty-first century that situation had stabilized, thanks to the introduction of needle-exchange programs and other special services for drug users. The growing incidence of hepatitis, especially Hepatitis C, has also raised concern among Nordic drug users. Drug-related deaths are also more common in Denmark and Norway—around 4 to 5 per every 100,000 deaths—than in the other Nordic countries.

Drug policy in the Nordic countries still rests on three main principles: control of supply and counteracting criminality; prevention of use and misuse; and treatment and harm reduction. In the early twenty-first century there seems to be a move toward an increased focus on substitution treatment or medicalization, even in those countries that traditionally maintained a restrictive drug policy. Substitution treatment is in some form part of the treatment offered to drug users in all Nordic countries. Even Sweden, which has taken the most restrictive stance on medically assisted treatment, introduced substitution treatment with buprenorphine in 1999. As well as running treatment services, measures are employed that seek to reduce drug-related harm in the group of drug users for whom a drug-free life seems unrealistic in either the short or long term. Harm reduction measures include such activities as outreach street work, low-threshold services at drop-in centers, low-threshold health-care centers, and syringe-exchange programs in most of the Nordic countries.

The major changes in the political structure of Eastern Europe and transformation of the former Soviet Union into Russia, however, also had consequences for the drug markets and drug supply in the Nordic countries. The most significant result has been—according to some observers—the increasing independence and size of the northern European illegal drug market, which formerly was an integral part of the broader European market. This has put pressure on the control side of drug policy.

Thus, even if substitution treatment and harm reduction measures have gained ground as responses to drug problems in the Nordic countries, there are no signs of downgrading the control measures. In Finland, for instance, policy has moved forward on a dual track of both increased control and increased harm-reducing measures. In the early twenty-first century Danish drug laws also became more restrictive while at the same time attempting to uphold the strong tradition of substitution treatment and harm reduction. Systems for substitution treatment and harm reduction developed notably in Norway since the late 1990s, with a new emphasis on the exchange of syringes and needles, experimental supervised injection rooms, and substitution treatment as well as specialized medical care.

ASSESSMENT

Consumption and policy regarding alcohol, tobacco, and illegal drugs exhibit both converging and diverging trends in the Nordic countries. On an individual level, drinking alcohol and smoking tobacco seem to be related activities, which the fears of restaurant owners on losing customers, as the result of bans on smoking in restaurants, bear witness to. Alcohol and other drugs are often seen by the greater public as substitutes for each other, but the concomitant use of alcohol and illegal drugs is, in fact, frequently the norm among drug users. On a broader level in terms of the general population, trends in alcohol and tobacco consumption do not coincide, as the use of alcohol has either increased or remained stable during the last several decades, whereas smoking has clearly diminished. Consumption trends in alcohol and other drugs are neither headed in the same direction nor going the opposite way.

In the early twenty-first century drinking alcohol is both legal and socially accepted in the Nordic countries, and traditional Nordic alcohol control has become weaker as more weight has been put on the individual's responsibility. European and global economic integration will in the future place even more weight on measures that affect the demand side of the alcohol equation and probably lead to further weakening of measures affecting the supply of alcoholic beverages as well as alcohol taxes and prices in the Nordic countries. Other drugs remain illegal and drug policy is somewhat restrictive, but that approach has been complemented with substitution treatment and harm reduction. The variations in drug policy among the Nordic countries seem to be smaller than was the case in the 1950s and 1960s. Smoking has become increasingly socially unacceptable and more heavily controlled with limits on advertising, establishment of age limits, and prohibition of smoking in public spaces, workplaces, and restaurants. These kinds of developments will no doubt continue as strict tobacco control also has become the norm on an international level, as exemplified in the Framework Convention on Tobacco negotiated under the auspices of the World Health Organization.

See also **European Union; Foreign Policy and Drugs, United States; International Drug Supply Systems.**

BIBLIOGRAPHY

Alko Ltd. (2007). *Nordic alcohol markets.* Helsinki, Finland: Author.

Anderson, P., & Baumberg, B. (2004). *Alcohol in Europe.* Brussels, Belgium: European Commission.

Bruun, K. (1971). *Alkohol i Norden (Alcohol in the Nordic countries).* Helsinki, Finland: Tammi.

Bruun, K., Edwards, G., Lumio, M., Mäkelä, K., Pan, L., Popham, R. E., et al. (1975). *Alcohol control policies in public health perspective.* Vol. 25. A Collaborative Project of the Finnish Foundation for Alcohol Studies, the World Health Organization Regional Office for Europe, and the Addiction Research Foundation of

Ontario. Forssa, Finland: Finnish Foundation for Alcohol Studies.

Hakkarainen, P. (2000). *Tupakka, nautinnosta ongelmaksi (Tobacco, from pleasure to problem)*. Vastapaino Tampere.

Hibell, B., Andersson, B., Bjarnason, T., Ahlström, S., Balakireva, O., Kokkevi, A., & Morgan, M. (2004). *The ESPAD report 2003*. Stockholm: Swedish Council for Information on Alcohol and Other Drugs.

Holder, H. D., Kühlhorn, E., Nordlund, S., Österberg, E., Romelsjö, A., & Ugland, T. (1998). *European integration and Nordic alcohol policies. Changes in alcohol controls and consequences in Finland, Norway and Sweden, 1980–1997*. Aldershot, U.K.: Ashgate.

Kouvonen, P., Skretting, A., & Rosenqvist, P. (2006). *Drugs in the Nordic and Baltic countries: Common concerns, different realities*. NAD Publication No. 48. Helsinki, Finland: Nordic Council for Alcohol and Drug Research.

Österberg, E., & Karlsson, T. (Eds.). (2002). *Alcohol policies in EU member states and Norway*. Collection of country reports. Helsinki, Finland: Stakes.

ESA ÖSTERBERG
PIA ROSENQVIST

NOREPINEPHRINE.

Also referred to as adrenaline, it is a catecholamine neurotransmitter known to be involved in the action of some addicting drugs. It is the biochemical product of dopamine and the enzyme dopamine-beta-hydroxylase. It is the major neurotransmitter for the sympathetic nervous system, as well as for several sets of long axon, multiple-branched neurons (nerve cells) of the central nervous system. After release from nerve terminals onto its receptors, much of it is recaptured or removed from extracellular spaces by an uptake mechanism, or transporter, located in the nerve terminal membrane. This transporter is an important drug target for antidepressants and psychostimulants. Monoamine oxidase is a well-known enzyme that breaks down norepinephrine.

Norepinephrine holds an important place in the history of drug studies. It was discovered as an active chemical in the body many years ago. The availability of pharmacological agonists and antagonists helped reveal its physiologic role in the body. Also the development of histochemical methods in the 1960s and 1970s for its direct light microscopic visualization led to a detailed understanding of the many neurons that contain it. Noradrenergic receptors, termed alpha and beta, can act independently or synergistically to mediate the activity of norepinephrine and related drugs. Brain noradrenergic neurons in the nucleus locus ceruleus are well characterized in general and are activated during withdrawal from addictive drugs.

See also **Dopamine; Neurotransmitters; Receptor, Drug.**

BIBLIOGRAPHY

Ordway, G. A., Schwartz, M. A., & Frazer, A., Eds. (2007). *Brain norepinephrine: Neurobiology and therapeutics..* Cambridge, U.K.: Cambridge University Press.

Sadock, B. J., & Sadock, V. A. (2007). *Kaplan and Sadock's synopsis of psychiatry: Behavioral sciences/clinical psychiatry*, 10th ed. Philadelphia, PA: Lippincott, Williams & Wilkins.

FLOYD BLOOM
REVISED BY MICHAEL J. KUHAR (2001)

NORWAY. *See* **Nordic Countries (Denmark, Finland, Iceland, Norway, and Sweden).**

NUCLEUS ACCUMBENS.

The nucleus accumbens is a group of neurons that is part of the limbic system and located near the midline in the frontal region, beneath the frontal lobe. Anatomically, it has been divided into the shell and core, with the shell perhaps being more important for the actions of drugs of abuse. It is one of the most important structures in the brain for studies of drug addiction because it is believed to be involved in reward, reinforcement, and unpredictably positive experiences. Nucleus accumbens is known to include neurons that contain GABA and acetylcholine and other neurotransmitters. It receives important input from dopaminergic neurons located in the ventral midbrain that are also involved in reward and reinforcement. It has output projections back to the ventral midbrain and other areas.

This nucleus is thought to be involved in the action of many different drugs of abuse, especially psychostimulants whose actions on the nucleus accumbens have been well studied. Destruction of neurons in this structure or its inputs disrupts psychostimulant self-administration by rodents, and psychostimulants and other drugs of abuse cause an efflux of dopamine from this structure. Because of its small size, it has been difficult to study, and, at this time, it is being studied in humans and nonhuman primates to determine its relevance to human drug and stimulant abuse.

See also **Limbic System; Reward Pathways and Drugs.**

BIBLIOGRAPHY

Lowinson, J. H. (2005). *Substance abuse: A comprehensive textbook.* Philadelphia, PA: Lippincott, Williams & Wilkins.

West, R. (2006). *Theory of addiction.* Malden, MA: Blackwell Publishing.

JAMES E. SMITH
REVISED BY MICHAEL J. KUHAR (2001)

Figure 1. Nutmeg. ILLUSTRATION BY GGS INFORMATION SERVICES. GALE, CENGAGE LEARNING

NUTMEG. Nutmeg, the common spice obtained from the aromatic seed of the tree *Myristica fragrans* (native to the Moluccas, the spice islands of the East Indies), has been used for centuries for food and medicinal purposes. It causes some hallucinogenic activity when consumed in large amounts. Since nutmeg is found in most kitchens, including food preparation areas found in prisons, it has been used by prisoners. Therefore, it has been removed from ready access in prisons to the tighter control of drugs of abuse; Malcolm X wrote about such use.

Nutmeg contains elemicin and myristicin, whose structures have some similarities to the hallucinogen mescaline as well as to the psychostimulant amphetamine. It has been hypothesized that elemicin and myristicin might be metabolized in the body to form an amphetamine- and/or mescaline-like compound, but this has not been proven. The effects of nutmeg have been reported to have some similarities to those produced by marijuana; however, the large amounts of nutmeg that must be ingested to elicit behavioral effects can cause dry mouth and thirst, increases in heart rate, vomiting and abdominal pain, severe headaches, agitation, and panic attacks.

See also **Lysergic Acid Diethylamide (LSD) and Psychedelics; Mescaline; Plants, Drugs From.**

BIBLIOGRAPHY

Max, B. (1992). This and that: The essential pharmacology of herbs and spices. *Trends in Pharmacological Science, 13,* 15–20.

Spinella, M. (2005). *Concise handbook of psychoactive herbs.* New York: Haworth Press.

Wills, S. (2005). *Drugs of Abuse.* London: Pharmaceutical Press.

DANIEL X. FREEDMAN
R. N. PECHNICK

OBESITY. The term *obesity* derives from the Latin *obesus*, meaning "to eat up," and it came into use in English in the early 1600s to mean a condition characterized by excessive bodily fat. Excess body weight is associated with the increased storage of energy in the form of adipose tissue. Standard criteria for obesity are (1) greater than 20 percent above ideal body weight (IDW) for a given height, as determined from actuarial tables; or (2) body mass index (BMI), defined as weight in kilograms divided by height in meters squared ($kg/m^2 =$ BMI), greater than 27 for men and greater than 25 for women.

The prevalence of obesity (in this case defined as having body fat in excess of 25 percent for males or 30 percent in females) is increasing worldwide, which varies substantially across ethnic groups and cultures and across age groups. In the United States, obesity is consistently more common among African American women than among white women; and tends to be more common among Hispanic women than among non-Hispanic women. Among men, race and ethnicity do not appear to play a significant role in the prevalence of obesity. Overall, approximately 90 million Americans are obese. In the early twenty-first century, the prevalence of obesity is leveling off in women but is increasing in men, children, and adolescents.

Obesity represents the upper end of a body-weight continuum rather than a qualitatively different state. Obesity can derive from a variety of causes (i.e., genetics, culture, nutritional intake, physical activity). Most notably, obesity is more prevalent (ten times more likely) in persons whose parents, brothers, or sisters are obese. Studies in identical twins have clearly demonstrated that genetics plays a major role. For example, nonidentical twins raised together were less similar in weight than identical twins raised apart. Environmental effects contribute to the rapid escalation and magnitude of the obesity epidemic in recent decades. The nature and nurture interactions for obesity are thought to occur after conception but before birth. Maternal nutritional imbalance and metabolic disturbances during pregnancy could affect gene expression and contribute to the development of obesity and diabetes mellitus of offspring in later life. Recent experiments have shown that nutritional exposures, stress or disease state after birth may also produce lifelong remodeling of gene expression.

Food ingestion is modulated by both peripheral and central signals. Peripheral hormone signals (e.g., ghrelin, cholecystokinin) that originate from the gut continually inform the brain about the status of acute hunger and satiety. The hypothalamus is a control center for appetite regulatory signals. The hunger peptide, ghrelin, normally increases during fasting. Ghrelin increases food intake and body weight by stimulating neurons in the hypothalamus. Its level is suppressed after a meal. Fasting ghrelin levels are lower in obese individuals and fail to decline after a meal, which may contribute to overeating. Obese individuals often have enlarged adipocytes with a reduced buffering capacity for fat storage. The dysfunction of adipose tissue plays an important role in the development and progression of insulin resistance. Adipocytes modulate influx of dietary fat and secrete a variety of hormones (e.g., leptin). Leptin communicates the level of body fat stores to the brain and induces weight loss by suppression of food intake and by stimulation of the metabolic rate. Leptin is involved in the neuroendocrine response to starvation, energy expenditure, and reproduction (i.e., the initiation of human puberty).

Common forms of obesity in humans are failure of elevated leptin levels in the brain to suppress feeding and mediate weight loss, which is defined as leptin resistance. Leptin resistance in the hypothalamus invokes the starvation pathway and promotes food intake. The hedonic pathway that includes the ventral tegmental area and nucleus accumbens makes food intake rewarding. The nucleus accumbens is also referred to as the pleasure center of the brain, which is responsive to alcohol, morphine, nicotine, and cocaine. Leptin resistance in the brain reward pathway makes food intake a more potent reward and promotes the intake of palatable food.

Some researchers and clinicians see similarities among certain patterns of overeating and other excessive behaviors such as drinking too much alcohol, compulsive gambling, engaging in too much sexual activity, and even exercising compulsively. Some ingredients in palatable food (e.g., sugar) can be substances of abuse and lead to a natural form of addiction. For example, ingestion of sugar induces the brain to release opioids and dopamine. Dopamine is a neurotransmitter known to play a role in motivation as well as in the experience of reward and pleasure. In rats, certain circumstances (e.g., intermittent excessive sugar intake) can produce behavioral and neurochemical changes that resemble the effects of drug dependence. Eating and craving palatable food are reflexive reactions to stimulation of the reward pathway as evidenced in human brain imaging studies. Exposure to palatable food that cannot be consumed in fasting humans is associated with increases in striatal extracellular dopamine. Brain imaging of obese individuals shows a reduction in striatal dopamine D2 receptors, which is similar to the reduction reported in drug-dependent subjects. These findings could explain why aberrant eating behaviors observed in obese individuals resemble behavior related to drug dependence. Other mechanisms that govern eating behavior, such as stress, also underlie the development of obesity. Human studies show that acute stress increases snacking of high energy-dense food.

It should be noted that not all persons whose weight is above average are obese (they may have excess muscle mass); not all who are obese eat excessively; not all who eat excessively become obese; and some individuals who have clinically recognized disorders centered on eating and body weight, such as bulimia, may or may not be obese.

The prevention and treatment of obesity should be comprehensive, including pharmacological and lifestyle modification (e.g., education concerning nutrition and exercise, intensive family-based psychological counseling, and effective stress reduction) and surgical treatment (if indicated), in order to prevent health problems linked to obesity, such as hypertension, stroke, and type 2 diabetes mellitus.

See also **Bulimia Nervosa; Overeating and Other Excessive Behaviors.**

BIBLIOGRAPHY

Adam, T. C., & Epel, E. S. (2007). Stress, eating and the reward system. *Physiology and Behavior, 91*(4), 449–458.

Avena, N. M., Rada, P., & Hoebel. B. G. (2008). Evidence for sugar addiction: Behavioral and neurochemical effects of intermittent, excessive sugar intake. *Neuroscience and Biobehavioral Reviews, 32*(1), 20–39.

Catalano, P. M., & Ehrenberg, H. M. (2006). The short- and long-term implications of maternal obesity on the mother and her offspring. *British Journal of Obstetrics and Gynaecology, 113*(10), 1126–1133.

Cummings, D. E., & Overduin, J. (2007). Gastrointestinal regulation of food intake. *Journal of Clinical Investigation, 117*(1), 13–23.

Gallou-Kabani C., Vigé, A., Gross, M. S., & Junien, C. (2007). Nutri-epigenomics: Lifelong remodeling of our epigenomes by nutritional and metabolic factors and beyond. *Clinical Chemistry and Laboratory Medicine, 45*(3), 321–327.

Myers, M. G., Cowley, M. A., & Münzberg, H. (2008). Mechanisms of leptin action and leptin resistance. *Annual Review of Physiology, 70,* 537–556.

Ogden, C. L., Carroll, M. D., Curtin, L. R., Mcdowell, M. A., Tabak, C. J., & Flegal, K. M. (2006). Prevalence of overweight and obesity in the United States, 1999–

2004. *Journal of the American Medical Association, 295*(13), 1549–1555.

Segal, N. L., & Allison, D. B. (2002). Twins and virtual twins: Bases of relative body weight revisited. *International Journal of Obesity-Related Metabolic Disorders, 26*(4), 437–441.

Snow, V., Barry, P., Fitterman, N., Qaseem, A., & Weiss, K.; Clinical Efficacy Assessment Subcommittee of the American College of Physicians. (2005). Pharmacologic and surgical management of obesity in primary care: A clinical practice guideline from the American College of Physicians. *Annals of Internal Medicine, 142*(7), 525–531.

Spear, B. A., Barlow, S. E., Ervin, C., Ludwig, D. S., Saelens, B. E., Schetzine, K. E., & Taveras, E. M. (2007). Recommendations for treatment of child and adolescent overweight and obesity. *Pediatrics, 120* (Suppl.), S254–S288.

Volkow, N. D., & Wise, R. A. (2005). How can drug addiction help us understand obesity? *Nature Neuroscience, 8*, 555–560.

TIMOTHY H. MORAN
REVISED BY GENE-JACK WANG (2009)

OPERATION INTERCEPT.

Described by government sources as the largest peacetime search-and-seizure operation in U.S. history, Operation Intercept was launched along the United States-Mexico border in September 1969. This unilateral program was instituted ostensibly to halt the flow of marijuana, heroin, and other dangerous drugs from Mexico into the United States. However, the actual goal of Intercept was not to interdict narcotics but to publicize the war on crime promoted by President Richard M. Nixon (served 1969–1974), who had taken office the previous January, and to force Mexican compliance with Washington's anti-drug campaign.

On September 16, 1968, presidential candidate Nixon had pledged to an Anaheim, California, audience that, if elected, he would move against the source of drugs and accelerate the development of tools and weapons to deter narcotics in transit. At the time, drug use per se did not elicit extreme concern from large segments of the population. According to a White House survey taken in May of 1969, people were more worried about racial problems, economic considerations, student unrest, and crime. In fact, among a substantial number of liberal-minded opinion leaders, some consensus was emerging that the prevailing 1950s-era drug legislation was too harsh, particularly with respect to marijuana. Nevertheless, among the Nixon constituency, the belief was common that drug use was increasing and that, with it, crime and antisocial behavior among youth was on the rise. Nixon's strategists must have seen narcotics control as an available strategy to move against crime and social unrest (both among minority populations and young people) and to divert attention from such problems as the war in Vietnam and the economy.

THE SPECIAL PRESIDENTIAL TASK FORCE

With John Ingersoll, the director of the Bureau of Narcotics and Dangerous Drugs, contending that the United States had "failed miserably" (*New York Times*, 1969, p. 23) in controlling narcotics abuse, Nixon chose to couple a highly publicized law-and-order campaign at home with an international offensive against foreign sources of heroin and marijuana. Attorney General John Mitchell was chosen to develop the program, and in April 1969 he and Treasury Secretary David M. Kennedy assembled a multiagency task force to form a plan to attack the importation into and illegal sale and use of illicit drugs in the United States. This Special Presidential Task Force Relating to Narcotics, Marijuana, and Dangerous Drugs consisted of two co-chairmen, an executive secretary, and twenty members drawn from various departments in the government: Justice; Treasury; Defense; Agriculture; Commerce; Labor; Health, Education and Welfare: Transportation; the Coast Guard; the Interstate Commerce Commission; and the White House staff. Conspicuously absent was any representative from the State Department.

The Task Force Report, submitted to the president in June, established a linear relationship between marijuana, deteriorating health, heroin usage, and increased crime. It devoted its first fifteen pages to this argument. The remaining twenty pages examined what could be done to stop the flow of (mainly) marijuana across the border from Mexico. The last page of the report urged the State Department (absent from the deliberations as noted) to engage in a "massive, continuous effort, directed by the highest officials of Mexico, [to] significantly curtail the production and refinement of marijuana and other dangerous drugs" (Special Presidential Task Force Report, 1969, p. 35). Officials noted further that (1) a significant percentage of the heroin was of Mexican origin; (2) substantial quantities of European heroin were being smuggled across the southern frontier; (3) Mexico served as an in-transit point for South American cocaine; and (4) considerable amounts of amphetamines and barbiturates entered the United States surreptitiously from Mexico. In the midst of so much smuggling, Mexico's resources and efforts remained inadequate. In the view of the task force report, both Mexican drug control statutes and the number of federal judicial police assigned to enforce them were insufficient. Mexican law enforcement authorities also lacked infrastructure and such technological resources as appropriate aircraft.

METHOD OF BORDER SURVEILLANCE

Something had to be done to elicit a concerted sustained anti-drug program from Mexico City. In July 1969 President Nixon sent a draft bill to Congress that would eventually become the Comprehensive Drug Abuse and Control Act of 1970. In August, the United States was flooded with media reports of a huge gathering of pot-smoking young music enthusiasts that would be remembered as Woodstock. In early September, the *New York Times* carried leaked reports of preparations for a spectacular operation to chokeoff cross-border smuggling from Mexico. On Sunday afternoon, September 21, 1969, at exactly 2:30 p.m. Pacific standard time, Operation Intercept was launched. Under the operational control of Myles Ambrose, the rather colorful commissioner of Customs, the operation was billed as "the largest search and seizure operation ever undertaken by civil authorities in peacetime" (*New York Times*, 1969, p. 29). Noting that the Mexican government had been kept "fully informed" of the operation, a U.S. Treasury Department news release termed Intercept a "coordinated effort" encompassing the law-enforcement resources of several branches of the federal government. Involving intensified land, sea, and air surveillance along the entire 1,945-mile U.S.–Mexico border, the effort would continue for an indefinite period, as everything and everyone, no matter their nationality or status, was thoroughly and painstakingly searched.

More than 4.5 million individuals and their belongings were ultimately inspected. Vehicles, their component parts, along with passengers' personal baggage, purses, books, lunch boxes, jackets, toys, and, in some cases, even blouses and hairdos were searched. The daily routine of life in Mexican border cities was radically altered, as traffic backed up for miles, car radiators boiled over, and tempers, both private and diplomatic, flared. No person or object, including diplomatic and consular officials, their children, possessions, and even their diplomatic cargo, was spared. In the process, the maneuver encompassed some two thousand personnel, intensified inspections, heightened air and sea surveillance, and the expenditure of some 30 million dollars.

On October 10, 1969, after some hasty negotiations with outraged Mexican officials (who did not feel that they had been fully informed), the administration announced that the border effort would be renamed Operation Cooperation. Surveillance was scaled back in return for a promise by Mexico to increase anti-marijuana enforcement and crop control.

Analyzed solely on the basis of drugs confiscated, Intercept surely was not worth the cost and effort it entailed. Seizures, however, were of minor importance.

In hindsight, the purpose of Operation Intercept appeared not to be to interdict drugs at the border but to press Mexico through economic denial. Seeking a politically expedient solution to the highly complex problem of domestic drug abuse and associated crime, the Nixon administration chose a course of action that, in effect, punished Mexico. Unfortunately, Intercept officials failed to gauge the impact of the blockage on the U.S. border economy. Highly dependent on shoppers and tourists from both sides of the border, U.S. and Mexican merchants reacted angrily and effectively through professional and civic groups. Pressure on the administration from border-state members of Congress was intense, and its impact increased as the project was prolonged. Along with diplomatic protests, this regional criticism proved crucial to Intercept's demise. The White House failed to recall the salient fact that Mexico is a foreign country and a friendly one at that.

Neglect of the State Department proved a serious blunder. Overlooked or overpowered by law-enforcement officials during Intercept's crucial formative stage, U.S. diplomats ultimately terminated the ill-advised project before it became an even greater diplomatic disaster. More important, if its supporters had managed to prolong the unilateral maneuver for an extended period, U.S. authorities probably would have never secured the level of cooperation they sorely needed to impair the cultivation of drugs in Mexico and the trafficking of drugs across the border.

Additionally, the operation was poorly timed; it came on the eve of *tapadismo*, the process through which Mexico chooses its next president, but before the Nixon administration's announcement of a Latin American policy. Furthermore, Mexico played host during the Intercept period to a regional meeting of the United Nations Commission on Narcotic Drugs and the thirty-eighth annual assembly of Interpol, thereby compounding its embarrassment over the blockade's indignities.

Yet despite its numerous shortcomings, Operation Intercept was not entirely void of accomplishments. Because of the tremendous publicity it engendered, the program made Mexican officials keenly aware of a reality heretofore ignored or slighted: its own burgeoning drug problem. Politicians and journalists became introspective and reluctantly admitted that the availability of domestically produced drugs posed a danger to the health of *nuestra juventud* (our youth) as well as providing an everyday pastime for *gringo jippies* (American hippies).

Intercept also helped spur a previously lagging Mexican campaign against the cultivation, manufacture, and shipment of illicit drugs of all kinds. As a corollary to this effort, cooperation between Mexican and U.S. narcotics officials improved during the 1970s, but the 1985 kidnapping and murder of DEA agent Enrique Camarena in Guadalajara, Mexico, was tragic evidence of the daring and impunity with which traffickers continued to operate in the border area.

See also **Border Management; Crime and Drugs; Crop Control Policies; Drug Interdiction; International Drug Supply Systems; Mexico; U.S. Government Agencies: U.S. Customs and Border Protection (CBP).**

BIBLIOGRAPHY

Astorga, L. (n.d.) *Drug trafficking in Mexico: A first general assessment.* Management of Social Transformation (MOST) Discussion paper No. 36. Available from http://www.unesco.org/most/astorga.htm.

Barona, L. J. (1976). *Mexico ante el reto de las drogas.* Mexico City: Impresiones Modernas.

Craig, R. B. (1978). La campana permanente: Mexico's antidrug campaign. *Journal of Interamerican Studies and World Affairs, 20,* 107–131.

Craig, R. B. (1980). Operation Intercept: The international politics of pressure. *Review of Politics, 42,* 556–580.

Epstein, E. J. (1977). *Agency of fear.* New York: Putnam.

Gooberman, L. A. (1974). *Operation Intercept: The multiple consequences of public policy.* New York: Pergamon.

Musto, D. F., & Korsmeyer, P. (2002). *The quest for drug control: Politics and federal policy in a period of increasing substance abuse, 1963–1981.* New Haven, CT: Yale University Press.

New York Times. (1969, Feb. 12), p. 23.

New York Times. (1969, Sept. 14), p. 29.

Schroeder, R. C. (1975). *The politics of drugs: Marijuana to mainlining.* Washington, DC: Congressional Quarterly.

Shannon, E. (1988) *Desperadoes: Latin drug lords, U.S. lawmen and the war America can't win.* New York: Viking.

Special Presidential Task Force Relating to Narcotics, Marijuana and Dangerous Drugs. (1969). *Task force report: Findings and recommendations.* Folder: Ex FG 221-28 Narcotics, Marijuana and Dangerous Drugs [1969-70], Box 5 FG 221 Task Forces, WHCF. Nixon Presidential Materials Staff. Washington, DC: National Archives.

RICHARD B. CRAIG
REVISED BY PAMELA KORSMEYER (2009)

OPIATES/OPIOIDS.

The *opiates* are central nervous system depressants that are found in opium or are derived from a substance found in opium, which is the juice of the opium poppy (*Papaver Somniferum*). The *opioids* include the opiates, along with totally synthetic agents, and naturally occurring peptides that bind to one or more opioid receptors found in a number of animal species. In general usage, both terms are often used interchangeably—but opioids is the larger grouping.

The effects of opium have been known for several thousand years. For most of this time it was not clear which of the ingredients in opium provide its analgesic (painkilling) and other therapeutic properties.

Figure 1. Opium poppy and pod. ILLUSTRATION BY GGS INFORMATION SERVICES. GALE, CENGAGE LEARNING

Regardless of their benefits, health care providers are often afraid to prescribe opiods for fear of psychological dependence and sale to illegal markets (Carver, 2000). Still, the medical community has been increasing the use of opioid analgesics (Increasing Use, 2000).

Morphine and codeine, two of the most abundant constituents of opium, were the first pure opiates isolated—morphine in 1806 and codeine in 1832. Chemical modifications were soon attempted in an effort to eliminate their problematic side effects. One of the first attempts (in the 1890s) produced 3,6-diacetylmorphine, which is commonly known as heroin. This agent did not eliminate the problems of tolerance, dependence, or abuse. Since then, extensive studies of the important components of morphine's structure have led to the development of a number of different classes of organic compounds. In 1939 and 1940, the first synthetics were discovered. The recent discovery of the opioid peptides have provided even more diversity in drug design.

AGONISTS, ANTAGONISTS, AND PARTIAL AGONISTS

Some drugs have very complex actions and many drugs act at specific receptor, locations on the surface of a cell. All the drugs that belong to the class of drugs called opioids act at opioid receptors on the surface of cells. Usually these cells are neurons, but there are also opioid receptors on white blood cells. Once a drug binds to a receptor, it can either turn it on (agonist) or do nothing (antagonist).

Even if a compound does nothing once it binds to the receptor, it still blocks the site and prevents an active compound from binding to the receptor. The situation is much like a key in a lock; some keys fit into the lock but will not turn, and as long as they remain in the lock they prevent the insertion of keys that would turn the lock. Finally, there are drugs known as *partial agonists*; these compounds bind to the receptor and turn it on but not nearly as well as pure agonists.

Again, using the key analogy, these partial agonists will turn in the lock, but only with some jiggling, lowering efficiency in opening the door. Pharmacologically, partial agonists have limited effects at the receptor, termed a *ceiling* effect. This means that increasing the dose further will not give a greater response. To further complicate understanding of these drug actions, it is important to recognize that the opioid receptors (and many other types of receptors as well) are actually families of similar but subtly different receptor types. Some opioids are agonists at one receptor type and partial agonists or even antagonists at another receptor type. These drugs are termed mixed agonist/antagonists and they can have complex pharmacological profiles. For this reason it can be difficult for pharmacists to determine conversion amounts (for example, to methadone) (Magill-Lewis, 2000).

RECEPTORS

Morphine and drugs with similar actions work through specific recognition sites, termed *receptors*, located on the outside of cells (see Table 1). A number of general classes of opioid receptors have now been identified and it is likely that even more will be discovered. The major types of opioid receptors have been designated mu, kappa, and delta. From the clinical perspective, the mu opioid receptors are the most important. This class, comprised of two subtypes, mu_1 and mu_2, have high affinity for morphine and most of the clinically used agents. Both mu subtypes mediate analgesia but through different mechanisms and locations within the brain and spinal cord. Mu receptors have been implicated in euphoria and mu agonists have often been abused. Equally important, activation of mu receptors depresses respiration and inhibits gastrointestinal transit. In addition to analgesia, euphoria, respiratory depression, and decreased activity in the stomach, mu agonist opioids produce some actions that are clinically useful, such as cough

Receptor	Agonists	Analgesia	Other action
Mu	Morphine		
mu$_1$		Supraspinal*	Prolactin release
			Acetylcholine turnover
mu$_2$		Spinal	Respiratory depression
			Inhibition of gastrointestinal transit
			Guinea pig ileum bioassay
Kappa			
kappa$_1$	Dynorphin A	Spinal	Diuresis
			Sedation (?)
			Rabbit vas deferens bioassay
kappa$_2$	Bremazocine		Pharmacology unknown
kappa$_3$	Nalorphine	Supraspinal	
Delta	Enkephalins	Spinal	Mouse vas deferens bioassay
			Dopamine turnover

*The supraspinal system is far more sensitive than the spinal one.

Table 1. Tentative receptor classification. ILLUSTRATION BY GGS INFORMATION SERVICES. GALE, CENGAGE LEARNING

suppression. However, most of their actions are considered unwanted side effects; for example, they affect endocrine function, constrict pupils, induce sweating, and cause nausea and vomiting. All mu agonist opioids also induce increasing tolerance and physical dependence in the user.

Kappa opioid receptors were defined using keto-cyclazocine, an experimental benzomorphan derivative, and subsequently with dynorphin A, an endogenous opioid, which is believed to be the natural ligand for at least one of the kappa receptor subtypes. Morphine has relatively poor affinity for kappa receptors, but other drugs, such as pentazocine and nalbuphine (analgesics in clinical use), interact with kappa receptors quite effectively. The importance of kappa mechanisms in their actions has only recently been appreciated. The pharmacology of kappa receptors in humans has not been extensively studied; however, animal studies indicate that the kappa receptors also can relieve pain through receptor mechanisms distinct for each of the subtypes. Many of the clinically used drugs active at kappa receptors are mixed agonists/antagonists. Although they are agonists at kappa receptors, they are antagonists or partial agonists at mu receptors. In contrast to mu agonists, which can produce mood elevations and euphoria, drugs that activate kappa agonists appear to produce weird feelings and dysphoria.

The discovery of the enkephalins—endogenous peptides with opioid properties—soon led to the identification of delta receptors. The clinical pharmacology of delta receptors is not well known, primarily because so few agents have been tested in humans. Again, animal testing indicates an important role of delta receptors in analgesia, which is supported by a few studies with humans. However, there are no pure delta agonists clinically available as of 2008.

Although all the various receptor subtypes examined can relieve pain, each receptor represents a different mechanism of action. Their sites of action within the brain differ; and most importantly, agents highly selective for a specific subtype do not show cross-tolerance. While tolerance develops with continued activation of any of the various receptors, tolerance to one does not lead to tolerance to another. For example, tolerance to morphine does not diminish the response to a kappa or delta drug. Similarly, mu agonists produce a characteristic variety of physical dependence, and there is cross-dependence among mu agonists (that is, people dependent on heroin will not experience withdrawal if given methadone.) However, there is no cross-dependence between mu agonists and kappa agonists.

All the various subtypes produce a number of actions other than analgesia. Most of the nonanalgesic actions of opiates can be explained by considering the receptors to which they interact. An excellent example is mu$_2$ receptors, which mediate respiratory depression and the constipation seen with morphine. Drugs that are agonists at these receptors also produce these side effects while compounds lacking affinity for these receptors do not. The role of multiple receptors is important clinically, primarily since few drugs are specific for one receptor. Even morphine, which is highly selective for mu receptors, interacts with two mu subtypes, and at higher doses with delta receptors as well.

CLASSES OF OPIOIDS

Opioids can be divided into a series of classes based upon their chemical structures, illustrated by prototypic compounds from each group (see Figure 1). These include morphine and its close analogs, the morphinans, the benzomorphans, the phenylpiperidines, and methadone. The pharmacology of agents within each category can be quite varied and often can be predicted from their affinity for various opioid-receptor subtypes. Most of the clinically relevant drugs will interact with more than one receptor. Thus their actions can be ascribed to the summation of a number of receptor actions.

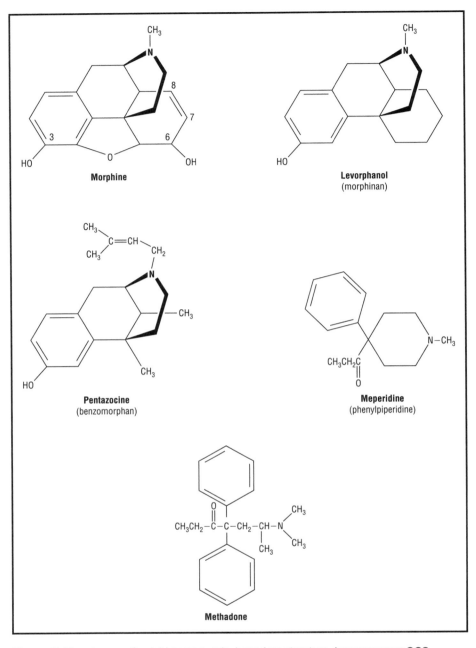

Figure 2. The classes of opioid compounds, based on structure. ILLUSTRATION BY GGS INFORMATION SERVICES. GALE, CENGAGE LEARNING

The importance of various regions of the morphine molecule has been well studied and a number of related compounds are widely used (see Figure 2). Early studies examined small changes in morphine's structure. One of the critical groups is the hydroxyl group at the 3-position on the molecule. Blockade of this position by adding chemical groups markedly reduces the ability of the drug to bind to opioid receptors. Although this may seem at odds with the analgesic activity of codeine, which lacks a free hydroxyl group at the 3-position, evidence indicates that codeine itself is not active and is metabolized to morphine, which is responsible for its actions. A similar situation exists for oxymorphone and oxycodone.

The morphine molecule has a single nitrogen atom. The substituent on the nitrogen in these

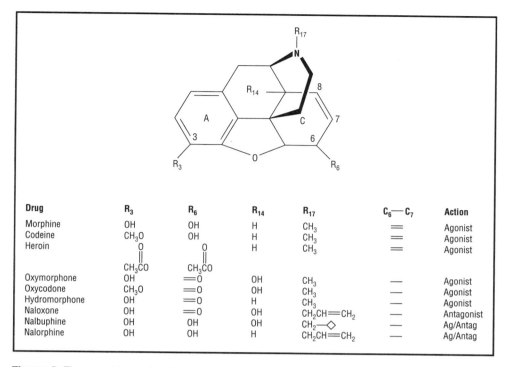

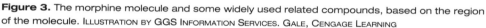

Drug	R_3	R_6	R_{14}	R_{17}	C_6—C_7	Action
Morphine	OH	OH	H	CH_3	=	Agonist
Codeine	CH_3O	OH	H	CH_3	=	Agonist
Heroin	O‖CH_3CO	O‖CH_3CO	H	CH_3	=	Agonist
Oxymorphone	OH	=O	OH	CH_3	—	Agonist
Oxycodone	CH_3O	=O	OH	CH_3	—	Agonist
Hydromorphone	OH	=O	H	CH_3	—	Agonist
Naloxone	OH	=O	OH	$CH_2CH=CH_2$	—	Antagonist
Nalbuphine	OH	OH	OH	CH_2—◇	—	Ag/Antag
Nalorphine	OH	OH	H	$CH_2CH=CH_2$	—	Ag/Antag

Figure 3. The morphine molecule and some widely used related compounds, based on the region of the molecule. ILLUSTRATION BY GGS INFORMATION SERVICES. GALE, CENGAGE LEARNING

series of opiates can have major effects on activity. Morphine and most of the mu agonists contain a methyl (CH_3-) group on the nitrogen, but a number of other compounds with different substituents have been developed. Replacing the methyl group with an allyl ($-CH_2CH=CH_2 2$) or methylcyclopropyl ($-CH_2CHCH_2CH_2$) group does not have much effect upon the ability of the compound to bind to opioid receptors, but it markedly changes what happens when they do bind. For example, oxymorphone, with its methyl group on the nitrogen, is a clinically useful analgesic many times more potent than morphine. Replacing the methyl group with an allyl group produces naloxone. Naloxone is an antagonist, a drug that blocks or reverses the actions of other opiates. Clinically, naloxone is used as an antidote to opiate overdose. This drug's structure shows how simple changes can profoundly influence the pharmacology of these agents.

Further investigations revealed that Ring C of morphine can be eliminated, enabling use of the benzomorphans—many of which are potent analgesics. The major drug in this group is pentazocine (Talwin). Even simpler structures produce potent analgesics, such as methadone. The phenylpiperidines comprise another large group of opioids. The first of these to be used clinically was meperidine, which was first prescribed in 1939 and which still is extensively used. Modifications of the phenylpiperidine structure led to a subgroup of drugs, with fentanyl as a prototype. Fentanyl is approximately 80-fold more potent than morphine, but its very short duration of action requires continual infusions. An advantage is that once the infusion is discontinued, the effects of the drug clear rapidly. This ability to quickly turn on or off the drug's actions, along with its great potency, has made this agent a valuable tool in anesthesia. This high potency has been exploited to develop skin patches that give a constant release of fentanyl into the body as the drug is absorbed through the skin. Other agents within this series, such as sufentanil and alfentanil, are even more potent than fentanyl. Two other members of this series, loperamide and diphenoxylate, have activity but very poor solubility. This property has led to their use as antidiarrheal agents since they cannot be made soluble and injected and are therefore less likely to be abused.

Together, these structure activity studies reveal that the basic requirements needed for opioid activity are quite simple. However, the wide variety

[Leu⁵]enkephalin	**Tyr-Gly-Gly-Phe-Leu**
[Met⁵]enkephalin	**Tyr-Gly-Gly-Phe-Met**
Dynorphin A	**Tyr-Gly-Gly-Phe-Leu**-Arg-Arg-Ile-Arg-Pro-Lys-Leu-Lys-Trp-Asp-Asn-Gln
Dynorphin B	**Tyr-Gly-Gly-Phe-Leu**-Arg-Arg-Gln-Phe-Lys-Val-Val-Thr
α-Neoendorphin	**Tyr-Gly-Gly-Phe-Leu**-Arg-Lys-Tyr-Pro-Lys
β-Neoendorphin	**Tyr-Gly-Gly-Phe-Leu**-Arg-Lys-Tyr-Pro
β$_h$-Endorphin	**Tyr-Gly-Gly-Phe-Met**-Thr-Ser-Glu-Lys-Ser-Gln-Thr-Pro-Leu-Val-Thr-Leu-Phe-Lys-Asn-Ala-Ile-Ile-Lys-Asn-Ala-Tyr-Lys-Lys-Gly-Glu
Dermorphin	Tyr-D-Ala-Phe-Gly-Tyr-Pro-Ser-NH$_2$

Table 2. Selected opioid peptides. ILLUSTRATION BY GGS INFORMATION SERVICES. GALE, CENGAGE LEARNING

of structures becomes even more intriguing since morphine and the other opioids act within the brain by mimicking naturally occurring peptides—the endogenous opioids. The enkephalins were the first such naturally occurring substances to be isolated and sequenced (Table 2). Initially, these results were somewhat confusing since the two enkephalins—both pentapeptides—contain the identical first four amino acids and differ only at the fifth. The complexity of these peptides became more clear with the subsequent isolation and characterization of β-endorphin, a 31-amino acid peptide derived from a larger protein, which also gives rise to active compounds, including ACTH and α-MSH. The first five amino acids in β-endorphin are identical to [met⁵]enkephalin, but [met]enkephalin and β-endorphin derive from different gene products. There are also a series of compounds containing the sequence of [Leu⁵]enkephalin, including dynorphin A, dynorphin B and α-neoendorphin. All these compounds (the enkephalins, endorphins, and dymorphine) have distinct genes and are expressed independently from one another. Thus, they comprise a family of similar but discrete neurotransmitters.

The opioid peptides are becoming important clinically. A major difficulty in the use of peptides is the fact that they are broken down when taken by mouth; thus most have very limited oral activity. However, new derivatives specifically designed to be more stable have been developed, which will provide new leads. The enkephalins are potent at delta receptors, and many of their derivatives are delta-selective. Some of the more recent derivatives label delta receptors more than 10,000-fold more selectively than others. Yet other peptides are very

much like morphine in terms of their pharmacology and receptor binding. Finally, peptides with opioid actions are now being identified in a variety of other tissues; for example, toad skin has dermorphin, a potent and stable opioid peptide.

See also **Addiction: Concepts and Definitions; Opioid Complications and Withdrawal; Pain, Drugs Used for.**

BIBLIOGRAPHY

Carver, A. (2000). Medical use and abuse of opioid analgesics. *Neurology Alert, 18,* 77.

Increasing use of opioid analgesics has not exacerbated addiction (2000). *Brown University Digest of Addiction Theory and Application, 19,* 1.

Jaffe, J. H. (1990). Drug addiction and drug abuse. In A. G. Gilman et al. (Eds.), *Goodman and Gilman's the pharmacological basis of therapeutics,* 8th ed. New York: Pergamon. (2005, 11th ed. New York: McGraw-Hill Medical.)

Jaffe, J. H., & Martin, W. R. (1990). Opioid analgesics and antagonists. In: A. G. Gilman et al. (Eds.), *Goodman and Gilman's the pharmacological basis of therapeutics,* 8th ed. New York: McGraw-Hill Medical. (2005, 11th ed.)

Lindesmith, A. R. (2008). *Addiction and opiates.* Piscataway, NJ: Aldine Transaction Publishers.

Lowinson, J. H. (2005). *Substance abuse: A comprehensive textbook.* Philadelphia, PA: Lippincott, Williams & Wilkins.

Magill-Lewis, J. (2000). How should opioids be converted? Pharmacists differ on approach. *Drug Topics, 144,* 53.

Sadock, B. J., & Sadock, V. A. (2007). Opioid-related disorders. In *Kaplan and Sadock's synopsis of psychiatry: Behavioral sciences/clinical psychiatry,* 10th ed. Philadelphia, PA: Lippincott, Williams & Wilkins.

Smith, H. S., Ed. (1996). *Opioid therapy in the 21st century.* New York: Oxford University Press USA. (2008, Oxford American Pain Library ed.)

Strain, E. C., & Stitzer, M. L. (2005). *The treatment of opioid dependence.* Baltimore, MD: The Johns Hopkins University Press.

Thorns, A., & Sykes, N. (2000). Opioid use in last week of life and implications for end-of-life decision-making. *Lancet, 356,* 398.

Will opium rear its smoky head yet again? (1999). *Psychopharmacology Update, 10,* 3.

GAVRIL W. PASTERNAK

OPIOID COMPLICATIONS AND WITHDRAWAL.

Opioids are frequently used in medicine for pain relief. The most commonly used opioids include morphine sulfate (Duramorph, MS Contin, Roxanol), meperidine (Demerol), hydromorphone (Dilaudid), oxymorphone (Numorphan), methadone (Dolophine), codeine phosphate and codeine sulfate, oxycodone (Percocet, Percodan), and hydrocodone (Hycodan, Vicodin). However, these substances are also among the most common drugs of abuse. When taken under medical supervision, opioid drugs have a low level of serious toxicity, with the most common side effects being nausea, drowsiness, and constipation. When self-administered, however, and not taken under medical supervision, their use is associated with a high incidence of untoward actions and side effects, as well as with a high death rate when used alone or in combination with other drugs (including alcohol).

A 2005 report by the Drug Abuse Warning Network (DAWN) estimated that heroin was involved in 164,572 emergency room visits in the United States in 2005. The DAWN report also found that in 2003 the rate of opiate-related drug abuse deaths in six states was in the range of 7.2 to 11.6 per 100,000 people.

RESPIRATORY DEPRESSION

It is generally believed that the most common life-threatening complication of opioid use, whether therapeutic or illicit, is respiratory depression, or loss of the ability to breathe automatically. Probably the most important action of morphine-like drugs in producing respiratory depression is the lessening of the sensitivity and responsiveness of the brain's medullary respiratory center to carbon dioxide (CO_2—the metabolic waste that circulates in the blood, derived from carbonic acid during animal respiration). Therefore, CO_2 becomes an inefficient respiratory stimulant, and automatic breathing ceases.

Administering a specific opioid antagonist such as naloxone to patients with severely depressed respiration frequently produces a dramatic increase in the rate of respiration and the volume of air taken in per breath. This occurs when a partial or completely re-sensitized respiratory center is confronted with high brain levels of CO_2. When the brain CO_2 levels dissipate as a consequence of the evoked excessive rate and volume of breathing (hyperpnea), the volume of air breathed per minute decreases. Yet when brain levels of the antagonist decrease, the respiratory depressant action of the opioid may again assert itself. Naloxone is a relatively short-acting antagonist (blocker). Patients who, for example, have received an overdose of long-acting opioids (e.g., methadone) may experience a fatal respiratory depression following an initially successful treatment with naloxone because the administration of that drug was discontinued prematurely.

TOLERANCE AND PHYSICAL DEPENDENCE

Other complications associated with the chronic use of opioids are the development of tolerance and dependence.

Tolerance. The most common understanding of tolerance to opioid drugs is that following chronic administration of one of these drugs, its effects are diminished. Several mechanisms are involved in the development of tolerance to drugs, including: (1) the induction of drug-metabolizing enzymes, (2) the development of coping strategies, (3) the exhaustion or depletion of neurotransmitters, and (4) an alteration in the number of active and inactive receptors. However, these mechanisms have, by and large, failed to provide adequate explanations for tolerance to opioid drugs. This may stem in part from the complexity of the results of chronic administration of opioids, the involvement of multiple mechanisms, and the influence of the dose, route, and frequency of drug administration.

Opioids, for example, alter the functioning of some body mechanisms that maintain homeostasis (i.e., equilibrium), and apparent tolerance is related to the establishment of new equilibrium conditions. This is clearly evident in respiratory depression, where opioids depress both the sensitivity and the reactivity of the brain-stem respiratory CO_2 homeostat (the sensor involved in maintaining homeostasis), causing CO_2 to be a less effective respiratory stimulant. Yet when CO_2 accumulates because of depressed respiration, the increasingly higher concentrations will cause stimulation of respiration to the degree that the altered homeostat dictates. The ability of opioids to constrict pupils (i.e., make them smaller) is dose-related, and patients receiving opioids frequently have miosis (near maximally constricted pupils). It is therefore difficult to determine if tolerance develops to opioids' miotic effect. This has given rise to the commonly accepted view that tolerance does not develop to the miotic effects of opioids.

In former opioid addicts, morphine-like drugs produce dose-related feelings of enhanced self-image, of being more efficient and effective, and of well-being. These related subjective states form the essence of opioid-induced euphoria, which is produced in patients who are plagued by feelings of inadequacy. This can be quantitatively measured using the Morphine-Benzedrine Group scale of the Addiction Research Center Inventory (ARCI).

Tests in many normal subjects (nonabusers) who are not suffering from pain indicate that opioids do not produce euphoria. Instead, in sufficiently large doses, they produce feelings of apathy and ineffectiveness, which can be dispiriting (dysphoric). When opioids are administered chronically to addicts, the subjective effects they produce change from feelings of well-being to feelings of being withdrawn, tired, and weak. With regard to these effects of chronic opioid administration, the effects are not simply diminished but rather changed.

The development of tolerance can be a problem when opioids are used in the treatment of pain. Although some degree of tolerance to analgesic effects is expected when opioid drugs are used repeatedly, in practice there is a great deal of variability among patients. Some patients with cancer pain appear to derive satisfactory relief from the same dose of morphine or similar drugs over a period of many months. For these patients, a need to increase the dose can be a signal that the disease is progressing. Other patients with terminal disease can develop remarkable tolerance. There are reports of patients who have been given the equivalent of 1,000 milligrams of morphine per hour intravenously. This is an impressively large dose, since the usual starting therapeutic doses of morphine are 10 to 15 milligrams by injection every 4 to 6 hours, and doses of more than 60 milligrams by injection can cause potentially fatal respiratory depression in nontolerant individuals. It is not usually of much benefit to change to another opioid that acts at the same receptor. For example, morphine acts at the mu-opioid (or μ-opioid) receptor.

When tolerance develops to morphine, other opioids acting at mu receptors will be less effective, a phenomenon referred to as "cross-tolerance."

Physical Dependence and Withdrawal. Closely related to the phenomenon of tolerance is the phenomenon of physical dependence. Subjects given repeated doses of opioid agonists (which act on opioid receptors to trigger physiologic actions similar to the body's natural chemicals that act at those receptors) exhibit a syndrome when the drug is withheld or when the subject is administered an opioid antagonist. The resulting group of signs and symptoms is called the "withdrawal syndrome" or "precipitated abstinence syndrome." Subjects who exhibit an abstinence syndrome are said to be "physically dependent" on the opioid. The degree of physical dependence and the intensity of the abstinence syndrome are related to the dose of the opioid agonist chronically ingested. In general, the intensity of all signs and symptoms vary together.

The opioid withdrawal syndrome includes restlessness, weakness, chills, body and joint pains, gastrointestinal cramps, anorexia (loss of appetite), nausea, feelings of inefficiency, and social withdrawal. Signs of withdrawal are generally opposite those of the acute effects of a drug, and for opioids they include activation of the autonomic nervous system, yawning, lacrimation (tearing eyes), rhinorrhea (running nose), piloerection (gooseflesh), tachypnea (rapid breathing), mydriasis (dilated pupils), hypertension (high blood pressure), tachycardia (rapid heart beat), muscle spasms, twitching, restlessness, vomiting, and diarrhea. The waves of gooseflesh that occur during severe opioid withdrawal remind some observers of the look of a plucked "cold turkey," a term that has come to be used not only for any abrupt discontinuation of a drug, but also for sudden cessation of any habit or pattern of behavior. The twitching and kicking movements of the lower extremities that can occur during opioid withdrawal have given the English language another widely used term, "kicking the habit," which is used to denote the process of giving up any pattern of behavior or drug use.

The time of onset of opioid withdrawal depends on the length of activity for the dependence-producing opioid. The withdrawal syndrome of subjects dependent on morphine or heroin is well developed within 24 hours after the last dose of the opioid, peaks after 48 hours of abstinence, and gradually subsides thereafter. Signs of abstinence in patients dependent on methadone begin to emerge 24 to 48 hours after the last dose and may not peak for two weeks.

After this acute withdrawal syndrome subsides, a protracted abstinence syndrome emerges. This differs from the acute withdrawal syndrome in some ways but not in others. Subjects who are dependent on morphine or methadone show the following signs of protracted abstinence: a modest hypotension (low blood pressure), bradycardia (low heart rate), hypothermia (lower than normal body temperature), miosis (small, constricted pupils), and tachypnea. Other signs of protracted abstinence may include an inability to concentrate and a decrease in fine-motor control. Symptoms associated with protracted abstinence in patients who were dependent on methadone include feelings of tiredness and weakness, withdrawal from society, inefficiency, decreased popularity and competitiveness, and loss of self-control. Protracted abstinence persists for at least 25 weeks after withdrawal. Protracted abstinence following addiction to morphine has also been demonstrated in rats and in dogs.

The patterns of withdrawal and the time course of symptoms described above are seen when opioid drugs that have been used for weeks or months are discontinued. However, opioid withdrawal can also be observed when a drug-dependent person is given an opioid antagonist (a drug such as naloxone that competes with opioid agonists for the opioid receptor). In a matter of minutes, this will produce a precipitated abstinence syndrome that can be severe, with vomiting, cramps, and diarrhea. This precipitated abstinence is usually brief, however, because as soon as the antagonist is metabolized (usually less than an hour for naloxone), the opioids still in the body can again attach to the opioid receptors and suppress the abstinence syndrome.

The biological mechanisms that are responsible for the development of opioid physical dependence are set into motion with the very first doses of an opioid drug. If volunteer subjects are given standard doses of morphine (15 to 30 mg) and then, after an interval varying from 6 to 24 hours, they are given naloxone, they report nausea and other feelings of dysphoria and exhibit yawning, dilated pupils, tearing, sweating, and runny nose. Changes in endocrine levels are also seen that are similar, although not as extreme, as those seen when chronically administered opioids are abruptly discontinued.

SIDE EFFECTS OF OPIOIDS

As mentioned previously, there are a number of side effects commonly associated with the use of opioid analgesics, including nausea, constipation, itching, convulsions, and dysphoria.

Nausea and Vomiting. Nausea and vomiting are experienced following the administration of opioids orally, by injection, or by injection into the spinal canal (epidurally), and they are worsened by movement and the resulting stimulation of the vestibular system (inner ear organ responsible for balance). The site responsible for these actions of opioids is presumed to be a special area in the brain stem or medulla, the chemoreceptive trigger zone of the area postrema.

Constipation. Constipation, a common but undesirable effect of opioids, is sometimes a useful effect for which opioids can be prescribed. It is undesirable when opioids are used for the relief of pain and in opioid-dependence maintenance therapy. This effect of opioids can be used to advantage, however, to treat diarrhea. In fact, the oldest of the therapeutic actions of opiates is their anti-diarrheal and constipating effects.

It is now known that the extrinsic innervation (nerves leading from the central nervous system to the gut) and the intrinsic innervation (nerves within the wall) of the gastrointestinal (GI) tract are complex and vary from species to species. A variety of neurons with diverse neurotransmitters have been identified in the GI tract, including neurons and their processes that contain opioid peptides: the enkephalins, beta-endorphin, dynorphins, and other ligands derived from pro-opiomelanocortin. Further, mu and delta opioid receptors have been identified in the GI tract. The vagus nerve also has fibers that contain enkephalins, and the central nervous system has opioid mechanisms that modulate GI movement (motility).

Several influences must play a role in the constipating effects of opiate agonists, including increased segmental activity, decreased propulsive activity, and decreased secretory activity. Naloxone, even when administered in high doses for a long period of time in antagonist therapy of opioid abusers, does not produce an overt stimulation of the GI tract resulting in diarrhea. When opioid antagonists are administered to opioid-dependent subjects, however, GI cramps and diarrhea develop as classic opioid withdrawal signs.

Pruritus. The ability of morphine-like drugs to produce the sensation of itching (pruritus) is well known, and it is a discomforting complication when opioids are administered for therapeutic reasons. Further, many morphine-like drugs (e.g., codeine) release histamine from white blood cells that store it (mast cells and basophils). When morphine is administered intravenously, wheals (hives, or raised red lumps) may appear at the site of the injection and along the course of the vein. The wheals may be associated with the sensation of itching. Occasionally, large doses of morphine may produce generalized itching. Rarely, morphine produces pulmonary edema (fluid in the air sacs of the lung), bronchoconstriction (narrowing of the air tubes in the lungs), or wheezing. With the advent of the use of intrathecal and epidural morphine (injection of morphine into spinal fluid or around the lining of the spinal canal) in pain management, the incidence of morphine-induced pruritus has become greater. Under this circumstance, the distribution of itching may be segmental (limited to the part of the spinal cord involved). Itching remains an elusive phenomenon and is harder to define and investigate than pain. It is thought that it may be mediated by a subgroup of nociceptive (pain-carrying) C nerve fibers. Further, morphine's histamine-releasing property has been implicated in its ability to produce itching, as histamine does in allergic reactions.

Convulsions. Although most opiates produce convulsions when administered in very large doses, convulsions are most frequently observed when excessively large doses of meperidine (Demerol) or *d*-propoxyphene (Darvon) are administered. Emergent meperidine seizures are characterized by tremors and twitching, which may evolve into tonic-clonic (epileptic) convulsions. Focal and tonic-clonic seizures have been observed in patients overdosed with *d*-propoxyphene. The mechanisms whereby opioid drugs produce convulsive phenomena are not well understood and may involve several mechanisms, including: (1) direct and indirect dysinhibition of glycine and GABA-mediated inhibition, and (2) excitatory actions that are probably mediated by yet-to-be-classified receptors. The convulsant effects of *d*-propoxyphene can be readily antagonized by naloxone; however, meperidine's convulsant effects may be more resistant. Meperidine probably has a convulsant effect in its own right when administered in very large doses acutely, yet convulsant phenomena seen following the administration of multiple doses of meperidine are produced by the accumulation of a metabolite, normeperidine.

Dysphoria, Delusions, and Hallucinations. It is rare for morphine-like analgesics to produce psychotic reactions. In patients with severe pain and discomfort and in opiate addicts, single doses of morphine-like drugs most commonly produce feelings of well-being. In normal subjects with no pain or with only modest levels of discomfort, morphine produces feelings of apathy and enervation, which are somewhat dysphoric. The drug *d*-propoxyphene (Darvon) has been reported to produce bizarre reactions—delusions and hallucinations—particularly when taken chronically in large doses and when used to suppress opioid abstinence. Some agonists-antagonists (e.g., pentazocine [Talwin], nalorphine, and cyclazocine) produce feelings of apathetic sedation, perceptual distortions, anxiety, delusion, and hallucinations.

STREET DRUGS

The complications described in the preceding sections are most commonly associated with pure, unadulterated opioids. When street drugs, which are typically diluted by the seller with quinine, lactose, or other powdered materials, are injected by the user in an unhygienic manner—in doses that vary significantly—the range of complications widens. Among the complications of heroin use reported in the medical literature are strokes, inflammation of cerebral (brain) blood vessels, toxic amblyopia (painless loss of vision caused by a toxic insult to the optic nerve), bacterial meningitis (infection and/or inflammation of the tissue covering the brain), aneurysms (bulging blood vessel) and brain abscesses (area of localized infection in the brain), disorders of peripheral nerves, impairment of segments of the spinal cord, and widespread injury to muscle tissue (rhabdomyolysis)—which by releasing muscle protein can cause damage to the kidneys.

OTHER MEDICAL COMPLICATIONS

Medical complications of opioid addiction may result from unsanitary administration of the drug, from overdosing, from intoxicated behavior (e.g., accidents, unsafe sex), or from the chemical properties of opioids themselves.

Lungs. Opioid addiction may lead to pneumonia, aspiration pneumonitis (inflammation of the lung tissue from inhaling vomit or other secretions), lung abscess (an area of localized infection within the lung), or septic emboli in the lungs (an infection that starts in the cardiovascular system but spreads via the blood stream and lodges in the lung tissue). It also decreases the vital capacity and diffusion capacity of lung tissue. Opioid addicts who also smoke tobacco are at increased risk of lung infections.

Liver. Opioid addicts frequently develop viral hepatitis (types A, B, and C). In addition, addicts who are also heavy drinkers have a high incidence of cirrhosis and other disorders of liver function.

Immune System. Hypergammaglobulinemia (an abnormally high level of gamma globulin in the blood) develops in about 90 percent of opioid addicts. It is unclear whether this change in the immune system is caused by infections or by daily injections of foreign substances. It diminishes in addicts on methadone maintenance. In addition to hypergammaglobulinemia, opioid addicts are at a very high risk of contracting HIV infection from shared needles.

Muscles and Bones. Osteomyelitis (inflammation of bone and the bone marrow caused by bacterial infection) is a common complication of opioid addiction. Drug abuser's elbow is a complication in which the muscles of the lower arm are damaged by repeated needle punctures and tears.

Skin and Lymphatic System. Opioid addicts frequently develop skin abscesses and ulcerated areas from injecting heroin under the skin ("skin popping"). Using contaminated needles may result in cellulitis (an infection of the skin), lymphangitis (inflammation and infection of the lymphatic system), lymphadenitis (infection of the lymph nodes), and phlebitis (inflammation of a major vein).

Pregnancy and Lactation. Because both heroin and methadone cross the placental barrier, infants of opioid-addicted mothers are born physically dependent on the drug. They may also acquire HIV infection or hepatitis from an infected mother. Pregnant addicts should be encouraged to enter a methadone maintenance program rather than attempt complete withdrawal, because withdrawal in the last trimester of pregnancy may cause early labor. Mothers on methadone can nurse infants without harm to the child, because breast milk will not contain large amounts of methadone. Buprenorphine is an opioid partial agonist that is approved for the treatment of opioid dependence. Because the use of buprenorphine in pregnancy is less well studied than that of methadone, the latter is presumed to be safer.

THE TREATMENT OF OPIOID WITHDRAWAL (DETOXIFICATION)

The opioid withdrawal syndrome varies in severity depending on the amount of opioid used and the duration of use. For the average user of illicit opioids, withdrawal is rarely severe because the amount of drug used typically is not high. The withdrawal syndrome from such a level of use can be uncomfortable, but it is not life threatening in otherwise healthy individuals. However, death can occur if severe withdrawal is left untreated in individuals who are weakened by other medical conditions.

The process of treating someone who is physically dependent so that acute withdrawal symptoms are controlled and the state of physical dependence is ended is usually referred to as detoxification. For opioid drugs, this process can be managed on an ambulatory (outpatient) basis or in a hospital or other residential (inpatient) setting. The most common approach to easing the severity of opioid withdrawal is to slowly lower the dose of opioid over a period of days or weeks. In the United States, however, if the drug is heroin, a substitution technique is used instead. Since virtually all opioids that are abused act as agonists at the mu-opioid receptor, any mu agonist could be a suitable substitute, but the only full agonists to be approved for this purpose in the United States are methadone and LAAM (L-alpha-acetylmethadol). These medical agents are effective when taken by mouth. Methadone can completely suppress the opioid abstinence syndrome. This capacity of one opioid to prevent the manifestations of physical dependence from another is called cross-dependence. LAAM, however, was recently withdrawn from the market because of deaths linked to a toxic action of the drug on cardiac function, which was thought to cause sudden death in some patients. Buprenorphine, a partial mu agonist, has also been approved for the treatment of opioid withdrawal.

Outpatient detoxification using methadone typically involves using doses of 20 to 40 milligrams per day for a few days and then gradually reducing the dose over several weeks. Because so many patients return to illicit drug use as the dose of methadone approaches zero, government regulations controlling methadone permit a long period (up to 180 days) of slow dose reduction.

When detoxification takes place in a hospital or other residential setting, where the patient is presumably not as likely to be exposed to environmental cues that elicit craving for opioids, dose reductions of methadone can be more rapid (e.g., over 8 to 10 days), although the intensity of discomfort will be higher.

Buprenorphine (Suboxone, Subutex) a partial mu agonist, and L-alpha-acetylmethadol have also been used satisfactorily to facilitate detoxification. The opioid withdrawal syndrome can also be modified and reduced in severity by treatment with medications that do not act at the mu receptor, but instead act on some of the physiological systems that cause hyperactivity as part of the syndrome. The use of the antihypertensive medication clonidine (Catapres) is an example. Additional supportive pharmacotherapies have been aimed at reducing withdrawal symptoms through peripheral routes, such as dicyclomine (Bentyl) for abdominal cramping, loperamide (Immodium) for diarrhea, and methocarbamol (Robaxin) for muscle cramping. Psychopharmacologic agents, such as atypical antipsychotics, may be used in patients with a serious co-occurring psychiatric disorder in order to reduce anxiety, insomnia, mood instability, and psychosis during withdrawal.

The opioid antagonist naltrexone can be used to detoxify patients rapidly and to help detoxified addicts stay off opioids. Naltrexone binds more strongly than heroin to the specific brain receptors to which heroin binds. The withdrawal is usually more severe than that which comes from simply stopping the heroin, but it also has the effect of detoxifying the individual more quickly. Thus, a combination treatment of clonidine to suppress the intensity of withdrawal symptoms and naltrexone to accelerate the pace of withdrawal has been used for rapid detoxification. An ultrarapid detoxification procedure that uses opioid antagonists and other medications administered while the patient is under general anesthesia has been used to detoxify patients from opioids, but the safety, efficacy, and advantage of this method, compared to more conservative methods, has yet to be clearly demonstrated. Ultrarapid opioid detoxification remains controversial because it may be associated with increased morbidity and mortality.

Because opioid withdrawal is time-limited and rarely life threatening, many nonmedical treatments have also been used, including acupuncture and herbal medicines. Another nonmedical treatment that has been used in addicts is transcutaneous electrical nerve stimulation (TENS). It is thought that both acupuncture and TENS may be helpful because they stimulate the parts of the central nervous system that release natural opioids. At present, further research is needed because opioid addicts are very suggestible and may feel better after acupuncture or TENS because of the placebo effect.

See also **Addiction: Concepts and Definitions; Agonist; Agonist-Antagonist (Mixed); Antagonist; Brain Structures and Drugs; Complications; Drug Abuse Warning Network (DAWN); Drug Types; Heroin; L-Alpha-Acetylmethadol (LAAM); Memory, Effects of Drugs on; Methadone Maintenance Programs; Morphine; Naloxone; Naltrexone; Neurotransmitters; Opiates/Opioids; Opioid Dependence: Course of the Disorder Over Time; Opium: U.S. Overview; Pain, Drugs Used for; Physical Dependence; Pregnancy and Drug Dependence; Receptor, Drug; Tolerance and Physical Dependence; Treatment: An Overview of Drug Abuse/Dependence; Treatment, Pharmacological Approaches to: An Overview; Treatment, Pharmacological Approaches to: Buprenorphine; Treatment, Pharmacological Approaches to: Methadone; Treatment, Pharmacological Approaches to: Naltrexone; Treatment, Specialty Approaches to:**

Acupuncture; Wikler's Conditioning Theory of Drug Addiction; Withdrawal.

BIBLIOGRAPHY

Ballantyne, J. C., Loach, A. B., & Carr, D. B. (1988). Itching after epidural and spinal opiates. *Pain, 33*(2), 149–160.

Beers, M. H., Porter, R. S., & Jones, T.V. (Eds.). (2006). *The Merck manual of diagnosis and therapy* (18th ed.). Whitehouse Station, NJ: Merck Research Laboratories.

Collins, E. D., Kleber, H. D., Whittington, R. A., & Heitler, N. E. (2005). Anesthesia-assisted vs. buprenorphine- or clonidine-assisted heroin detoxification and naltrexone induction: A randomized trial. *Journal of the American Medical Association, 294*(8), 903–913.

Drug Abuse Warning Network. (2005). *National Estimates of Drug-Related Emergency Department Visits* (DAWN Series D-29, DHHS Publication No. SMA 07-4256). Rockville, MD.

Drug Abuse Warning Network. (2006). Opiate-Related Drug Misuse Deaths in Six States: 2003. *The New DAWN Report* 19. Available from http://dawninfo.samhsa.gov/.

Favrat, B., Zimmermann, G., Zullino, D., Krenz, S., Dorogy, F., Muller, J., et al. (2006). Opioid antagonist detoxification under anaesthesia versus traditional clonidine detoxification combined with an additional week of psychosocial support: A randomised clinical trial. *Drug & Alcohol Dependence 81*(2), 109–116.

Gilbert, P. E., & Martin, W. R. (1976). The effects of morphine- and nalorphine-like drugs in the nondependent, morphine-dependent and cyclazocine-dependent chronic spinal dog. *Journal of Pharmacology and Experimental Therapeutics, 198*(1), 66–82.

Gutstein, H. B., and Akil, H. (2005). Opioid analgesics. In L. L. Brunton, J. S. Lazo, and K. L. Parker (Eds.), *Goodman and Gilman's the pharmacological basis of therapeutics* (11th ed.). New York: McGraw-Hill Professional.

Haertzen, C. A. (1974). Subjective effects of narcotic antagonists. In M. C. Braude et al. (Eds.), *Narcotic antagonists.* Advances in Biochemical Psychopharmacology, vol. 8. New York: Raven Press.

Hurle, M. A., Mediavilla, A., & Florez, J. (1982). Morphine, pentobarbital and naloxone in the ventral medullary chemosensitive areas: Differential respiratory and cardiovascular effects. *Journal of Pharmacology and Experimental Therapeutics, 220*(3), 642–647.

Kleber, H. D. (1998). Ultrarapid opiate detoxification. *Addiction* 93(11), 1629–1633.

Kromer, W. (1988). Endogenous and exogenous opioids in the control of gastrointestinal motility and secretion. *Pharmacological Review, 40*(2), 121–162.

Martin, W. R., & Jasinski, D. R. (1969). Physiological parameters of morphine dependence in man: Tolerance, early abstinence, protracted abstinence. *Journal of Psychiatric Research, 7*(1), 9–17.

Martin, W. R., et al. (1973). Methadone—a reevaluation. *Archives of General Psychiatry, 28*(2), 286–295.

Mueller, R. A., et al. (1982). The neuropharmacology of respiratory control. *Pharmacological Review, 34*(3), 255–285.

O'Brien, C. P. (2005). Drug addiction and drug abuse. In L. L. Brunton, J. S. Lazo, and K. L. Parker (Eds.), *Goodman and Gilman's the pharmacological basis of therapeutics* (11th ed.). New York: McGraw-Hill Professional.

Raisch, D. W., Fye, C. L., Boardman, K. D., & Sather, M. R. (2002). Opioid dependence treatment, including buprenorphine/naloxone. *Annals of Pharmacotherapy, 36*(2), 312–321.

Wang, S. C., & Borison, H. L. (1952). A new concept of organization of the central emetic mechanism: Recent studies of the site of action of apomorphine, copper sulfate and cardiac glycosides. *Gastroenterology, 22*(1), 1–12.

Wang, S. C., & Glaviano, V. V. (1954). Locus of emetic action of morphine and hydergine in dogs. *Journal of Pharmacology and Experimental Therapeutics, 111*(3), 329–334.

WILLIAM R. MARTIN
REVISED BY ALBERT ARIAS (2009)

OPIOID DEPENDENCE: COURSE OF THE DISORDER OVER TIME.

Opioid is the term used to describe a chemical agent whether naturally derived or synthetic that activates opioid receptors in the brain and in other locations throughout the body. Examples of opioids include the naturally occurring products codeine and morphine as well as the semi-synthetic street drug heroin and the totally synthetic drug methadone. For the topic of opioid abuse and dependence, the most relevant receptors are those located in the reward circuitry of the brain and those located in the gastrointestinal tract. When opioids are ingested, these opioid receptors are activated. The response in the brain is a feeling of calm euphoria and a sense of wellbeing. The reinforcing effects promote repeated use. Simultaneously, the receptors in the GI tract are activated, which slows down propulsive movement and produces constipation. Although there are many other effects such as pain relief, constriction of the pupil of the eye, sedation and depressed breathing, the euphoric effects in the brain and the constipating effect in the gut are the most relevant to the development of addiction and the experience of withdrawal distress.

OPIOID DEPENDENCE DEFINED

Substance Related Disorders are classified in the *Diagnostic and Statistical Manual of Mental Disorders* (4th edition) referred to as DSM-IV. Opioid dependence describes the condition commonly known as *narcotic addiction*. This diagnosis is reserved for the condition in which a compulsive, repetitive, destructive cycle of drug use continues despite adverse consequences. The inconceivable situation in which a person who has achieved a period of abstinence, often after experiencing severe, painful withdrawal distress and making sincere pronouncements of intentions to quit for good, relapses to yet another bout of opioid abuse is perhaps the most frustrating aspect of attempts to understand this condition.

Opioid dependence is regarded by the American Medical Association (AMA) as a primary, chronic, progressive, relapsing, fatal disease. This conceptualization is in sharp contrast to the widespread view in the general population and the desperate desire among opioid addicts to believe that getting over an addiction is simply a matter of achieving abstinence from the drug. The course of opioid dependence over time is marked by an insidious decline into a destructive, compelling relationship with opioids. The recovery from this condition requires no less than a total commitment to a life that rejects all the activities and trappings associated with substance abuse.

EXPERIMENTATION AND TOLERANCE

No one experiments with opioids intending to develop an addiction, yet about 25 percent of those who try opioids even one time will do so. The path from experimentation to addiction begins with curiosity about the effects of the drug or possibly ingestion motivated by peer pressure. If the reward from this initial exposure exceeds the negative consequences, the individual may engage in subsequent use with continued reinforcing effects. Over

a period of weeks, months, or perhaps years, individuals continue a pattern of increasingly frequent use, being drawn back to the drug experience for its positive effects or because the drug relieves angst or emotional distress. Individuals may eventually become convinced that opioid use makes life more pleasant and its continued use becomes integrated into their pattern of life. Infrequent, occasional use yields to a regular pattern of self-administration, which leads to drug tolerance.

Tolerance, a physiological adaptation, in turn requires larger doses to achieve the desired effect. Although tolerance is always present in individuals with physical dependence, the two can be readily differentiated. The user who has progressed into the condition of physical dependence finds that reduced use is met with abdominal distress and general malaise along with the emotional discomfort of giving up a desired behavior. Those who progress to this stage in the course of dependence struggle repeatedly with attempts to cut down or control their opioid use. Some may even quit for a short time, suffering some level of withdrawal distress, and ironically, use this success to justify their denial of a problem. The relapse back to problematic opioid abuse is evidence that individuals are unable to sustain abstinence by their own force of willpower.

RELAPSE

Understanding relapse is key to understanding addiction, and the diagnostic feature of loss of control is central to the problem of relapse. During the weeks, months, and perhaps years of opioid abuse, individuals have resorted to opioid ingestion for pleasure or relief of discomfort. When the desire for pleasure or the need for stress relief arises, the tendency is for individuals naturally to resort to opioid use. The essence of loss of control is the inability to use opioids in moderation consistently. When persons return to opioid use, the inevitable struggle to manage it ensues. Unfortunately, the addicted brain is primed for this exposure and once joined, the battle is already lost.

FACTORS CAUSING INCREASED USE

Several factors have contributed to the spread of opioid addiction since the late 1980s. First, the purity of street heroin has increased while the price has declined. Analysis of street heroin seized by the U.S. Drug Enforcement Administration chronicles a dramatic change in the street market for heroin. In 1980 the average purity of street heroin was less than 5 percent. By 1998 the average purity had risen to over 40 percent, and street level purity over 60 percent was not rare. Over the same time period the average price for a pure milligram of heroin dropped from about $4 to less than $1. This cheap and highly pure heroin made its way to rural areas where young experimenters were able to experience powerful opioid effects from intranasal use (snorting). The elimination of the need for intravenous injection and the use of needles made heroin easy and attractive to use. Eventually many of these became intravenous users as their tolerance increased along with their desire for more intense effects. The end result was extreme tolerance and physical dependence to high-dose intravenous heroin.

The second factor contributing to increased levels of youth exposure to opioids was a tremendous increase in the prescription of opioids for pain management. Some evidence points to the large-scale diversion of prescription opioids. Whether young people were buying prescription opioids from illegal street vendors or pilfering medication from their households, in 2004, about 20 percent of teens nationally had tried prescription opioids, second only in prevalence to the percentage who had tried marijuana and exceeding the percentage who had used inhalants. At the close of the twentieth century, the United States was facing a burgeoning problem of opioid addiction and a constraint on its ability to provide treatment for this condition.

RISK FACTORS

Social research has identified risk factors that make some individuals more vulnerable to addiction than others and protective factors that provide some measure of risk reduction. It has long been known that genetic influences are at work in alcoholism. Thus while the general population risk of alcoholism is about 13 percent, this rate increases to 50 percent for sons of alcoholic fathers. The role of genetics in the acquisition of opioid addiction is not clear, but there is good evidence from family studies that opioid dependence is familial. Further, three recent linkage studies of opioid dependence have identified regions of chromosomes that are likely to harbor genes that increase risk of opioid

dependence. However in general, whereas poor social skills and early aggressive behavior are regarded as risk factors, positive relationships and self control are protective factors. Drug availability and lack of parental supervision increase vulnerability, whereas parental monitoring and support and anti-drug use policies in the school have the opposite effect. (Leshner, 1997, pp. 45–47).

THE ADDICTED BRAIN

Alan Leshner, past director of the National Institute on Drug Abuse (NIDA), wrote an article titled "Addiction Is a Brain Disease—and It Matters." In it he argues, on the basis of years of research studies and clinical reports, that the addicted brain functions differently from the non-addicted brain. He cites evidence for this conclusion, including the addict's behavioral and emotional reactions to visual, auditory, and olfactory stimuli that produce no reactions in the non-addicted individual. For instance, the smell of a burning match, the sight of a crack pipe, and the sound of crack cocaine being heated in the pipe spark visible brain changes in cocaine addicts but not in non-users.

Nora Volkow, the director of NIDA, conducted extensive brain imaging research demonstrating clearly that the addicted brain's response to stimuli is known to be associated with addicts' drug use behaviors. Thus, it is widely known as of 2008 that drug addiction has powerful physiological underpinnings that, once established, are terribly difficult to overcome. Every behavior associated with the procurement, preparation, and administration of one's drug of choice (in this case, opioids) is neurologically connected to the primitive reward circuitry of the brain. In the addict's brain, the use of opioids is hooked into the same survival circuitry that underlies other life sustaining behaviors such as eating, drinking, and sex.

The treatment of opioid dependence in the United States has a long and convoluted history, well described by David Musto in *The American Disease*. Modern treatment can draw on abstinence-oriented approaches that employ counseling, support group interventions, and medication therapy. The most powerful approach combines these elements into a comprehensive program of care and adds urine testing to identify episodes of drug use as another key element.

RECOVERY

Recovery from opioid dependence requires critical changes in one's thought processes as well as one's behavior. Change is difficult in any circumstance and is fraught with ambivalence. In the case of opioid dependence, the ambivalence is particularly powerful as the addict vacillates between the compulsion to use opioids and the need to quit.

The change process was described by researchers J. O. Prochaska and C. C. DiClemente (initially related to smoking cessation, but which has been applied to opioid dependence) using a model that identifies five stages (Prochaska et al., 1992). The first is *precontemplation* in which individuals are not considering making a change even when confronted by others. As their condition worsens, they may begin to feel that change would be good but are not ready to make a firm commitment to change. This second stage is called *contemplation*. Continued losses in the areas of interpersonal relations, productivity, self-esteem, and health make the desire for change more urgent, and addicts begin making concrete plans to change. During this third stage, called *preparation*, they may seek out information about treatment options, may consider the availability of medication therapy, and may make telephone calls to treatment programs or physicians who provide addiction services. When they enter the treatment system they have moved to the fourth stage of change called *action*. They begin to put into play the behaviors necessary to quit using opioids. The fifth stage is termed *maintenance*, which is perhaps the most difficult stage of change in that sustaining abstinence requires different thoughts, behaviors, and skills than does the initial act of quitting.

When abstinence is imposed abruptly, as in the case of incarceration, addicts have not had ample time to work through the psychological challenges that accompany the process of change. Thus, despite having achieved abstinence, relapse frequently occurs soon after release from detention. The same situation occurs when their treatment is imposed by an outside authority (e.g., parent, employer, court). Although abstinence can be sustained while the coercive forces are applied, unless the motivation for change is vigorously addressed in treatment and internalized by addicts, the likelihood of long-term recovery is low. Fortunately, for some individuals, the transition to self-motivated recovery does take place, and in such cases individuals entering treatment through coercion have good outcomes.

Paradoxically, the chronic progressive nature of addiction coupled with the psychological defense process called *denial* and the effects of almost constant drug intoxication makes spontaneous change unlikely. The tension between others recognizing the need for change and the addict who feels that change is unnecessary can reach an unbearable level. This predictable dynamic is the cause of much family strife whether the addict is a child, parent, or spouse.

TREATMENT OF ADDICTION AS A CHRONIC DISEASE

The importance of understanding addiction as a chronic disease applies not only to friends and family but also to the addict. The belief that opioid dependence is simply a drug problem leads many addicts on a desperate search to rid themselves of the drug as quickly as possible. If abstinence from illegal opioids is achieved without acknowledging the *brain disease* components of addiction, abstinence will be short lived. Staying engaged in treatment long enough to learn this information, absorb it, and assimilate it into one's life may be the most important factor in addiction treatment.

Medications have proven useful in opioid addiction treatment. Three prescription drugs approved by the U.S. Food and Drug Administration to treat opioid dependence are currently in use. They are methadone oral tablets and liquid, buprenorphine sublingual tablets, and naltrexone oral tablets. Methadone is perhaps the most well known of these medications. Its use for the treatment of opioid dependence is restricted by federal regulations to methadone programs. Methadone cannot be prescribed by private physicians for the purpose of opioid addiction treatment and can be legally obtained for this purpose exclusively through a licensed methadone program.

Buprenorphine (Suboxone, Subutex) can be prescribed by physicians who have completed at least a basic course in addiction medicine and are certified buprenorphine prescribers under the terms of the Drug Addiction Treatment Act passed by the U.S Congress in 2000. Federally authorized physicians for buprenorphine treatment can be found online. Buprenorphine prescriptions can be dispensed by community pharmacies. One advantage of buprenorphine over methadone lies in its wider availability, especially relevant for opioid dependent individuals living in rural areas where methadone clinics are unavailable and the burden of travel is great. The unique pharmacology of buprenorphine makes it less likely to be abused by opioid addicts, especially in the naloxone-containing formulation called Suboxone.

The hurdle of opioid withdrawal distress is a barrier to abstinence for many opioid addicts. Both methadone (a full agonist) and buprenorphine (a partial agonist) activate opioid receptors and reverse the effects of opioid withdrawal. The immediate relief of withdrawal sickness is an attractive property of these agents. These medications make the entry into treatment less onerous by removing this stumbling block. Either of these medications can be effectively used in doses that first stabilize the patient's condition and then are tapered off, leaving the individual free of opioids at the conclusion of medication therapy. It has been said that "[w]ithdrawal services are essentially acute services with short-term outcomes, whereas heroin dependence is a chronic relapsing condition, and positive long-term outcomes are more often associated with longer participation in treatment" (Vorrath, 2001, p. 30). Engagement into treatment may be facilitated by medication therapy, but medications alone are insufficient intervention for the long-term management of the disease.

Maintenance treatment recognizes the limitation of medical withdrawal and employs the use of methadone or buprenorphine for months or years rather than days or weeks. The patient's physical dependence is sustained but since the medications are provided through legitimate channels in formulations that have low abuse potential and diminished reinforcing effects, the destructive elements of drug seeking behaviors are eliminated. A single daily dose of either medication produces a stable effect rather than the highs and lows of multiple daily doses of illicit opioids. This stabilizing effect on opioid physical dependence is one goal of maintenance therapy. Keeping patients attached to treatment services, including those that address disabilities that accompany, but are not central to, opioid dependence (e.g., family, social, educational, and general health problems) is another.

Multiple studies have demonstrated the therapeutic benefit of maintenance treatment with both methadone (Ball & Ross, 1991) and buprenorphine on multiple dimensions of patients' lives. Reduced opioid abuse and other criminal activity, improved interpersonal relationships, increased employment, and better physical and mental health are some of the consistently measured beneficial outcomes of maintenance therapy.

While engaged in maintenance therapy, patients optimally are simultaneously immersed in recovery activities with the goals of changing the way they think and the way they act. Successful patients learn new ways of responding to the elements of daily life that were woven into their addiction. People entering recovery find that while they want to change, the world around them is essentially the same. They continue being exposed to the environments in which they bought and used opioids; friends with whom they shared drug experiences continue calling; negative emotions that prompted opioid use have not been resolved. Maintenance therapy keeps patients engaged in treatment long enough to deal with these challenges and provides a measure of protection against unplanned opioid ingestions.

Naltrexone (Trexan) is a medication that has effects opposite those of methadone and buprenorphine. Naltrexone is an opioid receptor antagonist (blocker) and offers no relief from withdrawal distress, but if taken regularly it prevents opioids from accessing and activating the body's opioid receptors. In doing so, naltrexone prevents opioid effects in the brain or other locations in the body. Whereas a person abusing opioids today can begin a course of treatment with methadone or buprenorphine tomorrow, one complication of naltrexone is that a person must be free of opioids for least seven to ten days prior to beginning its use, since it precipitates a severe withdrawal reaction in individuals who are physically dependent on opioids. Another weakness of naltrexone is the low rate of adherence among those for whom it is prescribed.

New science, better clinical techniques, and advances in medication therapy have made opioid addiction more clearly understood and more effectively treated. Continuing challenges in the United States revolve around attempts to prevent opioid abuse through strategies that either reduce the demand for opioids or restrict their supply on the street. The creation of new scientific and clinical knowledge can lead to improved programs of intervention and treatment. Effective implementation of sound policies can limit availability of opioids and expand access to treatment. Together, these efforts will hasten the nation's efforts to respond effectively to the problem of opioid abuse and addiction in modern times.

See also **Addiction: Concepts and Definitions; Britain; Coerced Treatment for Substance Offenders; Conduct Disorder and Drug Use; Crime and Drugs; Opiates/Opioids; Opioid Complications and Withdrawal; Risk Factors for Substance Use, Abuse, and Dependence: An Overview; Wikler's Conditioning Theory of Drug Addiction.**

BIBLIOGRAPHY

American Psychiatric Association. (1994). *Diagnostic and statistical manual of mental disorders* (4th ed.). Washington, DC: Author.

Ball, J. C., & Ross, A. (1991). The effectiveness of methadone maintenance treatment. New York: Springer-Verlag.

Curran, J. J. (2005). *Prescription for disaster: The growing problem of prescription drug abuse in Maryland.* State of Maryland Office of the Attorney General.

Gelernter, J., Panhuysen, C., Wilcox, M., Hesselbrock, V., Rounsaville, B., Poling, J., et al. (2006). Genome-wide linkage scan for opioid dependence and related traits. *American Journal of Human Genetics, 78,* 759–769.

Glatt, S. J., Su, J. A., Zhu, S. C., Zhang, R., Zhang, B., Li, J., et al. (2006). Genome-wide linkage analysis of heroin dependence in Han Chinese: Results from wave one of a multi-stage study. *American Journal of Medical Genetics. Part B, Neuropsychiatriac Genetics, 141B*(6), 648–652.

Lachman, H. M., Fann, C. S., Bartzis, M., Evgrafov, O. V., Rosenthal, R. N., Nunes, E. V., et al. (2007). Genome-wide suggestive linkage of opioid dependence to chromosome 14q. *Human Molecular Genetics, 16*(11), 1327–1334.

Leshner, A. I. (1997). Addiction is a brain disease—and it matters. *Science, 278,* 45–47.

Merikangas, K. R., Stolar, M., Stevens, D. E., Goulet, J., Preisig, M. A., et al. (1998). Familial transmission of substance use disorders. *Archives of General Psychiatry, 5*(11), 973–979.

Musto, D. (1987). *The American disease: Origins of narcotic control* (expanded ed.). New York: Oxford University Press.

The science of drug abuse and addiction. National Institute on Drug Abuse. Available from http://www.nida.nih.gov/scienceofaddiction/addiction.html.

Prochaska, J. O., DiClemente, C. C., & Norcross, J. C. (1992). In search of how people change: Applications to the addictive behaviors. *American Psychologist, 47,*1102–1124.

Tsuang, M. T., Lyons, M. J., Meyer, J. M., Doyle, T., Eisen, S. A., Goldberg, J., et al. (1998). Co-occurrence of abuse of different drugs in men: The role of drug-specific and shared vulnerabilities. *Archives of General Psychiatry, 55,* 967–972.

Vorrath, E. (Ed.). (2001). National clinical guidelines and procedures for the use of buprenorphine in the treatment of heroin dependence. Available from http://www.nationaldrugstrategy.gov.au/.

ANTHONY C. TOMMASELLO

OPIUM: INTERNATIONAL OVERVIEW.

Throughout recorded history, opiates have occupied a central place in medicine, renowned for their ability to relieve pain, cough, and diarrhea and induce a sense of well-being. Since the early twentieth century, they have symbolized the problems with attempts to control drug use through legislation and enforcement. From the days of the Silk Road to the present, opium has been an important commodity in world trade. (Technically, opiates are a subset of opioids, which also include synthetic agents and naturally occurring peptides that bind to opioid receptors in the brain.)

EARLY USE AND CULTIVATION

From about 2000 BCE, poppy cultivation spread throughout the Middle East, as evidenced by references to opium in inscriptions of ancient Sumer and Egypt. The physician Galen, in the second century CE, noted that opium cakes were widely sold in Rome. For many centuries, the opium poppy (*Papaver somniferum*) was grown in semiarid parts of the Middle East and southern Asia, including dry or steep locales where other crops are difficult to cultivate. For traditional poppy farmers, opium was both a staple and cash crop that supplemented an agricultural livelihood. The entire plant was used: Poppy seeds were baked into breads; oil for cooking or fuel was extracted from them; and the body of the plant was fed to cattle. The labor-intensiveness of collecting the opium-containing exudate from excised seed pods meant that whole families were pressed into service at harvest time. From this region, opium was transported to distant points where it was enjoyed or used as a medicine to relieve such symptoms as pain and diarrhea. It was a commodity in the transcontinental market that brought spices and silks from India and China westward; opium moved eastward and Muslim traders brought it to China in the eighth century.

During the Middle Ages, the severing of ties between Europe and the Middle East cut off opium shipments to Europe. In the Middle East, however, the ancient Roman and Greek texts remained important sources of knowledge. In these Muslim countries, where alcohol was forbidden, both opium and cannabis were widely used. In the thirteenth century Europeans rediscovered the old texts in Arabic translation; their translation back into Latin helped spark the Renaissance. Opium came to Europe at about the same time that Galen, who had systematized humoral theory in his second-century writings, became recognized as an important medical authority in Europe. Physicians interpreted opium's effect on bodily fluids (by promoting sweat or relieving diarrhea) as affecting humors. Galen's views were challenged by the sixteenth-century Swiss physician Paracelsus, who favored chemical remedies (such as mercury) to herbal ones. Nevertheless, Paracelsus valued opium; he mixed alcohol, opium, and other ingredients to make laudanum (from the Latin for "praise") to suggest its superiority. The English physician Thomas Sydenham wrote in 1680: "Among the remedies which it has pleased Almighty God to give to man to relieve his sufferings, none is so universal and so efficacious as opium."

TRADE AND INDUSTRIALIZATION
As Europeans discovered ocean routes to Pacific and Asian ports, beginning in the sixteenth century, goods that had traveled over the Silk Road were now loaded onto sailing ships that plied global trade routes in a market which increasingly involved drugs as commodities. The Dutch brought tobacco and introduced smoking to Asian populations in the sixteenth century. By the early seventeenth century smokers had begun adding opium to the tobacco; in time, opium was smoked by itself.

An opium poppy. © EYE UBIQUITOUS/CORBIS.

This pattern of use was more social than medical, as men gathered to engage in the ritual of preparing the opium for smoking and together enjoying the languorous experience. Before long, some observers noted a pattern in which opium users steadily increased the amount they consumed and, if deprived of opium, exhibited symptoms of physiological and mental distress—what would later be called addiction. Concern about rising levels of use prompted the Chinese emperor to ban opium use in 1729; similarly, Southeast Asian countries banned the import and use of opium in the early nineteenth century. However, imports and use continued to rise.

In the eighteenth century the British became increasingly active in transoceanic trade, establishing the East India Company to manage trade in India. The British public expressed a persistent demand for Chinese products, especially tea, whereas the Chinese desired little in the way of imports from Great Britain, preferring payment in silver. The British sought to redress the resulting trade imbalance. Through triangular trade, the British satisfied the domestic demand for tea and reduced the silver drain by selling opium produced in India to the Chinese. By the 1830s opium was the dominant trade item between these countries. The Chinese government viewed the rising opium imports with growing alarm. Between 1838 and 1842, and again between 1856 and 1860, China and Britain fought two Opium Wars. The victorious British quelled China's attempts to prohibit the importation of opium, which continued to be an important cash generator in British overseas trade until the late nineteenth century. Use in China became widespread as domestic production in addition to imported opium increased the availability of the drug, prices dropped, and its purchase came within reach of poorer groups. By the early twentieth century its use was widespread.

Britain also experienced growing demand for opium over the course of the eighteenth and nineteenth centuries. Persons seeking to treat themselves for various aches or ailments, or wanting to relieve drudgery, sleeplessness, or simply a persistent cough, could buy pellets of opium from apothecaries. This pattern persisted throughout most of the nineteenth century, although by the late eighteenth century physician Thomas Trotter had described the effect of chronic opium consumption: If a habitual user stopped taking the drug, a clearly recognizable syndrome of symptoms ensued. These included runny nose, sweating, aches, tremor, vomiting, and diarrhea. This phenomenon was seen to a large extent as the unfortunate consequence of taking medicines; it was not portrayed as a unique and devastating problem that threatened the social fabric.

Industrialization caused profound social shifts in England in the first half of the nineteenth century. People whose families had worked on the land for generations became part of the first large-scale factory workforce. Working conditions were brutal; men, women, and children worked 14-hour days, six days a week. Working women often had to bring young children to the factory with them. For working people, opium was an easily available source of relief for many complaints of both adults and children. The nonmedical use of opium spread among working classes in the United States and western European countries as they industrialized.

The incidence of addiction worried some observers, and this phenomenon became increasingly visible in part as a result of new pharmacological discoveries and changing medical technology. In 1806 Frederich Serturner of Hanover, Germany, announced that he had isolated the chief active component of opium, which he named morphine, after Morpheus, the Greek god of sleep. As the first drug compound to be isolated from the plant that contained it, this discovery launched scientific pharmacology. Drug effects could not be precisely described and measured until individual compounds were isolated. The isolation of codeine followed in 1832. In time, the systematic modification of the molecular structure of such compounds would be an important source of new medications and the basis of the modern pharmaceutical industry. Invention of the hypodermic syringe in the 1850s added a faster, more powerful route for delivering drugs such as morphine to the bloodstream and the brain. In 1898 the Bayer Company of Germany began marketing the newly trademarked heroin, produced by modification of the morphine molecule. Heroin was an early example of a product of pharmaceutical innovation that was initially valued for perceived therapeutic benefits (cough relief in this case) but whose psychoactive properties stimulated nonmedical use. As heroin quickly proved to be addictive, some observers worried that the pharmaceutical industry's ability to develop ever new medications might portend a profusion of new psychoactives whose use would cross medical boundaries into popular use.

Meanwhile, changing conditions in the late 19th century influenced the patterns and prevalence of opium use in Asia and Europe. As labor opportunities in China dwindled, Chinese men emigrated in search of work, taking the custom of smoking opium with them. They typically worked in grueling conditions, sometimes in environments where they were exposed to intestinal parasites and disease. Not only did opium provide solace at the end of a workday, it also relieved pain and diarrhea. In the British and American cities where Chinese immigrants formed Chinatowns, opium dens became fixtures in working-class neighborhoods, and English bohemians and American laborers began frequenting them. In both countries, troubling new patterns of nonmedical use of opiates further energized reformers, who characterized opium dens as lairs of alien vice. In the

United States, compassion for middle-class white women who became addicted to morphine after being introduced to it by their physicians shifted to alarm as young men in working-class neighborhoods began sniffing, then injecting, heroin. In such a framework, opiate addiction appeared as a scourge to be eradicated.

EFFORTS TO CONTROL

Reformers took an international as well as domestic perspective. From their efforts evolved the modern system of drug control. Protestant reformers and missionaries in Britain and the United States criticized both the immorality of the opium trade and disturbing patterns of use in their own nations and abroad. Starting in the 1880s, the British Society for the Suppression of the Opium Trade sought to end Britain's involvement in the opium trade. Physicians continued to be concerned about patients who became addicted to opium or morphine, their use often beginning for medical reasons.

An international treaty emerged from conferences held in Shanghai and the Hague between 1909 and 1914; it marked the beginning of coordinated efforts to control global opiate production. In the early 1920s the League of Nations created an Opium Advisory Committee to advance this work. Opium-producing countries and the European nations where (during this period) most of the world's opium was refined into drugs such as morphine or codeine also cooperated, agreeing to limit supplies of the drug. This supply-side approach to drug control has characterized the drug policies of most countries ever since.

On the domestic side, countries adopted varying approaches to opiate control. In the United States, the Harrison Narcotics Act of 1914 criminalized the use, possession, and sale of opiates. Following its implementation, a number of American cities opened clinics to treat addicts; it was unclear whether their purpose was only to help addicts through withdrawal or to allow them to take regular doses of opiates so as to maintain a controlled addiction and avoid withdrawal. The question soon became moot as the federal government, interpreting Harrison as not permitting addiction maintenance, closed the clinics. From the 1930s to the early 1970s, except for those who could afford treatment in private clinics, addiction treatment was available only through two federally run narcotic clinics that also functioned as prisons. Meanwhile, the federal government and local governments built an enforcement infrastructure intended to arrest, convict, and incarcerate users, buyers, and sellers of opiates; it grappled with a growing illicit market in heroin.

The British, seeking to avoid stimulating an illicit market, opted for medicalization. Physicians could prescribe opiates to selected addicts, maintaining their addiction. Opiate use continued to be associated with a small group of affluent bohemians and patients addicted through legally prescribed medication. In this context, nonpunitive policies appeared appropriate. China had legalized opium use at the end of the second Opium War. In the 1930s China was estimated to have 40 million opium users and opium production was widespread in the countryside. After World War II the Communist government enacted a sweeping policy of detoxifying addicts and quashing production; by the early 1950s opium use had been all but eradicated in the Peoples Republic. In Indochina, the French had begun licensing opium dens in 1870. Over the ensuing decades, several Southeast Asian countries maintained government opium monopolies, controlling production and garnering profits.

During the course of the twentieth century, diversity in policy gave way to a single model: criminalization. The United States took the lead in urging other countries to adopt tough punitive policies toward drug users and traffickers. After World War II the United Nations assumed the coordinating functions that had been exercised by the League of Nations' Opium Advisory Committee.

Enforcement structures and illicit markets grew in tandem, especially after World War II as heroin use increased significantly in the United States. As law enforcement succeeded in disrupting production or trade in one part of the world, the market would shift to another. In the early twentieth century, a time when heroin was still an officially approved medicine in many countries, most illicitly sold heroin was diverted from pharmaceutical factories in Europe. As the multinational effort to limit opiate production to medical needs gained strength, and as heroin lost favor as a medicine, traffickers took over the processing of opium into heroin.

Before World War II disrupted global heroin markets, most heroin flowing to Europe and the United States originated in Turkey, whereas heroin production in Asia served intraregional markets. In the United States, the trade was managed by ethnic gangs that developed into alcohol-trafficking syndicates during Prohibition and shifted their attention to heroin following Repeal. Jewish gangs in the early twentieth century were succeeded by Sicilian gangs, which consolidated control over production, processing, and sales. After the war, Marseilles Corsicans' connections to Turkey and French Indochina made that city an important entrepôt for heroin smuggling. The United States persuaded Turkey to sharply curtail poppy production in the early 1970s; then, Southeast Asia became the world's leading producer. In the 1990s Afghanistan metamorphosed into the world's leading producer, with the insurgent Taliban encouraging production to finance its opposition to the Afghan government. Despite continuing international efforts to monitor the production and distribution of licit psychoactives, diversion from legitimate channels has persisted and contributed to rising levels of overdose.

On the demand side, the United States became the leading heroin-consuming country in the prosperous post-World War II era; while Congress enacted increasingly draconian punishments for drug trafficking, the drug issue simmered on a back burner in the national consciousness. Then, in the 1960s startling new patterns of drug use brought the issue to the mainstream in the United States and throughout Western Europe. Since the nineteenth century the leaders of American reform efforts aiming to curb drug use had couched their rhetoric as concern about use patterns among specific populations—foreigners or African Americans. In the 1960s many drug users were young, white, and middle-class. This new generation of drug users experimented with a range of drugs besides opiates.

Policymakers feared that rising levels of heroin addiction would fuel crime waves. As growing numbers of users developed dependence problems, the demand for treatment encouraged experimentation in new modalities (such as methadone maintenance) and expansion of treatment facilities (as in community-based residential or outpatient programs). The prevalence of stimulant use among the new generation of users challenged the prevailing definition of addiction, which had been based

on opiates and other depressants. Rather than focusing on tolerance and a physiologically overt withdrawal syndrome, a new definition emphasized behavior and loss of control. In the United States, as treatment facilities expanded in both the public and private sectors, a medical approach to addiction has coexisted with the longer-standing system of enforcement and incarceration. Factors such as socioeconomic status and race have influenced which users entered which system. Destabilization following the fall of the Soviet Union contributed to rising levels of heroin use—and HIV infection—in the former Soviet republics.

OTHER IMPACTS

Opiates and their users have been refracted through various lenses. Romantic poet Samuel Coleridge exalted the dreamy state opium produced in his poem "Kublai Khan." His contemporary Thomas DeQuincey recounted his early infatuation with opium and later struggles to give up the drug in *Confessions of an English Opium Eater*. Eventually, heroin addiction came to symbolize addiction more generally and the heroin addict, especially in the United States, was cast as a junkie: a criminally involved male who symbolized profound deviance. Some heroin addicts embraced this outlaw status as a place from which to criticize conformism and hypocrisy in mainstream society; William Burroughs's novel *Junky* exemplifies this stance. Rock 'n' rollers of the 1960s celebrated heroin use, whereas punk rockers of the 1970s used heroin as a platform for challenging affluent societies in which deindustrialization had left them facing chronic unemployment.

Addictive drugs, led by the opiates, created opportunities for scientists studying the workings of the brain. Decades of pharmacological attempts to devise a nonaddicting opioid analgesic created a library of compounds that enabled researchers to hypothesize about brain function and contributed to the discovery of receptor sites in the brain for morphine and, later, other psychoactive drugs. The research field of neuroscience developed from the study of receptor sites and the role of molecules in communicating signals from one neuron to another.

The realization, soon after the first AIDS cases were diagnosed in 1981, that the mysterious new disease could be transmitted through shared syringes sparked new public health initiatives focusing on the injectors of heroin and other drugs. The sense of emergency surrounding AIDS prompted activists in the Netherlands, Australia, Britain, the United States, and elsewhere to set up needle-exchange programs to distribute syringes to injectors and collect used ones for proper disposal. Working with active drug users challenged the assumption underlying most treatment modalities that abstinence (or stabilization on methadone) must precede any meaningful therapeutic engagement. However, needle-exchange activists discovered that their programs could engage participants in a range of services, including risk reduction education and referrals to drug treatment. From this work (and also from a public health approach to alcoholism) grew the philosophy of harm reduction. Rather than insisting that drug users must stop using drugs to receive other services, harm reduction values any behavioral change that reduces risk. Thus, using only sterile syringes, because it prevents the transmission of HIV, is a positive change even if the injection behavior continues. Initially controversial, in part because needle exchange was illegal where possession of syringes without a prescription was against the law, needle exchange has become increasingly—but not universally—accepted as an important public health measure to control the spread of infectious disease. In the early twenty-first century the development of harm reduction represents the latest significant change in policy approaches to dealing with the nonmedical use of opiates. Meanwhile, opiates remain important medications for the treatment of pain, cough, and diarrhea and critical tools for understanding the workings of the human brain.

See also **China; Golden Triangle as Drug Source; Harrison Narcotics Act of 1914.**

BIBLIOGRAPHY

Berridge, Virginia. (1998). *Opium and the people: Opiate use and opiate policy in 19th and early 20th century Britain.* London: Free Association Books.

Brook, T., & Wakabayashi, B. T. (Eds.). (2000). *Opium regimes: China, Britain, and Japan, 1839–1952.* Berkeley: University of California Press.

Burroughs, W. (2003). *Junky* (50th anniversary ed.). Edited and with an introduction by Oliver Harris. New York: Penguin. (Original work published 1953).

Dikötter, F., Laamann, L., & Zhou X. (2004). *Narcotic culture: A history of drugs in China.* Chicago, IL: University of Chicago Press.

McAllister, W. B. (2000). *Drug diplomacy in the twentieth century: An international history.* New York: Routledge.

McCoy, A. (1991). *The politics of heroin: CIA complicity in the global drug trade.* New York: Lawrence Hill Books.

Musto, D. F. (1987). *The American disease: Origins of narcotic control* (Expanded ed.). New York: Oxford University Press.

Trocki, C. A. (1999). *Opium, empire and the global political economy: A study of the Asian opium trade 1750–1950.* London: Routledge.

Walker, W. O. III, (1991). *Opium and foreign policy: The Anglo-American search for order in Asia, 1912–1954.* Chapel Hill: University of North Carolina Press.

CAROLINE JEAN ACKER

OPIUM: U.S. OVERVIEW.

Through much of American history, opiates have been central to an understanding of addiction, whether framed as a problem of medicine or public policy. From the Europeans' arrival to the late nineteenth century, opiates comprised one of the most important classes of medicines. In the 1900s, concerns about the nonmedical use of opiates shaped the development of American drug policy. In the late twentieth century, research on opiates provided a foundation for neuroscience, the study of brain function.

EARLY USES OF OPIUM

European settlers first brought opium to North America, where physicians administered it to relieve pain, cough, and diarrhea. A product of Asia, opium was a commodity in the shipping trade that connected the North American colonies with the rest of the world. As a medicine, opium was swallowed as pellets made from the exudate of the seed pods of the opium poppy (*Papaver somniferum*). Following the extraction of morphine and codeine from opium in the early nineteenth century, physicians relied more heavily on these compounds, though opium continued to be available for physicians to administer or patients to purchase.

In the first half of the nineteenth century, neither medications nor medical practice were regulated, and opiates were sold freely. During Andrew Jackson's presidency, the states repealed physician licensing requirements on the grounds that they created artificial elites. At the time, many people treated themselves or their families with homemade or purchased remedies. Taking charge of one's own medical care reflected the broadened democratic spirit of the Jacksonian Age.

Physicians also administered opiates generously as part of the "heroic" brand of therapy. Based on humoral theory, "heroic therapy" interpreted disease as an imbalance of bodily fluids and sought to restore balance through the administration of drugs whose visible effects provided evidence of their efficacy. Whether by producing sweat or inhibiting diarrhea, opiates demonstrated their efficacy in regulating bodily fluids. Physicians also valued opiates for their wide-ranging ability to relieve symptoms, including coughing and insomnia. For chronically weak patients, opiates improved spirits and energy, and they were thus considered to have a stimulant effect (although they are now classed as depressants).

The chief value of opiates, however, lay in their ability to relieve pain. This effect was enhanced with the introduction of the hypodermic syringe in the 1850s. Some American physicians were quick to adopt the syringe, using it to inject morphine under the skin to treat painful local conditions such as facial neuralgia. They valued the faster and stronger onset of the drug's effects this method produced, compared to oral administration. Morphine remained one of the most commonly injected drugs over the rest of the nineteenth century, and it was administered for a lengthening list of conditions. During the American Civil War (1861–1865), the combination of the more potent morphine, the hypodermic syringe, and wartime conditions contributed to widespread hypodermic morphine use. Wounded soldiers were given syringes and supplies of morphine to treat their own pain, and some became addicted. Following the war, many of these soldiers phased out opiate use as their wounds healed, but others continued using morphine for years.

THE POST-BELLUM PERIOD

The late nineteenth century witnessed the rise of a burgeoning market in medications advertised to the public through increasingly sophisticated methods. Opiate-containing preparations were pitched for women's ailments, children's colic, teething pain, and other similar uses. Labels made extravagant claims but frequently obscured the contents of these products. Morphine, with its ability to ease pain and induce calm, was a common ingredient in such medications. Men, women, and children consumed opiates, often unknowingly, as a normal part of maintaining health and managing moods. Use was especially high in the South. All of these factors made the late nineteenth century the period with the highest rates of opiate use in American history.

The most common pattern of opiate use—and addiction—in the late nineteenth century involved white middle-class women who began taking morphine as medicine. Most were introduced to morphine by their physicians, but opiates were also available from pharmacies or mail-order houses. Some women took morphine to relieve menstrual cramps, and they taught their adolescent daughters to do the same. Others were treated for a medical condition and found that morphine induced a powerful sense of well-being. At a time when such women were expected not to drink alcohol (and thus were deprived of a socially acceptable form of drug use to modulate emotion or ease social anxieties), some found morphine to be a reliable means of banishing worry. When what began as episodic use became habitual, such women found themselves burdened with addiction. The character of Mary Tyrone in Eugene O'Neill's play *Long Day's Journey into Night*, which is set in 1912, exemplifies this pattern, in which addiction was a source of shame.

Addicts often sought treatment in privately run clinics that promised anonymity and offered little more than a place to rest while they went through withdrawal. Some addicts, meanwhile, purchased purported cures that merely contained more opiates. Others continued to take opium or morphine, managing their responsibilities as long as their drug supply remained uninterrupted. Medical and moral views combined to frame addiction as a tragic loss of self-control that all too often it resulted from a physician's liberality in prescribing morphine.

In the early 1890s, physicians began to express concerns about rising levels of addiction. Some studied addiction as a medical problem termed *inebriety*. They believed that addiction to alcohol and to opiates reflected the same disease process. Psychiatrists established inebriety hospitals, modeled on insane asylums, for the treatment of alcoholics and morphine addicts. Other physicians urged their colleagues to reduce the prescribing of opiates. These concerns reflected the spirit of reform that was transforming medicine into an elite profession with epistemological foundations in the scientific laboratory. From this perspective, opiates' ability to relieve symptoms rather than attack the cause of disease cast them as old-fashioned. Addiction caused by a physician's actions tarnished the image these reformers sought for scientific medicine, and they urged that morphine use be restricted to a few conditions at minimal doses for short periods.

SHIFTING DEMOGRAPHICS OF USE

As industrialization, urbanization, and immigration transformed American society, new nonmedical patterns of opiate use arose. After 1850, Chinese laborers came to the American West to build the railroads and work at other forms of gang work. Some Chinese settled in Pacific coast cities, and they brought with them the practice of smoking opium to induce a two-to-three-hour state of dreamy relaxation. Whites, including laborers fearful of workplace competition, framed this practice as a sign of racial depravity. This racial linking, which demonized both a drug and its users, recurred repeatedly in the twentieth century.

From the 1880s until World War I, southern and eastern European immigrants came to America seeking jobs in the industrializing economy. They settled in crowded working-class neighborhoods in American cities, along with rural whites and, beginning in the early twentieth century, African Americans. The Americans who grew up in these neighborhoods encountered an emerging working-class entertainment scene that included dance and pool halls, brothels, and saloons. As young adults, they danced to early jazz, drank beer or whiskey, and sniffed cocaine or heroin. Bayer had introduced the latter drug in 1898 as a superior cough remedy, but thrill seekers found that crushing and sniffing the tablets produced a state of euphoria. Some of these users progressed to injecting heroin. The sale of both drugs remained unregulated, though some pharmacists exercised discretion in selling drugs. By 1910 the typical American opiate addict was a young man living and seeking amusement in a working-class neighborhood. Like the nineteenth-century matrons who injected morphine to relieve pain and assuage social anxieties, these men (and some women) used heroin from a mixture of motives: enjoyment with friends, relief of physical or emotional pain, and—when occasional use progressed to addiction—relief of withdrawal symptoms.

Heroin was a product of pharmaceutical research: A manipulation of the morphine molecule resulted in a semisynthetic compound whose effects were identical to those produced by morphine but came on faster and more intensely. As such, it exemplified an emerging trend in which pharmaceutical companies introduce new psychoactive compounds as medications. When users find them pleasurable, they incorporate them into nonmedical, social contexts of use.

THE PROGRESSIVE ERA AND EARLY LEGISLATION

By the early 1900s, opiates had become a physician's conundrum and a symbol of urban vice. Concerns about opiate addiction shifted from compassion for innocent victims of improper medication to fears of tough male heroin users. Physicians and Progressives responded with alarm and reform. Physicians worried about iatrogenic addiction and the unregulated sale of mislabeled, ineffective, or adulterated medicines. Progressives worried that opiate addiction undermined the middle-class virtues of thrift and hard work.

Concerns about adulteration, overdose, and addiction associated with an unregulated drug market became acute around 1900. In October 1905, *Collier's* magazine began publishing *The Great American Fraud*, Samuel Hopkins Adams's classic series of muckraking articles that excoriated the hawkers of ineffective or harmful medications. Adams singled out opiates, with their enslaving potential for addiction, as especially corrosive of civic virtue. His articles influenced passage of the 1906 Pure Food and Drug Act, the first federal legislation to regulate the sale of pharmaceuticals. Although it merely called for truth in labeling and proved difficult to enforce, the act foreshadowed the creation of the Food and Drug Administration.

Meanwhile, Progressive reformers responded to the new migration patterns with programs to assimilate immigrants to what they construed as "American ways." Motivated by concerns from airless tenements to wife-beating fueled by drinking sprees, they investigated deleterious conditions and recommended solutions. Alarm about high rates of syphilis and gonorrhea, which Progressive and medical observers linked to prostitutes, provoked a campaign to suppress prostitution. Cities appointed vice commissions to study prostitution, and their investigators reported widespread use of heroin and cocaine among denizens of brothels, among patrons of saloons where prostitutes picked up customers, and in the larger urban amusement districts. These investigators had discovered the new pattern of young male opiate addiction, and the civic leaders they reported to expressed alarm at the prospect of widespread addiction to drugs that seemed to vitiate the work ethic. Thus, parallel to the push to prohibit the sale of alcohol (except for medical use), a movement arose calling for the eradication of this newly perceived drug problem. Northern Progressives were joined by white southerners who brandished tales of cocaine-crazed Negroes committing violent crimes under the influence of that drug.

In the early 1900s, some states and localities restricted the sale of opiates. Congress did not take immediate action, because the Constitution left the regulation of medical practice to the states. In addition, even if they were being used in nonmedical ways, opiates were fundamentally understood to be medicines whose proper use was perverted by heroin-sniffing pool players and the like. However, pressure from another direction brought the issue of drug control before Congress. Protestant missionaries working in Asia believed the opium use they witnessed there contributed to what they perceived as economic backwardness. Between 1909 and 1914, reformers from around the world met at Shanghai and The Hague to urge worldwide control of opiate supplies so as to prevent nonmedical uses of the drugs. Some countries signed a treaty that marked the first attempt to develop a coordinated international system for controlling worldwide opiate supplies. The U.S. representatives to these meetings were embarrassed by the lack of federal legislation in the United States to control access to opiates.

The Harrison Act. A lobbying effort to bring American legislation into line with the goals of the Hague resolutions, combined with rising domestic concern about nonmedical use of opiates, led to passage of the 1914 Harrison Narcotics Act, the first U.S. law to control who could buy a drug. The act banned the sale of opiates, cocaine, and some other drugs, except as authorized by a physician. The American Medical Association (AMA), sensitive to charges that the overprescribing of opiates was the chief cause of addiction, supported the legislation. The Harrison Act set the basic course in drug policy that the United States has followed ever since, in that it sought to eradicate the use of proscribed drugs by controlling their supply. Attempts to reduce demand rather than supply—either by treating addicts or preventing drug use—have received less support.

Following implementation of the Harrison Act, health authorities in several American cities worried that the sudden lack of opiate supplies for addicts would create personal distress and a public crisis. They therefore opened clinics to dispense opiates to addicts so that they would not go suddenly into withdrawal when legal supplies were cut off. In many cases, however, the mission of the clinics was unclear. Were patients expected to wean themselves from opiates, for example, or would some be permitted to maintain their addiction with opiates supplied through such clinics? The U.S. Treasury Department, charged with enforcing the Harrison Act, moved vigorously to prosecute physicians who overprescribed opiates, arguing in court that the law specifically disallowed addiction maintenance. In 1919 the Supreme Court ruled that the wording of the Harrison Act meant that physicians could only prescribe opiates to addicts as part of a short-term detoxification program. Again, the AMA agreed. Armed with this legal support, the Treasury Department continued its enforcement against the clinics, and by the mid-1920s had closed them all. With the closure of the clinics, and as physicians became increasingly reluctant to treat drug users, opiate addicts faced drastically reduced treatment options.

THE ILLICIT MARKET AND LAW ENFORCEMENT

Opiate addicts, now forced to seek drugs in a growing illicit market, also faced a rising risk of arrest as government at various jurisdictional levels built an enforcement infrastructure. At the federal level, the creation of the Federal Bureau of Narcotics in 1930, with Harry Anslinger (1892–1975) as its head, moved drug enforcement out of the Prohibition Unit that oversaw enforcement of the 1919 Volstead Act. Following the repeal of alcohol prohibition in 1933, the Federal Bureau of Narcotics continued to enforce the prohibition of opiate use. Anslinger, a skillful administrator with a background in diplomatic service, oversaw American participation in the League of Nations' Opium Advisory Committee, which furthered the work on international control of opium supplies that had been initiated through the Hague Opium Treaty. On the domestic front, Anslinger managed an efficient team of nationwide enforcement officials. Believing that harsh and early punishment would be an effective deterrent, he supported increasingly severe punishments for drug offenders.

NEW RESEARCH INITIATIVES

Proponents of the Harrison Act had believed that cutting off opiate supplies would reduce the opiate problem to trivial levels, obviating the need for research. Earlier, the inebriety movement had led to a welter of research initiatives through the 1910s. While many of these efforts were inconclusive, a body of knowledge about drug effects, the nature of addiction, and treatment methods had accumulated. In the wake of drug and alcohol prohibition, such research was abandoned and what had been learned was quickly forgotten. However, new research initiatives emerged in the 1920s.

In 1923, as the problem of opiate addiction persisted into the era of Prohibition, the U.S. Public Health Service assigned psychiatrist Lawrence Kolb (1881–1972) to study opiate addiction. Kolb concluded that chronic addicts suffered from personality deficits that caused them to feel inordinate pleasure from opiates and thus become mired in addiction.

In the private sector, the Rockefeller-funded Bureau of Social Hygiene, founded to study prostitution, created a Committee on Drug Addictions in 1919 to study opiate use scientifically. Its work was linked through personal and professional connections to drug enforcement officials in Washington and representatives to the League of Nations' Opium Advisory Committee. The committee hired the physician Charles Terry, who had established an innovative morphine clinic in Jacksonville, Florida, to oversee its work. The committee set Terry to determining levels of opiate use in six American cities, in an effort to assess the legitimate medical need for opium imports to the United States. Rather than mailing out surveys, as previous

investigators had done, Terry traveled to each city and interviewed physicians, pharmacists, and others knowledgeable about the sale and use of opiates. The results constituted the first systematic attempt to determine levels of opiate use in a community setting. Terry and Margaret Pellens incorporated these findings, an exhaustive survey of research on opiates, with recommendations for a clinical approach to managing addiction, in *The Opium Problem*, a 1928 publication that remains a classic. The committee also sponsored a search for a non-addicting analgesic to replace morphine, on the grounds that eliminating medical need for morphine would make it possible to end opiate imports and eliminate nonmedical use.

These strands came together in the 1930s when the Public Health Service opened Narcotics Hospitals in Lexington, Kentucky, and Fort Worth, Texas. These institutions functioned as both hospitals and prisons where addicted federal prisoners, along with addicted probationers and voluntary admissions, underwent a therapeutic regimen intended to replace the bad habit of drug use with a regulated, wholesome routine. The Lexington hospital also housed the Addiction Research Center (ARC), which helped carry on the search for a nonaddicting opiate analgesic. A means of identifying addictiveness was necessary to determine whether the new analgesics being produced both by the Committee on Drug Addiction (now overseen by the National Research Council) and American and European pharmaceutical companies were, in fact, nonaddicting. Once an addictiveness assay was developed at the ARC, it became the world's clearinghouse for determining the addictiveness of new opioid compounds.

Meanwhile, as the cohort that had become addicted in the early years of the century aged and died, it was replaced by comparatively fewer new addicts. Thus, the "drug problem" faded to the background of public consciousness. The prevalence of addiction declined even further as World War II disrupted world heroin markets.

POSTWAR USAGE

Following World War II, heroin again flowed to the United States, mainly as Turkish opium refined and smuggled by Corsican gangs. Meanwhile, new populations and new patterns of entrenched and isolating poverty in American cities meant that heroin users were increasingly likely to be African American or Hispanic. A diversion of pills from the medical marketplace, including opiates, barbiturates, and amphetamines, also diversified patterns of use. Over the course of the 1950s, the age of first-time drug users fell as teenagers increasingly sampled ways to get high. Nonetheless, most Americans thought of heroin addiction as an exotic phenomenon associated with a city world of jazz and beatniks.

In policy circles, however, the heroin addict posed a serious symbolic threat. In the early years of the Cold War, when politicians fanned Americans' fears of Soviet spies masquerading as loyal Americans, a deviant identity like heroin addiction, which could be hidden from view, seemed particularly menacing. In this environment, Harry Anslinger inaccurately framed Communist China as a source of imported heroin intended to destroy the American spirit. Congress responded with the 1951 Boggs Act and the 1956 Narcotic Control Act, which imposed new, harsher penalties for heroin possession and sales. The Boggs Act included the first mandatory minimum sentences, marking a pattern in which judicial discretion, which had characterized Progressive Era criminal justice reforms, was steadily eroded. Not all agreed with ceding the drug problem to the criminal justice system, however. In 1958 the American Bar Association and American Medical Association jointly issued a report calling for less punitive responses to drug offenses and a greater emphasis on medical approaches to treating addicts.

THE 1960S
In the 1960s, startling new patterns of drug use brought the issue to mainstream consciousness. Since the 19th century, American reformers aiming to curb drug use had couched their rhetoric as concern about use among specific groups, such as the Chinese or black street criminals. Now, however, drug users were typically young, white, and middle-class.

The dramatic events of the 1960s prompted a generation raised during the prosperous 1950s to question the relatively calm and affluent world they had grown up in. The civil rights movement; the assassinations of President John Kennedy, Martin Luther King Jr., and presidential candidate Robert Kennedy; and the escalating War in Vietnam all had a profound effect on the youth culture of the 1960s. As they questioned adult authority, young people disregarded prohibitionist messages about illicit drugs. While they sought to forge new values, they also hoped to eliminate superficial and hypocritical aspects of American life. Marijuana and psychedelic drugs most closely symbolized the new spirit, but young people buying drugs on the illicit market and sharing lore about highs also encountered amphetamines and opiates.

In response to these trends, President Richard Nixon initiated the most significant changes in American drug policy since the passage of the Harrison Narcotic Act in 1914. The first legislative achievement was passage of the 1970 Controlled Substance Act, which established five schedules for ranking psychoactive drugs according to abuse potential and medical usefulness. When he became aware of a promising and inexpensive new treatment for heroin addiction, Nixon believed that it might reduce levels of heroin use and thus reduce crime levels as well. Beginning in 1963 in New York, Vincent Dole (1913–2006) and Marie Nyswander (1919–1986) had demonstrated that longtime heroin users, when stabilized on daily doses of oral methadone and supported with rehabilitative services, showed reduced criminal activity and improved functioning in social and employment areas. Nixon believed that methadone maintenance would provide a cost-effective means of reducing money-seeking crimes committed by street addicts. In 1972 he proposed, and Congress created, the National Institute on Drug Abuse (NIDA) to fund community-based drug treatment and coordinate research. The latter included studies of drug effects in the brain and contributed to the emerging field of neuroscience. Other inpatient and outpatient treatment modalities joined methadone maintenance as community-level resources for addicts. On the enforcement side, a new Drug Enforcement Administration replaced earlier agencies.

In addition, NIDA funded ethnographic studies of drug using. Inspired by the work of the sociologists Alfred Lindesmith (1905–1991) in the 1930s and Howard Becker (b. 1928) in the 1960s, as well as the work of sociologists at the Addiction Research Center at Lexington, a generation of ethnographers provided insights into social influences on drug-using behavior. Among the important studies done at this time was Lee Robins's work with Vietnam veterans. Robins (b. 1922) concluded that most veterans did not resume heroin use when they returned to their home communities.

NEW TREATMENT MODALITIES AND HARSHER PENALTIES

In the 1970s, under federal leadership, treatment programs were expanded and new ones created in cities across the nation. Increasingly, those running the programs encountered patients who did not fit the model of the criminally involved long-time heroin addict. Younger patients, women, and those using a variety of drugs reflected changing U.S. drug-use patterns, and opiates became just one group among many psychoactive drugs that were traded on the illicit market and used for recreational, lifestyle, political, or habitual reasons. As these other drugs (particularly cocaine) grabbed headlines, and as Americans' concerns focused on drug use by children as young as twelve, the national mood swung back in favor of harsh punishments for drug use. First Lady Nancy Reagan captured this mood with the slogan "Just Say No," and during Ronald Reagan's two terms as president, Congress again stiffened penalties for drug use and trafficking.

HIV, Drug Use, and Harm Reduction. Even as federal policy hardened, the advent of AIDS and the recognition of injection drug users among its earliest victims created opportunities for new public health perspectives on drug use. In the politicized context of AIDS, with its advocacy of patient activism, drug users and public health researchers directly addressed this risk. In the late 1980s, activists in a number of American cities began distributing sterile syringes to injectors to obviate the need for sharing, and thus prevent transmission of HIV. Studies established that these needle-exchange programs effectively deterred HIV transmission without increasing drug use. Over the ensuing years, localities and states used public health authority or changed laws to allow needle-exchange programs to operate with legal sanction. Needle exchange was a foundational policy initiative in the emerging movement of harm reduction.

As the possibility of HIV infection through sharing syringes became widely recognized, first-time heroin users increasingly sniffed the drug to avoid this risk. The market responded with a more potent form of heroin that was suitable for smoking. Nonetheless, many sniffers, as their tolerance rose, switched to injecting. In response to higher potency of heroin on the illicit market and the diversion of licit pharmaceuticals, such as a time-release formulation of oxycodone, overdose deaths rose dramatically. In response, harm reduction programs began overdose prevention trainings and distribution of naloxone, an opioid antagonist that reverses opioid overdoses.

In the harm reduction movement, unlike earlier initiatives to address drug problems, drug users were active in a public health movement addressing their own interests. But these initiatives faced opposition. Some treatment professionals believed that working in any way with drug users without engaging them in treatment for their drug dependence was counterproductive. Many of these individuals changed their minds as they saw the value of helping users avoid life-threatening disease until they became ready for treatment. Others, however, have opposed needle exchange on political grounds, viewing it as inconsistent with the overarching goal of federal drug policy to eradicate the nonmedical use of opiates and other illegal drugs. Still others have supported prohibition while arguing that reduction in drug-related harms constitutes a better measure of policy success than a reduction in the amounts of drugs used or numbers of users. While these debates continue, federal policy has remained committed to enforcement, with a lesser emphasis on treatment and prevention, and opposed to needle exchange and harm reduction.

See also **Foreign Policy and Drugs, United States; Harm Reduction; Harrison Narcotics Act of 1914; Opiates/Opioids; Opium: International Overview; World Health Organization Expert Committee on Drug Dependence.**

BIBLIOGRAPHY

Acker, C. J. (2002). *Creating the American junkie: Addiction research in the classic era of narcotic control.* Baltimore, MD: Johns Hopkins University Press.

Campbell, N. (2007). *Discovering addiction: The science and politics of substance abuse research.* Ann Arbor: University of Michigan Press.

Courtwright, D. T. (2001). *Dark paradise: A history of opiate addiction in America*. (Enlarged ed.). Cambridge, MA: Harvard University Press.

Jonnes, J. (1996). *Hep-cats, narcs, and pipe dreams: A history of America's romance with illegal drugs*. New York: Scribner.

Lindesmith, A. R. (1947). *Opiate addiction*. Bloomington, IN: Principia Press.

Morgan, H. W. (1981). *Drugs in America: A social history, 1800–1980*. Syracuse, NY: Syracuse University Press.

Musto, D. F. (1987). *The American disease: Origins of narcotic control*. (Expanded ed.). New York: Oxford University Press.

Terry, C., & Pellens, M., (1928). *The opium problem*. New York: Bureau of Social Hygiene.

CAROLINE JEAN ACKER

OVERDOSE, DRUG (OD).

Administration of a drug in a quantity that exceeds that which the body can metabolize or excrete before toxicity develops constitutes an overdose. Whether it is accidental or deliberate, drug overdose is a significant problem encountered by providers of emergency medical care. Accidental overdose is common among users of illegal substances of abuse, since little reliability can be placed on the potency, presence of adulterants, and even identity of the street substance. For example, heroin potency has been demonstrated to range from 3 to 90 percent. Overdoses and deaths from heroin are therefore common. The prevalence of comorbid disorders, particularly depression, in substance-abusing populations, has been found to be high. Thus, deliberate drug overdoses taken in the attempt to commit suicide are frequently encountered in this population. Also, people with a psychiatric illness but no drug-abuse problem most often attempt suicide with a drug overdose. Substances frequently implicated in drug overdose involve nonnarcotic analgesics (painkillers), benzodiazepines (tranquilizers), opiates, or antidepressants—often in combination with alcohol.

The treatment of a drug overdose begins by providing basic supportive care (i.e., ensuring that there is adequate ventilation and monitoring the heart), calling 911, an emergency medical service (EMS), or the Poison Control Center (see Appendix I in Volume 4). If little time has elapsed since ingestion, efforts may be made to prevent further absorption of the drug by such means as gastric lavage or by administration of activated charcoal. Other treatments include increasing the rate of excretion through forced diuresis or giving specific antidotes (e.g., naloxone for opiate overdose) when the substance is known or can be identified from the presenting clinical syndrome. Obtaining a careful drug history from the patient or accompanying individuals is of paramount importance in effectively treating and minimizing risks from a drug overdose, which often results in death.

See also **Drug Abuse Warning Network (DAWN); Drug Interactions and Alcohol.**

BIBLIOGRAPHY

Jaffe, J. H., Knapp, C. M., Ciraulo, D. A. (1997). Opiates: Clinical aspects. In J. H. Lowinson et al. (Eds.), *Substance Abuse: A Comprehensive Textbook*, 3rd ed. (pp. 158–166). Baltimore, MD: Lippincott, Williams, & Wilkins. (2004, 4th ed.)

Kosten, T. R., & Rounsaville, B. J. (1988). Suicidality among opioid addicts: 2.5-year follow-up. *American Journal of Drug and Alcohol Abuse, 14*, 257–369.

Linden, C. H., Rippe, J. M., & Irwin, R. S., Eds. (2005). *Manual of overdoses and poisonings*. Philadelphia, PA: Lippincott, Williams & Wilkins.

Olson, K. R. (2006). *Poisoning & drug overdose*, 5th ed. New York: McGraw-Hill Medical.

MYROSLAVA ROMACH
KAREN PARKER

OVEREATING AND OTHER EXCESSIVE BEHAVIORS.

Overeating is grouped together with substance abuse and dependence in a large group of disorders designated as behavioral (non-substance-related) addictions. The term *impulse control disorders* has been used by some clinicians to describe these behaviors. In this context the notion of *addiction* centers on the repetitiveness of the behavior and would include such behaviors as compulsive spending, compulsive gambling, excessive computer gaming, pathological overeating (bulimia), hypersexuality, kleptomania (repetitive, compulsive stealing when there is no need), as well as such miscellaneous obsessive-compulsive behaviors as tics and hair-pulling (trichotillomania).

Research into the neurobiology of these behaviors as of 2008 is in an early stage. Advances in understanding motivation, reward, and addiction have provided insight into the possible pathophysiology of these disorders. Some researchers have pointed out similarities among these disorders and speculate that there may be similar brain mechanisms involved in some of them. For example, it has been shown that dopamine levels in certain areas of the brain (such as the nucleus accumbens) are elevated by the smoking of reinforcing drugs, including cocaine, amphetamines, opioids, marijuana, and, to some degree, nicotine. However, increased dopamine levels in these same brain circuits have been shown to occur when animals anticipate food or sexual activity. Also, learning, conditioning, and reinforcement play important roles in these repetitive behavior disorders as well as in the more traditional chemical or substance abuse and dependence disorders. It has also been pointed out that treatments for nonchemical addictive disorders often follow principles used in substance use disorders; for example, identifying trigger and high-risk situations, teaching alternative coping behaviors, and emphasizing relapse prevention. Self-help groups using principles of Alcoholics Anonymous have also been organized, such as Overeaters Anonymous or Gamblers Anonymous. Some pharmacologic agents appear to alter both drug ingestion and obsessive-compulsive behaviors that are not drug-related. For example, selective serotonin reuptake inhibitors, used as antidepressant and antianxiety medications, seem to help some alcoholics decrease alcohol consumption and compulsive hair-pullers reduce that behavior.

Such broad definitions of addictive behaviors have disadvantages when they focus too much attention on the commonalities among the diverse behaviors while minimizing the differences and particularities. At a time when rapid progress is occurring in the understanding of the biological processes associated with substance dependence, focusing only on commonalities may obscure the value of therapeutic interventions aimed at specific disorders. For example, nicotine transdermal patches seem to have considerable value in treating tobacco dependence but are probably of no value for cocaine dependence or compulsive gambling.

The way society (or science) chooses to categorize behaviors—desirable or undesirable, repetitive or episodic—is determined in large measure by the objectives of developing the categorization. There are probably some circumstances in which it is helpful to think about a broad category of problematic excessive behaviors encompassing everything from substance abuse to excessive Internet gaming. There is also the risk that in doing so researchers convey the notion that excessive drug use is no more serious or refractory to intervention than Internet gaming. Certainly in the early twenty-first century, the social costs and medical consequences of the substance use disorders are so great that researchers should be cautious about embracing any conceptual scheme that tends to trivialize or make these problems seem less serious than they are.

See also **Addiction: Concepts and Definitions; Obesity; Research, Animal Model: An Overview; Risk Factors for Substance Use, Abuse, and Dependence: An Overview; Risk Factors for Substance Use, Abuse, and Dependence: Learning.**

BIBLIOGRAPHY

American Psychiatric Association. (2004). *Diagnostic and statistical manual of mental disorders* (4th ed., text revision). Washington, DC: Author.

Crockford, D. N., Goodyear, B., Edwards, J., Quickfall, J., & el-Guebaly, N. (2005). Cue-induced brain activity in pathological gamblers. *Biological Psychiatry, 58*(10), 787–795.

Rothemund, Y., Preuschhof, C., Bohner, G., Bauknecht, H. C., Klingebiel, R., Flor, H., et al. (2007). Differential activation of the dorsal striatum by high-calorie visual food stimuli in obese individuals. *Neuroimage, 37*(2), 410–421.

Schneider, J. P., & Irons, R. R. (2001). Assessment and treatment of addictive sexual disorders: relevance for chemical dependency relapse. *Substance Use and Misuse, 36*(13), 1795–1820.

Thalemann, R., Wölfling, K, & Grüsser, S. M. (2007). Specific cue reactivity on computer game-related cues in excessive gamers. *Behavior Neuroscience, 121*(3), 614–618.

Volkow, N. D., Fowler, J. S., Wang, G. J., Swanson, J. M., & Telang, F. (2007). Dopamine in drug abuse and addiction: Results of imaging studies and treatment implications. *Archives of Neurology, 64*(11), 1575–1579.

JEROME H. JAFFE
REVISED BY GENE-JACK WANG (2009)

OVER-THE-COUNTER (OTC) MEDICATION.

This class of medication can be purchased without a prescription. Which medications require prescriptions and which do not varies widely from country to country. Common examples of OTC medications in the United States include analgesics (aspirin, Tylenol), cough and cold products (Sinutab, Drixoral), allergy medications (Benadryl, Tavist), gastrointestinal products (Maalox), antidiarrheals (Imodium), and nicotine replacements (e.g., Nicorette gum, Nicoderm patch). Recently, a number of medications that previously were sold only by prescription have been made available over the counter. These include medications that block the production of gastric acid to relieve heartburn (Axid AR, Tagamet HB 200, Zantac 75) and nicotine gum (Nicorette CQ) and the nicotine patch (Nicotrol, Nicoderm CQ) for smoking cessation.

Prescription medications are labeled with patient-specific instructions determined by a physician whereas OTC products provide general information for use by consumers. OTC products *are drugs*, and as such they may cause side effects or adverse effects; or they may interact adversely with foods, alcohol, or other medications. Some of the more than 500,000 OTC products that are available have the potential to be misused or abused. Antihistamines, hypnotics, decongestants, analgesics, laxatives, and diet pills are often consumed in higher than recommended quantities; they have caused physical and/or psychological dependence. An epidemic of the early 1990s among adolescents has been "baby speed," the combining of OTC caffeine pills with the decongestant pills pseudoephedrine. Handfuls of these pills cost only a few dollars and are responsible for overstimulating the heart and central nervous system, causing strokes and death.

An estimated 28 percent of adults in the United States use all kinds of OTC products, often responsibly but also in combination with prescription medications or alcohol. The high cost of visits to a physician and stays in a hospital has generated heightened interest in self-medication, which has increased opportunities for pharmacists to counsel patients. This situation is also contributing to the increased availability of medications as products are transferred from prescription to OTC status. The legislation that controls OTC products is quite recent. It was in 1951 that the United States first separated drugs into the two categories—prescription and OTC. A drug that is available only on prescription cannot be made available as an OTC product until its relative safety and efficacy have been reviewed by the U.S. Food and Drug Administration (FDA).

See also **Drug Interactions and Alcohol; Legal Regulation of Drugs and Alcohol.**

BIBLIOGRAPHY

Berardi, R. R., et al. (2006). *Handbook of nonprescription drugs*, 15th ed. Washington, D.C: APhA Publications.

Graedon, J., & Graedon, T. (1985). *Joe Graedon's the new people's pharmacy*. New York: Bantam.

Kamienski, M. (2006). *Pharmacology demystified*. New York: McGraw–Hill Professional.

Palumbo, F. (1991). The impact of the prescription to OTC switch on practicing pharmacists. *American Pharmacy*, 4, 41–44.

PDR: *Physicians' desk reference for nonprescription drugs and dietary supplements*, 21st ed. (2001). Montvale, NJ: Medical Economics Data. (2007, 29th ed.)

MYROSLAVA ROMACH
KAREN PARKER

OXYCODONE.

Oxycodone is one of the most widely used opioid analgesics in the United States, and it is usually used in conjunction with the analgesics aspirin or acetaminophen. The combinations have proven effective and are in some ways superior to oxycodone alone, since they permit a lower dose of the opioid. They are therefore less likely to produce constipation, drowsiness, and nausea. Oxycodone is a derivative of oxymorphone, the relationship being the same as that between codeine and morphine. Like codeine, oxycodone is metabolized to oxymorphone, which is assumed to be responsible for its activity. Pharmacologically, the actions of oxycodone and oxymorphone are quite similar to those of morphine, so toxicity and addiction can occur. The availability of slow-release formulations (Oxycontin), containing larger quantities of the drug in each pill, has contributed to major problems with its diversion and abuse.

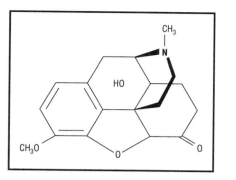

Figure 1. Chemical structure of oxycodone. ILLUSTRATION BY GGS INFORMATION SERVICES. GALE, CENGAGE LEARNING

See also **Opiates/Opioids; Opioid Complications and Withdrawal; Opioid Dependence: Course of the Disorder Over Time; Oxymorphone.**

BIBLIOGRAPHY

Reisine, T., & Pasternak, G. (1996) Opioid analgesics and antagonists. In J. G. Hardman et al. (Eds.), *The pharmacological basis of therapeutics* (9th ed., pp. 521–555). New York: McGraw-Hill.

GAVRIL W. PASTERNAK

OXYCONTIN. Prescription opioids, including oxycodone (OxyContin), are among the most commonly misused types of prescription drugs. OxyContin and Vicodin are the most frequently named pain relievers causing visits to hospital emergency rooms, being involved in 40 percent of such visits. OxyContin and Vicodin are more commonly associated with polydrug use than any other drugs. Approximately 75 percent of emergency room visits involving OxyContin and Vicodin also involve other drugs, such as alcohol and benzodiazepines, whereas approximately 50 percent of all drug abuse-related visits involve multiple drugs.

Of all opioids used nonmedically, OxyContin has raised the most concern among communities, researchers, and physicians for its abuse potential. OxyContin—also known as Oxy, killer, and hillbilly heroin—differs from other pain medication in that it contains a much larger amount of the active ingredient oxycodone. OxyContin is legally prescribed as a timed-release tablet, providing as many as 12 hours of relief from chronic pain. Abusers crush the tablet to disarm its timed-release action, which results in a quick, powerful high that has been compared to the euphoria associated with heroin. Once the tablet is crushed, the drug is administered by one of three methods: orally by swallowing; intranasally by sniffing; or intravenously after mixing it with water. Like other drugs that are administered intranasally or intravenously, OxyContin places users at risk for bloodborne pathogens such as hepatitis or HIV, as well as for overdose. Because its effects mimic heroin, an active black market has developed around OxyContin. A 40-milligram pill costs approximately US $4 by prescription, yet it may sell for $20 to $40 on the street. OxyContin is of particular concern because of its potency and its association with misuse, which could result in dependence, overdose, or death.

See also **Epidemics of Drug Abuse in the United States; Prescription Drug Abuse.**

BIBLIOGRAPHY

Drug Abuse Warning Network (DAWN), Substance Abuse and Mental Health Services Administration, Office of Applied Studies. (2004, July). *Oxycodone, hydrocodone, and polydrug use, 2002.* Rockville, MD: Substance Abuse and Mental Health Services Administration.

Substance Abuse and Mental Health Services Administration. (2006). *Results from the 2005 National Survey on Drug Use and Health: National findings* (Office of Applied Studies, NSDUH Series H-30, DHHS Publication No. SMA 06-4194). Rockville, MD: Author.

STEPHEN E. LANKENAU

OXYMORPHONE. Oxymorphone is a potent semisynthetic opioid analgesic derived from thebaine, one of the twenty alkaloids occurring naturally in opium. Oxymorphone is approximately fivefold more potent than morphine and has very similar actions and side effects. It is used to treat moderate to severe pain. Oral formulations are not available in the United States, but it is available by injection or by rectal suppository. Like morphine, continued use of oxymorphone leads to tolerance and physical dependence. It is interesting that oxymorphone shares the same basic chemical structure

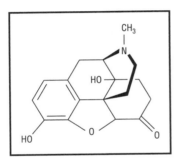

Figure 1. Chemical structure of oxymorphone. ILLUSTRATION BY GGS INFORMATION SERVICES. GALE, CENGAGE LEARNING

as the antagonists naloxone and naltrexone, the only difference being the substituent on the nitrogen. Neither naloxone nor naltrexone have analgesic activity; in contrast to oxymorphone, they are instead capable of blocking opiate actions.

See also **Alkaloids; Morphine; Naloxone; Opiates/ Opioids; Pain, Drugs Used for; Tolerance and Physical Dependence.**

BIBLIOGRAPHY

Freye, E. (2008). *Opioids in medicine: A comprehensive review of the mode of action and the use of analgesics in different clinical pain states.* New York: Springer.

Jaffe, J. H., & Martin, W. R. (1990). Opioid analgesics and antagonists. In A. G. Gilman et al. (Eds.), *Goodman and Gilman's the pharmacological basis of therapeutics,* 8th ed. New York: Pergamon. (2005, 11th ed. New York: McGraw-Hill Medical.)

GAVRIL W. PASTERNAK

PAIN: BEHAVIORAL METHODS FOR MEASURING ANALGESIC EFFECTS OF DRUGS.

Pain is a sensation produced by such potentially harmful stimuli as intense heat, stretching, cutting, or chemical irritation. The ways in which information about these stimuli is carried to the brain and the interpretation that results are very complex. Pain sometimes occurs in the absence of a harmful stimulus, such as in phantom limb pain (where the limb has long been missing). In other instances, pain is not even felt, although harmful stimuli are present. Thus pain is both a sensation and a response to that sensation. The response to pain can vary depending on the individual and the circumstances. Given this complexity, it is not surprising that pain can be modified in many ways—by a variety of drugs, by hypnosis, and by such stimulation as acupuncture.

PAIN TRANSMISSION

The transmission of pain involves two systems—an ascending and a descending neural system. Ascending neural systems carry information about potentially harmful stimuli from peripheral nerves to the spinal cord and from there to the brain, where information about the emotional and psychological aspects of painful stimuli is incorporated. In addition, the perception of painful stimuli is altered by descending neural systems, which send information from the brain back to the spinal cord. Pain transmission can be altered at any point in this loop. Drugs such as aspirin (an analgesic) relieve pain by reducing pain sensitivity in the periphery. Local anesthetics such as lidocaine (Xylocaine) and procaine (Novocaine) relieve pain by blocking nerve conduction in specific areas. Morphine and other opioids (narcotics) alter pain transmission by interfering with the processing of painful stimuli in the spinal cord and the brain.

MORPHINE AND OTHER OPIOIDS IN HUMAN PATIENTS

Among all the drugs that relieve pain, opium and its derivative morphine, are certainly the best known. When morphine is given to patients who are experiencing severe pain, they often say the pain is less intense or that it no longer exists. Other patients say the pain is still present, but it just does not bother them. Thus, morphine affects both the sensation of pain and the patient's response to the painful stimulus. It is generally believed that morphine acts on both the spinal cord and the brain. In the spinal cord, morphine inhibits the flow of information about painful stimuli from the spinal cord to the brain. In the brain, morphine alters pain perception by modifying activity in the descending pain-control system. In addition to relieving pain, morphine-like drugs produce a sense of pleasure (or euphoria) in some patients. Morphine and other opioids are the most effective drugs known for the relief of pain. Although their usefulness is sometimes limited by the fact that they can produce dependence, this factor is generally not a problem in clinical settings.

NONOPIOID ANALGESICS

Although the opioids are considered the most effective drugs for the treatment of pain, THC (delta-9-tetrahydrocannabinol), the active constituent of marijuana, has some pain-relieving properties, but it is not as effective as morphine in this respect. Very large doses of such drugs as alcohol and the barbiturates also appear to relieve pain; however, these effects do not represent true analgesia, since they occur only at doses of alcohol and the barbiturates that produce a loss of consciousness. Thus, the organism's lack of response to painful stimuli is simply an inability to respond.

STUDIES IN LABORATORY ANIMALS

To determine whether a newly-developed compound has pain-relieving properties, scientists use behavioral procedures developed in laboratory animals. In general, these procedures measure the time it takes an organism to respond to a painful stimulus, first when no drug is present and then after a drug is given. Morphine and other opioids consistently alter this and other measures of pain perception. For example, morphine increases the time it takes an animal to remove its tail from a warm water bath. It takes about 2 seconds for the monkey to remove its tail from a warm water bath if morphine is not given. A small amount of morphine increases tail-removal time to about 8 seconds; larger amounts of morphine increase the time to as much as 20 seconds. Modification of pain perception also depends on the intensity of the painful stimulus. If the water in the bath is very hot, only very large amounts of morphine will increase the time it takes animals to withdraw their tail, whereas a lesser amount of morphine will increase response time at lower temperatures. Similarly, some drugs such as buprenorphine are most effective in relieving pain when the pain is mild. Since buprenorphine also produces less dependence than morphine, it may be a very useful drug for treating mild forms of pain. By combining data about the pain-relieving effects of a drug with data about its likelihood of producing dependence, information is obtained about the usefulness of a new drug in a clinical setting.

See also **Addiction: Concepts and Definitions; Opiates/ Opioids; Pain, Drugs Used for.**

BIBLIOGRAPHY

Beecher, H. K. (1959). *Measurement of subjective responses.* New York: Oxford University Press.

Holdcroft, A., & Jaggar, S. (2005). *Core topics in pain.* Cambridge, U.K.: Cambridge University Press.

Wallace, M. S., & Staats, P. S. (2004). *Pain medicine & management.* New York: McGraw-Hill Professional.

Wasacz, J. (1981). Natural and synthetic narcotic drugs. *American Scientist, 69,* 318–324.

LINDA DYKSTRA

PAIN, DRUGS USED FOR. Pain is a sensation unique to an individual. Its perception depends on the injury or condition involved and the situation or context. A bruise obtained in a football game may not be appreciated at the time of the injury, yet in other circumstances the pain from a minor injury, such as stubbing a toe, may be overwhelming. The extent of the injury does not predict the amount of pain experienced, and it is this wide variability that makes the treatment of pain difficult.

Within the brain, there are two systems that can appreciate the sensation of pain. One deals with the objective component and tells the exact location of the injury and what type of injury it is. The other is more diffuse and comprises the subjective sense of hurting. Many people have experienced both types of pain. Touching a hot object or stubbing a toe is quickly followed by the appreciation that an injury has occurred, followed an instant later by the pain. It is this second pain that contains the *suffering*, the *hurt*, and the elimination of this second pain is the goal of analgesic therapy.

THREE CATEGORIES OF PAIN

Physicians have divided pains into three general categories. The first, and most common, *somatic pain*, results from tissue injury, such as a broken leg, metastases in the bone from cancer, muscle pulls, or ligament sprains. The second, *visceral pain*, results from activation of pain fibers in internal organs, typically in the abdomen or chest. This category includes discomfort associated, for example, with gall bladder disease, peptic ulcers, or pancreatitis. Unlike somatic pain, visceral pain is poorly localized. The most difficult pain to understand and to treat is *deafferentation*, or *neuropathic pain*, which is a consequence of injury to nerves. It is difficult for patients to describe these sensations, but they often use terms such as *burning, shooting,* or *electric*-like. This type of pain is commonly seen in cancer patients when tumors invade nerve bundles. It also is seen with mild damage to nerves.

The most common class of injury is the *peripheral neuropathies.* These disorders result from a wide variety of causes; they affect nerves as they course through the body. The longest nerves are most sensitive to injury, which explains why this type of pain is most likely to develop in the feet. Diabetes is one of the most common causes of neuropathy. A special type of pain also in this classification is *postherpetic neuralgia,* a burning and/ or shooting pain associated with herpes zoster, known as *shingles.*

ACUTE AND CHRONIC PAIN

Pain can be classified as either acute (short-term) or chronic (long-term). The duration of many kinds of pain can be anticipated. The acute pain associated with surgery is usually limited in duration and, over the period of several days, decreases markedly. Chronic pain, by contrast, is usually defined as pain that persists for six months or longer. There are two types of chronic pain: malignant and nonmalignant. Malignant pain is that caused by cancer. Chronic nonmalignant pain conditions include but are not limited to musculoskeletal pain, osteoarthritis, fibromyalgia (chronic widespread muscular aching, and heightened sensitivity and needle-like tingling of the skin), headache, sciatica (leg pain caused by compression or trauma of the sciatic nerve), and complex regional pain syndrome (characterized by severe burning pain and swelling and changes in the skin). Despite the sophistication of modern medicine, some types of chronic nonmalignant pain are difficult to classify, diagnose, or treat. In some cases, chronic pain may seem to have no cause. In many cases, patients need to see specialists who have received specific training and are board-certified in pain medicine.

GROUPS OF PAIN MEDICINES

Pain medicines (analgesics) are often divided into three major groups. The first group comprises the most commonly used drugs, acetaminophen and nonsteroidal anti-inflammatory drugs (NSAIDs). The second group includes the opioids (opiates). Some opioids are used for moderate pain whereas others are typically employed for more severe pain. Third, there are a number of drugs used either for specific pain syndromes or in conjunction with the first two groups. These agents, *adjuvant drugs,* include anticonvulsants (for neuropathic pain) and muscle relaxants (for back pain). The adjuvants are not discussed in this section because although they play a role in the treatment of pain, they are not considered as prototypic analgesics.

Table 1 lists different analgesics that are approved by the U.S. Food and Drug Administration as of 2008. They are divided into two major categories: non-opioids and opioids. Table 1 also provides typically recommended doses for acute pain (with two exceptions as noted) as well as frequency of dosing. The choice of analgesic is based on both the type of pain and its intensity.

Non-steroidal Anti-inflammatory Drugs (NSAIDs) and Acetaminophen. Most pain is treated in a standardized fashion. Initial therapy often utilizes acetaminophen and the NSAIDs, aspirin, ibuprofen, and naproxen. These non-opioid agents are available without prescription (i.e., over-the-counter, OTC) and can be very effective for mild to moderate types of pain. They have a number of properties that make them excellent analgesics. They all reduce fever and pain caused by muscle aches, the common cold, toothaches, menstrual cramps, and headaches. They also reduce pain caused by arthritis that is minor in nature. With the exception of acetaminophen, they also reduce inflammation. Their effectiveness against a wide variety of different types of pain and their oral dosage greatly enhance their utility.

Unfortunately, these OTC agents exhibit relatively low ceiling effects, which means that the maximal degree of analgesia that can be obtained by a drug can be limited, regardless of the dose. Several NSAIDs are only available by prescription and have greater analgesic potencies. Besides the prescribed NSAIDs listed in Table 1, others include fenoprofen (Nalfon), diflusanil (Dolobid), and piroxicam (Feldene). Primary indications for the prescribed NSAIDs include treatment of pain, tenderness, and swelling caused by rheumatoid arthritis, osteoarthritis, and other musculoskeletal ailments.

Typically, NSAIDs act at the site of injury, leading to their classification as peripherally acting drugs as opposed to centrally acting drugs, such as the opioids, which work within the brain and spinal cord. The analgesic and anti-inflammatory effects of NSAIDs are achieved through the inhibition of the cyclooxygenase (COX) enzyme. The COX enzyme converts arachidonic acid to cyclic prostanoids (e.g., prostaglandins, thromboxane). There are two forms of COX: COX-1 and COX-2. COX-1 is expressed in nearly all tissues and is responsible for platelet aggregation (thromboxane) and protection of the gastrointestinal mucosa (prostaglandins). COX-2, by contrast, is released in response to tissue injury and produces pain and inflammation. Nearly all NSAIDs are termed nonselective because they inhibit both forms of the COX enzyme. The analgesic and anti-inflammatory properties of NSAIDs are achieved through inhibition of COX-2, whereas undesired side effects in the gastrointestinal tract and kidneys (discussed below) are produced through the inhibition of COX-1. In 1999, the first NSAID to selectively inhibit COX-2 became available in the United States; COX-2 inhibitors selectively block the synthesis of the prostaglandins that produce inflammation and pain, while allowing for the synthesis of prostaglandins that protect the gastrointestinal tract.

All NSAIDs carry risks. With the exception of aspirin, both nonselective NSAIDs and selective COX-2 inhibiting NSAIDs may increase the chance of a heart attack or stroke. These risks increase with longer use, higher doses, and in people who have a history of heart disease. Unlike other NSAIDs, aspirin actually reduces the chance of heart attack and stroke by decreasing the production of thromboxane through the selective irreversible inhibition of COX-1. Another risk is gastrointestinal insult (e.g., gastric ulcers, bleeding). Therefore, aspirin and other nonselective NSAIDs should be avoided in patients with ulcer disease. Studies have demonstrated that the incidence of gastric ulcers is lower in patients who use selective COX-2 inhibitors than in patients who use nonselective NSAIDs, but the evidence is less convincing that non-ulcer gastrointestinal symptoms such as dyspepsia (chronic or recurrent pain or discomfort centered in the upper abdomen) are associated with less risk. As of 2008, there was only one FDA-approved COX-2 inhibitor available in the United States: celecoxib (Celebrex). In 2004, the manufacturers of a then widely prescribed COX-2 inhibitor, rofecoxib (Vioxx), withdrew their drug from the market.

The drug was associated with increased risk of heart attack and stroke associated with long-term, high dose use. Shortly thereafter in 2005, the FDA requested that the manufacturer of valdecoxib (Bextra) withdraw it from the market, due to its potential increased risk for serious cardiovascular adverse events and risk for serious skin reactions. Aspirin and other NSAIDs are also capable of producing renal (kidney) side effects, such as reductions in filtration rates.

Acetaminophen, the only non-opioid analgesic in Table 1 that is not an NSAID, does not irritate the gastrointestinal tract or produce renal side effects; however, it has its own potential problems. Although it is one of the safest drugs available when used as directed, overdoses with acetaminophen can be very dangerous, being associated with major damage to the liver, which can be life-threatening. Care must be taken to use only the recommended doses of acetaminophen.

Opioids. Opioids work within the brain and spinal cord to relieve the second pain—the hurt—described above. In this regard, they are highly effective since they take away pain without interfering with other sensations, unlike local anesthetics. It is this ability to selectively act on the hurt that makes them so valuable. There are a number of opioids that are used for the treatment of moderate to severe pain (see Table 1). Codeine is considered a *weak* opioid and is primarily indicated for moderate pain. It has a ceiling effect in that increasing the dose beyond a certain level does not confer greater analgesia, but only an increase in side effects. Propoxyphene is another weak opioid. Standard doses are not much more effective than aspirin or acetaminophen alone, and although still prescribed, prolonged use of it is discouraged, especially in the elderly, for a number of reasons, including the potential accumulation of a metabolite, norpropoxyphene, that can lead to pulmonary edema (abnormal accumulation of fluid in the lungs), cardiotoxicity (toxicity that affects the heart such as heart muscle damage), apnea (slowed or stopped breathing), and death.

The other opioids in Table 1 are prescribed for the treatment of moderate to severe pain. Tramadol is a unique opioid in that it also has serotonergic and noradrenergic actions. Special care must be taken with methadone because of its long, unpredictable

	Average oral dose (in milligrams)	Frequency of dosing (in hours)	Comment
Non-opioids			
Aspirin	325–650	4–6	NSAID; no prescription needed; maximum daily dose not to exceed 4000 mg for analgesia
Acetaminophen (Tylenol)	325–650	4–6	Reduces pain and fever, but not inflammation; no prescription needed; maximum daily dose not to exceed 4000 mg for analgesia
Ibuprofen (Motrin)	200–400	4–6	NSAID; no prescription needed; maximum daily dose not to exceed 1200 mg for analgesia
Naproxen (Naprosyn)	250–500	6–8	NSAID; no prescription needed; initially 500 mg, then 250 mg every 6–8 hours; maximum daily dose (naproxen base) not to exceed 1250 mg for analgesia; also available in controlled-release (CR) form
Diclofenac (Cataflam)	50	6	NSAID; prescription needed; indicated for acute pain, ankylosing spondylitis, primary dysmenorrhea, acute and chronic treatment of osteoarthritis and rheumatoid arthritis; dose listed is for treatment of acute pain and primary dysmenorrhea; maximum daily dose not to exceed 150 mg for acute pain and primary dysmenorrhea; also available in CR form
Meloxicam (Mobic)	7.5	24	NSAID; prescription needed; indicated for osteoarthritis and rheumatoid arthritis; maximum daily dose not to exceed 15 mg
Celecoxib (Celebrex)	200	24	NSAID; prescription needed; selective inhibitor of the COX-2 enzyme; indicated for ankylosing spondylitis, osteoarthritis, rheumatoid arthritis, acute pain, and primary dysmenorrhea; 200 mg/day dose refers to use for treatment of osteoarthritis, different doses used for analgesia or rheumatoid arthritis
Opioids			
Codeine	32–65	4–6	Often used in combination with acetaminophen (Tylenol#3)
Propoxyphene napsylate	100	4	Used alone (Darvon-N) or with acetaminophen (Darvocet)
Oxycodone	5–10	6	Often used in combination with acetaminophen (Percocet), and also available in CR form (OxyContin)
Hydrocodone	5–10	4–6	Often used in combination with acetaminophen (Vicodin, Lortab)
Tramadol	50–100	4–6	Used alone (Ultram) or in combination with acetaminophen (Ultracet), and also available in CR form (Ultram ER)
Meperidine	50–100	5	Not very effective orally, not recommended for chronic use
Morphine	10–30	4–6	Also available in controlled-release formulations
Fentanyl	see comment for dosing	72	Potent synthetic agonist in a CR transdermal system (Duragesic) used for relief of moderately severe to severe pain (dosage range: 12–100 mcg/h), and also available in oral (Actiq) and sublingual form (Fentora) for breakthrough pain
Hydromorphone (Dilaudid)	4–8	4–6	Potent analgesic that tends to be prescribed for severe pain
Methadone (Dolophine)	5–20	8	Very effective analgesic; also used as a substitution pharmacotherapy for opioid addiction
Levorphanol (Levo-Dromoran)	2–4	4–6	Potent analgesic that tends to be prescribed for cancer pain
Oxymorphone CR (Opana)	5–10	12	Doses listed are initial doses for opioid-naïve individuals, also available in IR formulation

Table 1. Food and Drug Administration (FDA)-approved analgesics. ILLUSTRATION BY GGS INFORMATION SERVICES. GALE, CENGAGE LEARNING

half-life that could result in drug accumulation and toxicity and because of its potential interaction with other drugs that could either lead to inappropriately low or high blood levels of methadone. Several opioids are available by themselves (i.e., a single entity product) or combined in a formulation that also includes a peripherally acting, non-opioid analgesic (e.g., acetaminophen). The peripheral actions of the non-opioid and the central actions of the opioid complement each other, in that pain is reduced by two separate processes.

Several of the opioids are available in a controlled-release (CR) formulation and are prescribed for the treatment of chronic pain. The product is formulated in such a way that the opioid is slowly released into the bloodstream and can, therefore, provide stable levels of analgesia for a prolonged period of time, ranging from twelve to thirty-six hours. There is another benefit of CR formulations: Patients do not have to awaken during the night to take their medication, unlike many chronic pain patients who are prescribed immediate-release (IR), short-acting opioids. Just as the non-opioids have risks, so too do opioids. These risks are usually described as *side effects*. Potential side effects include nausea and vomiting, pruritis (itchy skin), mental clouding, constipation, and respiratory depression (decreased breathing). Profound respiratory depression can lead to death.

In hospitals, many patients receive opiates by injection or intravenously. Doses need to be adjusted to compensate for differing distributions and metabolism, but these changes are relatively straightforward for physicians working in the area of pain. Special devices are also available that permit patients to dose themselves, as needed, within specified guidelines. This approach is termed *patient controlled analgesia* (PCA). Even more sophisticated routes of administration are available. Some medications can be injected deep in the back, adjacent to the spinal canal (epidurally) where they can act primarily on the spinal cord. Localizing the medication to the spinal cord can minimize the side effects produced in the brain, such as nausea and respiratory depression.

The chronic use of opioids leads to a lessening of potency, which is termed *tolerance*. To overcome this effect, it may be necessary to increase the dose to maintain a constant level of pain relief (e.g., analgesia). However, many chronic pain patients on long-term opioid therapy can be maintained on a given dose for long periods of time without requiring an increase in the dose. All patients taking sufficient quantities of opioids for an extended time become physically dependent; that is, they experience some withdrawal if the drug is stopped. It is important to distinguish between this physiological process and the process of addiction. A chronic pain patient may be physically dependent on an opioid but not be addicted to the opioid. In the medical community, it is thought that most patients on chronic opioid therapy with no prior history of substance abuse are not addicted; that is, they do not exhibit impaired control over their opioid use, do not use compulsively, and do not crave opioids. However, it is also acknowledged that misuse and abuse does occur in some chronic pain patients. One known risk factor for abuse of opioids in chronic pain patients is a history of substance abuse. That does not preclude such patients from long-term opioid therapy but does necessitate closer and more frequent monitoring of the patient on the part of the medical caregiver. Such

monitoring could involve urine toxicology screening and behavioral contracting.

In the late 1990s, drug abuse epidemiological networks detected increasing prevalence of nonmedical use of prescription opioids. This pattern was ascertained independently by drug abuse surveys, the number of emergency room visits associated with nonmedical use, and the number of admissions to drug abuse treatment facilities. As of 2006 (the most recent year as of 2008 for which epidemiological data are available), the prevalence of nonmedical use of prescription opioids remained substantially elevated and was of great concern to those in the medical, public health, drug abuse prevention, and law enforcement fields.

The nonmedical use is seen in all age groups, including children and adolescents. In 2006, 5 percent and 10 percent of U.S. high school seniors reported taking OxyContin (controlled-release formulation of oxycodone) and Vicodin (hydrocodone/acetaminophen), respectively, that was not prescribed to them. The increase in nonmedical use was thought to be related to increased medical use of the prescription opioids. For many years pain was grossly undertreated in the United States, but through educational efforts and public health initiatives, including mandating that patients be asked about their pain in hospitals, pain is being treated more aggressively, with increased prescribing of opioids when such drugs are indicated. The increased use of opioids for licit purposes, though, increases the amount of opioids available for diversion to nonmedical use.

The means by which prescription opioids are diverted are many and include a family member or friend giving them to other people, a person stealing another person's medication from the medicine cabinet, doctor shopping (a practice, or more aptly put a *scam*, in which a person not necessarily in pain gets opioid prescriptions from multiple doctors by complaining of a painful condition in which opioids might be indicated), and pharmacy and warehouse thefts. There is no simple solution to the problem of nonmedical use of prescription opioids. Reducing the amounts of opioids that are available for medical use might decrease the prevalence of nonmedical use but would deprive patients who need these medications for adequate pain relief. As of 2008, some pharmaceutical companies were working to develop opioids that may have less abuse liability by altering their formulation, but such attempts remained in preliminary phases. It was anticipated that nonmedical use of prescription opioids would continue to be a serious problem in the United States for some years to come.

See also **Abuse Liability of Drugs: Testing in Humans; Addiction: Concepts and Definitions; Controlled Substances Act of 1970; Pain: Behavioral Methods for Measuring Analgesic Effects of Drugs; Tolerance and Physical Dependence.**

BIBLIOGRAPHY

Aronoff, G. M., Gallagher, R. M., & Patel, J. G. (2002). Pharmacological management of chronic pain: A review. In C. D. Tollison, J. R. Satterthwaite, & Tollison, J. W. (Eds.), *Practical pain management* (3rd ed., pp. 253–277). Philadelphia: Lippincott Williams & Wilkins.

Barkin, R. L., Barkin, S. J., & Barkin, D. S. (2006). Propoxyphene (dextropropoxyphene): A critical review of a weak opioid analgesic that should remain in antiquity. *American Journal of Therapeutics, 13,* 534–542.

Beaver, W. T. (1984). Combination analgesics. *American Journal of Medicine, 77*(Suppl. 3A), 38–53.

Bruera, E., & Sweeney, C. (2002). Methadone use in cancer patients with pain: A review. *Journal of Palliative Medicine, 5,* 127–138.

Burke, A., Smyth, E. M., & FitzGerald, G. A. (2006). Analgesic-antipyretic and anti inflammatory agents; Pharmacotherapy of gout. In L. L. Brunton, J. S. Lazo, & K. Parker (Eds.), *Goodman and Gilman's the pharmacological basis of therapeutics* (11th ed., pp. 671–716). New York: McGraw-Hill.

Gilson, A. M., Ryan, K. M., Joranson, D. E., & Dahl, J. L. (2004). A reassessment of trends in the medical use and abuse of opioid analgesics and implications for diversion control: 1997–2002. *Journal of Pain & Symptom Management, 28,* 176–188.

Gutstein, H. B., & Akil, H. (2006). Opioid analgesics. In L. L. Brunton, J. S. Lazo, & K. L. Parker (Eds.), *Goodman and Gilman's the pharmacological basis of therapeutics* (11th ed., pp. 547–590). New York: McGraw-Hill.

Inciardi, J. A., Surratt, H. S., Kurtz, S. P., & Cicero, T. J. (2007). Mechanisms of prescription drug diversion among drug-involved club- and street-based populations. *Pain Medicine, 8,* 171–183.

Johnston, L. D., O'Malley, P. M., Bachman, J. G., & Schulenberg, J. E. (2007). *Monitoring the Future national results on adolescent drug use: Overview of key findings, 2006.* (NIH Publication No. 07–6202). Bethesda, MD: National Institute on Drug Abuse.

Passik, S. D., & Kirsch, K. L. (2004). Opioid therapy in patients with a history of substance abuse. *Central Nervous System Drugs, 18,* 13–25.

Portenoy, R. K., Farrar, J. T., Backonja, M. M., Cleeland, C. S., Yang, K., Friedman, M., et al. (2007). Long-term use of controlled-release oxycodone for non-cancer pain: Results of a 3-year registry study. *Clinical Journal of Pain, 23,* 287–299.

Reid, M. C., Engles-Horton, L. L., Weber, M. B., Kerns, R. D., Rogers, E. L., & O'Connor, P. G. (2002). Use of opioid medications for chronic noncancer pain syndromes in primary care. *Journal of General Internal Medicine, 17,* 173–179.

Savage, S. R., Joranson, D. E., Covington, E. C., Schnoll, S. H., Heit, H. A., & Gilson, A. M. (2003). Definitions related to the medical use of opioids: Evolution towards universal agreement. *Journal of Pain and Symptom Management, 26,* 655–667.

Substance Abuse and Mental Health Services Administration. (2007). Results from the 2006 National Survey on Drug Use and Health: National findings. (Office of Applied Studies, NSDUH Series H-32, DHHS Publication No. SMA 07-4293) Rockville, MD.

Wall, P., & Melzack, R. (1994). *Textbook of pain.* Edinburgh: Churchill Livingstone.

Zacny, J., Bigelow, G., Compton, P., Foley, K., Iguchi, M., & Sannerud, C. (2003). College on Problems of Drug Dependence taskforce on prescription opioid nonmedical use and abuse: Position statement. *Drug and Alcohol Dependence, 69,* 215–232.

GAVRIL W. PASTERNAK
REVISED BY JAMES P. ZACNY (2009)

PAKISTAN. *See* **India and Pakistan.**

PAPAVER SOMNIFERUM. Poppy plants, of the genus *Papaver*, are long-stalked flowers of varying colors encompassing approximately 140 species. Of the many types of poppy plants, *Papaver somniferum* is known as the opium poppy. It has white or blue-purple flowers and is widely cultivated in Asia, India, and Turkey, which supply much of the world's opium. Cultivation requires a tropical or subtropical climate without excessive rainfall. In the Northern Hemisphere, the plant flowers in late spring, after which the petals fall in a short time. Flowering is followed by the rapid growth of the capsules (the plant's ovaries) for about two weeks. Incisions are carefully made in the capsule to obtain the milky juice, which is then dried as a gum that yields opium. The yield of opium can vary widely, but is typically about five pounds (2.25 kilograms) per acre.

The opium serves as a source of morphine, codeine, and thebaine and is widely used in the production of important painkillers (analgesics).

Typically, morphine comprises 10 percent of opium. Most of the morphine used in medicine is obtained by purifying opium.

Illicit uses of opium are also widespread. In many parts of the world, opium is still smoked or eaten. Morphine extracted from opium may in turn be converted to heroin in clandestine laboratories. Heroin is the major opioid used illicitly in the United States. To prevent the collection and sale of opium for illicit conversion to heroin, new ways of processing the poppy plant have been developed. The most widely used consists of mowing the poppy fields before the pods are ripe enough to yield opium. The mowed stems, immature pods, and plant matter, referred to collectively as poppy "straw," are then shipped in bulk to large processing centers where the active alkaloids are extracted under careful supervision.

Other species of *Papaver* also contain alkaloids that can be converted into potent opioids. For example, *Papaver bracteatum* contains high concentrations of thebaine, which can be used to produce compounds several hundred times more potent than morphine.

See also **Crop Control Policies; Golden Triangle as Drug Source; International Drug Supply Systems; Opiates/Opioids; Pain, Drugs Used for.**

BIBLIOGRAPHY

Lewis, W. H. (2005). *Medical botany: Plants affecting human health.* Hoboken, NJ: John Wiley & Sons.

Reisine, T., and Pasternak, G. (1996) Opioid analgesics and antagonists. In J. G. Hardman et al. (Eds.), *The Pharmacological Basis of Therapeutics*, 9th ed. (pp. 521–555). New York: McGraw-Hill Medical. (2005, 11th ed.)

Van Wyk, B. (2004). *Medicinal plants of the world: An illustrated scientific guide to important medicinal plants and their uses.* Pretoria, South Africa: Briza Publications.

GAVRIL W. PASTERNAK

PARAPHERNALIA, LAWS AGAINST.

Drug paraphernalia includes equipment, products, and materials that facilitate or enable the making, using, or concealing of illicit drugs. Some paraphernalia, such as hypodermic syringes for heroin and pipes for smoking marijuana, are used by consumers of drugs. Equipment such as scales, vials, and baggies, as well as chemicals used to dilute drugs, are examples of paraphernalia used by dealers of illicit drugs. The Federal Drug Paraphernalia Act, which is part of the Controlled Substances Act, makes it illegal to possess, sell, transport, import, or export drug paraphernalia as defined by the statute. In addition, laws prohibiting the possession and use of paraphernalia have been adopted in every state. Though constitutional objections have been raised against these laws, the U.S. Supreme Court has declined to strike down such statutes.

The first drug-paraphernalia laws, prohibitions against possessing opium pipes, were enacted by western states in the late nineteenth century as part of broad statutory efforts to suppress opium smoking by Chinese immigrants. During the first third of the twentieth century, some states, in conjunction with a legislative attempt to criminalize the nonmedical use of opiates and cocaine, also prohibited the possession of hypodermic syringes without a medical prescription. By 1972, when the National Commission on Marijuana and Drug Abuse conducted a survey of state drug laws, about twenty states had adopted some type of drug-paraphernalia prohibition.

Commercialization of drug paraphernalia, especially through so-called head shops, in the early 1970s triggered a new generation of paraphernalia prohibitions, many of which criminalized the sale as well as possession of these articles. Such laws attempted to enforce comprehensive bans on drug-related devices or articles intended for use with illicit drugs.

The drug-paraphernalia industry responded to the enactment of these laws by challenging their constitutionality on grounds of vagueness and overbreadth. In most cases, courts struck down the laws as unconstitutionally vague. First, they applied to objects that had lawful as well as unlawful

Crack cocaine pipe. © BETTMANN/CORBIS.

uses, so these laws failed to provide fair notice of prohibited conduct. Second, the lack of explicit standards left police with discretion to enforce these laws in an arbitrary and discriminatory manner.

Since the late nineteenth century, the federal and state governments have enacted laws to regulate the possession and sale of drug paraphernalia, like the crack pipe pictured in Figure 1.

In 1979 the U.S. Drug Enforcement Administration (DEA) responded to these legal defeats by drafting a model law that could withstand constitutional scrutiny and at the same time effectively combat the drug-paraphernalia trade. The DEA drafted the Model Drug Paraphernalia Act (MDPA), which explicitly requires prosecutors to prove that the defendant knew the alleged paraphernalia would be used with illegal drugs. The addition of this intent requirement was designed to alleviate the fair-warning concern associated with the earlier generation of statutes. In addition, the MDPA attempts to provide a more specific definition of drug paraphernalia by listing objects included within the category and by providing factors that judges should consider in determining whether an object falls within the definition. Finally, the act prohibits placement of an advertisement when one knows, or "reasonably should know," that it is intended to promote the sale of objects "designed or intended for use as drug paraphernalia."

During the 1980s, most states enacted the MDPA or an equivalent statute, and legal challenges soon followed. In 1982 the Supreme Court upheld a local ordinance that required businesses to obtain a license in order to sell articles designed to be used with illegal drugs. Although this law did not involve a criminal statute prohibiting sale or possession of paraphernalia, lower courts subsequently upheld criminal laws modeled after the MDPA against vagueness and overbreadth challenges. In 1994 the Court addressed many of the MDPA issues when it reviewed the constitutionality of the Mail Order Drug Paraphernalia Control Act, which was part of the Anti-Drug Abuse Act of 1986.

This federal statute, which is modeled on the MDPA provisions, makes it a crime to use the U.S. mail to facilitate the sale and distribution of drug paraphernalia. The Court held that the statute was not unconstitutionally vague and that the seller need only be aware that customers in general are likely to use the merchandise with drugs. This reading of the intent requirement was a victory for law enforcement.

In the wake of the HIV/AIDS epidemic, another feature of traditional drug-paraphernalia laws has become controversial. In an effort to reduce the risk of transmission of the human immunodeficiency virus (HIV) and other blood-borne diseases among needle-sharing illicit drug users, state and local public-health authorities have sought to establish clean-needle exchange programs, usually through hospitals and clinics. To implement these programs, lawmakers have had to repeal the paraphernalia laws or prosecutors have agreed not to enforce them in this context. Many states and local governments have refused to support needle-exchange programs, and the federal government has not funded them due to concerns that dispensing needles will encourage illicit drug use. However, the National Academy of Sciences has concluded that these programs reduce the risk of HIV transmission and has found no evidence that they encourage drug use.

In general, drug-paraphernalia laws represent a type of drug legislation aimed mainly at declaring and symbolizing society's intolerance of illicit drug use. However, in 2003 the federal government's Operation Pipedream led to numerous criminal charges against eighteen companies selling drug paraphernalia. These companies accounted for annual sales of $250 million. With the decriminalization or reduction in severity of criminal sanctions for possession of small amounts of marijuana, local law enforcement agencies have used paraphernalia laws as a way of exacting heavier criminal penalties. These laws are subject to highly discretionary enforcement and can have unintended costs or ramifications.

See also **Legal Regulation of Drugs and Alcohol; Needle and Syringe Exchanges and HIV/AIDS; Parent Movement, The; Substance Abuse and AIDS.**

BIBLIOGRAPHY

Corcoran, A. M., & Helm, J. (1973). Compilation and analysis of criminal drug laws in the 50 states and five territories. *Technical papers of the second report of the National Commission on Marijuana and Drug Abuse.* Washington, DC: U.S. Government Printing Office.

Courtwright, D. T. (2004). The Controlled Substances Act: How a "big tent" reform became a punitive drug law. *Journal of Drug and Alcohol Dependence, 76*(1), 9–15.

Gable, L., Garmharter, K., & Gostin, L. (2007). *Legal aspects of HIV/AIDS: A guide for policy and reform.* Washington, DC: World Bank Publications.

RICHARD J. BONNIE
REVISED BY FREDERICK K. GRITTNER (2009)

PAREGORIC. Paregoric is a camphorated opium tincture. Tinctures of opium are alcoholic extracts of opium, widely used in the treatment of diarrhea. Paregoric contains powdered opium, anise oil, benzoic acid, camphor, glycerin, and diluted alcohol. With only 0.4 milligrams per milliliter of morphine in 45 percent alcohol, it is more dilute than opium tincture—and the taste of the camphorated formula is generally disliked, helping to minimize excessive use or abuse.

Although paregoric is not indicated for bacterial or parasitic causes of diarrhea, it can be very helpful for other causes. Taken orally, it effectively slows down the gastrointestinal transit of wastes and enhances resorption of fluid from the intestine. Doses that effectively treat diarrhea typically do not cause euphoria or analgesia; however, excessive doses can be abused and can lead to dependence.

See also **Dover's Powder; Laudanum; Opiates/Opioids.**

BIBLIOGRAPHY

Brunton, L. L. (1996). Agents affecting gastrointestinal water flux and motility; Emesis and antiemetics; Bile acids and pancreatic enzymes. In J. G. Hardman et al. (Eds.), *The Pharmacological Basis of Therapeutics*, 9th ed. New York: McGraw-Hill Medical. (2005, 11th ed.)

Ruiz, P., Strain, E. C., & Langrod, J. G. (2007). *The substance abuse handbook.* Philadelphia, PA: Lippincott, Williams & Wilkins.

GAVRIL W. PASTERNAK

PARENT MOVEMENT, THE. Several national organizations trace their origins to the Parent Movement of the 1970s and 1980s. As of 2008, the most prominent was National Families in Action whose founder, Sue Rusche, remained active in efforts to prevent drug use and abuse among young teenagers and pre-teens. The grassroots movement began with a group of concerned parents in then-president Jimmy Carter's home state of Georgia in 1976. At the time, these people believed children's drug use, particularly marijuana smoking, had reached unprecedented levels and officials and agencies of the Carter administration were communicating an attitude of complacence with respect to so-called recreational drug use that the parents found offensive and frightening.

Marsha Keith Schuchard and her husband, Emory University professor Ronald Schuchard, discovered that their eldest daughter and most of her friends were using drugs at the daughter's 13th birthday party. In response, the family organized the nation's first parent-peer group. Such groups consisted of parents whose children were each other's friends. They came together to establish age-appropriate social and behavioral guidelines for their children to help them avoid unhealthy and destructive behavior. Marsha Keith Schuchard, using the name Marsha Manatt, later wrote about this experience in Parents, Peers and Pot, a book the National Institute on Drug Abuse published and distributed free to the more than one million people who requested it during the 1980s.

At first, the parents confronted public attitudes that were not in their favor. In August 1977, President Carter endorsed decriminalization of marijuana, and opinion polls registered widespread acceptance of the idea. Nevertheless in the fall of 1977, the group of Atlanta citizens, who had begun meeting the previous year, formed National Families in Action. Founders included Marsha Keith Schuchard and Sue Rusche, who later became the organization's executive director. This organization called attention to the social and environmental factors that seemed to promote the use of illicit drugs. Its purpose was twofold: 1) to replace commercial and societal messages that glamorize drug use with accurate information based on scientific research about drug effects, and 2) to help people put this information to use by organizing community-based parent drug-prevention groups.

One target of the founders of National Families in Action was the drug paraphernalia shops, called head shops (drug users called themselves heads, acid heads, pot heads, coke heads). These shops offered drug-themed magazines, books, and colorful and attractive gadgets that appeared to the concerned parents to appeal particularly to impressionable youth.

In January 1978, the Georgia State Legislature passed the nation's first laws banning the sale of drug paraphernalia, thanks in large part to the lobbying activities of National Families in Action. At about the same time, Otto and Connie Moulton, of Danvers, Massachusetts, founded Committees of Correspondence. Their goal was to alert citizens about the activities of drug-culture and drug-policy organizations that advocate the decriminalization and legalization of illicit substances. They began sending out packets they called Otto Bombs, detailing information about the local, state, and federal lobbying activities of drug-legalization organizations such as National Organization for the Reform of Marijuana Laws (NORML), whose board and advisory committee at the time consisted of many drug-paraphernalia manufacturers and publishers. Patterned after the original Committees of Correspondence founded before the Revolutionary War, the modern version sought to uphold the rights of citizens to be drug free. A periodic newsletter presented information from researchers and doctors refuting medical and scientific claims made by legalization proponents. Committees of Correspondence also tracked the lobbying efforts of other organizations (such as NORML) that advocated legalizing drugs.

In the spring of 1978, NORML began to make issue of a U.S. supported crop eradication program in Mexico that involved spraying drug crops with the poison, Paraquat. NORML threatened to sue the government on the basis that the program endangered the health of American marijuana smokers. That people who were willfully breaking the law deserved protection and that officials of the federal government were making overly sophisticated distinctions among which drugs were dangerous and which were not was just too much for many people and the tide of opinion began to change.

In April 1978, Thomas Gleaton invited Keith Schuchard and Sue Rusche to address the Fourth

Annual Southeast Regional Drug Conference. Gleaton held the conference for drug education professionals at Georgia State University, where he taught. He also invited officials from various federal agencies. Many accepted, particularly from the National Institute on Drug Abuse. The Parents' Resource Institute for Drug Education (PRIDE) was founded in the summer of 1978, following this conference. Publicity generated by the passage of Georgia's drug paraphernalia laws, by the Fourth Southeast Drug Conference, and, later, by the publication of *Parents, Peers and Pot,* brought requests for help from parents throughout the United States. These parents wanted to form groups to ban drug paraphernalia sales in their cities and states and to prevent substance abuse among local children. For the next several years, leaders from National Families in Action, PRIDE, Committees of Correspondence, and other national organizations, along with leaders of emerging groups from various states, traveled across the nation helping parents form prevention groups. Funding from the National Institute on Drug Abuse made it possible for parent group leaders to travel to communities that sought their help. One of the first groups to form outside Georgia was Naples (Florida) Informed Parents, led by Pat and Bill Barton. The Florida leaders joined those from Georgia and Massachusetts to help parents in other states form similar groups.

In the summer of 1978, Carter's health advisor and so-called drug czar, Peter Bourne, was forced to resign amid allegations that he had written a fraudulent prescription for a staff member and even that he, himself, had used cocaine. This event marked the end of an era although the shift would not be immediately apparent. Lee Dogoloff, Bourne's deputy and successor, was instrumental in raising the profile of the Parent Movement among federal officials and in supporting the movement's efforts to influence federal publications on drugs and drug-use prevention. He also helped carry the movement's message to members of Congress through testimony at a number of hearings.

In January 1979, Senator Charles Mathias (D-MD) held congressional hearings on the harmful effects of marijuana and invited many parent-group leaders, along with scientists, to Washington to testify. The parent leaders took advantage of this opportunity to be together for the first time; they discussed the need to form a Washington-based organization that could represent their interests with both Congress and the federal agencies that were making and implementing national drug policy. They agreed to meet at the Fifth Annual Southeast Regional Drug Conference, later known as the PRIDE conference, in Atlanta in the spring of 1979. There, they founded the National Federation of Parents for Drug-Free Youth. Pat and Bill Barton were elected as the group's co-presidents and a Maryland parent group leader, Joyce Nalepka, later became the Federation's executive director.

During the presidential election campaigns that began in the summer of 1979, parent groups worked hard to get drug-abuse prevention policy on the agendas of presidential candidates. After the inauguration of Ronald Reagan (January 1981), the parent movement found that it had natural allies in the White House: Both President Reagan and First Lady Nancy Reagan were sympathetic to its cause. The National Federation of Parents for Drug-Free Youth led a massive letter writing campaign to the president-elect asking him to bring Carlton Turner to the White House as his drug-policy advisor. Turner, of the University of Mississippi, was responsible for growing marijuana used in scientific research. He had devoted much time to educating parents at various conferences about the pharmacological effects of marijuana on the brain and body and had earned their trust. President Reagan acted on the Federation's appeals and selected Turner as his drug advisor. Shortly after the inauguration, Turner helped the federation arrange for parent-group leaders to brief Mrs. Reagan on the prevention movement and enlist her support for their cause. She responded positively and served informally as the national spokesperson for the parent drug prevention movement.

A few years later, President Reagan appointed parent-group leader Ian Macdonald, a pediatrician from Florida, to serve as administrator of the Alcohol, Drug Abuse, and Mental Health Administration (ADAMHA), the federal agency in the Department of Health and Human Services that was responsible for substance abuse and mental health research and services. One of Macdonald's legacies is the Center for Substance Abuse Prevention (then called the Office for Substance Abuse

Prevention, or OSAP), which he created as an office during his tenure at ADAMHA. Congress formally authorized OSAP as a center, changed its name to CSAP, and funded it in the Anti-Drug Abuse Act of 1986. Through this kind of concerted effort, parents were able to influence the appointments of key policymakers in the federal government to emphasize and implement their goals: to mitigate the use of illegal drugs (and alcohol and tobacco among underage individuals), to help drug users quit, and to find treatment for those who are addicted and cannot quit by themselves. Beginning in the late 1980s, the Center for Substance Abuse Prevention made demonstration grants available to support local, grass-roots, drug prevention efforts targeting high-risk youth, primarily in African American, Hispanic, Asian American, and Native American communities.

The Parent Movement struggled in the following decades. According to the Monitoring the Future survey funded by the National Institute on Drug Abuse, annual use of marijuana, cocaine, and heroin reached a low point in the early 1990s but rose among children at all grade levels at least until 1997 when it seemed to level off. Despite determined attempts at the end of that decade by the CSAP director at the time, Karol Kumpfer, to enlist support from parents, the response was mainly from people who had been involved in the original movement and were now grandparents. It seemed that the grass-roots style and zero-tolerance approach characteristic of the Parent Movement lacked appeal to a new generation of parents.

BIBLIOGRAPHY

Mannat, M. (1980). *Parents, peers, and pot.* Rockville, MD: National Institute on Drug Abuse.

Musto, D. F., & Korsmeyer, P. (2001). *The quest for drug control: Politics and federal policy in a period of increasing substance abuse, 1963–1981.* New Haven, CT: Yale University Press.

National Families in Action. Available from http://www.nationalfamilies.org.

O'Donnell, O. (1999). *Parents helping parents: A guide for action.* Rockville, MD: Center for Substance Abuse Prevention.

Resnick, M. D., Bearman, P. S., Blum, R. W., Bauman, K. E., Harris, K. M., Jones, J., et al. (1997). Protecting adolescents from harm: Findings from the National Longitudinal Study on Adolescent Health. *Journal of the American Medical Association, 278,* 823–832.

Rusche, S. (1995). Voluntary organizations. In R. H. Coombs & D. Ziedonis (Eds.), *Handbook on drug abuse prevention: A comprehensive strategy to prevent the abuse of alcohol and other drugs* (pp.181–195). Boston: Allyn and Bacon.

Rusche, S. (1997). *A guide to the drug legalization movement.* Atlanta, GA: National Families in Action.

SUE RUSCHE
REVISED BY PAMELA KORSMEYER (2009)

PATHOLOGICAL GAMBLING (PG). *See* Gambling.

PEMOLINE. Pemoline is a stimulant medication. Although not structurally similar to the amphetamines, pemoline has similar psychomotor stimulant effects but only minimal effects on the cardiovascular system. Pemoline is often used therapeutically (despite being less effective than amphetamine or methylphenidate) in the treatment of attention deficit/hyperactivity disorder (ADHD)—a syndrome that first becomes evident during childhood and is characterized by excessive activity and difficulty in maintaining attention. Pemoline has the advantage of a long half-life, which means that dosing can be once daily, but clinical improvement can be delayed by three to four weeks after initiation of pemoline therapy. In addiction, the likelihood for abuse of pemoline appears to be substantially less than that of the amphetamines.

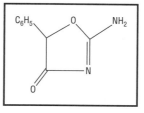

Figure 1. Chemical structure of pemoline. ILLUSTRATION BY GGS INFORMATION SERVICES. GALE, CENGAGE LEARNING

See also **Attention Deficit Hyperactivity Disorder; Psychomotor Stimulant; Schizophrenia.**

BIBLIOGRAPHY

Lowinson, J. H. (2005). *Substance abuse: A comprehensive textbook*. Philadelphia, PA: Lippincott, Williams & Wilkins.

Marangell, L. B., & Martinez, J. M. (2006). *Concise guide to psychopharmacology*, 2nd ed. Washington, D.C: American Psychiatric Publishing.

MARIAN W. FISCHMAN

PERCEPTION AND EFFECTS OF DRUGS. *See* Sensation and Perception and Effects of Drugs.

PERSONALITY DISORDERS. *Personality disorder* (PD) refers to a pattern of behavior and perception that deviates from the expected cultural norms and is "inflexible and pervasive across a broad range of personal and social situations" (*DSM-IV-TR*, p. 689). As with all DSM disorders, a diagnosis of a specific personality disorder requires that the symptoms cause significant distress or functional impairment. The diagnosis is made only in individuals who are at least 18 years old. In *DSM-IV*, diagnostic categories are intermittent syndromes characterized by a set of symptoms. *DSM-IV personality disorder* describes a set of traits that tend to be more stable over time than symptoms associated with other *DSM-IV* disorders. The *DSM-IV* describes ten independent categories of personality disorders, each containing a unique set of symptoms. The *DSM-IV* also provides a dimensional model in which the ten personality disorders are grouped into three clusters based on their similarities: odd-eccentric, dramatic-emotional, and anxious-fearful. The dimensional model of personality disorders posits that maladaptive personality traits are expressed on a continuum from normal personality to personality disorder. According to the dimensional model of personality disorders, many traits are shared among the personality disorder diagnostic categories. Table 1 provides PDs in each cluster and their shared characteristics.

PREVALENCE AND COMORBIDITY

The prevalence and comorbidity of PDs has been studied in patient groups and in the general population. In the 2001–2002 NIAAA *National Epidemiologic Survey on Alcohol and Related Conditions* (NESARC; Grant et al., 2004), 14.7 percent or 30.8 million adults reported at least one of the seven PDs assessed (paranoid, schizoid, antisocial, histrionic, avoidant, dependent, obsessive-compulsive). Obsessive-compulsive personality disorder was the most prevalent (7.9%) followed by paranoid (4.4%), antisocial (3.6%), schizoid (3.1%), avoidant (2.4%), histrionic (1.8%), and dependent (0.5%). Gender differences were evident, with women at significantly greater risk for avoidant, dependent, and paranoid PD, and men at significantly greater risk for antisocial PD. Blacks, Native Americans, Asians, and Hispanics were at significantly greater risk for schizoid PD than whites. Native Americans were at significantly greater risk for antisocial PD than whites (Grant et al., 2004). People with higher education (bachelor's degree or higher) were at lower risk for all PDs compared to those with lower levels of education. All seven PDs were highly associated with other PDs in each *DSM-IV* cluster as well as with other PDs (Grant et al., 2005). The high comorbidity across personality disorders suggests that each PD is a different manifestation of a shared underlying disorder, an approach that supports the dimensional model described above.

A NESARC study of personality disorders and Axis I comorbidity supported earlier findings from treatment studies of high rates of personality disorders among individuals with mood and anxiety disorders (Grant et al., 2005). Among NESARC respondents with a current mood or anxiety disorder, the prevalence of at least one PD was 46.8 percent and 41.8 percent, respectively. Among individuals with a mood or anxiety disorder, obsessive-compulsive, paranoid, and avoidant PDs were the most prevalent. Avoidant (ORs = 10.6–14.5) and dependent (ORs = 12.2–22.0) PDs were most strongly related to major depression, dysthymia, and mania. With respect to anxiety disorders, avoidant and dependent PDs were more strongly related to each of the anxiety disorders than any other PD (Grant et al., 2005). Nearly 53 percent of NESARC respondents who sought treatment for a mood disorder in the last 12 months had a personality disorder. Among those who sought treatment for an

Cluster	Personality disorder	Characteristics
A - odd-eccentric	Paranoid, Schizoid, Schizotypal	Suspicious, mistrustful, hypervigilant, easily offended, unfeeling toward others, withdrawn and isolated, odd and eccentric behavior
B - dramatic-emotional	Antisocial	A pervasive pattern of behavior that includes: lying, theft, violence, substance abuse, sexual promiscuity, spouse and/or child abuse, inconsistent work, legal conflicts, impulsivity and lack of remorse for antisocial acts
	Borderline	Unstable mood, behavior, relationships, and self-image; impulsive, self-destructive (e.g., suicide attempts, 'cutting,' substance abuse), chronic feelings of emptiness, low tolerance for being alone
	Histrionic, Narcissistic	Dramatic, emotional, erratic, seductive, attention-seeking, exaggerated sense of self-importance, feelings of entitlement, exploitation of others, lack of empathy, difficulty accepting criticism, disregard for social conventions.
C - anxious-fearful	Avoidant, Dependent, Obsessive-compulsive	Timid, extreme sensitivity to real or imagined rejection, socially withdrawn, low self-esteem; avoidance of assuming responsibility for life events and goals, dependence on others to make everyday decisions; passive, submissive, discomfort when alone; perfectionist, orderly, inflexible, indecisive, constricted emotions, obstinate, overly conscientious

Table 1. *DSM-IV* dimensional model for personality disorders. ILLUSTRATION BY GGS INFORMATION SERVICES. GALE, CENGAGE LEARNING

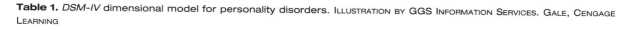

anxiety disorder, nearly 60 percent had a personality disorder (Grant et al., 2005). These high comorbidity rates are a concern to treatment providers because of conflicting evidence regarding the effects of co-occurring PDs on outcomes of treatment for mood and anxiety disorders. In earlier studies, PDs were found to complicate treatment outcomes (Alnaes & Torgersen, 1997; Baer et al., 1992; Turner, 1987) while subsequent studies showed that pharmacotherapy for major depression appears to improve PD symptomatology as well (Fava et al., 2002; Hirschfeld, 1999).

In the *Collaborative Longitudinal Personality Disorders Study* (CLPS; Gunderson et al., 2000) schizotypal, avoidant, borderline, and obsessive-compulsive PDs were assessed in treatment-seeking patients. In this study, the mean number of co-occurring personality disorders was 1.4, with 26 percent reporting borderline PD, 24 percent reporting avoidant PD, 23 percent reporting obsessive-compulsive PD, and 13 percent reporting schizotypal PD (Skodol et al., 2005). Borderline PD was significantly associated with substance use disorders and PTSD; and avoidant, borderline, and dependent PDs were associated with depression. When compared to Caucasian patients,

African American patients had proportionally higher rates of schizotypal PD and Hispanic patients had higher rates of borderline PD. Among individuals with borderline PD, there was a higher rate of substance abuse in men, and higher rates of Post Traumatic Stress Disorder (PTSD) and eating disorders in women.

TREATMENT

Strong empirical evidence supports psychotherapy, primarily psychodynamic and cognitive-behavioral approaches, as the treatment of choice for personality disorders when reduction in symptoms as well as improvement in social and occupational function are the targeted outcomes (Verheul & Herbrink, 2007). For psychotherapy conducted on an outpatient, individual basis, there is no evidence to support a difference in the efficacy between psychodynamic and cognitive-behavioral theoretical frameworks. Evidence for the efficacy of psychodynamic, long-term outpatient group psychotherapy is suggested in a number of studies but not as a stand-alone treatment for individuals with severe personality pathology who may have low tolerance for anxiety and frustration. For these patients, embedding group treatment into day-hospital treatment or adding individual sessions is recommended (Verheul & Herbrink, 2007). In terms of specific clusters of personality disorders, research suggests that short-term, psychodynamic psychotherapy in a day-hospital setting is more effective for Cluster C personality disorders than the disorders in the other clusters. It is suggested that day-hospital treatment be followed up with long-term individual or group psychotherapy to yield continued improvements in occupational and social functioning. Evidence suggests that inpatient psychotherapy is effective for all PDs and that a shorter inpatient phase (3–6 months vs. 12 months) followed by a long-term outpatient phase (e.g., 12 months) is preferable to a long-term inpatient phase with no outpatient follow-up. (For a thorough review of efficacy of modalities of psychotherapy for personality disorders, see Verheul & Herbrink, 2007.) Some research has begun to investigate the added value of psychopharmacological treatment with psychotherapy, but there is as of 2008 only limited evidence to support the use of medication as a treatment for personality disorder symptoms.

See also **Attention Deficit Hyperactivity Disorder; Conduct Disorder and Drug Use; Epidemiology of Drug Abuse; Risk Factors for Substance Use, Abuse, and Dependence: Personality.**

BIBLIOGRAPHY

Alnaes, R., & Torgersen, S. (1997). Personality and personality disorders predict development and relapse of major depression. *Acta Psychiatrica Scandinavica, 95,* 336–342.

American Psychiatric Association. (2000). *Diagnostic and statistical manual of mental disorders* (4th ed., text rev.). Washington, DC: Author.

Baer, K., Jenike, M., Black, D., Treece, C., Rosenfield, R., & Greist, J. (1992). Effect of axis II diagnoses on treatment outcome with clomipramine in 55 patients with obsessive-compulsive disorder. *Archives of General Psychiatry, 49,* 862–866.

Fava, M., Farabaugh, A. H., Sickinger, A. H., Wright, E., Alpert, J. E., Sonawalla, S., et al. (2002). Personality disorders and depression. *Psychological Medicine, 32,* 1049–1057.

Grant, B. F., Hasin, D. S., Stinson, F. S., Dawson, D. A., Chou, S. P., Ruan, W. J., et al. (2004). Prevalence, correlates, and disability of personality disorders in the United States: Results from the national epidemiologic survey on alcohol and related conditions. *Journal of Clinical Psychiatry, 65*(7), 948–958.

Grant, B. F., Hasin, D. S., Stinson, F. S., Dawson, D. A., Chou, S. P., Ruan, W. J., et al. (2005). Co-occurrence of 12-month mood and anxiety disorders and personality disorders in the U.S.: Results from the national epidemiologic survey on alcohol and related conditions. *Journal of Psychiatric Research, 39,* 1–9.

Grant, B. F., Stinson, F. S., Dawson, D. A., Chou, S. P., & Ruan, W. J. (2005). Co-occurrence of *DSM-IV* personality disorders in the United States: Results from the National Epidemiologic Survey on alcohol and related conditions. *Comprehensive Psychiatry, 46,* 1–5.

Gunderson, J. G., Shea, M. T., Skodol, A. E., McGlashan, T. H., Morey, L. C., & Stout, R. L. (2000). The Collaborative Longitudinal Personality Disorders Study: Development, aims, design, and sample characteristics. *Journal of Personality Disorders, 14*(4), 300–315.

Hirschfeld, R. M. A. (1999). Personality disorders and depression: Comorbidity. *Depression and Anxiety, 10,* 142–146.

Skodol, A. E., Gunderson, J. G., Shea, M. T., McGlashan, T. H., Morey, L. C., Sanislow, C. A., et al. (2005). The Collaborative Longitudinal Personality Disorders Study (CLPS): Overview and implications. *Journal of Personality Disorders, 19*(5), 487–504.

Turner, R. (1987). The effects of personality disorder diagnosis on the outcome of social anxiety symptom reduction. *Journal of Personality Disorders, 1,* 136–143.

Verheul, R., & Herbrink, M. (2007). The efficacy of various modalities of psychotherapy for personality disorders: A systematic review of the evidence and clinical recommendations. *International Review of Psychiatry, 19*(1), 25–38.

SHARON SAMET

PERU. Peru is a South American republic of about 500,000 square miles, bounded by the Pacific Ocean on the west, Ecuador and Colombia on the north, Bolivia and Brazil on the east, and Chile on the south. The country's varied elevation makes for three drastically different climatic zones. Along the west is a narrow and extremely dry desert; down the middle run two chains of the rugged Andes Mountains, with a high cold plateau between them; and to the east sprawls the hot, flat, forested headwaters of the Amazon. A variety of drugs have played important roles in the lives of the Peruvian people since ancient times. The little epidemiological data that exist are fragmentary and unreliable, while ethnographic studies are often richly detailed but only local in scope. However, much of the behavior associated with drugs in Peru in modern times is public and has been discussed by local writers.

COCA AND COCAINE

Coca is undoubtedly the most commonly used drug in Peru, and it plays a major role in the nation's culture. Cocaine, by contrast, is rarely used by Peruvians, but it is very significant in the illegal economy. Thus, the problems associated with coca do not derive from its traditional use but from the global market for its derivative, cocaine hydrochloride. Cocaine use and the big money and varied crimes associated with it have overshadowed the ancient origins and respectable cultural roots of coca (*Erythroxylon coca*). The coca bush grows best in a small subtropical portion of the eastern slopes of the Andes, and its leaves have been used and widely traded over a broad area for at least 1,000 years. Its early uses probably differed little from today's customary uses.

The leaves of the coca plant are routinely "chewed" (or, more accurately, sucked), and it is considered a refreshing dietary supplement. Its use is medicinal and healthful, as well as symbolic and mystical. Far removed from the derivative drug cocaine, coca produces neither the "rush" nor the "high" commonly associated with illicit drugs.

A cud, or quid, anywhere from the size of a peach pit to the size of a golf ball, can be gradually built up by tucking the plant's leaves into one's cheek. Throughout the day, the cud can occasionally be freshened by the addition of a few new leaves, or by the ingestion of a pinch of lime (i.e., ground shell or stone). Although it is mostly used by adult males, coca is by no means off-limits to others. Chewing coca leaves is most common among small-scale agriculturalists, but the habit has been brought to urban areas by migrants, where it is slowly being adopted as an occasional recreational activity.

Although the behavior of users shows little effect, scientific analysis supports subjective accounts that chewing coca helps to relieve hunger and thirst, as well as cold and fatigue. Calcium (from the lime), glucose, and a few vitamins that are lacking in the diet of the poor are beneficial, and there is no indication of any harms.

Coca leaves also have religious and magical uses among the native population. Coca is an ideal sacrifice or offering to the spirits and deities that are thought to inhabit the area and affect the lives of people. It is also used for divining by specialists who are said to know how to "read" scattered leaves. Such mystical associations strengthen support for coca, even among those who do not routinely chew it.

Tourists in Peru may occasionally be surprised to see coca tea offered in fancy hotels and restaurants, but this brew is said to be a cure or palliative for *sorroche*, the altitude sickness that newcomers often suffer when adjusting to a deficit of oxygen at high elevations. This condition is marked by heart palpitations and headache. Since about 2000, small amounts of coca have also been incorporated in some toothpastes, cookies, and other products, but these account for only a small portion of total production.

In addition to the legal market, coca growing has expanded for clandestine purposes, particularly since about 1980. The leaves are carried to the eastern lowlands, where, under the cover of the jungle, scattered encampments are devoted to production of cocaine paste. Soaking about a ton of coca leaves in kerosene or diesel fuel and sulphuric acid yields about twelve pounds of this paste, which in its crudest form is called *bazuco*. It is often mixed with tobacco in cigarettes (also called *bazuco*), and smoked by poor young people in urban slums throughout the country. This use is harmful to the individual smoker, but it is of negligible importance on the national scene. A more refined paste is generally flown clandestinely to Brazil or Colombia, where it is further processed to yield about one-third as much of the familiar white street drug, which is sold internationally to wealthy recreational users or desperate addicts.

ALCOHOLIC BEVERAGES

Not all Peruvian beverages that contain alcohol are habitually drunk with the aim or result of intoxication. For a significant portion of the population (notably Quechua and Aymara speakers), home-brewed beer is a dietary staple drunk by people of both sexes and all ages, often with meals or as a refreshing beverage at other times. Generically known as *chicha*, it is most often made from maize, although other grains, as well as various fruits and vegetables, may also be fermented. Regional and seasonal special *chichas* are greatly appreciated. With an alcohol content rarely above 4 percent, casual drinking is healthful because *chicha* is rich in some vitamins and nutrients that are scarce in the restricted diet of the nation's working class.

Most *chicha* is brewed at home in small batches for use as a basic food or for the celebration of special events. Some urban breweries produce larger batches, with more quality controls, but this is still for local consumption only, because the product spoils too rapidly to be transported for broader distribution. It also figures prominently in the Andean tradition of labor exchange. Often, a short period of pooled effort is required for work such as thatching a roof, sowing or harvesting a field, or threshing grain. People take turns working on each other's properties, with each individual alternating as host and guest for the chicha drinking that accompanies or follows such work.

In the wake of the Spanish Conquest, Catholic missionaries brought grapevines to the Americas in the hope of producing wine for ceremonial use by the native peoples, whom they hoped to convert. Grapes took root in Peru in the 1550s, but only in the twenty-first century have a few Peruvian vineyards begun to produce palatable wines, and these still have only a small internal market and are rarely exported.

Since refrigeration became affordable in commercial outlets, lager beer, which is produced by a few breweries throughout the country, has been an occasional refreshment, especially on hot days. However, this beverage plays little part in the lives of most Peruvians, as is also the case with a variety of distilled beverages. Such spirits were unknown in the area in pre-Columbian times, but they were introduced early in the colonial period (1500s). *Trago*, a crude rum distilled from sugarcane juice, is commonly used as a shortcut to drunkenness, and it is actively, though episodically, sought and appreciated by both males and females in many Indian communities, especially on religious holidays. Few claim to enjoy *trago*, but drinkers of the rum often boast of an almost mystical transcendence, and they habitually spill a little on the

ground or floor to share with Pachamama (the great Earth-Mother) before each drink. A form of whiskey is often passed off as various internationally famous brands and predominates in occasional celebratory drinking by wealthy urbanites. The local grape brandy, *pisco*, has gained some popularity among a few connoisseurs.

TOBACCO AND SNUFFS

Although this is one of the regions from which the plant containing nicotine (*Nicotiana spp.*) appears to have originated 3,000 years ago, local populations smoke little tobacco in cigarettes, cigars, or pipes. In the eastern lowlands there are many small groups of relatively isolated peoples (often called "indigenous" or "tribal" peoples), and it is customary for adult males to occasionally take snuffs in large doses. Often psychoactive, these snuffs have a number of ingredients derived from various plants of the tropical forest. There are minor variations in the means of administration, and in the effects they produce, but they are all used only on special occasions, and none of them result in addiction or in social, psychological, or other problems. Snuffs are sometimes used for artistic inspiration, predicting the future, or communicating with spirits that are thought to provide moral and religious guidance. Some of the alkaloids they contain are said to induce the sense of flying, while others produce visions of jaguars, but most result in immensely varied sensations that users interpret in diverse ways. A common theme is that of transcending ordinary reality.

In some populations in Peru, boys have a dramatic single exposure to such drugs at their initiation into adulthood, during which they first encounter the jungle animal that will be their ally or counterpart throughout life. More often, however, the use of these drugs is reserved for shamans, who are thought to have divinatory and supernatural powers. Because they supposedly can fly as well as communicate with animals, ancestors, and other spirits, shamans often serve as curers or fortune-tellers in public or private ceremonies.

One of the most popular snuffs is *ayahuasca*, or *yaje*, which is often called "the vine of souls." Its source is the jungle vine *Baniosteriopsis caapi*, and it contains both harmine and ibogaine alkaloids. Archeological remains show it was used 5,000 years ago, and it remains important today. Elaborate formal rituals accompany its ingestion, and a cult of "drug tourism" has grown up around it in the city of Iquitos. Shamans with specialized knowledge use it for the diagnosis and curing of disease, whereas dabblers claim that it bestows an incredible sense of transcendence.

Another of the more widespread snuffs is *ebene*, which is derived from the bark and resin of the tree *Virola theidora*. Mescaline, famous elsewhere as a derivative of peyote, is derived from the root of the San Pedro cactus (*Tricocereus pachanoi*), although cannabis, or marijuana, is strangely rare in Peru. *Huilca* (or *vilca*), which is derived from seed pods of the tree *Anadenanthera colubrina*, was at one time ingested via enema by the Inca, and it is still popular among many Amazonian groups. The deadly nightshade (*Atropa belladonna*) contains the mind-altering alkaloid scopolamine. One must be extremely careful when ingesting these last two substances, for only a minute difference in dosage could result in an agonizing death.

With few exceptions, the complex botany and chemistry of such preparations is still not fully understood, and scientists wonder at how so many and such complex concoctions could have been invented. Some contain several ingredients, each prepared in a special way and processed for a specific time. Others contain a single element that gives the blend its specific effect within the human body, while some others would be inactive (or deadly poisonous) if they were a few degrees warmer or cooler when ingested.

OTHER DRUGS

Coffee, tea, and chocolate (all of which contain caffeine) are commonplace refreshment drinks in urban settings, but no one in Peru thinks of them as drugs, and they are generally unimportant economically. In some parts of the eastern lowlands, the same is true of mate, or "Jesuit tea," which is brewed from *Ilex spp*.

As is true throughout much of the world, the most impoverished people in Peru often resort to mass-produced substances for relatively inexpensive (and physically dangerous) mind-altering experiences. The sniffing of gasoline, glue, dry-cleaning fluid, and other solvents and volatile chemicals takes a toll on many young people who roam in gangs through the streets of urban slums. As

important as such behaviors may be to those who participate, however, they have little significance at the national level.

At the middle and upper levels of society, it is similarly not uncommon for some people to use prescription drugs or "designer" drugs to alter their consciousness. A few ethnographic studies show that such experiences differ little from those in other countries, but there are virtually no epidemiological data available.

POLICIES AND INTERNATIONAL RELATIONS

Social and cultural contexts tell more about the importance of drugs than do the experiences of individual users. Coca and *chicha* figured prominently in trade and political alliances in pre-Columbian times, just as cocaine does today. Both Spanish colonial and republican governments displayed an ambivalence about alcohol and coca by alternating prohibitions with permissiveness (especially with respect to the "Indian" or native population). As is often the case in other countries, Peru has many laws and regulations that are supposed to reduce both the use of drugs and the problems that arise from their excessive use. But enforcement is sporadic, highly personalized, and influenced by political and economic corruption.

There is widespread resentment that members of the U.S. Drug Enforcement Agency and armed forces are actively involved in attempts to curb the growing and processing of coca. The widespread use of herbicides harms people, livestock, and other crops, and interference with the drug traffic is seen as economic oppression, an insult to national sovereignty, and an immediate danger to the lives and property of those few Peruvians who are involved. In the 1980s and 1990s the Maoist guerilla group Sendero Luminoso (Shining Path) consistently defended the peasantry who were growing and processing coca. This activity won popular support for the guerilla movement, even those who did not share their extreme leftist ideology.

In sum, drug use has a long and honored tradition in many of the varied populations that comprise contemporary Peru, and it plays integral and varied roles in their cultures. Drug abuse is rare, however, and the problems that are associated with drugs more often stem from outside influences, misunderstandings, and heavy-handed restrictive policies than from the drugs or their traditional uses.

See also **Brazil; Colombia; Foreign Policy and Drugs, United States; International Drug Supply Systems.**

BIBLIOGRAPHY

Allen, C. J. (1988). *The hold life has: Coca and cultural identity in an Andean community*. Washington, DC: Smithsonian Institution Press.

Dobkin de Rios, M. (1972). *Visionary vine: Psychedelic healing in the Peruvian Amazon*. San Francisco: Chandler.

Furst, P. T. (1976). *Hallucinogens and culture*. San Francisco: Chandler and Sharp.

Heath, D. B. (1982). Historical and cultural factors affecting alcohol availability and consumption in Latin America. In Institute of Medicine (Ed.), *Legislative approaches to prevention of alcohol-related problems* (pp. 128–160, 174–188). Washington, DC: National Academy Press.

Morales, E. (Ed.). (1986). *Drugs in Latin America*. Studies in Third World Societies, Publication No. 37. Williamsburg, VA: College of William and Mary, Department of Anthropology.

Morales, E. (1989). *Cocaine: White gold rush in Peru*. Tucson: University of Arizona Press.

Dwight B. Heath

PEYOTE. Peyote (or peyotl) is the common name for the cactus *Lophophore williamsii* or *Anhalonium lewinii*, which is found in the southwestern United States and northern Mexico. Although there are many compounds found in the cactus, some of which may be psychoactive, the principal hallucinogenic substance found in peyote is mescaline. As the other psychoactive substances may make some contribution to the psychedelic experience, there may be some slight difference in the behavioral effects produced by taking peyote and pure mescaline, but the overall effects of peyote are very similar to those produced by mescaline.

Peyote cactus, close-up, showing some small "buttons" on top. Custom Medical Stock Photo, Inc. Reproduced by permission.

Peyote, one of the oldest psychedelic agents known, was used by the Aztecs of pre-Columbian Mexico who considered it magical and divine. Its use spread to other Native American groups who used it to treat various illnesses, as a vehicle to communicate with the spirits, and in highly structured tribal religious rituals. For these rituals, the dried tops of the cactus—the buttons—are chewed or made into a tea. Since peyote may cause some initial nausea and vomiting, the participant may prepare for the ceremony by fasting prior to eating the buttons. Peyote is usually taken as part of a formalized group experience and over an extended period of time; the peyote ceremonies may take place at night and around a communal fire to increase the hallucinogenic effects and visions.

See also **Ayahuasca; Dimethyltryptamine (DMT); Psilocybin.**

BIBLIOGRAPHY

Efron, D. H., Holmstedt, B., & Kline, N.S., Eds. (1979). *Ethnopharmacologic search for psychoactive drugs*. New York: Raven Press.

Karch, S. B. (2006). *Drug abuse handbook*. Boca Raton, FL: CRC Press.

Lewis, W. H. (2005). Hallucinogens. In *Medical botany: Plants affecting human health*. Hoboken, NJ: John Wiley & Sons.

DANIEL X. FREEDMAN
R. N. PECHNICK

PHARMACODYNAMICS.

The study of the mechanism of how drugs act on the body is called pharmacodynamics. Most (but not all) drugs exert their action by binding to specific receptors. This binding may initiate changes that lead to the characteristic effects of the drug on body functions. An agonist is a drug that mimics the action of an endogenous ligand (e.g., a neurotransmitter or hormone) at a receptor. If various concentrations of an agonist are administered, the dose-response curve (see Figure 1) will show increased effects as one goes from left (low concentration) to right (high concentration). A full agonist is a drug that produces the maximal response. A partial agonist is a drug that provokes a response that is less than maximal. An antagonist is a drug that does not

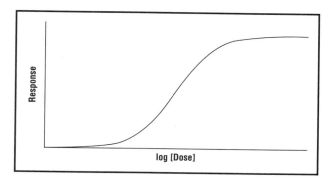

Figure 1. The shape of the dose-response curve. ILLUSTRATION BY GGS INFORMATION SERVICES. GALE, CENGAGE LEARNING

provoke a response by itself but that blocks agonist-mediated responses. An inverse agonist produces a response that is the opposite of the effect induced by an agonist.

A central question in drug therapy is identifying the proper dose of the drug that will produce a desired action without many harmful side effects. To clarify this problem, pharmacologists analyze the relationship between dose and response, in which the X-axis shows the concentration of a drug or a hormone and the Y-axis shows the response to the drug or hormone, which could be almost any type of measure. Most dose-response curves are sigmoidal (shaped like an S). The log-dose-response can be viewed as having four parameters: potency, slope, maximal efficacy, and variability. Potency describes the strength of drug effects. It is usually employed to calculate relative strengths among drugs of the same class. Slope refers to the central part of the curve that is approximately straight. It is used to analyze drug concentration (dose) from the observed corresponding responses. Maximal efficacy, or simply efficacy, is the greatest effect produced by the drug. This is one of the major characteristics of a drug. Efficacy and potency of a drug are not necessarily correlated, and the two characteristics should not be confused.

Many drugs, including drugs of abuse, produce tolerance, that is, it becomes necessary to take progressively larger doses to achieve the same drug effect or the same dose has a reduced effect. Sensitization involves the increase in the strength of a response to a stimulus induced by past experiences with the same or related stimuli. This increase represents adaptation, making the drug effect easier to elicit on future occasions. In some cases, the brain and other tissues on which a drug acts undergo adaptive changes (neuroadaptations) that tend to offset the drug effect. When a drug that produces neuroadaptation is withdrawn, the brain and other tissues have to readapt because they are no longer balanced by the drug effect. The adaptation produces a variety of signs and symptoms called the *withdrawal syndrome*. The severity of this syndrome depends on the degree of adaptive changes in the nervous system which, in turn, depends on the dose and the duration of exposure to the drug. The particular characteristics of the withdrawal syndrome depend on the pharmacological effects of the drug(s) and typically are opposite to the drug effects. For example, morphine constricts the pupil; the morphine withdrawal syndrome includes pupillary dilation.

Most drugs of abuse produce pleasant effects in humans. For example, some people use amphetamines or other stimulants (e.g., cocaine) to achieve a sense of well-being and euphoria. Some people use depressants—alcohol, opioids, or tranquilizers—to relax. Still others use either stimulants or depressants to relieve boredom or reduce anxiety or pain. The common feature is that people use drugs because somehow the drug is rewarding to the user, either by producing a feeling of well-being (e.g., euphoria, elation) or by taking away a negative feeling (e.g., anxiety).

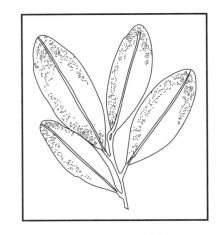

Figure 2. Coca leaf. ILLUSTRATION BY GGS INFORMATION SERVICES. GALE, CENGAGE LEARNING

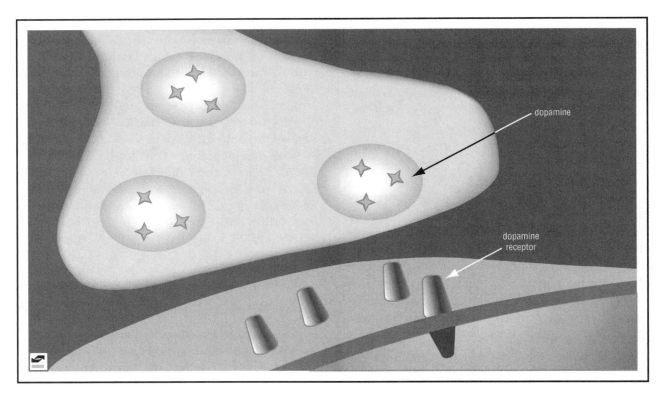

Figure 3. Dopamine neurotransmission. (Source: NIDA Notes, Vol. 13, No. 5, Feb. 1999. National Institute of Drug Abuse, National Institutes of Health, U.S. Department of Health and Human Services.) ILLUSTRATION BY GGS INFORMATION SERVICES. GALE, CENGAGE LEARNING

An extensive literature defines the role of dopamine (DA) in the motivational, rewarding and reinforcing effects of all drugs of abuse (Volkow et al., 2007). Alcohol, for example, activates DA release in the nucleus accumbens and surrounding extended amygdala (Heimer et al., 1997; Lyness et al., 1992; Weiss et al., 1993). The action of alcohol on the mesolimbic dopaminergic reward pathway is strongly associated with susceptibility to alcoholism (Noble, 1996); the development of craving and loss of control (Robinson & Berridge, 1993); and the acquisition of excessive motivational properties by alcohol-related cues. Brain dopaminergic systems are highly complex, with at least seven receptor subtypes, though most research has examined D2 dopamine receptors. Reduced levels of DA and of D2 receptors have been found in alcohol-preferring (P) rats during alcohol withdrawal. DA levels in P rats rise when the animals anticipate receiving alcohol (Weiss et al., 1992). Imaging studies in alcoholics also show a lower density of D2 receptors (Volkow et al., 2002a; Volkow et al., 2002b). The density of D2 receptors is also modulated by environmental factors (e.g., social hierarchy in monkeys; Morgan et al., 2002), suggesting that strategies could be developed to increase the expression of D2 receptors (Volkow et al., 2002c). Administration of a viral vector to deliver the gene encoding the D2 receptor to P and alcohol-non-preferring (NP) rats resulted in the overexpression of D2 receptors and a significant reduction in alcohol intake (Thanos et al., 2001). Imaging studies have shown that activation of DA in limbic and memory circuits (amygdala, dorsal striatum, and hippocampus) may contribute to craving, which can be associated with relapse in abstinent alcoholics (Volkow et al., 2002c). Increased D2 receptor activity was found in unaffected siblings of alcoholics, suggesting a protective effect of increased dopaminergic activity (Volkow et al., 2006). Furthermore, studies have shown that the high associated with cocaine results not only from the absolute increase in DA concentration but also from the rate at which DA increases. The faster the increase of DA, the more intense the reinforcing effects are (Volkow et al., 2007). Brain imaging studies show that in subjects dependent on cocaine there is a down-regulation (decrease) in D2 receptor density and of DA release in the nucleus accumbens, the reward center of the brain. Each of these decreases in function contributes to decreased sensitivity to naturally occurring rewards. The decreased sensitivity of reward circuits would lead to decreased interest in common environmental stimuli, possibly predisposing individuals to seek drug stimulation as a means to activate these reward circuits and forming the foundation of the transition from using cocaine (and other addictive drugs) to feel high to taking cocaine to feel normal. Cocaine, like other drugs, is much more potent in stimulating DA-regulated reward than are natural reinforcers; but unlike natural reinforcers, drugs are able to activate down-regulated circuits (Volkow et al., 2007). However, even addicting drugs have limited effectiveness, and a continual decrease in normal DA function could underlie the development of tolerance and the subsequent need to increase the dose of a drug such as cocaine to activate sufficient DA release from down-regulated reward center circuits.

See also **Receptor, Drug; Tolerance and Physical Dependence.**

BIBLIOGRAPHY

DiChiara, G. (1995). The role of dopamine in drug abuse viewed from the perspective of its role in motivation. *Drug and Alcohol Dependence, 38,* 95–137.

Heimer, L., Alheid, G. F., de Olmos, J. S., Groenewegen, H. J., Haber, S. N., Harlan, R. E., et al. (1997). The accumbens: Beyond the core-shell dichotomy. *Journal of Neuropsychiatry and Clinical Neurosciences, 9,* 354–381.

Lyness, W. H., & Smith, F. L. (1992). Influence of dopaminergic and serotonergic neurons on intravenous ethanol self-administration in the rat. *Pharmacology, Biochemistry, & Behavior, 42,* 187–192.

Morgan, D., Grant, K. A., Gage, H. D., Mach, R. H., Kaplan, J. R., Prioleau, O., et al. (2002). Social dominance in monkeys: Dopamine D2 receptors and cocaine self-administration. *Nature Neuroscience, 5*(2), 169–174.

Noble, E. (1996). The gene that rewards alcoholism. *Scientific American Science and Medicine, 3,* 52–61.

Robinson, T. E., & Berridge, K. C. (1993). The neural basis of drug craving: An incentive-sensitization theory of addiction. *Brain Research Reviews, 18,* 247–291.

Thanos, P. K., Volkow, N. D., Freimuth, P., Umegaki, H., Ikari, H., Roth, G., et al. (2001). Overexpression of dopamine D2 receptors reduces alcohol self-administration. *Journal of Neurochemistry, 78*(5), 1094–1103.

Urban, J. D., Clarke, W. P., von Zastrow, M., Nichols, D. E., Kobilka B., Weinstein, H., et al. (2007). Functional selectivity and classical concepts of quantitative pharmacology. *Journal of Pharmacology and Experimental Therapeutics, 320,* 1–13.

Volkow, N. D., Fowler, J. S., Wang, G. J., & Goldstein, R. Z. (2002a). Role of dopamine, the frontal cortex and memory circuits in drug addiction: Insight from imaging studies. *Neurobiology of Learning and Memory, 78,* 610–624.

Volkow, N. D., Wang, G. J., Maynard, L., Fowler, J. S., Jayne, B., Telang, F., et al. (2002b). Effects of alcohol detoxification on dopamine D2 receptors in alcoholics: A preliminary study. *Psychiatry Research, 116,* 163–172.

Volkow, N. D., Wang, G. J., Fowler, J. S., Thanos, P. P., Logan, J., Gatley, S. J., et al. (2002c). Brain DA D2 receptors predict reinforcing effects of stimulants in humans: Replication study. *Synapse, 46*(2), 79–82.

Volkow, N. D., Fowler, J. S., Wang, G. J., Swanson, J. M., & Telang, F. (2007). Dopamine in drug abuse and addiction: Results of imaging studies and treatment implications. *Archives of Neurology, 64*(11), 1575–1579.

Volkow, N. D., Wang, G. J., Begleiter, H., Porjesz, B., Fowler, J. S., Telang, F., et al. (2006). High levels of dopamine D2 receptors in unaffected members of alcoholic families: Possible protective factors. *Archives of General Psychiatry, 63*(9), 999–1008.

Weiss, F., Hurd, Y. L., Ungerstedt, U., Markou, A., Plotsky, P. M., & Koob, G. F. (1992). Neurochemical correlates of cocaine and ethanol self-administration. *Annals of the New York Academy of Sciences, 654,* 220–241.

Weiss, F., Lorang, M. T., Bloom, F. E., & Koob, G. F. (1993). Oral alcohol self-administration stimulates dopamine release in the rat nucleus accumbens: Genetic and motivational determinants. *Journal of Pharmacology and Experimental Therapeutics, 267,* 250–258.

Wise, R. A. (1982). Neuroleptics and operant behavior: The anhedonia hypothesis. *Behavior and Brain Science, 5,* 39–87.

Usoa E. Busto
Revised by George A. Kenna (2009)

PHARMACOKINETICS: GENERAL.

Pharmacokinetics describes quantitatively what the body does to drugs, including their absorption, distribution throughout the body, metabolism, and ultimate elimination. The rates of these processes are important in characterizing the fate of a medication in the body.

The actual percentage of a drug contained in a drug product that enters the circulation unchanged after its administration, combined with the rate of entry into the body, determines the bioavailability of a drug.

Once absorbed, most drugs are carried from their site of action and elimination by the circulating blood. Some drugs simply dissolve in serum water but many others are carried bound to proteins, especially albumin. Plasma protein binding influences the fate of drugs in the body, since only the free (unbound) drug reaches the site of drug action. This interaction with binding sites is reversible.

The intensity of drug action is most frequently related to the concentration of the drug at the site of action. The duration of drug effect is related to the persistence of its presence at this site. The time to reach maximum drug concentrations (or peak effects) is usually referred to as *tmax.*

Whenever the fate of a drug in the body is described by pharmacokinetic parameters, a model of the body is assumed. The fundamental principles of pharmacokinetics are based on the most elementary model. The body is considered a single compartment. Distribution of the drug is considered uniform. The volume in which the drug is distributed is referred to as the *volume of distribution* (Vd). It is typically expressed in liters per kilogram (L/kg).

Elimination of the drug is assumed to be exponential. The rate of elimination of a drug is usually described by its *half-life* ($t_{1/2}$), which is the time required for 50 percent elimination of the drug. This is typically expressed in hours (h). Another way to express drug elimination, and the most important pharmacokinetic parameter, is called clearance, which is the volume of plasma blood from which a drug is completely removed per unit time. The amount eliminated is proportional to the concentration of the drug in the plasma/blood. Clearance is usually expressed in milliliters per minute per kilogram (ml/min/kg) but can also be expressed in liters per hour per kilogram (L/h/kg).

An effect of a single dose of a drug may be characterized by its latency, the time needed for drug concentrations to reach maximum levels (tmax). Magnitude of peak effects and duration of action dosage and rates of absorption and

Drug	Dosage/route (mg)	Bioavailability (F) (%)	Protein binding (%)	t_{max} (h)	Mean $t_{1/2}$ (h) (range)	Vd (L/kg)	Cl (ml/min/kg)
Butorphanol	2/IV	100 (IM)	80	0.75	3–4	5	385
Codeine	60 oral/TIV	40–80 (oral)	7–53	1	3 (2.3–9.3)	2–6	15
Dextromethorphan		>50 (oral)	30–50	—	2–3 (estimated)	3–5	
Heroin (3,6 diacelylmorphine) (see morphine)							
Buprenorphine	4–16/IV	79 (oral)	—	—	3.0 minutes	—	31
	0.3/IV	40–90 (oral)	—	—	2–3	1–3	900–1,200 (ml/min)
Pentazocine	—	47 (oral)	65	—	4.5	7	17
Morphine	0.01/mg/kg	15–64 (oral)	35	<1	2–4	3–4	12–21
		100 (IM)					
		48 (rectal)					
		2 (epidural)					
Methadone	15–80	92 (oral)	40	<1	25 (13–47)	3.8	1.4
Meperidine	50–100/IM	50–60 (oral)	50–60	—	3–4	3–5	—
Propoxyphene	130	40–90 (oral)	—	1–2	2–15	—	—
Nalbuphine	—	16 (oral)	—	1–2	2–3	3–4	22
Naltrexone	—	5–40 (oral)	20	—	2–3	19	48

Vd = Volume of distribution
Cl = Clearance
IV = Intravenous
IM = Intramuscular

Table 1. Pharmacokinetic parameters of opioids. ILLUSTRATION BY GGS INFORMATION SERVICES. GALE, CENGAGE LEARNING

Drug	Dosage/route (mg)	Bioavailability (F) (%)	Protein binding (%)	t_{max} (h)	Mean $t_{1/2}$ (h)(range)	Vd (L/kg)	Cl (ml/min/kg)
Amphetamine	15–25/oral	—	23–26	1.25	14 (2–22)	6.1	0.2–0.6 (L/min)
Caffeine	1–5 mg/kg/oral	100 (oral)	15–40	0.5–1	5 (1–10)	0.6	1
Cocaine	30–100/IV;IN	28–51 (IN)	7	0.5–1.5	(0.3–1.5)	2	11
Nicotine	0.25–2 (mg/kg/min)/IV	30	5	—	2 (0.8–3.5)	1–2	18

Vd = Volume of distribution
Cl = Clearance
IV = Intravenous
IN = Intranasal

Table 2. Pharmacokinetic parameters of stimulant drugs. ILLUSTRATION BY GGS INFORMATION SERVICES. GALE, CENGAGE LEARNING

elimination are influenced by these parameters. As dosage increases, latency is reduced and peak effect increased without a change in the time of peak effect. Reduced elimination (long half-life, reduced clearance) results in an expected prolongation of drug effects and in some cases drug accumulation. Using more complex models than a single compartment model, physicians use pharmacokinetic data not only to characterize the fate of a drug in the body but also to calculate doses and frequency of drug administration for each particular patient. This determination is important because there are wide variations among individuals in the absorption, distribution, and elimination of drugs.

Tables 1 through 4 summarize the available data on the kinetic properties of alcohol and other abused drugs. Some of the drugs of abuse included in this summary are illicit drugs (e.g., cocaine), whereas others are therapeutic agents that have the potential for abuse (e.g., opioids).

Although some of the drugs included in the tables have been used for centuries (e.g., alcohol, caffeine), knowledge of their kinetics and metabolism

Drug	Dosage/route (mg)	Bioavailability (F) (%)	Protein binding (%)	t_{max} (h)	Mean $t_{1/2}$ (h) (range)	Vd (L/kg)	Cl (ml/min/kg)
Alcohol (ethanol)	—	80 (oral)	—	<1	0.25	0.5	124 mg/kg/h
Alprazolam	0.5–30/oral	90 (oral)	70	0.7–1.6	12 (6–18)	0.7–1.5	0.7–1.3
Bromazepam	0.25–3/oral	—	70	1	10–15	—	—
Chlordiazepoxide	20–50/oral IV, IM	100 (oral) PO or (IM)	95	0.5–3	10 (6–28)	0.3	0.5
Clobazam	10–20/oral	Good (oral)	90	1.3–1.7	25 (16–49)	0.9–1.8	0.36–0.63
Clonazepam	—	98	86	1–2	23 (20–80)	3.2	1.55
Clorazepate (see Desmethyldiazepam)	—	—	—	—	2.0	0.33	1.8
Desalkylflurazepam	—	—	—	1	75 (40–200)	22	4.5
Desmethyldiazepam	—	99	97	1–2	51 (51–120)	0.78	0.14
Diazepam	1–40/oral IM, IV	100 (oral) 50–60 (IM, rectal)	96	0.5–2	31 (14–61)	1 (0.9–3.0)	0.38–0.51
Flurazepam (see Desalkylflurazepam)	15–90/oral	—	97	—	—	—	—
Halazepam (see Desmelhyldiazepam)	—	—	—	—	—	—	—
Lorazepam	2–4/oral	93 (oral) 90 (IM)	90	1.5	13 (8–25)	0.8–1.6	1 (0.8–1.3)
Midazolam	5–15/oral IV, IM	44 (oral)	95	0.3–0.7	2 1.4–5	0.8–17	6
Nitrazepam	15–30/oral	78 (oral)	87	2	26 (16–48)	1.2–2.7	0.86
Oxazepam	15–45/oral	97 (oral)	98	3 (0.5–8)	7 (5.1–13)	0.5–2.0	0.6–2.9
Prazepam (see Desmethyldiazepam)							
Temazepam	10–30/oral	>80 (oral)	98	0.8–4.7	12 (7–17)	1.3–1.5	1.0–3.4
Triazolam	0.25–1.0/oral	44 (oral) 53 s.l.	90	1.6	2.5 (2–5)	1.1	3.7–8.8

Vd = Volume of distribution
Cl = Clearance
IV = Intravenous
IM = Intramuscular
s.l. = Sublingual

Table 3. Pharmacokinetic parameters of central nervous system depressants. ILLUSTRATION BY GGS INFORMATION SERVICES. GALE, CENGAGE LEARNING

Drug	Dosage/route (mg)	Bioavailability (F) (%)	Protein binding (%)	t_{max} (h)	Mean $t_{1/2}$ (h) (range)	Vd (L/kg)	Cl (L/min)
Marijuana (Δ^9-tetrahydrocannabinol)	0.5–30	8–24 (smoked) 4–12 (oral)	95–26	3–8 min	25 (19–57)	626(L)	0.2–1
Phencyclidine (PCP)	0.1–0.7/IV Inhaled	5–90	65	1.5	24 (7–51)	6.8	0.30 (0.14–0.77)

Vd = Volume of distribution
Cl = Clearance
IV = Intravenous

Table 4. Pharmacokinetic parameters of hallucinogens. ILLUSTRATION BY GGS INFORMATION SERVICES. GALE, CENGAGE LEARNING

is recent and in some cases still incomplete. This lack of information is due partly to their complex metabolism and partly to the difficulties of studying drugs of abuse in humans.

The tables show the route of administration, the type of subjects used in the study, the doses used, and the most important kinetic parameters, such as protein binding, half-life, volume of distribution, and clearance.

See also **Pharmacokinetics of Alcohol.**

USOA E. BUSTO
REVISED BY GEORGE A. KENNA (2009)

PHARMACOKINETICS: IMPLICATIONS FOR ABUSABLE SUBSTANCES.

Pharmacokinetics is the study of the movements and rates of movement of drugs within the body, as the drugs are affected by uptake, distribution, binding, biotransformation, and elimination. An understanding of the biological basis of the clinical actions of abused drugs depends, in part, on knowledge of their neurochemical and neuroreceptor actions that reinforce and sustain drug use (Hall et al., 1990). The pharmacokinetic properties of

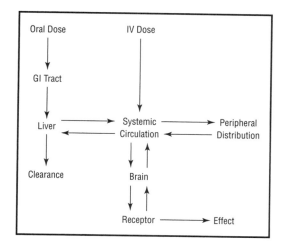

Figure 1. Schematic representation of physiological and pharmacokinetic events. These occur between administration of a centrally acting compound and the production of a pharmacological effect. If the medication is given orally, it must pass from the gastrointestinal (GI) tract to the portal circulation and to the liver before reaching the systemic circulation. Intravenous administration, however, yields direct access to the systemic circulation. Drugs of abuse may be taken by the intravenous route but are also taken by intranasal, intrabuccal, rectal, or inhalational routes, all of which will avoid the initial gastrointestinal–portal–hepatic exposure. ILLUSTRATION BY GGS INFORMATION SERVICES. GALE, CENGAGE LEARNING

abusable substances represent a second important component of the database. The discipline of pharmacokinetics applies mathematical models to explain and predict the time course of drug amounts (doses) and their concentrations in various body fluids (Greenblatt, 1991, 1992; Greenblatt & Shader, 1985). Pharmacokinetic principles can be used to provide quantitative answers to questions involving the relationship of drug dosage and route of administration to the amount and time course of the drug present in systemic blood and at the receptor site of action.

Before an orally administered psychoactive drug can exert a pharmacological effect through its molecular recognition site in the brain, a number of events must take place (see Figure 1). The drug must reach the stomach and dissolve in gastric fluid. The stomach empties this solution into the proximal small bowel, which is the site of absorption of most medications. The drug must diffuse across the gastrointestinal mucosal barrier, reach the portal circulation, and be delivered to the hepatic (liver) circulation. (The liver detoxifies chemicals, including drugs.) Before

reaching the systemic circulation, then, the absorbed drug must survive this initial exposure to the hepatic circulation, sometimes termed the *first-pass* through the liver (Greenblatt, 1993). After reaching the systemic blood, the drug is transported to the cerebral (brain) capillary circulation as well as to all other sites in the body that receive blood directly from the heart (cardiac output). The drug diffuses out of the cerebral capillary circulation, crosses the lipoidal (fatty) blood-brain barrier, and reaches the extracellular water surrounding the neuroreceptor site of action. Only then is the drug available to interact with its specific molecular recognition site.

All of these processes take time, and some may serve as obstacles that delay or prevent the drug from reaching its site of action. Pharmacokinetic models incorporate the physiology of these processes and can allow rational assessment of important clinical questions: How much drug reaches the brain? How fast does it get there? How long does it stay there?

DRUG ABSORPTION

The term *lag time* refers to the time that elapses between ingestion of an oral medication and its first appearance in the systemic circulation (see Figure 2). For most drugs, it generally falls between 5 and 45 minutes. For ethanol (drinking alcohol, which is also called ethyl alcohol), however, the lag time may be very short because the drug is already a liquid at the time it is ingested, and a significant component of absorption probably occurs across the gastric mucosa as well as in the proximal small bowel (Frezza et al., 1990). The physicochemical features of the drug contribute importantly to the time necessary for dissolution and, therefore, to the lag time. All else being equal, drugs in solution have shorter lag times than those administered in suspension form; they are, in addition, more rapidly absorbed than capsule preparations, tablet preparations and, finally, preparations intended to be used rectally. For any given solid dosage form, lag time and absorption rate are likely to be shorter if the drug particles are more finitely subdivided. Sustained-release (time-release) drug formulations are deliberately prepared to have long lag times and slow absorption rates, thereby avoiding drug effects associated with the peak concentration.

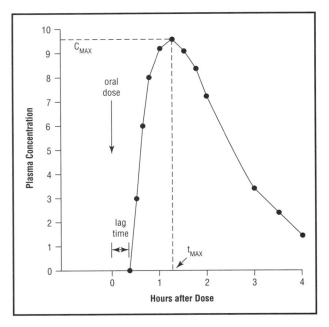

Figure 2. Schematic plot of plasma concentration versus time after oral dosage (given at time zero [arrow]). A lag time elapses between the time of administration and the beginning of appearance in the systemic circulation. Plasma levels then rise, reach a peak, and fall: c_{max} is the peak plasma concentration (9.6 units) and t_{max} is the time of peak concentration (1.25 hours after dosage). ILLUSTRATION BY GGS INFORMATION SERVICES. GALE, CENGAGE LEARNING

Absorption rate refers to the time necessary for the drug to reach the systemic circulation once the absorption process actually begins. Pharmacokinetic models can be applied to assign a half-life value to the process of absorption. Values of absorption half-life tend, however, to be of low statistical stability, and it is increasingly common to characterize the absorption process using the observed peak plasma concentration (cmax) and time of peak concentration (tmax). The tmax is actually a composite of the lag time plus the time necessary to reach peak concentration once absorption starts (Figure 2). In general, fast absorption implies a high value of cmax and a short value of tmax; slow absorption implies a long tmax and a low cmax. Again, sustained-release drug preparations are deliberately formulated to produce long lag times and slow absorption, thereby delaying and reducing the cmax after an oral dose. Drug absorption tends to be slower when medications are taken during or just after a meal, rather than in the fasting state (before a meal, on an empty stomach).

For these reasons, the ethanol in alcoholic beverages is relatively rapidly absorbed after oral ingestion. The popular lore that alcohol has a greater effect when taken on an empty stomach probably has a physiological basis, since peak concentrations are higher and earlier when alcohol is taken in the fasting state. Benzodiazepine derivatives (tranquilizers) clearly are not primary drugs of abuse and are seldom subject to misuse by the great majority of patients; however, benzodiazepines may be taken for non-therapeutic purposes by some substance abusers (Woods, Katz, & Winger, 1987, 1992; Shader & Greenblatt, 1993). The preference of specific benzodiazepines by drug abusers appears to be closely related to their rate of absorption. That is, rapidly absorbed benzodiazepines, leading to relatively high values of cmax shortly after dosage, appear to be preferred by drug abusers. The benzodiazepine diazepam (Valium), for example, is much more rapidly absorbed than is oxazepam (Serax or Serenid). In controlled laboratory settings, diazepam is more easily recognized as a potentially abusable substance by experienced drug users, and it is also preferred by this group to oxazepam (Griffiths et al., 1984a, 1984b). This preference also appears to be supported by epidemiological studies of prescription drug misuse (Bergman & Griffiths, 1986).

Some orally administered medications reach the systemic (blood) circulation in small or even negligible amounts relative to the dose ingested. Incomplete absorption from the gastrointestinal tract sometimes explains this. However, oral medications may be poorly available to the systemic circulation even if they are well absorbed. This is explained by the phenomenon termed *presystemic extraction*, which results from the unique anatomy and physiology of the gastrointestinal circulation (Greenblatt, 1993). Orally administered medications are absorbed into the portal rather than systemic circulation (Figure 3), and portal blood drains directly into the liver. Many drugs that are avidly metabolized in the liver may, therefore, undergo substantial biotransformation before reaching systemic blood. Some drugs may also be metabolized by the gastrointestinal (GI) tract mucosa. First-pass hepatic metabolism together with GI tract metabolism is collectively termed *presystemic extraction*. Cocaine, for example, is not favored as a drug of abuse by the oral route because of nearly complete presystemic extraction, allowing only small amounts of the intact drug to reach the systemic circulation (Jatlow, 1988; Jeffcoat et al., 1989).

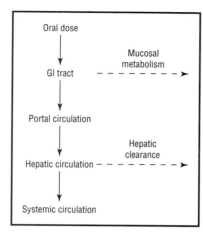

Figure 3. Possible mechanisms of presystemic extraction. Orally administered medications may undergo metabolism as they pass through the gastrointestinal tract mucosa (dashed arrow), which contains significant amounts of Cytochrome P45-3A4. Mucosal metabolism of cyclosporine appears to occur in humans (Kolars et al., 1991). Metabolism may also occur as the drug present in portal blood passes through the hepatic circulation (dashed arrow); this is termed "first-pass" metabolism. The net extent of presystemic extraction depends on the combination of mucosal metabolism and first-pass metabolism. ILLUSTRATION BY GGS INFORMATION SERVICES. GALE, CENGAGE LEARNING

DRUG DISTRIBUTION

The process of distribution is an important determinant of pharmacokinetic properties, as well as the time course of action, of most centrally acting drugs, including those that are subject to abuse. Drugs reversibly distribute not only to their site of action in the brain but also to peripheral sites such as adipose (fat) tissue and muscle, where they are not pharmacologically active (Figure 1). Only a small fraction of the total amount of a psychotropic drug in the body goes to the brain. An even smaller fraction actually binds to the specific molecular recognition site (receptor). The extent of distribution of a psychotropic drug is determined in part by lipid (fat) solubility (how well a substance dissolves in oils and fats; lipophilicity), which is related to molecular structure and charge. Most psychotropic drugs are highly lipid-soluble. Drug distribution is also determined by some characteristics of the organism: the relative amounts of adipose and lean tissue, blood flow to each individual tissue, and the extent of drug that binds to plasma protein. The overall extent of drug distribution throughout the body can be quantified by the pharmacokinetic volume of distribution, which is a ratio: the total

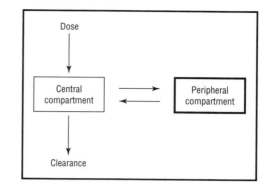

Figure 4. Schematic diagram of the Two-Compartment Model. It is assumed that medications are administered into and cleared from the central compartment only, and that only the central compartment (which includes blood) is accessible to measurement. Reversible distribution occurs between central and peripheral compartments. For most psychotropic drugs, high lipid solubility favors distribution to the peripheral compartment, producing a large apparent pharmacokinetic volume of distribution. ILLUSTRATION BY GGS INFORMATION SERVICES. GALE, CENGAGE LEARNING

amount of drug present in the body divided by the concentration in a reference compartment, usually serum or plasma. Lipid-soluble psychotropic drugs, as well as drugs of abuse, typically have very large pharmacokinetic volumes of distribution, which may exceed body size by tenfold or more. Although the drug cannot actually distribute to a space larger than the body, low plasma concentrations resulting from extensive uptake into peripheral tissues can yield a large apparent pharmacokinetic volume of distribution (Figure 4).

Drug distribution influences both onset and duration of drug action, as well as the observed value of elimination half-life. After an intravenous (IV) injection, lipid solubility allows for the rapid crossing of the lipoidal blood-brain barrier, leading to a rapid onset of pharmacological action (drug effect). In behavioral terms, then, drug-taking produces immediate reinforcement. The duration of a drug's action, however, is determined mainly by the extent of its peripheral distribution. Plasma levels of lipid-soluble psychotropic drugs will decline rapidly and extensively after a single intravenous dose because of peripheral distribution rather than elimination or clearance (Figure 5). A similar principle holds after oral administration of rapidly absorbed drugs (De Wit & Griffiths, 1991). Since duration of action after a single dose is determined more by distribution than by elimination or

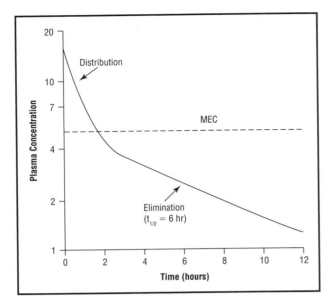

Figure 5. Plasma concentrations of a hypothetical lipid-soluble drug after intravenous injection. Disappearance from plasma is biphasic. The initial rapid phase is mainly due to drug distribution from central to peripheral compartments (see Figure 4). The slower phase of elimination is mainly due to clearance. For this drug, the elimination half-life in the postdistributive phase is 6 hours. If a plasma concentration of 5 units represents the minimum effective concentration (MEC) below which the drug exerts no detectable pharmacological effect, this drug in the dosage administered has a duration of action of approximately 2 hours. ILLUSTRATION BY GGS INFORMATION SERVICES. GALE, CENGAGE LEARNING

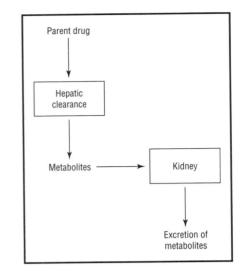

Figure 6. Psychotropic drugs: Most, including drugs of abuse, are cleared via the liver by hepatic biotransformation to metabolic products. The metabolites may then be released into the circulation and excreted by the kidney. ILLUSTRATION BY GGS INFORMATION SERVICES. GALE, CENGAGE LEARNING

clearance, it is generally not accurate to equate elimination half-life and duration of action.

CLEARANCE AND ELIMINATION

The terms *clearance* and *elimination half-life* are commonly used to describe the bodily process of drug removal or disappearance. These two concepts are related but are not identical. Clearance is the most important, since it is a unique independent variable that best describes the capacity of a given organism to remove a given drug from its system. Clearance has units of volume divided by time—for example, milliliters/minute (ml/min) or liters/hour (L/h)—and is the total amount of blood, serum, or plasma from which a substance is completely removed per unit of time. Clearance is not identical either to the rate of drug removal or to the elimination half-life. For most psychotropic drugs, clearance is accomplished by the liver via processes of biotransformation that change the administered drug into one or more metabolic products (Figure 6); this is commonly called *detoxification* by the liver. The metabolites may appear in the urine, but the liver is still the organ that affects clearance. For drugs cleared exclusively by the liver, the numerical value of clearance cannot exceed hepatic blood flow.

Elimination half-life is described in units of time; it can be seen as the time necessary for the plasma concentration to fall by 50 percent after distribution equilibrium has been attained. The elimination phase of drug disappearance—at which time the concept of elimination half-life is applicable—may not be attained until completion of an initial phase of rapid drug disappearance resulting from peripheral distribution (see Figure 5). As discussed earlier, the duration of action of a single dose of a psychotropic drug is not necessarily related to its elimination half-life.

Pharmacokinetic theory yields the following relationship between a drug's elimination half-life, volume of distribution (Vd), and clearance: Elimination half-life = 0.693 × Vd ÷ clearance. The independent variables, appearing on the right side of the equation, are Vd, the physicochemically determined property reflecting the extent of

Parent drug	Urinary metabolite
Marijuana (Tetrahydrocannabinol, THC)	11-nor-delta-9-THC-9-carboxylic acid
Cocaine	Benzoylecgonine
Heroin	Morphine glucuronide

Table 1. Principal urinary metabolites of potentially abusable drugs. ILLUSTRATION BY GGS INFORMATION SERVICES. GALE, CENGAGE LEARNING

distribution, and clearance, having units of volume divided by time, quantifying the capacity for drug removal. Elimination half-life is dependent on both of these. Note that a drug may have long elimination half-life, due either to a large Vd, a low clearance, or both.

PHARMACOKINETICS VERSUS PHARMACODYNAMICS

In contrast to pharmacokinetics or how the body acts on a drug, pharmacodynamics is the quantitative study of the time course of how a drug acts on the body. If drug distribution to the site of action occurs by passive diffusion from the systemic circulation, and if the intensity of drug action depends on the degree of receptor occupancy both in time and in quantity, then pharmacokinetics and pharmacodynamics are necessarily related. Kinetic-dynamic modeling, discussed in detail elsewhere (Greenblatt & Harmatz, 1993), addresses this relationship mathematically, by directly evaluating concentration versus effect. In the fields of psychopharmacology and substance abuse, kinetic-dynamic modeling is a major challenge, since (1) clinical drug effect (pharmacodynamic response) often is difficult to measure reliably and since (2) measured drug concentrations in systemic serum or plasma do not always parallel those at the central site of action. Nonetheless, certain advances in kinetic-dynamic modeling have significantly advanced the understanding of the relationship of the pharmacokinetics of psychotropic drugs to their pharmacodynamic effects.

ALTERED PHARMACOKINETICS ALTERS PHARMACODYNAMICS

Metabolic (i.e., pharmacokinetic) changes can result in changes in drug action. For example, differences in slow versus rapid metabolism can contribute to differences in dosing requirements and the need for lower

or higher doses (LaLovic et al., 2004). For example, Cytochrome P450 2D6 (CYP2D6) is a polymorphic enzyme that metabolizes many analgesics, antipsychotics, and antidepressants. Approximately 7 percent of Caucasians and 1 to 3 percent of other populations lack this enzyme and are classified as poor metabolizers (PMs). Poor metabolizers require lower dosages of a drug to achieve a therapeutic effect. Approximately 1 to 7 percent of European Caucasians have multiple copies of the gene and thereby produce more of this enzyme. These individuals are classified as ultrarapid metabolizers (UMs). The prevalence of UMs appears to be higher in some populations such as Saudi Arabians (20%) and Ethiopians (29%). When UMs are treated with typical doses of tricyclic antidepressants, for example, they have very low plasma concentrations and do not respond to the treatment. Codeine, hydrocodone, and oxycodone are activated by CYP2D6 (with codeine being converted to morphine by CYP2D6). Therefore, if the CYP2D6 enzyme is missing or inhibited by another drug such as paroxetine or fluoxetine, codeine does not work as an analgesic. Additionally, CYP2D6 PMs appear to be protected from dependence on these oral opioids (De Leon et al., 2003).

Physical changes in pharmacokinetics can also result in altered pharmacodynamics. For example, OxyContin tablets are designed to provide controlled delivery of oxycodone over 12 hours. Steady-state levels are achieved within 24 to 36 hours. OxyContin (10 mg) given every 12 hours compared to immediate-release oxycodone (5mg) given every 6 hours, are equivalent for area under the curve (AUC) and cmax, and similar for cmin (trough) concentrations. However, breaking, chewing or crushing OxyContin tablets eliminates the controlled delivery mechanism and results in the rapid release and absorption of the entire dose of oxycodone, potentially resulting in a fatal overdose of the drug. Additionally, because oxycodone is water soluble, crushed tablets can be dissolved in water and the solution injected. The rapid delivery of a large dose of oxycodone results in significant dopamine release in the nucleus accumbens via disinhibition of GABAergic control of the mesolimbic dopamine tract. Dependence occurs at least partially due to the rapid release of dopamine resulting in strong positive reinforcement and a disruption in allostasis (Koob & Le Moal, 2008). *Allostasis,* which means to maintain stability or homeostasis through

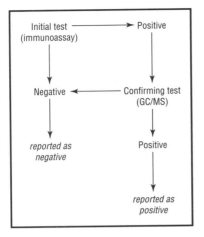

Figure 7. Urine-testing programs. Those for drugs of abuse typically use a two-tiered algorithm. An initial screening test is done with a relatively inexpensive, nonspecific, and insensitive immunoassay (such as enzyme-multiplied-, fluorescence-polarization-, or radio-immunoassay). If the initial test is negative, the result is reported as such, and no further testing is done. If the initial screen is positive, a second analysis is done on the same sample using a more accurate and specific method, such as gas-chromatography/mass-spectroscopy (GC/MS). If the confirmation test is negative, the result is reported as negative. If GC/MS confirms the initial screening test, the result is reported as positive. ILLUSTRATION BY GGS INFORMATION SERVICES. GALE, CENGAGE LEARNING

change, was introduced by Sterling and Eyer (1988) to describe how the cardiovascular system adjusts to resting and active states of the body.

As adapted by Koob and Le Moal (1997) for addiction, allostasis involves a continuous re-evaluation of drug need and re-adjustment of neurobiological mechanisms toward a new homeostasis. Oxycodone is well absorbed from OxyContin tablets with an oral bioavailability of 60 to 87 percent. The relative oral bioavailability of OxyContin to immediate-release oral dosage forms is 100 percent. This high oral bioavailability is due to low pre-systemic extraction. In normal volunteers, the half-life of absorption is 0.4 hours for immediate-release oral oxycodone. In contrast, OxyContin tablets exhibit a biphasic absorption pattern with two apparent absorption half-lives of 0.6 and 6.9 hours, which describes the initial release of oxycodone from the tablet followed by a prolonged release. When OxyContin is crushed or broken, individuals are at risk for overdose or death, as they receive a greater portion of the entire dose (e.g., 80 mg) due to increased bioavailability combined

with a more rapid half-life. Oxycodone is extensively metabolized and is eliminated primarily in the urine as both conjugated and unconjugated metabolites. The elimination half-life of oxycodone following the administration of OxyContin is 4.5 hours compared to 3.2 hours for immediate-release oxycodone.

OxyContin is not indicated for rectal administration. OxyContin tablets administered rectally result in an AUC 39 percent that is greater and a cmax 9 percent that is higher than tablets administered orally. Therefore, there is an increased risk of adverse events with rectal administration. Oxycodone binding to plasma protein at 37°C and a pH of 7.4 is about 45 percent. Oxycodone hydrochloride is extensively metabolized to noroxycodone, oxymorphone, and their glucuronides. The major circulating metabolite is noroxycodone, which is a considerably weaker analgesic than oxycodone. Oxymorphone, although possessing analgesic activity, is present in the plasma only in low concentrations. The correlation between oxymorphone concentrations and opioid effects was much less than that seen with oxycodone plasma concentrations. The analgesic activity profile of other metabolites is not known. The formation of oxymorphone, but not noroxycodone, is mediated by cytochrome P450 2D6 and, as such, its formation can, in theory, be affected by other drugs. Oxycodone and its metabolites are excreted primarily via the kidney. The total plasma clearance was 0.8 L/min for adults.

A comprehensive approach to understanding the biological bases of substance abuse must combine the neurochemical and molecular mechanisms that underlie the behavioral effects of these drugs with an understanding of their properties of absorption, distribution, and clearance. Advances initially made in the 1980s continued to be made as research techniques in both disciplines became increasingly refined.

BIBLIOGRAPHY

Agurell, S., Halldin, M., Lindgren, J. E., Ohlsson, A., Widman, M., Gillespie, H., et al. (1986). Pharmacokinetics and metabolism of delta-one-tetrahydrocannabinol and other cannabinoids with emphasis on man. *Pharmacological Reviews, 38*, 21–43.

Baselt, R. C., Chang, J. Y., & Yoshikawa, D. M. (1990). On the dermal absorption of cocaine. *Journal of Analytical Toxicology, 14*, 383–384.

Bergman, U., & Griffiths, R. R. (1986). Relative abuse of diazepam and oxazepam: Prescription forgeries and theft/loss reports in Sweden. *Drug and Alcohol Dependence, 16,* 293–301.

Burnett, D., Lader, S., Richens, A., Smith, B. L., Toseland, P. A., Walker, G., et al. (1990). A survey of drugs of abuse testing by clinical laboratories in the United Kingdom. *Annals of Clinical Biochemistry, 27,* 213–222.

De Leon, J., Dinsmore, L., & Wedlund, P. (2003). Adverse drug reactions to oxycodone and hydrocodone in CYP2D6 ultrarapid metabolizers. *Journal of Clinical Psychopharmacology, 23,* 420–421.

De Wit, H., & Griffiths, R. R. (1991). Testing the abuse liability of anxiolytic and hypnotic drugs in humans. *Drug and Alcohol Dependence, 28,* 83–111.

Elsohly, M. A. (1991). Urinalysis and casual handling of marijuana and cocaine. *Journal of Analytical Toxicology, 15,* 46.

Frezza, M., Di Padova, C., Pozzato, G., Terpin, M., Baraona, E., Lieber, C. S., et al. (1990). High blood alcohol levels in women: The role of decreased gastric alcohol dehydrogenase activity and first-pass metabolism. *New England Journal of Medicine, 322,* 95–99.

Friedman, H., & Greenblatt, D. J. (1986). Rational therapeutic drug monitoring. *Journal of the American Medical Association, 256,* 2227–2233.

Greenblatt, D. J. (1989). Urine drug testing: What does it test? *New England Law Review, 23,* 651–666.

Greenblatt, D. J. (1991). Benzodiazepine hypnotics: Sorting the pharmacokinetic facts. *Journal of Clinical Psychiatry, 52* (9, Suppl.), 4–10.

Greenblatt, D. J. (1992). Pharmacokinetic principles in clinical medicine (Clinical Therapeutics Conference). *Journal of Clinical Pharmacology, 32,* 118–123.

Greenblatt, D. J. (1993). Presystemic extraction: Mechanisms and consequences. *Journal of Clinical Pharmacology, 33,* 650–656.

Greenblatt, D. J., & Harmatz, J. S. (1993). Kinetic-dynamic modeling in clinical psychopharmacology. *Journal of Clinical Psychopharmacology, 13,* 231–234.

Greenblatt, D. J., & Shader, R. I. (1985). *Pharmacokinetics in clinical practice.* Philadelphia: Saunders.

Greenblatt, D. J., & Shader, R. I. (1990). Say "no" to drug testing. *Journal of Clinical Psychopharmacology, 10,* 157–159.

Griffiths, R. R., McLeod, D. R., Bigelow, G. E., Liebson, I. A., & Roache, J. D. (1984a). Relative abuse liability of diazepam and oxazepam: Behavioral and subjective dose effects. *Journal of Psychopharmacology, 84,* 147–154.

Griffiths, R. R., McLeod, D. R., Bigelow, G. E., Liebson, I. A., Roache, J. D., & Nowowieski, P. (1984b). Comparison of diazepam and oxazepam: Preference, liking and extent of abuse. *Journal of Pharmacology and Experimental Therapeutics, 229,* 501–508.

Hall, W. C., Talbert, R. L., & Ereshefsky, L. (1990). Cocaine abuse and its treatment. *Pharmacotherapy, 10,* 47–65.

Hayes, L. W., Krasselt, W. G., & Mueggler, P. A. (1987). Concentrations of morphine and codeine in serum and urine after ingestion of poppy seeds. *Clinical Chemistry, 33,* 806–808.

Jatlow, P. (1988). Cocaine: Analysis, pharmacokinetics, and metabolic disposition. *Yale Journal of Biology and Medicine, 61,* 105–113.

Jeffcoat, A. R., Perez-Reyes, M., Hill, J. M., Sadler, B. M., & Cook, C. E. (1989). Cocaine disposition in humans after intravenous injection, nasal insufflation (snorting), or smoking. *Drug Metabolism and Disposition, 17,* 153–159.

Kolars, J. C., Awni, W. M., Merion, R. M., & Watkins, P. B. (1991). First-pass metabolism of cyclosporin by the gut. *Lancet, 338,* 1488–1490.

Koob, G. F., & Le Moal, M. (1997). Drug abuse, hedonic homeostatic dysregulation. *Science 278,* 52–58.

Koob, G. F., & Le Moal, M. (2008). Addiction and the brain antireward system. *Annual Review of Psychology, 10*(5), 29–53.

LaFolie, P., Beck, O., Blennow, G., Boreus, L., Borg, S., Elwin, C. E., et al. (1991). Importance of creatinine analyses of urine when screening for abused drugs. *Clinical Chemistry, 37,* 1927–1931.

LaLovic, B., Phillips, B., Risler, L. L., Howald, W., & Shen, D. D. (2004). Quantitative contribution of CYP2D6 and CYP3A to oxycodone metabolism in human liver and intestinal microsomes. *Drug Metabolism and Disposition, 32,* 447–454.

Mikkelsen, S. L., & Ash, K. O. (1988). Adulterants causing false negatives in illicit drug testing. *Clinical Chemistry, 34,* 2333–2336.

Mikus, G., Bochner, F., Eichelbaum, M., Horak, P., Somogyi, A. A., & Spector, S. (1994). Endogenous codeine and morphine in poor and extensive metabolisers of the CYP2D6 (debrisoquine/sparteine) polymorphism. *Journal of Pharmacology and Experimental Therapeutics, 268,* 546–551.

Osterloh, J. (1993). Testing for drugs of abuse. *Clinical Pharmacokinetics, 24,* 355–361.

Schwarzhoff, R., & Cody, J. T. (1993). The effects of adulterating agents on FPIA analysis of urine for drugs of abuse. *Journal of Analytical Toxicology, 17,* 14–17.

Shader, R. I., & Greenblatt, D. J. (1993). Use of benzodiazepines in anxiety disorders. *New England Journal of Medicine, 328,* 1398–1405.

Sterling, P., & Eyer, J. (1988). Allostasis: A new paradigm to explain arousal pathology. In S. Fisher & J. Reason (Eds.), *Handbook of life stress, cognition and health* (pp. 629–649). New York: Wiley .

Sutherland, R. (1992). Mandatory drug testing: Boon for public safety or launch of a witch-hunt? *Canadian Medical Association Journal, 146,* 1215–1220.

Woods, J. H., Katz, J. L., & Winger, G. (1987). Abuse liability of benzodiazepines. *Pharmacological Reviews, 39,* 251–419.

Woods, J. H., Katz, J. L., & Winger, G. (1992). Benzodiazepines: Use, abuse, and consequences. *Pharmacological Reviews, 44,* 151–347.

DAVID J. GREENBLATT
REVISED BY GEORGE A. KENNA (2009)

PHARMACOKINETICS OF ALCOHOL.

The discipline known as *pharmacokinetics* deals with the way drugs are absorbed, distributed, metabolized, and eliminated by the body and how these processes can be described in quantitative terms. The pharmacokinetics of alcohol (ethyl alcohol or ethanol) is an important issue in forensic toxicology and clinical medicine, when the amount of alcohol in the body is estimated from the concentration measured in a blood sample.

The Swedish scientist Erik M. P. Widmark (1889–1945) made pioneering contributions to the knowledge about the pharmacokinetics of ethanol during the early decades of the twentieth century. Widmark observed that after the peak concentration in blood had been reached, the disappearance phase seemed to follow a near straight-line course, suggesting that the system for metabolizing alcohol was saturated (fully occupied), so that the amount of alcohol metabolized each hour did not depend on the amount in the blood. This situation is termed a *zero-order elimination process*. (Zero-order kinetics is contrasted with first-order kinetics, in which the metabolic system [e.g., the liver] is not saturated and in which the amount of drug metabolized per hour increases as the amount presented to the metabolic system increases.) Figure 1 (left frame) depicts zero-order elimination kinetics of ethanol after rapid intravenous infusion. Similar kinetics apply to the administration of alcohol, so, for example, if an individual drinks twelve standard drinks between 10 p.m. and 1 a.m., he or she will still have a detectable blood

alcohol concentration at 7 a.m. Zero-order kinetics means that the rate of metabolism is at the maximal capacity and has a constant rate of approximately 7 to 10 grams per hour (equivalent to about one standard drink per hour) regardless of how much alcohol is consumed (Swift, 2003).

Zero-order kinetics implies that the elimination rate of ethanol is independent of the blood alcohol concentration (BAC) and, therefore, k_β should be the same regardless of the dose of ethanol administered; however, subsequent studies have shown that the slope of the BAC decay phase is steeper after larger doses of ethanol are ingested. Furthermore, when the BAC declines below about 10 mg/dl (0.01 g%, 2.17 mmol/l) the elimination curve

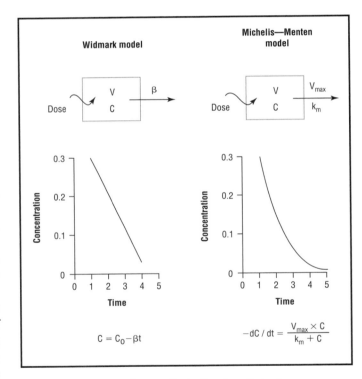

Figure 1. Schematic diagram illustrating the elimination kinetics of ethanol. The left frame shows Widmark's zero-order model. The right frame shows Michaelis–Menten (MM) capacity–limited kinetics. An intravenous bolus dose of ethanol enters a volume V to produce a concentration C; β is the zero-order elimination rate constant; V_{max} is the maximum velocity of the reaction; and k_m is the Michaelis constant—the concentration of ethanol at half maximum velocity. Concentration-time profiles are shown for zero-order and MM kinetics, and the mathematical expressions for the elimination rates are given. ILLUSTRATION BY GGS INFORMATION SERVICES. GALE, CENGAGE LEARNING

of ethanol from blood flattens out and changes into a curvilinear decay profile.

Two different methods are described in the literature to portray the pharmacokinetics of ethanol. The method of choice seems to depend on the professional interests, the scientific background, and the training of those concerned. Specialists in forensic medicine and toxicology, as well as other disciplines, favor the mathematical approach developed by Widmark. In contrast, scientists with their basic training in pharmacy and pharmacology prefer Michaelis-Menten (MM) kinetics, that is, saturable or capacity-limited enzyme kinetics. The MM model is depicted in Figure 1 (right frame) after intravenous input of ethanol. A pseudolinear phase is evident for most of the elimination profile, provided that the BAC remains sufficiently high (> 10 mg/dl). At low substrate concentrations (C), a hockey-stick shape develops when data are plotted on cartesian graph paper. Accordingly, when C is much greater than k_m, the elimination rate approaches its maximum velocity; $-dC/dt = V_{max}$ (Figure 1, right frame). When C is less than k_m the elimination rate is proportional to the substrate concentration; $-dC/dt = (V_{max}/k_m) C$ and the MM equation collapses into first-order kinetics. This collapsing of the model is a consequence of capacity-limited kinetics and does not reflect any sudden change in the order of the biochemical reaction.

ETHANOL AS A DRUG

Ethanol differs from most other drugs in the way it is absorbed into the blood, metabolized in the liver, and how it enters the brain and produces its pharmacological effect. Ethanol (CH_3CH_2OH) has a molecular weight of 46.05, mixes with water in all proportions and carries only a weak charge; this means that the molecules of ethanol easily pass through biological membranes, including the blood-brain barrier. After absorption into the portal blood, ethanol passes through the liver, where enzymes begin the conversion into acetaldehyde and acetate. The end products of ethanol metabolism are carbon dioxide and water. The concentrations of ethanol in biological specimens depend on the dose ingested, the time after drinking, and the water content of the materials analyzed. The concentration-time profiles of ethanol and the

pharmacokinetic parameters will differ depending on whether plasma, serum, urine, or saliva is the specimen analyzed. Several detailed reviews of ethanol pharmacokinetics are available and included in the bibliography.

Information about the absorption kinetics of ethanol is much less extensive than that about elimination kinetics. Unlike most other drugs, the dose of ethanol is not swallowed instantaneously because the drinking is usually spread over a period of time. For research purposes, however, ingestion of a bolus dose usually approximates drinking times of five to fifteen minutes. [The volume and concentration of ethanol, whether ingested as beer (3–6% w/v), wine (9–12% w/v), spirits (32–40% w/v), or as a cocktail (15–25% w/v), such that, for example, beer is less concentrated and consumed in greater volume than spirits, might influence the pharmacokinetic parameters. At lower alcohol concentrations, the portal blood concentration of alcohol is low, liver alcohol metabolizing enzymes are not saturated, and a higher proportion of alcohol is metabolized by the liver, leading to lower blood alcohol levels (Jones et al., 1997). Absorption of ethanol starts in the stomach where about 20 percent of the dose can become absorbed. The remainder is absorbed from the upper part of the small intestine. The speed of absorption of alcohol depends to a large extent on the rate of gastric emptying, which varies widely among different subjects. Because food in the stomach delays gastric emptying, food slows the rate of alcohol delivery to the intestine and the resulting peak blood alcohol level is lower. Food in the stomach acts this way by lowering the concentration of alcohol by dilution. This effect is more evident for small volumes of concentrated alcohol (spirits) than for larger volumes of more dilute alcohol (beer) (Roine et al., 1993). Assuming that the rate of absorption from the gut is a first-order process, one can represent the entire concentration-time profile of ethanol with a single equation: $C = C_o(1 - e^{-kt}) - k_\beta t$, where C = BAC at some time t after administration, C_o = initial BAC extrapolated BAC (see Figure 2), k = first-order absorption rate constant, k_β = zero-order elimination rate constant, and t = time after drinking. The peak BAC and the time of reaching the peak after drinking are important

Dose g/kg[1]	N	Peak BAC mg/dl		k_0 mg/dl h		Time to peak (min)[3]			
		mean	(range)	mean	(range)[2]	10	40	70	100
0.34	6	56	(43–67)	12	(9–14)	5	1	—	—
0.51	16	74	(54–91)	13	(10–14)	11	3	1	1
0.68	83	92	(52–136)	13	(9–17)	33	26	21	3
0.85	44	120	(83–178)	15	(12–18)	13	24	7	—

Maximum concentration of ethanol in capillary (fingertip) blood and the time of reaching the peak after end of drinking. The zero-order rate of elimination of ethanol from blood (k_0) is also given. The subjects drank neat whiskey within 15–25 minutes after an overnight 10-hour fast.
[1] g ethanol/kg = 0.036 oz ethanol/kg.
[2] Zero-order elimination rate.
[3] Number of subjects reaching their peak BAC at 10, 40, 70 and 100 min., measured from end of drinking.

Table 1. Peak blood alcohol concentration and time needed to reach the peak after end of drinking. ILLUSTRATION BY GGS INFORMATION SERVICES. GALE, CENGAGE LEARNING

aspects of the absorption kinetics. Table 1 gives examples of these parameters after healthy men drank undiluted whiskey (40% v/v or 80 proof) on an empty stomach. The absorption of ethanol occurs more slowly from the stomach than from the intestine owing to the enormous difference in the absorption surface available. The absorption of ethanol occurs progressively during a drinking binge or spree, and studies have shown that the BAC fifteen minutes after the last drink has reached about 80 percent of the final peak BAC. Because of the saturation-type kinetics, the peak BAC and the area under the curve (AUC) increase more than expected from proportional increases in the dose. The rate of delivery of ethanol to the liver determines the AUC for a given dose and vice versa. The systemic availability (bioavailability) of drugs such as ethanol with dose-dependent kinetics should not be calculated from the ratio of AUC after oral and intravenous administration.

THE WIDMARK EQUATION

Figure 2 gives examples of the concentration-time profiles of ethanol obtained from oral and intravenous administration of a moderate dose. The ratio of the dose administered (D) to the initial extrapolated concentration of ethanol in blood (C_o) is the apparent volume of distribution (V_d) having dimensions L/kg. This defines the relationship between the concentration of ethanol spread over the body weight (in kilograms, kg) and the concentration in the blood. $C_o = D/(kg \times V_d)$; $D = C_o \times kg \times V_d$ is known as the *Widmark equation*; it is widely used to estimate alcohol in the body from measurements of alcohol in

the blood. Widmark found that the average V_d for men was 0.68, with a range from 0.51–0.85, but in women the volume of distribution was less— with an average of 0.55 and a range of 0.44 to 0.66. These differences between the sexes stem from differences in body-tissue composition; proportionally, women carry more fat but less water than do men. Accordingly, women reach higher BACs than men if the same dose of ethanol is given according to body weight. A similar observation was made in studies of men with widely different ages because body water decreases in the elderly. By dividing the dose of ethanol administered (g/kg) by the time needed to reach zero BAC (time$_0$) one obtains an estimate of the rate of clearance of ethanol from the body. This calculation neglects the nonlinear phase of ethanol elimination beginning at BAC below 10 mg/dl but does include the contribution from any first-pass metabolism occurring in the liver and gut.

A second equation, $D = kg \times V_d \times (C + k_\beta t)$ can be used to estimate the amount (dose D) of alcohol a person has consumed from knowledge of his or her BAC (C). Similarly, a third equation, $C = D/(kg \times V_d) - (k_\beta t)$ allows estimating the BAC (C) that might exist after drinking a known amount of ethanol. For best results when using these equations, absorption and distribution of ethanol must be complete at the time of sampling blood. Owing to inter- and intra-individual variations in the pharmacokinetic parameters V_d and k_β the results obtained are subject to considerable uncertainty. This uncertainty should be allowed for when these calculations are made for legal purposes, for example, in trials concerned with driving under the

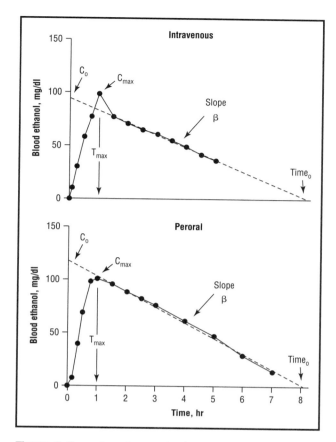

Figure 2. Examples of concentration-time profiles of alcohol taken by intravenous and oral routes of administration. Examples of concentration-time profiles of ethanol obtained after intravenous infusion of 0.4 g ethanol/kg body weight in 15 minutes (upper part) and after ingestion of 0.8 g/kg (lower part). Several key pharmacokinetic parameters are shown. ILLUSTRATION BY GGS INFORMATION SERVICES. GALE, CENGAGE LEARNING

influence of alcohol. A variability of ± 20 percent seems appropriate for most situations.

RESEARCH ON ADH

About 85 percent of the alcohol that enters the body is metabolized by hepatic enzymes responsible for ethanol oxidation (metabolism), but research has documented the existence of alcohol dehydrogenase (ADH)—the enzyme that transforms alcohol to ace-taldehyde—in the gastrointestinal mucosa. Gastric ADH seems to be less effective in oxidizing ethanol in women (than in men) and in alcoholics (than in moderate drinkers). When a moderate dose of etha-nol was ingested on an empty stomach, first-pass metabolism was negligible. This was explained by the ethanol bypassing gastric ADH, owing to rapid

absorption occurring. However, the quantitative significance of gut metabolism in the overall disposal of ethanol remains controversial.

ELIMINATION RATES AND ENZYMES

Differences in the rate of disappearance of ethanol from blood might depend on genetic and environmental factors influencing the catalytic activity of an individual's alcohol-metabolizing enzymes. In humans, the enzyme ADH occurs in multiple molecular forms, designated class I, II, and III. Class I enzymes are located mainly in the liver cytosol and have a low km for ethanol. Various isoenzymes (enzyme variations within a class) exist and β_1-ADH (class I) is predominant in Caucasians, whereas β_1-ADH (class II) is the most abundant isoenzyme in Asians. The rate of ethanol elimination in the various racial groups is not much different from the variations seen within a single racial group in well-designed studies that allow for racial differences in body composition—the proportion of fat-to-lean body mass.

Alcoholics have a greater capacity to eliminate ethanol than do moderate drinkers, though the tolerance seen in alcoholics is not fully explained on this basis. The liver microsomes contain enzymes capable of oxidizing ethanol as well as other drugs, organic solvents, and environmental chemicals. One particular form of the cytochrome P_{450} enzyme (denoted P450IIEI) metabolizes ethanol. This microsomal ethanol oxidizing system (MEOS) has a k_m of 40–60 mg/dl (8.7–13 mmol/l) compared with 2 to 5 mg/dl (0.4–1 mmol/l) for human ADH. More importantly, the P450IIEI isoenzyme becomes more active during prolonged exposure to ethanol—a process known as enzyme induction. Accordingly, because of continuous heavy drinking, alcoholics develop a high capacity for eliminating ethanol from the blood. Their enhanced capacity vanishes after a short period of abstinence, however, but liver disease (hepatitis, cirrhosis) in alcoholics does not seem to impair their ability to dispose of ethanol.

BEHAVIORAL EFFECTS OF ALCOHOL

Studies have shown that the behavioral effects of ethanol and its associated impairment of performance are more pronounced when the BAC is rising than when it is falling. This observation seems to depend, at least in part, on the distribution of ethanol between blood and tissue. The arterial blood concentration of ethanol pumped to the brain exceeds the concentration measured in the venous blood, which is returning to the heart from skeletal muscles. This arterial-venous difference is most pronounced shortly after drinking; it decreases as ethanol diffuses equally into all body fluids. It seems that this is not the whole story because some evidence points to the development of acute cellular tolerance to ethanol's effects—an aspect of tolerance that develops quickly.

Despite extensive studies of ethanol pharmacokinetics spanning many years, there are still a number of unsettled issues and areas of debate. Two such issues are (1) the practical advantages of Michaelis-Menten kinetics as opposed to Widmark's zero-order model and (2) the role of gastric ADH in the presystemic extraction of ethanol.

See also **Pharmacokinetics: Implications for Abusable Substances.**

BIBLIOGRAPHY

Holford, N. H. G. (1987). Clinical pharmacokinetics of ethanol. *Clinical Pharmacokinetics, 13,* 273–292.

Jones A. W., Jonsson, K. A., & Kechagias, S. (1997). Effect of high-fat, high-protein, and high-carbohydrate meals on the pharmacokinetics of a small dose of alcohol. *British Journal of Clinical Pharmacology, 44,* 521–526.

Roine, R. P., Gentry, R. T., Lim, R. T., Jr., Helkkonen, E., Salaspuro, M., & Lieber, C. S. (1993). Comparison of blood alcohol concentrations after beer and whiskey. *Alcoholism Clinical and Experimental Research, 17,* 709–711.

Swift R. (2003). Direct measurement of alcohol and its metabolites. *Addiction, 98*(Suppl. 2), 73–80.

Von Wartburg, J. P. (1989). Pharmacokinetics of alcohol. In K. E. Crow & R. D. Batt (Eds.), *Human metabolism of alcohol.* Boca Raton, FL: CRC Press.

Widmark, E. M. P. (1981). *Principles and applications of medicolegal alcohol determination.* Davis, CA: Biomedical Publications. (English translation of Widmark's 1932 monograph, in German).

Wilkinson, P. K. (1980). Pharmacokinetics of ethanol: A review. *Alcoholism: Clinical and Experimental Research, 4,* 6–21.

A. W. JONES
REVISED BY GEORGE A. KENNA (2009)

PHARMACOLOGY.

In its broadest sense, pharmacology can be defined as the science dealing with interactions between living systems and molecules—in particular, chemicals (i.e., drugs)—usually introduced from outside the system. This definition also includes medical pharmacology, which is the science of drugs used to prevent, diagnose, and treat disease. Also included are the important roles played by chemicals in the environment that can cause disease, as well as the use of certain chemicals as molecular probes for the study of normal biochemistry and physiology. Toxicology is the branch of pharmacology that deals with the undesirable (i.e., toxic) effects of chemicals in biological systems.

See also **Drug; Drug Metabolism; Drug Types; Pharmacodynamics; Pharmacokinetics: General; Poison.**

BIBLIOGRAPHY

Benet, L. Z., Mitchell, J. R., & Sheiner, L. B. (1990). General principles. In A. G. Gilman et al. (Eds.), *Goodman and Gilman's the pharmacological basis of therapeutics,* 8th ed. New York: Pergamon. (2005, 11th ed. New York: McGraw-Hill Medical.)

Kenakin, T. (2003). *A pharmacology primer: theory, application and methods.* New York: Academic Press.

NICK E. GOEDERS

PHENCYCLIDINE (PCP).

Phencyclidine is a recreational drug. Although phencyclidine (PCP) and drugs of similar chemical structure (arylcyclohexylamines) are often called hallucinogens, they rarely produce hallucinations, and the sensory distortions or apparent hallucinations that are produced are not the same type as LSD-induced hallucinations. Instead, phencyclidine belongs to a unique class of drugs called the dissociative anesthetics. Phencyclidine was developed in the 1950s as an anesthetic for veterinary medicine and later was tested in human surgical patients. There was great potential for PCP as an anesthetic because it produced minimal effects on the heart and did not suppress breathing. Unfortunately, the adverse side effects of PCP (e.g., dysphoria [unhappy, ill] and psychotic symptoms) led to a termination of the human clinical trials. The drug is no longer manufactured for veterinary use because supplies were stolen and the drug became widely abused in the 1970s. Ketamine, a drug chemically similar to PCP, is now used as a veterinary anesthetic and in special cases for anesthesia in humans. This drug is less powerful and shorter-acting than PCP.

Phencyclidine abuse, mainly in pill form, peaked in the late 1970s and markedly declined throughout the 1980s and 1990s. The most common route of administration in use in the 2000s was smoking. Phencyclidine is often added to marijuana cigarettes, and it is commonly used while people are also drinking alcoholic beverages. Street names for PCP are "angel dust" or "crystal"; it is called "space base" when combined with cocaine.

MECHANISM OF ACTION

Most investigators agree that the behavioral effects of PCP are mediated predominantly through receptors, which are proteins that are important for the normal functioning of cells within the body. Phencyclidine acts as an antagonist at the N-methyl-D-aspartate (NMDA) receptor-channel complex, which is one type of excitatory amino acid receptor that is selectively activated by the agonists NMDA and glutamate. By definition, agonists produce stimulation while antagonists block the effects of agonists. When either glutamate or NMDA bind to the receptor, a channel within the cell membrane, opens to allow sodium, calcium, and potassium ions to flow into and out of the cell. This movement of ions across the cell membrane causes a depolarization of the membrane, which, if sufficiently large, causes the cell to fire. When the cell fires, an electrical charge passes along its membrane and neurotransmitters (chemicals that allow cells to communicate with each other) are released. Thus, glutamate and NMDA are important for normal cell-to-cell communication within the body.

PCP, as well as TCP, ketamine, dizocilpine (MK-801), and SKF 10,047, is representative of compounds that act as noncompetitive antagonists at the NMDA-receptor complex. The binding site for PCP resides within the channel. Binding to this site physically prevents calcium and sodium ions from entering the cell while at the same time preventing potassium ions from leaving the cell. Blocking the movement of ions through the cell membrane in turn prevents the neuron from firing. In contrast to the noncompetitive antagonists, competitive antagonists such as CGS 19755, NPC 12626, CPP, and AP5 bind to the NMDA receptor itself without causing the ion channel to open. By simply occupying the receptor without activating it, competitive antagonists prevent NMDA from binding to and activating the receptor.

Unlike noncompetitive antagonists, competitive NMDA-antagonist effects can be surmounted by higher doses of the agonist. However, the end result of both noncompetitive and competitive antagonists is a reduction of neuronal firing.

PHARMACOKINETICS AND METABOLISM

PCP use in humans occurs through several routes of administration, including intranasal (snorted), intravenous, oral, and inhalation (smoked). When PCP is smoked in parsley cigarettes, approximately 70 percent of the total amount of PCP is inhaled. Of this amount, 38 percent is inhaled as PCP and 30 percent is inhaled as phenylcyclohexene, a by-product of PCP created when it is heated. Peak blood concentration of PCP occurs after only five to ten minutes, which is occasionally followed by a second peak one to three hours later. PCP is predominantly excreted in urine after intranasal, intravenous, and oral administration. The rate of PCP elimination through the kidneys depends on both urine pH and urine-flow rate. More specifically, PCP elimination occurs more rapidly when urine is acidic and when urine is passed rapidly.

DISCRIMINATIVE STIMULUS EFFECTS

One useful method of evaluating the pharmacological characteristics of PCP, as well as a variety of other drugs, is the drug-discrimination procedure. Typically, animals that are slightly food-restricted are trained to respond for food on one lever after drug administration and on another lever after saline. On days when the drug is administered before the session, responding on the drug-associated lever results in food delivery while responding on the saline-associated lever does not. Conversely, on days when saline is administered before the session, responding on the saline-associated lever results in food delivery while responding on the drug-associated lever does not. After a number of training days, animals learn to reliably respond on the drug lever after the drug injection and on the saline lever after saline injection. Once this discrimination has been established, a number of test drugs can be administered to determine whether or not they produce effects similar to the training drug. Test drugs that substitute for the training drug (i.e., cause responses on the drug-associated lever) are assumed to have discriminative stimulus effects that are similar to the training drug.

Using this procedure, several investigators have shown that PCP and other noncompetitive antagonists produce similar discriminative stimulus effects in a number of different species (see Willetts, Balster, & Leander, 1990 for a review). These results suggest that the mechanisms of action of PCP and such other noncompetitive antagonists as ketamine and dizocilpine, are similar. Furthermore, the discriminative stimulus effects of competitive antagonists such as CGS 19755, NPC 12626 and CPP were also similar to each other, which is again consistent with the notion that the mechanisms of action of competitive antagonists are similar. Given that competitive and noncompetitive antagonists both reduce neuronal firing, it was of interest to compare the discriminative stimulus effects of these two types of antagonists. In most species, the discriminative stimulus effects of competitive and noncompetitive antagonists are very different from each other.

Another difference between the competitive and noncompetitive antagonists lies in their abilities to antagonize the discriminative stimulus effects of NMDA. While both types of antagonist are effective in blocking the convulsant and lethal effects of NMDA, competitive antagonists in general are much more effective than noncompetitive antagonists in blocking the discriminative stimulus effects of NMDA. The noncompetitive antagonists partially antagonize NMDA but only at doses that produced substantial behavioral suppression. While most effects of NMDA are antagonized by both competitive and noncompetitive antagonists, the behavioral-suppressing effects of noncompetitive antagonists often interfere with their ability to antagonize the discriminative stimulus effects of NMDA.

Finally, another important finding with competitive and noncompetitive antagonists involve their interaction with other receptor systems. Studies show that the discriminative stimulus effects of competitive antagonists such as CPP and NPA 12626 are similar to those produced by the barbiturate pentobarbital. Under certain conditions, the discriminative stimulus effects of PCP and pentobarbital were also similar. In addition to the interactions of NMDA antagonists with barbiturate receptors, some investigators have found similarities between PCP and ethanol (alcohol). These studies have proven to be important in describing both the similarities and differences between the noncompetitive and competitive NMDA-receptor antagonists.

TOLERANCE

Tolerance to a drug occurs when increasingly higher doses are needed to produce a specific effect or if drug effects diminish after repeated administration of the same dose of the drug. It has not been possible to study tolerance to PCP in human subjects; but when interviewed, PCP users report that they increase the amount of PCP that they take over time (Carroll, 1990). Another indicator of tolerance development is that burn patients treated with ketamine for pain often require higher doses over time. It is easier to study tolerance to ketamine, PCP, and similar drugs in animals. Laboratory studies with rats have shown that tolerance developed to the effects of PCP on food-reinforced responding; to the effects of PCP and dizocilpine on steroid hormone (adrenocorticotropin and corticosterone) release; and to the cataleptic effects of ketamine. Supersensitivity, the opposite of tolerance, occurs when repeated drug exposure produces a greater effect at a given dose. Some investigators have found that tolerance develops to some effects of PCP, such as head weaving, turning, and backpedaling, while supersensitivity occurs with such other behaviors as sniffing, rearing, and ambulation. Although some scientists have hypothesized that PCP tolerance and supersensitivity are mediated through non-NMDA-receptor systems, others have suggested that PCP tolerance may be mediated through the NMDA receptor system. Repeated administration of dizocilpine, a PCP-like compound, produced a reduction in the number of NMDA receptors in the rat brain, and that was correlated with tolerance to some of the behavioral effects produced by dizocilpine. Further studies will clarify the role of different receptor systems in the development of tolerance to the effects of PCP and related compounds.

Studies indicate that there are interactions between PCP and other drugs with respect to tolerance and supersensitivity of drug effects. For example, dizocilpine blocked the development of tolerance to morphine's analgesic (painkilling) effects, but it did not alter the analgesic effects when morphine was administered acutely. Also, dizocilpine attenuated the development of tolerance to ethanol (alcohol), and it inhibited sensitization to amphetamine and cocaine (*DHHS Fourth*

Triennial Report to Congress on Drug Abuse and Drug Abuse Research, 1992).

DEPENDENCE

Physiological dependence on a drug is usually defined by a set of withdrawal symptoms that occur when steady use of the drug is discontinued. The withdrawal symptoms are typically the same for a given drug, and they follow a specific time course that ranges from about six to forty-eight hours, depending on the drug. The withdrawal symptoms may be rapidly reversed after one administration of the drug.

Most of what is known about PCP dependence is from experimental studies with animals. There are only limited reports of PCP withdrawal effects in humans. In 1981, Tennant and colleagues studied sixty-eight regular PCP users; they found that one-third of them had sought treatment or medication to relieve the effects of PCP withdrawal. Withdrawal symptoms that they commonly reported were depression, drug craving, increased appetite, and increased need for sleep. Another way PCP dependence has been documented in humans is in studies of babies born to PCP-using mothers. Withdrawal signs that have been noted are diarrhea, poor feeding, irritability, jerky movements, high-pitched cry, and inability to follow a stimulus visually.

In laboratory studies with monkeys, similar signs of PCP withdrawal have been noted. Balster and Woolverton (1980) gave rhesus monkeys continuous access to PCP directly into the blood stream for fifty days, using an intravenous cannula system. The monkeys were trained to respond on a lever for an infusion of PCP. When PCP was replaced with a salt and water solution used to dissolve the drug (vehicle), withdrawal signs were noted, such as poor feeding, weight loss, irritability, bruxism (grinding of the teeth), vocalizations, piloerection (hair standing up), tremors, less exploratory behavior in the cage, and poor motor coordination. The withdrawal syndrome began within four to eight hours, peaked between twelve and sixteen hours, and had disappeared by twenty-four to forty-eight hours. These results have been repeated in studies with rats. Some studies have reported PCP withdrawal effects after as little as two weeks of exposure. Thus long-term use of the drug may not be necessary to produce physical dependence.

Recent studies with animals have shown that not only a short period of exposure to PCP but low doses of PCP result in withdrawal effects when drug administration is discontinued. Operant conditioning experiments are used as sensitive tests of drug-withdrawal effects in animals. In these experiments, animals are trained to respond on a lever or push a button or other device to obtain a food reward. At the same time they are allowed to self-administer drugs orally or intravenously. When drug access is removed, a decrease in operant response to food is often seen, even when the drug dose is sufficiently low to produce no observable signs of withdrawal. These measures have also been used to demonstrate withdrawal effects from such drugs as cocaine, caffeine, and nicotine. When regular use of these drugs is discontinued there are no observable signs of withdrawal during abstinence. The most severe reductions in the operant behavioral baselines occur during the first forty-eight hours of drug withdrawal, a time during which physical signs occur when higher maintenance doses are used; however, the behavioral disruptions often last for long periods of time. During withdrawal, when animals will not respond on a lever for food, they readily consume hand-fed food. Thus, the decrease in feeding may not be due to illness but to a decrease in the motivation to work for food.

In the first study that demonstrated disruption in operant behavior during PCP withdrawal, Slifer and coworkers (1984) treated monkeys with continuous intravenous infusions for ten days. They were required to make 100 responses on a lever for each food pellet. When access to PCP was terminated, responding for food decreased substantially for up to seven days and did not return to normal levels until the monkeys were again allowed access to PCP. Similar results were found by other investigators using monkeys trained to self-administer orally delivered PCP. There was little difference in the results, depending on whether the PCP was self-administered or experimenter-administered. In the monkey studies, there was only a weak relationship between dose and the severity of the withdrawal effect; but in rats, PCP dose, blood levels, and magnitude of the withdrawal effect were closely related. Recent studies have shown that there is cross-dependence between drugs that are chemically similar to PCP—such as PCP and ketamine, dizocilpine, and the (+)isomer of SKF-10,047; however, cross-dependence was not demonstrated with either the racemate or (−)isomer of SKF-10,047 or with ethanol.

The PCP-withdrawal effect can be altered by changing schedules of reinforcement. In one study with monkeys, lever-press requirements or fixed ratios (FRs) for food were increased from 64 to 128 to 256 to 512 to 1024, and PCP-withdrawal effects were examined at each value. As the FR value increased, PCP withdrawal effects became more pronounced. At the two higher FRs, body weights declined and the severity of the withdrawal effect showed no further increases. To examine the effects of amount of food available, another experiment was conducted in which the FR was held constant at 1024 and the monkeys were either supplemented with 100 grams of hand-fed food or not. The amount of responding for earned food remained the same during supplemented and unsupplemented conditions, but when the effects of withdrawal were examined, a disruption in responding occurred only under the supplemented condition. When the monkeys had to earn their entire daily food ration, the withdrawal effect disappeared. These studies suggest that the severity of the PCP withdrawal effect is determined by the behavioral economics of food availability. The magnitude of PCP withdrawal increased as the price (FR of food) increased; but as the price became so high that body weight was lost, the PCP-withdrawal effect entirely disappeared. These data also suggest that PCP withdrawal is not necessarily an illness but a decreased level of motivation.

The use of drugs to treat the PCP-withdrawal syndrome has produced mixed results. When monkeys had access to orally delivered (+)SKF-10,047, the PCP-withdrawal-induced disruptions in food-maintained responding were reversed. This was not the case with (−)SKF-10,047 or the racemate (±)SKF-10,047. Injections of dizocilpine before PCP withdrawal, or two days into PCP withdrawal, greatly reduced or reversed, respectively, the disruptions in food-reinforced responding. Dizocilpine also dose-dependently reduced PCP self-administration. In contrast, while buprenorphine, a partial agonist at the mu-opiate receptor, also dose-dependently reduced PCP self-administration, it had no effect on PCP-withdrawal-induced disruptions in food-maintained responding. When PCP was self-administered concurrently with ethyl alcohol (ethanol) and then PCP access was removed, PCP-withdrawal effects were as severe as when ethanol had not been available. Thus ethanol did not alleviate the PCP withdrawal effect; although, as noted earlier, PCP and ethanol share discriminative stimulus effects (Grant et al., 1991). In other studies, PCP was self-administered concurrently with ethanol or caffeine. When PCP and the other drug were removed simultaneously, the withdrawal disruption was more severe than when PCP alone was withdrawn. (Further details of these withdrawal studies may be found in reviews by Carroll [1990] and by Carroll and Comer in the *DHHS Fourth Triennial Report to Congress on Drug Abuse and Drug Abuse Research*, 1992.)

REINFORCING EFFECTS
The reinforcing effects of a drug are determined by demonstrating that self-administration of the drug plus the solution it is dissolved in (vehicle) occurs in excess of self-administration of the vehicle alone. When drug-reinforced behavior is readily achieved in the animal laboratory, it is usually a good predictor that the drug has considerable abuse liability in the human population. The reinforcing effects of PCP have been studied using two animal models of self-administration, oral and intravenous. The intravenous route of self-administration requires the animal to make a specified number of responses on a lever or other manipulandum within a predefined time—then a fixed dose of the drug is delivered by an infusion pump via a catheter that is surgically implanted in a large vein that leads to the heart. Studies from various laboratories have demonstrated that intravenously delivered PCP functions as a reinforcer for rats, dogs, monkeys, and baboons.

Drugs that are chemically similar to PCP are also self-administered intravenously. These include drugs that have similar receptor-binding sites in the brain, such as ketamine, (+)SKF-10,047, dexoxadrol, and cyclazocine; and phencyclidinelike drugs that function as noncompetitive antagonists at the NMDA receptor, such as dizocilpine. Phencyclidine and dizocilpine self-administration is more reliably obtained when the animal has a history of self-administration of a drug with similar pharmacological or discriminative-stimulus effects. It has also been found that drugs that share discriminative-stimulus effect with PCP, such as (+)SKF-10,047, ketamine, PCE, TCP, and ethanol, are readily substituted for PCP in self-administration studies.

Oral PCP self-administration is established by presenting gradually increasing concentrations of PCP after the animal is given its daily food ration. After sufficient quantities of PCP are consumed, food is given after the drug self-administration session, and PCP consumption usually persists. This procedure provides a long-term stable baseline to examine variables that affect PCP-reinforced behavior. For example, alternative nondrug reinforcers, such as saccharin, reduce PCP-reinforced responding up to 90 percent of baseline if the FR for PCP is high or if the PCP concentration is very low. Free access to food decreases PCP self-administration, while even small reductions in the daily food allotment markedly increase PCP self-administration. Concurrent availability of ethanol also reduces PCP-reinforced responding.

A limited amount of information is available concerning drug pretreatment and PCP self-administration. Buprenorphine and dizocilpine pretreatment both resulted in dose-dependent decreases in PCP self-administration; however, potential treatment drugs such as fluoxetine and carbamazepine had no effect. Treatment with other drugs such as amphetamine or pentobarbital had a biphasic effect on PCP self-administration. Low doses of the pretreatment drugs increased PCP self-administration and high doses decreased PCP self-administration.

TOXICITY

There is little evidence that long-term PCP use in adult humans (Luisada, 1981) and monkeys (see *DHHS Fourth Triennial Report to Congress on Drug Abuse and Drug Abuse Research*, 1992) results in any detectable organ or cellular damage. In monkeys that had been self-administrating PCP for eight years, tests of all organ systems, clinical chemistries, physical exams, and X rays revealed no differences between PCP-experienced and control animals that were the same age but had little drug experience. In humans, the form of toxicity most commonly associated with PCP use is a change in behavior. There have been a few accounts of bizarre and/or violent behavior associated with

PCP use. Such reports have diminished since the preferred route of self-administration has shifted from oral (pill) to inhalation, which offers the users an ability to more carefully control the dose.

In monkeys, PCP produces a calming, tranquilizing effect. The immediate effects in humans are not seen in the hospital or clinic. Instead, the PCP user arrives in the emergency room several hours after PCP use, possibly while suffering acute withdrawal effects. Approximately twelve to fifteen hours after PCP was last taken, monkeys become agitated, violent, and aggressive. It is possible that many of the early reports of human violence and PCP-related homicides were related to the withdrawal effects. It is necessary to determine the time course of unusual behavior and important to know the time of drug intake, although this is difficult to establish because the patient often loses memory of the drug-taking event.

Another unusual aspect of PCP toxicity is that users often complain of unpleasant effects long after chronic use has stopped. These reports could be caused by the fact that PCP is highly fat-soluble and becomes stored for long periods of time in body fat. During periods of weight loss, there is subsequent mobilization of fat-stored PCP into blood and brain tissues. Recent laboratory research with rats supports this hypothesis by demonstrating the ability of food deprivation to increase PCP levels in blood and brain (Coveney & Sparber, 1990).

Increasing data have become available on the effect of drugs of abuse on the offspring of dependent mothers, and it appears that the offspring of PCP users may be more vulnerable to the adverse effects of PCP than their adult counterparts. Golden and coworkers (1987) studied ninety-four PCP-exposed newborns and ninety-four nonexposed controls; they found neurological abnormalities such as abnormal muscle tone and depressed reflexes in the exposed group. Another study followed twelve exposed infants for eighteen months and found a high percentage of medical problems (Howard et al., 1986). At six months the infants were irritable and hyperresponsive, and later they showed varying degrees of abnormalities in fine motor, adaptive, language and social skills. A recent study of the offspring of forty-seven PCP abusers and thirty-eight nonusers found that neurological dysfunction was common in the infants of PCP-abusing mothers (Howard, Beckwith, & Rodning, 1990). There was greater apathy, irritability, jitters, and abnormal muscle tone and reflexes. Follow-up interviews at six and fifteen months, using the Gesell Developmental Exam, revealed poor language development and a lower developmental quotient in general; however, the long-term outcome for PCP-exposed newborns is unknown.

TREATMENT

There are currently no PCP antagonists that are useful for treatment of PCP overdose. Symptomatic treatment may be given for suppressed breathing rates, fever, high blood pressure, and increased salivation. Convulsions are treated with diazepam. Elimination of the drug may be enhanced by making the urine more acidic and/or pumping stomach contents. Attempts to minimize environmental stimuli have helped to control violent and self-destructive behavior. Psychiatric care may be needed for an extensive psychotic phase that may follow overdose (Jaffe, 1989).

See also **Abuse Liability of Therapeutic Drugs: Testing in Animals; Addiction: Concepts and Definitions; Aggression and Drugs: Research Issues; Fetus, Effects of Drugs on the; Phencyclidine (PCP): Adverse Effects; Research, Animal Model: An Overview; Research: Drugs as Discriminative Stimuli; Tolerance and Physical Dependence.**

BIBLIOGRAPHY

Carroll, M. E. (1990). PCP and hallucinogens. *Advances in Alcohol and Substance Abuse, 9,* 167–190.

Conveney, J. R., & Sparber, S. B. (1990). Delayed effects of amphetamine or phencyclidine: Interaction of food deprivation, stress and dose. *Pharmacological and Biochemical Behavior, 36,* 443–449.

Golden, N. L., et al. (1987). Neonatal manifestations of maternal phencyclidine exposure. *Perinatal Medicine, 15,* 185–191.

Grant, K. A., et al. (1991). Ethanol-like discriminative stimulus effects of noncompetitive n-methyl-d-aspartate antagonists. *Behavioural Pharmacology, 2,* 87–95.

Hanson, G. R., Venturelli, P. J., & Fleckenstein, A. E. (2005). Hallucinogens (Psychedelics). In *Drugs and Society.* Sudbury, MA: Jones & Bartlett Publishers.

Howard, J., Beckwith, L., & Rodning, C. (1990). Adaptive behavior in recovering female phencyclidine/polysubstance abusers. *NIDA Research Monograph, 101,* 86–95.

Jaffe, J. H. (1989). Psychoactive substance abuse disorders. In H. I. Kaplan and B. J. Sadock (Eds.), *Comprehensive textbook of psychiatry,* 5th ed. Baltimore: Williams & Wilkins. (2004, 8th ed.)

Karch, S. B. (2006). *Drug abuse handbook.* Boca Raton, FL: CRC Press.

Maisto, S. A., Galizio, M., & Connors, G. J. (2007). *Drug use and abuse,* 5th ed. Belmont, CA: Thomson Wadsworth.

Marcovitz, H. (2005). *PCP.* San Diego, CA: Lucent Books.

Phencyclidine Hydrochloride (1999). *Clinical Reference Systems,* 1141.

Slifer, B. L., Balster, R. L., & Woolmerton, W.L. (1984). Behavioral dependence produced by continuous phencyclidine infusion in rhesus monkeys. *Journal of Pharmacology and Experimental Therapies, 230,* 339–406.

Willetts, J., Balster, R. L., & Leander, J. D. (1990). The behavioral pharmacology of NMDA receptor antagonists. *Trends in Pharmacological Sciences, 11,* 423–428.

MARILYN E. CARROLL
SANDRA D. COMER

PHENCYCLIDINE (PCP): ADVERSE EFFECTS.

Widely known as PCP, phencyclidine is an important drug of abuse in the United States, even though its use has declined since the 1980s. PCP is difficult to classify pharmacologically and is considered separately from the hallucinogens. The drug has not been studied systematically in animals, although research done in 1973 and 1980 indicated that it produces dependence in monkeys. Its effects on the human central nervous system are generally unpleasant. It produces a unique type of hallucinatory effect and is used both by smoking and ingestion. Persons under the influence of PCP experience mood changes, perceptual distortions, and feelings of dissociation from their surroundings. Since their judgment is impaired, they may take unnecessary risks. They may become unpredictable and violent. In certain individuals, PCP use, especially if repeated often, can result in the production of a mental disturbance referred to as PCP psychosis. It is not, however, known with certainty whether PCP itself, or a combination of factors involved in the lifestyle of PCP abusers, is the cause of brain damage or of long-term behavior impairment that also sometimes occurs in PCP abusers.

HISTORY

Phencyclidine was developed in the 1950s for use as an anesthetic, but its use was discontinued because patients developed delusions, severe anxiety, or frank psychosis after their operation. It was also used by veterinarians as an anesthetic for some years; at present, however, all PCP sold on the street is manufactured illegally. The initials "PCP" are derived from a nickname, "The Peace Pill." The history of PCP as a drug of abuse began in the United States in the mid-1960s, when it was primarily taken by ingestion; but the real epidemic of PCP abuse occurred in the 1970s, when smoking and insufflation ("snorting") became the more common forms of use (Burns & Lerner, 1976). Because it is not difficult for an experienced chemist to synthesize the drug, PCP and its abuse spread rapidly, peaking about 1978. After 1980, its prevalence declined—however, PCP abuse continues to occur precisely because the drug is relatively easy to make. National Institute on Drug Abuse surveys show that PCP abuse remains a significant public health problem. PCP abuse remains a significant public health problem. As of 2008, most PCP abusers either snort PCP powder, ingest PCP pills, or smoke it by sprinkling it on smoking material (mint leaves, parsley, marijuana, or tobacco). Users also dip cigarettes in liquid PCP and smoke them.

PSYCHOLOGICAL EFFECTS OF PCP

The psychological effects of PCP abuse can be discussed under three headings: (1) effects accompanying acute intoxication, (2) personality disturbances that can sometimes develop in PCP abusers, especially when associated with chronic use, and (3) possible neurobehavioral toxicity that may result from chronic use.

SIGNS AND SYMPTOMS OF PCP INTOXICATION

Low Dose. Dreamy carefree state, mood elevation, heightened or altered perception, impaired judgment, partial amnesia.

Intermediate Dose. Inebriation, motor incoordination, dissociation and depersonalization, confusion and disorientation, perceptual distortions and preoccupation with abnormal body sensations, diminished pain sensitivity, partial amnesia, and sometimes exaggerated mood swings and panic.

High Dose. Catatonia, "blank stare," drooling, nystagmus (eye-rolling), delirium and hallucinations, psychotic behavior, severe motor incoordination, total amnesia.

ACUTE PCP INTOXICATION

As with all drugs, the effects of PCP depend on the dose that is taken. The section above lists the typical effects of PCP at various doses. PCP abusers usually adjust their dosage to experience only the low-dose effects. High-dose effects are similar to a mild type of dissociative anesthesia.

Experienced drug abusers can readily distinguish the experience of PCP intoxication from that produced by other drugs such as marijuana, mescaline, and lysergic acid diethylamide (LSD). Users typically report a feeling of dissociation from the environment and abnormal body sensations and body image. The perceptual distortions often cause objects to appear far away or abnormal in size. Compared to LSD, the effects of PCP are not very psychedelic.

The most dangerous effects of PCP intoxication arise from the impaired judgment and altered perceptions that occur. People can engage in risk-taking behavior and harm themselves or others. Driving, swimming, or other activities requiring coordination and good judgment become extremely dangerous. Someone on PCP may also engage in casual but high-risk sexual behaviors. PCP users experience profound mood swings—in which what begins as a pleasant experience can turn into panic and terror—and their behavior is unpredictable. Sometimes these "bad trips" can lead to violent and uncharacteristic behaviors with disastrous results. In cases of high-dose intoxication, users can experience a toxic psychotic episode with delirium, profound hallucinations, and paranoia. In cases of severe overdose, seizures, stroke, or kidney failure may lead to death (Burns & Lerner, 1976).

MEDICAL TREATMENT

As of 2008, there is no medication that can serve as an antagonist to the effects of PCP or that can speed up its excretion. PCP is easily soluble in fats, thus can remain in the central nervous system for long periods. A patient who has overdosed on PCP must be placed on life support. Patients with anxiety or seizures can be given diazepam (Valium). Patients with psychotic episodes are usually treated with haloperidol (Haldol). Chlorpromazine (Thorazine) should *not* be given to patients who have taken PCP, as it may produce hypotension. Patients with severe hypertension due to PCP should be given diazoxide (Proglycem). Gastric lavage has been used successfully to treat patients who have ingested PCP directly.

PCP intoxication is considered a psychiatric emergency. It is recommended that these patients be placed in a secure room under observation. The health professional should not attempt to "talk the patient down." Physical restraints or a sedative such as lorazepam (Ativan) may be needed if the patient becomes violent.

LONG-TERM USE

In persons who abuse PCP in large amounts over a long period, or in those who have psychological problems that make them especially vulnerable, a chronic psychosis may develop. This PCP psychosis is evident even when abusers are not high on PCP, and it may be quite difficult to treat. The symptoms of PCP psychosis differ considerably from person to person; but patients may show many features of schizophrenia, including the appearance of a thought disorder, paranoid ideation, hallucinations, mood changes, and aberrant behavior. These patients often require psychiatric hospitalization and treatment with antipsychotic medications. In research studies in which PCP has been given repeatedly to animals, it has been possible to show the development of physical dependence (e.g., Balster & Woolverton, 1980). The doses required for dependence are quite high, so it may be that dependence in human PCP abusers is difficult to develop. There have been some clinical reports of withdrawal effects in heavy PCP abusers, but these do not appear to be present in most individuals needing treatment for PCP abuse. There are no specialized treatment methods for PCP abusers, and since many PCP abusers also abuse other drugs and/or alcohol, they are usually helped by the same counseling and psychotherapy programs that are used for other forms of drug abuse.

NEUROPSYCHOLOGICAL AFTEREFFECTS OF PCP ABUSE

It is not known for certain whether PCP causes brain damage or long-term neurological or behavioral impairment in chronic abusers. Although some

PCP abusers develop neurobehavioral impairment, controlled experiments of the type that would need to be carried out to show that PCP alone was the cause of the problems have not been done. PCP abusers typically abuse many other drugs in addition to PCP, which may contribute to their problems, and they may have lifestyles and health habits that lead to neuropsychological dysfunction. For example, while under the influence of PCP, they may be involved in an accident resulting in brain injury, so the risk factors that accompany PCP abuse may be responsible for the clinical problems sometimes seen in abusers. It should be pointed out that PCP was used in humans for medical research for a number of years, and ketamine—a close analog of PCP—is, even in the early twenty-first century, given to thousands of patients, though only under close supervision. No legacy of neuropsychological impairment is seen in these individuals.

Does this mean that chronic PCP abuse does not cause neuropsychological impairment? Certainly, PCP—like all drugs—must be considered as a possible source of neural damage. In animal testing, it was found that even a single injection of a fairly high dose of PCP produced reversible pathomorphological changes in neurons of the cingulate and retrosplenial cortex in the brains of rats (Olney, Labruyere, & Price, 1989). Although it is not known if PCP produces these effects in humans, it is possible that it does and that this could lead to adverse health effects. Another possibly important basis for concern comes from studies which show that PCP, and related drugs, impair learning and memory in various animal models. PCP's ability to do this may be greater than for other classes of drugs of abuse, possibly due to PCP's ability to interfere with specific brain mechanisms for learning that involve N-methyl-D-aspartate (NMDA) receptors.

PCP AND VIOLENCE

Many people associate the abuse of PCP with violence and aggression, so this concern deserves special mention. Those under the influence of PCP often behave erratically and exercise poor judgment. These effects of PCP could certainly lead to violent behavior, and there are certainly numerous examples of extremely violent acts being performed by persons under the influence of PCP. This raises the question of whether PCP is uniquely associated with the production of violence and aggression: Is someone intoxicated with PCP more likely to be violent than someone who is intoxicated with cocaine or alcohol?

Unfortunately, the answer to this question is not known. A great deal of criminal conduct in the United States is certainly carried out by people under the influence of alcohol or drugs. In addition, the public often associates drug use they do not understand with criminal and violent behavior. Every new drug epidemic is greeted with public concern that this drug causes violence. There is also the common practice of criminal attorneys using the defense of diminished capacity because of drug use to lessen the responsibility that their clients might bear for criminal conduct. All these factors undoubtedly contribute to the public attention focused on the relationship of PCP to violence.

Few good research studies have attempted to determine the specific role that PCP abuse may have in crime and violence. In one study (Wish, 1986) of nearly five thousand arrestees in New York City in 1984 who agreed to leave a urine specimen for drug analysis, it was found that 56 percent tested positive for at least one drug of abuse. For those who had used PCP recently, most had committed robbery, not bizarre violent offenses. In fact, assault was more common among arrestees who had not used PCP than among those who had. These results support the conclusion that PCP may be no more likely to cause violence than some other drugs of abuse—but clearly more research on this question is needed.

The National Institute on Drug Abuse estimates that as many as six million Americans have tried PCP at least once. The very large majority of these occasions of PCP use were not associated with violent acts; however, if some users prone to violence take PCP and are faced with a threatening situation, they may act unpredictably and violently. Although there is no scientific evidence that PCP actually increases muscular strength, PCP users unmindful of their own potential safety or injuries can be a formidable risk, so law enforcement personnel are on guard against these dangerous situations. Alternatively, it should not be assumed that most people who abuse PCP will become violent—nor should every inexplicable act of violence be casually or speculatively attributed to PCP abuse.

See also **Addiction: Concepts and Definitions; Amphetamine Epidemics, International; Complications: Mental Disorders; Crime and Drugs; Tolerance and Physical Dependence.**

BIBLIOGRAPHY

Balster, R. L., & Pross, R. S. (1978). Phencyclidine: A bibliography of biomedical and behavioral research. *Journal of Psychedelic Drugs, 10*, 1, 1–15.

Balster, R. L., & Woolverton, W. L. (1980). Continuous access phencyclidine self-administration by rhesus monkeys leading to physical dependence. *Psychopharmacology, 70*, 5–10.

Beers, M. H., & Berkow, R. (Eds.) (1999). *The Merck manual of diagnosis and therapy*, 17th ed. Whitehouse Station, NJ: Merck Research Laboratories. (2006, 18th ed.)

Bishop, M. L., Fody, E. P., & Schoeff, L. E. (2004). *Clinical chemistry: Principles, procedures, correlations,* 5th ed. Philadelphia, PA: Lippincott Williams & Wilkins.

Carroll, M. E. (1991). PCP: The dangerous angel. In S. H. Snyder (Ed.), *Encyclopedia of psychoactive drugs*, Vol. 8. New York: Chelsea House.

Clouet, D.H. (Ed.) (1986). *Phencyclidine: An update.* National Institute on Drug Abuse Research Monograph 64. DHHS Publication No. (ADM)86-1443.

Feldman, H. W., Agar, M. H., & Beschner, G.M., Eds. (1979). *Angel dust: An ethnographic study of PCP users.* Lexington, MA: Lexington Books.

Hardman, J. G., & Limbird, L.E. (Eds.) (1996). *Goodman and Gilman's The pharmacological basis of therapeutics*, 9th ed. New York: McGraw–Hill Medical (2005, 11th ed.)

Karch, S. B. (2006). *Drug abuse handbook.* Boca Raton, FL: CRC Press.

National Drug Intelligence Center. (2006). *PCP Fast facts: questions and answers.* NDIC Product number 2003-L0559-008.

National Institute on Drug Abuse (1991). *National household survey on drug abuse: Main findings 1990.* DHHS Publication No. (ADM)91-1788. Washington, DC: U.S. Government Printing Office.

Olney, J. W., Labruyere, J., & Price, M. T. (1989). Pathological changes induced in cerebrocortical neurons by phencyclidine and related drugs. *Science, 244*, 1360–1362.

Pollard, J. C., Uhr, L., & Stern, E. (1965). *Drugs and phantasy: The effects of LSD, psilocybin and Sernyl on college students.* Boston: Little, Brown.

Wish, E. (1986). PCP and crime: Just another drug? In D. H. Clouet, (Ed.) *Phencyclidine: An update*. National Institute on Drug Abuse Research Monograph 64. DHHS Publication No. (ADM)86-1443.

ROBERT L. BALSTER
REVISED BY REBECCA J. FREY (2001)
PUBLISHER (2009)

BIBLIOGRAPHY

Harvey, S. C. (1975). Hypnotics and sedatives. In L. S. Goodman & A. Gilman (Eds.), *The Pharmacological basis of therapeutics*, 5th ed. New York: Macmillan. (2005, 11th ed. McGraw-Hill Medical.)

Howland, R. D., & Mycek, M. J. (2006). *Pharmacology*, 3rd ed. Philadelphia, PA: Lippincott Williams & Wilkins.

SCOTT E. LUKAS

PHENOBARBITAL.

This is the prototypic barbiturate central nervous system (CNS) depressant. It is prescribed and sold as Luminal and was introduced into clinical medicine in 1912. It was used for a long period as a sedative-hypnotic drug but has now largely been replaced by the much safer benzodiazepines.

Phenobarbital's long duration of action makes it useful for treating many forms of general and partial seizure disorders, such as epilepsy. Chronic use can result in tolerance and physical dependence, so it is classified as a Schedule III drug under the Controlled Substances Act. Chronic treatment with phenobarbital can increase the activity of certain liver enzymes that metabolize other drugs. Thus a potential side effect is that other drugs (e.g., steroids, oral anticoagulants, digitoxin, beta-blockers, oral contraceptives, phenytoin, and others) are metabolized more quickly—and their effectiveness is reduced. Combinations of phenobarbital and other CNS depressants, such as alcohol (ethanol), can lead to severe motor impairment and reduced breathing.

See also **Drug Interactions and Alcohol; Drug Metabolism.**

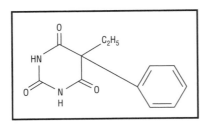

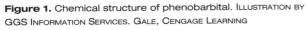

Figure 1. Chemical structure of phenobarbital. ILLUSTRATION BY GGS INFORMATION SERVICES. GALE, CENGAGE LEARNING

PHYSICAL DEPENDENCE.

Physical dependence is a state produced by repeated or prolonged drug exposure in which the presence of the drug in the body is required to maintain normal physiological function. This state is recognizable only by the occurrence of a withdrawal reaction when the drug is removed, which is reversed when the drug is again administered. Such dependence is believed to result from adaptive changes in the nervous system, opposite in direction to the drug effects, which offset these effects when the drug is present and produce a drug-opposite effect in its absence. Physical dependence is not synonymous with addiction and can occur in nonaddicted persons.

See also **Addiction: Concepts and Definitions; Models of Alcoholism and Drug Abuse; Tolerance and Physical Dependence.**

HAROLD KALANT

PHYSICIANS AND MEDICAL WORKERS, SUBSTANCE ABUSE AMONG.

Physicians and other health professionals (HPs) are not spared the ravages of addiction. In fact, some of history's most prominent physicians were addicted to drugs. Dr. William Halsted, known as the "Father of Modern Surgery," (innovator of blood transfusions, intravenous fluid therapy, and gall bladder surgery) was addicted to cocaine, while practicing, in the late 1800s. His friend, Sir William Osler, another prominent physician at Johns Hopkins University, attempted to wean Halsted off cocaine by using morphine.

Until the early twentieth century, medical practice went largely unregulated. As state medical regulatory boards evolved, their role was to assure that physicians received legitimate education and degrees. Not until the mid-1900s did medical boards begin to protect the public from impaired physicians.

Addicted HPs are excellent subjects to study because they are usually accessible both prior to and after treatment, and money is not a limiting factor in their receiving good treatment. The more than thirty types of licensed HPs include physicians, nurses, dentists, veterinarians, acupuncturists, massage therapists, social workers, and others; but all addicted HPs share the problem of substance abuse. Physicians have been studied the most; however, much of what is said about physicians applies to all HPs (Storr et al., 2000).

TERMINOLOGY

Historically, the word *impaired*, as in *impaired physician* or *impaired pharmacist*, became synonymous with *substance abusing*. This terminology is inaccurate because *impaired* actually means that one is unable to work with skill and safety. There are many causes for impairment unrelated to substance abuse (e.g., neurologic disorders, aging, psychiatric disorders, physical disability, or fatigue). Additionally, many HPs who have substance use disorders are not impaired at work, which is often the last place symptoms of addiction appear. Therefore, the word *impaired* should be limited to work-related impairment rather than used as a synonym for substance abuse.

EPIDEMIOLOGY

Substance use disorders (SUDs) are surprisingly common among physicians and other HPs. The lifetime prevalence among physicians is approximately 10–15 percent, similar to or slightly higher than the general population (Brewster, 1986; Talbott, 1987; Hughes et al., 1992b; Flaherty & Richmond, 1993). Nurses have a similar lifetime prevalence (Dunn, 2005). Physicians drink more alcohol than the general population, as do other members of higher socioeconomic groups. Substance abuse, disguised as *self-medication*, is especially common among physicians. As many as 11.4 percent of physicians have used benzodiazepines, and 17.6 percent have used opioids without valid prescriptions (Hughes et al., 1992b). Unauthorized use of prescription medications and alcohol abuse often begin in medical school, at an age when other groups also experience peak onset of substance

use. In one study 18 percent of students met criteria for alcohol abuse in the first two years of medical school (Clark et al., 1987). Alcohol and drug-related problems account for 14 to 21 percent of all disciplinary actions by state licensing boards (Morrison et al., 1998). This does not include most HPs receiving confidential assistance for SUDs offered by physician health programs (PHPs).

GENDER

Among physicians with SUDs, males predominate 7 to 1 (McAuliffe et al., 1991). Female physicians are more likely to be younger and have medical and psychiatric comorbidity, past or current suicidal thoughts, and suicide attempts (Bissell & Jones, 1976). Interestingly, women physicians with SUDs are subject to more severe sanctions by medical boards than their male counterparts (Morrison & Wickerson, 1998).

SPECIALTY

Anesthesiologists, emergency room physicians, psychiatrists, and, in some studies, family practitioners have higher rates of SUDs than other physicians (see Table 1). Approximately 5 percent of all physicians are anesthesiologists, but they account for a disproportionately high share (13–15%) of physicians in substance abuse treatment (Talbott, 1987). The Anesthesiology Task Force on SUDs suggested that anesthesiologists have higher rates of SUDs due to the following (Berry et al., 2008):

- higher addictive potential of anesthetic drugs, such as fentanyl/sufentanil
- ease of diverting small doses of highly potent fentanyl for illicit use;
- easy access to drugs
- being accustomed to giving large doses of mood-altering, parenteral substances with immediate results
- lack of "needle taboo"
- expectation of being in control
- curiosity about what drugs feel like for the patients
- more rapid identification of SUDs, because use of highly potent drugs is more obvious
- vigilance of specialty looking for addiction within itself

Authors of study	Type of study	Number of subjects studied	Over-represented specialties	Under-represented specialties
Bissell	Closed Survey	98	Psychiatry, Emergency Medicine	Surgery
Earley and Weaver	Treatment Records	618	Anesthesiology, Emergency Medicine	Pathology, Pediatrics, Radiology
Hughes	Survey	1785	Psychiatry, Emergency Medicine	Pediatrics, Pathology, Surgery
Ikeda and Pelton	PHP/MB*	247	Anesthesiology, Emergency Medicine, Family Practice	
Knight	PHP/MB*	120	Anesthesiology, Emergency Medicine	Pediatrics
McAullife et al.	Survey	489	Psychiatry, Anesthesiology	
Meyers and Weiss	Resident Survey	1805	Psychiatry, Anesthesiology	Community health, Emergency Medicine, Surgery, Pediatrics
Morrison and Wickersham	PHP/MB*	375	Anesthesiology, Psychiatry	Internal Medicine, Pediatrics
Shore	PHP/MB*	34	Psychiatry	
Talbott	Treatment Records	1000	Anesthesiology, Family Medicine / General Practice	

*Physician Health Program/Medical Board.

Table 1. Addiction rate by specialty. ILLUSTRATION BY GGS INFORMATION SERVICES. GALE, CENGAGE LEARNING

In addition to these factors, an important debate rages about whether opioid-addicted anesthesiologists should ever return to the operating room. An early study showed poor outcomes for addicted anesthesiologists in training, reporting only 34 percent successful re-entry for those using parenteral opioids and 26 deaths (14% of the 180 reported cases), half attributed to drug relapse (Menk et al., 1990, p. 3060). This oft-quoted study potentiated a pessimistic view about anesthesiologists returning to work. It has been criticized, however, because it was an opinion survey of program directors rather than a longitudinal study. A similar survey study by Collins (2005) of anesthesiology program directors reported comparable findings, noting a smaller but still significant number (9%) of anesthesiologists in training who died from substance abuse relapses (p. 1460). By contrast, longitudinal studies report far better outcomes. California's PHP (California Diversion Program) reported a 10-year follow-up involving all 255 physician participants that showed no difference in relapse rates for anesthesiologists (Pelton &

Ikeda, 1991, p. 429). Paris and Canavan (1999) compared 32 addicted anesthesiologists with 36 addicted non-anesthesiologist controls for an average of 7.5 years and showed no difference in relapse rates (p. 6). Domino and colleagues (2005) found no statistical difference in outcomes for the anesthesiologists and, strikingly, not a single episode of patient harm or anesthesiologist overdose death (pp. 1457–1458). Long-term follow-up studies of groups of physicians have shown no difference in outcome between anesthesiologists and other physicians. It appears the pessimism regarding anesthesiologists returning to work may not be warranted, although careful monitoring for early detection and deterrence of relapse is required.

DRUGS ABUSED

Alcohol is the most common substance of abuse by physicians, followed closely by opioids (Domino et al., 2005; Hughes et al., 1992b, 1999; Lutsky et al., 1993; McAuliffe et al., 1986, 1991; Talbott, 1981). Interestingly, family practice and OBGYN specialists have a higher probability of abusing less potent opioids (i.e., hydrocodone, oxycodone, codeine, and other oral opioids) (Hughes et al., 1992a).

Exposure to, and availability of, drugs in the workplace predisposes to abuse of that drug (Hughes et al., 1999). For example, cocaine-using professions (ophthalmology, head and neck surgery, plastic surgery, and otolaryngology) have higher rates of cocaine abuse (Hughes et al., 1999). To underline this point, when surgery residents abuse cocaine, it often comes from hospital sources. Similarly, psychiatrists have higher rates of benzodiazepine abuse, 26.3 percent using benzodiazepines in the past year compared with 11.4 percent by other physicians (Hyde et al., 1995, p. 30). Nonprescription drugs, such as heroin and marijuana, contribute minimally to use pattern among physicians (Hughes et al., 1992b).

Skipper and colleagues (2004), writing about emerging abuse of tramadol among HPs, hypothesized that physicians may be the "point men" (i.e., the first) to abuse newly introduced pharmaceutical drugs. This has certainly been the case historically for opioids such as morphine, meperidine, pentazocine, butorphanol, and others. Physicians also have earlier access to unusual addictive drugs, such as propofol (Wischmeyer et al., 2007) or ketamine (Moore & Bostwick, 1999).

ETIOLOGY

Drug Access. Availability is a key factor preceding drug use in any population, including physicians. Despite ethical codes and state laws prohibiting self-prescribing, it is a common practice (Valliant et al., 1972). The particular drugs abused change over time due largely to changing patterns of availability. Hughes et al. (1992b) noted that many physicians began abusing benzodiazepines and opioids immediately after receiving their own prescribing privileges. Demerol, once the most commonly abused opioid (Talbott, 1987), dropped to 10 percent by 2004 as hydrocodone became the most frequent (40%) (Skipper et al., 2004, p. 1818).

Personality. Personality and character disorders are often consequences of drug use rather than causes of addiction. Nevertheless, certain personality factors may place physicians at risk for addictive diseases. "Sensation seeking" (McAullife, 1986), novelty seeking,

intense experience seeking (Hughes et al., 1999), perfectionism, and high class rank (Bissell & Jones, 1976), "emotionally barren childhood" (Vaillant et al., 1972), childhood parental deprivation (Johnson & Connolly, 1981), sense of omnipotence or invulnerability regarding drug use, and knowledge of pharmacology may all be important risk factors for substance abuse among physicians.

Stress and Emotional Issues. Physicians in treatment for SUDs report that the stress of medical school, combined with social isolation and a lack of support, provided the backdrop for the development of addiction. They are taught in medical school and residency (and often in their childhoods) at all costs to appear in control and competent. The addiction undermines the physician's external appearance of competence. A physician falling deeper into addiction becomes more secretive and dishonest. Emotional regression and dysregulation are intensified by the secrecy and escalating stress.

CO-OCCURRING DISORDERS

Psychiatric. As in the general population, emotional and psychiatric problems appear with higher frequency in relation to substance abuse disorders, both as cause and result of substance abuse. Psychiatric problems, including depression, anxiety (including obsessive-compulsive disorder), and bipolar disorders are seen as frequently in addicted physicians as in other addicted groups. In recent years identified psychiatric comorbidity has increased, likely due to more careful evaluation rather than increased prevalence (Angres et al., 2003).

Chronic Pain. PHPs report working with an increasing number of physicians suffering from chronic pain. These cases pose diagnostic, treatment, and management difficulties. Regulatory enigmas further cloud the pain treatment of addicted physicians. Should a formerly addicted physician on opioids for pain be allowed to practice? If not, should any physician on opioids be allowed to practice? These can be perplexing questions.

IDENTIFICATION AND MANAGEMENT

Identification. Substance abuse is detected over a broad spectrum of symptom severity, from a self-report of alcoholism while in couple's therapy to finding a physician unconscious or dead on the operating room floor. Physicians with SUDs have often had years of familial and social discord while struggling to maintain acceptable work performance. In addition, families (and medical partners) often codependently protect the addicted income earner. As soon as symptoms of substance abuse appear at work, the addiction is usually advanced. Denial, shame, and fear of reprisal often keep the HP from seeking needed care until significant external consequences occur (Centrella, 1994).

A confidential and effective PHP promotes early reporting and protects public health by offering physicians a safe haven for confronting substance abuse problems. By contrast, some patient advocacy groups claim that all HPs with a history of SUDs should be publicly identified. Most experts in physicians' health, however, believe that confidential PHPs promote early identification as opposed to the alternative, in which public stigma causes substance abusing physicians to hide their problems until disasters occur.

Other factors that work in concert with PHPs to encourage early reporting include the establishment in 2001 of new standards for physician health awareness by hospital accrediting agencies. Additionally, many states have *snitch laws* that require peers to report substance-abusing colleagues. PHPs collaborate with hospitals and rely on these laws, combined with their rehabilitative non-punitive approaches, to motivate early reporting that ultimately protects both patients and physicians alike.

Intervention. PHPs have become skilled at conducting professional interventions, often by telephone. Using the telephone for interventions may be actually less threatening and more practical. The immediate goal of the intervention is to get the HP to stop working and into an evaluation program. An HP who resists is informed that failure to comply will very likely result in a report to the regulatory board. PHP staff, often recovering HPs themselves, become skilled at gently coercing their troubled colleagues into needed evaluations.

Evaluation. Most PHPs utilize independent expert evaluation teams, selected for their credibility with the HP and with the regulatory board, which may later become involved. Most PHPs have established criteria and maintain an authorized list of evaluators (see Table 2). The opportunity for a thorough evaluation is uniquely valuable and, if mismanaged, can result in failure of the entire process.

Ideally, at the conclusion of evaluation, recommendations are presented to the HP patient in a formal meeting. Family members, particularly spouses, are commonly involved, as are PHP personnel. Such secondary interventions decrease confusion and "splitting" regarding the final recommendations. PHP personnel can answer questions about alternatives or consequences of noncompliance with evaluation recommendations. Finally, the evaluation team sends a written, comprehensive, integrated report to the PHP and other relevant parties, such as the referring hospital, if necessary.

Physicians as Patients. Treatment of physicians can be difficult, so good boundaries and experience are critical (Graham, 1980; Howard, 1983; Nace, 1995). Typically, physicians resist becoming patients, seek general medical check-ups and consultation visits less often than controls, and wait longer before seeking consultation for serious symptoms (Edelstein, 1984). They tend to diagnose and treat themselves, request "hallway" medical consultations regarding symptoms, get treatment from professional friends, and receive less than objective medical treatment. All of these factors inhibit an ill or impaired physician from seeking timely and effective treatment (Stoudemire & Rhoads, 1983).

Treatment. Approximately a dozen addiction treatment programs in the U.S. have extensive experience and recognized expertise in treating addicted physicians. These programs usually have a full-time medical director, a highly sophisticated capability for evaluation, expertise and familiarity with PHPs and Licensing Boards, and specialized treatment components for HPs, such as groups where return-to-work issues are discussed (Skipper, 1997). In many ways these are model programs for what substance abuse treatment should be for everyone.

Because the initial treatment is typically long-term (6–12 weeks), and requires the physician to be off work, some think of treatment as limited to acute episodes. When physicians leave the treatment setting, whether outpatient or residential, three weeks or six months later and return to work, the PHP vernacular is that they have completed treatment. For the next five

Component	Component type	Purpose of component*
Addiction Medicine Evaluation	Critical	Determine existence and extent of any type of addictive disorder
Addiction Psychiatry Evaluation	Critical	Determine comorbid Axis I and II disorders that interact with the addictive disease and impede treatment
History and Physical and Review of Medical Records	Critical	Determine existence and extent of medical consequences of substance use. Evaluate comorbid medical conditions (chronic pain, etc)
Psychological testing	Critical	Correlate with psychiatric evaluation, determine interaction of personality and treatment
Neuropsychological testing	Critical	Determine if cognitive deficits exist and ultimately, the physician's ability to practice
Family assessment	Critical	Determine how the evaluatee's family of origin and current nuclear family contributes to psychological, psychiatric, and addiction problems
Collection of collateral information	Critical	Evaluate effects of addiction on the workplace, family and social life. Behavioral observations that correlate with personality problems.
Hair and Body Fluid drug testing	Critical	Correlate with addiction history from multiple sources. Determine honesty of self disclosures.
Spiritual History	Critical	Assess past involvement with spiritual and religious pursuits. Determine potential pitfalls with twelve step programs.
Forensic Interview	Suggested	Determine level of honesty on a broad base of issues
Polygraph testing	Suggested	Address honesty on key issues of the evaluatee's history (Must have a list of specific questions prepared for polygrapher)
Pain evaluation	Suggested	Determine the interaction between an acute or chronic pain disorder and the addictive process. Distinguish between pseudo-addiction and addiction
Milieu interaction	Suggested	Evaluate physician for social abilities, personality issues. Help physician enter the patient role.
Sexual issues evaluation	Suggested	Evaluate need for sexual compulsivity treatment, predator treatment, or special sexual issues therapy.

*All components of the evaluation contribute to determining if an addictive disease exists, the level of care needed, and treatment planning for eventual care.

Table 2. Suggested components of a comprehensive physician addiction assessment.
ILLUSTRATION BY GGS INFORMATION SERVICES. GALE, CENGAGE LEARNING

years, however, they receive far more intense treatment than members of the general public usually receive during their primary treatment. This typically includes weekly group therapy sessions, peer support groups, aftercare groups, individual counseling or psychotherapy, self-help group attendance, drug testing, worksite monitoring reports, and more. In essence, PHP-managed treatment for health professionals actually lasts more than five years because the distinction between treatment and monitoring is blurred.

Ultimately, HPs need to receive the best possible treatment because hospitals, malpractice carriers, regulatory boards, health insurance companies, family, and friends all have high expectations for continual abstinence. Relapse for an HP can and does carry harsh consequences professionally and often within the family.

The following are important components of treatment for HPs:

1. Intensive day or residential treatment

2. Personnel experienced in setting firm limits and boundaries with physician-patients

3. Regular contact with a peer (HP) support group facilitated by a physician during assessment and/or treatment

4. Opportunity for extended treatment for patients who need additional time before returning to work (2–6 month program)

5. Comprehensive family program for family and associates

6. Availability of neuropsychiatric assessment to substantiate ability to return to work

7. Availability of staff to conduct assessments, handle treatment, and advocate for the HP to return to work

8. Personnel capable of addressing needs post-discharge (Skipper, 1997).

Most HPs have work-related triggers (e.g., drug access at work, prescription pads, or locations in the office or hospital where use occurred); therefore trigger management skills and relapse prevention plans are developed prior to discharge. HPs receive minimal pharmacological treatment for addiction. About one-third of physicians in treatment receive antidepressants. Naltrexone, an opioid-blocking drug, is occasionally used in opioid-addicted physicians.

PHYSICIAN HEALTH PROGRAMS (PHPS)

History. The physician's health movement can be traced to the founding of International Doctors in Alcoholics Anonymous (IDAA) by Clarence Pearson, MD, in 1949. IDAA grew from 24 physicians, meeting in Dr. Pearson's garage in Cape Vincent, New York, to an international organization attracting thousands of physicians. On the regulatory side, the Federation of State Medical Boards called for a model probation and rehabilitation process for addicted physicians in 1958; however, no meaningful change occurred until 1973 with the publication of the watershed article from the *Journal of the American Medicine Association* titled "The Sick Physician. Impairment by Psychiatric Disorders, including Alcoholism and Drug Dependence" (Council on Mental Health, 1973). The AMA held its first conference on physician impairment in 1975. State medical societies organized committees on physician impairment, resulting in the state-by-state emergence of PHPs. Currently, all but two states in the U.S. have a formal PHP, ranging in size from one employee and a $20,000 budget to a $1.5 million budget and 19 full-time employees. Over 9,000 physicians are now in monitoring in the United States. (Skipper et al., 2004, p. 1818). Although most PHPs (85%) address other psychiatric disorders and disruptive behavior, SUDs remain the most common problems.

Education and Referral. PHPs strongly emphasize education aimed at early detection of all impairments, not just SUDs. Educational programs afford PHP staff the opportunity to network with medical leadership throughout their state. Public relations/ training efforts help individuals and institutions understand and trust PHPs, which in turn promotes early referral of potentially impaired HPs.

Abstinence Monitoring. Monitoring has become more sophisticated in recent years and includes hair testing, flexible variations in drug testing panels, new markers for alcohol, medical devices to detect alcohol exposure, and software to track results more efficiently. All PHPs use random drug testing (most frequently, urine testing, but at times hair, saliva, sweat, or blood analysis). Screens commonly taper in frequency over the course of monitoring, for a period of five or more years.

Drug testing in physician populations requires considerable expertise, resourcefulness, and accuracy. Addicted physicians can use their knowledge to evade detection. Most drug panels test for 20 to 25 drugs, including a wide variety of opioids and other prescribed controlled substances (Skipper et al., 2004). Observed collection at the lab is often required to reduce the risk of cheating. Some PHPs perform periodic hair or saliva tests because these tests are less vulnerable to deception. Special screenings for fentanyl are necessary for some recovering physicians. Hair testing for fentanyl is best as these anesthesia drugs have very brief half-lives, but are readily detected in hair. Because physicians occasionally abuse more unusual drugs (e.g., ketamine, propofol, or dextromethorphan) personalized drug test panels are sometimes necessary.

In 2002 PHPs began using ethylglucuronide (EtG), a metabolite of alcohol that persists for several days or more after drinking, for early detection and deterrence of alcohol relapse (Skipper et al., 2004). Previous tests for alcohol use were inadequate due to the short half-life of alcohol in the body. Negative EtG tests, often better proof of abstinence, are needed before HPs return to work. One problem with EtG testing, however, is false-positives. The test cannot differentiate drinking from incidental alcohol exposure to various foods, hygiene products, over-the-counter medications, or topical products containing alcohol (especially if excessive alcohol vapors are inadvertently inhaled). Thus, HPs under EtG monitoring must avoid exposure to products containing alcohol, and PHPs must use care in interpreting low positive EtG results.

Recovery Support. In addition to drug testing, PHPs utilize group-facilitated psychotherapy (Caduceus groups, similar to twelve-step meetings). Unlike Alcoholics Anonymous meetings, direct feedback (*cross-talk*) is encouraged. Newcomers often obtain sponsors or guidance from Caduceus members. In one survey, "A.A. was perceived by respondents as the most potent element of their recovery" (Galanter et al., 1990, p. 63). Most PHP treatment programs strongly encourage or require Alcoholics Anonymous or Narcotics Anonymous attendance.

Relapse Management. Some PHPs have formalized models of assessing relapse with categories based upon severity:

- Level I relapse consists of missing therapy meetings, support groups, or engaging in dishonesty or other behavioral infractions (without relapse to substance use).

- Level II relapse involves use of unauthorized drugs or alcohol, but outside the context of medical practice.

- Level III relapse involves drug or alcohol use within the context of medical practice with potential risk to patients.

If managed properly, singular episodes of relapse, detected early, are not necessarily indicators of failed treatment. Unfortunately, consequences of relapse can be severe for physicians, including loss of license, arrest, and damage to professional reputation. Once a physician is in monitoring, patients run little risk even if relapse occurs, because under the careful scrutiny of PHPs, relapse is rapidly detected. Ultimately, even relapsing PHP participants have excellent long-term prognoses.

Typical responses to a relapse include:

- Reevaluation by an addiction specialist to identify the cause and suggest remedial actions to prevent future relapses

- Reexamination of the HP'S psychiatric status for psychiatric disorder, character disorder, or past unresolved trauma

- Reassessment of HP'S family dynamics and physician's support system

- Evaluation of the physician's ability to practice

- Determination of the need to repeat primary residential treatment (or to treat other elements of the addiction).

HPs who have difficulty maintaining abstinence are often removed from the workforce for extended periods until treatment providers are confident that they can safely practice. The physician's treatment provider and the monitoring PHP decide when a physician can return to work. The medical board and the public at large place pressure on all parties, so great care must be exercised in returning substance abusing HPs to work.

Outcomes. Physicians have been the subject of multiple outcome studies. Success rates have been remarkably high (Gallegos et al., 1992), with good outcomes for 91 percent over five years (Ganley et al., 2005, pp. 10–11), and low relapse rates of 25 percent (Domino et al., 2005, p. 1458) and 21 percent defined as *any* unauthorized substance use. Long-term monitoring with random drug testing under a signed PHP contingency contract may be the most important procedure accounting for their high success rates. Satisfaction surveys of PHPs by participants have generally been favorable (Fletcher & Ronis, 2005).

CONCLUSION

By utilizing the highest level of evaluation and treatment and by careful long-term monitoring with meaningful consequences for noncompliance or relapse, the nation's PHPs have achieved excellent outcomes with reduced risk to patients. PHPs are distinctive programs of care management that actively pursue early detection of SUDs prior to overt impairment at work and have high success rates with very low risk to patients, and thus should be supported.

BIBLIOGRAPHY

Angres, D. H., McGovern, M. P., Shaw, M. F., & Rawal, P. (2003). Psychiatric comorbidity and physicians with substance use disorders. *Journal of Addictive Disorders, 22*(3), 79–97.

Berry, A. J., Bogard, T. D., Harter, R. L., Hanlon, P. R., Katz, J. D., & Jackson, S. H. (2008). *Curriculum on drug abuse and addiction for residents in anesthesiology.* Occupational Health Task Force, American Society of Anesthesiologists. Available from http://www.asahq.org/.

Bissell, L., & Jones, R. W. (1976, October). The alcoholic physician: a survey. *American Journal of Psychiatry, 133*(10), 1142–1146.

Brewster, J. M. (1986, April 11). Prevalence of alcohol and other drug problems among physicians. *Journal of the American Medical Association, 255,* 1913–1920.

Centrella, M. (1994). Physician addiction and impairment—current thinking: A review. *Journal of Addictive Diseases, 13*(1), 91–105.

Clark, D.C., Eckenfels, E. J., Daugherty, S. R., & Fawcett, J. (1987, June 5). Alcohol-use patterns through medical school: A longitudinal study of one class. *Journal of the American Medical Association,, 257*(21), 2921–2926.

Collins G. B., McAllister, M. S., Jensen, M., Gooden, T. A. (2005). Chemical dependency treatment outcomes of residents in anesthesiology: results of a survey. *Anesthesiology and Analgesia, 101*(5), 1457–1462.

Council on Mental Health. (1973, February 5). The sick physician: Impairment by psychiatric disorders, including alcoholism and drug dependence. *Journal of the American Medical Association, 223*(6), 684–687.

Dilts, S. (1994). The Colorado Physician Health Program: Observations at 7 years. *American Journal on Addictions, 3*(4), 337–345.

Domino, K. B., Hombein, T. F., Polissar, N. L., Renner, G., Johnson, J., & Aberti, S. (2005, March 23). Risk factors for relapse in health care professionals with substance use disorders. *Journal of the American Medical Association, 293*(12), 1453–1460.

Dunn, D. (2005, October). Substance abuse among nurses: Defining the issue. *AORN Journal in Health, 82*(4), 573–582.

Edelstein, E. L. (1984). Physicians as patients: A comparative study of attitudes of physicians and non-physicians. *Psychopathology, 17,* 213–216.

Flaherty, J. A., & Richman, J. (1993). A. substance use and addiction among medical students, residents, and physicians: Recent advances in addictive disorders. *Psychiatric Clinics of North America,16*(1), 189–195.

Fletcher, C. E., & Ronis, D. L. (2005). Satisfaction of impaired health care professionals with mandatory treatment and monitoring. *Journal of Addictive Diseases, 24*(3), 61–75.

Gabbard, G. O. (1985, November 22–29). The role of compulsiveness in the normal physician. *Journal of the American Medical Association, 254*(20), 2926–2929.

Galanter, M., Talbott, G. D., Gallegos, K., & Rubenstone, E. (1990, January). Combined Alcoholics Anonymous and professional care for addicted physicians. *American Journal of Psychiatry,147*(1), 64–68.

Gallegos, K. V., Lubin, B. H., Bowers, C., Blevins, J. W., Talbott, G. D., Wilson, P. O. (1992, April). Relapse and recovery: five to ten year follow-up study of chemically addicted physicians—the Georgia experience. *Maryland Medical Journal, 41*(4), 315–319.

Ganley, O. H., Pendergast, W. J., Wilkerson, M. W., & Mattingly, D. E. (2005). Outcome study of substance impaired physicians and physician assistants under contract with the North Carolina Physicians Health Program for the period 1995–2000. *Journal of Addictive Diseases, 24*(1), 1–12.

Gold, M. S., Melker, R. J., Dennis, D. M., Morey, T. E., Baipai, L. K., & Pomm, R. (2006). Fentanyl abuse and dependence: further evidence for secondhand exposure hypthesis. *Journal of Addictive Diseases, 25*(1), 15–21.

Graham, J. R. (1980). Risk to self, patients, and profession: Physician health problems. *Colorado Medicine, 7*(5), 167–172.

Howard, R. B. (1983). Physicians as patients: The lessons of experience. *Postgraduate Medicine, 74*(2), 15–16.

Hughes, P. H., Baldwin, D. C. Jr., Sheehan, D. V., Conard, S., & Storr, C. L. (1992a, October). Resident physician substance use by specialty. *American Journal of Psychiatry, 149*(10), 1348–1354.

Hughes, P. H., Brandenburg, N., Baldwin, D. C. Jr., Storr, C. L., Williams, K. M., & Anthony, J. C., & Sheehan, D. V. (1992b, May). Prevalence of substance use among U.S. physicians. *Journal of the American Medical Association, 267*(17), 2333–2339.

Hughes, P. H., Storr, C. L., Brandenburg, N. A., Baldwin, D. C. Jr., Anthony, J. C., & Sheehan, D. V. (1999). Physician substance use by medical specialty. *Journal of Addictive Diseases, 18*(2), 23–37.

Hyde, G. L., & Wolf, J. (1995). Alcohol and drug use by surgery residents. *Journal of the American College of Surgeons, 181,* 1–5.

Johnson, R. P., & Connelly, J. C. (1981 January 16). Addicted physicians. A closer look. *Journal of the American Medical Association, 245*(3), 253–257.

Khantzian, E. J. (1985, July 12). The injured self, addiction, and our call to medicine. Understanding and managing the addicted physician. *Journal of the American Medical Association, 254*(2), 249–252.

Knight, J. R., Sanchez, L. T., Sherritt, L., Bresnahan, L. R. & Fromson, J. A. (2007, January).Outcomes of a monitoring program for physicians with mental and behavioral health problems. *Journal of Psychiatric Practice, 13*(1), 25–32.

Lutsky, I., Hopwood, M., Abram, S. E., Jacobson, G. R., Haddox, J. D., & Kampine, J. P. (1993, October). Psychoactive substance use among American anesthesiologists: A 30-year retrospective study. *Canadian Journal of Anaesthesia, 40*(10), 915–921.

McAuliffe, W. E., Rohman, M., Santangelo, S., Feldman, B., Magnuson, E., & Sobol, A. (1986, September 25). Psychoactive drug use among practicing physicians and medical students. *New England Journal of Medicine, 315*(13), 805–810.

McAuliffe, W. E., Rohman, M., Breer, P., Wyshak, G., Santangelo, S., & Magnuson, E. (1991, February). Alcohol use and abuse in random samples of physicians and medical students. *American Journal of Public Health, 81*(2), 177–182.

Menk, E. J., Baumgarten, R. K., Kingsley, C. P., Culling, R. D., & Middaugh, R. (1990, June 13). Success of reentry into anesthesiology training programs by residents with a history of substance abuse. *Journal of the American Medical Association, 263*(22), 3060–3062.

Moore, N. N., & Bostwick, J. M. (1999, July–August). Ketamine dependence in anesthesia providers. *Psychosomatics, 40*(4), 356–359.

Morrison, J., & Wickersham, P. (1998, June 17). Physicians disciplined by a state medical board. *Journal of the American Medical Association, 279*(23),1889–1893.

Nace, E. P. (1995). *Achievement and addiction: A guide to the treatment of professionals.* Chicago: Brunner/ Mazel.

Notman, M. T., & Khantzian, E. J. (1987). Psychotherapy with the substance-dependent physician: pitfalls and strategies. *American Journal of Psychotherapy, 41*(2),220–230.

O'Connor, P. G., & Spickard, Jr., A. (1997). Physician impairment by substance abuse. *Medical Clinics of North America, 81*,1037–1052.

Paris, R. T., & Canavan, D. I. (1999). Physician substance abuse impairment: anesthesiologists vs. other specialties. *Journal of Addictive Diseases, 18*(1), 1–7.

Pelton, C., & Ikeda, R. M. (1991, October–December). The California Physicians Diversion Program's experience with recovering anesthesiologists. *Journal of Psychoactive Drugs, 23*(4), 427–431.

Shaw, M. F., McGovern, M. P., Angres, D. H., & Rawal, P. (2004, September). Physicians and nurses with substance use disorders. *Journal of Advanced Nursing, 47*(5), 561–71.

Skipper, G. E. (1997). Treating the chemically dependent health professional, *Journal of Addictive Diseases, 16*(3), 67–74.

Skipper, G. E., Fletcher, C., Rocha-Judd, R., & Brase, D. (2004). Tramadol abuse and dependence among physicians. *Journal of the American Medical Association, 292*(15), 1818–1819.

Skipper, G. E., Weinmann, W., Theirauf, A., Schaefer, P., Wiesbeck, G., & Allen, J. P. (2004). Ethyl Glucuronide: A biomarker to identify alcohol use by health professionals recovering from substance use disorders. *Alcohol & Alcoholism, 39,* 445–449.

Storr, C. L., Trinkoff, A. M., & Hughes, P. (2000, August). Similarities of substance use between medical and nursing specialities. *Substance Use & Misuse, 35*(10),1443–1469.

Stoudemire, A, & Rhoads, J. M. (1983). When the doctor needs a doctor: Special considerations for the physician-patient. *Annals of Internal Medicine, 98*(Part 1), 654–659.

Talbott, G. D., Gallegos, K. V., Wilson, P. O., Porter, T. L. (1987). The Medical Association of Georgia's Impaired Physician Program. Review of the first 1,000 physicians: analysis of specialty. *Journal of the American Medical Association, 257,* 2927–2930.

Smith, P. C. (1991). Treatment outcomes of impaired physicians in Oklahoma. *Journal of Oklahoma State Medical Association. 84*(12), 599–603.

Vaillant, G. E., Sobowale, N. C., & McArthur, C. (1972, August 24). Some psychologic vulnerabilities of physicians. *New England Journal of Medicine, 287*(8), 372–375.

Wischmeyer, P. E., Johnson, B. R., Wilson, J. E., Dingmann, C., Bachman, H. M., & Roller, E., et al. (2007, October). A survey of propofol abuse in academic anesthesia programs. *Anesthesia & Analgesia,105*(4),1066–1071.

Wunsch, M. J., Knisely, J. S., Cropsey, K. L., Campbell, E. D., & Schnoll, S. H. (2007). Women physicians and addiction. *Journal of Addictive Diseases, 26*(2), 35–43.

GREGORY E. SKIPPER
ROBERT L. DUPONT

PLANTS, DRUGS FROM.

Humans have used their local plants for medicinal effects since prehistoric times. They gathered and ate plants and noticed the effects that some offered—whether therapeutic, mind-altering, or toxic. From trial and error they fashioned associations between cause and effect, keeping certain mushrooms, roots, barks, leaves, or berries for certain situations—the treatment of accidents, ill health, childbirth, coughs, fevers, rashes, and so on. Over the centuries, people established herbal medicine, as it is now called; they had also found certain plants that produced immediate and mind-altering effects, many of which were relegated to religious ritual. By the nineteenth century, Europeans had developed the science of chemistry to the point at which they could isolate and concentrate the activator in many plants.

If experimentation with plant materials has led to such cures as quinine for malaria or digitalis for heart disease, it has also led to the discovery of unpleasant effects or the discovery of poisons. From the literally thousands of substances that have been self-administered over the centuries, only a few continue to be used for nonmedicinal purposes. Even fewer have given rise to serious problems of chronic use and dependence. The legal and readily available drugs that are found naturally in plants (e.g., nicotine, caffeine) or are derived from plants (e.g., alcohol) will be described here first because the use and abuse of these drugs is more widespread than all the other abused drugs combined. The health problems associated with the chronic use of alcohol and tobacco are therefore a very serious problem in our society, not only because of the large number of people who suffer and die each year from the direct toxic effects of these drugs but also because of the costs—the absenteeism from work and the unnecessary health care costs. The illegal drugs will be discussed next; although the illicit use of marijuana, cocaine, opioids, and psychedelics remains a major social, legal, financial, and health problem in the United States today, the proportion of the population physically dependent on these drugs is actually relatively low—only a small fraction of a percent. Finally, it is important to note that people often do not restrict their drug use to a single type. Alcohol users typically smoke cigarettes and may sometimes use other drugs as well. Heroin users may also smoke and consume alcohol, marijuana, coffee or colas, and in some instances various stimulants. Multiple drug use is therefore a relatively common occurrence.

ALCOHOL

Alcohol is perhaps the most widespread drug in use worldwide. It forms naturally by the fermentation process of plant materials and has been produced on purpose since at least Neolithic times, when grains were first farmed, harvested, stored, and processed into gruels, porridges, puddings, and so forth. Often these spoiled, forming a fermented base. Alcohol is made as well from other starchy or sugary plant materials, such as fruits, canes, roots, and such. Fermentation (also called anaerobic respiration, or glycolysis) is the chemical process by which living cells, such as yeast, use sugar in the absence of air to produce part or even all of their energy requirements. In fermentation, sugar molecules are converted to alcohol and lactic acid. Beer, wine, and cheese production, as well as certain modern commercial processes, require fermentation by specific kinds of yeast, bacteria, and molds.

Ethyl alcohol, also called ethanol, is the type of alcohol that is usually produced for human consumption. In its pure form, alcohol is a clear liquid with little odor. People drink it primarily in three kinds of beverages: (1) beers, which are made from grains through brewing and fermentation and normally contain from 3 to 8 percent alcohol; (2) wines, which are fermented from fruits, such as grapes, and naturally contain from 8 to 12 percent alcohol (up to 21% when fortified by adding more ethanol); (3) beverages or spirits, which are distilled from a fermented base, such as whiskey, gin, or vodka. Spirits contain about 40 to 50 percent alcohol, on average (often expressed in proof, so that 40% equals 80 proof; 50% is 100 proof).

NICOTINE AND TOBACCO

Tobacco is a tall herbaceous plant, the leaves of which are harvested, cured, and rolled into cigars, shredded for use in cigarettes and pipes, and processed for chewing or snuff. Tobacco has become a commercial crop in almost all tropical countries as well as in many temperate ones. The main source of commercial tobacco is *Nicotiana tabacum*, although *Nicotiana rustica* is also grown and is used in Asian tobaccos. Tobacco has been developed to yield a wide range of morphologically different types, from the small-leaved aromatic tobaccos to the large broad-leaved cigar tobaccos. Tobacco is native to South America, where it was used in a drink for ritual purposes long before inhaling the smoke of the dried plant material was first documented by the Maya more than 2,000 years ago. Tobacco was then traded and grown in Central America; it moved into Mexico and the Caribbean and eventually into North America by about 800 CE. The Arawaks of the Caribbean smoked tobacco; during Columbus's voyage of 1492, he found the Arawaks smoking loosely rolled cigars. The Spanish took tobacco seeds to Europe, where Jean Nicot, France's ambassador to Portugal, sent tobacco to Paris in 1560 and gave the plant the name of its genus (*Nicotiana*). In England, Sir Walter Raleigh began the popularization of pipe smoking in 1586, and the cultivation and consumption of tobacco spread with each voyage of discovery from Europe. Two kinds of tobacco were traded between Europe and America: "Spanish," from the West Indies and South America, and "Virginia," from the British plantations in their

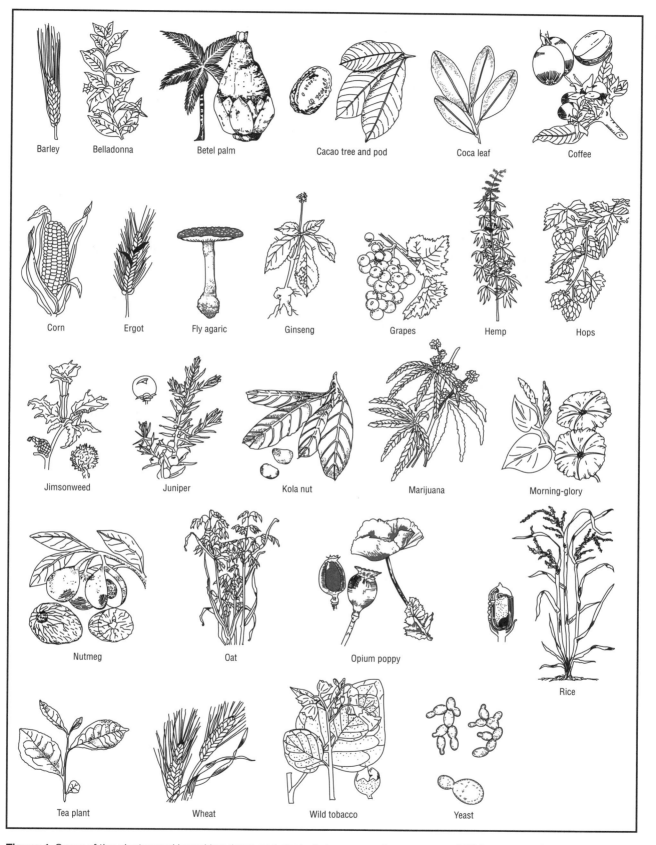

Figure 1. Some of the plants used in making drugs and alcoholic beverages. ILLUSTRATION BY GGS INFORMATION SERVICES. GALE, CENGAGE LEARNING

colony of Virginia. Despite its popularity in England, King James I forbade its production there since he vehemently disapproved of tobacco. Europeans at first smoked their tobacco in pipes, and later in cigars. It was often provided free to drinkers of coffee in coffee houses and cafés, as was the new product sugar. (Both remain strongly associated with coffee drinking.) Cigarettes spread in popularity only after the Crimean War (1854–1856), and their spread was especially aided by the first cigarette-making machine, developed in the United States in 1881.

Nicotine is the most powerful ingredient of the tobacco plant, found primarily in the leaves. Nicotine is an extremely poisonous, colorless, oily alkaloid that turns brown upon exposure to air. Nicotine can affect the central nervous system, resulting in respiratory failure and general paralysis. Nicotine can also be absorbed through the skin. Only two to three drops—less than 50 milligrams—of the pure alkaloid placed on the tongue can be rapidly fatal to an adult. A typical cigarette contains 15 to 20 milligrams of nicotine; however, the actual amount that reaches the bloodstream (and therefore the brain) through normal smoking is only about 1 milligram. Nicotine is responsible for most of the short-term as well as the long-term effects of smoking and plays a major role in the reinforcing properties.

CAFFEINE

Caffeine is an odorless, slightly bitter, alkaloid chemical found in coffee beans, tea leaves, and kola nuts, and several other plants used by humans such as cacao (chocolate) and maté (a South American holly used as a popular drink). In small amounts, caffeine acts as a mild stimulant and is harmless to most people. In large amounts, however, caffeine can result in insomnia, restlessness, and cardiac irregularities.

Tea. Tea is the beverage made when the processed leaves of the tea plant are infused with boiling water. Native to Southeast Asia, the tea plant, *Camellia sinensis*, is a small shrub-like evergreen tree that belongs to the family Theaceae. The seeds of the tea plant contain a volatile oil, and its leaves contain the chemicals caffeine and tannin. Although second to coffee in commercial value, tea ranks first as the most frequently consumed beverage. More

than 50 percent of the world's population drink some form of tea every day. Many also use tea medicinally as a stimulant. The tea plant originated in the region encompassing Tibet, western China, and northern India. According to ancient Chinese legend, the emperor Shen-Nung learned how to brew the beverage in 2737 BCE, when a few leaves from the plant accidentally fell into water he was boiling. Tea leaves began to be processed in China (dried, smoked, fermented, pressed, etc.) and were sold in cakes of steamed leaves, as powder, or in leaf form. Tea was introduced by Chinese Buddhist monks into Japan (9th to 13th centuries), where the preparation and consumption of tea developed into the ritual tea ceremony called *cha no yu*. Tea culture then spread into Java, the Dutch East Indies, and other tropical and subtropical areas. British merchants formed the East India Company (1600–1858) and introduced teas from China and India into England, the American colonies, and throughout the British Empire.

Coffee. The coffee bean is the world's most valuable legal agricultural commodity. In 1982, for example, the coffee-importing bill for the United States alone was 2.537 billion dollars. Of the many varieties of the genus *Coffea* (family Rubiaceae) known to exist, only two species have significant commercial importance—*C. arabica* and *C. robusta* together constitute 99 percent of production. Coffee is native to the Ethiopian highlands and has been cultivated and brewed in Arab countries for centuries. The drink was introduced into Europe in the mid-seventeenth century and European colonial plantations were established in Indonesia, the West Indies, and Brazil, soon making coffee cultivation an important element in imperialist economies. Today, Latin America and Africa produce most of the world's coffee. The United States is the largest importer, having broken with the British tea tradition during the Revolutionary War to maintain the new American drink of coffee instead (purchased from non-British sources). In 2006 the United States imported 24 million bags of coffee, 25 percent of the world's supply.

MARIJUANA

Marijuana is the common name given to any drug preparation derived from the hemp plant, *Cannabis sativa*. Two varieties of this plant are *Cannabis sativa* variety *indica* and variety *americana*. The several forms of this drug are known by various names throughout the world, such as *kif* in Morocco, *dagga* in South America, and *ganja* in India. Hashish refers to a dried resinous substance collected from the flowering tops of the plant (also known as *charas* in Asia). In Western culture, cannabis preparations have acquired a variety of slang names, including grass, pot, tea, reefer, weed, and Mary Jane or MJ. Cannabis has been smoked, eaten in baked goods, and drunk in beverages. In Western cultures, marijuana is prepared most often from the dried leaves and flowering shoots of the plant as a tobaccolike mixture that is smoked in a pipe or rolled into a cigarette. As one of the oldest known drugs, cannabis was acknowledged as early as 2700 BCE in a Chinese manuscript. Throughout the centuries, it has been used both medicinally and as an intoxicant. The major psychoactive component of this drug, however, was not known until the mid-1960s. This ingredient is tetrahydro-cannabinol, commonly known as THC. Psychoactive compounds (cannabinoids) are found in all parts of the male and female plants, with the greatest concentrations found in the flowering tops. The content of these compounds varies greatly from plant to plant, depending on genetic and environmental factors.

COCAINE

Cocaine is an alkaloid drug found in the leaves of the coca plant, the common name of a shrub, *Erythroxylum coca*, of the coca family, Erythroxylaceae. Coca is densely leaved and grows to heights of 8 feet (2.5 m). It is cultivated in its native South America but also in Africa, Southeast Asia, and Australia for the narcotic alkaloids of its leaves, particularly cocaine. Whole or powdered dried leaves, usually mixed with lime (calcium carbonate), have been chewed by the people of what is now Colombia, Bolivia, and Peru for centuries, to dull the sense of hunger and to lessen fatigue. The coca shrub should not be confused with the cacao tree, the source of cocoa and chocolate.

Cocaine was first used in Western medicine as a local anesthetic. In 1884 it was used by Carl Koller, an ophthalmologic surgeon. Historically, the chief medical use for cocaine has been as a local anesthetic, especially for the nose, throat, and cornea, because of its effectiveness in depressing nerve endings. Cocaine has been largely replaced by less toxic, synthetic local anesthetics. Used systemically, cocaine stimulates the central nervous system, producing feelings of excitation, elation, well-being, enhanced physical strength and mental capacity, and a lessened sense of fatigue. It also results, however, in increases in heart rate, blood pressure, and temperature, and its use can result in death. Cocaine use became popular because of its stimulating properties. In Western countries, it is frequently ingested by sniffing its fine white powder, often called snow. It is sometimes injected intravenously, although repeated injections can result in skin abscesses, hepatitis, and the spread of AIDS. Cocaine can also be inhaled (smoked) once it has been converted to its freebase form; some preparations of freebase cocaine are known as rock or crack. Crack cocaine gained popularity in the late 1980s and early 1990s because it is relatively inexpensive as a single dose, (e.g., $10 to $20 per "hit"); usually smoked in a special pipe, it produces an intense euphoria as it is rapidly absorbed from the lungs and carried by the blood directly to the brain.

OPIUM

Opium is a drug obtained from the juice of the immature seed pods of the oriental poppy, *Papaver somniferum*. There are over 20 natural alkaloids of opium, including codeine and morphine. Morphine is the largest component and it contributes most significantly to opium's physiological effects. Heroin (diacetylmorphine) was derived from morphine and is the most important drug synthesized from opium's natural alkaloids. As a folk medicine, opium has been used to relieve pain, reduce such drives as hunger and thirst, induce sleep, and ease anxiety and depression. Opium and some of its derivatives are highly addictive, and their use has led to abuse and serious drug problems. Drugs derived from opium are still used widely in medicine, despite the development of such synthetic opioid drugs as meperidine (Demerol). The therapeutic effects of the opioids include pain relief, suppression of the cough reflex, slowing of respiration, and slowing of the action of the gastrointestinal tract. Opium's constipating effect led to its initial use, in the form of paregoric, in treating diarrheas and dysenteries. The main producers and exporters of opium are located in India and Turkey. About 750 tons (680 metric tons) of opium are annually needed to meet medical uses worldwide.

Opioids have been used since ancient times both for medicinal purposes and for pleasure. Opium was taken orally as a pill or added to beverages for centuries in the Middle East, India, and Asia. Addiction did not become a widespread problem until the practice of opium smoking was introduced by the British from India into China in the late seventeenth century (in an effort to gain a trade opening to the "closed" empire of China). China attempted to deal with the problem by restricting the cultivation and importation of opium in the nineteenth century. This restriction led to the Opium Wars (1839–1842), since the opium trade became highly profitable to the British East India Company. Britain won over China, and opium was sold to the Chinese through treaty ports until the twentieth century.

In Europe and North America in the eighteenth century, opioids became widely used as most effective and reliable analgesics (painkillers). Heroin was developed in Germany in the 1890s and used from 1898 as a cough suppressant and analgesic with the hope that it would not lead to addiction, as did morphine (from which it was derived). From the first year or two after introduction, some clinicians agreed that it did not show addictive properties. A few even suggested that it might be useful in treating people addicted to morphine. Within a few years it became clear that, like morphine, the use of heroin could lead to addiction comparable in gravity to that of morphine.

On the street, opium is sold as a dark brown chunk of gum (from the pod of the opium poppy) or in dried powdered form. It is smoked, eaten, and drunk or injected as a solution for medicinal and recreational purposes. Indian and Chinese immigrants brought the practices with them, but the number of users is not great. During the early phases of addiction, opium produces a feeling of euphoria or well-being. With time, one may become dependent through physical and emotional factors. Tolerance develops and larger and larger doses of the drug are required to produce the same effect. If denied access to the drug, an addict will experience severe withdrawal symptoms; sudden withdrawal in a heavily dependent person has occasionally been fatal.

MESCALINE

Peyote, or mescal, is the common name of the small spineless cactus *Lophophora williamsii*, found in the southwestern United States and northcentral Mexico. Peyote is used in Native American religious rituals, primarily for its hallucinogenic effects. At the end of the nineteenth century, Arthur Heffter demonstrated that mescaline (3,4,5-trimethoxyphenethylamine) is responsible for peyote's pharmacological effects. Mescaline is related to the amphetamines. When ingested, it can produce hallucinations, frequently of a visual nature, characterized by vivid colors, designs, and a distorted space perception. It stimulates the autonomic nervous system and can cause nausea, vomiting, sweating, tachycardia (rapid heartbeat), pupillary dilation, and anxiety. The use of peyote in Native American ritual, referred to as Peyotism, was documented by Europeans in the sixteenth century. The modern practice of the peyote-based religion began in the late nineteenth century, was widely practiced by Native Americans in the southwestern United States, and was incorporated as the Native American Church in 1918. This church claimed more than 200,000 members in the 1960s. From the church member's point of view, peyote symbolizes spiritual power; the peyote "button"—the dried top of the cactus—is eaten as a sacrament to induce a hallucinogenic trance (of a few hours duration) for communion with God.

PSILOCYBIN

Psilocybin is the active substance contained in the fruiting bodies of the *Psilocybe mexicana* mushroom (called the magic mushroom); it is a potent hallucinogen that can cause psychological disturbances. Taken orally or injected, the drug produces effects similar to those of the chemically unrelated LSD (lysergic acid diethylamide), and cross-tolerance has been experienced between psilocybin, LSD, and mescaline. The use of psilocybin is illegal in the United States, except for the direct consumption of mushrooms by a few religious groups as part of their ritual.

OTHER SUBSTANCES

Throughout the world, many other natural plant substances are used for mind- and mood-altering effects. These include the use of the KAVA root (*Piper methysticum*) for an intoxicating drink in the South Pacific; indole-containing snuff (distilled from indigo, genus *Indigofera*) among the Amazonian Indians of Brazil; khat leaves of a bush indigenous to East Africa containing an amphetamine-like drug (cathinone); betel nut derived from the betel palm (*Areca catechu*) and widely used throughout the Pacific rim; and fly agaric (a toxic mushroom, *Amanita muscaria*) among the Uralic-speaking tribes of Siberia.

See also **Alcohol: History of Drinking (International); Ginseng; Ibogaine; Jimsonweed; Morning Glory Seeds; Nutmeg; Opiates/Opioids; Paregoric; Tobacco: Tobacco Industry.**

BIBLIOGRAPHY

Bloom, F. E. (1988). Neurobiology of alcohol action and alcoholism. *Annual Review of Psychiatry, 8,* 347–360.

Lewis, W. H. (2005). *Medical botany: Plants affecting human health.* Hoboken, NJ: John Wiley & Sons.

O'Brien, C. P. (1996). Drug addiction and drug abuse. In J. G. Hardman et al. (Eds.), *The Pharmacological basis of therapeutics,* 9th ed. New York: McGraw-Hill Medical. (2005, 11th ed.)

Reisine, T., & Pasternak, G. (1996) Opioid analgesics and antagonists. In J. G. Hardman et al. (Eds.), *The Pharmacological basis of therapeutics,* 9th ed. New York: McGraw-Hill Medical. (2005, 11th ed.)

Schultes, R. E. (1981). Coca in the northwest Amazon. *Journal of Ethnopharmacology, 3,* 173–194.

Schultes, R. E. (1969). Hallucinogens of plant origin. *Science, 163,* 245–247.

Siegel, R. K. (2005). *Intoxication: The universal drive for mind-altering substances.* Rochester, VT: Park Street Press.

Spinella, M. (2005). *Concise handbook of psychoactive herbs.* New York: Haworth Press.

Spinella, M. (2001). *The psychopharmacology of herbal medicine: Plant drugs that alter mind, brain, and behavior.* Cambridge, MA: MIT Press.

NICK E. GOEDERS

POISON. A substance that, when introduced into the body in relatively small quantities, causes destruction or malfunction of some tissues and organs. Depending on the quantity in the body (the dose), a poison can kill. The word *poison* usually implies that a substance has no healthful use and is to be considered dangerous even in small quantities. Most common household substances are poisonous, including bleach, ammonia, drain cleaners, paint supplies, and so on.

SUBSTANCES CAUSING DEATHS FROM ACCIDENTAL POISONING

DRUGS

Analgesics and antipyretics
Sedatives and hypnotics
Tranquilizers
Antidepressants
Other psychotropic agents
Other drugs acting on the nervous system
Antibiotics and other antimicrobial agents
Cardiovascular drugs
Hormones
Hematological agents
Other drugs

OTHER SUBSTANCES

Alcohols
Cleaning and polishing agents and paint
Petroleum products
Pesticides
Corrosives and caustics

GASES

Utility gas
Carbon monoxide
Nitrogen oxides
Freon
Other gases

In the practice of medicine, many useful drugs, such as antibiotics for treating infections or antihypertensive drugs for treating high blood pressure, can be poisonous or toxic in higher doses. Almost all drugs that are abused can be poisonous or toxic; some, even at relatively low doses.

A few drugs that are commonly used in medicine in small amounts to produce important therapeutic effects are also used in other contexts as poisons. For example, the drug warfarin is used medically as an anticoagulant (to increase the time it takes blood to clot), an important effect for people who have had strokes or heart-valve replacement—but warfarin is also used as rat poison, because when rats eat it in large amounts they die soon after from massive hemorrhages. The same mustard gas (nitrogen mustards) that, as poison gas, caused much death and suffering in World War I, actually has medical use in the treatment of certain leukemias. Similarly, a series of extremely potent chemicals were developed during World

War II as nerve gases for warfare, which act by flooding the body with excess acetylcholine (a body substance necessary for synaptic transmission), causing muscle paralysis and death. Consequently, close chemical relatives of some of the most potent nerve gases ever developed are being used to treat such medical disorders as myasthenia gravis, in which there is not enough acetylcholine in nerve endings.

Treatment of someone who has been poisoned may require removal of the poison from the body (e.g., with the use of a stomach pump for ingested poisons), administration of an antidote if one exists, or simply support in repairing the damage done to the body. Many cities have a telephone "hot line" or poison-control center number where information about poisons, antidotes, and actions to take in case of poisoning can be obtained; often, the staff will alert emergency medical service (EMS) units to arrive in mere minutes. In case of a poisoning, including a drug overdose, it is essential to call for expert medical help as quickly as possible to minimize damage to the victim.

See also **Complications: Medical and Behavioral Toxicity Overview; Drug Types; Inhalants.**

BIBLIOGRAPHY

Klaassen, C. D. (1996). Principles of toxicology and treatment of poisoning. In J. G. Hardman et al. (Eds.), *The Pharmacological basis of therapeutics*, 9th ed. New York: McGraw-Hill Medical. (2005, 11th ed.)

Klaassen, C. D. (Ed.) (2007). *Casarett & Doull's toxicology: The basic science of poisons*, 7th ed. New York: McGraw-Hill.

MICHAEL J. KUHAR

POLYDRUG ABUSE. This term refers to the common observation that individuals who are considered drug abusers often abuse more than one type of drug. Almost all drug abusers smoke nicotine cigarettes and a large proportion consume alcoholic beverages, but many of them do not consider the co-occurrence of these two forms of drug use as an instance of polydrug abuse.

There are several types of polydrug abusers. They include those who abuse two or more substances but have a definite preference for one; only when they are not able to get supplies of their preferred drug do they abuse other types of drugs. These other types of drugs may be either from the same pharmacological class (e.g., heroin abusers may abuse such other narcotics as codeine or Demerol) or from different pharmacological classes (e.g., stimulant abusers—such as cocaine abusers—may also use heroin, a narcotic). Some polydrug abusers do not necessarily have a favorite drug but instead may select different drugs for consumption at different times (e.g., stimulants in the morning, sedatives at night) or under different conditions.

Polydrug abuse can also refer to the consumption of a drug to counteract an unpleasant effect produced by another drug or by withdrawal from another drug. For example, individuals who take enough stimulants to become highly agitated and aroused may take a tranquilizer to counteract the unpleasant side effects. Finally, polydrug abuse can refer to the consumption of different drugs simultaneously (e.g., speedballs). The assumption is that the different drugs in combination constitute more than the sum of their individual parts, producing a unique, highly reinforcing effect.

See also **Barbiturates; Barbiturates: Complications; Drug Abuse Warning Network (DAWN); Drug Interactions and Alcohol; Prescription Drug Abuse; Sedatives: Adverse Consequences of Chronic Use.**

BIBLIOGRAPHY

Frances, R. J., Miller, S. I., & Mack, A. H. (Eds.) (2005). *Clinical textbook of addictive disorders*, 3rd ed. New York: Guilford Press.

Landry, M. J. (2004). *Understanding drugs of abuse: The processes of addiction, treatment, and recovery*. Washington, D.C.: American Psychiatric Publishers.

CHRIS-ELLYN JOHANSON

PREGNANCY AND DRUG DEPENDENCE. Drug use is most prevalent during the reproductive years. A report from the American College of Obstetricians and Gynecologists (ACOG) reported that among women age 15 to 44 nearly 90 percent have used alcohol, 4 percent have used marijuana, and 14 percent have used cocaine (ACOG, 1994). Although a reduction in substance use may occur during pregnancy, a large number of fetuses are exposed to illicit substances in utero. Based on the Substance Abuse and Mental Health Services Administration's National Survey on Drug Use and Health (NSDUH) among pregnant women, 18 percent reported smoking tobacco, 10 percent reported drinking alcohol, and 4 percent reported using at least one illicit drug in the past month (SAMHSA, 2005). According to this survey, pregnant white women and pregnant Hispanic women had lower rates of past month illicit drug use (4.4 and 3.0%, respectively) than pregnant black women (8%). Further, the rates of illicit drug use during pregnancy were higher among women age 15 to 25 (1.6%) as compared with women age 26 to 44. From the public health perspective the impact of substance use during pregnancy extends far beyond maternal health to that of a large number of the unborn population.

Maternal prenatal substance abuse became an issue for public health debate in the mid-1980s when heightened attention came in response to the emergence of a perceived "crack" epidemic (Lester, Andreozzi & Appiah, 2004). During this time, drug use by pregnant women was seen by some as a moral as well as a public health issue. Since then, there has been an onslaught of attention and research in this area. There have been a number of large-scale studies that have examined substance use during pregnancy, including the National Institute on Drug Abuse's National Pregnancy and Health Survey, the National Center for Health Statistics' National Maternal and Health Survey, and the National Longitudinal Survey.

EXPERIENCE OF SUBSTANCE-USING PREGNANT WOMEN

Substance-using pregnant women are often stigmatized, which in turn may cause them to deny their drug use, to not acknowledge its possible harmful effects, and to not seek help. Fear of negative repercussions may limit their use of medical and social welfare systems. Women who are chronic heroin, marijuana, or cocaine abusers are often already in sufficiently poor health, compromising the growth and well-being of the fetus. The most frequently encountered medical complications in women who abuse drugs during pregnancy include anemia and various infections such as pneumonia, hepatitis, urinary tract infections, and sexually transmitted diseases. In addition, these women are at risk for infection with human immunodeficiency virus (HIV).

HIV has been increasingly linked to drug use. The practice of sharing contaminated needles to inject heroin or cocaine, the practice of prostitution in order to procure money for drugs, or the direct sex-for-drugs transaction associated with crack smoking have all contributed to this serious international health crisis. Although the exact risk of an infected mother passing the disease to her offspring is not precisely known, it is estimated that in the absence of detection and treatment, the rate of perinatal HIV transmission is approximately 25 percent (Olges et al., 2007). In addition to many potential medical problems, the lifestyle of pregnant addicts is burdensome. Associated risks include unemployment, poverty, prostitution, physical abuse, stress, depression, and lack of social support.

IMPACT ON FETAL WELFARE

Teratology is the study of perinatal developmental injury or abnormal development, and of the causative factors which include birth accidents and genetic mutations that increase the risk of developmental injury. Behavioral teratology investigates the developmental impact of exposure to exogenous agents (e.g., illicit substances) or of events during different critical periods on the developing brain, and hence, on the child's psychological development. The impact of individual exposures is assessed using varying levels of analysis (e.g., behavioral, neuropsychological, neurochemical, neuropathological) and at varying distances in time starting from the initial fetal exposure. There are ten basic principles central to behavioral teratology investigation (Mayes & Ward, 2003; Vorhees & Mollnow, 1987; Wilson, 1973, 1977):

1. Delineate the possible mechanisms of teratogenic effect.
2. Define the specific teratogenic agent.
3. Specify the timing of the exposure (there are differing windows of vulnerability in the developing fetus).
4. Define the nature of the exposure (route, amount, and duration).
5. Delineate the range of susceptibility and response relationships.
6. Select those groups at greater or lesser risk for exposure.

7. Consider the environmental context and conditions most related to the exposure.

8. Define the outcomes most likely to be related to the mechanism of action of the exposure agent or event (it may be that the context of drug abuse greatly alters the child's care giving environment).

9. Consider when exposure-related outcomes are most likely to become apparent (not all effects are apparent in the perinatal period).

10. Take into account those conditions that ameliorate or exacerbate any exposure-related functional outcomes (effects may be exacerbated or ameliorated by other exposures or environmental conditions).

Fetal exposure to illicit substance use, like other exogenous agents, is neither specific nor discrete; the outcomes are not uniformly present even with documented exposure, and the severity or extent of the deformity or developmental abnormality is variable. Abuse of one or multiple drugs rarely occurs independent of other developmentally salient variables. Parental health during pregnancy is usually compromised and more often than not, substance-using mothers receive little or no prenatal care. Exposure to nearly all illicit substances during pregnancy may at the very least influence fetal growth and contribute to intrauterine growth retardation and perhaps prematurity. Important covariates include those broadly describing postnatal parental/care-giving function. Indeed, variables such as ongoing parental substance use, neglect and abuse, parental depression, exposure to violence as witness or victim, homelessness, parental separation, and parental loss are common events for children growing up in substance-using families.

In sum, a difficulty in evaluating the effects of illicit drugs is the range of sociodemographic, psychosocial, behavioral, and biological risk factors associated with both illicit drug use and adverse pregnancy outcomes. It is challenging to determine the extent to which adverse outcomes are due to the direct effects of the drug versus the surrounding social conditions (Mayes & Ward, 2003). The accumulation of numerous risk factors appears to have a greater negative impact on child development than any single risk factor. As such, complex models that include interactions between the exposure agent and the environment are essential.

IMPACT OF OPIOIDS, COCAINE, AND MARIJUANA

Opioids. Newborns that have been prenatally exposed to opiates (heroin or methadone) are born passively addicted to the drug and exhibit withdrawal symptoms in the first days to weeks after delivery. Numerous studies have also replicated the finding that prenatal opioid exposure reduces birth weight and head circumference (e.g., Hans, 1992). Prenatal exposure to opiates also contributes significantly to an increased incidence of sudden infant death syndrome (SIDS). In some studies the incidence of SIDS is eight times that reported for non-opiate-exposed infants (Rosen & Johnson, 1982; Hans, 1992).

Neurobehavioral assessments in the newborn period found that opiate-exposed infants are more easily aroused and more irritable (Jeremy & Hans, 1985). They exhibit less time in quiet sleep compared to active sleep and show increased muscle tone and poor motor control (e.g., tremulousness and jerky movements). Opiate-exposed infants are less often in alert states and are more difficult to bring to an alert state. The dramatic neurobehavioral abnormalities seen in the newborn period generally diminish during the first month of life for the majority of infants, and are thus assumed to reflect the transitory symptoms of narcotic withdrawal rather than evidence of permanent neurological dysfunction (Jeremy & Hans, 1985).

Infancy studies have shown some persistent problems in poor motor coordination, high activity level, and poor focused attention among opiate-exposed infants in the first year of life (Hans, 1992). These state and motor regulatory difficulties make it hard for even a well-functioning adult in a relatively low-stress environment to care for the infant, and present significant problems for an opiate-addicted adult who is experiencing his or her own state and attentional regulatory difficulties.

Follow-up studies through the early childhood of opiate-exposed children compared with non-opiate-exposed children have reported few or no differences in cognitive performance. However, opiate-exposed school-age children show higher activity levels, are often impulsive with poor self-control, show poor motor coordination, and have more difficulty with tasks requiring focused attention (Wilson, 1989).

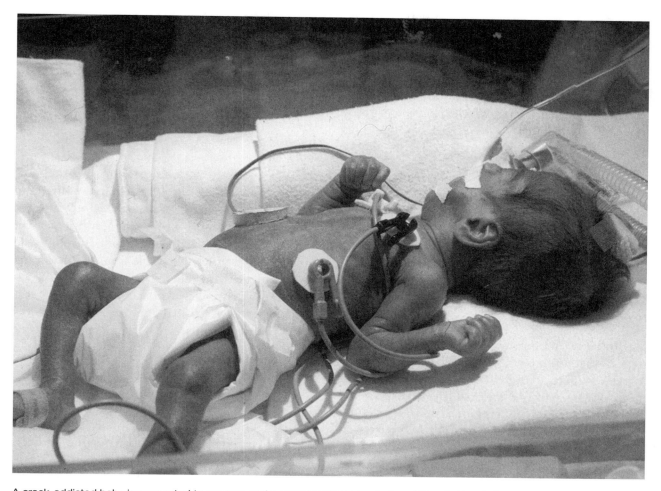

A crack-addicted baby is connected to sensors and a respirator in an incubator at Lincoln Hospital in New York. Crack-addicted babies usually exhibit irritability, nasal congestion, respiratory distress, seizures, and often have knee and nose abrasions. JOHN CHIASSON/GETTY IMAGES.

There are few studies past the years of early childhood of the long-term effects of prenatal opiate exposure. Data suggest that, by adolescence, opiate-exposed children exhibit an increased incidence of behavior and conduct problems including impulsivity, involvement in criminal activities or in early substance abuse, more antisocial behavior, and increased school dropout. It is not clear how much these problems in conduct and impulse regulation are attributable to persistent effects of prenatal opiate exposure and how much they are the consequence of cumulative exposure to the discord and dysfunction often characterizing substance-abusing households. In addition, the potential exists for these behaviors to reflect an inherited predisposition to conduct disorder and antisocial personality disorder, both of which are highly associated with substance dependence.

Cocaine. Cocaine has been studied extensively because of a rapid rise in its use during the 1980s and public concern over the purported "crack baby" phenomenon. The chemical properties of cocaine allow it to cross the placenta easily and enter the fetus. The passage from maternal circulation to the fetus is enhanced by the injection or smoking of cocaine. In addition, because of acid/base balance issues and low levels of certain enzymes, which usually metabolize the drug, accumulation of cocaine in the fetus occurs. Furthermore, the "binge" pattern commonly associated with cocaine use may lead to even higher levels of cocaine in the fetus. Transfer of cocaine appears to be greatest in the first and third trimesters of pregnancy. In the first trimester, prenatal cocaine exposure may have a direct effect on neuronal migration and brain structure formation whereas in the third trimester the effect may be on synaptogenesis (i.e., the formation of new synapses between nerve cells) in specific brain regions (Hadeed & Siegel, 1989).

The use of cocaine by the mother may also affect the course of labor. Crack appears to directly increase contractions of the uterus and may thus precipitate the onset of premature labor. Higher rates of early fetal loss and third-trimester separations of the placenta appear to be major complications of maternal cocaine use. Increased blood pressure and increased body temperature caused by cocaine may be responsible for early fetal loss and later separation of the placenta. The latter is hazardous to the fetus and the mother because of associated bleeding, shock, and the chance of death for both, if an emergency cesarean section is not performed (Hadeed & Siegel, 1989).

In terms of outcomes it now appears that early reports that portrayed children who were exposed to cocaine in utero as irreparably doomed and damaged were exaggerated. Although still inconclusive on many crucial issues, published studies to date nonetheless reveal evidence of cocaine-related effects on the neuropsychological functions subserving arousal and attention regulation and reactivity to stressful conditions (Mayes et al., 1998). In studies of newborns and 3- to 6-month-old cocaine-exposed infants, impairments have been reported in startle-responsiveness, auditory information processing, habituation, recognition memory, and reactivity to novelty. Studies suggest persisting problems into school-age, specifically, small deficits in intelligence and academic skills including poor sustained attention, more disorganization, and less abstract thinking.

Infants prenatally exposed to cocaine are often also exposed to a number of other risk factors that may also contribute to impaired development. First, these may include exposure to other substances of abuse including alcohol and tobacco as well as opiates, marijuana, and amphetamines. Second, infants postnatally exposed to cocaine that continue to be exposed to ongoing parental substance abuse are more often neglected and abused, and they have parents who are more frequently depressed and have higher overall stress and anxiety. Adults who are under the influence of cocaine are less able to respond adequately to their children at any given age. Third, the psychological/personality factors that lead an adult to substance abuse may have genetic implications for the fetus. These factors alone or in conjunction influence the observed developmental outcomes including attentional and arousal regulatory functions, language development, and emotional regulation (Mayes & Truman, 2002).

Marijuana. After alcohol, marijuana is the most commonly abused drug in the United States, and like alcohol, marijuana abuse cuts across different socioeconomic groups and strata. Marijuana has an indirect effect on fetal oxygenation through the high level of carbon monoxide found in marijuana smoke (higher than that in cigarette smoke), which in turn results in fetal hypoxia. This type of effect may influence fetal growth, particularly in instances of heavy marijuana use.

Characteristics of newborns exposed to heavy maternal marijuana use are tremors and increased startle in the first 7 to 14 days of life (Levy & Koren, 1992). Changes in sleep patterns have also been reported. Longer-term studies of the outcome of prenatal marijuana exposure are few in number. There is limited support for an impact on IQ in childhood. Behaviorally, children exposed to marijuana prenatally may show increased impulsivity and difficulties with sustained attention (Fried et al., 1992). There is a suggestion that by early adolescence those children exposed to marijuana prenatally may have more difficulty with complex visual processing, though follow-up through adolescence is warranted to determine the course of this effect.

Each of these presumed effects relating prenatal drug exposure to neurobehavioral and developmental dysfunctions must be viewed in the context of the postnatal substance-abusing environment in which many prenatally drug-exposed children remain. As already described, postnatal drug use carries a number of risks to children's development. These include exposure to extreme, often chronic violence, virtual homelessness, poverty, parental neglect and abuse, and parental depression and associated psychopathology. Each of these factors in turn influences the parenting behaviors of adults who are also substance abusers.

AMELIORATING THE EFFECTS

There is no clear empirical evidence as to what treatment modality is best for substance-using mothers. However, there is a general consensus that providing comprehensive multidisciplinary drug-treatment services and prenatal care for addicts will significantly reduce the medical and psychological problems and the death rate in both mothers and infants (Bauer et al., 2002). Comprehensive care may include specialized treatment in a perinatal center where the mother can be provided with comprehensive addictive and obstetrical care, psychosocial counseling, and supportive services (e.g., drug abuse treatment, medical and psychiatric care, public assistance, day care, housing, and vocational counseling). Clinicians must work as part of a well-coordinated team that closely monitors mothers' and children's progress.

Specific to substance use, supportive psychotherapy typically includes counseling, group therapy, lifestyle-change training, exercise, and self-help groups such as Narcotics Anonymous. Relapse prevention methods, which use peer support and learning principles, are directed toward avoiding situations that elicit conditioned cravings for and abuse of substances and toward developing better coping skills. Selective pharmacologic therapy is an important treatment modality. A prime example is methadone, which has been widely used for years in treating opiate dependence during pregnancy. Methadone maintenance reduces the risk of relapse and enhances retention in treatment and prenatal programs. Furthermore, methadone treatment among pregnant women who are opiate-dependent has been shown to improve perinatal outcome (Dashe et al., 2002). Other forms of pharmacologic maintenance therapy are not currently accepted during pregnancy.

To target children's developmental outcomes, maternal-infant attachment should be given special emphasis. After children are born, substance abuse has the potential to disrupt parenting behavior, as the use of illicit drugs can impede awareness of and sensitivity to environmental cues, interfere with emotion regulation, judgment, and aspects of executive functioning, and impair motor skills. All of these abilities are necessary to provide stable, timely, and responsive parenting. Growing evidence suggests that the quality of care in the home environment during the first five years can have a significant impact on children's developmental outcomes such as capacities for self-regulation, autonomy, and evolving expectations for relationships. Thus, the first five years of life represent a window of opportunity within which therapeutic interventions with drug-dependent parents are critical to promote optimal child development. Programs that have demonstrated promise focus on improving the quality of the mother-child relationship. Parenting intervention in this relational approach emphasizes the emotional quality of the relationship between parent and child as the mechanism that promotes optimal child development. These interventions aim to (a) foster flexibility and emotional openness in mothers' mental representations of their children, (b) foster a greater capacity to make accurate inferences about their children's emotional needs, and (c) foster sensitive responses to children's emotional needs (Suchman et al., 2006). This focus on the emotional aspects of the care-giving relationship is critical to sustained improvements in children's long-term psychosocial development.

Care of substance-using pregnant women is complex, difficult, and often demanding. Providers must be aware of the unique psychological and social needs, and the related legal and ethical ramifications surrounding substance use during pregnancy (Lester, Andreozzi, & Appiah, 2004). The goal of comprehensive perinatal care should be to promote safe and healthy pregnancies, improve perinatal outcome, enhance the development of children exposed to illicit substances, and keep the patients from substance abuse after the pregnancy.

See also **Alcohol- and Drug-Exposed Infants; Fetal Alcohol Syndrome; Fetus, Effects of Drugs on the; Injecting Drug Users and HIV; Opioid Complications and Withdrawal; Substance Abuse and AIDS.**

BIBLIOGRAPHY

American College of Obstetricians and Gynecologists. (1994). Substance abuse in pregnancy. *ACOG Technical Bulletin, 195*, 825–831.

Bauer, C. R., Shankaran, S., Bada, H. S., Lester, B., Wright, L. L., Krause-Steinrauf, et al. (2002). The maternal lifestyle study: Drug exposure during pregnancy and short-term maternal outcomes. *American Journal of Obstetrics and Gynecology, 186*, 487–495.

Bendersky, M., Alessandri, S., Gilbert, P., & Lewis, M. (1996). Characteristics of pregnant substance abusers in two cities in the northeast. *American Journal of Drug and Alcohol Abuse, 22*, 349–362.

Dashe, J., Sheffield, J. S., Olscher, D. A., Todd, S. J., Jackson, G. L., & Wendel, G. D., Jr. (2002). Relationship between maternal methadone dosage and neonatal withdrawal. *American Journal of Obstetrics and Gynecology, 100*, 1244–1249.

Feldman, J. G., Minkoff, L., McCalla, S., & Salwen, M. (1992). A cohort study of the impact of perinatal drug use on prematurity in an inner-city population. *American Journal of Public Health, 82*, 726–728.

Fried, P. Watkinson, B., & Gray, R. (1992). A follow-up study of attentional behavior in 6-year-old children exposed prenatally to marijuana, cigarettes, and alcohol. *Neurotoxicology & Teratology, 14*, 299–311.

Hadeed, A. J., & Siegel, S. R. (1989). Maternal cocaine use during pregnancy: Effect on the newborn infant. *Pediatrics, 84*, 205.

Hans, S. L. (1992). Maternal opioid use and child development. In I. S. Zagon & T. A. Slotkin (Eds.), *Maternal Substance Abuse and the Developing Nervous System* (pp. 177–214). Boston: Academic Press.

Jeremy, R. J., & Hans, S. L. (1985). Behavior of neonates exposed in utero to methadone as assessed on the Brazelton scale. *Infant Behavior and Development, 8*, 323–336.

Jones, H. E. (2006). Drug addiction during pregnancy. *Current Direction in Psychological Science, 15*, 126–130.

Lester, B. M., Andreozzi, L., & Appiah, L. (2004). Substance use during pregnancy: Time for policy to catch up with research. *Harm Reduction Journal, 1*, 1–44.

Levy, M., & Koren G. (1992). Clinical toxicology of the neonate. *Seminars in Perinatology, 16*, 63–75.

Mayes, L. C., Grillon, C., Granger, R., & Schottenfeld, R. (1998). Regulation of arousal and attention in preschool children exposed to cocaine prenatally. *Annals of the New York Academy of Science, 846*, 126–143.

Mayes, L. C., & Truman, S. D. (2002). Substance abuse and parenting. In M. H. Bornstein (Ed.), *Handbook of parenting. Volume 4: Social conditions and applied psychology* (pp. 329–360). Mahwah, NJ: Erlbaum.

Mayes, L. C., & Ward, A. (2003). Principles of neurobehavioral teratology. In D. Cicchetti, & E. Walker (Eds.), *Neurodevelopmental mechanisms in psychopathology* (pp. 3–33). New York: Cambridge University Press.

National Institute on Drug Abuse (1996). *National Pregnancy and Health Survey. Drug use among women delivering live births, 1992.* Rockville, MD: National Institutes of Health Publication No.: 96–3819.

National Institute on Drug Abuse (1995). *Drug use among racial/ethnic minorities.* Washington, DC: National Institutes of Health Publication No. 95–3888.

Olges, J. R., Murphy, B. S., Caldwell, G. G., & Thornton, A. C. (2007). Testing practices and Knowledge of HIV among prenatal care providers in a low seroprevalence state. *AIDS Patient Care and STDs, 21*, 187–194.

Rosen, T. S., & Johnson, H. L. (1982). Children of methadone-maintained mothers: Follow-up to 18 months of age. *Journal of Pediatrics, 101*, 192–196.

Substance Abuse and Mental Health Services Administration (2005). *Substance use during pregnancy: 2002 and 2003 update.* Rockville, MD.

Suchman, N., Pajulo, M., DeCoste, C., & Mayes, L. (2006). Parenting interventions for drug-dependent mothers and their young children: The case for an attachment-based approach. *Family Relations, 55*, 211–227.

Vorhees, C. V., & Mollnow E. (1987). Behavioral teratogenesis: Long-term influences on behavior from early exposure to environmental agents. In J. Osofsky (Ed.), *Handbook of infant development* (pp. 913–971). New York: Wiley.

Wilson, G. S. (1989). Clinical studies of infants and children exposed prenatally to heroin. *Annals of the New York Academy of Science, 562*, 183–194.

Wilson, J. G. (1973). *Environment and birth defects.* New York: Academic Press.

Wilson, J. G. (1977). Current status of teratology—General principle and mechanisms derived from animal studies. In J. G. Wilson & F. C. Fraser (Eds.), *Handbook of teratology, vol. 1* (pp. 47–74). New York: Plenum.

Zuckerman, B. (1988). Marijuana and cigarette smoking during pregnancy: Neonatal effects. In I. Chasnoff (Ed.). *Drugs, Alcohol, Pregnancy, and Parenting* (pp. 73–89). London: Kluwer.

LORETTA P. FINNEGAN
MICHAEL P. FINNEGAN
GEORGE A. KANUCK
REVISED BY LINDA C. MAYES (2009)
ELIZABETH K. REYNOLDS (2009)

PRESCRIPTION DRUG ABUSE. Prescription drugs have become as of 2008 a major category of abused substances, and the prevalence of prescription drug abuse may soon overtake that of illicit drugs. Abuse of prescription medications may result from the inappropriate dosing or route of administration or use for reasons other than those for which the prescription is indicated. Some classes of prescription drugs act, either directly or indirectly, upon the same brain systems affected by illicit addictive drugs; therefore, their nonmedical use may result in abuse and addiction.

Prescription drug abuse may be classified under the diagnostic criteria given to substance abuse or substance dependence (addiction) patterns. Commonly abused classes of prescription drugs are opioids, central nervous system depressants, and stimulants.

OPIOIDS

Prescription opioids are commonly prescribed because of their effective pain-relieving properties, and are mostly administered orally. Morphine is often used before or after surgery to alleviate severe pain. Codeine is used for milder pain and severe coughing. Other examples of opioids that can be prescribed to alleviate pain include oxycodone (OxyContin, an oral, controlled release form of the drug), propoxyphene (Darvon), hydrocodone (Vicodin), hydromorphone (Dilaudid), and meperidine (Demerol). In addition to their effective pain-relieving properties, some medications in this class, such as diphenoxylate (Lomotil), can be used to relieve severe diarrhea.

Opioids act on the brain and body by attaching to specific proteins known as opioid receptors. These receptors are located in the central nervous system (the brain and the spinal cord), and the attachment of the prescription drug to the receptor blocks the perception of pain. In the short-term, opioids can produce drowsiness, nausea, and constipation; large, single doses may cause severe respiratory depression that can lead to death. Opioid drugs also can induce euphoria by affecting the brain regions that mediate the perception of pleasure and may be intensified when administered through nonprescribed routes. For example, OxyContin often is snorted or injected to enhance its euphoric effects. Long-term use of opioids can lead to physical dependence and addiction. Withdrawal symptoms include restlessness, insomnia, vomiting, muscle and bone pain, diarrhea, cold flashes, and involuntary leg movements. Opioids are known to interact with other substances, including those that cause central nervous system (CNS) depression (including alcohol, antihistamines, barbiturates, benzodiazepines, and general anesthetics). Since these substances slow breathing, their combined effects can lead to life-threatening respiratory depression. Options for effectively treating addiction to prescription opioids are drawn from research on treating addiction to heroin (an illicit opioid).

Pain-relieving prescription drugs are the most widely abused class. Attention was drawn to this class around 2000, following a rapid rise in the prescribing of OxyContin and reports of users crushing time-release capsules to allow for the entire dose to be dissolved quickly. In 2002, Drug Abuse Warning Network data ranked prescription opioids fourth among emergency room mentions and first among drug-associated deaths.

CENTRAL NERVOUS SYSTEM DEPRESSANTS (SEDATIVES AND TRANQUILIZERS)

CNS depressants can slow normal brain function. Because of this property, some CNS depressants, including sedatives and tranquilizers, are useful in the treatment of anxiety and sleep disorders. In higher doses, some CNS depressants can become general anesthetics. There are many CNS depressants, and most act on the brain in similar ways. This class of drugs increases the neurotransmitter gamma-aminobutyric acid (GABA), which then acts by decreasing brain activity. Although different classes of CNS depressants work in unique ways, the commonality is their ability to increase GABA activity to produce a drowsy or calming effect.

Results of short-term use of CNS depressants include initial drowsiness and a feeling of uncoordination. Effects of long-term use include the potential for physical dependence and addiction. Tolerance may occur, as larger doses may be needed to achieve therapeutic effects. When use is eventually reduced or stopped, withdrawal may occur. Because CNS depressants work by slowing the brain's activity, a potential consequence of abuse is that the brain's activity can rebound to the point that seizures can occur once the drug is discontinued. Often the abuse of CNS depressants occurs in conjunction with the abuse of another substance, such as alcohol or cocaine. When used in combination, CNS depressants may have additive effects, which can slow the heart or respiration and may be fatal. Therefore, CNS depressants should not be combined with any medication or substance that causes drowsiness, including prescription pain medicines, certain over-the-counter cold or allergy medications (which can contain alcohol or antihistamines), or beverage alcohol.

Most CNS depressants can be divided into groups, based on their chemistry and pharmacology.

Among the medications that are commonly prescribed for these purposes are barbiturates and benzodiazepines.

Barbiturates, such as mephobarbital (Mebaral) and pentobarbital sodium (Nembutal), are used to treat anxiety, tension, and sleep disorders. Although barbiturates are more or less obsolete as tranquilizers and sleeping tablets, addiction to them continues to be encountered as of 2008. Tolerance and physical dependence can rapidly occur during therapy, and abrupt withdrawal can result in a severe and life-threatening withdrawal state. Studies in abusers show them to greatly prefer barbiturates to benzodiazepines, which have replaced them pharmacologically and are discussed below. Meprobamate, a carbonate used as a tranquilizer, is similar in many ways to the barbiturates, including its abuse potential.

Clinically, patterns of nonmedical use of nonopioids vary greatly; large quantities can be injected into a vein or muscle, often producing abscess formation. Other users take large amounts by mouth, on a binge or spree basis, the most popular being pentobarbital, amylbarbital, quinalbarbital, and Tuinal, the amylbarbital/quinalbarbital combination. Some users become permanently intoxicated and totally engrossed in maintaining their supply, licit or illicit. Polydrug use, which combines these drugs with amphetamines or opioids, is common.

Withdrawal can be hazardous, with the risk of seizures or psychotic features, when discontinuing chronic usage of 500 milligrams a day or more. Withdrawal delirium (similar to delirium tremens, DTs) is common and often difficult to treat; a chronic state with hallucinations may ensue.

Benzodiazepines, such as diazepam (Valium), chlordiazepoxide (Librium), and alprazolam (Xanax), are prescribed to treat anxiety, acute stress reactions, and panic attacks. The more sedating benzodiazepines, such as triazolam (Halcion) and estazolam (ProSom) are prescribed for short-term treatment of sleep disorders. Usually, benzodiazepines are not prescribed for long-term use and therefore increasing therapeutic levels are uncommon. The benzodiazepines supplanted the barbiturates because they seemed to be at least as effective, with few side effects and less likelihood of producing addiction. However, they have been used as drugs of abuse, either as the main drug of abuse or as part of a polydrug-abuse pattern. Abusers have found that the effect of benzodiazepines is enhanced through interaction with a number of other drugs. Within polydrug abuse, the benzodiazepine is used to eke out the supply of opioid or to ease the crash from the high euphoria of cocaine use.

In the 1990s, flunitrazepam (Rohypnol) was a benzodiazepine sold as a hypnotic in many countries around the world. Reports surfaced that it was being added to the alcoholic drinks of unsuspecting women by their dates, resulting in an intoxication so profound the woman is unable to remember recent activities. It became widely known as the *date-rape drug*. In 1997, the manufacturer changed the formulation of the pill so that when it dissolves in a drink it produces a characteristic color.

A new generation of non-benzodiazepine anxiolytics (e.g., zolpidem and zaleplon) has emerged with the hopes of avoiding the difficulties that arose with benzodiazepines' abuse. While early investigations showed little evidence of abuse or dependence, several subsequent studies demonstrated that these medications do have significant abuse potential, particularly at high doses and in patients with a history of substance dependence.

STIMULANTS

Stimulants enhance brain activity, causing an increase in alertness, attention, and energy. They have also been found to raise mood, increase the sense of well-being, and decrease appetite. Stimulants historically were used to treat asthma and other respiratory problems, obesity, neurological disorders, and a variety of other ailments. As their potential for abuse and addiction became apparent, the medical use of stimulants began to wane. As of 2008, stimulants are prescribed for the treatment of only a few health conditions, including narcolepsy, attention deficit hyperactivity disorder (ADHD), and depression that has not responded to other treatments. This class of medication—which as of 2008 includes dextroamphetamine (Dexedrine and Adderall) and methylphenidate (Ritalin and Concerta)—has a chemical structure that is similar to that of a family of key brain neurotransmitters called *monoamines*, which include norepinephrine and dopamine. Stimulants enhance the effects of these chemicals in the brain. The result is increased blood pressure and heart rate, constriction of blood vessels, increased blood glucose, and an opening of the pathways of the respiratory system.

Additional short-term side effects include suppressed appetite and sleep deprivation. In addition, the increase in dopamine is associated with a sense of euphoria that can accompany the use of stimulants, sometimes resulting in dependence or addiction. Withdrawal symptoms associated with discontinuing stimulant use include fatigue, depression, and disturbance of sleep patterns. Repeated use of some stimulants over a short period or high doses can lead to feelings of hostility or paranoia. Further, taking high doses of a stimulant may result in a dangerously high body temperature and an irregular heartbeat. There is also the potential for cardiovascular failure or lethal seizures.

Intravenous amphetamine produces euphoria, similar to but more sustained than that following the use of cocaine. As abuse of prescription amphetamines was recognized in the 1960s and 1970s, physicians prescribed less of the drugs for medical conditions such as depression and obesity. Clandestine laboratories manufacturing amphetamine emerged and continued to be active into the 2000s. Their preferred substance is methamphetamine, which can be synthesized easily. Since intravenous use of methamphetamine is usual, and tolerance quickly occurs, larger and more frequent doses become required to achieve the desired effect. Toxic effects supervene, with repetitive face and hand movements and stereotyped behavior; for example, the user assembling and dismantling mechanical objects. A full-blown paranoid type of psychosis may develop, with loss of reality and delusions of persecution. Individual susceptibility to these toxic effects varies greatly. Polydrug abuse of amphetamines is common; co-administration of amphetamine with heroin (speedball) or a barbiturate is believed to optimize the pleasurable effects while minimizing the toxic ones.

The most common indication for the prescription of stimulants is ADHD, and prescription drug treatment for this condition has been steadily increasing over the past years, especially in adolescents and college students. Newer preparations have emphasized delayed-release mechanisms and other methods of lengthening the duration of therapeutic serum drug levels in attempts to overcome the limitations of those stimulants with short-half lives. Of all prescription medications, methylphenidate has the highest prevalence of nonmedical use among adolescence. Misuse of prescription stimulants typically involves short-acting formulations.

In August 2006, the FDA called for new warnings on stimulants used for ADHD. Treatment of addiction to prescription stimulants, such as methylphenidate, is often based on behavioral therapies that have proven effective in treating cocaine and methamphetamine addiction. Overdose is frequently cited as a reason for stimulant-related emergency department visits. Antidepressants may enhance the effects of a stimulant, and stimulants in combination with over-the-counter cold medicines containing decongestants may cause blood pressure to become dangerously high or lead to irregular heart rhythms. Therapeutic doses are lower than doses that are abused. For example, the doses of methylphenidate used for attention deficit disorder are typically below the level expected to produce reinforcement. However, higher doses and intravenous use can result in a rapid development of dependence.

Appetite suppressants cover a range of compounds, from the decongestant phenylpropanolamine (often available without prescription), to powerful amphetamine analogues (chemical variants). Most are stimulants, although one, fenfluramine, is quite sedative. As with the amphetamines, patterns of use and abuse vary a great deal, from chronic daily ingestion of a therapeutic dose to binge or spree use of large quantities. The appetite suppressants that act as amphetamines are more likely to be abused. Withdrawal symptoms include tiredness, dysphoria (emotional discomfort), and depression. In the early to mid-1990s, two prescription diet drugs, fenfluramine (often taken with phentermine and popularly known as fen-phen) and dexfenfluramine (Redux) grew in popularity. These drugs stimulated production of the brain chemical serotonin, creating a feeling of satiety. In 1997, reports of heart valve disease in women taking fen-phen or Redux began to surface. By September 1997, the drugs dexfenfluramine and fenfluramine were withdrawn from the U.S. market by their manufacturer, American Home Products. Phentermine (Fastin, Adipex, Ionamin) remains available in the market as its use alone has not been associated with the adverse health effects of the fenfluramine-phentermine combination.

EPIDEMIOLOGY AND TRENDS
Prescription drug abuse is widespread in the general population, and research in the 2000s has

focused on ascertaining its prevalence and correlates, including common comorbid psychiatric disorders. Historical evaluation of prescription drug abuse has been limited by the inconsistent definition of abuse and dependence, lack of drug-specific data, and lack of data on comorbid conditions, The prevalence of nonmedical use of prescription drugs remains highest for opioids and amphetamines; these two drug categories are also associated with the highest rates of abuse and dependence in the general population. Rates of prescription drug abuse and dependence tend to be higher among men than women. In addition, prescription drug abuse and dependence frequently begins with stimulant abuse and during adolescence. Numerous epidemiologic surveys have also found consistent associations of such abuse with alcohol use disorders, as well as mood, anxiety, and personality disorders. Thus, treatment of prescription drug abuse may require a comprehensive psychiatric assessment, including the evaluation of comorbid substance use and psychiatric disorders. Research has also demonstrated that abuse of prescription drugs is highly disabling but frequently remains untreated, despite highly effective and available treatment options.

Several factors may be contributing to the availability of prescription drugs that may result in abuse. The most common methods of diversion of controlled prescription drugs include: (1) "doctor shopping" (an individual visits several physicians who write a prescription for a controlled substance, which the individual then fills at different pharmacies), (2) illegal online pharmacies, (3) purchasing from drug dealers, (4) receiving from friends and family, (5) and negligent/intentional overprescribing by physicians or other practitioners. Prescription drug manufacturers have taken steps to minimize the potential harms of prescription drug abuse. National plans for addressing the rising prevalence of prescription drug abuse includes the establishment of a national All Schedule Prescription Electronic Reporting Program, a nationwide registry of all substances prescribed for an individual. In addition, the federal government has set up the Drug Abuse Warning Network (DAWN), which collects data on drug-related crises from several hundred hospital emergency rooms in metropolitan areas around the country.

See also **Iatrogenic Addiction; Obesity.**

BIBLIOGRAPHY

Arria, A. M., & Wish, E. D. (2006). Nonmedical use of prescription stimulants among students. *Pediatric Annals, 35*(8), 565–571.

Ator, N. A., & Griffiths, R. R. (1987). Self-administration of barbiturates and benzodiazepines: A review. *Pharmacology, Biochemistry, and Behavior, 57,* 391–398.

Blanco, C., Alderson, D., Ogburn, E., Grant, B. F., Nunes, E. V., Hatzenbuehler, M. L., et al. (2007). Changes in the prevalence of non-medical prescription drug use and drug use disorders in the United States: 1991–1992 and 2001–2002. *Drug and Alcohol Dependence, 90*(2–3), 252–260.

Caplan, J. P., Epstein, L. A., Quinn, D. K., Stevens, J. R., & Stern, T. A. (2007). Neuropsychiatric effects of prescription drug abuse. *Neuropsychology Review, 17*(3), 363–380.

Compton, W. M., Thomas, Y. F., Stinson, F. S., & Grant, B. F. (2007). Prevalence, correlates, disability, and comorbidity of *DSM-IV* drug abuse and dependence in the United States: Results from the national epidemiologic survey on alcohol and related conditions. *Archives of General Psychiatry, 64*(5), 566–576.

Gardin, J. M., Schumacher, D., Constantine, G., Davis, K. D., Leung, C., & Reid, C. L. (2000). Valvular abnormalities and cardiovascular statistics following exposure to dexfenfluramine or phentermine. *Journal of the American Medical Association, 283,* 1703–1709.

Hertz, J. A., & Knight, J. R. (2006). Prescription drug misuse: A growing national problem. *Adolescent Medicine Clinics, 17*(3), 751–769; abstract, xiii.

Huang, B., Dawson, D. A., Stinson, F. S., Hasin, D. S., Ruan, W. J., Saha, T. D., et al. (2006). Prevalence, correlates, and comorbidity of nonmedical prescription drug use and drug use disorders in the United States: Results of the National Epidemiologic Survey on Alcohol and Related Conditions. *Journal of Clinical Psychiatry, 67*(7), 1062–1073.

Hurwitz, W. (2005). The challenge of prescription drug misuse: A review and commentary. *Pain Medicine, 6*(2), 152–161.

Ksir, C., Hart, C. L., & Ray, O. (2006). *Drugs, society and human behavior* (11th ed.) New York: McGraw Hill.

Manchikanti, L. (2006). Prescription drug abuse: What is being done to address this new drug epidemic? Testimony before the Subcommittee on Criminal Justice, Drug Policy, and Human Resources. *Pain Physician, 9*(4), 287–321.

Manchikanti, L. (2007). National drug control policy and prescription drug abuse: Facts and fallacies. *Pain Physician, 10*(3), 399–424.

Martell, B. A., O'Connor, P. G., Kerns, R. D., Becker, W. C., Morales, K. H., Kosten, T. R., et al. (2007). Systematic review: Opioid treatment for chronic back pain, prevalence, efficacy, and association with addiction. *Annals Internal Medicine, 146*(2), 116–127.

McCabe, S. E., Cranford, J. A., & Boyd, C. J. (2006). The relationship between past-year drinking behaviors and nonmedical use of prescription drugs: Prevalence of co-occurrence in a national sample. *Drug and Alcohol Dependence, 84*(3), 281–288.

National Institute on Drug Abuse. (2005). *Prescription drugs: Abuse and addiction, research report, 2005.* Available from http://www.nida.nih.gov/.

Simoni-Wastila, L., & Strickler, G. (2004). Risk factors associated with problem use of prescription drugs. *American Journal of Public Health, 94*(2), 266–268.

Substance Abuse and Mental Health Services Administration. (2008). *Results from the 2006 National Survey on Drug Use and Health: National findings, 2007.* Available from http://oas.samhsa.gov/.

Turunen, J. H., Mäntyselkä, P. T., Kumpusalo, E. A., & Ahonen, R. S. (2005). Frequent analgesic use at population level: Prevalence and patterns of use. *Pain, 115*(3), 374–381.

Volkow, N. D., & Swanson, J. M. (2003). Variables that affect the clinical use and abuse of methylphenidate in the treatment of ADHD. *American Journal of Psychiatry, 160*(11), 1909–1918.

Wesson, D. R., & Smith, D. E. (1977). *Barbiturates: Their use, misuse, and abuse.* New York: Human Sciences Press.

Wilens, T. E., Adler, L. A., Adams, J., Sgambati, S., Rotrosen, J., Sawtelle, R., et al. (2008). Misuse and diversion of stimulants prescribed for ADHD: A systematic review of the literature. *Journal of American Academy of Child and Adolescent Psychiatry, 47*(1), 21–31.

LISA WEISS

PRESCRIPTION DRUG MONITORING PROGRAM.

In the fiscal year (FY) 2002, the U.S. Congress appropriated funds to support the Prescription Drug Monitoring Program (PDMP) as a part of the U.S. Department of Justice Appropriations Act (Public Law 107–77). According to the Department of Justice, PDMPs are designed to help states prevent or detect the diversion and abuse of controlled pharmaceuticals at the retail level. These programs can easily collect and analyze prescription data using a state-level data collection and analysis system, thus enhancing the ability to use this data and facilitating the exchange of data between states.

To receive funding and implement the program, states or territories must have legislation or regulations in place or pending that require the submission of dispensing data to a centralized database and authorize or designate a state agency to implement and administer the program. Planning grants and enhancement grants are also available. Technical assistance in the development of this legislation is provided by the Prescription Drug Monitoring Project of the National Alliance for Model State Drug Laws (NAMSDL). NAMSDL provides access to model state laws and policy resources for planning, implementing, or enhancing PDMPs. These efforts include maintaining a listserv, monitoring legislation and regulatory changes, and distributing bimonthly PDMP updates.

As of November 2007, 20 states had implemented such programs and 23 states were in the implementation process, which excludes Arkansas, Delaware, Georgia, Maryland, Nebraska, South Dakota, and Wisconsin. Maryland introduced legislation during the 2008 session, but it did not pass. In an evaluation of state PDMPs conducted by Simeone Associates in 2006, researchers assessed both indirect and direct routes that may be used by these programs to decrease (regulate prescribing behavior) or hold steady (regulate dispensing behavior) the supply of controlled pharmaceuticals and thus decrease their abuse. They found that PDMPs that included Schedule II pain relievers and stimulants reduced the per capita supply of these drugs, which, in turn, reduced the probability of their abuse. In addition, states that were proactive in their use of a PDMP were more effective than those that were reactive.

COMPONENTS AND DATA ELEMENTS

Although all states and territories must apply for funding using the same process, the type of PDMP and the drugs covered can vary from Schedule II to Schedule V. PDMPs may be either reactive or proactive, which means that they can be used to generate reports in response to specific inquiries or to conduct investigations that generate unsolicited reports whenever suspicious behavior is detected.

The NAMSDL identified seven components for a strong prescription monitoring statute/program, which are listed below and described on its Web site.

1. Drugs monitored should include all state and federally controlled substances and other drugs

of concern documented to demonstrate a potential for abuse by law enforcement and addiction treatment professionals.

2. The monitoring system should proactively provide information to law enforcement and occupational licensing officials to support prescription drug-related investigation. Information without identifying information should also be provided to researchers, policymakers, and educators to support research, prevention, and other efforts.

3. The system should enable specific individuals, such as dispensers, physicians and other prescribers, law enforcement, and occupational licensing officials, to request specific information.

4. Individuals receiving information from the system should demonstrate that they know how to responsibly and properly use it.

5. An evaluation should be conducted to identify cost benefits and recommended improvements.

6. Statutory provisions should include confidentiality protections to prevent the improper use of the system or the information received from it.

7. Statutory provisions, regulations, or interstate agreements should be implemented to prevent interstate misuse and abuse of prescription drugs.

The data elements most commonly found in PDMPs are: name/ID and/or address of practitioner/dispenser/pharmacy; practitioner's/prescriber's and/or dispenser's DEA registration number; date prescription/medication filled or dispensed; name/address for the patient/recipient; patient's/recipient's data of birth; national drug code number of the controlled substance dispensed; and the quantity of the controlled substance prescribed or dispensed. All of these items are captured by the PDMPs of ten or more states. Other, rarer items collected include: the pharmacy number, prescription number, prescription form number, patient's/recipient's ID number, and the dosage or strength of the controlled substance prescribed.

OTHER USES FOR PRESCRIPTION DRUG MONITORING PROGRAMS

PDMPs can be used to track specific types of drugs or activities. For instance, 13 of the 20 states operating PDMPs as of 2008 require out-of-state mail-order pharmacies delivering or dispensing drugs into their states to enter data into the PDMP. Three states do not require this participation, and the remaining four lack the laws necessary to require the participation of mail-order pharmacies. Other innovations include a Web portal implemented by the Maine PDMP to increase users' ability to input and access the data. Texas has used data from its PDMP to support investigations into *pill mills*. And, licensure boards and law enforcement in Kentucky use data from their PDMP to produce geographic information system (GIS) maps that identify locations of controlled substance use by geographic area and increases and decreases in use over time.

Other types of electronic monitoring systems have also been developed or were pending as of 2008 such as pseudoephedrine monitoring systems and Department of Health and Human Services (DHHS) drug monitoring systems. The National All Schedules Prescription Electronic Reporting Act of 2005 requires that the DHHS award grants to establish or improve electronic drug monitoring programs. However, as of 2008, no funds had been appropriated for this effort, and it remained unclear how this act would relate to the original PDMPs. During FY2008, some states began to develop electronic tracking systems to monitor compliance with existing restrictions on the sale and purchase of pseudoephedrine products. NAMSDL was working with these states to ensure that these systems are interoperable with other systems such as PDMP.

See also **Prescription Drug Abuse; U. S. Government Agencies.**

BIBLIOGRAPHY

Bureau of Justice Assistance, Office of Justice Programs. *Harold Rogers prescription drug monitoring.* Available from www.ojp.usdoj.gov.

National Alliance for Model State Drug Laws. *Prescription drug monitoring project.* Available from www.natlalliance.org/.

Simeone, R., & Holland, L. (2006, September). *An evaluation of prescription drug monitoring programs.* Simeone Associates, Inc.: Albany, NY.

E. ERIN ARTIGIANI

PREVENTION. Prevention of substance abuse is generally defined as either *demand reduction* through education and behavior change strategies to reduce precursor risk factors or to increase protective factors; or *supply reduction* through increasing taxes and penalties, better enforcement, and interdiction. However, in some countries, prevention also includes *harm reduction approaches*, such as designated drivers, overdose prevention hotlines, checking drugs at raves, and providing clean needles. *Primary prevention* approaches are used before individuals begin regular use, *secondary prevention* approaches reduce use through screening and early intervention, and *tertiary prevention* approaches include treatments to stop drug use and associated problems. In 1995 the area of *primary* prevention was further divided by the Institute of Medicine (IOM) into three types: (a) *universal prevention* targeting low-risk general populations (e.g., students, families, or communities through media campaigns); (b) *selective prevention* targeting at-risk groups of individuals (e.g., children of substance abusers or prisoners or Native American children); and (c) *indicated prevention* targeting those with identified or diagnosed precursors of alcohol or drug abuse such as aggression, conduct disorders, thrill-seeking, or delinquency.

The length or dosage (number of contact hours) of these prevention approaches differs for each of these three primary prevention types. Namely, indicated primary prevention programs are generally longer and address more risk and protective factors than do those for general populations of low-risk youth in schools. Programs conducted for all youth or families in a school or community are universal prevention programs and are generally shorter in number of sessions and time per session than selective or indicated programs.

Sometimes indicated prevention approaches identify and prevent greater drug use in individuals who are experiencing early signs of substance use; technically, this should be defined as secondary prevention. Recently the White House Office of National Drug Control Policy (ONDCP) began stressing secondary prevention approaches in its Demand Reduction Themes because non-dependent users do not perceive the negative consequences of drug use and introduce friends to drugs. This type of secondary prevention will require effective early identification and intervention programs by school, workplace, social service, justice, and primary health-care settings. In February 2008 the president released the 2008 National Drug Control Strategy of the White House ONDCP, its goals being to reduce drug use in America by stopping use before it starts, healing America's drug users, and disrupting the market for illegal drugs (ONDCP, 2008).

PREVENTION APPROACHES

Prevention of substance abuse is now a sophisticated science. It has moved beyond less effective approaches of the 1970s and 1980s that included scare tactics, one-time drug-prevention assemblies, and "Just Say No" campaigns. Because taxpayers and state and federal agencies require accountability, prevention practitioners are using a wide variety of evidence-based prevention programs to match the needs of different participants. Lists of programs that have been studied for effectiveness can be found at these websites: the National Institute of Drug Abuse (NIDA, http://www.nida.nih.gov/), the Substance Abuse and Mental Health Administration (SAMHSA) Model Programs list (http://www.modelprograms.samhsa.gov), the White House Helping America's Youth guide (http://guide.helpingamericasyouth.gov), the Office of Juvenile Justice and Delinquency Prevention's (OJJDP) Strengthening America's Families at the University of Utah (http://www.strengtheningfamilies.org), or BluePrints at the University of Colorado (http://www.colorado.edu/cspv/blueprints/model/overview.html).

A number of these evidence-based programs, especially comprehensive ones targeting the family and community, also reduce other behavioral problems such as delinquency, family violence, child abuse, teenage pregnancy, and school failure. Hence, investment in these programs can have additional positive effects.

COST BENEFITS

Most research-based prevention programs are cost beneficial. For each dollar spent, they save at least $4 in costs for drug abuse treatment and counseling. Considering other costs to society, such as crime, unemployment, and health costs, the cost effectiveness of good drug abuse prevention is even greater. Aos and associates' (2004) analysis showed positive cost/benefit ratios ranging from $102.29 saved for every dollar spent for the *Minnesota Smoking Prevention Program* to a low of $3.43 for the *All Stars Program*. Only two programs produced losses—*D.A.R.E.* and *S.T.A.Rs for Families*. Not all substance abuse prevention programs are listed in this category, since some fall into the Youth Development section, such as the *Seattle Social Development Project* ($3.14/$1 spent), *Guiding Good Choices* ($11.07/$1 spent), and the *Strengthening Families Program for Youth 10–14 Years* ($7.82/$1 spent), which were developed and tested for drug use prevention. The highest cost-benefit ratios of all educational and social services programs are for substance abuse prevention programs. Their ratios are much higher than Pre-school Education Programs (highest was $2.34/$1), Child Welfare/Home Visitation Programs (highest was $2.88/$1 for the *Nurse Home Visitation Program*), Teen Pregnancy Prevention Programs, or many Juvenile Offender Programs. Some had spectacularly negative results. For example, the *Scared Straight* program cost $54 per youth but resulted in increased costs of over $11,000 per offender. Not all prevention programs work, so states and agencies should invest in programs that studies show to have a high level of effectiveness.

SELECTING THE BEST PREVENTION APPROACHES

Because there is not one best program, practitioners should conduct a needs assessment of their target population first. They should determine the most salient risk or protective factors and then select the best prevention approaches to address those needs. The Center for Substance Abuse Prevention (CSAP) recommends standardized needs assessment instruments for states to determine how to best use their Block Grant funds for prevention. A number of communities and states also use the *Communities That Care* (Hawkins & Catalano, 1999) student needs assessment survey and matching system to select evidence-based prevention programs.

A number of factors should go into selecting the best program for a local population: age of children, ethnicity and language, length of program, cost, staff required, outcomes improved, and level of clients' dysfunction (e.g., low-risk universal families, selective high-risk families, or indicated in-crisis families). In addition, Web sites or reports that include meta-analyses enable practitioners to pick the most effective program for their investment. Factors to consider are the quality of the research, the amount of research, and the replication of program by independent researchers (Flay et al., 2005). After narrowing the search to two or three programs, focus groups of

parents or staff can review the materials. Other considerations include the availability of training, technical assistance, and evaluation services as well as the costs.

PRINCIPLES OF EFFECTIVE PREVENTION PROGRAMS

Characteristics of effective prevention programs, called *principles of prevention*, can be used to judge the potential effectiveness of different programs. Both NIDA and ONDCP have published lists of principles for substance abuse prevention programs. Nation and colleagues (2003) used a "review of reviews" approach to extract effectiveness principles from research articles on prevention programs in four content areas—substance abuse, risky sexual behavior, school failure, and juvenile delinquency and violence. Nine program characteristics were consistently associated with effective prevention programs: theory-driven, comprehensive, appropriately-timed, socio-culturally relevant, sufficient dosage, varied teaching methods, positive relationships, well-trained staff, and outcome evaluation.

WHAT WORKS IN PREVENTION PROGRAMS

What works in prevention, according to ONDCP, are approaches that are primarily punitive: drug testing in schools and workplaces, community coalitions with *supply reduction* strategies (e.g., increasing taxes, using restrictive zoning, increasing sting operations, and passing local regulations to restrict outlet licenses), drug courts, threats to remove children from drug-using parents, brief screening interventions, and referrals to treatment (ONDCP, 2008). Few randomized control trials of these environmental approaches exist to prove these approaches work. No mention is made of positive youth development or family programs, although prevention researchers, expert review committees of federal departments (NIDA, NIAAA, SAMHSA's NREPP, CDC), and expert review groups (e.g., the Cochrane Collaboration Reviews in Medicine and Public Health at Oxford University) found these primary *demand reduction* approaches effective.

Most research on preventing alcohol and drug abuse has focused on junior-high-school-aged students, because most individuals initiate substance use during this time. Less is known about other developmental periods; however, this entry discusses what is known about the most effective approaches for both children and adolescents.

To increase accountability and positive outcomes, substance abuse funding agencies are increasingly requiring that funding be used only or primarily for evidence-based programs (EBPs). Best practices are those with research evidence showing decreased substance use, delayed age of use onset, improved protective factors, and decreased risk factors related to later use. Research literature contains many evidence-based programs (EBPs) with sufficient effectiveness as tested in large-scale, randomized, controlled intervention trials to warrant dissemination and adoption by schools and communities. Effective EBP prevention approaches have been identified by federal review committees and are listed on the Web sites of federal agencies. Syntheses of best practices in evidence-based prevention practices have been published by the Institute of Medicine (IOM, 1995), CSAP (1998), NIDA *Preventing Drug Use Among Children and Adolescents* (NIDA, 2008), and researchers (Hawkins & Catalano, 1999; Kumpfer & Alder, 2003).

Different approaches generally included in a comprehensive prevention plan are family-focused approaches, child-only approaches, and community- or school-change approaches. These are briefly reviewed below in order of effectiveness according to meta-analyses of amount of positive change.

Parenting and Family Focused Approaches.
Strong families are key to preventing adolescent drug use problems. For instance, youth report on the PRIDE survey (2006) that parent disapproval is the major reason *not* to use drugs. Also almost three-fourths of parents believe they are the most effective deterrent. However, they fail at monitoring youth behaviors and dramatically underestimate the percentage of youth using alcohol versus the percentage actually reporting use (11% versus 42%) (PRIDE, 2006). The general logic of a family-focused approach is that by teaching parents to be better parents, improving their parent/child relationships, and increasing effective discipline and monitoring, children will have better developmental outcomes in all areas, including tobacco, alcohol, and drug use. Family programs appear to be the most effective prevention programs for many adolescent problems.

Several attempts have been made to classify the different types of family-focused approaches for prevention. Researchers in this area disagree, however, about definitions of family-focused approaches. The CSAP Prevention Enhancement Protocols System (PEPS, 1998) review of family-focused approaches defined eight approaches, but found only four approaches with sufficient research evidence to prove they worked for substance abuse prevention: (a) behavioral parent training, (b) family skills training, (c) family therapy, and (d) in-home family case management or support programs. Since this 1998 CSAP review, the low-cost *Family Matters* program of involving parents in substance-abuse-prevention homework assignments with their children is showing promise as a cost effective approach (Bauman et al., 2001).

Kaminski and associates (2008) at the Centers for Disease Control (CDC) have analyzed the critical core components of EBP family interventions from 77 studies of programs for 0–7-year-olds. Because the presence of conduct disorders in early life often precedes later delinquent, aggressive, and risky behaviors in adolescence, they reasoned that effective parenting could reverse this trend. The *core components* of effective parenting and family interventions include:

1. Practice time for parents to interact with their children while therapists or group leaders are available for coaching.

2. Teaching parents to interact positively with children (e.g., showing enthusiasm and attention for good behavior and letting children take the lead in play activities).

3. Increasing parental attention and praise for children's positive behaviors, explaining children's normal development to promote realistic expectations for children's behaviors, improving family communication (e.g., increasing active listening and reducing criticism and sarcasm), and teaching effective and consistent discipline (e.g., time-outs).

4. Teaching children social skills, so they get along better with parents, peers, and teachers.

5. Assigning and encouraging home practice assignments to improve generalization of new behaviors at home.

(For additional reviews of effective family-strengthening approaches, see Kumpfer & Alvarado

[2003] and the OJJDP Strengthening America's Families Web site).

A national review of family-strengthening approaches conducted in 2000 found about 35 evidence-based practices (Kumpfer & Alvarado, 2003). However, only 14 family programs have been tested in randomized control trials, and only seven were independently replicated, thus meeting the criteria for the highest level of evidence of effectiveness, Exemplary I Programs. The Exemplary I family programs for ages 0–5 include *Helping the Noncompliant Child* and *The Incredible Years*. The only Exemplary I program for ages 6–12 is Kumpfer's *Strengthening Families Program*. The only pre-teen and adolescent programs included in this category are *Functional Family Therapy, Multisystemic Family Therapy, Preparing for the Drug Free Years* (now called *Guiding Good Choices*), and *Treatment Foster Care*. According to the Cochrane Collaboration Reviews in Medicine and Public Health meta-analysis of all school-based universal alcohol-prevention programs, the *Strengthening Families Program for 10–14 Year Olds* is twice as effective as the next best program, *Preparing for the Drug-Free Years* (Foxcroft et al., 2003).

Overall, family-focused approaches averaged effect sizes (as measured by Cohen's d and measuring amount of change) were nine times larger than child-only prevention approaches (d = 0.96 ES versus d = 0.10ES) as shown in Table 1 below (Kumpfer, Alvarado, & Whiteside, 2003). Effect sizes measure the amount of change in the treatment group compared to the control group. A d effect size of 1 is about equivalent to one standard deviation of change or a large change. A small change is under d=.20. In selecting the best family-focused program, the prevention practitioner must consider the target population's need for a universal, selective, or indicated prevention program as well as the age of the child, ethnicity, and special needs. A matrix of these programs by prevention level and age is available on the Strengthening America's Families Web site (http://www.strengtheningfamilies.org) along with program descriptions and links to the program developer's Web sites.

The United Nations Office of Drugs and Crime has developed with Kumpfer an updated search for

School-based affective	−.05
Knowledge plus affective	.05
Life or social skills training	.28
Average ES youth-only programs	**.10 ES**
Parent skills training	.31
Family therapy	.45
Family skills training	.82
In-home family support	1.62
Average ES family interventions	**.96 ES**

Table 1. Average effect sizes of youth-only and family prevention interventions for substance abuse prevention. ILLUSTRATION BY GGS INFORMATION SERVICES. GALE, CENGAGE LEARNING

evidence-based parenting and family programs worldwide and identified 185 noteworthy programs. A protocol with steps for culturally adapting these EBPs can be found on their Web site (http://www. unodc.org/) along with a publication by Kumpfer and associates (2008) on steps for local and cultural adaptations.

Youth-only Prevention Approaches. The most rigorously tested and effective approaches include social skills and life skills training programs, which are implemented in many settings (e.g., schools, community centers, churches, and youth clubs). Other child-only school or community agency approaches for reducing substance abuse include mentoring, tutoring, and providing alternative activities, recreation and leisure programs, wilderness challenge programs, and community service programs. However, little research has been done on these programs. Additionally the most well-researched mentoring program, *Big Brothers/Big Sisters*, costs about the same as its benefits—a $1.01 benefit per $1.00 spent (Aos et al., 2004). School-based programs are most successful in reducing tobacco use, followed by drug use, and then alcohol use.

Critical core components of effective school-based programs include involvement with positive role models or mentors, sufficient number of contact hours, interactive/cooperative learning, and booster sessions. Interventions run by mental health clinicians are two to three times more effective than programs implemented by peers, teachers, police officers, or others (Tobler et al., 2000). The effect size (ES) in reducing substance use varies considerably by type of child-only approach.

Life Skills Training Programs have the highest positive results as measured by average effect size or amount of change. These Life Skills programs include refusal skills, life skills (e.g., communication, problem-solving, coping, social/dating, goal-setting, stress management, and media literacy), and public commitments not to use. The average effect size for these child-only programs (N=206) was 0.10, which is quite small; however, the most effective programs were Botvin's *Life Skills Training* (LST) (Botvin, 1995) and Schinke's and associates (2000) *Smart Moves for Native Americans*, which had higher effect sizes averaging 0.28. One of the first to study the use of computer technology in substance abuse prevention, Schinke and associates (2004) tested a 10-session computer-based (CD-ROM) version of his life skills program with and without parental involvement (30-minute video tape and two newsletters on effective parenting). They found that parental involvement improved the outcomes for alcohol use, but both versions were more effective for drug and tobacco use reductions compared to a no-treatment control.

The least effective program, which produced slight negative effects, was the combination of *Knowledge-only* and *Affective Education* programs that were popular in the early 1980s. The widely promoted *D.A.R.E.* program (a social skills program based on the effective SMART program) failed to prevent drug use (Harrington et al., 2000). One possible reason for the failure of *D.A.R.E.* is that police officers tend to lecture and tell stories. Prevention programs using interactive, skills training methods to change behaviors as opposed to didactic lecture methods to change knowledge are more effective, particularly for minority youth. A new version of *D.A.R.E.* is being developed and tested by Sloboda. However, the initial cost-benefit ratio for *D.A.R.E.* is estimated at a net loss of $99 per student (Aos et al., 2004), because there are minimal positive outcomes (d = 0.03 or very small) (Tobler et al., 2000).

Community Coalition or Environmental Change.

Community coalition approaches are currently popular with the federal government. Most funding for community prevention grants provided by ONDCP and SAMHSA CSAP goes for the Antidrug Communities Support Program, which funds 750 coalitions for about 90 million total. In 2008

they funded about 150 new community coalitions at $125,000 each. However, the United States has about 4,000 drug prevention coalitions. These coalitions typically follow a comprehensive community approach that changes the total community climate and norms. They can only spend 20 percent of their federal budget to implement multiple prevention strategies, including individual, school, workplace, and family prevention approaches. The bulk of the funding is used for advocacy, media campaigns, meetings, and environmental policy change.

Examples of evidence-based community partnership or coalition approaches include the *Midwestern Prevention Program*, *Project Northland*, and the *Communities That Care (CTC)* model (Hawkins & Catalano, 1999). Research on *Communities That Care* is being conducted on 41 matched communities in seven participating states (Hawkins, Catalano, & Arthur, 2000). This project tracks the history of risk- and protection-focused prevention planning and assesses the effectiveness of the CTC coalition model in reducing risk factors, increasing protective factors, and decreasing youth substance abuse. The CTC community coalition model is based on six phases: (a) needs assessment using standardized CTC school and community leaders surveys, (b) prioritization of risk and protective factors for intervention, (c) selection of tested interventions to address needs, (d) implementation of science-based prevention interventions, (e) monitoring of changes in targeted risk and protective factors, and (f) adjustment of interventions as indicated by performance data.

Evaluations found that community coalitions were effective if they were organized in areas with a high degree of community readiness, progressed from planning to implementation within the first two years, implemented proven prevention strategies, and had strong, empowering leaders who promoted a shared vision, utilized members' talents, and avoided or resolved conflict (Yin & Ware, 2000). An analysis of 10 percent of the more than 250 CSAP-funded community coalitions found community coalitions were effective in reducing alcohol and drug abuse in eighth and tenth grade boys and adult males as compared to matched communities without coalitions. Community coalitions were not effective for girls or women and, in fact, resulted in increases in drug use in eighth grade girls (Yin et al., 1997). Because coalitions typically focus on implementing environmental policies, such as access to tobacco and alcohol, they often do not include funding for school- and family-strengthening approaches, which have more impact on reducing drug abuse in girls.

Policy Change Strategies. Community coalitions generally are most effective in changing community policies and laws related to age of legal purchase, cost of tobacco or alcohol, availability of products, density of outlets, keg registration, server training, counter-advertising, legislating warning labels, and other environmental changes. Many alcohol-misuse interventions are implemented through an overall community coalition mobilization. Some examples of effective alcohol-prevention coalitions include the *Community Trials Project, Saving Lives,* and *Project Northland.*

Because states have less funding for substance abuse prevention services, they turn to policy change strategies, which cost less and can generate increased tax dollars. Despite a recent upswing in the popularity of policy approaches, only a few policy approaches, such as increasing the age of purchase and boosting taxes and cost of tobacco or alcohol, are effective in reducing substance use (Wagenaar & Toomey, 2002). Sting operations to reduce sales of tobacco or alcohol have not reduced adolescent use, although they are effective in reducing sales to minors. Sting operations staffed by coalition youth along with increased enforcement and limiting licenses resulted in a reduction in sales to minors of about 50 percent to 20 percent between 1997 and 2000. However, during that time tobacco use did not decrease in minors. Teens get adults to purchase for them or steal cigarettes.

The effects of community-based alcohol prevention are modest, even though great effort and funds have been expended on them. Cost-benefit studies are needed to help communities understand how much improvement they can expect. Increasing the cost of alcohol and increasing the legal drinking age or maintaining it at 21 years appears to be an effective approach to reducing consumption among youth.

COLLEGE AGED YOUTH PREVENTION

Despite documented risks, few prevention strategies aimed at college-age drinking have been successful (NIAAA, 2000). The Department of Education's Fund for the Improvement of Postsecondary Education (FIPSE) was successful in funding drug prevention centers on college campuses nationwide. Many colleges continued these prevention centers when the seed funding ended. Primary prevention approaches adopted in colleges are media campaigns, alcohol and drug policy revisions, early identification, and referrals to counseling. Changing the perception that most college students are substance users through published needs assessment surveys is also effective.

Little research exists on prevention strategies that work for college students. The NIAAA Task Force in 2002 suggested that generalized strategies effective with adults should work (e.g., increasing taxes and cost of alcohol, increasing enforcement and consequences of violating minimum legal drinking age laws and driving under the influence, and instituting policies and training for servers of alcoholic beverages). Strategies recommended specifically for college/university students include normative education and stress/coping strategies as well as correcting false beliefs about the effects of alcohol and increasing motivation to reduce drinking. Combining approaches into a comprehensive campus-wide approach should be more effective. More information on the NIAAA Task Force's report can be found on their website.

COCHRANE COLLABORATION REVIEWS

The World Health Organization Cochrane Collaboration Reviews in Medicine and Public Health has conducted several meta-analyses of substance abuse prevention programs. One of the first was of school-based alcohol prevention (Foxcroft et al., 2003). Of 56 studies, 20 had no or negative results. They concluded that the *Strengthening Families Program 10 to 14 Years* (Kumpfer, Molgaard, & Spoth, 1996) was twice as effective for preventing alcohol use after at least a two-year follow-up. The next best program was also a parenting program, *Preparing for the Drug-free Years* (PFDY). The next most effective programs were Schinke's (2000) *Smart Moves for Native Americans* and Botvin's (1995) *Life Skills Training* (LST). A 2006 meta-analysis of drug abuse prevention also found SFP to be one of only two promising programs, the other being a social marketing media approach (Gates et al., 2006). BluePrint program reviewers found positive results in evidence-based programs depend heavily on fidelity

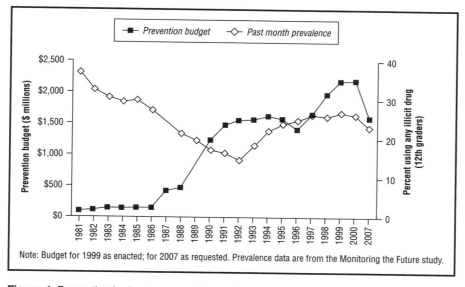

Figure 1. Prevention budget and prevalence of drug use among 12th graders, 1971–2007.
ILLUSTRATION BY GGS INFORMATION SERVICES. GALE, CENGAGE LEARNING.

to the original model and high quality implementation (Elliott & Mahalic, 2004).

FUNDING FOR PREVENTION AND TREATMENT

Funding for drug treatment and prevention has not kept pace with the need. Despite increased recognition of the cost effectiveness of prevention programs, Dr. Sloboda, President of the Society for Prevention Research, noted funding difficulties (Sloboda, 2008). She said in her presidential address at SPR, "In a squeeze, budgets for prevention have been easy targets for cash-strapped governments. In the U.S., prevention funding had already been *cut by up to 25 percent* when investments in interdiction that are not working have increased. Investments to support the Safe and Drug-Free Schools and Communities Act, for example, fell from $346 million in 2001 to $270 million last year."

According to ONDCP, the percentage of the total federal budget for prevention was 12 percent in 2008, compared to 14 percent in 2000. The National Drug Control Budget rose 57 percent from $12.2 billion to $19.2 billion between 1994 and 2001, but dropped to 12.9 billion in 2007. During the rise from 1994 to 2001, prevention and treatment funding increased only 33 percent and 44 percent respectively, while international efforts increased 175 percent, interdiction efforts increased by 68

percent, and domestic law enforcement by more than 60 percent. Without increased funding for drug prevention and treatment, it is difficult to reduce the demand for drugs (see Figure 1).

Despite these increases in total federal funding over the last two decades, the "War on Drugs" has been criticized for its failure to reduce drug use or to produce a consistent and fair legal policy (Battin et al., 2007). Overall, about 90 percent of U.S. funding for the War on Drugs goes for supply reduction, including funding for interdiction, crop eradication, and border patrols, and not for demand reduction or prevention. Despite this, adolescents report in the *Monitoring the Future* surveys that drugs are as available as in the late 1980s or early 1990s, depending on the drug (Johnston, O'Malley, Bachman, & Schulenberg, 2007). What emerges from this picture is an erosion of funding for prevention in America, which can only lead to increased substance use in the future. Citizens must become more vocal and involved in local and national substance abuse prevention policy making. They should promote increased prevention funding and support prevention programs that work to promote not just reductions in illegal drug use but also in many other associated social and health problems.

See also **Crime and Drugs; Gangs and Drugs; Prevention, Education and.**

BIBLIOGRAPHY

Aos, S., Lieb, R., Mayfield, J., Miller, M., & Pennucci, A. (2004). Benefits and costs of prevention and early intervention programs for youth. *Washington State Policy Institute.* Available from http://www.wsipp. wa.gov/.

Battin, M. P., Luna, E., Lipman, A. G., Gahlinger, P. M., Rollins, D. E., Roberts, J. C., et al. (2007). *Drugs and justice: Seeking a consistent, coherent, comprehensive view.* New York: Oxford University Press.

Bauman, K. E., Foshee, V. A., Ennett, S. T., Hicks, K. A., & Pemberton, M. (2001). Family matters: A family-directed program designed to prevent adolescent tobacco and alcohol use. *Health Promotion and Practice* 2(1), 81–96.

Botvin, G. J. (1995). Drug abuse prevention in school settings. In G. J. Botvin, S. Schinke, & M. A. Orlandi (Eds.), *Drug abuse prevention with multiethnic youth* (pp. 169–192). Thousand Oaks, CA: Sage Publications.

Center for Substance Abuse Prevention. (1998). *Preventing substance abuse among children and adolescents: Family-centered approaches. Prevention Enhancement Protocols System (PEPS).* (DHHS Publication No. SMA 3223-FY 98). Rockville, MD: National Clearinghouse for Alcohol and Drug Information.

Elliott, D., & Mahalic, S. (2004). Issues in disseminating and replicating effective prevention programs. *Prevention Science,* 5(1), 47–53.

Flay, B. R., Biglan, A., Brouch, R., Castro, P., Gottfredson, D., Kellam, S., et al. (2005). Standards of evidence: Criteria of efficacy, effectiveness, and dissemination. *Prevention Science,* 6(3), 151–175.

Foxcroft, D. R., Ireland, D., Lister-Sharp, D. J., Lowe, G., & Breen, R. (2003). Longer-term primary prevention for alcohol misuse in young people: A systematic review. *Addiction,* 98, 397–411.

Gates, S., McCambridge, J., Smith, L. A., & Foxcroft, D. R. (2006). Interventions for prevention of drug use by young people delivered in non-school settings. *The Cochrane Database of Systematic Reviews* (Issue 1) Art. No.: CD005030. DOI: 10.1002/14651858.CD005030. pub2.

Harrington, N., Hoyle, R., Giles, S., & Hansen, W. (2000). The All-Stars Prevention Program. In W. B. Hansen, S. M. Giles, & M. D. Fearnow-Kenney (Eds.), *Improving prevention effectiveness.* Greensboro, NC: Tanglewood Research.

Hawkins, D., & Catalano, R. (1999). *Communities that care.* (2nd ed.). San Francisco, CA: Jossey-Bass.

Hawkins, D., Catalano, R., & Arthur, M. (2000). *Diffusion Consortium Project briefing for federal funding agencies.* Washington, DC: Social Development Research.

IOM, Institute of Medicine. (1995). *Reducing risks for mental disorders: Frontiers for preventive intervention research.* In P. J. Mrazek & R. J. Haggerty (Eds.), Washington, DC: National Academy Press.

Johnston, L. D., O'Malley, P. M., Bachman, J. G., & Schulenberg, J. E. (2007). *Monitoring the Future national survey results on drug use, 1975–2006. Secondary school students.* (Vol. I). (NIH Publication No. 07-6205). Bethesda, MD: National Institute on Drug Abuse, p. 699, Figure 8.4.

Kaminski, J. W., Valle, L. A., Filene, J. H., & Boyle, C. L. (2008). A meta-analytic review of components associated with parent training program effectiveness. *Journal of Abnormal Psychology,* 36, 567–589.

Kumpfer, K. L., & Alder, S. (2003). Dissemination of research-based family strengthening interventions for the prevention of substance abuse. In Z. Sloboda & W. Bukoski (Eds.), *Handbook for drug abuse prevention, theory, science, and practice* (pp. 75–100). New York: Kluwer Academic/Plenum.

Kumpfer, K. L, & Alvarado, R. (2003). Family strengthening approaches for the prevention of youth problem behaviors. *American Psychologist,* 58(6/7), 457–465. [PMID: 12971192]

Kumpfer, K. L. Alvardo, R., & Whiteside, H. (2003). Family-based interventions for substance use and misuse prevention. *Substance Use and Misuse,* 38(11), 1759–1787.

Kumpfer, K. L., Molgaard, V., & Spoth, R. (1996). The Strengthening Families Program for prevention of delinquency and drug use in special populations. In R. DeV. Peters & R. J. McMahon (Eds.), *Childhood disorders, substance abuse, and delinquency: Prevention and early intervention approaches* (pp. 241–267). Newbury Park, CA: Sage Publications.

Kumpfer, K. L., Pinyuchon, M., de Melo, A., & Whiteside, H. (2008). Cultural adaptation process for international dissemination of the Strengthening Families Program (SFP). *Evaluation and Health Professions.* 33(2), 226–239.

Nation, M., Kumpfer, K. L., Crusto, C. A., Wandersman, A., Seybolt, D., Morrissey-Kane, E., et al. (2003). What works in prevention: Principles of effective prevention programs. *American Psychologist,* 58(6/7), 449–456 [PMID: 12971191].

National Institute on Alcohol Abuse and Alcoholism (NIAAA). (2000). Community-based prevention approaches. Rockville, MD: NIAAA, 397–411.

National Institute on Alcohol Abuse and Alcoholism (NIAAA). (2002). College Drinking—Changing the Culture. Available from http://www.collegedrinkingprevention.gov/.

National Institute on Drug Abuse (NIDA). (2008). *Preventing drug use among children and adolescents* (2nd ed.). Available from http://www.drugabuse.gov/.

Office of National Drug Control Policy (ONDCP). (2008). *Prevention Programs*. Available from www.whitehouse drugpolicy.gov/.

PRIDE Surveys (2006, June 20). Parents, kids, alcohol and drugs: A disconnect? Available from www.pridesurveys. com/.

Schinke, S. P., Schwinn, T. C., DiNoia, J., & Cole, K. C. (2004). Reducing the risk of alcohol use among urban youth. *Journal of Studies on Alcoholism, 65*(4), 443–449.

Schinke, S. P., Tepavac, L., & Cole, K. C. (2000). Preventing substance use among Native American youth: Three-year results. *Addictive Behaviors, 25*, 387–397.

Sloboda, Z. (2008, May). *Presidential address.* Annual conference of the Society for Prevention Research, San Francisco, CA.

Tobler, N. S., Roona, M. R., Ochshorn, P., Marshall, G. D., Streke, A. V., & Stackpole, K. M. (2000). School-based adolescent drug prevention programs: 1998 meta-analysis. *Journal of Primary Prevention, 20*, 275–337.

Wagenaar, A. C., & Toomey, T. L. (2002). Effects of minimum drinking age laws: Review and analysis of the literature from 1960 to 2000. *Journal of Studies on Alcoholism*, Supp., 14, 206–225.

Yin, R. K., Kaftarian, S., Yu, P., & Jansen, M. (1997). Outcomes from CSAP's Community Partnership Program: Findings from the National Cross-site Evaluation. *Evaluation Program Planning, 20*, 345–355.

Yin, R., & Ware, A. (2000). Using outcome data to evaluate community drug prevention initiatives: Pushing the state-of-the-art. *Journal of Community Psychology, 28*, 323–338.

KAROL KUMPFER

PREVENTION, EDUCATION AND.

In its broadest sense, prevention refers to the reduction of the supply of drugs through law enforcement actions and the demand for drugs through public health and education programs. Prevention can occur throughout the life span and in five distinct domains: individual, family, peer, school, and community. Public health and education prevention programs reduce the demand for drugs by stopping use or abuse after it starts or providing people with the resources and support they need to avoid using them in the first place. Thus, such programs may be designed to reach individuals before they initiate use (primary prevention), provide screening and early intervention (secondary prevention), or prevent the progression of an existing drug problem (tertiary prevention). Successful programs help participants strengthen existing, and develop new, protective factors (e.g., strong neighborhood or familial attachments) while reversing or reducing modifiable risk factors (e.g., early aggressive behavior or lack of parental supervision) and can operate on three levels. Universal programs target a general population, selective programs target a subset of the general population known to be at risk, and indicated programs target individuals already experimenting with drugs. The higher the level of risk of the target population, the younger the participants should be when they initiate the program and the more intensive the program should be. Research has shown that successful programs are also developmentally appropriate and culturally sensitive.

In 1997 the National Institute on Drug Abuse (NIDA) produced a research-based guide to prevention programs for parents, educators, and community leaders that lists the principles of effective research-based prevention programs and provides guidance on thinking about, planning, selecting, and delivering community-based prevention programs. The second edition, released in October 2003, provided 16 principles derived from NIDA-funded research on the origins of drug-abuse behaviors and effective prevention programs:

1. Prevention programs should enhance protective factors and reverse or reduce risk factors.

2. Prevention programs should address all forms of drug abuse, alone or in combination.

3. Prevention programs should address the type of drug-abuse problem in the local community, target modifiable risk factors, and strengthen identified protective factors.

4. Prevention programs should be tailored to address risks specific to population or audience characteristics, such as age, gender, and ethnicity, to improve program effectiveness.

5. Family-based prevention programs should enhance family bonding and relationships and include parenting skills; practice in developing, discussing, and enforcing family policies on substance abuse; and training in drug education and information.

6. Prevention programs can be designed to intervene as early as preschool to address risk factors for drug abuse, such as aggressive behavior, poor social skills, and academic difficulties.

7. Prevention programs for elementary school children should target improving academic and social-emotional learning by building self-control, emotional awareness, and communication and social problem-solving skills.

8. Prevention programs for middle or junior high and high school students should increase academic and social competence by building study habits, communication skills, peer relationships, self-efficacy and assertiveness, drug resistance skills, antidrug attitudes, and personal commitments against drug abuse.

9. Prevention programs aimed at general populations at key transition points, such as the transition to middle school, can produce beneficial effects even among high-risk families and children. Such interventions do not single out risk populations and, therefore, reduce labeling and promote bonding to school and community.

10. Community prevention programs that combine two or more effective programs, such as family- and school-based programs, can be more effective than a single program alone.

11. Community prevention programs reaching populations in multiple settings—for example, schools, clubs, faith-based organizations, and the media—are most effective when they present consistent, communitywide messages in each setting.

12. When communities adapt programs to match their needs, community norms, or differing cultural requirements, they should retain core elements of the original research-based intervention including structure, content, and delivery.

13. Prevention programs should be long-term with repeated interventions (i.e., booster programs) to reinforce the original prevention goals. Research shows that the benefits from middle school prevention programs diminish without follow-up programs in high school.

14. Prevention programs should include teacher training on good classroom management practices, such as rewarding appropriate student behavior. Such techniques help to foster students' positive behavior, achievement, academic motivation, and school bonding.

15. Prevention programs are most effective when they employ interactive techniques, such as peer discussion groups and parent role-playing, that allow for active involvement in learning about drug abuse and reinforcing skills.

16. Research-based prevention programs can be cost-effective. Similar to earlier research, recent research shows that for each dollar invested in prevention, a savings of up to $10 in treatment for alcohol or other substance abuse may be seen.

NATIONAL APPROACH TO PREVENTION: CENTER FOR SUBSTANCE ABUSE PREVENTION

The Substance Abuse and Mental Health Services Administration's (SAMHSA) Center for Substance Abuse Prevention (CSAP) works with states and local communities to develop comprehensive prevention systems that promote communities with healthy, drug- and crime-free environments at work and in school, supportive neighborhoods, and connections with families and friends. To further this mission, CSAP has developed a strategic prevention framework and a registry of proven and promising programs. It maintains four funding streams to support state and local efforts to implement the framework and programs.

Strategic Prevention Framework. The Strategic Prevention Framework (SPF) is a five-step data-driven strategic planning and community development process. It promotes youth development and builds assets and resilience while reducing risk-taking and other problem behaviors across the life span. In this way, CSAP ensures that implemented prevention programs are grounded in evidence-based research and that the outcomes of those programs are regularly monitored.

The five steps in the SPF are assessment, capacity building, planning, implementation, and evaluation. Assessment uses data to define and quantify substance use and its consequences. It enables states and communities to prioritize substance-abuse problems to determine how to focus future steps in the process. The second step is to build the capacity of the state or community to address these problems by engaging key stakeholders and mobilizing communities and resources. Once priority problems are identified and the state or community has the capacity to address them, the planning phase begins. Comprehensive interventions are designed to impact specific risk and protective factors. Then the plans are implemented and evaluated.

The evaluation of a program should involve monitoring both the progress of the implementation and impact of the program over time. SAMHSA has identified 14 prevention measures in eight domains as a part of National Outcomes Measures (NOMs) to provide uniform measures for all federally funded programs. The domains are reduced morbidity, employment and education, crime and criminal justice, social connectedness, retention, access and capacity, use of evidence-based programs and strategies, and cost-effectiveness. Baseline reports on the NOMs for each state are based largely on national data sets, such as the National Survey on Drug Use and Health.

Sustainability and cultural competence make up the backbone of this process and are ongoing efforts throughout the process. Sustainability refers to the ability to maintain positive outcomes by making the SPF steps the norm and integrating them in the ongoing operations of state and local agencies. Sustainability is vital to ensuring that necessary resources (financial and otherwise) are secured to establish and maintain prevention values, processes, and partnerships over the long term. Cultural competence is the ability to communicate with participants from diverse geographic, ethnic, racial, cultural, economic, social, and linguistic backgrounds. Culturally competent programs are effective because they eliminate disparities between services and participants. They meet the needs of the people they serve.

Funding Mechanisms to Support Local Prevention Efforts. Currently CSAP maintains four grant programs to support states and communities implementing the SPF: The SPF State Incentive Grant (SIG), drug-free community grants, HIV grants, and methamphetamine grants. The SPF SIG is an infrastructure grant designed to support the implementation of the strategic prevention framework described above by states and federally recognized tribes and tribal organizations. The infrastructure provides a solid foundation for preventing the onset and reducing the progression of substance abuse and substance-abuse-related problems in communities. Thirty-seven SIGs were operating across the nation in 2008.

The cornerstone of the SPF SIG is the State Epidemiology Outcomes Workgroup (SEOW). The SEOW is responsible for completing the first step of the SPF by conducting both statewide and community level needs assessments. As of 2008, SEOWs were funded in all 50 states. The mission of the SEOW in Maryland, for instance, is to monitor the use of alcohol, tobacco, and other drugs and the consequences of their use in Maryland and its localities in order to identify and prioritize the prevention needs of the state and its local jurisdictions. To achieve this end, the Maryland SEOW will oversee the collection, interpretation, and dissemination of statewide and local data that quantify substance use and its consequences for Maryland. The reports prepared by the SEOW will be used to complete the remaining steps of the SPF process.

Drug-free community grants are a part of the Drug Free Communities Program that is run jointly by SAMHSA and the White House Office of National Drug Control Policy (ONDCP). In the most recent round of funding as of 2008, new grants were awarded to 90 communities and continuation grants were awarded to 646 communities in 49 states, the District of Columbia, Puerto Rico, and the Virgin Islands. These grants support community organizations that act as catalysts to increase citizen participation in substance prevention efforts directed at youth.

HIV grants were initially awarded in 2004. At that time, SAMHSA awarded more than $111 million to support states implementing the SPF to develop local capacity to address substance abuse by individuals (especially racial and ethnic minorities) living with and affected by HIV/AIDS. These funds have been used for mental health, treatment, prevention, outreach, training, and studying the costs associated with delivering integrated care. In FY2005, 25 states, the District of Columbia, and the Virgin Islands received funding to implement the SPF for substance-abuse and HIV/hepatitis prevention in targeted minority populations. In the most recent funding cycle, SAMHSA planned to support up to 46 cooperative agreements for community-based substance-abuse and HIV/AIDS prevention programs for at-risk racial or ethnic minority populations based on the SPF.

In response to increases in methamphetamine abuse across the country, SAMHSA awarded methamphetamine grants in FY2006 and FY2007. These grants were designed to support infrastructure development and/or methamphetamine prevention interventions. The goal is to prevent, reduce, or delay the use of methamphetamine. Like the other SAMHSA/CSAP grants, this grant encourages the use of the SPF to build local capacity and implement evidence-based programs. Programs in eight states received awards in FY2006, and programs in Corona, California, and San Antonio, Texas, received grants in FY2007.

ASSESSMENT

The science of prevention has made great progress since the mid-1990s. Substance-abuse prevention programs have been shown to be cost-effective. Research-based estimates demonstrate that every dollar invested in prevention saves $10 in treatment and other expenses. SAMHSA/CSAP has established a strategic prevention framework with standards for evidence-based programs and measures to assess outcomes. The National Registry of Evidenced-Based Programs and Practices, for instance, includes 35 proven substance-abuse prevention and treatment programs and 92 legacy (effective or promising) programs to address co-occurring disorders, mental health, prevention, and treatment. The NOMs, described in an earlier section, ensure that the impacts of these programs are measured consistently and regularly. In spite of this continuing progress in understanding prevention and implementing effective programs, the George W. Bush administration's drug control budget continued to emphasize supply reduction programs over demand reduction programs. Funding for supply reduction programs increased 57 percent from FY2002 to FY2009, while funding for demand reduction programs grew by only 2.7 percent and prevention funding actually decreased 25 percent. This trend appears to be counter to current research and has made it increasingly difficult for federal, state, and local agencies to effectively implement the current prevention framework.

See also **Adolescents and Drug Use; Families and Drug Use; Homelessness, History of Association with Alcohol and Drugs; Models of Alcoholism and Drug Abuse; Parent Movement, The; Prevention.**

BIBLIOGRAPHY

Abadinsky, H. (2001). *Drugs: An introduction* (4th ed.). Chapter 10. Belmont, CA: Wadsworth.

Akers, R. L. (1992). *Drugs, alcohol, and society: Social structure, process, and policy.* Chapter 8. Belmont, CA: Wadsworth.

Aos, S., Phipps, P., Barnoski, R., & Lieb, R. (2001). *The comparative costs and benefits of programs to reduce crime.* Volume 4. Olympia: Washington State Institute for Public Policy.

Ashery, R. S., Robertson, E. B., & Kumpfer, K. L. (Eds.) (1998). *Drug abuse prevention through family interventions.* NIDA Research Monograph No. 177. Washington, DC: U.S. Government Printing Office.

Battistich, V., Solomon, D., Watson, M., & Schaps, E. (1997). Caring school communities. *Educational Psychologist, 32*(3), 137–151.

Botvin, G. J., & Botvin, E. M. (1992). 69: School-based and community-based prevention approaches. In J. H. Lowinson, P. Ruiz, & R. Millman (Eds.), *Substance abuse: A comprehensive textbook* (2nd ed.). Baltimore, MD: Williams & Wilkins.

Botvin, G., Baker, E., Dusenbury, L., Botvin, E., & Diaz, T. (1995). Long-term follow-up results of a randomized drug-abuse prevention trial in a white middle class population. *Journal of the American Medical Association, 273,* 1106–1112.

Carnevale Associates. (February 2008). *Policy brief: Federal drug budget trend.* Gaithersburg, MD: Author.

Chou, C., Montgomery, S., Pentz, M., Rohrbach, L., Johnson, C., Flay, B., & Mackinnon, D. (1998). Effects of a community-based prevention program in decreasing drug use in high-risk adolescents. *American Journal of Public Health, 88,* 944–948.

Conduct Problems Prevention Research Group. (2002). Predictor variables associated with positive Fast Track outcomes at the end of third grade. *Journal of Abnormal Child Psychology, 30*(1), 37–52.

Dishion, T., Kavanagh, K., Schneiger, A. K. J., Nelson, S., & Kaufman, N. (2002). Preventing early adolescent substance use: A family centered strategy for the public middle school. *Prevention Science, 3*(3), 191–202.

Hawkins, J. D., Catalano, R. F., & Arthur, M. (2002). Promoting science-based prevention in communities. *Addictive Behaviors, 90*(5), 1–26.

Hawkins, J. D., Catalano, R. F., Kosterman, R., Abbott, R., & Hill, K. G. (1999). Preventing adolescent health-risk behaviors by strengthening protection during childhood. *Archives of Pediatric and Adolescent Medicine, 153,* 226–234.

Ialongo, N., Poduska, J., Werthamer, L., & Kellam, S. (2001). The distal impact of two first-grade preventive interventions on conduct problems and disorder in early adolescence. *Journal of Emotional and Behavioral Disorders, 9,* 146–160.

Johnston, L. D., O'Malley, P. M., & Bachman, J. G. (2002). *Monitoring the future National Survey results on drug use, 1975–2002. Volume 1: Secondary school students.* Bethesda, MD: National Institute on Drug Abuse.

National Institute on Drug Abuse. (October 2003). *Preventing drug use among children and adolescents: A research-based guide for parents, educators, and community leaders* (2nd ed.). Bethesda, MD: U.S. Department of Health and Human Services, National Institutes of Health.

Oetting, E., Edwards, R., Kelly, K., & Beauvais, F. (1997). Risk and protective factors for drug use among rural American youth. In E. B. Robertson, Z. Sloboda, G. M. Boyd, L. Beatty, & N. J. Kozel (Eds.), *Rural substance abuse: State of knowledge and issues* (pp. 90–130). NIDA Research Monograph No. 168. Washington, DC: U.S. Government Printing Office.

Office of National Drug Control Policy. (2008). Drug free communities support program. Available from http://www.ondcp.gov/.

Pentz, M. A. Costs, benefits, and cost-effectiveness of comprehensive drug abuse prevention. In W. J. Bukoski & R. I. Evans (Eds.), *Cost-benefit/cost-effectiveness research of drug abuse prevention: Implications for programming and policy* (pp. 111–129). NIDA Research Monograph No. 176. Washington, DC: U.S. Government Printing Office.

SAMHSA. (2008). Center for substance abuse prevention. Available from http://www.prevention.SAMHSA.gov/.

SAMSHA. (2008). National registry of evidence-based programs and practices. Available from http://www.nrepp.samhsa.gov/.

SAMHSA. (2008). State data: National outcomes measures. Available from http://www.nationaloutcomemeasures.samhsa.gov/.

Scheier, L., Botvin, G., Diaz, T., & Griffin, K. (1999). Social skills, competence, and drug refusal efficacy as predictors of adolescent alcohol use. *Journal of Drug Education, 29*(3), 251–278.

Sloboda, Z. (1999). The prevention of drug abuse: Interrupting the paths. In M. D. Glantz & C. R. Hartel (Eds.), *Drug abuse: Origins and interventions.* Washington, DC: American Psychological Association.

Spoth, R. L., Redmond, D., Trudeau, L., & Shin, C. (2002). Longitudinal substance initiation outcomes for a universal preventive intervention combining family and school programs. *Psychology of Addictive Behaviors, 16*(2), 129–134.

Substance Abuse and Mental Health Services Administration Center for Substance Abuse Prevention. *A life in the community for everyone.* Available from http://www.download.ncadi.samhsa.gov/.

Webster-Stratton, C. (1998). Preventing conduct problems in Head Start children: Strengthening parenting competencies. *Journal of Consulting and Clinical Psychology, 66,* 715–730.

Webster-Stratton, C., Reid, J., & Hammond, M. (2001). Preventing conduct problems, promoting social competence: A parent and teacher training partnership in Head Start. *Journal of Clinical Child Psychology, 30,* 282–302.

E. ERIN ARTIGIANI

PREVENTION OF ALCOHOL RELATED HARM: THE TOTAL CONSUMPTION MODEL.

The total consumption model of alcohol is an important concept for anyone who wishes to understand the underpinnings of modern policy efforts to prevent heavy drinking and alcohol-related harm. The point of departure for this concept is a set of observations about how alcohol consumption is distributed in human societies and how the total, or mean, consumption per drinker is related to excessive drinking and alcohol-related harm.

The distribution of alcohol consumption in a population can be shown as a distribution curve in a diagram where the number of drinkers in a population is on the *y*-axis and the annual amount of alcohol intake is on the *x*-axis. This distribution curve could—a priori—take on different shapes. A popular assumption that normal drinkers and alcoholics (or "abnormal drinkers") constitute distinct categories of drinkers would imply that they are populations separated on the consumption scale and that the distribution of consumption occurs in two parts. If that were the case, the distribution of alcohol consumption

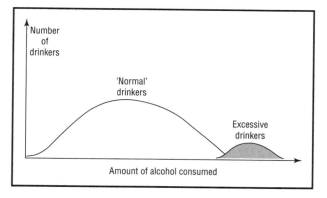

Figure 1. Hypothetical distribution curve of alcohol consumption. ILLUSTRATION BY GGS INFORMATION SERVICES. GALE, CENGAGE LEARNING

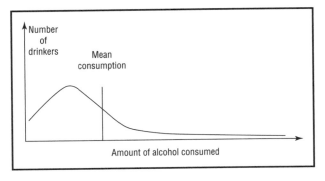

Figure 2. Example of empirical distribution of alcohol consumption. ILLUSTRATION BY GGS INFORMATION SERVICES. GALE, CENGAGE LEARNING

could take the shape illustrated in Figure 1. Starting on the left are the majority of normal drinkers, with a few people drinking very little in a year, then moving to an increasing number drinking greater amounts but less than the average amount, and finally, a declining number drinking more than the average amount, until the graph reaches the normal drinkers who drink much more than the average—and these are relatively few in number. In addition, there are a minority of "abnormal" drinkers; their drinking distribution also might be plotted as a bell-shaped curve, but this curve is shifted to the right of the distribution for normal drinkers. The two peaks in the distribution (one for normal and one for abnormal drinking) create a bi-modal distribution.

A large number of empirical studies in various populations have demonstrated, however, that the distribution of alcohol consumption does not resemble such a bi-modal distribution. The observed distributions in different populations with varying mean consumption do, in fact, display the same kind of distribution curve, which is *unimodal* (having one peak) and very skewed with a long tail toward high consumption levels. Such a skew distribution implies that the majority of drinkers consume less than the population average (see Figure 2). Moreover, this distribution implies that there is no clear separation between normal drinkers and excessive drinkers or alcoholics.

BACKGROUND

The relationship between total consumption (or mean consumption) and prevalence of excessive drinking was first noted by the French demographer Sully Ledermann (1956; 1964), and hence

the model is also known as the Ledermann model. Ledermann's work on the distribution of alcohol consumption began in his earlier studies showing a significant co-variation in space and time between per capita alcohol consumption and mortality. This led to the assumption that the mean (per capita) alcohol consumption in a population is closely connected to the prevalence of excessive drinkers, who have an elevated risk of premature death. Ledermann proposed that the consumption distribution is a one-parameter lognormal distribution. A lognormal distribution means that the distribution is skewed with a long tail to the right and that, when plotted on a natural logarithmic consumption scale, the distribution is normal with a bell-shaped form. A one-parameter distribution means that there is constant relationship between the mean and the dispersion of the distribution; hence, it is also called a single-distribution model.

The critics of Ledermann have demonstrated, however, that the mathematical properties of the distribution of consumption are not as strict as he suggested (Bruun et al., 1975; Skog, 1985; Lemmens, 1991). For instance, the relationship between the mean and the dispersion of the distribution is not—as Ledermann suggested—constant, but varies to some extent, and the dispersion tends to be somewhat higher in populations with a low mean consumption (Bruun et al., 1975). Consequently, the distribution of consumption and the prevalence of excessive drinking in a population is not precisely predicted by the Ledermann model. It should also be noted that the distribution of alcohol may, under certain conditions, deviate significantly from the Ledermann model. According to Thor Norström (1987), this was the case in Sweden during the period of individual rationing of spirits from around 1920 to 1955 when Swedish men were allowed, depending on marital and social status and social stability, a maximum purchase of 1, 2, 3, or 4 liters of spirits per month. Under the rationing, consumption distribution displayed distinct peaks corresponding to the categories of maximum individual rations, and the relative dispersion of consumption was much lower compared to the period after the rationing was abolished. A significant redistribution of alcohol consumption among Swedes occurred after the rationing system ended; the skewness of the distribution increased markedly, revealing a large increase in the prevalence of excessive drinkers.

Ledermann's work has been followed by a large number of empirical studies demonstrating two essential aspects of the distribution of alcohol consumption: (1) that alcohol consumption in various populations and in various eras is indeed very skewed, and (2) that the prevalence of heavy drinkers is linked to the average level of consumption (Bruun et al., 1975; Skog, 1985; Lemmens, 1991;). The strong link between prevalence of excessive drinking and mean consumption in the population implies that the mean consumption is an *indicator* of the prevalence of excessive drinking. Thus, when per capita consumption is high, the prevalence of excessive drinkers is high as well and vice versa. Kettil Bruun and colleagues proposed in 1975 that the proportion of heavy alcohol consumers is approximately proportional to the square of the mean consumption. Consequently, if mean consumption in one population is twice as high as another, a fourfold higher prevalence of heavy alcohol consumers can be expected.

Ledermann did not offer much to explain *why* consumers are distributed along the alcohol consumption scale with such a degree of regularity. (Skog, 1985; Lemmens, 1991). The Norwegian scientist Ole-Jørgen Skog proposed in 1985 a theory of alcohol-consumption distribution: a theory of the collectivity of drinking cultures, founded on two basic hypotheses about human drinking behavior. First, the factors influencing a person's drinking behavior tend to combine multiplicatively, implying that a change in consumption is proportional to the initial consumption level. And second, social interaction is one of the most important mechanisms regulating individual drinking behavior. Based on a large number of surveys from various drinking cultures with a large variation in mean consumption, Skog in 1985 demonstrated that both the prevalence of excessive drinkers (e.g., those consuming above 10 centiliters of pure alcohol per day) and the consumption in all other consumer groups were strongly associated with the mean consumption of the population. Even the consumption among alcoholics co-varied with the mean consumption in the population. He concluded that there is a strong collective component in human drinking behavior and, consequently, when mean consumption in a population changes, all consumer groups move in

concert along the consumption scale. This has also been illustrated by longitudinal data. In 2002 Pia Mäkelä analyzed panel data from Finland covering the years 1968–1969. At that time mean alcohol consumption in Finland increased by 46 percent in one year due to a significant increase in availability of alcohol. Mäkelä found that all consumer groups increased their consumption and those with higher initial consumption, more so. Whether similar changes also occur in all consumer groups when the total (or mean) consumption decreases is, however, less well studied.

IMPLICATIONS FOR PREVENTION
Ledermann's work has been an important point of departure in the effort to understand the relationship between the total consumption of alcohol in a society and the prevalence of excessive alcohol use. From a prevention point of view, it is relevant that a reduction in the mean consumption will reduce the number of excessive or "at risk" drinkers and reduce the overall amount of alcohol-related harm. The prevention of alcohol-related harms, however, is not only about reducing consumption among the heaviest drinkers and those with the highest risks. For several types of alcohol-related harms—particularly acute harms, such as accidents and violence—the majority of cases are not found among the relatively few excessive drinkers, but mainly among low- or moderate-risk drinkers according to Skog's 2006 study. In such cases the potential impact of population-based prevention strategies is larger than that of strategies aimed at a small group of high-risk individuals. In 1981 Geoffrey Rose referred to this as the *prevention paradox*.

Based on what is known about the total consumption model and the prevention paradox, good arguments can be made for applying prevention strategies to reduce total consumption (or mean consumption) of alcohol in a population. Not only will reduced total consumption imply less harm as excessive drinkers become fewer, but it will also imply less harm among the light and moderate drinkers, because these groups will also drink less. The empirical evidence to support these assumptions is found in numerous studies demonstrating that some population-based prevention strategies (those that affect all consumers), such as price and availability of alcohol, are effective in reducing not only total consumption but also the amount of alcohol-related harm, according to work by Thomas Babor et al. in 2003. Mäkelä, Ingeborg Rossow, and Kalle Tryggvesson present further evidence for the effectiveness of such strategies among heavy drinkers in their 2002 review of differential effects of alcohol policies in the Nordic countries. Many studies indicate that, when availability of alcohol changes, those with an initially high level of consumption are most affected.

As Babor and his colleagues pointed out in 2003, several decades of research have clearly shown that the amount of alcohol-related harm in a population is not only proportional to the total consumption of alcohol but also to the way in which alcohol is consumed. Thus, in 2002 Norström and others indicated that the same amount of alcohol may cause more harm in a population with a drinking pattern characterized by relatively few, but heavy, drinking occasions as compared to a population where the intake is less per occasion and spread over a larger number of drinking occasions. Thus effective strategies to prevent heavy drinking occasions and to prevent drinking in risky contexts are important supplements to those aimed at reducing total consumption.

BIBLIOGRAPHY

Babor, T., Caetano, R., Casswell, S., Edwards, G., Giesbrecht, N., Graham, K., et al. (2003). *Alcohol: No ordinary commodity. Research and public policy.* Oxford, U.K.: Oxford University Press.

Bruun, K., Edwards, G., Lumio, M., Mäkelä, K., Pan, L., Popham, R. E., et al. (1975). *Alcohol control policies in public health perspective.* (Vol. 25). Forssa, Finland: Finnish Foundation for Alcohol Studies.

Ledermann, S. (1956). *Alcool, alcoolisme, alcoolisation: Données scientifiques de caractère physiologique, economique et social.* (Cah No. 29). Paris: Presses Universitaires de France (Institut National d'Études Démographiques: Travaux et Documents).

Ledermann, S. (1964). *Alcool, alcoolisme, alcoolisation: Mortalité, morbidité, accidents du travail.* (Cah. No. 41). Paris: Presses Universitaires de France (Institut National d'Études Démographiques: Travaux et Documents).

Lemmens, P.H.H.M. (1991). *Measurement and distribution of alcohol consumption.* Maastricht, The Netherlands: University of Limburg.

Mäkelä, P. (2002). Whose drinking does the liberalization of alcohol policy increase?: Change in alcohol consumption by the initial level in the Finnish panel survey in 1968 and 1969. *Addiction, 97,* 701–706.

Mäkelä, P., Rossow, I., Tryggvesson, K. (2002). Who drinks more or less when policies change?: The evidence from 50 years of Nordic studies. In R. Room, (Ed), *The effects of Nordic alcohol policies: What happens to drinking and harm when alcohol controls change?* Helsinki: Nordic Council for Alcohol and Drug Research. NAD publication 42.

Norström, T. (1987). The abolition of the Swedish alcohol rationing system: Effects on consumption distribution and cirrhosis mortality. *British Journal of Addiction, 82,* 633–641.

Rose, G. (1981). Strategy of prevention: lessons from cardiovascular disease. *British Medical Journal, 282,* 1847–1851.

Skog, O. J. (1985). The collectivity of drinking cultures: A theory of the distribution of alcohol consumption. *British Journal of Addiction, 80,* 83–99.

Skog, O. J. (2006). Alcohol and the so-called prevention paradox: How does it look today? *Addiction, 101,* 155–158.

BRYAN M. JOHNSTONE
REVISED BY INGEBORG ROSSOW (2009)

PRISM. The Psychiatric Research Interview for Substance and Mental Disorders (PRISM) (Hasin et al., 1996; 2006) is a semi-structured diagnostic interview designed expressly to assess DSM-IV psychiatric disorders in individuals who abuse alcohol and drugs. The PRISM is most useful when a psychiatric diagnosis is needed for research purposes, intake assessment, or treatment planning. One challenge in psychiatric diagnosis has been to design a measure to differentiate three conditions: (a) expected effects of intoxication and withdrawal, (b) psychiatric disorders occurring during periods of heavy substance use, and (c) psychiatric disorders that are clearly independent from substance use. In the PRISM, a substance-induced diagnosis is given if the episode co-occurs with heavy substance use and the individual experiences symptoms that are greater than the expected effects of intoxication or withdrawal. The instrument's strength is in differentiating primary psychiatric disorders, such as major depression, from psychiatric syndromes that overlap with periods of heavy substance use or withdrawal.

The PRISM provides current and lifetime diagnoses that commonly occur with heavy substance use: mood and anxiety disorders. Modules are also provided to assess psychotic disorders, eating disorders, and antisocial and borderline personality disorders. Special assessment procedures are included for disorders that can mimic intoxication and withdrawal states (depression, mania, dysthymia, psychosis, panic, generalized anxiety) to rule out physiological symptoms associated with heavy substance use.

The substance modules consist of a brief screening for use of alcohol and seven drug categories (cocaine, heroin, cannabis, hallucinogens, sedatives, stimulants, and opiates), chronic intoxication and binge use, and the time period in which substance use occurred (last 12 months, prior to last 12 months). If the respondent passes screening for alcohol or drugs (drank or used at least six times in a year), abuse and dependence are assessed independently. Ages of lifetime onset, remission, recurrence, and offset of the most recent episode are obtained for substance-specific abuse and dependence diagnoses.

A number of features were incorporated into the PRISM to reduce the lengthy administration time associated with standardized diagnostic interviews:

- Diagnostic sections are modular so that the instrument can be tailored to fit specific treatment or research needs.

- The Overview section covers basic demographics and a brief history of treatment. Demographic information is limited to marital, educational, housing, military, legal, and employment status. Medical and psychiatric treatment items inquire about lifetime major medical conditions, and earliest and most recent psychiatric and substance abuse treatment.

- The substance screening module is placed at the beginning of the interview to provide a background for the assessment of co-occurring psychiatric disorders, thereby limiting substance-related questions in later sections.

- Consumption questions in the substance screening module do not seek detailed information about lifetime patterns of use. Questions are limited to determine if the respondent used a substance at least six times in a single year and whether he or she ever experienced chronic intoxication or binge use.

- Assessment of Major Depressive Disorder begins with the most recent episode. If this episode meets DSM-IV criteria for major depression, a potential earlier substance-induced episode is also explored. Conversely, if the most recent episode is determined to be substance-induced, a potential earlier primary episode is also explored. This way, time is not spent assessing the same type of depressive episode (primary or substance-induced) more than once.

The complete PRISM takes approximately two hours to administer but the time required varies with the complexity of the diagnosis, the number of drugs used, the experience of the interviewer, and the respondent's reporting style. Individuals with clinical experience are better equipped to administer the interview but lay interviewers with proper training and supervision can obtain reliable diagnoses in a timely manner.

RELIABILITY

The PRISM has been subjected to reliability and validity testing. A reliability study (N=285) in which heavy substance users were interviewed twice (each time by a different interviewer) showed good-to-excellent reliability for most substance dependence diagnoses (Hasin et al., 2006). Reliability was also good to excellent for current and lifetime primary (independent) major depression and substance-induced major depression. The reliability of current and lifetime primary anxiety disorder (any anxiety disorder) was fair to good; however, the reliability of substance-induced panic and substance-induced generalized anxiety disorder (GAD) was poor. The reliability of substance-induced generalized anxiety disorder appeared to have been reduced by inconsistencies in reporting of major depressive disorder in the first and second interviews, which led to inconsistent skipping out of the GAD module. Reliability of any current primary or substance-induced psychotic disorder was excellent. An independently conducted validity study compared diagnoses formulated using a Spanish version of the PRISM (Torrens et al., 2004), the Structured Clinical Interview for DSM-IV Diagnosis (SCID-IV), and expert diagnosis made by an experienced clinician using all available data (LEAD [longitudinal expert, all data]; Spitzer, 1983). In that study, concordance between the PRISM and LEAD diagnoses for current depression, past substance-induced major depression, and borderline personality disorder was better than the concordance between the LEAD procedure and the SCID. Concordance of the three methods for substance dependence was good to excellent. As with all self-report measures, the credibility of the information obtained using the PRISM is susceptible to the respondent's mood at the time of the interview and other cognitive biases.

The PRISM has been used in cross-sectional and longitudinal studies that require the differential diagnosis of primary and substance-induced disorders. Populations of these studies include first-break psychotic patients interviewed in emergency departments (Caton et al., 2005; 2006; 2007), substance abuse patients in inpatient and outpatient treatment settings (Hasin et al., 2002; Aharonovich et al., 2002, 2005; Nunes et al., 2006), Spanish drug abusers in a detoxification unit of a general hospital (Nocon et al., 2007), an HIV-infected cohort (Morgello et al., 2006), Spanish heroin users aged 18 to 30 outside the healthcare system (Rodriguez-Llera et al., 2006), jail recidivists (Chandler & Spicer, 2006), and patients with co-occurring alcohol dependence and depression (Kranzler et al., 2006).

The English paper version of the PRISM and training information can be downloaded at http://www.columbia.edu/~dsh2/prism. A computer-assisted version administered by the interviewer will include marijuana withdrawal (in preparation of DSM-V), and modules for nicotine-related disorders, pathological gambling, and attention deficit hyperactivity disorder (ADHD) (available in 2008). Translated paper versions are available in Spanish (Spain) and Norwegian.

See also **Addictive Personality and Psychological Tests; Alcohol Use Disorder Identification Test (AUDIT); Alcohol, Smoking and Substance Involvement Screening Test (ASSIST); Drug Abuse Screening Test (DAST); Michigan Alcoholism Screening Test (MAST).**

BIBLIOGRAPHY

Aharonovich, E., Liu, X., Nunes, E., & Hasin, D. S. (2002). Suicide attempts in substance abusers: effects of major depression in relation to substance use disorders. *American Journal of Psychiatry, 159*(9), 1600–1602.

Aharonovich, E., Liu, X., Samet, S., Nunes, E., Waxman, R., & Hasin, D. (2005). Postdischarge cannabis use and its relationship to cocaine, alcohol, and heroine use: A

prospective study. *American Journal of Psychiatry, 162*(8), 1507–1514.

Caton, C. L., Drake, R. E., Hasin, D. S., Dominguez, B., Shrout, P. E., Samet, S., et al. (2005) Differences between early-phase primary psychotic disorders with concurrent substance use and substance-induced psychoses. *Archives of General Psychiatry, 62*(2), 137–145.

Caton, C. L., Hasin, D. S., Shrout, P. E., Drake, R. E., Dominguez, B., Samet, S., et al. (2006). Predictors of psychosis remission in psychotic disorders that co-occur with substance use. *Schizophrenia Bulletin, 32*(4), 618–625. Epub 2006, July 27.

Caton, C. L., Hasin, D. S., Shrout, P. E., Drake, R. E., Dominguez, B., First, M. B., et al. (2007). Stability of early-phase primary psychotic disorders with concurrent substance use and substance-induced psychosis. *British Journal of Psychiatry, 190*, 105–111.

Chandler, D. W., & Spicer, G. (2006). Integrated treatment for jail recidivists with co-occurring psychiatric and substance use disorders. *Community Mental Health Journal, 42*(4), 405–425.

Hasin, D. S., Liu, X., Nunes, E., McCloud, S., Samet, S., & Endicott, J. (2002). Effects of major depression on remission and relapse of substance dependence. *Archives of General Psychiatry, 59*, 375–380.

Hasin, D. S., Trautman, K. D., Miele, G. M., Samet, S., Smith, M., & Endicott, J. (1996). Psychiatric Research Interview for Substance and Mental Disorders (PRISM): Reliability for substance abusers. *American Journal of Psychiatry, 153*(9), 1195–1201.

Hasin, D., Samet, S., Nunes, E., Meydan, J., Matseoane, K., & Waxman, R. (2006). Diagnosis of comorbid psychiatric disorders in substance users assessed with the Psychiatric Research Interview for Substance and Mental Disorders for *DSM-IV. American Journal of Psychiatry, 163*(4), 689–696.

Kranzler, H. R., Mueller, T., Cornelius, J., Pettinati, H. M., Moak, D., Martin, P. R., et al. (2006). Sertraline treatment of co-occurring alcohol dependence and major depression. *Journal of Clinical Psychopharmacology, 26*(1), 13–20.

Morgello, S., Holzer, C. E., III, Ryan, E., Young, C., Naseer, M., Castellon, S. A., et al. (2006). Interrater reliability of the Psychiatric Research Interview for Substance and Mental Disorders in an HIV-infected cohort: Experience of the National NeuroAIDS Tissue Consortium. *International Journal of Methods in Psychiatric Research, 15*(3), 131–138.

Nocon, A., Bergé, D., Astals, M., Martín-Santos, R., & Torrens, M. (2007). Dual diagnosis in an inpatient drug-abuse detoxification unit. *European Addiction Research, 13*(4), 192–200.

Nunes, E., Liu, X., Samet, S., Matseoane, K., & Hasin, D. (2006). Independent versus substance-induced major depressive disorder in substance-dependent patients: Observational study of course during follow-up. *Journal of Clinical Psychiatry, 67*(10), 1561–1567.

Rodriguez-Llera, M. C., Domingo-Salvany, A., Brugal, M. T., Silva, T. C., Sanchez-Niubo, A., & Torrens, M. (2006). ITINERE Investigators. Psychiatric comorbidity in young heroin users. *Drug and Alcohol Dependence, 1, 84*(1), 48–55.

Spitzer, R. L. (1983). Psychiatric diagnosis: Are clinicians still necessary? *Comprehensive Psychiatry, 24,* 399–411.

Torrens, M., Serrano, D., Astals, M., Perez-Dominguez, G., & Martin-Santos, R. (2004). Diagnosing comorbid psychiatric disorders in substance abusers: Validity of the Spanish versions of the Psychiatric Research Interview for Substance and Mental Disorders and the Structured Clinical Interview for *DSM-IV. American Journal of Psychiatry, 161*(7), 1231–1237.

SHARON SAMET

PRISONS AND JAILS.

Jails are typically operated by municipalities or counties and used to confine people on a pre-trial basis or for short sentences, usually for minor offenses. Prisons are operated by state and federal governments and house inmates who have been sentenced for more than a year and who have generally committed offenses that are more serious. Jails and prisons have grown significantly in the past 20 years because of increased drug-related arrests, mandatory sentencing guidelines, and the erosion of community services. The jail population in the United States increased from 405,000 in 1990 to 723,000 in 2008, and the prison population increased from 793,000 to 1,596,000 during this same period (Warren, 2008). The United States has historically imprisoned a large proportion of its population and now has the highest incarceration rate in the world (Sheldon, 2004; Walmsley, 2007). Approximately 2.3 million people were incarcerated in federal or state prisons and local jails in 2008, amounting to an incarceration rate of 1 in every 100 adults (Warren, 2008). Over 3 percent of the U.S. adult population is under some form of correctional supervision, including probation and parole.

Drug offenders account for approximately half of the recent growth in U.S. jails and prisons (Harrison & Beck, 2006) and have high rates of recidivism and reincarceration. Substance use disorders do not resolve simply through forced abstinence in jails and prisons, and incarceration appears to have little effect in reducing drug use and drug-related crime. In fact, states with higher rates of incarceration also tend to have higher rates of drug use (Schiraldi, Holman, & Beatty, 2000). Within the first year after release, 85 percent of offenders with substance use disorders return to drug use, and 95 percent return to drug use within three years (Inciardi, Martin, & Butzin, 2004).

A disproportionate number of people incarcerated on drug offenses are African American and an increasing number are women (Beatty, Petteruti, & Ziedenberg, 2007; Harrison & Beck, 2006). Many drug offenders do not have extensive criminal records and are incarcerated for minor offenses (e.g., drug possession, sales of small quantities of drugs) that do not involve violence or sophisticated criminal activity. Drug offenders are often imprisoned because of the enforcement of minimum mandatory sentences, and many could be placed in less restrictive settings; however, there is an absence of community diversion programs that involve supervision and treatment (Peters & Wexler, 2005).

EXPENSE OF INCARCERATION

The costs associated with expanding jail and prison capacity in the United States are substantial. Total spending on state corrections rose from $12 to $49 billion from 1987 to 2007, and these costs are expected to rise by another $25 billion by 2011 (Warren, 2008). The average cost for incarcerating someone is from $20,000 to $23,000 (Office of National Drug Control Policy, 2001). The costs for incarceration are over six times higher than the costs for providing probation or parole supervision in the community (Administrative Office of the U.S. Courts, 2005). Almost 80 percent of correctional costs are linked to substance abuse, representing approximately 10 times the amount that states currently spend on substance abuse treatment, prevention, and research (National Center on Addiction and Substance Abuse, 2001; Office of National Drug Control Policy, 2001).

RATE OF DISORDERS

At least half of all inmates have a lifetime history of substance use disorders, including a significant proportion that has a diagnosable substance dependence disorder (Mumola & Karberg, 2006; Peters et al., 1998). These rates are significantly higher than in the general population. Rates of mental disorders, HIV/AIDS, hepatitis, and tuberculosis are also significantly higher among offenders. Many offenders have not previously received adequate treatment for substance abuse, mental health, dental, or other health-care problems, and a significant number have acute and severe health-care needs. Incarceration in jail or prison provides a critically important opportunity to address these health-care issues through treatment services that promote significant lifestyle change and that encourage abstinence, gainful employment, and successful reentry to society.

TREATMENT SERVICES IN JAILS AND PRISONS

In recent years there has been an emerging gap between the need for substance abuse treatment in jails and prisons and the services provided in these settings. Although correctional treatment services have increased during this period, they have not kept pace with the rapid influx of drug offenders, the vast majority of whom are in need of these services. Only a fraction of incarcerated offenders who need these services receives drug treatment. Recent surveys indicate that only 33 percent of jails and 56 percent of prisons provide any type of substance abuse treatment services (Substance Abuse and Mental Health Services Administration, 2000, 2002). When correctional treatment is provided it is often not comprehensive in scope and, it is frequently not provided in treatment units that are isolated from the general inmate population. One of the most significant gaps in services occurs following release from jail or prison, or reentry to the community—a particularly vulnerable time when offenders are exposed to various risks for relapse, and stress associated with reengagement with family, and full-time work (Peters & Bekman, 2007; Peters & Wexler, 2005). Few jails and prisons currently provide reentry services for offenders who are in need of substance abuse services (Cropsey, et al., 2007; Peters, Matthews, & Dvoskin, 2005).

Incarceration in jail or prison provides an opportune time to intervene with drug-involved offenders. Arrest and incarceration often precipitate a crisis in the offender's life and can provide additional motivation to initiate lifestyle changes that have been neglected in the past. The lengthy period of incarceration also provides sufficient time to engage inmates in assessment, treatment, and reentry planning. An important challenge in providing treatment in jails and prisons is that security issues often receive priority over rehabilitation and treatment needs in these settings (Peters, Matthews, & Dvoskin, 2005). Jails and prisons are also not architecturally designed to provide treatment and may have limited space in which to provide these services.

Research indicates that jail and prison treatment can significantly reduce substance abuse, criminal recidivism, and recommitment to prison, particularly when in-custody treatment is coupled with post-release treatment in the community (Inciardi, Martin, & Butzin, 2004; Prendergast et al., 2004). A growing body of research demonstrates that effective drug treatment services for offenders combines behavioral and pharmacological approaches, and encourages sustained involvement over time to address the chronic, relapsing nature of substance use disorders (National Institute on Drug Abuse, 2000).

See also **Crime and Drugs; Criminal Justice System, Treatment in the; Prisons and Jails, Drug Treatment in; Shock Incarceration and Boot-Camp Prisons; Treatment Accountability for Safer Communities (TASC).**

BIBLIOGRAPHY

Administrative Office of the U.S. Courts. (2005). *FY 2004 cost of incarceration and supervision.* The Third Branch: Newsletter of the federal courts, 37(5).

Beatty, P., Petteruti, A., & Ziedenberg, J. (2007). *The vortex: The concentrated racial impact of drug imprisonment and the characteristics of punitive counties.* Washington, DC: Justice Policy Institute.

Cropsey, K. L., Wexler, H. K., Melnick, G., Taxman, F. S., & Young, D. W. (2007). Specialized prisons and services: Results from a national survey. *The Prison Journal, 87*(1), 58–85.

Harrison, P. M., & Beck, A. J. (2006). *Prisoners in 2005.* Washington, D.C: U.S. Department of Justice, Bureau of Justice Statistics.

Inciardi, J. A., Martin, S. S., & Butzin, C. A. (2004). Five-year outcomes of therapeutic community treatment of drug involved offenders after release from prison. *Crime and Delinquency, 50*(1): 88–107.

Inciardi, J. A., Martin, S. S., Butzin, C. A., Hooper, R. M., & Harrison, L. D. (1997). An effective model of prison-based treatment for drug-involved offenders. *Journal of Drug Issues, 27,* 261–278.

Mumola, C. J., & Karberg, J. C. (2006). *Drug use and dependence, state and federal prisoners, 2004.* Washington, DC: U.S. Department of Justice, Bureau of Justice Statistics.

National Center on Addiction and Substance Abuse. (2001). *Shoveling up: The impact of substance abuse on state budgets.* New York: Columbia University.

National Institute on Drug Abuse. (2000). *Principles of drug abuse treatment for criminal justice populations—a research-based guide.* Rockville, MD: Author.

Office of National Drug Control Policy. (2001). *Drug treatment in the criminal justice system.* Washington, DC: Author.

Peters, R. H., & Bekman, N. M. (2007). Treatment and reentry approaches for offenders with co-occurring disorders. In R. B. Greifinger, J. Bick, & J. Goldenson (Eds.), *Public health behind bars: From prisons to communities* (pp. 368–384). New York: Springer Publishers.

Peters, R. H., Greenbaum, P. E., Edens, J. F., Carter, C. R., & Ortiz, M. M. (1998). Prevalence of *DSM-IV* substance abuse and dependence disorders among prison inmates. *American Journal of Drug and Alcohol Abuse, 24*(4), 573–587.

Peters, R. H., Matthews, C. O., & Dvoskin, J. A. (2005). Treatment in prisons and jails. In J. H. Lowinson, P. Ruiz, R. B. Millman, & J. G. Langrod (Eds.), *Substance abuse: A comprehensive textbook–fourth edition* (pps. 707–722). Baltimore, MD: Williams and Wilkins Publishers.

Peters, R. H., & Wexler, H. K. (Eds.). (2005). *Substance abuse treatment for adults in the criminal justice system.* Treatment Improvement Protocol (TIP) #44. Rockville, MD: Substance Abuse and Mental Health Services Administration, Center for Substance Abuse Treatment.

Prendergast, M., Hall, E., Wexler, H., Melnick, G., & Cao, Y. (2004). Amity prison-based therapeutic community: Five-year outcomes. *Prison Journal, 84*(1), 36–60.

Schiraldi, V., Holman, B., & Beatty, P. (2000). *Poor prescription: The cost of imprisoning drug offenders in the United States.* Washington, DC: Justice Policy Institute.

Sheldon, R. G. (2004). The imprisonment crisis in America: Introduction. *Review of Policy Research, 21*(1), 5–12.

Substance Abuse and Mental Health Services Administration. (2000). *Substance abuse treatment in adult and juvenile correctional facilities: Findings from the Uniform Facility Data Set 1997 Survey of Correctional Facilities.* Rockville, MD: Author.

Substance Abuse and Mental Health Services Administration. (2002). *Substance abuse services and staffing in adult correctional facilities.* Rockville, MD: The Drug and Alcohol Services Information System. Available from http://www.samhsa.gov/.

Walmsley, R. (2007). *World prison population list: Seventh edition.* London, England: International Centre for Prison Studies.

Warren, J. (2008). *One in 100: Behind bars in America 2008.* Public Safety Performance Project. PEW Center of the States.

ROGER PETERS
JANINE KREMLING

PRISONS AND JAILS, DRUG TREATMENT IN.

Prison and jail populations in the United States have swelled to over two million as a result of a significant increase in arrest and incarceration of drug offenders (Warren, 2008). The vast majority of inmates have significant substance abuse problems, and over one-fourth are arrested for drug offenses (James, 2004; Harrison & Beck, 2004; Peters & Wexler, 2005). Lifetime prevalence rates for substance use disorders among prisoners are between 68 and 74 percent, including 46 percent for drug dependence and 37 percent for alcohol dependence (Karberg & James, 2005; National Institute of Justice, 2000). Additionally, as many as 15 percent of inmates have major mental disorders, rates that are significantly higher than in the general population (Ditton, 1999; National GAINS Center, 2004). Approximately two-thirds of drug-involved offenders are rearrested within three years of release from custody (Langan & Levin, 2002).

As of 2008, a growing gap existed between the need for drug treatment in correctional settings and the scope of the services provided. Among inmates with substance use disorders only 17 percent received treatment in prisons or jails, with only 7 percent receiving treatment in jails (Karberg & James, 2005). Fewer than 40 percent of all correctional facilities provide substance abuse treatment (Substance Abuse and Mental Health Services Administration, 2000), and less than 6 percent of state and federal prison budgets as of 2008 was spent on substance abuse treatment. Of significant concern is the absence of reentry or transition services for substance-involved inmates who are returning to the community (Travis, Solomon, & Waul, 2001), a period marked by elevated risk for relapse and recidivism.

Many prison and jail substance-abuse programs are provided in settings that are not conducive to effective treatment, are not comprehensive in approach, and are poorly staffed (Peters, Matthews, & Dvoskin, 2005). For example, many such programs rely on volunteers, non-licensed staff, or inmate counselors. Similarly, staff/inmate ratios are quite low in many correctional drug treatment programs, averaging 1:25 in state prisons (Substance Abuse and Mental Health Services Administration, 2002). A survey conducted through CJ-DATS network of the National Institute on Drug Abuse (NIDA) indicates that while specialized prison-based treatment programs are available, a significant proportion of assessment and treatment services for substance-involved inmates are "generic" and inadequate in scope and quality (Cropsey et al., 2007).

Correctional drug treatment programs were first developed in the United States in the late 1920s for opiate addiction. During the 1960s several states enacted civil commitment statutes that provided substance abuse treatment in secure residential settings. A common modality of correctional residential treatment that emerged at this time was the therapeutic community (TC), which is based on a social learning model and engages professional staff and a peer recovery community to promote behavior change. There is considerable evidence to support the effectiveness of prison TCs in treating substance use disorders (Pearson & Lipton, 1999).

Subsequently, some jails and prisons developed multitiered substance abuse treatment services that include outpatient, intensive outpatient, short-term residential, and reentry/transition programs, in addition to TCs (Peters, Matthews, & Dvoskin, 2005). For example, the Federal Bureau of Prisons and a number of state prison systems developed a continuum of treatment services that vary in length and intensity to meet the needs of substance-involved offenders (Peters, Matthews, & Dvoskin, 2005; Weinman & Dignam, 2002). Several specialized correctional programs were also developed for inmates with co-occurring substance use and mental disorders (Peters & Bekman, 2007). Correctional treatment programs introduced in other countries include *harm reduction* approaches and treatment interventions (e.g., cognitive-behavioral and psychosocial skills programs) that are designed for

application with a broader inmate population (Jacob & Stover, 2000; Lightfoot, 1999). Most comprehensive substance abuse treatment programs in jails and prisons employ the following types of evidence-based services: (1) screening and assessment, (2) motivational interviewing, (3) cognitive skills training and criminal thinking, (4) relapse prevention, and (5) re-entry and transition planning.

Several challenges arise in providing substance abuse treatment in prisons and jails. Jails house many unsentenced inmates for short periods of time who may be reluctant to accurately disclose information that could adversely influence their pending case and who may be less interested in treatment than in a favorable judicial disposition. Noise levels and lack of adequate space present barriers to effective treatment in many correctional facilities. In addition, the primary focus for most correctional systems is inmate security and punishment rather than rehabilitation of substance use disorders. In times of budget cutbacks, substance abuse services are often among the first to be eliminated. Prisons and jails vary widely in the resources allocated for substance abuse treatment and are often influenced by cyclical patterns of political support for either punishment or rehabilitation of offenders.

Considerable evidence indicates that correctional treatment reduces drug use and criminal activity. Research indicates that these programs lead to significant reductions in arrests, recommitment to prison, and substance abuse during 12- and 24-month follow-up periods, although positive gains related to prison treatment are not typically maintained during three- and five-year follow-up periods (Martin et al., 1999; Prendergast et al., 2004; Wexler et al., 1999a, 1999b). However, long-term positive outcomes have been found among offenders who participate in prison treatment that is followed by aftercare treatment in the community (Inciardi, Martin, & Butzin, 2004; Martin et al., 1999; Prendergast et al., 2004). Research also indicates that providing a continuum of offender substance abuse treatment services during custody and in the community effectively reduces costs associated with crime and incarceration (McCollister et al., 2003).

While the courts have consistently rejected a general constitutional right to drug treatment in prisons and jails, case law indicates that some services are legally mandated. For example, inmates have the right to medical treatment to address withdrawal (i.e., detoxification) and other serious, life-threatening medical problems associated with substance abuse. A number of professional standards have also been developed to guide the implementation of correctional substance abuse treatment services, including those developed by the National Commission on Correctional Health Care (NCCHC, 2008) and by the American Correctional Association (ACA). Essential substance abuse treatment services described in professional standards for both jails and prisons include management of intoxication and withdrawal and a comprehensive health assessment that includes a substance abuse history.

See also **Coerced Treatment for Substance Offenders; Treatment, Stages/Phases of: Aftercare.**

BIBLIOGRAPHY

Cropsey, K. L., Wexler, H., Melnick, G., Taxman, F. S., & Young, D. W. (2007). Specialized prisons and services. Results from a national survey. *Prison Journal, 87*(1), 58–85.

Ditton, P. M. (1999). Mental health and treatment of inmates and probationers. Washington, DC: U.S. Department of Justice, Office of Justice Programs, Bureau of Justice Statistics.

Harrison, P. M., & Beck, A. J. (2004). *Prisoners in 2004.* Washington, DC: U.S. Department of Justice, Office of Justice Programs, Bureau of Justice Statistics.

Inciardi, J. A., Martin, S. S., & Butzin, C. A. (2004). Five-year outcomes of therapeutic community treatment of drug-involved offenders after release from prison. *Crime and Delinquency, 50*(1), 88–107.

Jacob, J., & Stover, H. (2000). Drug use, drug control, and drug services in German prisons: Contradiction, insufficiencies and innovative approaches. In D. Shewan & J. Davies (Eds.), *Drugs and prisons* (pp. 57–88). London: Harwood Academic.

James, D. J. (2004). *Profile of jail inmates.* Washington, DC: U.S. Department of Justice, Office of Justice Programs, Bureau of Justice Statistics.

Karberg, J. D., & James, D. J. (2005). *Substance dependence, abuse, and treatment of jail inmates, 2002* (Special Report). Washington, DC: U.S. Department of Justice, Office of Justice Programs, Bureau of Justice Statistics.

Langan, P. A., & Levin, D. J. (2002). Recidivism of prisoners released in 1994 (Special Report). Washington, DC: U.S. Department of Justice, Office of Justice Programs, Bureau of Justice Statistics.

Lightfoot, L. O. (1999). Treating substance abuse and dependence in offenders: A review of methods and outcomes. In E. Latessa (Ed.), *Strategic solutions: The International Community Corrections Association examines substance abuse* (pp. 43–80). Lanham, MD: American Correctional Association.

Martin, S., Butzin, C. A., Saum, C. A., & Inciardi, J. A. (1999). Three-year outcomes of therapeutic community treatment for drug-involved offenders in Delaware: From prison to work release to aftercare. *Prison Journal, 79*(3), 294–320.

McCollister, K. E., French, M. T., Inciardi, J. A., Butzin, A. C., Martin, S. S., & Hooper, R. M. (2003). Post-release substance abuse treatment for criminal offenders: A cost-effectiveness analysis. *Journal of Quantitative Criminology, 19*(4), 389–407.

National Commission on Correctional Health Care. (2008). *Standards for correctional health services.* Chicago: Author.

National GAINS Center for People with Co-Occurring Disorders in the Justice System. (2004). *The prevalence of co-occurring mental illness and substance use disorders in jails* (Fact Sheet Series). Delmar, NY: Author.

National Institute of Justice. (2000). *1999 annual report on drug use among adult and juvenile arrestees: Arrestee Drug Abuse Monitoring Program.* Washington, DC: U.S. Department of Justice.

Pearson, F. S., & Lipton, D. S. (1999). A meta-analytic review of the effectiveness of corrections-based treatments for drug abuse. *Prison Journal, 79*(4), 384–410.

Peters, R. H., & Bekman, N. M. (2007). Treatment and reentry approaches for offenders with co-occurring disorders. In R. B. Greifinger, J. Bick, & J. Goldenson (Eds.), *Public health behind bars: From prisons to communities* (pp. 368–384). New York: Springer.

Peters, R. H., Matthews, C. O., & Dvoskin, J. A. (2005). Treatment in prisons and jails. In J. H. Lowinson, P. Ruiz, R. B. Millman, & J. G. Langrod (Eds.), *Substance abuse: A comprehensive textbook* (4th ed., pp. 707–722). Baltimore: Williams and Wilkins.

Peters, R. H., & Wexler, H. K. (Eds.). (2005). *Substance abuse treatment for adults in the criminal justice system* (Treatment Improvement Protocol [TIP] No. 44). Rockville, MD: Substance Abuse and Mental Health Services Administration, Center for Substance Abuse Treatment.

Prendergast, M. L., Hall, E. A., Wexler, H. K., Melnick, G., & Cao, Y. (2004). Amity prison-based therapeutic community: 5-year outcomes. *Prison Journal, 84*(1), 36–59.

Substance Abuse and Mental Health Services Administration. (2000). *Substance abuse treatment in adult and juvenile correctional facilities: Findings from the Uniform Facility Data Set 1997 Survey of Correctional Facilities.* Rockville, MD: Author.

Substance Abuse and Mental Health Services Administration. (2002). *Substance abuse treatment and staffing in adult correctional facilities*. Rockville, MD: Author. Available from http://www.samhsa.gov/.

Travis, J., Solomon, A. L., & Waul, M. (2001). *From prison to home: The dimensions and consequences of prisoner reentry*. Washington, DC: Urban Institute, Justice Policy Center.

Warren, Jennifer. (2008). *One in 100: Behind bars in America 2008* (The Pew Charitable Trusts. Pew Center of the Streets and the Public Safety Performance Project). Available from http://www.pewcenteronthestates.org/.

Weinman, B. A., & Dignam, J. T. (2002). Drug-abuse treatment programs in the Federal Bureau of Prisons: Past, present, and future directions. In C. G. Leukefeld, F. M. Tims, & D. Farabee (Eds.), *Treatment of drug offenders: Policies and issues* (pp. 91–104). New York: Springer.

Wexler, H., DeLeon, G., Thomas, G., Kressler, D., & Peters, J. (1999a). The Amity prison TC evaluation. *Criminal Justice and Behavior, 26*(2), 147–167.

Wexler, H., Melnick, G., Lowe, L., & Peters, J. (1999b). Three-year reincarceration outcomes for Amity in-prison therapeutic community and aftercare in California. *Prison Journal, 79*(3), 321–336.

ROGER H. PETERS
JANINE KREMLING

PRISONS AND JAILS, DRUG USE AND HIV/AIDS IN.

Human immunodeficiency virus and acquired immunodeficiency syndrome, commonly abbreviated as HIV/AIDS, have had a serious impact on U.S. prisons and jails since the 1980s and represent a dangerous health threat among all inmate populations and for the general public when offenders are released from custody. Of the approximately 2.3 million persons in U.S. prisons and jails, between 1 to 2 percent are estimated to be infected with HIV (Hammett, Harmon, & Maruschak, 1999; Maruschak, 2008). These rates are significantly higher than in the U.S. general population (Bick, 2007; Maruschak, 2008).

INFECTED INCARCERATED PERSONS AND THEIR TREATMENT

An estimated 25 percent of HIV-infected persons in the United States are incarcerated in prison or jail during a given year (Hammett, Harmon, & Rhodes, 2002; Spaulding et al., 2002). HIV/AIDS prevalence rates in prisons and jails vary widely by geographic area and gender, with the highest rates (3.6%) reported in the Northeast and the lowest rates in the Midwest and West. HIV/AIDS is more frequently detected among female inmates (2.4%) than male inmates (1.6%), and disproportionately affects minorities (Foundation for AIDS Research, 2008; Maruschak, 2008). The number of HIV/AIDs cases and the mortality rate in prisons decreased in the late 1990s and early 2000s, reflecting similar trends in the general population (Bick, 2007; Maruschak, 2008).

Advances in medication therapy have significantly reduced AIDS-related mortality rates in prisons and jails, reflecting declines in the general population (Baham et al., 2002). Inmates have a constitutional right to HIV treatment and other medical care for life-threatening illnesses. However, in some settings, inmates are treated for HIV and related disorders by staff who do not have specialized training related to HIV/AIDS, drug treatment, mental health services, or reentry services (Foundation for AIDS Research, 2008). Privatization of correctional healthcare services and rising costs for correctional medical treatment have also presented barriers to implementation of effective services (DeGroot, Hammett, & Scheib, 1996).

DRUG ABUSE, HIV/AIDS, AND PREVENTION STRATEGIES

There is a strong connection between drug abuse and HIV/AIDS in correctional settings, affecting strategies for both prevention and treatment. Inmates have higher rates than the general population of sexually transmitted diseases, other infectious disease (e.g. hepatitis, tuberculosis), substance use, and mental disorders that facilitate the spread of HIV (Foundation for AIDS Research, 2008). For example, as many as three-fourths of offenders have diagnosable substance use disorders (Karberg & James, 2005), including many who have a history of IV drug use and risky sexual behavior that is related to drug use. Drugs are widely available in prisons and jails, and HIV is often spread through injection drug use in these settings. Two other major routes of HIV transmission in correctional settings are sexual behavior and tattooing (Zack, 2007).

The often lengthy period of incarceration offers significant opportunities to prevent HIV through medications, substance abuse treatment, and other means (Beckwith et al., 2006). Inmates often come from impoverished, medically underserved neighborhoods, and have not frequently engaged in drug treatment, received HIV screening or other prevention services, or received HIV treatment (Foundation for AIDS Research, 2008, Peters & Wexler, 2005; Zack, 2007). Although drug treatment is available in many prisons and jails, these services are provided to only a small proportion of those inmates who have substance use disorders (Karberg & James, 2005). When correctional drug treatment is available, services are not typically prioritized for inmates with HIV/AIDs, and HIV prevention practices are often not comprehensively addressed.

Substance abuse treatment has been shown to be effective in reducing drug and alcohol use and risky sexual behavior among offenders and to prevent HIV infection (Prendergast, Urada, & Podus, 2001; Sorensen & Copeland, 2000; World Health Organization, 2004) and is clearly an underused prevention strategy. Substance abuse treatment has significant positive effects on knowledge, attitudes, and beliefs related to HIV prevention; sexual behavior; and particularly on risk reduction skills (Prendergast et al., 2001). Research indicates that methadone maintenance also has a significant impact on HIV risk behaviors and helps to prevent HIV infection (Sorensen & Copeland, 2000). Drug testing in correctional settings provides additional deterrence for intravenous (IV) and other drug use and can help to identify offenders who are in need of treatment and supervision.

Other important HIV prevention and treatment strategies implemented in prisons and jails include routine HIV screening, which has proven to be cost-effective in prisons and other settings (Bick, 2007; Sanders et al., 2005; Varghese & Peterman, 2001). Identification of HIV status through screening can facilitate referral to counseling, promotion of testing for others who may be at risk, and can reduce HIV risk behaviors (Centers for Disease Control and Prevention, 2000). Mandatory HIV testing is provided by almost half of the state prison systems (Bick, 2007). However, this approach has been criticized due to the potential for discrimination and segregation of HIV-infected inmates (World Health Organization, 2006), leading to reduced access to housing options and educational and job opportunities. In jails, the lengthy period of time required to test blood samples for HIV and to return results can be problematic for a significant number of inmates who are released within two weeks of arrest.

INTERVENTIONS FOR POST-CUSTODY POPULATIONS

Several HIV interventions have proven effective in reducing post-custody HIV risk behaviors (Wolitski, 2006; Zack, 2007), including educational services, development of risk reduction plans, and reentry services (e.g., case management, housing, employment). Basic information about HIV is an important first step in educating inmates about prevention approaches and is often provided in jail booking or general confinement settings and at the time of prison reception. However, educational approaches are insufficient to generate changes in HIV risk behaviors, and lasting behavior change requires use of professional staff and interventions focused on rehearsal, modeling, and feedback related to specific HIV prevention skills (Zack, 2007). A number of *harm reduction* approaches (e.g., condom distribution, syringe exchange) have been successfully used in European prisons to prevent HIV transmission (Dolan, Rutter, & Wodak, 2003), although these are only used in a few U.S. prisons and jails. In general, opportunities to participate in HIV education, prevention, and treatment interventions should be provided throughout the course of incarceration.

The vast majority of prison and jail inmates eventually return to the community. However, release from custody is often associated with worsening of HIV/AIDS symptoms and reengagement in risky behaviors (Stephenson & Leone, 2005). Most jails and prisons do not provide adequate reentry services, leading to resumption of HIV risk behaviors, transmission of HIV, and re-arrest (Health Resources and Services Administration; HRSA, 2007; McLean et al., 2006). Difficulties in reinstating medical benefits and lack of access to health insurance present additional barriers to effective community reentry. Correctional discharge planning and reentry services are of critical importance to ensure continuity of HIV treatment, engagement in substance abuse and mental health services, and access to housing and educational/vocational services (United Nations Office on Drugs and Crime/World Health Organization, 2006; Zack, 2007). Demonstration projects developed by several state prison systems have provided a combination of pre-release planning, life skills training, substance abuse treatment, peer support, housing and employment support, assertive case management, and linkage to community treatment (HRSA, 2007). Correctional transition planning and case management programs have been shown to significantly reduce risky sexual behavior and criminal recidivism and to facilitate involvement in substance abuse treatment and healthcare services among offenders with HIV (Bick, 2007; Myers et al., 2005; Rich et al., 2001, Wolitski, 2006).

See also **See also Alcohol and AIDS; Injecting Drug Users and HIV; Risk Factors for Substance Use, Abuse, and Dependence: An Overview; Substance Abuse and AIDS.**

BIBLIOGRAPHY

Baham J., Bick, J. A., Giannoni, D., Harris, D., & Ruiz, J. (2002). *Trends in an HIV infected incarcerated population: An autopsy review*. 40th Annual Meeting of the Infectious Diseases Society of America.

Beckwith, C. G., Zaller, N., & Rich, J. D. (2006). Addressing the HIV epidemic through quality correctional healthcare. *Criminology and Public Policy, 5*(1), 149–156.

Bick, J. A. (2007). HIV and viral hepatitis in corrections: A public health opportunity. In R. B. Greifinger, J. Bick, & J. Goldenson (Eds.), *Public health behind bars: From prisons to communities* (pp. 103–126). New York: Springer.

Centers for Disease Control and Prevention. (2000). Adoption of protective behaviors among persons with recent HIV infection and diagnosis—Alabama, New Jersey, and Tennessee, 1997–1998. *Morbidity and Mortality Weekly Report, 49*(23), 512–515.

DeGroot, A. S., Hammett, T. M., & Scheib, R. (1996). Barriers to care of HIV-infected inmates: A public health concern. *AIDS Reader, 6*(3), 78–87.

Dolan, K., Rutter, S., & Wodak, A. D. (2003). Prison-based syringe exchange programs: A review of international research and development. *Addiction, 98,* 153–158.

Foundation for AIDS Research. (2008). *HIV in correctional settings: Implications for prevention and treatment policy* (Issue brief No. 5). New York: Author.

Hammett, T. M., Harmon, P., & Maruschak, L. M. (1999). *1996–1997 update: HIV/AIDS, STDs and TB in correctional facilities*. Washington, DC: U.S. Department of Justice, Office of Justice Programs, National Institute of Justice.

Hammett, T. M., Harmon, P., & Rhodes, W. (2002). The burden of infectious diseases among inmates of and releasees from U.S. correctional facilities, 1997. *American Journal of Public Health, 92*(11), 1789–1794.

Health Resources and Services Administration. (2007). *Opening doors: The HRSA-CDC Corrections Demonstration Project for People Living with HIV/AIDS*. Rockville, MD: U.S. Department of Health and Human Services, HRSA HIV/AIDS Bureau.

Karberg, J. D., & James, D. J. (2005). *Substance dependence, abuse, and treatment of jail inmates, 2002* (Special Report). Washington, DC: U.S. Department of Justice, Office of Justice Programs, Bureau of Justice Statistics.

Maruschak, L. M. (2008). *HIV in prisons, 2006*. Washington, DC: U.S. Department of Justice, Office of Justice Programs, Bureau of Justice Statistics.

McClean, R. L., Robarge, J., & Sherman, S. G. (2006). Release from jail: Moment of crisis or window of opportunity for female detainees? *Journal of Urban Health, 83*(3), 382–393.

Myers, J., Zack, B., Kramer, K., Gardner, M., Rucobo, G., & Costa-Taylor, S. (2005). Get Connected: An HIV prevention case management program for men and women leaving the California prisons. *American Journal of Public Health, 95*(10), 1682–1684.

Peters, R. H., & Wexler, H. K. (Eds.). (2005). *Substance abuse treatment for adults in the criminal justice system* (Treatment Improvement Protocol [TIP] No. 44). Rockville, MD: Substance Abuse and Mental Health Services Administration, Center for Substance Abuse Treatment.

Prendergast, M. L., Urada, D., & Podus, D. (2001). Meta-analysis of HIV risk-reduction interventions within drug abuse treatment programs. *Journal of Consulting and Clinical Psychology, 69*(3), 389–405.

Rich, J. D., Holmes, L., Sales, C., Macalino, G. D., Ryczek, D. J., & Flanigan, T. (2001). Successful linkage of medical care and community services for HIV positive offenders being released from prison. *Journal of Urban Health, 78,* 279–289.

Sanders, G. D., Bayoumi, A. M., Sundaram, V., Bilir, P., Neukermans, C. P., Rydzak, C. E., et al. (2005). Cost-effectiveness of screening for HIV in the era of highly active antiretroviral therapy. *New England Journal of Medicine, 352*(6), 570–585.

Sorensen, J. L., & Copeland, A. L. (2000). Drug abuse treatment as an HIV prevention strategy: A review. *Drug and Alcohol Dependence, 59,* 17–31.

Spaulding, A. C., Stephenson, B., Macalino, G., Ruby, W., Clarke, J. G., & Flanigan, T. P. (2002). Human immunodeficiency virus in correctional facilities: A review. *Clinical Infectious Diseases, 35*(3), 305–312.

Stephenson, B., & Leone, P. (2005). HIV care in prison: The potential and challenge. *AIDS Community Research Initiative of America Update, 14*(4), 7–11.

United Nations Office on Drugs and Crime and the World Health Organization. (2006). *HIV/AIDS prevention, care, treatment, and support in prison settings: A framework for an effective national response.* Vienna: Author.

Varghese, B., & Peterman, T. A. (2001). Cost-effectiveness of HIV counseling and testing in U.S. prisons. *Journal of Urban Health, 78*(2), 304–312.

Wolitski, R., & the Project START Writing Group for The Project START Study Group. (2006). Relative efficacy of a multi-session sexual risk-reduction intervention for young men released from prisons in four states. *American Journal of Public Health, 96*(10), 1854–1861.

World Health Organization (2004). *Policy brief: Reduction of HIV transmission through drug dependence treatment.* Geneva: Author.

World Health Organization (2006). *HIV testing and counseling: The gateway to treatment, care and support.* Available from http://www.who.int/.

Zack, B. (2007). HIV prevention: Behavioral interventions in correctional settings. In R. B. Greifinger, J. Bick, & J. Goldenson (Eds.), *Public health behind bars: From prisons to communities* (pp. 156–173). New York: Springer.

JANINE KREMLING
ROGER H. PETERS

PROCESSES OF CHANGE MODEL.

Traditionally, changing an addictive behavior was assumed to be the same as taking action. People with addictions were viewed as changing when they quit abusing substances. Action-oriented therapies have been readily available and have dominated the ways in which individuals and addiction practitioners perceive behavioral change. In other words, motivation to change was seen as a *fixed* state; individuals who were motivated to change could make changes, and intervention was unlikely to be effective among those who were not motivated.

FIVE STAGES FOR BEHAVIORAL CHANGE

Based on smoking cessation research conducted in the 1970s, James Prochaska and Carlos DiClemente (1983; 1984; 1998) proposed a model of behavioral change: the Transtheoretical Model (TTM). According to this model, behavioral change is a process, which unfolds over time and involves progress through five stages of change: Precontemplation, Contemplation, Preparation, Action, and Maintenance. "The underlying perspective of the stages of change is that there is a multidimensional process of intentional behavior change that extends from the establishment of a stable pattern of abuse to the achievement of significant sustained change of the addictive behavior" (DiClemente et al., 2004, p. 104). The word *intentional* underlines the important role that motivation plays at each stage of change. Since the inception of TTM, it has received substantial empirical support that applies to a wide range of behavior, populations, and settings.

Precontemplation State and Stage Matching.

In the Precontemplation stage, individuals do not intend to take action in the foreseeable future. They may or may not be aware of their problem behavior and have little or no interest in change. Families, friends, or employers, however, are often well aware that precontemplators have problems. When precontemplators present for addiction treatment, they often do so because of pressure from others. These individuals are at risk of dropping out of treatment quickly and prematurely. The research of Prochaska and colleagues has shown that if therapists match interventions to the individual's stage, precontemplators will complete treatment at the same rate as those in the Preparation stage.

Stage matching begins by setting realistic goals. If precontemplators are pressured into immediate action, they are more likely to drop out of treatment. In contrast to traditional action-oriented treatment in which therapists tend to label such individuals as unmotivated or noncompliant, the TTM provides a different approach in conceptualizing behavioral change to meet the needs of these individuals.

The goal of addiction treatment with precontemplators is to help them progress to Contemplation. This initial goal produces success early in treatment. Consciousness-raising (see Table 1) is frequently used to help individuals become more aware of why

Process	Definitions: Interventions
Consciousness raising	Increasing information about self and problem: observations, confrontations, interpretations, bibliotherapy
Self-reevaluation	Assessing how one feels and thinks about oneself with respect to a problem: value clarification, imagery, corrective emotional experience
Self-liberation	Choosing and commitment to act or belief in ability to change: decision-making therapy, New Year's resolutions, logotherapy techniques, commitment–enhancing techniques
Counterconditioning	Substituting alternatives for problem behaviors: relaxation, desensitization, assertion, positive self-statements
Stimulus control	Avoiding or countering stimuli that elicit problem behaviors: restructuring one's environment (e.g., removing alcohol or fattening foods), avoiding high–risk cues, fading techniques
Reinforcement management	Rewarding one's self or being rewarded by others for making changes: contingency contracts, overt and covert reinforcement, self-reward
Helping relationships	Being open and trusting about problems with someone who cares: therapeutic alliance, social support, self-help groups
Dramatic relief	Experiencing and expressing feelings about one's problems and solutions: psychodrama, grieving losses, role playing
Environmental reevaluation	Assessing how one's problem affects physical environment: empathy training, documentaries
Social liberation	Increasing alternatives for nonproblem behaviors available in society: advocating for rights of repressed, empowering, policy interventions

Table 1. Titles, definitions, and representative interventions of the processes of change. (Source: Prochaska, DiClemente, & Norcross, 1992.) ILLUSTRATION BY GGS INFORMATION SERVICES. GALE, CENGAGE LEARNING

they are not ready to change problem behavior. As precontemplators become more aware of why they are resistant to change, they are more likely to consider the pros of treatment. As the pros of change increase, individuals are more likely to progress into Contemplation.

Contemplation. In the Contemplation stage, awareness of the pros of change increase, but the cons also increase. The pros and cons of behavioral change, conceptualized as decisional balance in the TTM, produce a profound ambivalence that causes some individuals to procrastinate. This ambivalent attitude toward using substances can sometimes mislead addiction practitioners into assuming that these individuals are ready for immediate action. For individuals to progress to Preparation, their perception of the cons of quitting must change. They need to reevaluate how they think and feel about themselves as an addict and how they imagine themselves free from addiction.

Individuals' cons of change have to decrease only about half as much as their pros increase; therefore, in stage-matched treatments researchers place twice as much emphasis on the benefits of changing. Typically, there are more than forty scientific benefits to becoming free from an addiction. One of a few strategies to enhance motivation is to become aware of how much of one's body, self, social relations, and society benefit from such major changes.

Preparation. Individuals in the Preparation stage are convinced the pros of changing outweigh the cons. They are generally ready to take immediate action within thirty days and often have a plan for action. However, they might not be fully committed to their plan due to a number of reasons such as low self-efficacy (lack of confidence in the ability to change across problem situations). For these individuals, action-oriented treatment programs may effectively help them progress to the next stage.

Action. In the Action stage, individuals take specific steps to implement their plans for changing their substance use behavior. Individuals need to be prepared for how long action will last. Biologically, going through the symptoms of withdrawal is relatively quick. Behaviorally, however, people have to be prepared to work on changing their behavior for about six months.

Maintenance. Individuals progress into the Maintenance stage when the new behavior becomes the norm. In this stage, individuals establish a new pattern of behaviors for at least six months, and this change eventually can lead to termination of the change process. Evidence suggests that the Maintenance stage lasts four to five years. With smoking, for example, the national data in the 1990 *Surgeon General's Report* indicated that after 12 months of not a single puff, the percentage of smokers who resume regular smoking is about 40 percent. After

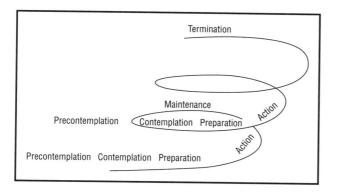

Figure 1. A spiral model of the stages of change. (Source: Prochaska, DiClemente, & Norcross, 1992.) ILLUSTRATION BY GGS INFORMATION SERVICES. GALE, CENGAGE LEARNING

five years of total abstinence, the relapse rate drops to 5 percent.

DIFFERENT PATHS FOR CHANGE

A spiral model of the Stage of Change is presented in Figure 1 to illustrate how most individuals travel through the stages of change. Behavioral change in this model is viewed as a process: "Current stage status represents a changeable state rather than a static trait" (DiClemente et al., 2004, p. 108). The duration in which each individual occupies each stage can vary. For example, after learning about the death of a friend from liver failure, an individual who is in Precontemplation about reducing alcohol consumption today could be in the Preparation or Action stage tomorrow.

Furthermore, individuals can move through stages in both linear and nonlinear fashions, with nonlinear being more common. When individuals go back to an earlier stage of change, regression occurs. In general, people can regress from any stage to an earlier stage. One form of regression is relapse, which involves regression from Action or Maintenance to an earlier stage. In a study examining smoking behavior (Prochaska & DiClemente, 1986), only about 15 percent of participants regressed all the way to the Precontemplation stage. The vast majority of participants regressed to the stage of Contemplation or Preparation. According to the TTM, relapse is perceived as a positive opportunity, rather than a failure to change problem behavior: "Movement back and forth, as well as recycling through the stages, represents a successive learning process whereby the individual continues to redo the tasks of various stages

in order to achieve a level of completion that would support movement toward sustained change of the addictive behavior" (DiClemente et al., 2004, p. 104).

In addition to Stages of Change, Prochaska and colleagues (1992) proposed that ten covert and overt processes need to be implemented to successfully progress through the stages of change and attain the desired behavioral change (see Table 1). These processes of change aim to explain how changes in cognition, emotion, and behavior take place. These ten processes can be divided into two groups: cognitive and affective experiential processes and behavioral processes. Experiential processes refer to consciousness raising, dramatic relief, environmental reevaluation, social-liberation, and self-reevaluation. Behavioral processes include counterconditioning, stimulus control, reinforcement management, helping relationship, and environmental evaluation. To understand how and when behavioral change occurs, Prochaska and colleagues (1992) integrated both processes and stage of change in their research. For example, for smoking cessation and weight loss, they found that individuals who were in Precontemplation used eight of the change processes significantly less than those who were in any other stages.

ASSESSMENT OF CORE CONSTRUCTS

Between the late 1970s and the early 2000s, Prochaska and DiClemente developed measures to assess core constructs of the TTM: the stages of change, decisional balance, processes of change, temptations, and self-efficacy. Critics raised questions regarding the validity of this model, particularly in how to assess stage status of individuals with different substance abuse problems and in different types of treatment programs. In an effort to address these concerns, DiClemente and colleagues (2004) identified key issues in assessing stage status. For example, one key issue is the difficulty in capturing stage status, given that it signifies a changeable state and not a static trait. In addition, they highlighted the importance of understanding motivation in terms of the stages of change:

> The stages of change specify motivational demands by segmenting the change process into specific tasks to be accomplished and goals to be achieved, if movement toward successfully sustained change is to occur. Each of the multiple tasks encountered on the road to recovery requires effort, energy, and

'motivation' on the part of the addicted individual. Successful change of an addiction represents a resolution of each stage's tasks in a way that supports engagement in the tasks of the next stage. (DiClemente et al., 2004, p. 104)

DiClemente and colleagues recommended that more research is needed to develop better assessments as well as enhance the understanding of subtasks at each stage.

See also **Treatment, Behavioral Approaches to: An Overview.**

BIBLIOGRAPHY

DiClemente, C. C., & Prochaska, J. O. (1998). Toward a comprehensive, transtheoretical model of change: Stages of change and addictive behavior. In W. R. Miller & N. Heather (Eds.), *Treating addictive behaviors* (2nd ed., pp. 3–24). New York: Plenum.

DiClemente, C. C., Schlundt, D., & Gemmell, L. (2004). Readiness and stage of change in addiction treatment. *American Journal of Addiction, 13,* 109–113.

Prochaska, J. O., & DiClemente, C. C. (1983). Stages and processes of self-change of smoking: Toward an integrative model of change. *Journal of Consulting and Clinical Psychology, 51,* 390–395.

Prochaska, J. O., & DiClemente, C. C. (1984). *The transtheoretical approach: Crossing the traditional boundaries of therapy.* Malabar, FL: Krieger.

Prochaska, J. O., & DiClemente, C. C. (1986). Toward a comprehensive model of change. In W. R. Miller & N. Heather (Eds.). *Treating Addictive Behaviors: Processes of change.* (pp. 3–27). New York: Plenum.

Prochaska, J. O., DiClemente, C. C., & Norcross, J. C. (1992). In search of how people change: Applications to addictive behavior. *American Psychologist, 47,* 1102–1114.

JAMES O. PROCHASKA
REVISED BY SHARON H. HSU (2009)
G. ALAN MARLATT (2009)

PRODUCTIVITY: EFFECTS OF ALCOHOL ON.

Alcohol is the most commonly used and abused substance in the United States. As with workforce drug use, besides affecting productivity, the depressant effects of alcohol impact workplace safety because its use may reduce an individual's reaction time, and impair judgment and memory. Its use also affects workplace morale because of attendance and coworker relationship problems. Its use also adds to the health costs of employers. The impact from alcohol occurs not only as a consequence of intoxication, but also because of carry-over effects in the short term such as a hangover, and chronic health effects such as alcoholism or liver disease.

In 2000 the National Household Survey on Drug Abuse revealed that for the reported workforce of over 108 million people aged 18 to 48, about 8 percent reported they had been drinking heavily (five or more drinks on five or more occasions) during the past month and 7.4 percent of these workers were dependent on or abusing alcohol. Heavy drinking is more than three times as prevalent among male workers than it is among female workers, and it is most prevalent in semiskilled or male-dominated occupations such as construction, mining, precision production and craft, and operators and fabricators. Younger workers (aged 18 to 25) are over two times more likely to be heavy drinkers than older workers (aged 35 to 49) (The George Washington University Medical Center, 2002).

Problem drinkers (individuals who are not necessarily alcoholics but are heavy or binge drinkers prone to causing harm or conflict while under the influence) and alcoholics are more likely than other workers to have major difficulties in the workplace; however, the cost to employers is not limited to problem drinkers and alcoholics, it is also affected by non-drinking employees (The George Washington University Medical Center, 2002). According to the National Institute on Alcohol Abuse and Alcoholism, there are two types of problem drinkers: chronic and situational. Chronic drinkers have been heavy drinkers (2 or more drinks per day on average per year) for many years (FTN Centers For Disease Control And Prevention). Binge drinkers are defined as drinking that corresponds to "5 or more drinks on a single occasion for men or 4 or more drinks on a single occasion for women, generally within about 2 hours" (FTN National Institute of Alcohol Abuse and Alcoholism). Situational abusers may develop a drinking problem later in life, often because of negative life events (failing health, death of a loved one, loneliness) wherein alcohol may initially bring "relief" but may later turn into a problem.

The impact of alcohol use off the job extends to the workplace and affects the user's functionality. Employees who drink heavily off the job are more likely to experience hangovers causing them to be absent, to show up late or leave early; to feel sick at work; to sleep on the job; to perform poorly; or to initiate conflict with their coworkers.

An estimated 500 million workdays are lost annually due to alcoholism (National Association of Treatment Providers, 1991).

> Problems related to alcohol and drug abuse cost American businesses over $134 billion annually in lost productivity, and work performance drops significantly (The George Washington University Medical Center, 2002).
>
> Up to 40 percent of industrial fatalities can be linked to alcohol abuse and alcoholism and the individuals who consume alcohol are more likely to cause injuries to themselves or others while on the job (Baker, 1987; Bureau of National Affairs, 1986).
>
> People with alcoholism and problem drinkers are more likely than other workers to have had three or more employers during the last year, to have missed work more than two days in the past month because of illness or injury, and to have skipped work more than two days in the past month, according to the findings of a National Survey on Drug Use and Health taken in 2000. People with alcoholism use twice as much sick leave as other employees (The George Washington University Medical Center, 2002).
>
> Employees who regularly use alcohol are five times more likely to file workers' compensation claims (The George Washington University Medical Center, 2002); nearly half of all workers' compensation claims are related to substance abuse (National Council on Compensation Insurance, 2008).
>
> Employees who use alcohol and other drugs cost their employers about three times as much in medical claims as do employees who do not use drugs or alcohol (Bureau of National Affairs, 1980).

Sixty percent of alcohol-related job performance problems are caused by people who are *not* alcoholics or problem drinkers; they are employees who occasionally drink too much at lunch or the night before. Twenty percent of workers reported that they have been injured, had to cover for a coworker, or had to work harder because of other employees' alcohol consumption (The George Washington University Medical Center, 2002).

As with drugs, many employers implemented workplace alcohol-testing programs using breath alcohol protocols. The Nuclear Regulatory Commission (NRC) and the Department of Transportation (DOT) require alcohol testing as a part of their substance abuse prevention efforts. Because of the rapid elimination of alcohol from the human body, the deterrent nature of alcohol testing is significantly less in these programs than those for drug testing, because evidence of recent drug use remains in the system for a day or more depending on the drug, and frequency and intensity of use. Positive rates for alcohol testing by the NRC and DOT remain low, as is true for most other employers. A more reliable method of alcohol testing is for-cause testing because there is a greater likelihood of recent alcohol use.

See also **Accidents and Injuries from Alcohol; Complications: Medical and Behavioral Toxicity Overview; Economic Costs of Alcohol and Drug Abuse; Industry and Workplace, Drug Use in; Social Costs of Alcohol and Drug Abuse.**

BIBLIOGRAPHY

Baker, T. E. (1987). *Strategic planning for the workplace drug abuse programs.* National Institute on Drug Abuse.

Bureau of National Affairs (BNA). (1980, 1986). *Alcohol and other drugs in the workplace: Costs, controls and controversies.*

FTN Centers for Disease Control and Prevention. *Alcohol fact sheet.* Available from http://www.cdc.gov/.

FTN National Institute of Alcohol Abuse and Alcoholism. (2004). NIAAA council approves definition of binge drinking. *NIAAA Newsletter, 3:3.*

The George Washington University Medical Center (GWUMC). (2002). *Alcohol problems cost American businesses.*

National Association of Treatment Providers. (1991). *Treatment is the answer: A white paper on the cost-effectiveness of alcoholism and drug dependency treatment.* Laguna Hills, CA: National Association of Treatment Providers.

National Council on Compensation Insurance. (2008). As referenced in *What does employee alcohol and drug use cost your business?* DWI Resource Center. Available from http://www.dwiresourcecenter.org/.

National Household Survey on Drug Abuse. (2002). *Substance use, dependence or abuse among full-time workers.* Office of Applied Studies.

National Survey on Drug Use and Health, U.S. Dept. of Health and Human Services. (1994, 1997). Office of Applied Studies.

DICK BUCHER

PRODUCTIVITY: EFFECTS OF DRUG USE ON. *See* **Industry and Workplace, Drug Use in.**

PROFESSIONAL CREDENTIALING.

Myriad health-care professionals and paraprofessionals provide treatment for substance-abuse (or SA) disorders. They include, but are not limited to, physicians, psychologists, social workers, nurses and nurse practitioners, clergy, and addiction or drug-abuse counselors. Institutions and programs that train these professionals are accredited, and such individuals, after undergoing training, may obtain credentials from a professional or state body.

Although accreditation applies to programs or institutions and does not cover substance-abuse counseling, credentials apply to individuals and do cover this subspecialty. Institutions that offer training in substance-abuse counseling design their programs to meet the requirements outlined by the state or by potential employers so that graduates can obtain certification. Graduates must then pass tests certifying that they have a specific level of proficiency in the theoretical and practical aspects of substance-abuse treatment. For example, in Michigan the Department of Public Health and other interested organizations initiated a program for the professional development of counselors that is based on education, experience, supervised practical training, professional recommendation, testing and review, ethics, and residence. Michigan requires that persons undergo a three-tier testing process covering the theoretical and practical aspects of substance-abuse treatment to become certified addiction counselors (CACs). The first test covers the fundamental knowledge of substance-abuse

counseling; the second, applications to specific populations; and the third, the oral presentation of a case. Certification is for a specific term and renewal requires additional education. Once certified, a person may provide addiction treatment in states other than the one that awarded certification, through a reciprocity agreement that covers states with membership in the International Certification Reciprocity Consortium.

In addition to certification by the state, professional credentialing may also be obtained through professional organizations. For example, the American Society of Addiction Medicine, under the auspices of the American Medical Association, certifies physicians who wish to treat substance abuse. The association offers courses that review topics in addiction theory and practice, examines candidates who wish to obtain credentials, and certifies their advanced knowledge and skills in this area. Other professional associations such as the American Psychological Association are currently developing procedures and mechanisms for providing substance-abuse-treatment credentials to their members who supply mental health services in this area.

Both accreditation and certification work to improve the quality of the education and specialty training that individuals receive and to assure the quality of the services provided. As a safeguard, consumers of substance-abuse services may determine whether the professional delivering the services was trained in a program accredited by the appropriate professional organization in a university or college and accredited by the appropriate regional accrediting board. Consumers may also determine if the professional holds credentials as a substance-abuse counselor, as these credentials certify that a person has met certain educational requirements and displayed the level of knowledge and skill deemed necessary in the profession.

Professional substance-abuse-treatment credentialing is somewhat murky in many states, as professionals who hold a license or certification within their initial discipline (e.g., social work, counseling, or psychology) rarely need to obtain additional substance-abuse certification in order to provide those services. The upshot of this is that many more persons provide substance-abuse services to clients than there are credentialed substance-abuse providers in the United States.

In a 2003 Substance Abuse and Mental Health Services Administration (SAMHSA) Alcohol and Drug Services (ADSS) study, it was reported that between 45 and 72 percent of those providing substance-order services are specifically credentialed to do so, and nearly all are degreed or licensed in related disciplines. In a large-scale study Harwood (2002) found that slightly more than half of the staff at agencies or facilities surveyed were credentialed or licensed specifically as substance-abuse service providers; of those, nearly 60 percent held a master's degree. Among those substance-abuse service providers without credentials or licenses, few had graduate degrees, and nearly two-thirds less than a college education. Roughly one-fourth of the personnel surveyed were neither credentialed nor were they pursuing the process to become so. Among the substance-abuse counselors included in the Harwood study, 15,500 were neither licensed nor certified, and 16,700 of the general behavioral health service providers lacked the credentials to provide substance-abuse counseling services.

The SAMSHA results were similar, indicating that less than half of the staff providing direct substance-abuse counseling and treatment possessed specific credentials for doing so. However, their data indicated significant variation by type of treatment facility, with outpatient, nonmethadone clinics having the highest rate of credentialed or certified staff and methadone-specific clinics the fewest. However, methadone clinics are federally required to have the most staff with medical training, based on their mission. Overall, significantly higher percentages of credentialed substance-abuse counselors were employed by private, not-for-profit or for-profit agencies than by public agencies and facilities. The fewest certified or credentialed substance-abuse counselors were employed by community mental health centers, according to the ADSS/SAMHSA data.

In 2003 the National Association of Alcoholism and Drug Abuse Counselors (NAADAC) reported that 79 percent of its membership were licensed, certified, or credentialed to provide substance-abuse services. It also reported that 31 percent of its membership were licensed professional counselors (LPCs or LPCCs), 22 percent licensed clinical social workers (LCSWs or LISWs), and 16 percent licensed mental health counselors (LMHCs). No statistics were reported on how many of the members hold more than one license or certification, that is, are credentialed in more than one discipline—that percentage is likely to be significant, based on the SAMHSA and Harwood data.

Unlike many of the helping professions, the substance-abuse counseling credentialing process is quite often competency- or experience-based rather than educationally based. For as long as rigorous educational or training standards are not required for service provision, the workforce in the field will lack uniformity of service provision. It would benefit substance-abuse clients significantly to be served by providers who are truly skilled and trained in the field of addiction treatment.

See also **American Society of Addiction Medicine (ASAM).**

BIBLIOGRAPHY

American Association of Marriage and Family Therapy. (Oct. 2001). *Practice research network survey report.* Alexandria, VA: Author.

American Counseling Association. (2001, September). *Practice research network report.* Alexandria, VA: Author.

American Psychological Association. (2001). *Substance abuse treatment survey final report.* Washington, DC: Author.

Annie Casey Foundation. (2003). *The unsolved challenge of system reform: The condition of the frontline human services workforce.* Baltimore, MD: Author.

Harwood, H. J. (2002, November) Survey on Behavioral Health Workplace. *Frontlines.* Washington, DC: Academy Health.

Keller, D. S., & Dermatis, H. (1999). Current status of professional training in the addictions. *Substance Abuse, 20*(3), 123–140.

Substance Abuse and Mental Health Services Administration. (2003). *Alcohol and Drug Services Study (ADSS). The national substance abuse treatment system: Facilities, clients, services, and staffing.* Rockville, MD: Office of Applied Studies.

M. Marlyne Kilbey
Amy L. Stirling
Revised by Pamela V. Michaels (2009)

PROHIBITION OF ALCOHOL. The Eighteenth Amendment to the Constitution of the United States, passed by Congress in 1917, had its origins in temperance reformers' efforts to eliminate the vice and social destruction they believed stemmed from the sale of alcoholic beverages, particularly alcohol sold at saloons. The amendment prohibited the "manufacture, sale and transportation of intoxicating liquors" and became effective one year after its ratification by the states. It outlawed only the manufacture, transport, and sale of liquor; it did not criminalize the possession of alcohol for personal use, nor did it make purchase of liquor from bootleggers a criminal offense, nor did it define "intoxicating" liquors. To implement the amendment, Congress passed the National Prohibition Act, better known as the Volstead Act. The Volstead Act allowed alcohol to be produced and transported for scientific and other commercial purposes. It also defined an intoxicating liquor as any beverage containing more than 0.5 percent alcohol. It could have set the permissible level higher and allowed the production, transportation, and sale of beer, but it did not. Prohibition became effective in 1920.

The Treasury Department established a Prohibition Bureau to carry out the provisions of the law. Under the Volstead Act, Treasury agents could obtain a search warrant only if they could prove that alcohol was being sold, thus precluding searches of individual homes, no matter how much liquor might be there. Some wealthy people, given ample notice that Prohibition was coming, laid in enough alcoholic beverages to last them through most of the following decade. The law also had the effect of allowing manufacture for personal use. Such home production sometimes became part of a cottage industry contributing to the supplies distributed by bootleggers. Even committed Prohibitionists appeared to believe that the public would not tolerate any effort to criminalize the act of drinking itself. The Volstead Act, unlike some state laws, permitted the manufacture of beer as long as the beer contained no more than 0.5 percent alcohol (near beer).

EFFECTS OF PROHIBITION

Given the common belief that Prohibition failed to alter the consumption of alcohol or its adverse effects on health, it is appropriate to ask: To what extent did the law reduce alcohol use in the United States? First, there is no question that it succeeded in eliminating 170,000 saloons, even if it did not change the attitudes of most Americans about the morality of drinking. And, although some writers have asserted that

Patrons of a speakeasy enjoy their drinks, which were illegal under the Volstead Act. © Bettmann/Corbis.

drunkenness actually increased during Prohibition, most available records point to the opposite conclusion (Aaron & Musto, 1981; Lender & Martin, 1987). The most consistent findings on the impact of Prohibition come from statistics on medical problems linked to alcohol consumption, especially excessive alcohol consumption. Among these problems were hospital admissions for alcoholism and admissions to state mental institutions for alcoholic dementia and alcoholic psychosis. Striking decreases were observed in New York and Massachusetts, two states that did not have restrictions on alcohol consumption prior to 1920. Massachusetts state mental hospital admissions for alcoholic psychosis fell from 14.6 per 100,000 in 1910 to 6.4 in 1922 and were 7.7 in 1929; in New York, such admissions fell from 11.5 in 1910 to 3.0 in 1920, rising again to 6.5 in 1931 (Aaron & Musto, 1981).

Deaths from alcohol-related diseases also fell. National statistics showed that the number of deaths from cirrhosis (about 14.8 per 100,000 in 1907) were only 7.9 in 1919, 7.1 in 1920, and did

PROHIBITION, 1910 – 1929

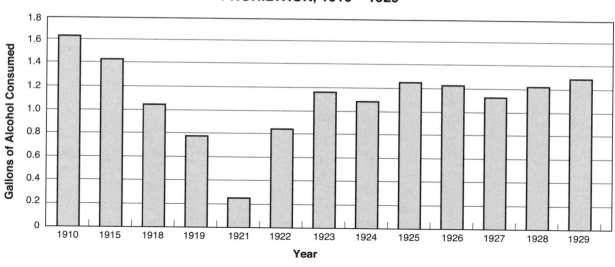

Bar graph showing gallons of alcohol consumed per capita during Prohibition, 1910–1929. ILLUSTRATION BY GEORGE BARILLE. GALE, CENGAGE LEARNING.

not rise above 7.5 during the 1920s. There were decreases in arrests for drunkenness and in costs of jailing public inebriates. Commander Evangeline Booth of the Salvation Army asserted that not only had drinking fallen off sharply, especially among the poor, but there were fewer broken homes because of wages lost to drinking or violence related to drinking.

Paul Aaron and David Musto state, "Observers . . . have been unanimous in concluding that the greatest decreases in consumption occurred in the working class . . . In large measure, intoxicants priced themselves out of the market" (Aaron & Musto, 1981, p. 165). A quart of beer and a quart of gin were each five to six times more expensive in 1930 than they were prior to Prohibition. Prohibition defenders asserted that instead of purchasing liquor in saloons, workers were putting their earnings into cars and refrigerators. Admittedly, the impact on alcohol consumption was greatest in the early years of Prohibition. As bootlegging increased in the late 1920s, medical problems linked to alcohol use rose again, but they did not reach the high levels experienced before 1920. Other data on per capita alcohol consumption immediately after repeal in 1934 indicated that there had been a drastic decline in average alcohol consumption during the Prohibition years.

BOOTLEGGING

Undoubtedly, crime associated with bootlegging increased. Many bootleggers became quite wealthy. Some who were involved in illegal activities prior to Prohibition used the wealth flowing from bootlegging to extend and further develop organized criminal enterprises, some of which later became involved with trafficking in illicit drugs. One of the most notorious figures associated with organized crime was Al Capone, who came to national attention because of his Chicago-based criminal activities. Aaron and Musto point out, however, that organized rackets existed in large cities before Prohibition and that the homicide rate increased most sharply between 1900 and 1910.

Unquestioned, also, is the unreliable quality of bootlegged liquor, much of which was produced by diverting or hijacking industrial alcohol. Some industrial alcohol could be flavored and sold as scotch, gin, or bourbon. Much of it, however, had been mixed with methanol (methyl alcohol) or other chemicals to render it undrinkable—denatured. Bootleggers hired chemists to remove the denaturants by redistillation (*washing*). Inadequate processing, which was not uncommon, produced a liquor that could be toxic or even lethal. The liquor produced in England and Canada and smuggled in by ship or truck was of a higher quality. One smuggler who brought in such quality liquor, Bill McCoy, was responsible for the term still used to describe an authentic product—the "real McCoy."

CRITICISM OF PROHIBITION

The continued criticism of Prohibition and the frustration of enforcing the Volstead Act led many of its advocates to become increasingly defensive and hostile to non-supporters. Concern for the drunkard sharply diminished. According to Lender and Martin, "Many crusaders began labeling rehabilitation as nothing more than a waste of time and energy; prohibition, they promised would make such work unnecessary" (Lender & Martin, 1987). Groups interested in treatment declined. The Association for the Study of Inebriety dissolved in the mid-1920s. Volstead Act advocates became more hostile toward alcoholics as criticism of Prohibition increased. Some suggested amending the act to make drinking itself a criminal offense. One such suggestion came from an official in the Prohibition Unit of the Treasury Department, Harry J. Anslinger, then the Assistant Commissioner of Prohibition. Thus the 19th century concerns of the Temperance Movement for the physical and spiritual health of alcoholics turned, in the 1920s, to calls for stiffer jail terms, or even exile, for chronic alcoholics. In the context of these attitudes, the harsh penalties meted out under the leadership of the Treasury Department for mere possession of illicit drugs become somewhat more comprehensible.

The enforcement of the Volstead Act had been vested in the Treasury Department's Prohibition Unit within the Internal Revenue Bureau. The first National Prohibition Administrator and head of the Prohibition Unit was John F. Kramer. The Narcotics Division, headed by Levi G. Nutt, a pharmacist by training, was part of the Prohibition Unit. The Narcotics Division became an independent unit in the Treasury Department in 1930 when the Prohibition Unit was transferred to the Department of Justice. Harry J. Anslinger was appointed first Commissioner of Narcotics.

CHANGES TO THE VOLSTEAD ACT

Despite growing criticism, Prohibition, according to Aaron and Musto, was still alive and well when Herbert C. Hoover was elected president by a large margin in 1928. An overwhelming majority of both houses of Congress and nearly all the state governors supported the Eighteenth Amendment. Even opponents of Prohibition did not realistically expect to see it repealed. But the onset of the Great Depression in 1929 dramatically changed the situation. Opponents of Prohibition no longer argued for its repeal because of its demoralizing effects on civil liberty, but argued instead that the revival of the liquor industry would provide jobs and tax revenue. In the 1932 campaign for the presidency, Franklin D. Roosevelt promised to repeal Prohibition. Almost immediately after his inauguration, he introduced changes in the Volstead Act to legalize the sale of beer.

In 1933 the Twenty-first Amendment to the Constitution was ratified. It was brief and to the point: "Section 1. The Eighteenth Article of Amendment to the Constitution of the United States is hereby repealed." The federal government, however, retained responsibility to regulate and tax beverage alcohol and to prevent its illegal production. Section 2 of the Amendment allowed the states to continue Prohibition under state laws if they so desired. Some states did so; many states adopted alcohol beverage control laws (ABC laws) to curb the abuses that had characterized the production and sale of alcohol prior to prohibition. Among other provisions, ABC laws restricted the hours when alcohol could be sold (to make taverns and bars less attractive) and banned liquor sales on Sundays and election days. Some ABC laws created state-operated monopolies for the sale of packaged beverages. The federal laws dealing with control of alcohol remained the responsibility of various federal agencies. It was not until 1972 that they were brought together and responsibility for overseeing them was assigned to a single agency—the Bureau of Alcohol, Tobacco, and Firearms (BATF) in the Department of the Treasury.

Author Richard Hamm has observed that the Eighteenth Amendment had long-term consequences for American law and constitutionalism. The amendment both facilitated the growth of the law-enforcement establishment within the federal government, and it directly influenced the shape of the constitutional system "by specifying a seven-year time limit for ratification." Time limits such as this became the order of the day, allowing the opponents of amendments "to translate delay into defeat" (Hamm, 2001, p. 218).

See also **Alcohol: History of Drinking in the United States; Temperance Movement; Woman's Christian Temperance Union.**

BIBLIOGRAPHY

Aaron, P., & Musto, D. F. (1981). Temperance and prohibition in America: A historical overview. In M. Moore & D. Gerstein (Eds.), *Alcohol and public policy: Beyond the shadow of Prohibition*. Washington, DC: National Academy Press.

Behr, E. (1997). *Prohibition: Thirteen years that changed America*. New York: Arcade Publishing.

Burnham, J. C. (1993). *Bad habits: Drinking, smoking, taking drugs, gambling, sexual misbehavior, and swearing in American history*. New York: New York University Press.

Hamm, R. F. (1995). *Shaping the Eighteenth Amendment: Temperance reform, legal culture, and the polity, 1880–1920*. Chapel Hill: University of North Carolina Press.

Hamm, R. F. (2001). Eighteenth Amendment. In P. Boyer (Ed.), *The Oxford Companion to United States History* (pp. 217–218). Oxford and New York: Oxford University Press.

Kerr, K. A. (1985). *Organized for Prohibition: A new history of the Anti-Saloon League*. New Haven: Yale University Press.

Lender, E. M., & Martin, J. K. (1987). *Drinking in America*. New York: Free Press.

Lerner, M. A. (2008). *Dry Manhattan: Prohibition in New York City*. Cambridge and London: Harvard University Press.

Musto, D. F. (1987). *The American disease: Origins of narcotic control*. (Expanded ed.). New York: Oxford University Press.

Pegram, T. R. (1999). *Battling demon rum: The struggle for a dry America, 1800–1933*. Chicago: Ivan R. Dee.

Rorabaugh, W. J. (1996). Reexamining the Prohibition Amendment. *Yale Journal of Law and the Humanities, 8*, 285–294.

Szymanski, A.-M. E. (2003). *Pathways to Prohibition: Radicals, moderates, and social movement outcomes*. Durham, NC: Duke University Press.

Tice, P. M. (1992). *Altered states: Alcohol and other drugs in America*. Rochester: The Strong Museum.

Tyrell, I. (1997). The U.S. Prohibition experiment: Myths, history, and implications. *Addiction, 92*, 1405–1409.

JEROME H. JAFFE
REVISED BY SARAH W. TRACY (2009)

PROPOXYPHENE. *d*-Propoxyphene (Darvon) is an opioid drug that is structurally related to methadone. It is used clinically to produce analgesia when the level of pain is not severe. Its popularity rests largely on the belief that propoxyphene is less likely to cause addiction than codeine, a drug that is also used for relief of moderate levels of pain. Propoxyphene is typically used in combination with aspirin or acetaminophen. Its analgesic effects are synergistic with those of aspirin and other nonsteroidal anti-inflammatory agents.

When it was introduced into clinical medicine in the early 1960s, propoxyphene was not subject to special narcotic regulatory control. This fact may explain its early popularity, which was probably due to clinicians' unrealistic fears about the addictive potential of codeine and to the inconvenience of prescribing it under the narcotic regulations that were in effect before the the Controlled Substances Act of 1970 was passed.

Although propoxyphene has only one-half to two-thirds the potency of codeine, it has been used to control symptoms of the opioid withdrawal syndrome. It is not commonly abused because it produces unpleasant toxic effects at high doses.

See also **Opiates/Opioids.**

BIBLIOGRAPHY

Barkin, R. L., et al. (2006). Propoxyphene (dextropropoxyphene): A critical review of a weak opioid analgesic that should remain in antiquity. *American Journal of Therapeutics, 13*, 6, 534–542.

Howland, R. D., & Mycek, M. J. (2006). *Pharmacology*, 3rd ed. Philadelphia, PA: Lippincott, Williams & Wilkins.

Reisine, T., & Pasternak, G. (1996) Opioid analgesics and antagonists. In J. G. Hardman et al. (Eds.), *The Pharmacological Basis of Therapeutics*, 9th ed. New York: McGraw-Hill Medical. (2005, 11th ed.)

JEROME H. JAFFE

PSILOCYBIN. Psilocybin is an indole-type hallucinogen, found naturally with another hallucinogen in a variety of mushrooms—the most publicized being the Mexican or magic mushroom, *Psilocybe mexicana*, as well as other *Psilocybe* and *Conocybe*

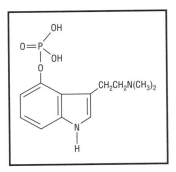

Figure 1. Chemical structure of psilocybin. ILLUSTRATION BY GGS INFORMATION SERVICES. GALE, CENGAGE LEARNING

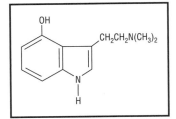

Figure 2. Chemical structure of psilocin. ILLUSTRATION BY GGS INFORMATION SERVICES. GALE, CENGAGE LEARNING

species. These mushrooms have long been consumed by Native Americans, especially in Mexico and the southwestern United States, as part of religious rites.

Psilocybin produces effects similar to lysergic acid diethylamide (LSD), but it is less potent and is metabolized in the body to form psilocin, another hallucinogenic compound. Both of these compounds have been synthesized in clandestine laboratories and made available on the streets.

See also **Hallucinogenic Plants; Peyote; Plants, Drugs From.**

BIBLIOGRAPHY

Karch, S. B. (2006). *Drug abuse handbook.* Boca Raton, FL: CRC Press.

Spinella, M. (2005). *Concise handbook of psychoactive herbs.* New York: Haworth Press.

Weil, A. (1972). *The natural mind: An investigation of drugs and the higher consciousness.* Boston: Houghton Mifflin. (1998, rev. ed.)

DANIEL X. FREEDMAN
R. N. PECHNICK

PSYCHIATRIC RESEARCH INTERVIEW FOR SUBSTANCE AND MENTAL DISORDERS (PRISM). *See* PRISM.

PSYCHOACTIVE. *Psychoactive* is a general term that came into use about 1961. It describes a substance that affects the central nervous system, producing changes in mental activity and/or behavior. A psychoactive substance or process may affect the way an individual thinks or the manner in which the environment is perceived or experienced; it may also change the behavior of an individual in a given situation.

See also **Psychopharmacology.**

BIBLIOGRAPHY

Inaba, D. S., & Cohen, W. E. (2007). *Uppers, downers, all-arounders: Physical and mental effects of psychoactive drugs,* 6th ed. Medford, OR: CNS Publications.

Julien, R. M. (2001). *A primer of drug action: A concise, non-technical guide to the actions, uses, and side effects of psychoactive drugs,* rev. ed. New York: MacMillan.

NICK E. GOEDERS
REVISED BY NICHOLAS DEMARTINIS (2001)

PSYCHOACTIVE DRUG. Any of a group of drugs (also called psychotropic drugs) that act upon the central nervous system, producing changes in mental activity and/or behavior. Psychoactive drugs are among the most widely used group of pharmacologically active agents, with extremely important clinical applications, including anesthesia for surgery and analgesia for relief of pain. They are also used for nonmedical purposes, such as to alter consciousness, improve performance, and as elements in cultural and religious rituals (alcohol and peyote are examples). Some psychoactive drugs produce an effect in those who suffer from a mental or medical disorder, but have no effect on normal individuals. The antidepressants, for example, have little or no effect on normal individuals other than side effects. Other psychoactive drugs, such as the sedative-hypnotics, produce effects in all individuals.

Psychoactive drugs are used to suppress disorders of movement and to treat anxiety disorders, depression, bipolar disorder (manic depression), and schizophrenia, among other mental illnesses. In addition, drugs used primarily to treat disorders in peripheral organs can also affect the central nervous system (e.g., beta-blocking agents, used to treat high blood pressure or disorders of heart rhythm; or steroid hormones, used to control inflammation). The psychoactive effects of these drugs are generally considered side effects, although some are used for their psychoactive properties as well.

Culturally approved nonmedical psychoactive drugs include alcohol, nicotine (tobacco), and caffeine. Psychoactive drugs that have been determined to have a high potential for harm and little medical benefit include heroin, hallucinogens, and some older sedative-hypnotics such as methaqualone. Marijuana has traditionally been placed in this category, but research has demonstrated potential effectiveness for medical problems including glaucoma, nausea, and weight loss associated with cancer or AIDS.

See also **Alcohol; Caffeine; Nicotine; Pain, Drugs Used for; Peyote; Sedative-Hypnotic; Tobacco.**

BIBLIOGRAPHY

Inaba, D. S., & Cohen, W. E. (2007). *Uppers, downers, all-arounders: Physical and mental effects of psychoactive drugs*, 6th ed. Medford, OR: CNS Publications.

Julien, R. M. (2001). *A primer of drug action: A concise, non-technical guide to the actions, uses, and side effects of psychoactive drugs*, Rev. ed. New York: MacMillan.

Meyer, J. S., & Quenzer, L. F. (2004). *Psychopharmacology: Drugs, the brain and behavior.* Sunderland, MA: Sinauer Associates.

NICK E. GOEDERS

PSYCHOANALYSIS.

Psychoanalysis is an analytic technique originated by Sigmund Freud (1856–1939), an Austrian neurologist. It has been altered by his students and their students, in turn, throughout the twentieth century. Psychoanalysis is a theory of the way the mind works: (1) Sequences of thoughts are determined—they do not occur by chance; (2) Much of our thinking takes place out of awareness—it is unconscious and not easily recovered; (3) The experiences of early childhood, particularly those with important caretakers, continue to have an impact (often unconsciously) on our daily lives; (4) Feelings, both sexual and aggressive, are present at birth and affect behavior. Psychoanalytic theory helps us understand something of addicts' complex motivations and of their inner experiences and behaviors.

Psychoanalysis is also a method: It attempts to understand mental processes by free association (following thoughts wherever they lead without selection or censoring) and by the analysis of dreams, fantasies, and behaviors. Psychoanalysts apply this method as a therapy or treatment for certain forms of mental disability.

See also **Freud and Cocaine.**

BIBLIOGRAPHY

Brenner, C. (1973). *An elementary textbook of psychoanalysis.* New York: International Universities Press.

Renik, O. (2006). *Practical psychoanalysis for therapists and patients.* New York: Other Press.

WILLIAM A. FROSCH

PSYCHOMOTOR EFFECTS OF ALCOHOL AND DRUGS.

The psychomotor effects of alcohol and other drugs are costly. Thirty-nine percent of traffic fatalities are associated with alcohol. Twenty-five percent are associated with other drugs (Kaplan, Kraner, & Paulozzi, 2006, pp. 1293–1296). The majority of these fatalities can be linked to a driver under the influence. However, alcohol or drug use by pedestrians also contributes to the fatality statistics in a substantial manner.

PSYCHOMOTOR PERFORMANCE

Driving a car, crossing a street, or working on an assembly line are psychomotor tasks. Over many decades, researchers have examined the effects of drugs on the performance of these and other tasks or tasks that closely approximate them. Researchers have also examined drug effects on stimulus perception time, memory retrieval time, and other information processing activities that are commonly engaged by many tasks. Although the information provided by available research is already extensive, the vast range of possible tasks, as well as the large number of available drugs, doses, and combinations means that research in this area must continue if our goal is to understand the impairing properties of alcohol and other drugs under all relevant circumstances.

Interpreting the psychomotor effects of a drug is complicated by a number of factors. The most obvious factor is the state of the subject when exposed to the drug. For example, some stimulant drugs, including caffeine and nicotine, will affect psychomotor performance only when the subject is sleep-deprived or fatigued but will have minimal effects at other times. In part this is simply a measurement issue: a subject who is already performing at his/her best has little room for improvement and will respond minimally to a performance-enhancing drug. Similarly, a subject performing at his/her worst will show minimal deterioration when confronted with a drug expected to impair performance. The individual's experience in performing the task and the degree to which the task can be performed with minimal (automatic) versus substantial cognitive effort will also determine whether task performance is drug sensitive.

In addition to these factors, variation in the response to a drug is related to traits (enduring characteristics) of the people under study. Some characteristics (e.g., genetic differences) may be unknown or unknowable and may produce different responses from one individual to the next. Other characteristics may be knowable but may confuse the interpretation of the results. For example, consider a study in which the research subjects are college students. Most college students have above-average intelligence, good problem solving skills, and no history of medical or psychiatric complications. As a result of their higher baseline function, they may be capable of exerting more cognitive effort or have the cognitive flexibility and motivation to adopt an alternate problem-solving strategy when a task becomes too difficult. Accordingly, when confronted with a drug challenge, they may show less performance impairment than subjects with less cognitive reserve.

A final example of a characteristic that can modify responsiveness is previous exposure to the drug. If the level of exposure is sufficient, then a neurophysiological adaptation may occur. This neuroadaptation is known as *tolerance*. Tolerance is indicated when repeated administrations of the same dose of the drug no longer evoke the same response and a higher dose than the original is required to reinstate the original response. Tolerance can be a powerful determinant of responsiveness. For example, police reports include many examples of alcohol-dependent drivers with blood alcohol levels sufficient to incapacitate or kill a nonalcoholic, and yet these individuals were capable of walking, talking, and driving before they were arrested.

ALCOHOL

The effects of alcohol obviously depend upon the dose and the rate of administration. Among non-alcoholics, blood-alcohol concentrations above the legal limit for driving, 80 mg/dL, depress many cognitive and motor skills. At lower concentrations, the effects of alcohol become task-dependent. Tasks that require the discrimination of one stimulus from another based upon simple visual (e.g., color) or auditory (e.g., pitch) cues are notoriously insensitive to alcohol concentrations below the legal limit, according to studies reviewed by Lance O. Bauer (2001). It is likewise true that tests of working memory or sustained vigilance are insensitive to the effects of an alcohol challenge unless the dose is large. Indeed, Tilman Schulte, Eva M. Müller-Oehring, Hans Strasburger, Hans Warzel, and Bernhard A. Sabel (2001) note that in many studies described in the literature over several decades, alcohol does not reliably impair performance when attention is focused on a single attribute.

In general, tests of divided attention and simulated driving are optimal for detecting the performance-impairing effects of alcohol (Liu & Fu, 2007; Moskowitz, Burns, & Williams, 1985; Ogden, & Moskowitz, 2004). In a dose-related manner, alcohol impairs visual search behavior during simulated driving; specifically, it increases fixation duration, decreases eye movements, slows saccade onset, and produces eye tremor (nystagmus) during visual tracking. It impairs steering accuracy and the maintenance of a constant following distance. Low doses of alcohol have also been shown to degrade performance on tasks that require inhibition of a powerful response tendency. A real world example of this impairment is failing to override the impulse to look at an interesting scene (e.g., a car crash) as one drives by.

A notable and obvious effect of alcohol is its ability to impair balance and gross motor skills (Goebel, Dunham, Rohrbaugh, Fischel, Stewart, & Hanson, 1995). Alcohol impairs balance and coordination in a dose-dependent manner: as the dose increases, the level of impairment increases proportionately.

Although many studies demonstrate adverse effects of alcohol on the performance of psychomotor tasks presented in a laboratory, caution is needed when generalizing results to settings outside of the laboratory. Yet, it remains possible that impaired performance on some laboratory tests would generalize. For example, one laboratory task affected by alcohol involves measuring accelerator pedal release time during simulated driving. Under specific circumstances, such as driving in heavy traffic, a slight delay in releasing the accelerator pedal and applying the brakes can cause an accident and bodily harm (e.g., a 0.2 second delay in applying the brakes at 65 mph increases the stopping distance by 19 feet). Under other circumstances, such as driving in light traffic, the increase in stopping distance would have no impact. Similar scenarios can be envisioned that enhance the danger associated with impaired balance/motor coordination (e.g., operating a motorcycle at higher speed) or divided attention (e.g., negotiating an exit from a busy parking lot after an athletic event while hundreds or thousands of other drivers exit the same parking lot). When contemplating findings from laboratory studies, one must be mindful that an intoxicated subject will not be at risk for accidents at all times under all circumstances. The threat to personal or public safety associated with alcohol may be constrained by individuals' specific occupations and activities. If a subject becomes intoxicated and is then confronted by a specific high-risk circumstance, then these otherwise minor psychomotor impairments may prove significant.

DRUG-ALCOHOL INTERACTIONS

Although many people believe that the adverse effects of alcohol can be antagonized, or reversed, by stimulant drugs, the evidence in support of this belief is remarkably weak. For example, although caffeine (Marczinski & Fillmore, 2003) and nicotine can, under some circumstances, successfully antagonize the slowing of reaction time caused by alcohol, they do not antagonize alcohol's adverse effects on executive control and balance/coordination or

alcohol's propensity to increase risk taking. Beliefs regarding the psychomotor effects of caffeine or nicotine on alcohol intoxication can sometimes be a more powerful determinant than their actual effects, according to a 2002 study done by Mark T. Fillmore, Emily L. Roach, and Julietta T. Rice.

In the majority of cases, the use of alcohol and another drug together is more detrimental to performance than either drug administered alone. When doses are large, severe sedation or loss of consciousness may result, leading to obvious impairment in task performance. When doses are in the small-to-moderate range, interactions are detectable and occasionally specific to a certain task or skill.

ALCOHOL AND BENZODIAZEPINES

When taken at the proper dosage, benzodiazepines have a low potential for acute toxicity. However, when taken with alcohol (ethanol), their sedative properties can be magnified (Simpson & Rush, 2002) and may pose a serious medical risk. Taken together, benzodiazepines and alcohol increase the perception of drunkenness and impair balance and cognitive flexibility more than when either drug is taken alone. A notable and profound effect of the drug combination is its ability to impair learning and memory. Benzodiazepines, in particular, cause state-dependent learning—an impairment wherein information acquired in the intoxicated state is less easily recalled in the sober state (or vice-versa). This is one reason that benzodiazepines are commonly administered during surgical procedures.

ALCOHOL AND CANNABIS

The acute effects of cannabis (marijuana) on psychomotor performance are modest. Apart from its documented ability to impair short-term memory and recognition/recall performance, low doses of cannabis have negligible effects on reaction time in simple and complex settings. Although cannabis is detrimental to psychomotor performance at higher doses, its effects remain less profound than those of alcohol and some other drugs. Furthermore, it appears that cannabis affects a different set of performance skills than those affected by alcohol.

ALCOHOL AND OPIATES

The acute effects of opiates on psychomotor performance have not been studied extensively. The most notable and reproducible decrement is an impaired ability to perceive and discriminate visual stimuli. This decrement might be wholly attributable to pupillary constriction and blurred vision. Yet, Zacny, Conley, and Galinkin (1997) have shown that it may reflect a central reduction in attention and in the ability to accurately perceive and encode stimuli in any modality, visual or otherwise. Greater performance declines have been reported following buprenorphine than morphine.

Opiates produce sedation. They can thereby impair the ability to maintain alertness during long vigils, such as driving along a highway for an extended distance. These adverse effects can combine with the sedative effects of alcohol or sleep deprivation to increase risk for performance failures (e.g., motor vehicle accidents).

See also **Accidents and Injuries from Alcohol; Accidents and Injuries from Drugs; Antagonists of Alcohol and Drugs; Benzodiazepines; Blood Alcohol Concentration; Driving, Alcohol, and Drugs; Drug Interactions and Alcohol; Marijuana (Cannabis); Memory, Effects of Drugs on; Opiates/Opioids; Productivity: Effects of Alcohol on.**

BIBLIOGRAPHY

Bauer, L. O. (2001). Electroencephalographic studies of substance use and abuse. In M. J. Kaufman (Ed.). *Brain imaging in substance abuse.* Totowa, NJ: Humana Press, 77–112.

Fillmore, M.T., Roach, E. L., & Rice, J. T. (2002). Does caffeine counteract alcohol-induced impairment? The ironic effects of expectancy. *Journal of Studies on Alcohol and Drugs. 63,* 745–754.

Goebel, J. A., Dunham, D. N., Rohrbaugh, J. W., Fischel, D. G., Stewart, P. A., & Hanson, J. M. (1995). Dose-related effects of alcohol on dynamic posturography and oculomotor measures. *Acta Oto-Laryngologica Supplement, 520*(1):212–215.

Kaplan, J., Kraner, J., & Paulozzi, L. (December 8, 2006). Alcohol and other drug use among victims of motor-vehicle crashes—West Virginia, 2004–2005. MMWR: *Morbidity and Mortality Weekly Report, 55*(48), 1293–1296.

Liu, Y. C., & Fu, S. M. (2007). Changes in driving behavior and cognitive performance with different breath alcohol concentration levels. *Traffic Injury Prevention, 8,* 153–161.

Marczinski, C. A., & Fillmore, M.T. (2003). Dissociative antagonistic effects of caffeine on alcohol-induced impairment of behavioral control. *Experimental and Clinical Psychopharmacology, 11,* 228–236.

Moskowitz, H., Burns, M. M., & Williams, A. F. (1985). Skills performance at low blood alcohol levels. *Journal of Studies on Alcohol, 46,* 482–485.

Ogden, E. J., & Moskowitz, H. (2004). Effects of alcohol and other drugs on driver performance. *Traffic Injury Prevrevention, 5*(3), 185–198.

Schulte, T., Müller-Oehring, E. M., Strasburger, H., Warzel, H., & Sabel, B. A. (2001). Acute effects of alcohol on divided and covert attention in men. *Psychopharmacology* (Berlin), *154*(1), 61–69.

Simpson, C. A., & Rush, C. R. (2002). Acute performance-impairing and subject-rated effects of triazolam and temazepam, alone and in combination with ethanol, in humans. *Journal of Psychopharmacology. 16,* 23–34.

Zacny J. P., Conley, K., & Galinkin, J. (1997). Comparing the subjective, psychomotor, and physiological effects of intravenous buprenorphine and morphine in healthy volunteers. *Journal of Pharmacology and Experimental Therapeutics, 282,*1187–1197.

LANCE BAUER

PSYCHOMOTOR STIMULANT.

This term is used to describe drugs that act as central nervous system (CNS) stimulants. Such drugs generally are appetite suppressants, decrease sleep and fatigue, increase energy and activity, and at higher doses can cause convulsions and death.

Ingestion typically results in increased wakefulness and a decreased sense of fatigue; increased speech and motor activity; alertness; and frequently elevation of mood. Many of the drugs in this class have a potential for abuse, with reports of euphoria at higher doses. Although users often report improved performance on physical and mental tasks, this is rarely the case, but they do restore performance that has been impaired by fatigue.

Prolonged use of most of these drugs can result in tolerance to many of their effects. Repeated high doses can result in distorted perception and overt psychotic behavior.

See also **Amphetamine; Cocaine; Tolerance and Physical Dependence.**

BIBLIOGRAPHY

Karch, S. B. (2006). *Drug abuse handbook.* Boca Raton, FL: CRC Press.

Roach, S. S., & Ford, S. M. (2006). Central nervous system stimulants. In *Introductory clinical pharmacology*, 8th ed. Philadelphia, PA: Lippincott, Williams & Wilkins.

MARIAN W. FISCHMAN

PSYCHOPHARMACOLOGY.

Psychopharmacology is that branch of science that involves the study of the effects of interactions between drugs that affect the central nervous system (i.e., psychoactive drugs) and living systems. Behavioral and neurobiological effects as well as the mechanisms of actions and side effects of drugs are often examined. Preclinical studies of psychoactive drugs using animal models and tissue preparations are an important aspect of psychopharmacology, contributing to our understanding of the mechanisms involved in disorders of the central nervous system and mental illness. Clinical psychopharmacological investigations include examining the effects of drugs used in treating psychiatric disorders (such as anxiety, depression, schizophrenia, and mania), as well as other dysfunctions within the central nervous system (such as movement disorders, Alzheimer's disease). Also included is study of the effects of psychoactive drugs used nonmedically to induce altered states of consciousness, to improve mood, or to otherwise affect the mental status and/or behavior of the individual. A growing area of research in psychopharmacology addresses disorders of addiction or dependence to some of these drugs. New treatments for alcoholism (naltrexone), opioid dependence (buprenorphine), and smoking cessation (bupropion) have resulted from these efforts, and many more treatments are under development. Some of the drugs used for treatment of depression and anxiety are also being investigated for potential usefulness in treating substance dependence, since it is often accompanied by these comorbid conditions.

Psychopharmacology is an interdisciplinary field of science. Psychopharmacologists may be physicians trained in psychiatry or neurology; psychologists with extra training in pharmacology; or pharmacologists with special training in psychology and behavior.

BIBLIOGRAPHY

Bloom, F. E., & Kupfer, D., Eds. (1995). *Psychopharmacology: the fourth generation of progress.* New York: Raven Press.

Meyer, J. S., &amp: Quenzer, L. F. (2004). *Psychopharmacology: Drugs, the brain and behavior.* Sunderland, MA: Sinauer Associates.

Nemeroff, C. B., & Schatsberg, A. F., Eds. (1998). *The American Psychiatric Press Textbook of Psychopharmacology.* Washington, D.C.: American Psychiatric Press.

Sadock, B. J., & Sadock, V. A. (2007). Psychopharmacology and other biologic therapies. In *Kaplan and Sadock's synopsis of psychiatry: Behavioral sciences/clinical psychiatry*, 10th ed. Philadelphia, PA: Lippincott, Williams & Wilkins.

NICK E. GOEDERS
REVISED BY NICHOLAS DEMARTINIS (2001)

PUBLIC INTOXICATION.

In 1606 England first made simple public intoxication a criminal offense. This English precedent was reflected in laws in the American colonies as well as in city, county, and state laws enacted after the American Revolution. By the early 1960s about 2 million arrests occurred annually for simple public intoxication, representing about 33 percent of all arrests in the United States.

Since then, changes have occurred in the handling of public intoxication. Through initial efforts in the judicial/court system and later through federal and state legislation, the handling of public intoxication was transferred from the criminal-justice system to the more humane and effective public-health care system. Major obstacles to further progress, however, have been the lack of adequate funding and the struggle to find effective alcohol abuse and alcoholism treatments.

INITIAL COURT CHALLENGES

Beginning in 1964, lawyers argued that alcoholics could not lawfully be punished for public intoxication. First, they argued that alcoholics did not have the *mens rea* (Latin, guilty mind or intent) required for conviction of a crime, because public intoxication was a symptom of the disease of alcoholism. Second, they argued that punishing an alcoholic for exhibiting symptoms of a disease was cruel and unusual punishment, prohibited by the U.S. Constitution.

In lower court cases these arguments prevailed. In 1968, however, in the case of *Powell v. Texas,* the U.S. Supreme Court handed down a split decision on this issue. Four justices deemed it cruel and unusual punishment to convict Powell, an admitted alcoholic, for public intoxication. Four others determined that the matter should be decided on a state rather than a constitutional level. The ninth and controlling justice said that, because Powell had a home, he could properly be held responsible for being intoxicated in public, so he was convicted. This opened the question of whether a homeless alcoholic could also be convicted.

ENACTMENT OF FEDERAL STATUTES

Faced with a stalemate in the Supreme Court, advocates for reforming public-intoxication laws turned to Congress. In spite of a large number of federal public health statutes, none referred explicitly to the problems of intoxication and alcoholism. Congress responded by enacting the Alcoholic Rehabilitation Act of 1968, which recognized alcoholism as a major health and social problem and recommended handling public intoxication as a health problem rather than a law-enforcement matter. The Comprehensive Alcohol Abuse and Alcoholism Prevention, Treatment, and Rehabilitation Act of 1970 (also called the Hughes Act) followed. It created the National Institute on Alcohol Abuse and Alcoholism to administer all alcoholism programs under the authority of the U.S. Department of Health, Education, and Welfare (now the U.S. Department of Health and Human Services). These new federal laws for the first time provided a national focus for handling intoxication on a public-health basis.

CHANGES IN STATE STATUTES

Following the legal developments in the courts and in Congress, state and local laws rapidly changed. Initially in the District of Columbia and in Maryland, and subsequently throughout other parts of the country, criminal statutes prohibiting simple public intoxication were repealed and replaced with new laws establishing detoxification programs for intoxicated persons and rehabilitation programs for chronic alcoholics.

Federal and state laws now provided a firm foundation for handling public intoxication as a public-health problem rather than as a matter for the criminal-justice system. Relatively little additional change

In response to the costs of transporting and detaining public inebriates, some communities have instituted "sobering centers" where intoxicated individuals can safely spend the night and receive treatment referrals. AP IMAGES

could be accomplished solely by further litigation or legislation, but two additional obstacles arose. First, the competition for federal and state health funds became intense. Other important health needs, including basic health care for the needy and treatment for people with acquired immunodeficiency syndrome (AIDS), made it difficult for public officials to devote adequate resources to expanding public-health programs for alcoholism. The problem was compounded by uncertainty as to the best method for preventing or treating intoxication and alcoholism. A low rate of rehabilitation led many public health officials to conclude that scarce public resources could be more effectively devoted to other illnesses, especially communicable diseases. Without additional investment, the police remain deeply involved in identifying and responding to intoxicated individuals, and their response is not necessarily limited to transporting individuals to sobering-up stations.

Progress in the prevention and treatment of intoxication and alcoholism has therefore been slow. Unless and until the American public places a higher priority on public intoxication as a public-health matter or medical science finds more effective methods to prevent and treat this problem, this situation is unlikely to change.

Two developments in the last decade of the twentieth century illustrate the public concern and frustration with the continuing problems of public intoxication and alcoholism. First, publicity about the substantial death and destruction caused by people driving under the influence of alcohol has led to more stringent penalties and stricter enforcement against this behavior. Second, tragic deaths caused by binge drinking on college campuses have led to an increase in the drinking age from 18 to 21 as well as stricter enforcement in college towns throughout the country.

CHRONIC PUBLIC INEBRIATION (CPI) AND SOBERING CENTERS

In the absence of an optimal treatment and prevention program or unlimited funds to administer such a system, individuals will continue to become intoxicated; some will be termed chronic public inebriates (CPI). To keep down the staggering costs of emergency department or law enforcement personnel transporting intoxicated individuals to detention facilities for sobering up, many states have created *sobering centers*. These nonmedical, non-detention centers allow intoxicated persons to safely spend the night (or other brief interval). They also provide food, showers, and referrals to treatment or rehabilitation facilities. Individuals can stay the night to sleep off the effects of alcohol, or they can stay for several days to engage in assessment and programming activities. In many sobering centers, clients are encouraged to attend self-help or twelve-step meetings and to consider referral to longer-term treatment facilities. Typically, sobering centers are based on the philosophy that many alcoholics also have mental health disorders (co-occurring disorders), so they offer screening and referral for behavioral health (mental health and substance abuse) problems. Many sobering centers offer intensive case management services, housing referrals, and other public assistance along with detoxification and assessment protocols.

See also **Alcohol: History of Drinking; Homelessness, Alcohol and Other Drugs, History of; Temperance Movement; Treatment, Stages/Phases of: Non-Medical Detoxification; Treatment, Stages/Phases of: Medical Detoxification; Treatment: An** Overview of Alcohol Abuse/Dependence; Treatment: A History of Treatment in the United States.

BIBLIOGRAPHY

Arfken, C. L., Klein, C., Di Menza, S., & Schuster, C. R. (2001). Gender differences in problem severity at assessment and treatment retention. *Journal of Substance Abuse Treatment, 20*, 53–57.

Arfken, C. L., Borisova, N., Klein, C., Di Menza, S., & Schuster, C. R. (2002). Women are less likely to be admitted to substance abuse treatment within 30 days of assessment. *Journal of Psychoactive Drugs, 34*, 33–38.

Bendtsen, P., Dahlstrom, M., & Bjurulf, P. (2002). Sociodemographic gender differences in patients attending a community-based alcohol treatment centre. *Addiction Behavior, 27*, 21–33.

Greenfield, S. F., Kolodziej, M. E., Sugarman, D. E., Muenz, L. R., Vagge, L. M., & He, D. Y. (2002). History of abuse and drinking outcomes following inpatient alcohol treatment: A prospective study. *Drug and Alcohol Dependence, 67*, 227–234.

Hesselbrock, M. N., & Hesselbrock, V. M. (1997). Gender, alcoholism, and psychiatric comorbidity. In R. W. Wilsnack & S. C. Wilsnack (Eds.), *Gender and alcohol: Individual and social perspectives* (pp. 49–71). New Brunswick, NJ: Center of Alcohol Studies, Rutgers University.

Marsh, J. C., Cao, D., & D'Aunno, T. (2004). Gender differences in the impact of comprehensive services in substance abuse treatment. *Journal of Substance Abuse Treatment, 27*, 289–300.

Mojtabai, R. (2005). Use of specialty substance abuse and mental health services in adults with substance use disorders in the community. *Drug and Alcohol Dependence, 78*, 345–354.

Room, R., Matzger, H., & Weisner, C. (2004). Sources of informal pressure on problematic drinkers to cut down or seek treatment. *Journal of Substance Use, 9*, 280–295.

Weisner, C., & Schmidt, L. A. (2001). Rethinking access to alcohol treatment. In M. Galanter (Ed.), *Recent developments in alcoholism: Services research in the era of managed care* (Vol. 15). (pp. 107–136). New York: Kluwer Academic/Plenum Press.

PETER BARTON HUTT
REVISED BY PAMELA V. MICHAELS (2009)

RACIAL PROFILING.

Profiles, formal and informal, are common in law enforcement, particularly in narcotics law enforcement. They consist of general characteristics, features, and behaviors that might make a law enforcement officer suspicious. In some instances, law enforcement agencies formulate and disseminate formal profiles to officers to guide their investigative actions. Even when profiles are not formally maintained, however, officers inevitably rely on their past experience to generate informal profiles to help them determine who to follow more closely, approach, stop, or question. There is much controversy regarding profiling as a general practice. When race becomes a factor in a profile, however, serious constitutional and ethical issues arise.

STATISTICS ON RACIAL TARGETING

Racial profiling is the use of racial of ethnic generalizations or stereotypes as a basis for stopping, searching, questioning, or detaining an individual. Racial profiling has received a great deal of attention in the United States, beginning in the late 1990s with a series of prominent incidents and the release of data on police practices from several jurisdictions. The data consistently showed that African Americans and Hispanics are disproportionately targeted by law enforcement for stops, frisks, and searches. Court records showed, for example, that in Maryland African Americans made up 70 percent of those stopped and searched by the Maryland State Police from January 1995 through December 1997, on a road on which 17.5 percent of the drivers and speeders were African American. A 1999 report by the New Jersey attorney general found that 77 percent of those stopped and searched on New Jersey highways were African American or Hispanic, even though, according to one expert, only 13.5 percent of the drivers and 15 percent of the speeders on those highways are African American or Hispanic.

An *Orlando Sentinel* analysis of 1,000 videotapes of Florida state trooper traffic stops in 1992 showed that on a road where 5 percent of the drivers were African American or Hispanic, 70 percent of those stopped and 80 percent of those searched by the Florida state police were African American or Hispanic. Although matters had improved somewhat by the start of the twenty-first century in terms of racial percentages at traffic stops, there has been little change in what occurs *after* the initial stop. According to Bureau of Justice statistics, Blacks, Hispanics and Whites are pulled over with roughly equal frequency, but Blacks and Hispanics are far more likely to be questioned, searched, handcuffed, detained, or arrested than their White peers. For every three White people subjected to more than a simple traffic stop, at least 10 Blacks and 11 Hispanics were searched.

Racial targeting need not be expressly invited by a profile. Consider, for example, the U.S. Drug Enforcement Agency's (DEA) drug courier profile for airports. All the factors listed below have been identified by DEA agents in court testimony as part of the DEA's drug courier profile:

- Arrived late at night.
- Arrived early in the morning.
- Arrived in afternoon.

- One of first to deplane.
- One of last to deplane.
- Deplaned in the middle.
- Bought coach ticket.
- Bought first-class ticket.
- Used one-way ticket.
- Used round-trip ticket.
- Paid for ticket with small denomination currency.
- Paid for ticket with large denomination currency.
- Made local telephone call after deplaning.
- Made long-distance telephone call after deplaning.
- Pretended to make telephone call.
- Traveled from New York to Los Angeles.
- Traveled to Houston.
- Traveled to Detroit.
- Traveled to Miami.
- Carried no luggage.
- Carried brand-new luggage.
- Carried a small bag.
- Carried a medium-sized bag.
- Carried two bulky garment bags.
- Carried two heavy suitcases.
- Carried four pieces of luggage.
- Overly protective of luggage.
- Disassociated self from luggage.
- Traveled alone.
- Traveled with a companion.
- Acted too nervous.
- Acted too calm.
- Made eye contact with officer.
- Avoided making eye contact with officer.
- Wore expensive clothing and gold jewelry.
- Dressed casually.
- Went to restroom after deplaning.
- Walked quickly through airport.
- Walked slowly through airport.
- Walked aimlessly through airport.
- Left airport by taxi.
- Left airport by limousine.
- Left airport by private car.
- Left airport by hotel courtesy van.

- Suspect was Hispanic.
- Suspect was African American female.

Even without the last two factors, this profile describes so many travelers that it does not so much focus an investigation as provide DEA officials a ready-made excuse for stopping whomever they please. The profile for terrorists is quite similar, with the addition of *Muslim* as a race/ethnicity.

Although statistical data alone do not conclusively establish that officers are engaged in racial profiling, they provide strong circumstantial evidence. Many police officers, moreover, admit that all other things being equal, they are more suspicious of, for example, young African American men than elderly White women. Nor is such thinking irrational. Criminologists generally agree that young (African American) men are more likely to commit crime than elderly (White) women, because at least with respect to some crime, young people commit more crime than old people, men commit more crime than women, and African Americans commit more crime than Whites. Indeed, it is precisely because the use of race as a generalization is not irrational that racial profiling is such a widespread phenomenon.

USE IN DRUG LAW ENFORCEMENT

In some areas, however, there is evidence that the use of racial profiles is irrational. The strongest evidence is with respect to drug law enforcement. Much of the racial profiling that occurs on the nation's highways is conducted for drug law enforcement purposes. Officers use the pretext of a traffic infraction to stop a car and then ask for consent to search the car for drugs. The U.S. Supreme Court has expressly approved this tactic.

Yet studies show that officers get virtually the same "hit rates" for Whites and African Americans when they conduct traffic stops for drugs. In other words, officers are no more likely to find drugs on an African American driver than a White driver. Consistent with these results, the U.S. Public Health Service has found, based on confidential self-report surveys, that African Americans and Whites use illegal drugs in rough proportion to their representation in the population at large. Because most users report having purchased drugs from a dealer of the same race, drug dealing is also likely to be fairly evenly represented demographically. Thus, the supposition that African

Americans are more likely to be carrying drugs is sharply contradicted by the data.

UNLAWFUL AND UNWISE

In any event, even where demographic data suggests that the practice of racial profiling may not be irrational, it is both unconstitutional and unwise. Because of the pernicious history of racial classifications in the United States, the Supreme Court forbids official reliance on racial generalizations—even accurate ones—except when there is no other way to achieve a compelling government end. The usual argument police officers advance in defense of profiling is that it recognizes the unfortunate fact that minorities are more likely than nonminorities to commit crime. Although this may be true with respect to *some* crimes, however, the generalizations are significantly overinclusive, even where those crimes are concerned. The fact that African Americans are more likely than Whites to engage in violent crime, for example, does not mean that most African Americans commit violent crime. Most African Americans, like most Whites, do not commit any crime; annually, at least 90 percent of African Americans are not arrested for anything. On any given day, the number of innocent African Americans is even higher. In addition, when officers focus on minorities, they lose sight of White criminals. Race is a grossly inaccurate indicator of crime.

Most important, relying on race as a factor for suspicion violates the first principle of criminal law: individual responsibility. The state's authority to take its citizens' liberty—and in extreme cases, lives—turns on the premise that all are equal before the law. Racial generalizations fail to treat people as individuals. As a result, policies that tolerate racial profiling undermine the criminal law's legitimacy. As any good leader knows, and many criminologists have confirmed, legitimacy is central to getting people to follow the rules. If people believe in the legitimacy and fairness of the system, they are much more likely to abide by the rules than if they see the system as unjust. Thus, racial profiling may indeed contribute to crime by corroding the legitimacy of the criminal law.

TERRORISM AND NEW RACIAL PROFILING

The terrorist attacks on American soil on 9/11, along with the attacks on Spain's railway system and the London transportation system, effectively reversed the antiprofiling trend. It added another group to be profiled, potential terrorists, and another racial/ethnic group to scrutinize: young Middle Eastern or Muslim-appearing males.

In addition to the ethical dilemmas inherent in search and seizure based on statistically determined racial or ethnic profiles is the logic flaw sharply exemplified by the twenty-first-century terrorist attacks: The persons who committed the violence were able to blend into the cultures in which they operated before their final acts. They didn't look substantially different than those around them, and they moved comfortably within the societies they targeted, whether in the United States, Spain, or the United Kingdom. Ethnic identity, or the appearance thereof, can be changed. In London, the members of the jihad cell shifted their assumed identities to East African to avoid being profiled as Pakistani or Arab.

Thus far, there is no convincing, empirical evidence that racial or ethnic profiling achieves the desired ends: eradicating crime or preventing acts of terror. When groups become aware that they are being profiled, they shift identities to assimilate (persons of African descent transform themselves into Jamaicans or Caribbeans, Mexicans become Spaniards, persons from the Middle East become African, etc.). When metal detectors were installed in airports a few decades ago, terrorists shifted from metal weapons to liquid and plastic explosives. Hijackings decreased, but bombings increased dramatically. These are called substitution effects.

Most counterterrorists are convinced that the way to combat terrorism is to effectively limit terrorist resources through the use of proactive counterterrorism activities and through the use of intelligence (informational resources). General Mier Dagan, the former head of the Bureau of Counterterrorism in the Office of the Prime Minister of Israel stated, "Investments in intelligence are invisible, whereas increased security is visible but often wasteful. The first priority must be placed on intelligence, then on counterterrorism operations, and finally on defense and protection."

See also **African Americans, Ethnic and Cultural Factors Relevant to Treatment for; Crime and Drugs; Driving Under the Influence (DUI); Hispanic Americans, Alcohol and Drug Use Among.**

BIBLIOGRAPHY

Banks, R. R. (2001). Race-based suspect selection and colorblind equal protection: Doctrine and discourse. *UCLA Law Review, 48,* 1075.

Borooah, V. K. (2001). Racial bias in police stops and searches: An economic analysis. *European Journal of Political Economy, 17,* 17–37.

Borooah, V. K. (2002). Economic analysis of police stops and searches: A reply. *European Journal of Political Economy, 18,* 607–608.

Cole, D. (1999). *No equal justice: Race and class in the American criminal justice system.* New York: New Press.

Dominitz, J., & Knowles, J. (2005, February 18). *Crime minimization and racial bias: What can we learn from police search data?* (PIER Working Paper 05-019.) Available from http://ssrn.com/.

Enders, W., & Sandler, T. (2004). What do we know about the substitution effect in transnational terrorism? In A. Silke & G. Ilardi (Eds.), *Researching terrorism: Trends, achievements, failures.* London: Frank Cass.

Faria, J. R. (2006). Terrorist innovations and anti-terrorist policies. *Terrorism and Political Violence, 18,* 47–56.

Gladwell, M. (2006, February 6). Troublemakers: What pit bulls can teach us about profiling. *The New Yorker.* Available from http://www.newyorker.com/.

Harcourt, B. E. (2004). Rethinking racial profiling: A critique of the economics, civil liberties, and constitutional literature, and of criminal profiling more generally. *The University of Chicago Law Review, 71,* 1275–1381.

Harcourt, B. E. (2006, March). Muslim profiles post-9/11: Is racial profiling an effective counterterrorist measure and does it violate the right to be free from discrimination? (University of Chicago Law & Economics, Olin Working Paper No. 288). Available from http://ssrn.com/.

Harcourt, B. E. (2007). *Against prediction: Profiling, policing and punishing in an actuarial age.* Chicago: University of Chicago Press.

Harris, D. (1999). *Driving while black: Racial profiling on our nation's highways.* New York: American Civil Liberties Union.

Harris, D. (1999). The stories, the statistics, and the law: Why driving while black matters. *Minnesota Law Review, 84*(2), 265–326.

Knowles, J., Persico, N., & Todd, P. (2001). Racial bias in motor vehicle searches: Theory and evidence. *Journal of Political Economy, 109,* 203–229.

Persico, N. (2002). Racial profiling, fairness, and effectiveness of policing. *American Economic Review, 92,* 1472–1497.

Posner, E., & Vermeule, A. (2006). Should coercive interrogation be legal? *Michigan Law Review, 104*(4), 671–707.

Smith, M., Makarios, M., & Alpert, G. (2006, June). Differential suspicion: Theory specification and gender effects in the traffic stop context. *Justice Quarterly, 23.*

Sperry, P. (2005, July 28). When the profile fits the crime. *New York Times.* Available from http://www.nytimes.com/.

DAVID D. COLE
REVISED BY PAMELA V. MICHAELS (2009)

RAVE. Raves in the United States in the twenty-first century are similar in nature to those that emerged in the 1980s: Large parties held into the early hours of the morning characterized by loud electronic music, people socializing and dancing, and widespread substance use. While raves started out as *underground* parties held in clandestine locations known to the few, *raving* generally morphed into *clubbing*, which often occurs in legitimate, regulated venues attended by many people across the nation every weekend (Sanders, 2006; Hobbs et al., 2003; Thornton, 1995). No doubt underground raves still exist, and occasional super parties held in stadiums, convention centers, and open fields are billed and thought of as *raves* or *festivals*, but socializing to electronic dance music in semi-public venues while using one of a number of substances has become commonplace, another option within the leisure spectrum of many U.S. cities (Sanders, 2006; Presdee, 2000; Rojeck, 2000).

Underground raves and those who attend them are differentiated from *mainstream* club scenes and clubbers in terms of style, culture, musical preference, and other characteristics, but raving, festivals, clubbing, and the like in the early twenty-first century are, in the main, fundamentally commercial enterprises (Sanders, 2006; Thornton, 1995). This entry describes common forms of clubbing or raving, all of which is henceforth referred to as electronic dance parties (EDPs), so as not to confuse them with underground raves.

CLUB DRUGS AND THEIR USERS
To be sure, not all those who attend EDPs use drugs (National Institute on Drug Abuse, 2006). Certain types of drugs, collectively known as *club drugs,*

however, are commonly used at EDPs (Fendrich & Johnson, 2005). The drug ecstasy, which is often associated with MDMA (3,4-methylenedioxy-N-methylamphetamine), in particular, has been considered ubiquitous at EDPs (Beck & Rosenbaum, 1994; Sanders, 2006; Colin & Godfrey, 1997; Redhead, 1993; Shapiro, 1999). The drug, in a similar vein to other so-called club drugs—magic (psilocybin) mushrooms, and LSD (acid)—*fit* with the music and overall theme of the events (Sanders, 2006). The pulse of the beat, with names like *jungle, trance, hard house,* and *drum and bass,* work with the stimulant and hallucinatory effects of these drugs and are thought to enhance the visual effects of the lasers, disco balls, and general party atmosphere created by the venue and its punters (Reynolds, 1997). Other club drugs, such as ketamine (Special K), a *dissociative* anesthetic widely used in veterinary practices, and GHB, a simple carbohydrate which has been used by bodybuilders as a supplement, are also associated with EDPs (National Institute on Drug Abuse, 2006; Lankenau, 2006). Even the potent sedative, Rohypnol, was considered a club drug at one point (Maxwell, 2005). The uses of drugs such as powder cocaine and crystal methamphetamine (crystal) are, however, not uncommon at EDPs (Green, 2006; Kelly & Parsons, 2006; Kelly, Parsons & Brooke, 2006). Other powerful hallucinogens, known as tryptamines (DMT) and phenethylamines (2C-B), have also been reported at EDPs (Kelly, 2006; Sanders, 2006; Sanders et al., 2008). Again, both stimulants and hallucinogens work with the overall atmosphere produced at EDPs. If *club drugs* are those drugs used within such venues, then other substances fall in this category.

Individuals who use drugs are thought of *marijuana users, heroin users, ecstasy users,* and the like. These terms may capture particular drug consumption patterns. However, at EDPs, many individuals use multiple drugs, either sequentially or simultaneously (Lankenau & Clatts, 2005; Kelly, Parsons, & Wells, 2006; Klein, Sterk, & Elifson, 2006; Sanders, 2006). People attending EDPs are likely to use several substances over the course of the event, as opposed to sticking with one. Moreover, alcohol is prominent since many EDPs are held in venues that sell alcohol (Measham & Brain, 2005). The following example certainly does not apply to all who attend EDPs, but it does provide some insight into the potential for using a variety of substances while attending an event.

This example is derived from a slightly altered amalgamation of several ethnographic accounts of drug consumption at EDPs in the United States (Green, 2006; Navarez, 2001; Perrone, 2006). Friends meet up at a bar around 10 p.m. for a couple drinks. An hour later, they go to an EDP. Prior to entering the venue, they smoke a little cannabis. They enter the EDP buzzing from the alcohol and cannabis mixture. Around 12:30, they decide to take an ecstasy pill. Alcohol is sold in the venue, and these individuals decide to have a few drinks during their three-hour ecstasy high. At 3:30 a.m., their ecstasy buzz is wearing off, but the party does not stop for another couple of hours. Fortunately, they brought cocaine and crystal with them, and each sniffs a small amount of *trail mix,* a combination of both drugs. The trail mix keeps them going until 7 a.m., and when the party stops, they rally to a friend's house for a *chillout* session. To help them *comedown* from the ecstasy, cocaine, and crystal, they smoke some more cannabis, and have a few drinks. Despite the alcohol and strong, hydroponically grown cannabis, the trail mix keeps them going for a bit longer than expected. As a remedy, each takes a Vicodin prior to going to bed sometime in the late morning, 12 hours after they first headed out.

EDP ATTENDEES AND THEIR RISK OF LEGAL PROBLEMS

Individuals who attend EDPs are part of the workforce and attend EDPs in order to release tension and stress after a week's work (Green, 2006; Perrone, 2006; Sanders, 2006). These youth, in the main, lead normal, productive lives. Youth who attend EDPs en masse are not outlaws, not drug-crazed addicts, and evidence generally does not indicate that such individuals are more prone to crime and delinquency than their non-attending EDP counterparts (Sanders, 2006). To be clear, many punters may be chemically addicted and/or suffer from serious health problems related to their substance use, and accounts of overdose or drug-related negative health outcomes or death do occur at or around EDPs. But substance use consumption patterns among punters at EDPs appear largely recreational, and the youth who attend these events, in the main, have meaningful lives (Green, 2006; Perrone, 2006). These youth have generally not opted out of society and are not the *double failures* as drug users were described generations ago (Cloward & Ohlin, 1960; Merton, 1957). Attendees at EDPs may be considered part of a broadly defined *subculture* to the extent that they enjoy similar forms of music, have a tolerance for drug use, and like to socialize during the early morning hours. However, beyond these preferences, such youth are remarkably different from one another and do not constitute a segment of the population otherwise distinct from everyone else (Presdee, 2000; Rojeck, 2000; Sanders, 2006; Thornton, 1995).

Criminal justice and public health reactions to EDPs are at odds with one another: The former seeks to curtail drug use at EDPs through sanctions and prosecution, whereas the latter attempts to make substance use safer for the evening's punters (Sanders, 2006). Dancesafe, for instance, is an organization largely run by those who enjoy EDPs. Dancesafe has offered pill-testing services by providing punters with testing kits in order to have their ecstasy tablets checked for content. Among other activities, Dancesafe has set up small booths in or around EDPs in order to provide information about drugs commonly used within such venues. While pill testing may be "harm minimization gone too far" (Winstock, Wolf, & Ramsey, 2005), it represents a unique public health approach towards reducing the potential of adverse affects related to recreational youthful substance use.

The contrast there is opposition to illicit substance use at EDPs. In 2002, for instance, the R.A.V.E Act was introduced (R.A.V.E stood for Reducing Americans' Vulnerability to Ecstasy). The act would make it illegal to use illicit drugs on venue premises, and if anyone was caught doing so, the owner and manager of the venue, and the night's promoters, as well as the offending punter, could all be subject to criminal prosecution. While the RAVE Act was never passed, its central tenets were incorporated into another bill—the Illicit Drug Anti-Proliferation Act of 2003—that eventually became law. The difficulty is in effectively policing this law (Measham, Alrdridge, & Parker, 2001). If EDPs are subject to closure as a consequence of one punter using illicit drugs inside the venue, then EDPs are surely doomed. Substance use—whether illicit or not—is common at most

EDPs and may be seen as *normalized* within such settings (Measham et al., 2001). Shutting down illicit substance use at EDPs threatens their existence. This, in turn, not only jeopardizes a multi-million-dollar-a-year industry but may also serve to push EDPs further underground, away from regulated nightclubs and venues. If this occurs, then punters may become unnecessarily exposed to the public health hazards of clandestine EDP locations (Sanders, 2006).

The future of EDPs in the United States is not known. Youth at EDPs are exposed to a broad range of illicit substances, and, regardless of whether they decide to use them or not, most wake up the following morning and get on with their (largely) law-abiding lives. Substance-using youth may get caught in the legal system, which, in turn, can detrimentally affect the remainder of their lives. If attending EDPs and using drugs may be part of a fad or fashion that many youth pass through, then people need to think carefully about their responses to these criminal aspects of their otherwise productive, respectable and obedient young lives.

See also **Club Drugs; Cocaine; Lysergic Acid Diethylamide (LSD) and Psychedelics; Marijuana (Cannabis); MDMA; Media; Methamphetamine; Music; Psilocybin; Rohypnol.**

BIBLIOGRAPHY

Beck, J., & Rosenbaum, M. (1994). *Pursuit of ecstasy: The MDMA experience.* Albany: State University of New York Press.

Cloward, R., & Ohlin, L. (1960). *Delinquency and opportunity: A theory of delinquent gangs.* London: Collier-Macmillan.

Collin, M., & Godfrey, J. (1997). *Altered state: The story of ecstasy culture and acid house.* London: Serpent's Tail.

Degenhardt, L., Copeland, J., & Dillion, P. (2005). Recent trends in the use of club drugs: An Australian review. *Substance Use and Misuse, 40,* 1241–1256.

Fendrich, M., & Johnson, T. P. (2005). Editors' introduction (special issue on club drug epidemiology). *Substance Use and Misuse, 40,* 1179–1184.

Green, A. I. (2006). "Chem friendly": The institutional basis of club drug use in a sample of urban gay men. In B. Sanders (Ed.), *Drugs, clubs, and young people: Sociological and public health perspectives* (pp. 67–76). Aldershot, Hampshire, England: Ashgate.

Hobbs, D., Hadfield, P., Lister, S., & Winlow, S. (2003). *Bouncers: Violence and governance in the night-time economy.* Oxford, England: Oxford University Press.

Kelly, B. C. (2006). Conceptions of risk in the lives of ecstasy-using youth. In B. Sanders (Ed.), *Drugs, clubs and young people: Sociological and public health perspectives* (pp. 50–66). Aldershot, Hampshire, England: Ashgate.

Kelly, B. C., & Parsons, J. T. (2006, November). *Resurgence of cocaine among club-going young adults.* Paper presented at the American Public Health Association Annual Meeting, Boston.

Kelly, B. C., Parsons, J. T., & Wells, B. E. (2006). Prevalence and predictors of club drug use among club-going young adults in New York City. *Journal of Urban Health, 83*(5), 884–895.

Klein, H. A., Elifson, K. W., & Sterk, C. E. (2006, November). "Garbage Heads": High-end polydrug abusing ecstasy users and their involvement in HIV risk behaviors. Paper presented at the American Public Health Association Annual Meeting, Boston.

Lankenau, S. E. (2006). On ketamine: In and out of the k hole. In B. Sanders (Ed.), *Drugs, clubs and young people: Sociological and public health perspectives* (pp. 77–87). Aldershot, Hampshire, England: Ashgate.

Lankenau, S. E., & Clatts, M. C. (2005). Patterns of polydrug use among ketamine injectors in New York City. *Substance Use and Misuse, 40,* 1381–1398.

Maxwell, J. C. (2005). Party drugs: Properties, prevalence, patterns, and problems. *Substance Use and Misuse, 40,* 1203–1240.

Measham, F. (2004). The decline of ecstasy, the rise of binge drinking and the persistence of pleasure. *Probation Journal, Special Edition: Rethinking drugs and crime, 51*(4), 309–326.

Measham, F., Aldridge, J., & Parker, H. (2001). *Dancing on drugs: Risk, health, and hedonism in the British club scene.* London: Free Association Books.

Measham, F., & Brain, K. (2005). Binge drinking, British alcohol policy, and the new culture of intoxication. *Crime, Media, Culture: An International Journal, 1*(3), 262–283.

Merton, R. K. (1957). *Social theory and social structure* (Revised and enlarged ed.), London: Glencoe Free Press.

Narvaez, R. (2001, July). *MDMA in combination: Trail mix and other powdered drug combinations.* Paper presented at MDMA/Ecstasy Research: Advances, Challenges, Future, Bethesda, MD.

National Institute on Drug Abuse. (2006). NIDA Info Facts: Club drugs. National Institute on Drug Abuse, National Institutes of Health, U.S. Department of Health and Human Services. Available from http://www.nida.nih.gov/.

Perrone, D. (2006). New York City club kids: A contextual understanding of club drug use. In B. Sanders (Ed.) *Drugs, clubs and young people: Sociological and public health perspectives* (pp. 26–49). Aldershot, Hampshire, England: Ashgate.

Presdee, M. (2000). *Cultural criminology and the carnival crime.* London: Routledge.

Redhead, S. (1993). The politics of ecstasy. In *Rave off: Politics and deviance in contemporary youth culture* (pp. 7–28). Aldershot, Hampshire, England: Avebury.

Reynolds, S. (1997). Rave culture: Living dream or living death? In S. Redhead (Ed.) with D. Wynne & J. O'Connor, *The club-cultures reader: Readings in popular cultural studies.* Oxford, England: Blackwell.

Rojek, C. (2002). *Leisure and culture.* London: Macmillan.

Sanders, B. (2006). Young people, clubs, and drugs. In B. Sanders (Ed.), *Drugs, clubs, and young people: Sociological and public health perspectives* (pp. 1–12). Aldershot, Hampshire, England: Ashgate.

Sanders, B., Lankenau, S. E, Jackson Bloom, J., & Hathazi, D. (2008). 'Research chemicals': Tryptamine and phenethylamine use amongst high-risk youth. *Substance Use and Misuse, 43*(3), 389–402.

Shapiro, H. (1999). Dances with drugs: Pop music, drugs and youth culture. In N. South (Ed.), *Drugs: Cultures, controls and everyday life* (pp. 17–35). London: Sage.

Thornton, S. (1995). *Club cultures: Music, media, and subcultural capital.* Middletown, CT: Wesleyan University Press.

Winstock, A. R., Wolff, K., & Ramsey, J. (2001). Ecstasy pill testing: Harm minimization gone too far? *Addiction, 96,* 1139–1148.

BILL SANDERS

RECEPTOR, DRUG.

A receptor is a molecular site, specific for a drug or its class, with which the drug must combine to produce its effect. If a drug is in the body but cannot bind to the receptor, then there is no effect. A receptor can be thought of as the button or switch that the drug must activate in order to produce a physiologic effect.

Receptors for drugs are the same receptors used in the brain by naturally occurring compounds called neurotransmitters. Neurotransmitters are chemical signaling messengers in the brain that work by binding to specific receptors; a wide variety of drugs of abuse bind to these same receptors. In this sense, drugs of abuse insert themselves into natural and normal systems found in the brain and take over normal pathways in abnormal ways. Receptors are essential for normal functioning of the body and are therefore of great interest and importance in physiology and medicine.

Receptors can be stimulated by compounds called agonists, or blocked by compounds called antagonists. Antagonists prevent the action of agonists. For example, naltrexone, an antagonist, will prevent morphine, an agonist, from having any effect.

A major achievement of research in drug abuse over the past thirty years has been the identification and study of almost all receptors for drugs of abuse. Receptors are generally classified into two types: an ion channel type and a coupled type receptor or "G protein." Nicotine acts at one of the former and morphine at one of the latter. However, sometimes the initial molecular site where a drug acts is not one of these two classical types of receptors. For example, cocaine acts at another kind of molecule called a transporter for dopamine; after cocaine binds at this site, dopamine transport in the brain is blocked, which then results in increased actions at the dopamine receptor. Since receptors are the initial molecular sites of binding of drugs, they are clearly of interest in understanding how drugs produce their effects and how we might develop medications to treat drug abuse.

See also **Agonist; Agonist-Antagonist (Mixed); Neurotransmitters.**

BIBLIOGRAPHY

Kenakin, T. (2000) *The pharmacology of functional, biochemical, and recombinant receptor systems.* New York: Springer.

NICK E. GOEDERS
REVISED BY MICHAEL J. KUHAR (2001)

RECEPTOR: NMDA (N-METHYL D-ASPARTIC ACID).

The NMDA receptor is a protein on the surface of neurons (nerve cells). When the major excitatory neurotransmitter, glutamate, binds to this protein, the central pore of the NMDA receptor channel opens—then cations (the ions of sodium, potassium, and calcium) are able to cross the cell membrane. The movement of cations through the pore results in neuronal excitation.

The NMDA receptor is one of several cell receptor surface proteins activated by glutamate. The hallucinogen phencyclidine (PCP) blocks the open channel of the NMDA receptor, preventing cation flow. It is believed that overactivation of the NMDA receptor could be responsible for the neuronal cell death observed following some forms of stroke; it may even be involved in the cell death associated with neurodegenerative diseases.

See also **Neurotransmission; Receptor, Drug.**

BIBLIOGRAPHY

Choi, D. (1988). Glutamate neurotoxicity and diseases of the nervous system. *Neuron, 1*, 623–634.

Collingridge, G., & Lester, R. (1989). Excitatory amino acid receptors in the vertebrate central nervous system. *Pharmacology Reviews, 40,* 2, 145–210.

Mayer, M. L., & Westbrook, G. L. (1987). The physiology of excitatory amino acids in the vertebrate central nervous system. *Progress in Neurobiology, 28,* 197–276.

VanDongen, A. (2008). *Biology of the NMDA receptor.* Boca Raton, FL: CRC Press.

GEORGE R. UHL
VALINA DAWSON

RECEPTOR ANTAGONIST. *See* **Antagonist; Antagonists of Alcohol and Drugs.**

REINFORCEMENT.

Although the term reinforcement has many common uses and associated meanings, its meaning is precise when used by behavior analysts and behavior therapists. The act or process of making a reinforcer contingent on behavior is termed positive reinforcement. A reinforcer is any object or event that, when delivered following some behavior, increases the probability that the behavior will occur again. A typical example might be observed in a laboratory experiment with rats. A rat is placed in a small plastic chamber. The rat can press a lever located on one wall of the chamber. When the rat presses the lever, a small food pellet drops into a dish. If the rat returns to the lever and continues to press it would be said that the food pellet functions as a reinforcer and that the behavior is maintained by positive reinforcement.

There is often confusion between positive reinforcement and negative reinforcement. Negative reinforcement occurs when a behavior results in terminating an aversive stimulus. In the case of the rat, the negative stimulus might be a loud noise. A lever press turns off the stimulus. If the rat continues to press the lever, it would be said that loud noise functions as a negative reinforcer and the behavior is maintained by negative reinforcement. Thus, both positive and negative reinforcement refer to increases in behavior, but differ in whether a pleasant stimulus is presented as the result of some behavior (positive reinforcement). Negative reinforcement is also referred to as escape (if the response turns off the stimulus each time it appears) or avoidance (if the response can postpone presentation of the stimulus).

It is important to note that reinforcement is a concept that refers to the relationship between behavior and its consequences. Stimuli or events are not assumed to have inherent reinforcing effects. For example, although most people like money and will continue to exhibit behavior that results in obtaining money, it cannot be assumed that money functions as a reinforcer for everyone. For example, money might not serve as a reinforcer for a monk devoted to an ascetic lifestyle. The defining characteristic of reinforcement depends on how a behavior is changed and not on the types of things that serve as reinforcing events (Morse & Kelleher, 1977). Factors that help determine whether a given object or event is reinforcing or punishing for a given individual include that individual's previous experiences and other features of the environment that coexist and are associated with the object or event. The upshot is that different things may function as reinforcers for different people.

Drugs can serve as reinforcers that maintain drug-seeking and drug-taking behaviors. This fact can be observed in the prevalence of drug use among humans and has also been shown in laboratory research with animals. In a typical laboratory experiment, an animal such as a rat or monkey has a catheter placed in a vein and connected to a pump-driven syringe. The animal can press a lever to activate the pump, and this results in a dose of a drug such as cocaine, heroin, nicotine, or alcohol being infused into the vein. If the animal continues to press the lever to obtain the drug, then the drug is said to serve as a reinforcer. Interestingly, those drugs which lead to addiction in humans also serve as reinforcers in animals. The only exception is marijuana (THC), which is used fairly extensively by humans but does not function as a reinforcer in animals. It should be noted that drugs that serve as reinforcers under one condition may not serve as reinforcers under other conditions. For example, nicotine serves as a reinforcer only at low doses and when doses are properly spaced. Nevertheless, the observation that drugs of abuse generally function as reinforcers in experimental animals has brought the study of drug-seeking behavior and drug abuse into a framework that allows carefully controlled behavioral analyses and the application of well-established and objective behavioral principles (Schuster & Johanson, 1981).

The acquisition of drug use in humans predominantly involves positive reinforcement, whereas the maintenance of drug use can involve both positive and negative reinforcement. The ability of a drug to serve as a positive reinforcer is usually associated with its pleasurable subjective effects (e.g. a "rush," a "high," or other feelings of intoxication). But again, given the definition of reinforcement, it is not necessary for a drug to be subjectively reinforcing or pleasurable in order for it to maintain behavior. Many drugs are also associated with symptoms of withdrawal when abstinence is initiated following a period of regular use. In this case, taking the drug again may terminate the aversive state of withdrawal; in this way, drug use is maintained by negative reinforcement. Drug use can also be influenced by sources of reinforcement other than the direct effects of the drug. For example, social encouragement and praise from a peer group can play an important role in the development of drug use by teenagers. Biological factors may also come into play. For example, some individuals may be more or less susceptible than others to feeling and recognizing the pleasurable effects of drugs. When drug use is viewed as a behavior maintained by the reinforcing effects of drugs, it suggests that this behavior is not amoral or uncontrolled but rather that it is the result of normal behavioral processes.

See also **Addiction: Concepts and Definitions; Research, Animal Model: An Overview; Risk Factors for Substance Use, Abuse, and Dependence: Learning; Wikler's Conditioning Theory of Drug Addiction.**

BIBLIOGRAPHY

Flora, S. R. (2004). *The power of reinforcement.* Albany, NY: State University of New York Press.

Morse, W. H., & Kelleher, R. T. (1977). Determinants of reinforcement and punishment. In W. K. Honig & J. E. R. Staddon (Eds.), *Handbook of operant behavior.* Englewood Cliffs, NJ: Prentice Hall.

Schuster, S. R., & Johanson, C. E. (1981). An analysis of drug-seeking behavior in animals. *Neuroscience and Biobehavioral Reviews, 5,* 315–323.

MAXINE STITZER

RELAPSE. Although specific definitions of *relapse* vary across behaviors and diagnoses, the term in general refers to a return to a problematic behavior. Relapse is used to describe outcomes and stages in many fields, including substance use, sexual behaviors, eating disorders, mood disorders, and medical conditions. While each of these disciplines may assign some variation to the consideration of relapse, much consensus exists regarding its antecedents, process, and interventions.

Generally, after individuals have made a change regarding a problematic behavior (e.g., reduced or abstained from drinking alcohol, stopped pathological gambling, established a healthy diet), they are at risk for a return to the previous behavior. A brief, minor, or transient return is typically referred to as a lapse. Following this situation, one of two outcomes may follow. If individuals reestablish their goals and return to a positive change state, prolapse has occurred. If, by contrast, individuals reengage in the problematic activities, returning to pre-change behavior, they experience a relapse.

Due to varying definitions of *relapse* in research, relapse rates are difficult to generalize among substance abusers, let alone across fields. Some studies have indicated that relapse rates are relatively high among individuals seeking abstinence either with or without formal treatment. For example, studies have indicated that up to 60 percent of alcoholics, heroin addicts, and smokers relapse within three months of the end of treatment.

The cognitive-behavioral model of relapse originally proposed a linear series of antecedents and outcomes (if/then relationships) based on high-risk situations and individual predispositions. Subsequently, this theory evolved to incorporate a dynamic relationship between tonic processes, or chronic vulnerabilities, and phasic responses, or transient states. The interactions between these vulnerabilities and states either increases or decreases the risk of relapse for individuals in any given situation. For example, poor coping skills may interact with a temporary increase in negative affect and positive expectancies, resulting in a relapse. Conversely, significant social support may mediate risks related to dependence and family history, thus avoiding a relapse. This model considers the interaction of diverse influences such as physical withdrawal, cognitive processes, affective states, coping behaviors, family history, social support, and expectancies.

The dynamic model of relapse incorporates many previously disparate theories on the determinants of relapse. For example, high-risk situations are not limited to external events or circumstances (e.g., passing by a location where drugs are bought or used), but also incorporate enduring personal characteristics (e.g., low self-efficacy). A family history of substance abuse may increase risk of relapse, but its effects can only be fully understood under the broader context of high-risk situations. Furthermore, the consideration of affective states incorporates psychopathology and mood disorders, such as relationships between depression and relapse. Reactions to major life events are included through phasic affective states (e.g., grief) and cognitive processes (e.g., repetitive thoughts). Even classic learning theories and conditioning models are incorporated through the inclusion of withdrawal symptoms or cues paired with expectancies associated with engaging in the previous behavior (e.g., "I will feel less anxious/angry/sad if I drink").

Following exposure to a high-risk situation, individuals may successfully avoid or limit the problematic behavior, leading to an increase in self-efficacy and a lower risk of future relapse.

Conversely, if a lapse occurs, individuals are likely to experience either prolapse or relapse. Prolapse is associated with external, specific, and transient attributions of the lapse. For example, drinking after a stressful day at work will be attributed to the specific stresses experienced that day and a poor decision to drive by the local tavern. In this case, individuals are likely to learn from the mistake and take steps to increase future success. Conversely, relapse is associated with internal, global, and stable attributions referred to as the abstinence violation effect (AVE). In this case, the stressful day at work is seen as evidence that change is not possible due to inability to deal with any stress. The lapse is viewed as a personal failure, self-efficacy is diminished, and motivation to change is confounded by hopelessness (e.g., the conclusion that the lapse proved that the individual has no will power.)

Relapse prevention (RP) is a widely accepted and used treatment in each of the fields previously listed. Although RP looks different on the surface between treatment for cocaine dependence and treatment for depression, for example, the underlying theory remains consistent. RP seeks to identify potential high-risk situations as well as successful coping strategies. Given the infinite number of interactions for any individual, generalization is required to both identify high-risk situations and to avoid relapse. RP has substantial support in the literature both in its traditional cognitive-behavioral model as well as more recent combinations, including acceptance and mindfulness-based relapse prevention. Meanwhile, researchers continue as of 2008 to identify what works best for whom in which situations.

See also **Abstinence Violation Effect (AVE); Treatment, Behavioral Approaches to: Cognitive-Behavioral Therapy.**

BIBLIOGRAPHY

Larimer, M. E., Palmer, R. S., & Marlatt, G. A. (1999). Relapse prevention: An overview of Marlatt's cognitive-behavioral model. *Alcohol Research and Health, 23*(2), 151–160.

Marlatt, G. A., & Gordon, J. R. (Eds.). (2005). *Relapse prevention: Maintenance strategies in the treatment of addictive behaviors* (2nd ed.). New York: Guilford Press.

McKay, J. R. (1999). Studies of factors in relapse to alcohol, drug, and nicotine use: A critical review of methodologies and findings. *Journal of Studies on Alcohol, 60,* 566–576.

Witkiewitz, K., & Marlatt, G. A. (2007). Modeling the complexity of post-treatment drinking: It's a rocky road to relapse. *Clinical Psychology Review, 7,* 724–738.

Witkiewitz, K., & Marlatt, G. A. (Eds.). (2007). *Therapist's guide to evidence-based relapse prevention.* London: Academic Press.

DIANE E. LOGAN
G. ALAN MARLATT
REVISED BY DIANE E. LOGAN (2009)
G. ALAN MARLATT (2009)

RELIGION AND DRUG USE. Drug use and religion have been intertwined throughout history, but the nature of this relationship has varied over time and from place to place. Alcohol and other drugs have played important roles in the religious rituals of numerous groups. For example, among a number of native South American groups, tobacco was considered sacred and was used in religious ritual, including the consultation of spirits and the initiation of religious leaders. Similarly, wine, representing the blood of Christ, has been central in the Holy Communion observances of both Roman Catholic and some Protestant churches. Considered divine by the Aztecs of ancient Mexico, the peyote cactus (which contains a number of psychoactive substances, including the psychedelic drug mescaline) is used today in the religious services of the contemporary Native American Church (Goode, 1984).

Although tobacco, alcohol, peyote, and other drugs have been important in the religious observances and practices of numerous groups, many religious teachings have opposed either casual use or the abuse of psychoactive drugs—and some religious groups forbid any use of such drugs, for religious purposes or otherwise. Early in America's history, Protestant religious groups were especially prominent in the temperance movement. Many of the ministers preached against the evils of drunkenness, and such well-known Protestant leaders as John Wesley, called for the prohibition of all alcoholic beverages (Cahalan, 1987). The Latter-day Saints' (Mormons) leader Joseph Smith prohibited the use of all common drugs, including alcohol, tobacco, and caffeine (in cola drinks, coffee, or tea), as did other utopian groups founded during the Second Great Awakening of the early 1800s. Religious groups and individuals were also active in America's early (1860s–1880s) antismoking movement (U.S. Department of Health and Human Services, 1992). In contemporary American society, certain religious commitments continue to be a strong predictor of either use of or abstinence from drugs, whether licit or illicit (Cochran et al., 1988; Gorsuch, 1988; Payne et al., 1991). For example, Islam forbids alcohol and opium use but coffee, tea, tobacco, khat, and various forms of marijuana are not prohibited because they came into the Islamic world after the prohibitions were laid down. Indulgence in any debilitating substance is, however, not considered proper or productive. Christianity, Judaism, and Buddhism may not prohibit specific drugs, but they and most other widespread mainstream religious traditions also caution against indulgence in most substances. In our society, many who have indulged have sought the help of Alcoholics Anonymous (AA) or Narcotics Anonymous (NA)—both self-help groups founded on strong spiritual underpinnings.

This discussion is limited to conditions in the United States, focusing on potentially dangerous, abusive, and/or illicit patterns of drug use. Since such drug use is widely disapproved by most religious teachings and leaders, it is not surprising to find that those with strong religious commitments are less likely to be drug users or abusers. Moreover, research findings clearly show that religious involvement has been a protective factor, helping some adolescents resist the drug epidemics of the 1970s and 1980s.

Because religion has been found to be a protective factor against drug use and dependence and because our society is concerned with drug use among young people, much of the research linking religion with drug use focuses on adolescents and young adults. This age range is particularly important for several reasons. First, it is the period during which most addiction to nicotine begins; the majority of people who make it through their teens as nonsmokers do not take up the habit during their twenties or later (Bachman et al., 1997). Second, adolescence and young adulthood is the period during which abusive alcohol consumption is most widespread. Third, recent epidemics in the use of illicit drugs have been most pronounced

among teenagers and young adults. Fourth, during this portion of the life span, many changes, opportunities, and risks occur; thus the structures and guidelines provided by religious commitment may be especially important in helping young people resist the temptation to use and abuse drugs. Finally, evidence that religious conversion is most likely to occur during adolescence (Spilka, 1991) makes this period particularly appropriate for research on the link between religion and drug use.

THE RELATIONSHIP BETWEEN RELIGIOUS COMMITMENT AND DRUG USE

Research investigating the relationship between religious commitment and drug use consistently indicates that those young people who are seriously involved in religion are more likely to abstain from drug use than those who are not; moreover, among users, religious youth are less likely than nonreligious youth to use drugs heavily (Gorsuch, 1988; Lorch & Hughes, 1985; Payne et al., 1991).

Figure 1 shows how drug use was related to religious commitment among high school seniors in 1979, 1989, and 1999. Individuals with the highest religious commitment were defined as those who usually attend services once a week or more often and who describe religion as being very important in their lives; individuals with low commitment are those who never attend services and rate religion as not important. Figure 1 clearly indicates that those with low religious involvement were more likely than average to be frequent cigarette smokers, occasional heavy drinkers, and users of marijuana and cocaine; conversely, those highest in religious commitment were much less likely to engage in any of these behaviors. Other analyses have shown that similar relationships exist for other illicit drugs (Bachman et al., 1986) and for other age groups (Cochran et al., 1988; Gorsuch, 1988).

Trends in Drug Use and Religious Commitment. Figure 1 presents data from three points in time, separated by ten-year intervals. It is obvious in the illustration that between 1979 and 1989, the proportion of high school seniors using the illicit drugs marijuana and cocaine declined markedly; also during that decade, the proportion reporting instances of heavy drinking declined appreciably, as did the proportion of frequent smokers. Between

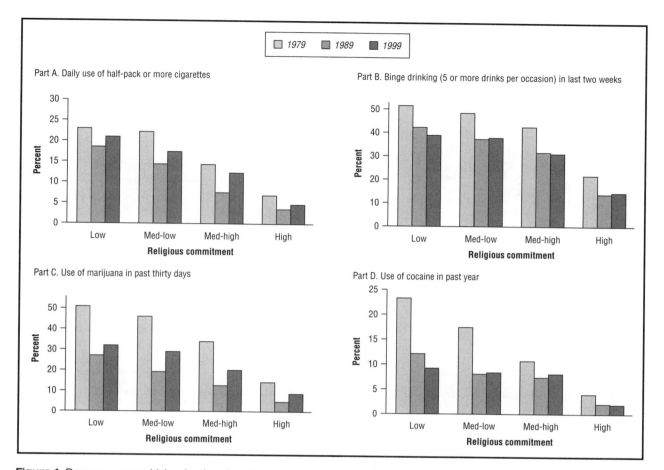

Figure 1. Drug use among high school seniors shown separately for four levels of religious commitment. ILLUSTRATION BY GGS INFORMATION SERVICES. GALE, CENGAGE LEARNING

1989 and 1999, the proportion of cigarette users and marijuana users rose somewhat; for year-to-year changes in substance use, see Johnston et al., (2000). For the present purposes, the most important finding in Figure 1 is that religion was linked to drug use at all three times, although the relationships appear a bit more dramatic during periods of heavier use.

Because high religious commitment is associated with low likelihood of drug use, it is reasonable to ask whether any of the decline in illicit drug use during the 1980s could be attributed to a heightened religious commitment among young people during that period. The answer is clearly negative, as illustrated in Figure 2. The same annual surveys that showed declines in drug use also indicated that religious commitment, rather than rising during the 1980s, was actually declining among high school seniors. It thus appears that other factors accounted for the declines

in illicit drug use, factors such as the increasing levels of risk and the heightened disapproval associated with such behaviors (Bachman et al., 1988, 1990; Johnston, 1985; Johnston et al., 2000). Moreover, Figure 2 shows that religious commitment—especially ratings of importance—actually rose slightly during the 1990s, so it does not appear that the rise in use of some drugs during the 1990s is attributable to any further drop in religiosity.

Religion as a Protective Factor. The most plausible interpretation of the relationship between religion and drug use during recent years, in our view, is that religion (or the lack thereof) was not primarily responsible for either the increases or the subsequent decreases in illicit drug use. Rather, it appears that those with the strongest religious commitment were least susceptible to the various epidemics in drug use. Figure 3 (adapted from

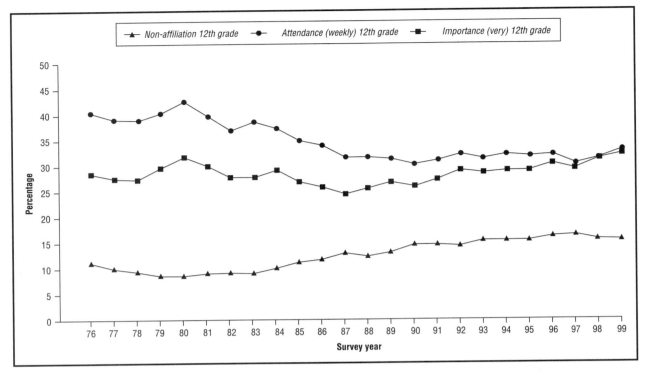

Figure 2. Trends in American youth religiosity. ILLUSTRATION BY GGS INFORMATION SERVICES. GALE, CENGAGE LEARNING

Bachman et al., 1990) provides one example in support of that interpretation. The figure illustrates trends in cocaine use from 1976 through 1988, distinguishing among the four different degrees of religious commitment. Cocaine use roughly doubled between 1976 and 1979 among high school seniors and began to decline sharply after 1986. But the most important pattern in the figure for present purposes is that these historical trends in cocaine use were much more pronounced among those with little or no religious commitment. Put another way, it seems that strong religious commitment operated as a kind of protective factor, sheltering many youths from the waves of drug use sweeping the nation.

Denominational Differences. There are important differences among religious groups in the emphasis placed on drug use (Lorch & Hughes, 1988). In particular, the more fundamentalist Protestant denominations, as well as Latter-day Saints (Mormons) and African American Muslims, rule out the use of alcohol and tobacco and disdain illicit drug use. Research examining differences in drug use among young people finds that those who belong to fundamentalist denominations are more likely to

abstain from drug use than are youth who belong to more liberal denominations (Lorch & Hughes, 1985). Analyses of the data on high school seniors (Wallace & Forman, 1998) corroborate the findings of earlier research; the number of young people strongly committed to fundamentalist denominations (e.g., Baptists) who use drugs is much lower than average and lower than the percentages for those strongly committed to other religious traditions.

Changes During Young Adulthood. Panel surveys that followed high school seniors up to fourteen years after graduation revealed that substance use often increases in response to such new freedoms as leaving high school and moving out of parents' homes, whereas use often decreases in response to such new responsibilities as marriage, pregnancy, and parenthood (Bachman et al., 1997). Additional analyses of these data reveal that religion continues to be strongly related to various forms of drug use during the late teens, twenties, and early thirties. These analyses reveal that religious attendance and importance change rather little for most individuals; but when changes in religiosity occur, there tend to be corresponding

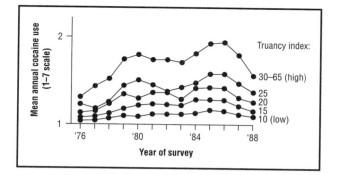

Figure 3. Trends in annual cocaine use shown separately for five levels of truancy among high school seniors. ILLUSTRATION BY GGS INFORMATION SERVICES. GALE, CENGAGE LEARNING

changes in substance use. Specifically, increases in religious commitment are correlated with declines in the use of alcohol and illicit drugs. Smoking behavior, on the other hand, is linked with religiosity during high school and thus also during young adulthood. However, after high school, smoking behavior is relatively little affected by changes in religiosity—presumably because by the time of young adulthood, most individuals who continue to smoke have become dependent on nicotine and find it very difficult to quit.

POSSIBLE CAUSAL PROCESSES

Since religious commitment is negatively related to drug use, it becomes important to understand the possible causal processes underlying that relationship. Wallace and Williams' socialization influence model (1997) specifies a number of possible mechanisms through which religious commitment might operate to influence adolescent drug use. The model postulates that health-compromising behaviors like drug use are the result of a dynamic socialization process that begins in childhood and extends throughout the course of life. According to the model, the family is the primary and first socialization influence, and a continuing source of socialization into the norms and values of the larger society. The model hypothesizes that religion, peer networks, and other contexts in which young people find themselves (e.g., schools) operate as key secondary socialization influences that impact drug use primarily indirectly through their influence on key socialization mechanisms, including social control, social support, values, and individual and group identity. Below, we describe some of the ways in which religion, parents, peers, and other

potential causes might overlap to influence adolescent drug use. The socialization influence model further suggests that key aspects of adolescent religiosity, particularly denominational affiliation and religious attendance, are often under the control of parents and reflect the types of doctrinal beliefs, teachings, and adult and peer models to which parents want their children exposed.

Content of Religious Teaching. One possible causal process seems obvious: Most religious traditions teach followers to avoid the abuse of drugs. Restrictions vary, of course, from one tradition to another; and the greater emphasis on prohibition in fundamentalist denominations seems the most likely explanation for the lower levels of use among adherents. But even in traditions that do not explicitly or completely ban drug use, there is still much teaching ranging from respect for one's own body to family responsibilities to broader social responsibilities, all arguing against the abuse of drugs. Because all drugs, including cigarettes and alcohol, are illicit for minors, young people who are strongly committed to religion may abstain from drug use simply in obedience to the laws of the nation; but even more important, they are likely to act in obedience to what they perceive to be God's laws.

Parental Examples and Precepts. In addition to the direct teachings associated with attendance at religious services, young people raised in religious traditions are likely to be exposed to parents and other relatives who follow such teachings. Thus, part of the explanation for less drug use among religiously involved young people may be that their families reinforce the religious structures against use and abuse. A further factor may simply be availability; religious parents who do not drink, smoke, or use drugs will not have these substances in their homes, thus reducing the opportunity for young people to experiment with them.

Peer Group Factors. The dynamics operating within the family probably have their parallel in broader social contacts. That is, those who are strongly committed to religion probably associate with others holding similar views. Thus, the strongly religious are less likely to belong to peer groups that encourage experimentation with cigarettes, alcohol, and other drugs and more likely to participate in

Measure	Response[1]	Percent of substance use in the past month			
		Illicit drugs[2]	Marijuana	Cigarettes	Binge alcohol[3]
Religious beliefs very important part of life	Yes	7.6	4.8	7.9	8.1
	No	17.1	13.0	18.7	17.8
Religious beliefs influence decision making in life	Yes	6.9	4.2	7.0	7.2
	No	15.7	11.9	17.8	17.1
Important to share religious beliefs with friends	Yes	6.3	3.3	6.1	6.2
	No	11.6	8.4	12.8	12.6

[1]Illicit drugs include marijuana/hashish, cocaine (including crack), heroin, hallucinogens, inhalants, or prescription-type psychotherapeutics used nonmedically.
[2]Illicit drugs include marijuana/hashish, cocaine (including crack), heroin, hallucinogens, inhalants, or prescription-type psychotherapeutics used nonmedically.
[3]Binge alcohol use is defined as drinking five or more drinks on the same occasion (i.e., at the same time or within a couple of hours of each other) on at least 1 day in the past 30 days.

Table 1. Past month use of selected substances by measure of religious beliefs among persons aged 12 to 17, by percentage, 2006. (Source: National Survey on Drug Use and Health, 2006, Office of Applied Studies, Substance Abuse and Mental Health Services Administration, U.S. Department of Health and Human Services.) ILLUSTRATION BY GGS INFORMATION SERVICES. GALE, CENGAGE LEARNING.

peer networks and activities that do not involve drugs. Given the strong relationship between drug use by peers and an adolescent's own drug use, the norms of the peer group are especially important as predictors of whether a particular teenager will start using drugs (Jessor & Jessor, 1977).

Overlaps with Other Causes. Religious commitment among young people is correlated with a number of other factors known to relate to drug use. In particular, students who achieve good grades, who plan to go to college, and who are not truant are also less likely to use drugs as well as more likely to display high levels of religious commitment. These various factors are closely interrelated in a common syndrome (Dryfoos, 1990; Jessor & Jessor, 1977), and thus it is difficult to disentangle causal processes. Indeed, it could be argued that religious commitment is probably one of the root causes contributing to both educational success and the avoidance of drug use. Analyses of possible multiple causes of drug use (or abstention) have shown that religious commitment overlaps with other predictors, but only partially. In other words, although religious commitment may be part of a larger syndrome, it also appears to have some unique (i.e., nonoverlapping) impact on drug use.

RELIGION AND DRUG USE: CONCLUSION
The relationship between religion and drug use among young people is not completely straightforward. On the one hand, a considerable amount of research indicates that young people who are strongly committed to religion are less likely than their uncommitted counterparts to use drugs. On the other hand, data presented here and elsewhere suggest that religion has had relatively little impact on recent national declines in drug use among young people. Further examination of this relationship reveals that America's drug epidemic occurred primarily among those not affected by religion; highly religious youth were relatively immune to the plague that infected a significant portion of the nation's youth. Accordingly, we conclude that religious commitment has been, and continues to be, an effective deterrent to the use and abuse of licit and illicit drugs.

This work was supported by Research Grant No. 3 R01 DA 01411 from the National Institute on Drug Abuse. We thank Dawn Bare for her contribution to data analysis and figure preparation and Tanya Hart for her editorial assistance.

See also **African Americans, Ethnic and Cultural Factors Relevant to Treatment for; Jews and Alcohol; Prevention.**

BIBLIOGRAPHY

Bachman, J. G., Johnston, L. D., & O'Malley, P. M. (1986). *Change and consistency in the correlates of drug use among high school seniors: 1975–1986.* (Monitoring the Future Occasional Paper No. 21.) Ann Arbor: University of Michigan, Institute for Social Research.

Bachman, J. G., Johnston, L. D., & O'Malley, P. M. (1990). Explaining the recent decline in cocaine use among young adults: Further evidence that perceived risks and disapproval lead to reduced drug use. *Journal of Health and Social Behavior, 31*, 2, 173–184.

Bachman, J. G., Johnston, L. D., O'Malley, P. M., & Humphrey, R. H. (1988). Explaining the recent decline in marijuana use: Differentiating the effects of perceived risks, disapproval, and general lifestyle factors. *Journal of Health and Social Behavior, 29*, 92–112.

Bachman, J. G., Wadsworth, K. N., O'Malley, P. M., Johnston, L. D., & Schulenberg, J. (1997). *Smoking, drinking and drug use in young adulthood: The impacts of new freedoms and new responsibilities.* Mahwah, NJ: Lawrence Erlbaum Associates.

Bartkowski, J., & Xu, X. (2007). Religiosity and teen drug use reconsidered: A social capital perspective. *American Journal of Preventive Medicine, 32*, 6, S182–S194.

Benda, B. B., & McGovern, T. F. (2006). *Spirituality and religiousness and alcohol/other drug problems: Treatment and recovery perspectives.* London: Routledge.

Bock, E. W., Cochran, J. K., & Beeghley, L. (1987). Moral messages: The relative influence of denomination on the religiosity-alcohol relationship. *Sociological Quarterly, 28*, 1, 89–103.

Cahalan, D. (1987). *Understanding America's drinking problem.* San Francisco: Jossey-Bass.

Cochran, J. K., Beeghley, L., & Bock, E. W. (1988). Religiosity and alcohol behavior: An exploration of reference group theory. *Sociological Forum, 3*, 2, 256–276.

Dryfoos, J. G. (1990). *Adolescents at risk: Prevalence and prevention.* New York: Oxford University Press.

Goode, E. (1984). *Drugs in American society*, 2nd ed. New York: Knopf. (2007, 7th ed.)

Gorsuch, R. L. (1988). Psychology of religion. *Annual Review of Psychology, 39*, 201–221.

Jessor, R., & Jessor, S. L. (1977). *Problem behavior and psychosocial development: A longitudinal study of youth.* New York: Academic Press.

Johnston, L. D. (1985). The etiology and prevention of substance use: What can we learn from recent historical changes? In C. L. Jones & R. J. Battjes (Eds.) *Etiology of drug abuse: Implications for prevention.* Washington, DC: U.S. Government Printing Office.

Johnston, L. D., O'Malley, P. M., & Bachman, J. G. (2000). *National survey results on drug use from the Monitoring the Future study, 1975–1999. Volume I: Secondary school students. Volume II: College students and young adults.* Rockville, MD: National Institute on Drug Abuse.

Lorch, B. R., & Hughes, R. H. (1988). Church, youth, alcohol, and drug education programs and youth substance abuse. *Journal of Alcohol and Drug Education, 33*, 2, 14–26.

Lorch, B. R., & Hughes, R. H. (1985). Religion and youth substance use. *Journal of Religion and Health, 24*, 3, 197–208.

Miller, W. R., & Bogenschutz, M. P. (2007). Spirituality and addiction. *Southern Medical Journal, 100*, 4, 433–436.

Payne, I. R., Bergin, A. E., Bielema, K. A., & Jenkins, P. H. (1991). Review of religion and mental health: Prevention and the enhancement of psychosocial functioning. *Prevention in Human Services, 9*, 2, 11–40.

Spilka, B. (1991). Religion and adolescence. In R. M. Lerner et al. (Eds.), *Encyclopedia of adolescence.* New York: Garland.

U.S. Department of Health and Human Services. (1992). *Smoking and health in the Americas.* Atlanta: Public Health Service, Centers for Disease Control, National Center for Chronic Disease Prevention and Health Promotion, Office of Smoking and Health.

Wallace, J. M., Jr., & Forman, T. A. (1998). Religion's role in promoting health and reducing risk among American youth. *Health Education and Behavior 25*, 6, 721–741.

Wallace, J. M., Jr., & Williams, D. (1997). Religion and adolescent health-compromising behavior. In J. Schulenberg, J. Maggs, K. Hurrelmann (Eds.), *Health risks and developmental transitions during adolescence.* New York: Cambridge University Press.

JERALD G. BACHMAN
JOHN M. WALLACE JR.

REMOVE INTOXICATED DRIVERS (RID-USA, INC.).

The organization Remove Intoxicated Drivers (RID-USA, Inc.) was founded in 1978 by Doris Aiken. This volunteer grassroots organization is devoted to deterring impaired driving, providing a variety of supports to victims and their families, monitoring court proceedings involving impaired or intoxicated drivers, influencing the development of nationwide legislation regarding alcohol use, and educating the public on the scope of impaired-driving and binge-drinking tragedies.

In November 1977, a young drunk driver in upstate New York killed Karen and Timothy Morris, who were 17 and 19 years old, respectively. When a local TV talk show host named Doris Aiken learned that the district attorney did not plan to prosecute the crime, she decided to form an organization to represent people affected by alcohol-related crimes. She learned that plea-bargaining in alcohol-related automobile accidents generally enabled impaired drivers to remain on the road for more than three years before reaching the conviction and sentencing stages. In the late 1970s, an average of 25,000 people died annually in alcohol-related motor vehicle accidents, and the surviving drivers were, more often than not, allowed to retain their licenses and continue to operate motor vehicles. Aiken was able to obtain a start-up grant from the National Highway Traffic Safety Administration (NHTSA), and by 1982 her organization, RID-USA, had 75 chapters across 22 states.

RID-USA's victim-support activities, which are free, include providing long-term emotional support to victims of drunk-driving crashes (and to victims' families), counseling victims and accompanying them throughout all phases of the criminal prosecution of the offender, assisting victims in obtaining compensation, and referring victims and their families to appropriate supportive agencies. Court monitoring and research activities include monitoring the efforts of police, prosecutors, magistrates, and judges in drunk-driving cases through research and analysis of local court records, and then reporting these findings to the public.

RID-USA's public awareness and education activities are extensive. Members organize public meetings; present educational talks to community and religious organizations; participate in forums, exhibits, and media events; supplement high school driver-education classes; and support Students Against Destructive Decisions (SADD; originally named Students Against Driving Drunk) and other similar student groups. They also study and report on alcohol-related vehicle and traffic laws, support concepts such as designated-driver and alcohol-server education, and promote the Sane National Alcohol Policy (SNAP) campaign, which advocates raising taxes on alcohol, curbing campus beer promotions, and airing public-service advertising to counter broadcast alcohol commercials. Among its media campaigns, RID-USA has developed and implemented a multimedia public awareness and education program about binge drinking and alcohol poisoning, particularly among underage drinkers. RID-USA, which celebrated its 30th anniversary in 2008, is organized into autonomous chapters, with more than 150 chapters in 41 U.S. states and a national group in France.

See also **Accidents and Injuries from Alcohol; Alcohol; Crime and Alcohol; Dramshop Liability Laws;** **Driving, Alcohol, and Drugs; Driving Under the Influence (DUI); Mothers Against Drunk Driving (MADD).**

BIBLIOGRAPHY

Aiken, D. (2002). *My life as a pit bull: Collaring the drunk driver.* Lincoln, NE: Writers Club Press.

Hanson, D. J. (1996). *Alcohol education: What we must do.* Westport, CT: Praeger.

McGowan, R. (1997). *Government regulation of the alcohol industry: The search for revenue and the common good.* Westport, CT: Quorum Books.

Slavin, S. (Ed.). (1995). *U.S. women's interest groups: Institutional profiles.* Westport, CT: Greenwood Press.

FAITH K. JAFFE
REVISED BY PAMELA V. MICHAELS (2009)

RESEARCH

This entry includes the following essays:
AIMS, DESCRIPTION, AND GOALS
CLINICAL RESEARCH
DEVELOPING MEDICATIONS TO TREAT SUBSTANCE ABUSE AND DEPENDENCE
DRUGS AS DISCRIMINATIVE STIMULI
MEASURING EFFECTS OF DRUGS ON BEHAVIOR
MEASURING EFFECTS OF DRUGS ON MOOD
MOTIVATION

AIMS, DESCRIPTION, AND GOALS

There has always been interest in information related to drugs and alcohol and their effects. Reports on the use of psychoactive substances first appear in ancient manuscripts. The properties of marijuana were first described in 2732 BCE in a Chinese book on pharmacy. A description of the effects of opium has been found in an Egyptian papyrus scroll dating from about 1550 BCE. In almost every culture, the uses of alcohol are documented in both oral and written traditions, often going back to antiquity—the Bible, for example, mentions both the use and abuse of wine. Although people have made observations on these substances for thousands of years, much of that information is regarded as *anecdotal*, that is, based on the observation of specific incidents rather than from any systematic evaluation of the facts. The problem with anecdotal observation is that it cannot always be generalized, that is, it cannot be used reliably to predict future events or behavior.

Scientific research, by contrast, employs the techniques of the *scientific method* to generate knowledge. When researchers use the scientific method, they may begin with an anecdotal observation to formulate their initial hypothesis, but from there the process changes. Instead of generalizing from the anecdotal evidence, the scientific researcher designs an experiment to test the prediction generated from the observation, performs the experiment, collects and analyzes the data, and only then arrives at a conclusion. The goal of current research into substance abuse, then, is to apply the techniques of the scientific method to solving the problems related to the use of both alcohol and drugs of abuse. Of course, there are limits to the use of the scientific method when studying human beings. For example, scientists cannot ethically conduct experiments in which some women are exposed to cocaine while pregnant and others are not. They must instead use animal models for these experiments, which can only approximate, rather than reproduce exactly, what occurs in humans. Other experiments are not economically or practically feasible. For example, a researcher may want to follow research subjects (people who have agreed to participate in a research experiment) over a period of five years to learn about the long-term effects of a medication. Unfortunately, each additional visit a subject makes to the clinic adds to the expense of the project and in the meantime the subjects themselves may no longer be available to complete the visits. The constraints of the situation may result in only a brief period of follow-up and thus limit the conclusions that may be drawn from the data.

Substance abuse research is no different from any other sort of scientific endeavor: The process is not always orderly. Critical observations by clinicians frequently provide basic researchers with important insights, which guide the research into new channels. Observations in one science often lead to breakthroughs in other areas. It is important to understand that the benefits of research may not be immediately obvious. Some research that seems promising may lead to a disappointing dead-end, whereas other lines of research may yield surprising results. Often, the research process is much like that of assembling a jigsaw puzzle: Many scientists contribute pieces to the puzzle, creating snapshots of parts of the problem, until one individual assembles them into a coherent picture that answers a larger question. The physicist Sir Isaac Newton modestly noted that his own theories came from standing on the "shoulders of giants," that is, he built on the work of scientists who preceded him. No less is true of early-twenty-first-century substance abuse research.

WHAT WE NEED TO KNOW

Most substance abuse research is a consequence of public health and social concerns. With millions of people using and abusing many different substances, and because of the close association between acquired immune deficiency syndrome (AIDS) and drug abuse, as well as between drug use and crime, it is imperative to know just how dangerous—or not dangerous—any given drug is to public health and safety. For economic as well as medical reasons, it is essential to find the most effective ways to use health-care resources to prevent and treat substance abuse. So many questions still exist that no one scientific discipline can answer them all. The answers must be found through studies in basic chemistry, molecular biology, genetics, pharmacology, neuroscience, biomedicine, physiology, behavioral science, epidemiology, psychology, economics, social policy, and even international relations. From a social standpoint, the first question for research must be: How extensive is the problem?

Surveys and other indicators of drug and alcohol use are the tools used by epidemiologists to determine the extent and nature of the problem, or to find out how many people are abusing exactly which drugs, how often, and where. As the dimensions of the problem are defined, basic scientists begin their work, trying to discover the causes and effects of substance abuse at every level, from the movement of molecules to the behavior of entire human populations. Chemists determine the physical structure of abused substances, and then molecular biologists study how they interact with the subcellular structures of the human body. Geneticists try to determine which components, if any, of substance abuse are inherited. Pharmacologists determine how the body handles abused substances and, in turn, the effects of those substances on the body. Neuroscientists examine the effects of drugs and alcohol on the cells and larger anatomical structures of the brain and other parts of the nervous system. As these structures control human thoughts, emotions, learning, and perception, psychologists and behavioral pharmacologists study the drugs' effects on these functions. Cardiologists and liver and pulmonary specialists study the responses of heart, liver, and lungs, respectively, to drugs and alcohol. Immunologists examine the consequences of substance abuse for the immune system, a study made critical by the AIDS epidemic. The conclusions reached through these basic scientific inquiries guide clinicians in developing effective treatment programs.

In considering drug abuse, people have long wondered why so many plants contain substances that have such profound effects on the human brain and mind. Surely, people were not equipped by nature with special places on their nerve cells (called receptors) for substances of abuse—on the off chance that they would eventually smoke marijuana or take cocaine or heroin. The discovery in the late 1960s that animals would work to obtain injections or drinks of the same drugs that people abuse was an important scientific observation; it contributed to the hypothesis that there must be a biological basis for substance abuse.

These observations and this reasoning led scientists to look for substances produced by people's own bodies (endogenous substances) that behave chemically and physiologically like those that people put into themselves from the outside (exogenous substances), such as alcohol, nicotine, marijuana, cocaine, and other drugs of abuse. When receptors for endogenous substances were discovered—first for the opiates and then later for PCP, cocaine, marijuana, and LSD—their existence helped establish the biological basis for drug abuse. So did the evidence supporting a genetic component for certain types of alcoholism. These discoveries by no means negate the extensive behavioral and social components of substance abuse, but they do suggest a new weapon in dealing with the problem—that is, the possibility of using medication, or a biological therapy, as an adjunct to psychosocial therapies. Asserting a biological basis for substance abuse also removes some of the social stigma attached to drug and alcohol addiction. Since drug dependence is a disorder with strong biological components, society begins to understand that it is not merely the result of weak moral fiber. Armed with information that was derived initially from basic research, clinical researchers in hospitals and clinics can test and compare treatment modalities, looking for the best balance of pharmacological and psychosocial methods to rehabilitate individuals suffering from addiction. Finding the right approach for each type of patient is an important goal of treatment research, because patients frequently have a number of physical and mental problems besides substance abuse. The development of new medications to assist in the treatment process is an exciting and complex new frontier in substance abuse research.

The best way to prevent the health and social problems associated with substance abuse has always been an important research question. Insights gained from psychological and social research enable us to design effective prevention programs targeted toward specific populations that are particularly vulnerable to substance abuse for both biomedical and social reasons. Knowing the consequences of substance abuse often helps researchers to formulate prevention messages. For example, the identification of fetal alcohol syndrome (FAS), a pattern of birth defects among children of mothers who drank alcohol heavily during pregnancy, was a major research contribution to the prevention message aimed specifically at pregnant women.

Drug abuse prevention research has assumed a new urgency with the realization, brought about by epidemiologists and others, that the human immunodeficiency virus (HIV) is blood-borne—spread by sexual contact and by drug abusers who share contaminated syringes and needles. HIV-positive drug users then spread the disease through unprotected sexual intercourse. Public education about drug abuse and AIDS must use the most powerful and carefully targeted means to reach the populations at greatest risk for either disease, and these means can be determined only by the most careful social research and evaluation methods.

METHODS
The range of methods employed by scientists studying substance abuse is as wide as the range of methods in all of the biological and social sciences. One important method is the use of animal models of

behavior to answer many of the questions raised by drug and alcohol use. Animal models are used in virtually every field of biomedical research, but the discovery that animals will, for the most part, self-administer alcohol and drugs of abuse meant that there was great potential for behavioral research uncontaminated by many of the difficult-to-control social components of human research. The results of animal studies have been verified repeatedly in human research and in clinical observation, thus validating an animal model of human drug-seeking behavior.

Another important method is controlled clinical trials, in which one treatment method is compared to another. In controlled clinical trials, research subjects are randomly assigned to one of two or more treatment situations, allowing comparisons to be drawn that are not confounded by other factors. For example, patients can be assigned randomly to treatment with a medication, counseling, both medication and counseling, or neither medication nor counseling. Comparison of the groups' response to treatment can determine the efficacy of the medication both alone and in the context of counseling.

Drug and alcohol abuse research is conducted by individuals with many different qualifications, but mostly by physicians and people with doctoral degrees in a variety of disciplines. They work with animals and with patients in university and federally funded laboratories, as well as in privately funded research facilities, in offices, and in clinical treatment centers. Other sites include hospitals, clinics, and sometimes schools, the streets, and even advertising agencies when prevention research is being conducted.

FUNDING

Who pays for substance abuse research has always been an important issue. Most of the drug and alcohol abuse research in the world is supported by the U.S. government. One of the federally funded National Institutes of Health—the National Institute on Drug Abuse (NIDA)—funds the majority of drug abuse research conducted in the United States and abroad. In 2007 this amounted to nearly $1 billion, which supported NIDA's own intramural research at the Addiction Research Center and the research done in universities under grants awarded by the institute. NIDA's sister institute, the National

Institute on Alcohol Abuse and Alcoholism (NIAAA), plays a parallel role in funding alcohol abuse research. In 2007 it funded $436 million of alcohol research.

Many other U.S. government agencies also have important roles in sponsoring and conducting substance abuse research. For the most part, state and local governments do not sponsor substance abuse research, although they distribute much of the funds for treatment and prevention programs. Other countries, most notably Canada, sponsor basic clinical and epidemiological substance abuse research within their own universities and laboratories, but none does so on a scale that is comparable to that of the United States. Private foundations and research institutions such as the Salk Institute for Biological Studies, Rockefeller University, and the Scripps Clinic and Research Foundation use their own funds, as well as federal grant support, to pay for their research endeavors. Pharmaceutical companies also support some substance abuse research—mostly clinical work related to medications being developed for use in the treatment of drug and alcohol abuse. The U.S. government also sponsors much of the work of medications development for substance abuse.

See also **National Survey on Drug Use and Health (NSDUH); Research, Animal Model: An Overview; Substance Abuse and AIDS; U.S. Government; U.S. Government Agencies.**

BIBLIOGRAPHY

Barinaga, M. (1992). Pot, heroin unlock new areas for neuroscience. *Science, 258,* 1882–1884.

Cooper, J. R., Bloom, F. E., & Roth, R. H. (2002). *The biochemical basis of pharmacology* (8th ed.). New York: Oxford University Press.

Gershon, E. S., & Rieder, R. D. (1992). Major disorders of mind and brain. *Scientific American, 267*(3), 126–133.

National Institute on Alcohol Abuse and Alcoholism. (2000). *Alcohol and health: Tenth special report to the U.S. Congress.* Washington, D.C. Available from http://pubs.niaaa.nih.gov/.

National Institute on Drug Abuse. (1999). *Drug abuse and addiction research: Sixth triennial report to Congress.* Washington, D.C. Available from http://www.drug abuse. gov/.

National Institute on Drug Abuse. (2007). *Fiscal year 2008 budget information.* Department of Health and Human Services. Available from http://www.nida .nih.gov/.

National Institute on Alcohol Abuse and Alcoholism. (2008). *NIAAA director's report on institute activities to 117th meeting of the national advisory council.* Available from http://www.niaaa.nih.gov/.

CHRISTINE R. HARTEL
REVISED BY LEAH R. ZINDEL (2009)

CLINICAL RESEARCH

Clinical research consists of multiple approaches seeking to describe, understand, predict, and/or change human health and behavior. Although the focus here is limited to research with humans, experiments with animals frequently lay the foundation for human studies. Furthermore, although clinical research methods are widely used in all branches of medical science, we will review the primary types of clinical research relevant to alcohol and drug abuse: social and behavioral research, brain studies, genetic and epidemiological studies, psychotherapeutic interventions, clinical drug trials, and combinations of these strategies. While many studies employ a large sample size and traditional quantitative methodology, case studies and phenomenological/qualitative research procedures also expand our knowledge and contribute to the scientific literature. We will begin with a discussion of ethics in clinical research and conclude with the dissemination and practical applications of findings.

Ethical issues are paramount in human research. Such issues are important whether a study involves participants answering personal questions anonymously or undergoing invasive experimental surgery. Most research is subject to review by an Institutional Review Board (IRB) prior to implementation to ensure the protection of its participants. Even exempt studies are typically required to obtain their exemption through an IRB. Although the specific IRB changes based on the funding mechanism and where the research will take place, some general guidelines apply across reviews. The Belmont Report (*Ethical Principles and Guidelines for the Protection of Human Subjects of Research*), created in 1979, embodies the three main principles that guide protections for human subjects in the United States: respect for persons, beneficence, and justice. Respect for persons requires that participants' autonomy be protected, that they are treated with respect, and that they provide informed consent for participation. The IRB ensures that volunteers understand their rights, the research's potential risks and benefits, and understand what to do should they need assistance or additional information. Although consent applies to legally competent adults, assent (or permission) is typically sought from participants under 18 years of age or those deemed legally incompetent to make medical decisions. Beneficence requires that the benefits of the research are maximized, while the risks to the research subjects are minimized. Often, laboratory results or pilot studies are required to demonstrate potential benefits and risks as well as to support the scientific merit of the proposal. Justice requires that the costs and benefits of the research be distributed equally throughout the population. Finally, the IRB monitors the study in an ongoing way, requiring approval for modifications, while ensuring the continued safety of participants.

Some types of research seek to simply observe and record behavior. Many social and behavioral studies use an observational approach to define, identify, and log types of behavior. These studies provide a foundation for further studies by illustrating problematic (or beneficial) behaviors, providing frequency estimates, and developing a baseline of natural occurrences. These studies can vary from naturalistic observation to nationally representative questionnaires. In addition to recording behavior, investigators often manipulate a variable to explore alternate behaviors. These studies test hypotheses related to understanding and predicting behaviors. For example, a social experiment might explore individual reactions to criticism while in a relaxed versus a stressed state. Understanding how external stimuli relate to behavior can ultimately provide opportunities to change behavior.

Brain imaging research is another area of investigation that seeks to describe or identify factors related to behavior. Advances in neuroimaging have allowed investigators to isolate the brain structures involved in specific activities. Functional magnetic resonance imaging (fMRI), for example, has greatly increased knowledge of brain regions that are activated in relation to specific mood states, behaviors, etc. Areas of the brain that could have only been viewed in animals or on postmortem examinations are now detectable in healthy functioning individuals. These studies combine biology and psychology, and can provide empirical evidence of changes within or between individuals.

Genetic and epidemiological studies extend description and seek causes or correlates of disease. Epidemiological studies, in general, focus on a specific disorder and attempt to identify risk factors. For example, alcohol use disorders are associated with many exposures and behaviors in adolescence, even if the disorder does not present until decades later. Genetic studies are a specific type of epidemiology, looking at the role of biological markers in risk for disease. There continues to be much debate about the role of genetics in many disorders, even with increases in technology and the ability of investigators to examine genetic influences. The Human Genome Project and subsequent large-scale efforts to understand the role of genetics in human health and disease have resulted in a veritable explosion of new knowledge in this area.

INTERVENTIONAL STUDIES

Studies that seek to manipulate the occurrence or trajectory of a disorder fall into the category of clinical trials. Other types of clinical trials can include prevention, diagnostic, screening, and quality of life trials, although the focus here is limited to treatment trials. Two primary types of clinical trials are considered: behavioral (psychotherapeutic) and medical (drug) interventions. While many of the same goals and requirements apply to each, the nature of the study designs can vary. Both types of studies are bound by the same ethical guidelines and requirement for IRB approval. Study designs also tend to be similar in these trials, with emphasis placed on randomized studies with adequate sample size to allow for valid conclusions. One clear difference between study designs is the ease with which a blinded study can be conducted. In a double-blind study, common in drug trials, neither the participant nor the investigator is aware of whether the substance administered is the active drug or a placebo. In psychotherapy research, it is virtually impossible for a provider to not know which treatment is being provided. Rather than using a blinded design, psychotherapy research typically includes a comparison group to account for natural progression or improvement. In either case, ethics require that participants be made aware of the potential to be assigned to either group as well as any risks they might endure if assigned to each of the specific groups.

Psychotherapy research attempts to identify, standardize, and test psychotherapeutic interventions for efficacy and effectiveness. These studies focus on changing or modifying behavior. Efficacy refers to the internal validity of an intervention; it scientifically evaluates a specific treatment for a specific population. These studies, referred to as randomized controlled trials (RCT), lead to the identification of empirically supported treatments (EST) or empirically validated treatments (EVT). These studies will randomly assign an adequate number of screened participants with a specific disorder to receive either the intervention that is being tested, an alternate intervention, and/or a no-treatment or wait-list control group. For example, participants meeting criteria for drug dependence might be randomized to receive a brief cognitive-behavioral (CBT) intervention, a twelve-step program, or an attention-control (i.e., one in which the participant receives comparable attention, but not the specific intervention being evaluated). The interventions in these studies are typically standardized and therapist adherence is monitored. Outcomes of these studies frequently inform healthcare practices and insurance coverage for services. These closely monitored and rigorous studies are more likely to receive and maintain funding as well as have their findings published in prestigious journals. Although the benefits of efficacy studies are great, the role of effectiveness studies is equally important. At this stage, studies are typically transferred from a controlled setting to the "real world." With the addition of covariates such as comorbid conditions, the specificity and ability to detect change based on the intervention are typically lessened, while issues of practical application and generalizability are increased. The dissemination of research and applicability to practice will be discussed below.

Clinical trials testing drugs or other medical interventions also seek to identify ways to change or manipulate behaviors or conditions. Drug trials progress through four individual phases, which occur after animal testing shows the drug to be safe enough for human administration. Phase I studies assess the safety of a drug by testing it in a small number of healthy individuals and provide a range of doses that are well tolerated in humans. Phase II is concerned with initial efficacy in affected individuals and may take months to years to complete. This phase of the study involves randomized and blinded conditions with several hundred participants. If a drug has been determined to be safe and potentially efficacious, it progresses to Phase III and is tested in several hundred to several thousand participants. Studies in this phase, which can last several years, are also typically randomized and blinded, and inform a decision by the Food and Drug Administration (FDA) in the United States or similar regulatory agencies in other countries concerning the suitability of the drug for use in the general population. Phase IV studies are employed to test a drug against other drugs on the market, to monitor long-term effects, and/or to establish cost-effectiveness. Specific examples of Phase IV studies are the clinical trials of naltrexone for the treatment of alcohol dependence, after the medication had been approved for the treatment of opiate dependence.

In the early twenty-first century many studies combine different types of research, and funding agencies increasingly encourage collaboration. For example, the COMBINE study included medications, behavioral interventions, and combinations of each to identify the effectiveness of each treatment independently and together. Large studies such as this, with adequate sample sizes, can also incorporate epidemiological and demographic factors to determine what works best and which intervention or combination is efficacious for which participants.

DISSEMINATION AND PRACTICAL APPLICATIONS

Of the myriad clinical research studies ongoing at any given time, the results from only a small proportion of them ever reach clinical practitioners, and a smaller number are distributed to the general public. Given the importance placed on rigorous design, some studies are deemed unsuitable for publication in peer-reviewed journals. In addition, regardless of the design, the results of studies that do not find significant outcomes are often not published. These situations can lead to an exaggerated opinion of the effectiveness of treatment methods. There are also concerns that a conflict of interest or bias could influence the distribution of specific findings. For example, pharmaceutical companies typically fund their own studies, and they have a financial interest in having favorable outcomes disseminated. Although much behavioral research is financed by government agencies and other sources, an investigator may be biased by a conflict of interest related to ongoing support from public or private sources. Double-blind studies and control groups can reduce an investigator's influence on outcomes, and peer-review or government analysis can regulate the consistency and rigor of design. Nonetheless, conflicts of interest in clinical research, particularly treatment studies, have begun to take center stage in academic and regulatory affairs.

Even when a study passes all of the required levels of review, is completed, and its findings are accepted for publication in a peer-review journal, many barriers to implementation exist. Clinical research should not only further the science underlying the diagnosis and treatment of addictive disorders, but must also be designed to inform practice. Effectiveness trials of behavioral interventions and Phase IV drug trials are crucial to transferring research into practice.

IN SUMMARY

Clinical research employs a variety of methods, from observation to intervention. The role of clinical research is to inform practice by improving our understanding of the mechanisms of disease and its diagnosis, and efficacious treatment. There are many ethical considerations in the conduct of clinical research, and IRB review provides a system of checks and balances to ensure informed consent by participants and their ongoing protection throughout the research process. Advances in technology will continue to improve our capacity to identify biological and genetic factors that underlie addictive behavior and disorders, and epidemiological studies, including clinical trials, will continue to inform interventions to improve the health and welfare of addicted individuals.

See also **Abuse Liability of Drugs: Testing in Humans; Abuse Liability of Therapeutic Drugs: Testing in Animals; Brain Structures and Drugs; Clinical Trials Network; Diagnosis of Substance Use Disorders: Diagnostic Criteria; Epidemiology of Alcohol Use Disorders; Imaging Techniques: Visualizing the Living Brain.**

BIBLIOGRAPHY

Cacioppo, J. T., Berntson, G. G., & Nusbaum, H. C. (2008). Neuroimaging as a new tool in the toolbox of psychological science. *Current Directions in Psychological Science, 17,* 62–67.

CenterWatch Web site. Available from http://www.centerwatch.com/.

Clinical Trials Web site, National Institutes of Health. Available from http://www.clinicaltrials.gov/.

Jablensky, A. (2002). Research methods in psychiatric epidemiology: An overview. *Australian and New Zealand Journal of Psychiatry, 36*, 297–310.

Office of Human Subjects Research Web site, National Institutes of Health. *The Belmont report: Ethical principles and guidelines for the protection of human subjects of research.* April 18, 1979. Available from http://www.ohsr.od.nih.gov/.

Prathikanti, S., & Weinberger, D.R. (2005). Psychiatric genetics—the new era: Genetic research and some clinical implications. *British Medical Journal, 73,* 107–122.

Zechmeister, J. S., Zechmeister, E. B., & Shaughnessy, J. J. (2001). *Essentials of research methods in psychology.* New York: McGraw-Hill.

DIANE E. LOGAN

DEVELOPING MEDICATIONS TO TREAT SUBSTANCE ABUSE AND DEPENDENCE

Dependence on drugs, alcohol, or tobacco is difficult to treat, and practitioners have tried many approaches in their attempts to arrive at successful treatments. One approach is to develop medications, or pharmacological treatments. This approach is most effective when the medication is given along with behavioral treatments. These behavioral treatments help the individual cope with the underlying etiology of his or her drug use and the problems associated with drug use; they may also help to ensure compliance in taking the medication that is prescribed.

PERPETUATION OF DRUG ABUSE: EUPHORIA AND WITHDRAWAL

Many people who are drug or alcohol dependent want to stop their habit, but typically they have a difficult time doing so. There are at least two reasons for this difficulty. First, the drugs produce pleasant or euphoric feelings that the user wants to experience again and again. Second, unpleasant effects can occur when the drug use is stopped. The latter effect, commonly known as withdrawal, has been shown after prolonged use of many drugs, including alcohol, opiates (such as heroin), sedative hypnotics, and anxiety-reducing drugs. Other drugs, such as cocaine and even caffeine (coffee and cola drinks), nicotine (cigarettes), and marijuana, are also believed to be associated with withdrawal effects after prolonged use. These unpleasant

withdrawal effects are alleviated by further drug use. Thus drugs are used and abused because they produce immediate pleasant effects (positive reinforcement) and because the drug reduces the discomfort of withdrawal (negative reinforcement).

The symptoms of withdrawal are fairly specific for each drug and include physiological effects and psychological effects. For example, alcohol withdrawal can be associated with shaking or headaches, and opiate withdrawal with anxiety, sweating, and increases in blood pressure, among other effects. Withdrawal from cocaine may cause depression or sadness, withdrawal from caffeine is associated with headaches, and withdrawal from nicotine often produces irritability. All drug withdrawals are also associated with a strong craving to use more drugs. Much work has been done to document the withdrawal effects from alcohol, opiates, benzodiazepines, and tobacco; however, as of 2008 withdrawal from cocaine or other stimulant drugs has been less well documented.

NEURAL CHANGES WITH CHRONIC DRUG USE

Both withdrawal and the pleasant or euphoric effects from drug use occur, in part, as a result of the drug's action on the brain. The immediate or acute effects of most drugs of abuse involve areas of the brain that have been associated with reward or pleasure. These drugs stimulate areas normally aroused by natural pleasures such as eating or sexual activity. Long-term, or chronic, drug use alters these and other brain areas. Some brain areas will develop tolerance to the drug effects, so that greater and greater amounts are needed to achieve the original effects of the drug. Some examples of drug effects to which tolerance develops are the analgesic, or painkilling, effect of opiates and the euphoria or pleasure-producing effect of most drugs of abuse, which are probably related to their abuse potential.

Because some brain areas may also become sensitized, an original drug effect will either require a lesser amount of the drug to elicit the effect when the drug is used chronically or the effect becomes greater with chronic use. This phenomenon has been studied most extensively in cocaine and other stimulant use. Stimulants are associated with behavioral sensitization of motor activity in animals, and paranoia (extreme delusional fear) in humans. There are physiological effects that develop tolerance or sensitization as well. For example, the chronic use of cocaine sensitizes some brain areas so that seizures are more easily induced, an effect that is called *kindling*. Other health risks of drug use are addressed below.

In addition to these more direct acute and chronic drug effects, another phenomenon occurs with long-term drug use. This phenomenon is the conditioned drug effect, in which the environmental or internal (mood states) cues commonly presented with drug use become conditioned or psychologically associated with drug use. For example, when angry, a drug addict may buy or use drugs in a certain place with certain people. After frequently taking drugs under similar conditions, the individual can experience a strong craving or even withdrawal when in the environment in which he or she has taken drugs or feels angry. When the individual tries to stop using drugs, exposure to these conditioned cues can often lead to relapse because the craving and withdrawal effects are so powerful. Very little research has been done as of 2008 on the neural bases of the conditioned withdrawal; thus, it is not known whether these conditioned effects are mediated by similar or different neural mechanisms than the primary pharmacological withdrawal from these drugs.

RESEARCH ON DRUG EFFECTS

Many of these acute and chronic effects of drugs on the brain have been investigated in animal research, which allows greater control over the research, including manipulations of drug exposure. A number of animal models are used to assess drug preferences, and, since most drugs that humans abuse are also preferred by animals, these models are useful for understanding human drug abuse. Moreover, animal research allows scientists to directly study the various areas of the brain that are involved in drug use. In addition, recent technological advancements in non-invasive imaging have allowed scientists to look at pictures of the brains of humans while they are being administered drugs or while they are withdrawing from drugs. This human work has provided information about the drug effects on the brain and validated the information gained from animal research.

Another useful line of research in assessing the effects of drugs involves human laboratory studies. In one type of study, research volunteers who have had experience with the abused drugs are given a specific drug (e.g., morphine), and various psychological and physiological measurements are obtained. The psychological measurements can include reports from the subject on the effects of the drug as well as more sophisticated behavioral measures that tell the experimenter how much the drug is preferred. Another type of human laboratory research entails the study of the effects of drug withdrawal. For opiates, withdrawal can be precipitated by an opiate antagonist drug (e.g., naltrexone), and withdrawal signs and symptoms are measured. For other drugs (such as cocaine), withdrawal is more difficult to measure because little is known about their withdrawal syndromes.

Some of what scientists have learned from such studies includes delineating specific brain areas as well as the neurotransmitters (the chemicals released by the brain cells) involved in drug use and withdrawal. Thus, when specific neurotransmitters are identified as playing an important role in drug use or withdrawal, scientists can administer experimental drugs that act on these neurotransmitters to see if the animals will alter their drug preference or show less severe withdrawal signs. Researchers can also give these experimental drugs to human research volunteers to see if the medication alters the subjects' perception of or behavior toward the abused drug, or if it alleviates withdrawal symptoms. If the results from these animal and human laboratory studies are promising, then these agents can be tested on treatment-seeking, drug-dependent individuals in clinical trials. This latter type of research is more time-consuming and expensive than the laboratory studies, but it helps provide an answer to the ultimate question: Does this medication help an individual stop abusing drugs?

APPROACHES TO DEVELOPING MEDICATIONS FOR DRUG ABUSE

Researchers can use the knowledge gained from animal and human studies of the effects of drugs on the brain as they develop medications for alcohol and drug dependence. Most likely, one medication will be needed to help detoxify the drug-dependent individual and a second medication to help sustain abstinence from drug use. This two-phase medication regimen is used for opiate and alcohol treatment, and it may ultimately be the approach used for countering dependency on other drugs, such as cocaine, sedatives, and nicotine. In theory, a pharmacological treatment agent or medication would block or reduce either the acute, rewarding effect of the drug or the discomfort of withdrawal. In practice, few treatment drugs have been found to be very effective in sustaining abstinence from drugs or alcohol.

Any pharmacological agent should be able to be given orally, as this is much easier than other routes of administration, such as injections. The agent itself must be medically safe and not enhance any of the health risks associated with illicit drug use, since the individual may illicitly use drugs while being maintained on the treatment agent. Finally, the pharmacological treatment agent must be acceptable to the patient. That is, if the agent causes undesirable side effects, individuals tend not to take it.

Research in the early twenty-first century on the effects of alcohol and drugs on the brain and on treatment outcome holds great promise for the identification of effective pharmacological agents. This search process will necessarily include the animal and human laboratory studies mentioned as well as medicinal chemistry research. Medicinal chemistry research is used to develop new compounds that have similar but slightly altered chemical structures to the abused drugs or to the neurotransmitters that mediate the drug or alcohol effects. These new compounds are then tested in animals to see if they produce therapeutic effects. These effects include having a low potential for abuse and attenuating the effects of the abused drug under study, preferably in a way that would lead to decreased drug abuse.

EXAMPLES OF MEDICATIONS USED TO TREAT DRUG ABUSE

Several types of medications have been developed for countering various kinds of dependencies.

Opiate Dependence. Some of the best examples of pharmacotherapies for drug abuse were developed for opiate addicts. One of the first pharmacological agents used to treat opiate addicts is methadone. Methadone itself is an opiate drug and effectively reduces or blocks the withdrawal discomfort brought on by discontinuing use of heroin or other illegal opiates. Although methadone is itself addictive, it is delivered to the opiate-dependent patients in a facility with psychological and other medical and support treatments and services. Methadone is safer

than opiates obtained illegally, in part because it is given orally.

Because illegal opiates are often injected by addicts, they can lead to many diseases, including AIDS and hepatitis, if the needles are shared with an infected person. Illegal drug use is expensive, and many addicts steal to support their habit. Moreover, since drugs obtained illegally vary in their quality and purity, there is a greater chance of getting an overdose that produces severe medical problems and, perhaps, death. Thus methadone decreases the need to use illegal opiates, as a result of its ability to relieve withdrawal as well as to block the effects of other opiates by cross-tolerance. Moreover, it reduces the health risks and social problems associated with illegal opiate use.

Another treatment drug that was developed for opiate dependence and abuse is naltrexone. This agent blocks the ability of the opiate drug to act on the brain. Thus, if a heroin addict maintained on naltrexone injects heroin, he or she will not feel the pleasant or other effects of the heroin. The principle behind this approach is based on research suggesting that drug use is continued, despite the dire consequences, because of the euphoria associated with its use. Once maintained on naltrexone, the addict may forget this association because the drug can no longer produce these effects. Unfortunately, although naltrexone works well for some, others simply discontinue using the naltrexone in order to get high from drugs again.

Before opiate abusers can be maintained on the medication naltrexone, they must be detoxified from the opiate drugs in their systems. Although abstaining (going cold turkey) from heroin use for several days accomplishes detoxification, the withdrawal process is difficult because of the physical distress it causes. Thus, another detoxification method was developed in which the withdrawal is precipitated, or triggered, with naltrexone, while the symptoms are treated with another medication, clonidine.

When withdrawal is precipitated, the symptoms are worse than that seen with natural withdrawal, but the symptom course is much briefer. Moreover, clonidine helps alleviate the symptoms, to make this shorter-term withdrawal process less severe. Finally, buprenorphine is a medication that is effective in reducing opiate use, and at higher doses is able to block the *high* or pleasant effects of opiates like heroin. Buprenorphine is effective in initiating acute withdrawal and suppressing withdrawal symptoms.

Alcohol Dependence. An example of another type of medication is one used to treat alcoholism: disulfiram. The basis for this agent's therapeutic effect is different from that of methadone or naltrexone. When someone is maintained on disulfiram, alcohol ingestion causes stomach distress and, possibly, vomiting because the disulfiram prevents the breakdown of a noxious alcohol metabolite by the liver. Patients maintained on disulfiram should come to forget the pleasant effects of alcohol use, which is similar to the psychological basis of naltrexone maintenance. Moreover, they should begin to develop an aversion to alcohol use. Another similarity to the use of naltrexone is that disulfiram treatment of alcoholism has not been very successful because the patient who wants to use alcohol again can simply stop using disulfiram.

Some pharmacological agents have been tested to reduce craving for alcohol and thus help the alcoholic abstain from drinking. As of 2008, there were four medications approved by the U.S. Food and Drug Administration for the treatment of alcohol dependence: disulfiram, naltrexone, acamprosate, and a long-acting injectable formulation of naltrexone. Naltrexone may be beneficial in preventing a return to heavy drinking because its effects, like those of most drugs of abuse, are believed to be mediated, in part, through the brain's natural opiate system (e.g., endorphins). Other medications that have been studied for treatment of alcohol dependence include serotonergic medications and anticonvulsants, including topiramate. However, as in the treatment of opiate abuse, alcoholics must be detoxified before any of these medications are used as maintenance agents.

Tobacco Dependence. One commonly used pharmacological treatment for tobacco dependence is nicotine gum (Nicorette). The main reason to quit smoking is that it is linked to lung cancer, emphysema, and other serious illnesses. Yet the active ingredient in cigarettes, nicotine, is associated with pleasant effects and with withdrawal discomfort, thereby making it an extremely addicting drug. Providing smokers with nicotine replacement in

the form of a gum helps them avoid the health risks associated with cigarettes. One problem with nicotine gum is that it is difficult to chew correctly; people need to be shown how to chew it in order to get the therapeutic effect. A patch is also available that is placed on the arm and automatically releases nicotine. This method shows good treatment potential. Other forms of nicotine replacement therapy include: lozenges, inhalers, and nasal spray. The patch, gum, and lozenge are available for over-the-counter purchase.

The first non-nicotine treatment approved to treat nicotine dependence is the antidepressant bupropion. The medication varenicline also became available as an effective smoking cessation treatment. Bupropion may have beneficial effects by increasing availability of the neurotransmitter dopamine. Varenicline reduces craving and withdrawal symptoms following cessation or reduction in nicotine consumption. It also has been shown to reduce the satisfied feeling gained through smoking. Detoxification from nicotine may also be facilitated with the medication clonidine, the same agent used to help alleviate opiate withdrawal symptoms.

Stimulant Dependence. Developing pharmacological treatment agents for stimulant (e.g., cocaine) dependence is a difficult task but has been the focus of a great deal of research. One of the difficulties in treating cocaine abuse is that cocaine affects many different neurotransmitter systems in various ways. Thus one approach may be to develop a treatment drug or regimen of drugs that affects a variety of neurotransmitter systems. However, the exact nature of the neural effects of cocaine was not entirely understood as of 2008.

Another difficulty is that it is not clear what approach to take in developing a treatment drug. One obvious technique in developing a medication for cocaine abuse is to use an agent that blocks the rewarding aspects of cocaine use. This type of drug would, presumably, decrease cocaine use because the rewarding effects are no longer experienced. However, this approach is similar to having opiate addicts use naltrexone, which has not been well accepted by heroin addicts. Clinical work with some treatment agents that were suggested to block the rewarding effects of cocaine did not prove to be useful in the treatment of abuse and dependence. Whether this lack of treatment effect resulted from a flaw in the method or from the limited knowledge of cocaine's effects on neurotransmitter systems is not clear. One problem is that the potential blocking agents for cocaine may produce dysphoria, or an unpleasant feeling.

Another approach to treating cocaine abuse and dependence is based on a premise similar to that of methadone for opiate abuse. That is, a pharmacological agent similar in its effects to cocaine, but one that is not addicting, may be a useful anticraving agent. Just as methadone helps alleviate drug withdrawal, an agent of this type for cocaine abuse may alleviate the distress and craving associated with abstinence from cocaine. Several medications of this type have been tried, including bromocriptine and amantadine. As of 2008, these and other agents have shown some limited treatment promise.

Most of the approaches to developing pharmacological treatments for cocaine abuse have been based on research suggesting that one specific neurotransmitter (dopamine) is important for cocaine's rewarding effects. Yet other neurotransmitters are activated during cocaine use and may be better targets for developing new treatment drugs. That is, although dopamine is critical for the rewarding aspects of cocaine use, other neurotransmitter systems may be more important in withdrawal distress. Although withdrawal distress from cocaine has been difficult to document, depression is thought to be one important consequence of abstaining from chronic cocaine use. Antidepressant medications, such as desipramine and imipramine, have shown limited treatment potential, as have some anticonvulsant medications (e.g., tiababine and topiramate), antinarcoleptics (modafinil), and antihypertensives (selegiline).

Sedative Dependence.

Treatments for sedative dependence as of 2008 include detoxification agents, not anticraving agents. Detoxification is accomplished by tapering the dosage of benzodiazepines over two to three weeks. Carbamazepine, an antiseizure analgesic medication, has shown promise in relieving sedative withdrawal symptoms. Future work with agents that block the actions of benzodiazepines may hold promise as a maintenance or anticraving agent to help the sedative abuser abstain from drug abuse.

Marijuana Dependence.

Although marijuana is the most commonly used illicit drug in the United States, there are no FDA-approved medications for the treatment of cannabis dependence. Withdrawal symptoms, such as negative mood, muscle pain, chills, and weight loss following daily use of marijuana quite likely play a role in relapse to marijuana use and impede abstinence efforts. Antidepressants and other mood stabilizers, as well as oral THC (a cannabinoid agonist) have been tested in clinical studies to reduce withdrawal symptoms. However, marijuana dependence appears to be as difficult to treat as other drug dependence and thus other options are needed.

One of the great lessons learned from the practice of giving medications to drug-abusing individuals is that these medications must be accompanied by psychological and social treatments and support. Medications do not work by themselves. Moreover, medications that are developed based on principles of altering or blocking the drug's effects in the brain may not be useful in practice to treat drug abuse and dependence because the premises on which the pharmacological treatment was developed may not be valid. Yet the largest research challenge is to understand the etiology and mechanisms of drug abuse. Thus, more research in many fields is needed to identify potential medications in order to develop more effective treatments for the difficult problems of drug abuse and dependence.

See also **Addiction: Concepts and Definitions; Imaging Techniques: Visualizing the Living Brain.**

BIBLIOGRAPHY

Galanter, M., & Kleber, H. D. (Eds.). (2008). *Textbook of substance abuse treatment* (4th ed.). Washington, DC: American Psychiatric Press.

Gardner, T. J., & Kosten, T. R. (2007). Therapeutic options and challenges for substances of abuse. *Dialogues in Clinical Neuroscience, 9,* 143–155.

Hart, C. (2005). Increasing treatment options for cannabis dependence: A review of potential pharmacotherapies. *Drug and Alcohol Dependence, 80,* 147–159.

Kranzler, H. R., & Ciraulo, D. A. (Eds.). (2005). *Clinical manual of addiction psychopharmacology*. Washington, DC: American Psychiatric Publishing.

Lowinson, J. H., Ruiz, P., Millman, R. B., & Langrod, J. G. (Eds.). (2005). *Substance abuse: A comprehensive textbook* (4th ed.). Philadelphia: Lippincott Williams & Wilkins.

THERESE A. KOSTEN
REVISED BY THERESE A. KOSTEN (2009)
TRACIE J. GARDNER (2009)

DRUGS AS DISCRIMINATIVE STIMULI

Human behavior is influenced by numerous stimuli in the environment. Those stimuli acquire behavioral control when certain behavioral consequences occur in their presence. As a result, a particular behavioral response becomes more or less likely to occur when those stimuli are present. For example, several laboratory experiments have demonstrated that it is possible to increase a particular response during a stimulus (such as a distinctively colored light) by arranging for reinforcement (such as a preferred food or drink) to be given following that response when the stimulus is present; when that stimulus is absent, however, responses do not produce the reinforcer. Over a period of time, responding will then occur when the stimulus is present but not when it is absent. Stimuli that govern behavior in this manner are termed *discriminative stimuli* and have been widely used in behavioral and pharmacological research to better understand how behavior is controlled by various stimuli, and how those stimuli, in turn, might affect the activity of various drugs.

It is important to recognize that there are differences between discriminative stimuli that merely set the occasion for a response to be reinforced and other types of stimuli that directly *produce* or *elicit* responses. Discriminative stimuli do not coerce a response from the individual in the same way that a stimulus such as a sharp pierce evokes a reflexive withdrawal response. Instead, discriminative stimuli may be seen as providing guidance to behavior because of the unique history of reinforcement that has occurred in their presence.

DRUGS AS DISCRIMINATIVE STIMULI

Although the stimuli that typically govern behavior are external (i.e., located in the environment outside the skin), it is also possible for internal or subjective stimuli to influence behavior. One of the more popular methods to emerge in the field of behavioral pharmacology has been the use of drugs as discriminative stimuli. The procedure consists of establishing a drug as the stimulus, in the presence of which a particular response is reinforced. Typically, to establish a drug as a discriminative stimulus, a single dose of a drug is selected and, following its administration, one of two responses are reinforced; with rodents or nonhuman primates, this usually entails pressing one of two simultaneously available levers, with reinforcement being scheduled intermittently after a fixed number of correct responses. Alternatively, when saline or a placebo is administered, responses on the other device are reinforced. Over a number of experimental sessions, a discrimination develops between the administration of the drug and saline, with the interoceptive (subjective) stimuli produced by the drug seen as guiding or controlling behavior in much the same manner as any external stimulus, such as a visual or auditory stimulus. Once the discrimination has been established, as indicated by the selection of the appropriate response following either the training drug or the saline administration, it is possible to investigate aspects of the drug stimulus in the same way as one might investigate other physical stimuli. It is thus possible to determine gradients of intensity or dose-effect functions with the training drug as well as generalization functions aimed at determining how similar the training drug dose is to a different dose or to another drug substituted for the training stimulus.

BASIC EXPERIMENTAL RESULTS

One of the more striking aspects of the drug discrimination technique is the strong relationship that has been found between the stimulus-generalization profile and the receptor-binding characteristics of the training drug. For example, animals trained to discriminate between a benzodiazepine anxiolytic, such as chlordiazepoxide, and saline solution typically respond similarly to other drugs that also interact with the receptor sites for benzodiazepine ligands. Anxiolytic drugs that produce their effects through other brain mechanisms or receptors do not engender responses similar to those occasioned by benzodiazepines. This suggests that it is activity at a specific receptor that is established when this technique is used and not the action of the drug on a

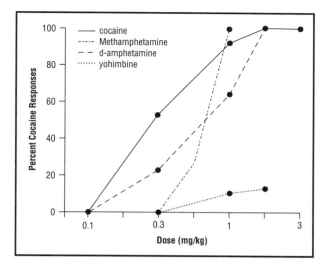

Figure 1. Discriminative stimuli. Effects of establishing a dose of 1.7 mg/kg cocaine, administered intramuscularly, as a discriminative stimulus in pigeons. Following the administration of the training dose of cocaine, 30 consecutive pecks on one illuminated response key resulted in food reinforcement, whereas following the administration of saline, 30 consecutive pecks on a different key produced food. Once the discrimination was established, various doses of other drugs were substituted for cocaine. The discriminative stimulus effects of cocaine were dose-dependent, with doses from 0.1 to 1.7 producing increases in responding on the key correlated with the training dose of cocaine. Similarly, d–amphetamine and methamphetamine also resulted in responding on the cocaine key, thereby showing that these drugs have some of the same subjective stimulus properties and presumably neuropharmacological effects as cocaine. A drug that does not produce generalization, yohimbine, an α2-adrenoreceptor antagonist, resulted only in modest levels of responding on the cocaine-associated response key, which suggests that this is not a mechanism by which cocaine produces its subjective behavioral and pharmacological effects. (Adapted from Johnson & Barrett, 1993.) ILLUSTRATION BY GGS INFORMATION SERVICES. GALE, CENGAGE LEARNING

hypothetical psychological construct such as anxiety (Barrett & Gleeson, 1991).

Several studies have examined the effects of drugs of abuse by using the drug discrimination procedure, and they have established cocaine and numerous other drugs—such as an opiate, phencyclidine (PCP), or marijuana—as a discriminative stimulus in an effort to help delineate the neuropharmacological or brain mechanisms that contribute to the subjective and abuse-liability effects of these drugs. As an example, Figure 1 shows the results obtained in pigeons trained to discriminate a 1.7 milligram per kilogram (mg/kg) dose of cocaine from saline. The dose-response

function demonstrates that doses below the training dose of cocaine yielded a diminished percentage of responses on the key correlated with cocaine administration, which suggests that the lower doses of cocaine were less discernible than the training dose. In addition, other psychomotor stimulants such as amphetamine and methamphetamine also produced cocaine-like responses, and this suggests that these drugs share some of the neurochemical properties of cocaine. In contrast, other drugs, such as the α_2-adrenoreceptor antagonist yohimbine, along with several other drugs such as morphine, PCP, or marijuana (that are not illustrated) do not produce responding on the key correlated with cocaine administration—thereby suggesting that the mechanisms of action underlying those drugs, as well as their subjective effects, are not similar to those of cocaine and the other psychomotor stimulants in this figure.

IMPLICATIONS

The use of drugs as discriminative stimuli has provided a wealth of information on the way drugs are similar to more conventional environmental stimuli in their ability to control and modify behavior. The procedure has also increased our understanding of the neuropharmacological mechanisms that operate to produce the constellation of effects associated with those drugs. The technique has wide generality and has been studied in several species, including humans—in whom the effects are quite similar to those of nonhumans.

Because it is believed that the subjective effects of a drug are critical to its abuse potential, the study of drugs of abuse as discriminative stimuli takes on added significance. A better understanding of the effects of drugs of abuse as pharmacologically subjective stimuli provides a means by which to evaluate possible pharmacological as well as behavioral approaches to the treatment of drug abuse. For example, a drug that prevents or antagonizes the discriminative-stimulus effects (and presumably the neuropharmacological actions) of an abused drug might be an effective medication to permit individuals to diminish their intake of abused drugs, because the stimuli usually associated with its effects will no longer occur. Similarly, although little work has been performed on the manipulation of environmental stimuli correlated with the drug stimulus, it might be possible to design innovative treatment strategies in which other stimuli compete with the subjective discriminative-stimulus effects of the abused drug. Thus, a basic experimental procedure such as drug discrimination has provided a useful experimental tool for understanding the behavioral and neuropharmacological effects of abused drugs.

Further work may help design and implement novel treatment approaches to modifying the behavioral and environmental conditions surrounding the effects of abused drugs and thus result in diminished behavioral control by substances of abuse.

See also **Abuse Liability of Therapeutic Drugs: Testing in Animals; Drug Types; Research, Animal Model: An Overview.**

BIBLIOGRAPHY

Barrett, J. E., & Gleeson, S. (1991). Anxiolytic effects of 5-HT$_{1A}$ agonists, 5-HT$_3$ antagonists and benzodiazepines. In R. J. Rodgers & S. J. Cooper (Eds.), *5-HT$_A$ agonists, 5-HT$_3$ antagonists and benzodiazepines: Their comparative behavioral pharmacology.* New York: Wiley.

Frieman, J. (2001). *Learning and adaptive behavior.* Belmont, CA: Wadsworth Publishing.

Johanson, C. E., & Barrett, J. E. (1993). The discriminative stimulus effects of cocaine in pigeons. *Journal of Phamacology and Experimental Therapeutics, 267,* 1–8.

Mazur, J. E. (2006). *Learning and behavior,* 6th ed. Upper Saddle River, NJ: Prentice Hall.

McKim, W. (2006). *Drugs and behavior: An introduction to behavioral pharmacology,* 6th ed. Upper Saddle River, NJ: Prentice Hall.

JAMES E. BARRETT
JUNE STAPLETON

MEASURING EFFECTS OF DRUGS ON BEHAVIOR

People throughout the world take drugs such as heroin, cocaine, and alcohol because these drugs alter behavior. For example, cocaine alters general activity levels; it increases wakefulness and decreases the amount of food an individual eats. Heroin produces drowsiness, relief from pain, and a general feeling of pleasure. Alcohol's effects include relaxation, increased social interactions, marked sedation, and impaired motor function. For the most part, the scientific investigations of the ways drugs alter behavior began in the 1950s, when chlorpromazine was introduced as a treatment for schizophrenia. As a result of this discovery, scientists became interested in the development of new medications to treat behavioral disorders as well as in the development of procedures for studying behavior in the laboratory.

HOW IS BEHAVIOR STUDIED?

The simplest way to study the effects of drugs on behavior is to pick a behavior, give a drug, and observe what happens. Although this approach sounds very easy, the study of a drug's effect on behavior is not so simple. Like any other scientific inquiry, research in this area requires careful description of the behaviors being examined. If the behavior is not carefully described, it is difficult to determine whether a change in behavior following drug administration is actually due to the drug.

Behavior is best defined by describing how it is measured. By specifying how to measure a behavior, an *operational definition* of that behavior is developed. For example, to study the way in which a drug alters food intake, the following procedure might be used: First, select several people and present each with a box of cereal, a bowl, a spoon, and some milk after they wake up in the morning. Then measure how much cereal and milk they each consume within the next thirty minutes. To make sure the measurements are correct, repeat the observations several times under the same conditions (i.e., at the same time of day, with the same foods available). From these observations, determine the average amount of milk and cereal consumed by each person. This is the baseline level. Once the baseline level is known, give a small amount of drug and measure changes in the amount of milk and cereal consumed. Repeat the experiment, using increasing amounts of the drug. This concept of baseline level and change from baseline level is common to many scientific investigations.

In addition to defining behavior by describing how it is measured, a good behavioral procedure is also (1) sensitive to the ways in which drugs alter behavior and (2) is reliable. Sensitivity refers to whether a particular behavior is easily changed as the result of drug administration. For example, food consumption may be altered by using cocaine, but other behaviors may not be. Reliability refers to whether a drug produces the same effect each time it is taken. In order to say that cocaine reliably alters the amount of food consumed, it should decrease food consumption each time it is given, provided that the experimental conditions surrounding its administration are the same.

WHAT FACTORS INFLUENCE A DRUG'S EFFECTS ON BEHAVIOR?

Although good behavioral procedures are necessary for understanding a drug's effects on behavior, pharmacological factors are also important determinants of a drug's effect. Pharmacological factors include the amount of drug given (the *dose*), how quickly the drug produces its effects (its *onset*), the time it takes for its effects to disappear (its *duration*), and whether the drug's effects are reduced (*tolerance*) or increased (*sensitivity*) if it is taken several times. Although this point may seem obvious, it is often overlooked. It is impossible to describe the behavioral effects of a drug on the basis of just one dose of the drug, since drugs can have very different effects, depending on how much of the drug is taken. Moreover, the probability that a drug will produce an effect also depends on the amount taken. As an example, consider Figure 1, which shows the risk of being involved in a traffic accident as a function of the amount of alcohol in a person's blood.

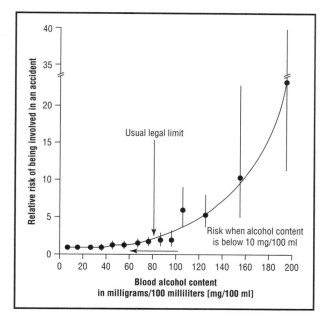

Figure 1. Risk of being involved in a traffic accident as a function of the amount of alcohol in the blood. ILLUSTRATION BY GGS INFORMATION SERVICES. GALE, CENGAGE LEARNING

The way in which a drug is taken is also important. Cocaine can be taken by injection into the veins, by smoking, or by sniffing through the nose. Each of these routes of administration can produce different effects. Environmental factors also influence a drug's effect. Cocaine might change the amount of cereal and milk consumed in the morning but it might not change the amount consumed at a different time of day or if other types of food are available. Finally, individual factors also influence the drug effect. These include such factors as how many times an individual has taken a particular drug; what happened the last time it was taken; or what one may have heard from friends about a drug's effects.

HOW IS BEHAVIOR STUDIED IN THE LABORATORY?

Human behavior is very complex, and it is often difficult to examine. Although scientists do conduct studies on people, many investigations of drug effects on behavior are carried out using animals. With animals, investigators have better control over the conditions in which the behavior occurs as well as better information about the organism's past experience with a particular drug. Although animal experiments provide a precise, controlled environment in which to investigate drug effects, they also have their limitations. Clearly, they cannot research all the factors that influence human behavior. Nevertheless, many of the effects that drugs produce on behavior in animals also occur in humans. Moreover, behavioral studies sometimes require a large number of subjects with the same genetic makeup or with no previous drug experience. It is easier to meet these requirements in animal studies than in studies with people.

Since animals are often used in research studies, it is important to remember that behavioral scientists are very concerned about the general welfare of their animals. The U.S. Animal Welfare Act set standards for handling, housing, transporting, feeding, and veterinary care of a wide variety of animals. In addition, all animal research in the United States is now reviewed by a committee that includes a veterinarian experienced in laboratory-animal care. This committee inspects animal-research areas and reviews the design of experiments to ensure that the animals are treated well.

WHAT APPROACHES ARE USED TO EXAMINE DRUG EFFECTS?

In general, there are two ways to examine drug effects on behavior in the laboratory. One approach relies on observation of behavior in an animal's home cage or in an open area in which the animal (or person) can move about freely. When observational approaches are used, special precautions are necessary. First of all, the observer's presence should not disrupt the experiment. Television-monitoring systems and videotaping make it possible for the observer to be completely removed from the experimental situation. Second, the observer should not be biased. The best way to ensure that the observer is not biased is to make the observer "blind" to the experimental conditions; that is, the observer does not know what drug is given or which subject received the drug. If the study is done in human subjects, then they also should be blind to the experimental conditions. An additional way to make sure observations are reliable is to use more than one observer and compare observations. If these precautions are taken, observational approaches can produce interesting and reliable data. Indeed, much of what is known about drug effects on motor behavior, food or water intake, and some social behaviors comes from careful observational studies.

Another approach uses the procedures of classical and operant conditioning. This involves training animals to make specific responses under special conditions. For example, in a typical experiment of this sort, a rat is placed in an experimental chamber and trained to press a lever to receive food. The number and pattern of lever presses are measured with an automatic device, and changes in responding are examined following drug administration. These procedures have several advantages. First, they produce a very consistent measure of behavior. Second, they can be used with human subjects as well as with several different animal species. Third, the technology for recording behavior eliminates the need for a trained observer.

WHAT BEHAVIORS DO DRUGS ALTER?

Some of the behaviors that drugs alter are motor behavior, sensory behavior, food and water intake, social behavior, and behavior established with classical and operant conditioning procedures. By combining investigations of these behaviors, scientists classify drugs according to their prominent behavioral effects.

For example, drugs such as amphetamine and cocaine are classified as psychomotor stimulants because they increase alertness and general activity in a variety of different behavioral procedures. Drugs such as morphine are classified as analgesics because they alter the perception of pain, without altering other sensations such as vision or audition (hearing).

Motor Behavior. Most behaviorally active drugs alter motor behavior in some way. Morphine usually decreases motor activity, whereas with cocaine certain behaviors occur over and over again (that is, repetitively). Other drugs, such as alcohol, may alter the motor skills used in driving a car or operating various types of machinery. Finally, some drugs alter exploratory behavior, as measured by a decrease in motor activity in an unfamiliar environment. Examination of the many ways in which drugs alter motor behavior requires different types of procedures. Some of these procedures examine fine motor control or repetitive behavior; others simply measure spontaneous motor activity.

Although changes in motor behavior can be observed directly, most studies of motor behavior use some sort of automatic device that does not depend on human observers. One of these devices is the running wheel. The type of running wheel used in scientific investigations is similar to the running wheel in pet cages. This includes a cylinder of some sort that moves around an axle when an animal walks or runs in it. The only difference between a running wheel in a pet cage and a running wheel in the laboratory is its size and the addition of a counter that records the number of times the wheel turns. Another device for measuring motor behavior uses an apparatus that is surrounded by photocells. If the animal moves past one of the photocells, a beam of light is broken and a count is produced. Yet another way to measure motor behavior is with video tracking systems. An animal is placed in an open area and a tracking system determines when movement stops and starts as well as its speed and location. This system provides a way to look at unique movement patterns such as repetitive behaviors. For example, small amounts of amphetamine increase forward locomotion, whereas larger amounts produce repetitive behaviors such as head bobbing, licking, and rearing. Until recently, this type of repetitive behavior was measured by direct observation and description.

Percent blood alcohol	Behavioral effect
0.05	alertness reduced
0.10	reaction time prolonged
0.20	motor function impaired
0.30	severe motor impairment
0.40	consciousness lost

Table 1. Blood alcohol level and behavioral effect. ILLUSTRATION BY GGS INFORMATION SERVICES. GALE, CENGAGE LEARNING

Although technology for measuring motor behavior is very advanced, it is important to remember that how much drug is given, where it is given, and the type of subject to whom it is given will also influence a drug's effect on motor behavior. Whether a drug's effects are measured at night or during the day is an important factor. The age, sex, species, and strain of the animal is also important. Whether food and water are available is another consideration as well as the animal's previous experience with the drug or test situation. As an example, see Table 1, which shows how the effects of alcohol on motor behavior differ depending on the amount of alcohol in a person's blood.

Sensory Behavior. The integration and execution of every behavior an organism engages in involves one or more of the primary senses, including hearing, vision, taste, smell, and touch. Obviously, a drug can affect sensory behavior and thereby alter a number of different behaviors. For example, drugs such as lysergic acid diethylamide (LSD) produce visual abnormalities and hallucinations. Phencyclidine (PCP) produces a numbness in the hands and feet. Morphine alters sensitivity to painful stimuli.

It is difficult to investigate drug effects on sensory behavior, since changes in sensory behavior cannot be observed directly. In order to determine whether someone hears a sound, one must report having heard it. In animal studies, rats or monkeys are trained to press a lever when they hear or see a given stimulus. Then a drug is given and alterations in responding are observed. If the drug alters responding, it is possible that the drug did so by altering sensory behavior; however, care must be taken in coming to this conclusion since a drug might simply alter the motor response used to measure sensory behavior without changing sensory behavior at all.

One area of sensory behavior that has received considerable attention is pain perception. In most procedures for measuring pain perception, a potentially painful stimulus is presented to an organism and the time it takes the organism to respond to that stimulus is observed. Once baseline levels of responding are determined and considered reliable, a drug is given. If the time it takes the organism to respond to the stimulus is longer following drug administration and if this change is not because the animal is too sedated to make a response, then the drug probably has altered pain perception.

Among the most common procedures used to measure pain perception is the tail-flick procedure in which the time it takes an animal to remove its tail from a heat source is measured prior to and after administration of a drug such as morphine. Another commonly used procedure measures the time it takes an animal to lick its paws when placed on a warm plate or to remove its tail from a container of warm water. Thus, an alteration in pain perception is operationally defined as a change in responding in the presence of a painful stimulus. It is also important to note that the animal, not the experimenter, determines when to respond or remove its tail. Also, these procedures do not produce long-term damage or discomfort that extends beyond the brief experimental session.

Food and Water Intake. The simplest way to measure food and water intake is to determine how much an organism eats or drinks within a given period of time. A more thorough analysis might also include counting the number of times an organism eats or drinks in a single day, or measuring the time between periods of eating and periods of drinking. Several factors are important in accurately measuring food and water intake. For example, how much food or water is available to the organism and when is it available? Is it a food the organism likes? When did the last meal occur?

In animals, food intake is often measured by placing several pieces of pelleted food of a known weight in their cages. The food that remains after a period of time is weighed and subtracted from the original amount to get an estimate of how much was actually eaten. Water intake is usually measured with calibrated drinking tubes clipped to the front of the animal's cage or with a device called a drinkometer, which counts the number of times an animal licks a drinking tube. An accurate measure of fluid intake also requires a careful description of the surrounding conditions. For example, was fluid intake measured during the day or during the night? Was food also available? What kind of fluid was available? Was there more than one kind of fluid available? These procedures are also used to examine drug intake. If rats are presented with two different drinking tubes, one with alcohol, another with water, they will generally drink more alcohol than water; however, the amount they drink is generally not sufficient to produce intoxication or physical dependence. Rats will drink a large amount of alcohol as well as other drugs of abuse such as morphine and cocaine when these drugs are the only liquid available. Indeed, most animals will consume sufficient quantities to become physically dependent on alcohol or morphine.

Social Behavior. Behaviors such as aggression, social interaction, and sexual behavior are usually measured by direct experimenter observation. Aggressive behavior can be measured by observing the number of times an animal engages in attack behavior when another animal is placed into its cage. In some cases, isolation is used to produce aggressive behavior. Sexual behavior is also measured by direct observation. In the male rat or cat, the frequency of behaviors such as mounting, intromission, and ejaculation are observed. Another interesting procedure for measuring social behavior is the social interaction test. In this procedure, two rats are placed together and the time they spend in active social interaction (sniffing, following, grooming each other) is measured under different conditions. In one condition, the rats are placed in a familiar environment; in another condition, the environment is unfamiliar. Rats interact more when they are in a familiar environment than when they are in an unfamiliar environment. Moreover, antianxiety drugs increase social interaction in the unfamiliar area. These observational techniques can produce interesting data, provided that they are carried out under well-controlled conditions, the behavior is well-defined, and care is taken to make sure the observer neither disrupts the ongoing behavior nor is biased.

Classical Conditioning. Classical conditioning was made famous by the work of the Russian

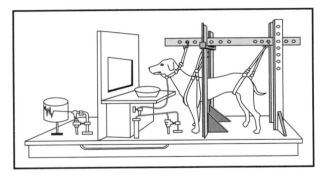

Figure 2. Diagram of Pavlov's classical conditioning experiment. A tube is attached to the dog's salivary duct, and saliva drops into a device that records the number of drops. ILLUSTRATION BY GGS INFORMATION SERVICES. GALE, CENGAGE LEARNING

scientist Ivan Pavlov in the 1920s. In those experiments, Pavlov used the following procedure. First, dogs were prepared with a tube to measure saliva, as shown in Figure 2. Then Pavlov measured the amount of saliva that was produced when food was given. The amount of saliva not only increased when food was presented but also when the caretaker arrived with the food. From these careful observations, Pavlov concluded that salivation in response to the food represented an inborn, innate response that did not require any learning. Because no learning was required, he called this an unlearned (unconditioned) response and the food itself an unlearned (unconditioned) stimulus. The dogs did not automatically salivate, however, when the caretaker entered the room; but after the caretaker and the food occurred together several times, the presence of the caretaker was paired with (or conditioned to) the food. Pavlov called the caretaker the *conditioned stimulus* and he called the salivation that occurred in the presence of the caretaker a *conditioned response*.

Events in the environment that are paired with or conditioned to drug delivery can also produce effects similar to the drug itself, much in the same way that Pavlov's caretaker was conditioned to food delivery. For example, when heroin-dependent individuals stop taking heroin, they experience a number of unpleasant effects, such as restlessness, irritability, tremors, nausea, and vomiting. These are called withdrawal or abstinence symptoms. If an individual experiences withdrawal several times in the same environment, then events or stimuli in that location became paired with (or conditioned to) the withdrawal syndrome. With time, the environmental events themselves can produce withdrawal-like responses, just as the caretaker produced salivation in Pavlov's dogs.

Operant Conditioning. About a decade after Pavlov's discovery of classical conditioning, another psychologist, B. F. Skinner, was developing his own theory of learning. Skinner observed that certain behaviors occur again and again. He also observed that behaviors with a high probability of occurrence were behaviors that produced effects on the environment. According to Skinner, behavior "operates" on the environment to produce an effect. Skinner called this process *operant conditioning.* For example, people work at their jobs because working produces a paycheck. In this situation, working is the response and a paycheck is the effect. In other situations, a person does something to avoid a certain effect. For example, by driving a car within the appropriate speed limit, traffic tickets are avoided and the probability of having a traffic accident is reduced. In this case, the response is driving at a given speed and the effect is avoiding a ticket or an accident.

If the effect that follows a given behavior increases the likelihood that the behavior will occur again, then that event is called a *reinforcer.* Food, water, and heat are common reinforcers. Drug administration is also a reinforcer. It is well known that animals will respond on a lever to receive intravenous injections of morphine, cocaine, and amphetamine, as well as a number of other drugs. Not all drugs are self-administered, however. For example, animals will respond to avoid the presentation of certain nonabused drugs such as the antipsychotics (medications used in the treatment of schizophrenia). Because there is a good correlation between drugs that are self-administered by animals and those that are abused by people, the self-administration procedure is often used to examine drug-taking behavior.

In most operant conditioning experiments, animals perform a simple response such as a lever press or a key peck to receive food. Usually the organism has to make a fixed number of responses or to space responses according to some temporal pattern. The various ways of delivering a reinforcer are called *schedules of reinforcement.* Schedules of reinforcement produce very consistent and reliable patterns of responding. Moreover, they maintain behavior for long periods of time, are easily adapted for a number of different animals, and provide a very accurate measure of behavior. Thus, they provide a well-defined, *operational measure* of behavior, which is used to examine the behavioral effects of drugs.

Motivation, Learning, Memory, and Emotion. One of the biggest challenges for behavioral scientists is to develop procedures for measuring drug effects on processes such as motivation, emotion, learning, or memory since these behaviors are very difficult to observe directly. Drugs certainly alter processes such as these. For example, many drugs relieve anxiety. Other drugs produce feelings of pleasure and well-being; still others interfere with memory processes. Given the complexity of devised procedures, they are not described in detail here; however, it is important to emphasize that the approach for examining the effects of drugs on these complex behaviors is the same as it is for any behavior: First, carefully define the behavior and describe the conditions under which it occurs. Second, give a drug and observe changes in the behavior. Third, take special care to consider pharmacological factors, such as how much drug is given, when the drug is given, or the number of times the drug is given. Fourth, consider behavioral factors, such as the nature of the behavior examined, the conditions under which the behavior is examined, as well as the individual's past experience with the behavior.

RESEARCH: MEASURING EFFECTS OF DRUGS ON BEHAVIOR: SUMMARY

To find out how drugs alter behavior, several factors are considered. These include the pharmacology of the drug itself as well as an understanding of the behavior being examined. Indeed, the behavioral state of an organism, as well as the organism's past behavior and experience with a drug contribute as much to the final drug effect as do factors such as the dose of the drug and how long it lasts. Thus, the examination of drug effects on behavior requires a careful description of behavior with special attention to the way in which the behavior is measured. Behavioral studies also require a number of experimental controls, which assure that changes in behavior following drug administration are actually due to the drug itself and not the result of behavioral variability.

See also Addiction: Concepts and Definitions; Aggression and Drugs: Research Issues; Pharmacodynamics; Psychomotor Effects of Alcohol and Drugs; Reinforcement; Research, Animal Model: An Overview; Risk Factors for Substance Use, Abuse, and Dependence: An Overview; Sensation and Perception and Effects of Drugs; Tolerance and Physical Dependence.

BIBLIOGRAPHY

Carlton, P. L. (1983). *A primer of behavioral pharmacology.* New York: W. H. Freeman.

Domjan, M., & Burkhard, B. (1982). *The principles of learning and behavior.* Pacific Grove, CA: Brooks/ Cole Publishing Co. (2005, 5th ed.)

Greenshaw, A. J., & Dourish, C. T., Eds. (1987). *Experimental psychopharmacology.* Clifton, NJ: Humana Press.

Grilly, D. M. (1989). *Drugs and human behavior.* Boston: Allyn & Bacon. (2005, 5th ed.)

Julien, R. M. (1988). *A primer of drug action.* New York: W. H. Freeman. (2007, 11th ed.)

McKim, W. A. (1986). *Drugs and behavior.* Englewood Cliffs, NJ: Prentice-Hall. (2006, 6th ed.)

Meyer, J. S., & Quenzer, L. F. (2004). *Psychopharmacology: Drugs, the brain and behavior.* Sunderland, MA: Sinauer Associates.

Myers, D. G. (1989). *Psychology.* New York: Worth. (2006, 8th ed.)

Ray, O., & Ksir, C. (1987). *Drugs, society, & human behavior.* St. Louis: Times Mirror/Mosby. (2006, 12th ed.)

Seiden, L. S., & Dykstra, L. A. (1977). *Psychopharmacology: A biochemical and behavioral approach.* New York: Van Nostrand Reinhold.

LINDA A. DYKSTRA

MEASURING EFFECTS OF DRUGS ON MOOD

Subjective effects are feelings, perceptions, and moods that are the personal experiences of an individual. They are not accessible to other observers for public validation and, thus, can only be obtained through reports from the individual. Subjective-effect measures are used to determine whether the drug is perceived and to determine the quantitative and qualitative characterization of what is experienced. Although subjective effects can be collected in the form of narrative descriptions, standardized questionnaires have greater experimental utility. For example, they may be used to collect the reports of individuals in a fashion that is meaningful to outside observers, can be combined across subjects, and can provide data that are reliable and replicable. The measurement of subjective effects through the use of questionnaires is scientifically useful for determining the pharmacologic properties of drugs—including time course, potency, abuse liability, side effects, and therapeutic utility. Many of the current methods used to measure subjective effects resulted from research aimed at reducing drug abuse.

HISTORY
Drug abuse and drug addiction are problems that are not new to contemporary society; they have a long-recorded history, dating back to ancient times. For centuries, various drugs including alcohol, tobacco, marijuana, hallucinogens, opium, and cocaine, have been available and used widely across many cultures. Throughout these times, humans have been interested in describing and communicating the subjective experiences that arise from drug administration. Although scientists have been interested in the study of pharmacology for many centuries, reliable procedures were not developed to measure the subjective effects of drugs until recently.

Throughout the twentieth century, the U.S. Government has become increasingly concerned with the growing problem of drug abuse. To decrease the availability of drugs with significant abuse liability, the government has passed increasingly restrictive laws concerning the possession and sale of existing drugs and the development and marketing of new drugs. The pressing need to regulate drugs that have potential for misuse prompted the government to sponsor research for the development of scientific methodologies that would be useful in assessing the abuse liability of drugs.

Two laboratories that made major contributions to the development of subjective-effect measures were Henry Beecher and his colleagues at Harvard University and the government-operated Addiction Research Center (ARC) in Lexington, Kentucky. Beecher and his colleagues at Harvard conducted a lengthy series of well-designed studies that compared the subjective effects of various drugs—opiates, sedatives, and stimulants—in a variety of subject populations that included patients, substance abusers, and normal volunteers and highlighted the importance of studying the appropriate patient population. Additionally, this group laid the foundation for conducting studies with solid experimental designs, which include double-blind and placebo controls, randomized dosing, and characterization of dose-response relationships. Investigators at the ARC conducted fundamental studies of both the acute (immediate) and chronic (long-term) effects of drugs, as well as physical dependence and withdrawal symptoms (e.g., Himmelsbach's opiate withdrawal scale). A number of questionnaires and procedures now in use to study the subjective effects of drugs were developed, including the Addiction Research Center Inventory and the Single Dose Questionnaire. Although many of the tools and methods developed at the ARC are still in use, other laboratories have since modified and expanded subjective-effect measures and their applications.

MEASURES

Question Format. Subjective-effects measures are usually presented in the form of groups of questions (questionnaires). These questions can be presented in a number of formats, the most frequently used of which are ordinal scales and visual analog scales. The ordinal scale is a scale of ranked values in which the ranks are assigned based upon the amount of the measured effect that is experienced by each individual. Subjects are usually asked to rate their response to a question on a 4- or 5-point scale (e.g., to rate the strength of the drug effect from 0 to 4, with 0 = not at all; 1 = a little; 2 = moderately; 3 = quite a bit; and 4 = extremely). A visual-analog scale is a continuous scale presented as a line without tick marks or sometimes with tick marks to give some indication of gradations. A subject indicates the response by placing a mark on that line, according to a particular reference point; for example, lines are usually anchored at the ends with labels such as "not at all" and "extremely." Visual-analog scales can be unipolar (example: "tired," rated from no effect to extremely), or they may be bipolar (example: "tired/alert," with "extremely tired" at one end, "extremely alert" at the other, and "no effect" in the center). Another frequently used format is the binomial scale, usually in the form of yes/no or true/false responses, such as the Addiction Research Center Inventory. A fourth format utilizes a nominal scale, in which the response choices are categorical in nature and

mutually exclusive of each other (e.g., drug class questionnaire).

Questionnaires. Frequently used subjective-effect measures include investigator-generated scales, such as adjective-rating scales, and standardized questionnaires, such as the Profile of Mood States and the Addiction Research Center Inventory. A description of a number of questionnaires follows; however, this list is illustrative only and is not meant to be exhaustive.

Adjective Rating Scales. These are questionnaires on which subjects rate a list of symptoms, describing how they feel or effects associated with drug ingestion. The questionaires can be presented to subjects with either visual-analog or ordinal scales. Items can be used singly or grouped into scales. Some adjective-type scales are designed to measure global effects, such as the strength of drug effects or the subject's liking of a drug, while other adjective rating scales are designed to measure specific drug-induced symptoms. In the latter use, the adjectives used may depend on the class of drugs being studied and their expected effects. For example, studies of amphetamine include items such as "stimulated" and "anxious," while studies of opioids include symptoms such as "itching" and "talkative." To study physical dependence, symptoms associated with drug withdrawal are used; for example, in studies of opioid withdrawal, subjects might rate "watery eyes," "chills," and "gooseflesh." Most adjective-rating scales have not been formally validated; investigators rely on external validity.

Profile of Mood States (POMS). This questionnaire was developed to measure mood effects in psychiatric populations and for use in testing treatments for psychiatric conditions such as depression and anxiety. It is a form of an adjective-rating scale. This scale was developed by Douglas McNair, Ph.D., and has been modified several times. It exists in two forms—one consisting of sixty-five and another of seventy-two adjectives describing mood states that are rated on a five-point scale from "not at all" (0) to "extremely"

(4). The item scores are weighted and grouped by factor analysis into a number of subscales, including tension-anxiety, depression-dejection, anger-hostility, vigor, fatigue, confusion-bewilderment, friendliness, and elation. This questionnaire has been used to measure acute drug effects, usually by comparing measures collected before and after drug administration. Its use in drug studies has not been formally validated; however, it has been validated by replication studies in normal and psychiatric populations and in treatment studies.

Single Dose Questionnaire. This was developed in the 1960s at the ARC to quantify the subjective effects of opioids. It has been used extensively and has been modified over time. This questionnaire consists of four parts; (1) a question in which subjects are asked whether they feel a drug effect (a binomial yes/no scale); (2) a question in which subjects are asked to indicate which among a list of drugs or drug classes is most similar to the test drug (a nominal scale); (3) a list of symptoms (checked yes or no); and (4) a question asking subjects to rate how much they like the drug (presented as an ordinal scale). The list of drugs used in the questionnaire includes placebo, opiate, stimulant, marijuana, sedative, and other. Examples of symptoms listed are turning of stomach, skin itchy, relaxed, sleepy, and drunken. While this questionnaire has not been formally validated, it has been used widely to study opioids, and the results have been remarkably consistent over three decades.

Addiction Research Center Inventory (ARCI). This is a true/false questionnaire containing more than 550 items. The ARCI was developed by researchers at the ARC to measure a broad range of physical, emotive, and subjective drug effects from diverse pharmacological classes. Subscales within the ARCI were developed to be sensitive to the acute effects of specific drugs or pharmacological classes (e.g., morphine, amphetamine, barbiturates, marijuana); feeling states (e.g., tired, excitement, drunk); the effects of chronic drug administration (Chronic Opiate Scale); and drug withdrawal (e.g., the Weak Opiate Withdrawal and Alcohol Withdrawal Scale). The ARCI subscales most frequently used in acute drug-effect studies are the Morphine-Benzedrine Group (MBG) to measure euphoria; the Pentobarbital-Chlorpromazine-Alcohol Group (PCAG) to measure apathetic sedation; and the Lysergic Acid Diethylamide Group (LSDG) to measure dysphoria or somatic discomfort. The use of the MBG, PCAG, and LSDG scales has remained standard in most studies of abuse liability. Subscales on this questionnaire were developed empirically, followed by extensive validation studies.

Observer-rated Measures. These may frequently accompany the collection of subjective effects and are often based on the subjective-effect questionnaires. Ratings are made by an observer who is present with the subject during the study, and items are limited to those drug effects that are observable. Observer-rated measures may include drug-induced behaviors (e.g., talking, scratching, activity levels, and impairment of motor function), as well as other drug signs such as redness of the eyes, flushing, and sweating. Observer-rated measures can be designed using any of the formats used in subject-rated measures. Examples of observer-rated questionnaires that have been used extensively are the Single Dose Questionnaire, which exists in an observer-rated version, and the Opiate Withdrawal Scale developed by Himmelsbach and his colleagues at the ARC.

USES OF SUBJECTIVE-EFFECT MEASURES

The methodology for assessing the subjective effects of drugs was developed, in large part, to characterize the abuse liability, the pharmacological properties, and the therapeutic utility of drugs. *Abuse liability* is the term for the likelihood that a drug will be used illicitly for nonmedical purposes. The assessment of the abuse-liability profile of a new drug has historically been studied by comparing it with a known drug, whose effects have been previously characterized. Drugs that produce euphoria are considered more likely to be abused than drugs that do not produce euphoria.

Subjective-effects measures may also be used to characterize the time course of a drug's action (such

	Global effects	ARCI	POMS	Adjectives
Sedatives	Drug effect Liking High	PCAG	Fatigue (increase) Vigor (decrease)	Tired Sleepy Relaxed Drunk
Stimulants	Drug effect Liking High	MBG	Vigor (increase) Fatigue (decrease)	Stimulated Nervous Thirsty Jittery
Opiates	Drug effect Liking High	MBG PCAG		Nauseous Itchy Nodding Energetic

Table 1. Typical response profiles for sedatives, stimulants, and opiates on selected subjective-effect measures. ILLUSTRATION BY GGS INFORMATION SERVICES. GALE, CENGAGE LEARNING

as time to drug onset, time to maximal or peak effect, and the duration of the drug effect). These procedures can provide information about the pharmacological properties of a particular drug, such as its drug class, whether it has agonist or antagonist effects, and its similarity to prototypic drugs within a given drug class. Subjective-response reports are also useful in assessing the efficacy (the ability of a drug to produce its desired effects), potency (amount or dose of a drug needed to produce that effect), and therapeutic utility of a new drug. Subjective reports provide information regarding the potency and efficacy of a new drug in comparison to available treatment agents. Subjective-effect measures may be useful in determining whether a drug produces side effects that are dangerous or intolerable to the patient. Drugs that produce unpleasant or dysphoric mood-altering effects may have limited therapeutic usefulness.

DESCRIPTION OF MAJOR FINDINGS OBTAINED WITH DIFFERENT DRUG CLASSES

Drugs of different pharmacological classes generally produce profiles of subjective effects that are unique to that class of drugs and that are recognizable to individuals. The subjective effects of major pharmacological classes have been characterized using the questionnaires described above. Table 1 lists some major pharmacological classes and their typical effects on various instruments. While global measures provide quantitative information regarding drug effects, they tend not to differentiate among different types of drugs. Nevertheless, the more specific

subjective-effect measures, such as the ARCI and the Adjective Rating Scales, yield qualitative information that can differentiate among drug classes.

RESEARCH: MEASURING EFFECTS OF DRUGS ON MOOD: CONCLUSION

Measures of the subjective effects of drugs have been extremely useful in the study of pharmacology. Questionnaires have been developed that are sensitive to both the global effects and the specific effects of drugs; however, research is still under way to develop even more sensitive subjective-effect measures and new applications for their use.

See also **Addiction: Concepts and Definitions; Drug Types; Risk Factors for Substance Use, Abuse, and Dependence: An Overview.**

BIBLIOGRAPHY

Beecher, H. K. (1959). *Measurement of subjective responses: Quantitative effects of drugs.* New York: Oxford University Press.

DeWit, H., & Griffiths, R. R. (1991). Testing the abuse liability of anxiolytic and hypnotic drugs in humans. *Drug and Alcohol Dependence, 28*, 11, 83–111.

Earleywine, M. (2005). *Mind-altering drugs: The science of subjective experience.* New York: Oxford University Press USA.

Foltin, R. W., & Fischman, M. W. (1991). Assessment of abuse liability of stimulant drugs in humans: A methodological survey. *Drug and Alcohol Dependence, 28*, 1, 3–48.

Hofer, A., et al. (2007). Subjective response and attitudes toward antipsychotic drug therapy during the initial treatment period: A prospective follow-up study in patients with schizophrenia. *Acta Psychiatrica Scandinavica, 116*, 5, 354–361.

Martin, W. R. (1977a). *Drug addiction I.* Berlin: Springer-Verlag.

Martin, W. R. (1977b). *Drug addiction II.* Berlin: Springer-Verlag.

Preston, K. L., & Jasinski, D. R. (1991). Abuse liability studies of opioid agonist-antagonists in humans. *Drug and Alcohol Dependence, 28*(1), 49–82.

KENZIE L. PRESTON
SHARON L. WALSH

MOTIVATION

Motivation is a theoretical construct that refers to the neurobiological processes responsible for the initiation and selection of such goal-directed patterns of behavior as are appropriate to the physiological needs or psychological desires of the individual. *Effort* or *vigor* are terms used to describe the intensity of a specific pattern of motivated behavior. Physiological "drive" states, caused by imbalances in the body's homeostatic regulatory systems, are postulated to be major determinants of different motivational states. Deprivation produced by withholding food or water is used routinely in studies with experimental animals to establish prerequisite conditions in which nutrients or fluids can serve as positive reinforcers in both operant and classical conditioning procedures. In more natural conditions, the processes by which animals seek, find, and ingest food or fluids are divided into appetitive and consummatory phases. Appetitive behavior refers to the various patterns of behavior that are used to locate and bring the individual into direct contact with a biologically relevant stimulus such as water. Consummatory behavior describes the termination of approach behavior leading subsequently to ingestion of food, drinking of fluid, or copulation with a mate.

Incentive motivation is the term applied to the most influential psychological theory that explains how the stimulus properties of biologically relevant stimuli, and the environmental stimuli associated with them, control specific patterns of appetitive behavior (Bolles, 1972). According to this theory, the initiation and selection of specific behaviors are triggered by external (incentive) stimuli that also guide the individual toward a primary natural incentive, such as food, fluid, or a mate. Drugs of abuse and electrical brain-stimulation reward can serve as artificial incentives. In a further refinement of this theory, Berridge and Valenstein (1991) defined incentive motivation as the final stage in a three-part process. The first phase involves the activation of neural substrates for pleasure, which in the second phase are associated with the object giving rise to these positive sensations and the environmental stimuli identified with the object. The critical third stage involves processes by which salience is attributed to subsequent perceptions of the natural incentive stimulus and the associated environmental cues. It is postulated that this attribution of "incentive salience" depends upon activation of the mesotelencephalic dopamine systems. The sensation of pleasure and the classical associative learning processes that mediate stages one and two respectively are subserved by different neural substrates.

In the context of drive states as the physiological substrates of motivation, the level of motivation is manipulated by deprivation schedules in which the subject is denied access mainly to food or water for fixed periods of time (e.g., 22 hours of food deprivation). An animal's increased motivation can be inferred from measures such as its running speed in a runway to obtain food reward. Under these conditions, speed is correlated with level of deprivation. Another measure of the motivational state of an animal is the amount of work expended for a given unit of food, water, or drug. Work here is defined as the number of lever presses per reinforcer. If one systematically obtains an increase in the number of presses, one can identify a specific ratio of responses per reward beyond which the animal is unwilling to work. This final ratio is called the break point. In the context of drug reinforcement, the break point in responding for cocaine can be increased or decreased in a dose-dependent manner by dopamine agonists and antagonists respectively.

Appetitive behavior also can be measured directly in animal behavior studies either by an animal's latency (the time it takes) in approaching a source of food or water during presentation of a conditioned stimulus predictive of food, or simply by measuring the animal's latency approaching a food dispenser when given access to it. The fact that these appetitive behaviors are disrupted by dopamine antagonists has been interpreted as evidence of the role of mesotelencephalic dopamine pathways in incentive motivation.

In extending these ideas to the neural bases of drug addiction, Robinson and Berridge (1993) emphasized the role of sensitization, or enhanced behavioral responses to fixed doses of addictive drugs, that occurs after repeated intermittent drug treatment. Neurobiological evidence indicates that sensitization is directly related to neuroadaptations in the mesotelencephalic dopamine systems. As a result of these neural changes, a given dose of amphetamine, for example, causes enhanced levels of extracellular dopamine and an increase in the behavioral effects of the drug. Given the role proposed for the mesotelencephalic dopamine systems in incentive salience, it is further conjectured that craving, or exaggerated desire for a specific object or its mental representation, is a direct result of drug-induced sensitization. In this manner, repeated self-administration of drugs of abuse, such as amphetamine, produce neural effects that set the stage for subsequent craving for repeated access to the drug.

See also **Brain Structures and Drugs; Research, Animal Model: An Overview; Risk Factors for Substance Use, Abuse, and Dependence: An Overview.**

BIBLIOGRAPHY

Beck, R. C. (2003). *Motivation: Theories and principles.* Upper Saddle River, NJ: Prentice Hall.

Berridge, K. C., & Valenstein, E. S. (1991). What psychological process mediates feeding evoked by electrical stimulation of the lateral hypothalamus? *Behavioral Neuroscience, 105,* 3–14.

Bolles, R. C. (1992). Reinforcement, expectancy and learning. *Psychological Review, 79,* 394–409.

Robinson, T. E., & Berridge, K. C. (1993). The neural basis of drug craving: An incentive-sensitization theory of addiction. *Brain Research Reviews, 18,* 247–291.

ANTHONY G. PHILLIPS

RESEARCH, ANIMAL MODEL: AN OVERVIEW.

Since the 1970s, research using experimental animals has made major contributions to understanding the etiology of drug abuse. Indeed, one can view the sequence of historical development of this knowledge as paralleling much of what now appears to be the sequence of the development of addiction. That sequence is:

1. Assessment of the rewarding nature of the drug upon initial intake.

2. Possible sensitization of the drug effect with continued intake.

3. Linking of the drug reward to originally neutral external stimuli.

4. Addiction, or compulsive drug-taking.

The following review will examine the history of this research and present the current consensus view of the etiology of drug abuse, with particular reference to landmark studies with experimental animals. First, however, a few comments on terminology are in order.

Experimental analyses of drug effects on behavior began in laboratories using the methods of operant, or instrumental, conditioning. Early investigators not only used the methods of operant conditioning, they also adopted the terminology of operant conditioning, which developed in the 1920s and dominated American psychology until the end of the 1960s. To illustrate, this terminology can be applied to a situation of acquisition in which the pressing of a lever results in intravenous delivery of a drug to a rat. First, the rat would spontaneously *emit* movements, or *responses*, some of which would include lever-presses. If each lever-press resulted in the intravenous injection of the drug, and if the frequency of lever pressing increased over time, the drug would be called a *positive reinforcer*. Notice that there is no statement about the rat "liking" the drug. In fact, the word *reward* was not used to describe the drug because, as originally used by Thorndike (1911), that term referred to a "satisfying state of affairs." The language of operant conditioning, in an attempt to be more scientific, would not refer to the unknown internal state of the rat.

If one asked an investigator using the terminology of operant conditioning why the rat self-administered the drug, the investigator would say that because the rate of lever-pressing increased once the drug infusion was made contingent upon the response, the drug must, by definition, be a positive reinforcer. This approach was, of course, criticized as being a tautology. Why was the drug a positive reinforcer? Because delivery of it contingent upon a response resulted in an increase in the occurrence of that response. Why did the responding increase? Because the drug was a positive reinforcer.

In an odd way, the operant view of drug addiction coincided with the medical view of drug addiction during the same historical period. The medical view said very little about the etiology of addiction. Rather, a person simply became an addict (perhaps because of a weak will) and was then physically dependent on the drug (defined by the occurrence of somatic withdrawal signs when the drug was discontinued). The problem was how to get the person to stop taking the drug. In the medical view, drug taking was maintained by avoidance of the aversive state of withdrawal. The operant conditioning approach to this view was that drug taking was maintained by *negative reinforcement;* that is, the response of drug administration removed the noxious state of withdrawal.

The conceptual and semantic worlds of the operant conditioning laboratory and the medical clinic were similar in emphasizing the behavior of the addict and saying little about the internal state of the addict. Those worlds began to change as a result of an experiment reported in 1954.

THE IDEA OF A REWARD SYSTEM IN THE BRAIN

Olds and Milner reported in 1954 that rats would press levers to deliver brief electrical stimulation to electrodes chronically implanted in their brains. They named the phenomenon intracranial self-stimulation (ICSS). Studies in the ensuing 15 years mapped the brains of rats and other animals for ICSS and found the greatest response rates and lowest current thresholds to be in the posterior hypothalamus and ventral midbrain regions. Stein (1964) found that experimenter-administered amphetamine potently increased ICSS responding, and Crow (1972) reported high rates of responding from electrodes in the region of the dopaminergic cell bodies of the ventral midbrain. By 1982 the "dopamine hypothesis" of ICSS reward, and indeed all reward, had been proposed (Wise, 1982). This hypothesis was particularly attractive because it explained not only ICSS, but psychostimulant reward as well, in terms of a single brain "reward system." Note that with the entry of more neuroscience-oriented research, the term *reward* began to be used interchangeably with, or instead of, *positive reinforcement.*

The discovery of ICSS led to the idea of a brain reward system being the substrate of drug reward and drug abuse. The earlier emphasis on the behavior of the addict as an attempt to stave off withdrawal was replaced with a view of addictive behavior as being based on the hedonic value of the drug.

ASSESSING DRUG REWARD IN EXPERIMENTAL ANIMALS

The argument is often made that if a drug increases ICSS responding, or particularly if it decreases the current threshold for ICSS, that drug will most likely be a drug of abuse. This procedure, however, does not directly measure the reward of the drug itself. Instead, it assesses the modulatory effect of the drug on a separate rewarding stimulus, the electrical stimulation of the brain. Thus, procedures that more directly measure the reward of the drug must be viewed as being closer to the world of the human drug addict. Two procedures are commonly used to assess the reward value of a drug in experimental animals: conditioned place preference (CPP), which is almost exclusively used with rat subjects, and intravenous self-administration (IVSA), which is used with rats and, to a more limited extent, with monkeys.

Conditioned Place Preference (CPP). Conditioned place preference utilizes classical (Pavlovian) conditioning. In the simplest version, the rat is placed in a chamber divided into two easily discriminable compartments that differ in the brightness of the walls, the texture of the floor, and sometimes in their odor. Ideally, in the initial 15-minute test, the rat will not evince a preference for either compartment. On subsequent training sessions, the rat is injected with the drug of interest or the drug vehicle and confined in one of the compartments, typically for 30 minutes. One compartment is paired with the drug for two to four sessions, and the other compartment is paired with the vehicle for two to four sessions (typically these alternate). Finally, in the test session, the rat is allowed to freely move about the chamber without having been injected before the session. If the rat spends more time in the drug-paired chamber than the vehicle-paired chamber (compared with pre-drug testing), the drug is declared to be rewarding. If the rat avoids the drug-paired chamber, the drug is deemed aversive.

CPP has various benefits. It is easy to do, for one thing, and many animals and drugs can be tested in this way. It also has limitations, however. First, humans typically administer a drug to themselves, even the first time they try it. While the classical conditioning aspect of CPP clearly happens in humans—as in the case of the "needle freak," for whom the act of intravenous injection is rewarding—the fact is that after initial use, both the addict-to-be and the addict seek out the drug. Second, the single, rather crude measure of time in the drug-associated compartment does not provide much in the way of the "texture" of behavior. Regardless, this approach has been very widely used.

Intravenous Self-Administration (IVSA). Intravenous self-administration (IVSA), in contrast, utilizes operant (instrumental) conditioning. A catheter is implanted into a vein (usually the jugular) of the rat, leading to a port on the animal's head or back. After minimal initial training using food reward, the rat is allowed to press a lever or "nose-poke" (into a hole in the wall, breaking a light beam) to activate a syringe pump that delivers a fixed amount of drug solution into the vein via the catheter. Work with monkeys has the advantage of more available veins (typically in the back); the monkey wears a vest covering the catheter.

In the simplest version of IVSA, each response results in a drug infusion. This is a fixed-ratio 1 (FR1) schedule of reinforcement. In an attempt to generate more behavior to better examine the effect of a manipulation on the drug taking, the schedule may be shifted to a partial reinforcement version. For the FR schedule, this might be FR2, FR4, and so on. Many studies have been done examining the effect of difference schedules of reinforcement (FR, variable-interval, fixed-interval, etc.) on drug-reinforced responding. The use of schedules in which the drug is not delivered upon each lever-press is thought to better measure the reinforcing or rewarding value of the drug, and thus may be closer to a human's "craving" for the drug.

Perhaps the major difficulty with the IVSA procedure is in the interpretation of the results. If a manipulation (e.g., brain lesion, systemic drug injection, social deprivation) results in an increased rate of IVSA of a drug, does that mean the drug has become more or less rewarding? An increase in the dose per injection of most drugs of abuse results in a lower response rate by the animal. A decrease in the dose per injection results in a higher response rate. The interpretation is that the animal is titrating the concentration of drug in the bloodstream— too low is not rewarding enough, and too high is aversive. Therefore, if a manipulation decreases the response rate, that manipulation has probably increased the reward of the drug.

This explanation is mostly likely accurate using an FR1 schedule, in which each response delivers the drug. The use of a partial reinforcement schedule of drug delivery may make it more difficult for the animal to achieve the desired blood level, and thus the incentive value of the drug rises in importance. A commonly used method to decrease the role of the response rate in IVSA is to use a progressive-ratio (PR) schedule of reinforcement. In this procedure, a trained animal must meet the criterion of a progressively increasing response requirement (e.g., the exponential series 1, 2, 4, 6, 9, 12, ... 251, 331 ...) within a self-administration session. The variable of interest is the "breakpoint," or when the animal ceases to complete a ratio requirement. Higher breakpoints are interpreted as indicating a higher reward value for the drug.

The IVSA procedure has its benefits. One can test the animal over and over again, varying the conditions (dose, presence of other drugs, etc.), and it is the method most similar to the human situation, in which people actively seek out and self-administer the drug. However, it also presents a major challenge in that it is difficult to do—the catheter must be flushed with an anticoagulant to prevent clogging, the animal must not overdose, and infections can be a worry. In general, drugs that produce a CPP are drugs that support IVSA. There are exceptions, but more agreements than exceptions.

A DOPAMINE SYSTEM AS THE BASIS OF PSYCHOSTIMULANT DRUG REWARD

Studies using CPP and IVSA conducted between 1975 and 1985 rapidly accumulated evidence that the neurotransmitter dopamine is crucial to psychostimulant (amphetamines and cocaine) reward. Systemic injection of dopamine receptor antagonists reduced the efficacy of psychostimulants to produce a CPP. Low doses of dopamine receptor antagonists increased the rate of IV self-administration of psychostimulants. The increased responding was interpreted as a compensatory response for the decreased reward, and high doses of the same antagonists decreased or abolished responding. Increased responding at low doses was crucial, because high doses of these antagonists induce a Parkinson's-like state, (Parkinson's disease is largely caused by degeneration of dopamine-releasing neurons in the brain), obscuring whether the reduced responding at high doses was due to blunted reward or motor impairment.

Soon after the demonstrations using systemically administered antagonists, the question was asked: Which dopamine system? Chemical neuroanatomists had defined a number of dopamine-using sets of neurons in the mammalian brain. Two prominent systems, containing approximately 95 percent of total brain dopamine, were identified. Both have neuronal cell bodies located in the mesencephalon (*midbrain* in English) and terminals in the forebrain. One is the *nigrostriatal* system, with cell bodies in the substantia nigra pars compacta and dopamine-releasing terminals in the dorsal striatum (composed of the caudate and putamen nuclei in primates, but fused as a caudate-putamen in rodents). Sometimes the nigrostriatal system is referred to as the *mesostriatal* system. The second is the mesocorticlimbic system, with cell bodies in the ventral tegmental area of Tsai (VTA) and major terminal fields in the nucleus accumbens septi and prefrontal cortex. This entry will term these subdivisions of the mesocorticolimbic system the *mesoaccumbens* and *mesofrontal* systems, respectively.

The studies to answer the question of which dopamine system is involved were all carried out using rats, due to the numbers of subjects needed and the necessity of intracranial manipulations, which are more difficult in primates. Selective destruction of the nigrostriatal system was achieved using intra-nigral injections of the neurotoxin 6-hydroxydopamine (6-OHDA). For anatomical reasons, midbrain injections of 6-OHDA could not be used to destroy the mesocorticolimbic system (they would also damage the nigrostriatal system), so injections were made into the forebrain terminal fields.

Studies using CPP and IVSA of psychostimulants agreed that the nigrostriatal and mesofrontal dopamine systems did not seem necessary for the rewarding effect, and that the mesoaccumbens system seemed crucial for the reward effect. These results converged with another, much less used, approach, in which rats self-administered amphetamine solution in extremely small volumes directly into the nucleus accumbens but not into the dorsal striatum. Finally, additional work, using CPP with both 6-OHDA and intracerebral injection, indicated that another, smaller dopamine system originating in the VTA and terminating in the ventral pallidum formed a *mesopallidal* reward system for psychostimulant reward (Gong et al., 1996a).

INDIVIDUAL DIFFERENCES IN PSYCHOSTIMULANT REWARD

For any drug of abuse, a minority of those sampling it move on to addiction. By the beginning of the 1990s, it was clear that while considerable progress had been made in determining the neurochemical and neuroanatomical bases of psychostimulant reward, possible neurobiological bases of individual differences in the development of addiction were unknown. Work with humans over a number of decades had resulted in numerous debates over postulated "addictive personalities," but work with nonhuman animals had been scarcely investigated.

A paper by Piazza and colleagues, published in 1989, initiated studies on an animal model of differences in addiction vulnerability that continue to the present. These investigators screened rats for their locomotor response to a novel environment (an activity-measuring chamber where the rats had never been). Using a median split, they separated the rats into high-responder (HR) and low-responder (LR) groups. When these rats were subsequently implanted with IV catheters and allowed to nose-poke respond for injections of a low dose of amphetamine, the HR rats acquired self-administration but the LR rats did not.

The debate about why humans are attracted to psychostimulants goes back decades. Some assume that these individuals are basically depressed and taking the drug to elevate their mood (self-medicate), while others believe them to be "sensation-seekers," for whom the drug emulates the biological state accompanying "thrills." The results of Piazza and colleagues were interpreted as being consistent with the "thrill-seeking" or "sensation-seeking" argument.

A steady production of research results by the Piazza group and others has clarified the nature of the HR-LR difference. The Piazza group found the elevation of the "stress hormone" corticosterone (the primate version is cortisol) by a mild stressor lasted longer in HR than LR rats. They also reported that HR, but not LR, rats would intravenously self-administer corticosterone. This finding, which does not appear to have been replicated, is nonetheless consistent with a large literature indicating that elevated corticosterone, whether induced via injection or stressor, enhances self-administration of psychostimulants (Goeders, 2003). This work is very exciting because it opens up the possibility that humans under stressful environmental conditions (e.g., poverty) are more responsive to the rewarding effect of psychostimulants, and thus more likely to become addicted.

Some peculiarities of the HR-LR difference may shed further light on the nature of the difference. First, although a number of laboratories have replicated the faster acquisition of IVSA of psychostimulants by

HR rats compared to LR rats, those who have used the CPP method have not found an HR-LR difference for amphetamine (Erb & Parker, 1994) or cocaine (Gong et al., 1996b). Second, a critical article by Mitchell and colleagues (2005) reported that while HR rats acquired lever-pressing at a higher rate with IV cocaine or food pellets, and that while this rate correlated with their locomotor activity in a novel environment, the correlation between locomotion and responding for cocaine disappeared if the rats were pretrained to lever-press for food. This seemed to show that in a free-operant procedure without pre-exposure to the apparatus, HR rats acquire lever-pressing for cocaine at a faster rate simply because they are more active in novel environments, not because the reward of the cocaine is greater than in LR rats.

As noted by Marinelli (2005), the procedure used by Mitchell and colleagues was unusual. They used a very brief (15 minute) locomotor screening (the usual is 30–120 minutes), and acquisition of lever-pressing was done with an FR5 schedule (the usual is FR1). Furthermore, studies have shown HR-LR differences in psychostimulant IVSA after acquisition, and that HR rats previously trained on FR1 will respond more than LR rats on a progressive-ratio schedule (Grimm & See, 1997).

Another unusual observation is that when IVSA of psychostimulants in HR and LR rats is compared across a range of doses, the usual "inverted-U" dose-response curve is seen, but it is displaced upward in the HR relative to the LR rats (Piazza et al., 2000; Belin et al., 2008). The expectation is that if HR rats are more sensitive to the reward of psychostimulants, their dose-response curve should be shifted to the left of that of the LR rats. Instead, it is shifted vertically. The interpretation of the vertical shift has been contentious.

Aspects of behavioral differences in HR and LR rats in nondrugged conditions may afford some insight into the above peculiarities of the HR-LR difference. In particular, HR rats seem to find novel environments less aversive. Kabbaj and colleagues (2000), using standard rodent tests of anxiety and fear, found HR rats to be less fearful than LR rats. Presumably, this is why they show more locomotor activity in a novel environment. Decades of work with rats has indicated that locomotor activity in a novel environment is determined by the competing tendencies to explore the environment or to withdraw for safety. One can interpret the higher locomotor activity of the HR rats as a heightened tendency to explore or a decreased tendency to withdraw.

The French group who originally described the HR/LR distinction has leaned toward the heightened tendency to explore (the "sensation-seeking" argument previously described), suggesting that the stress of the novel environment triggers the release of corticosterone, and that corticosterone is rewarding in HR rats (Piazza & Le Moal, 1996). On the other hand, Kabbaj and colleagues (2000) found less messenger RNA (mRNA) for corticotrophin-releasing hormone (CRH) in the central nucleus of the amygdala and less mRNA for the CRH receptor in the hippocampus of HR rats as compared to LR rats. CRH was first discovered as a chemical signal released by the hypothalamus. This signal travels via vasculature to activate the release of adrenocorticotrophic releasing hormone by the pituitary; the pituitary signal then evokes the release of corticosterone into the general circulation. However, CRH is also a transmitter, released within the brain by some cells, which acts via CRH receptors on other neurons. Because an extensive literature relates amygdala activity to fear and anxiety, a lower number of CRH receptors in the amygdala of HR rats is consistent with the idea that although HR rats may show a greater corticosterone response in the blood to stress, they may also show a lower activation of brain systems for fear and anxiety than LR rats.

Psychostimulants are well known to produce anxiety—even panic—in a subset of people who take them. A series of experiments by Ettenberg has measured this in rats. Rats are trained to traverse an alley where the reward at the end is an intravenous or intracerebroventricular (into the brain ventricular system) infusion of cocaine. Ettenberg's group (e.g., Guzman & Ettenberg, 2007) found that, with both routes of administration, higher doses of the drug cause the animals to exhibit approach-avoidance behavior, which they can measure.

The vertical shift in the psychostimulant dose-response curves seen in HR rats may be a consequence of their having less of an anxiety component in their response to these drugs than do LR rats. Indeed, this may be a major part of why they more rapidly acquire psychostimulant IVSA than LR rats.

SENSITIZATION

It has been known for a very long time that repeated administration of many psychoactive drugs results in tolerance, or a progressive decrease in response to a drug. Human abusers of psychostimulants and opiates can eventually consume quantities that would be lethal for nontolerant users. Thus, it was a great surprise when it was reported that repeated administration of amphetamine to rats resulted in a progressively greater increase in locomotor activity and stereotyped behaviors. Initially termed *reverse tolerance*, this phenomenon has now become known as *sensitization* (Stewart & Vezina, 1988; Everitt & Wolf, 2002). As will be subsequently examined, the neural mechanisms of sensitization have been intensively investigated. However, for understanding the relevance of this work to human drug abuse, the question of whether sensitization occurs for the rewarding effect of a drug is crucial.

It is virtually impossible to investigate possible sensitization of drug reward using humans. To do such a study, a group of people not previously exposed to the drug would be repeatedly administered the drug, and the psychological and behavioral effects would be investigated in a longitudinal fashion. For both ethical and legal reasons this cannot be done, and one must look to research with other animals. The closest approximation in work with humans has been investigations of paranoid thinking induced by psychostimulants, which has been reported to show sensitization (e.g. Bartlett et al., 1997).

Experimenter-delivered pre-exposure to cocaine facilitates the acquisition of IVSA (Schenk & Partridge, 2000) and increases breakpoints on a progressive ratio schedule (Covington & Miczek, 2001). Work from the laboratory of D. C. S. Roberts (Morgan et al., 2006) has investigated sensitization in rats using self-administered cocaine. In their procedure, rats were given access to cocaine by insertion of a response lever into the test chamber once every 15 minutes. A lever-press resulted in a single drug infusion followed by retraction of the lever. This procedure was in place 24 hours a day (the rats lived in the test chambers) for 10 consecutive days, followed by 7 days of forced abstinence. No lever was present during the period of abstinence. The advantage of this method was that, unlike previous experiments in which the animal was allowed access 24 hours a day, drug intake could be limited to avoid the signs of toxicity noted with the previous approach. When the animals were retested on a progressive ratio schedule using cocaine self-administration after the abstinence period, the breakpoint of responding was greatly increased. Roberts and colleagues interpreted these results as modeling the "binge-abstinence" pattern of cocaine administration seen in human users, and they noted the resulting sensitization.

Neurobiological work has been carried out with the goal of determining the cellular and molecular mechanisms of psychostimulant sensitization. Virtually all of this work has involved the most easily measured behavioral effects of locomotor activity and stereotypy (continuous repetition of a particular action). Locomotor activity is typically measured via a chamber with infrared light beams, which are invisible to the rat, crossing just above the floor. Advanced software can measure not only the number of beams broken by the rat's locomotion, but the sequence of beam breaks, allowing determination of the animal's path. This is particularly important if stereotypy is involved, because then the rat locomotes relatively little, typically staying in one region of the chamber to lick an area, gnaw the floor, or some similar action. Locomotor activity is a low-dose phenomenon and stereotypy is a high-dose phenomenon.

Induction of sensitization can be carried out in various ways. One method is to inject the animal with a constant dose every few days and measure the resulting increase in locomotion or stereotypy. Another is to administer a constant or escalating dose for a number of consecutive days, stop administration, then measure the locomotion or stereotypy at a later time (e.g., a week later). In all cases, the behavioral response to the drug increases.

The psychostimulants amphetamine and cocaine increase transmission for the monoaminergic transmitters dopamine, norepinephrine, and serotonin. Studies in the 1970s using receptor antagonists revealed that the increased locomotion and stereotypy produced by psychostimulants is largely due to the effect on dopamine. This was followed by work to determine which sets of dopaminergic terminals were responsible. Studies using local brain injections of dopamine receptor antagonists, selective neurotoxins, and amphetamine and cocaine themselves led to the conclusion that the locomotor effect of psychostimulants is caused by increased dopaminergic transmission in the ventral pallidum—and particularly in the nucleus accumbens—whereas the stereotypy is caused by similar transmission in the dorsal striatum.

Not surprisingly, sensitization of the locomotor effect of psychostimulants seems to take place within the system originating in the VTA and terminating in the nucleus accumbens. Sensitization of the stereotypic effect seems to take place within the system originating in the SNPC and terminating in the dorsal striatum. Most studies have involved measuring locomotor activity, because this can readily be done using automated equipment.

The major questions, of course, have been: "Where in each system does sensitization occur?" and "What is the mechanism of this sensitization?" We will consider the *mesoaccumbens* component of the mesocorticolimbic system, with locomotor activity as the measure. The development of sensitization can be blocked by the systemic administration of drugs that are antagonists at the N-methyl-D-aspartic acid (NMDA) subtype as well as the alpha-amino-3-hydroxy-5-methyl-4-isoxazolepropionic acid (AMPA) subtype of receptor for the neurotransmitter glutamate. These results indicate a significant involvement of glutamate in the phenomenon. A considerable amount of experimental evidence has implicated glutamatergic synapses in the regions of the dopaminergic cell bodies in the midbrain, particularly in the VTA. These results include: (1) injection of NMDA receptor antagonists into the VTA does not affect the locomotor response to systemically administered amphetamine, but it does prevent amphetamine sensitization from occurring, (2) injection of AMPA agonists into the VTA produces sensitization even though the rat has not previously been exposed to amphetamine, and (3) intra-VTA injection of a drug that facilitates the action of glutamate at NMDA receptors sensitizes rats to amphetamine. Other chemicals also seem to be involved. The "stress hormone" corticosterone is reported to enhance amphetamine sensitization via an action on glutamate transmission. Dopamine, released from dendrites of VTA neurons, appears to act via the D1 subtype of dopamine receptor to facilitate, via glutamate, amphetamine sensitization within the VTA.

Putting the above together, the current thinking is that stress, whether via the environment or a psychostimulant, elevates circulating corticosterone, and, with dopamine within the VTA, brings about a lasting facilitation at glutamatergic synapses on VTA dopaminergic neurons. This lasting facilitation is manifest as sensitization.

Considerable work at the cellular level supports the hypothesis that psychostimulant sensitization utilizes an extremely well-studied mechanism of synaptic plasticity called *long-term potentiation*, or *LTP*. The most basic LTP mechanism works in the following way. Transmission at a glutamatergic synapse acts on the AMPA subtype of glutamate receptor to depolarize the cell. If stronger depolarization occurs, either via a transient greater glutamate release or via another transmitter acting on the same cell, a simultaneous action of glutamate at a glutamate receptor of the NMDA subtype opens a channel in the cell membrane allowing the entry of calcium into the cell. The calcium cannot enter unless the membrane has been sufficiently depolarized by the action at the AMPA (which mimics effects of glutamate) or nonglutamate receptor. Entry of the calcium triggers an intracellular cascade of biochemical reactions, resulting in the insertion of more AMPA receptors than before into the cell membrane. These AMPA receptors remain, and glutamatergic transmission at that synapse is strengthened, meaning that a given amount of glutamate now results in greater membrane depolarization than before.

The LTP mechanism, or variants on it, are currently considered the best candidates for the mechanism of long-term or permanent memory at the cellular level. Just as it has been proposed that the rewarding effect of psychostimulants may result from a "hijacking" of the brain mechanisms for natural reward, it has been proposed that sensitization to psychostimulants may result from a hijacking of the cellular mechanisms for memory formation (see Hyman et al., 2006; Kaver & Malenka, 2007).

It has also been proposed that the glutamate in the VTA which effects LTP may be released by an axonal projection from the prefrontal cortex to the VTA or by another set of neurons that, activated by the prefrontal cortex, release glutamate upon the VTA. Studies in rats have shown that electrical stimulation of the prefrontal cortex induces firing of VTA neurons via glutamate release upon the VTA, and that glutamate release in the VTA is greatly increased by psychostimulant administration. A number of research papers from different laboratories have reported that surgical damage to the prefrontal cortex greatly reduces or abolishes psychostimulant sensitization of locomotor activity in rats (e.g., Cador et al., 1999). It has also been reported that electrical stimulation of the prefrontal cortex induces sensitization in the absence of prior drug exposure.

RELAPSE

Relapse is one of the major, or perhaps *the* major, problem of drug addiction. Many therapies have been developed to treat addiction, but in the end, the value of most is diminished by extremely high rates of relapse. Work with experimental animals has shown that neutral stimuli can be paired with a drug, and that, via classical conditioning, those stimuli can evoke drug-taking, even if the drug-taking response has been extinguished. This can be seen if the drug is paired with stimuli or if withdrawal from the drug is paired with stimuli. After significant advances during the 1970s and 1980s in understanding the rewarding nature of many drugs of abuse, and after advances in the 1980s and 1990s concerning sensitization, work with experimental animals in the 1990s began to concentrate on the relapse phenomenon, particularly the neurobiological correlates.

Work with rats clearly shows three classes of stimuli that trigger the relapse of drug-taking behavior: (1) re-exposure to the drug, (2) presentation of stimuli previously associated with the drug, and (3) stress (Shaham et al., 2003).

Relapse Caused by Drug Re-exposure. In work from the laboratory of Dr. Jane Stewart (Mueller & Stewart, 2000), it has been shown that a conditioned place preference (CPP) to an environment paired with intraperitoneally administered cocaine can be reactivated after extinction via a cocaine injection. These investigators noted the surprising robustness of the CPP, which endured for weeks after conditioning, and the ease with which a single cocaine injection reactivated the CPP. This work is

an example of relapse induced by contextual cues, although it was not known which of the many cues (brightness of wall, texture of floor, etc.) was linked to the drug state.

Dr. Peter Kalivas and colleagues have consistently used the intravenous self-administration procedure to examine relapse. In Kalivas's method, rats are trained to self-administer cocaine intravenously, and then subjected to response extinction by replacing the drug solution with saline. After responding is reduced to 10 percent or less of the drug-responding level for three sessions, a cocaine-priming dose is administered intraperitoneally before a session and responding with saline infusions is measured. A marked increase in responding typically results, which is viewed as a relapse.

A series of studies by Kalivas and colleagues has revealed the brain system necessary for this model of relapse. The method of finding the system consisted of the intracranial injection of a drug cocktail of GABA (gama-amino-butyric acid, the major inhibitory transmitter in the brain) agonists, which transiently suppresses neural activity in the injected region, just before the intraperitoneal administration of cocaine. The results of this method have shown that inactivation of the more dorsal components of the medial prefrontal cortex, the core of the nucleus accumbens, and the ventral pallidum substantially suppresses relapse responding. In other studies, this group has shown that the cocaine-priming dose induces glutamate release in the nucleus accumbens, and that this effect is decreased by inactivation of the medial prefrontal cortex. In addition, intra-accumbens administration of an antagonist for the AMPA, but not the NMDA, subtype of glutamate receptor suppresses relapse responding. Kalivas and colleagues explain all of the above by a model in which the activation of prefrontal neurons induces glutamate release in the core of the nucleus accumbens, which then effects relapse responding via an output to the ventral pallidum.

Interestingly, the Kalivas group has not found that antagonism of dopamine receptors in the nucleus accumbens prevents relapse responding. They suggest that cocaine-priming affects the prefrontal cortex, which then—via a glutamate signal—affects the accumbens. Furthermore, they report that the rise in extracellular glutamate in the accumbens is only seen in animals that lever-press in the relapse test. Yoked controls that have not been trained to lever-press show a rise in accumbal dopamine in response to the relapse-inducing cocaine injection, but they do not exhibit a rise in glutamate.

Perhaps the most surprising result of the findings of Kalivas and colleagues is that the anatomical system necessary for cocaine relapse seems only partially responsible for the reward of the drug. Rats will more readily self-inject cocaine into the shell than the core of the accumbens. But relapse involves the core, not the shell. Damage to the medial prefrontal cortex of rats results in more robust responding, with higher breakpoints, for cocaine than is normally seen, yet this damage reduces cocaine-primed relapse. Finally, if one hypothesizes that the priming injection produced a state similar to that of self-administration, and thus results in a return of extinguished responding, the expectation would be that antagonism of dopamine, not glutamate receptors, in the accumbens would reduce relapse responding, and that prefrontal inactivation would be ineffective. However, the experimental results seem to be the opposite of this expected result.

One interpretation is that, rather than inducing a drug state that acts as a reminder, cocaine-priming affects a system for "impulse control." An enormous literature, stretching back decades, has implicated the prefrontal cortex in impulse control, and now it is receiving attention in human cocaine addicts (e.g., Ray Li et al., 2008). Norepinephrine and dopamine are both released within the prefrontal cortex, and that transmission should be enhanced by psychostimulants. Indeed, this is perhaps the dominant hypothesis at present to account for why psychostimulants such as amphetamine and methylphenidate are useful in the treatment of Attention-Deficit Disorder (ADD) and Attention-Deficit Hyperactivity Disorder (ADHD). Poor impulse control is a major component of these disorders. Kalivas and colleagues have found that an injection of a broad-spectrum dopamine antagonist into the prefrontal cortex blocks relapse due to cocaine re-exposure.

Relapse Caused by Drug-Associated Cues. There are of two types of drug-associated cues: discrete cues, such as a sound or light, and contextual cues, such as a test chamber. In humans, the discrete cues are thought to correspond to drug paraphernalia, while the contextual cues are thought to correspond to

location. In this view, both kinds of cues evoke a "craving" state and lead to relapse.

The most straightforward way to model cue-evoked relapse is to pair the cue or cues with drug administration, institute a number of extinction sessions in which responses are ineffective or result in the delivery of saline until responding is very low, then subsequently examine the ability of the cue or cues to evoke responding. When this has been done, the results show that the presentation of a light or sound associated with drug infusion evokes responding (or relapse). On the neurobiological side, lesions of the basolateral amygdala (BLA) were reported to abolish the ability of the cues to evoke relapse. This is consistent with a large literature, particularly from fear conditioning, showing the role of the BLA in the linkage of a neutral stimulus with an emotional state. Transient inactivation of the rostral BLA has been found to be more effective in blocking cue-induced reinstatement than inactivation of the caudal BLA (Kantak et al., 2002). Given that the rostral BLA sends axons to the core of the accumbens (discussed above as being crucial for drug-induced reinstatement), cue-induced reinstatement may, in the end, activate the same subcortical system as drug-induced reinstatement.

It has been suggested that dopamine receptors of the D1 subtype within the BLA are important, because intra-BLA injection of a D1 (but not D2) antagonist blocks the reinstatement of responding by a drug-associated cue. These results are consistent with the finding that dopamine release increases in the BLA upon presentation of a drug-associated cue. Interestingly, BLA injections of antagonists at glutamate receptors (of both the AMPA and NMDA subtypes) are ineffective in affecting cue-evoked reinstatement. Much of the above is reviewed by Kalivas and McFarland (2003).

A much more limited number of experiments indicate that environmental context is linked to the drug state via the hippocampus, specifically the dorsal hippocampus. The hippocampus is an ancient cortex, pushed into a subcortical location by the growth of neocortex. An extremely extensive literature relates hippocampal function to spatial memory, and perhaps contextual memories in general, in rats. In humans, the hippocampus seems necessary for the formation of "declarative" memories, which are accessible to conscious retrieval. Inactivation of the dorsal hippocampus, but not the basolateral amygdala, impairs reinstatement of cocaine self-administration in rats. The hippocampus sends axonal projections to the nucleus accumbens, particularly the shell component, so it reproduces the amygdalo-accumbens projection, while presumably carrying contextual rather than cue-related information.

Relapse Caused by Stress. The primary method used in these studies has been to train the rat to self-administer cocaine intravenously, then institute an extinction procedure for a number of sessions until responding is very low, and then administer an inescapable electric shock to the floor beneath the rat's feet (footshock). The result is a robust reinstatement of responding.

The brain systems involved in stress-evoked reinstatement seem to be different from those of drug-evoked and cue-evoke reinstatement (McFarland et al., 2004). Within the amygdala, the central nucleus (CeA), not the BLA, seems important. Transient inactivation of the CeA, or pharmacological blockade of receptors for norepinephrine in it, attenuate stress-evoked reinstatement. These findings make sense, because stressors increase the release of norepinephrine within the amygdala. The bed nucleus of the stria terminalis (BNST) is another forebrain structure that receives a norephinephrine-releasing input, and for which there is a large literature relating it to stress. Consistent with this, pharmacological blockade of noradrenergic receptors of the *beta* subtype in the BNST attenuates stress-induced reinstatement. Finally, an axonal projection from the CeA to the BNST is known to release the stress-associated peptidergic transmitter corticotropin-releasing hormone (CRH), and antagonism of CRH receptors in the BNST attenuates stress-induced relapse.

Comparison of the Neurobiology of Drug-, Cue-, and Stress-Evoked Relapse. While there is some overlap, the apparently distinct nature of the neural pathways for the three methods of inducing relapse is notable, at least for cocaine. Drug-induced relapse appears to depend on a circuit originating in the medial prefrontal cortex, projecting to the core of the accumbens, and thence to the ventral pallidum. The projection from cortex to accumbens utilizes glutamate as the transmitter and acts via the AMPA subtype of

receptor in the accumbens. The amygdala does not seem particularly involved in this type of relapse. Cue-evoked relapse appears to depend on a circuit for which the basolateral amygdala is a central component. A glutamate-releasing projection from the BLA to the accumbens core is very important for this form of relapse, suggesting that, in the end, cue-evoked relapse activates the same "downstream" circuitry as drug-evoked relapse. Finally, the major components of stress-evoked relapse include the central nucleus of the amygdala and the bed nucleus of the stria terminalis. Release of norepinephrine in both structures, and the peptide CRH in the bed nucleus, appears crucial for stress-evoked relapse.

DRUG-ASSOCIATED STIMULI AS REWARDS

A considerable amount of work—rather than testing relapse directly—has been done to measure the ability of drug-related stimuli to maintain responding in the absence of the drug. It is thought that this taps into the mechanism of relapse, even though relapse itself is not tested.

Psychologists have a long history of talking about operant (instrumental) conditioning in two ways. On the one hand, when a stimulus follows a behavior and increases the probability of that behavior, that stimulus is, ipso facto, a positive reinforcer. On the other hand, the same stimulus can be considered as having "incentive" properties, thus energizing further responding. The "reinforcement" view emphasizes the ability of the stimulus to "stamp in" a response. The "incentive" view emphasizes the ability of the stimulus to facilitate additional responding, even for behaviors that did not precede the stimulus (e.g., exploration). Incentive-oriented theorists think the ability of a drug-associated stimulus to induce "craving" reflects an incentive-motivational property of the stimulus.

A theoretical paper on the neural basis of drug craving, written by Terry Robinson and Kent Berridge and published in 1993, has had a major impact on the incentive-oriented approach to drug addiction—and indeed on drug addiction studies in general. Basing their thinking largely on experimental and neurobiological studies with nonhuman animals, Robinson and Berridge considered both the negative reinforcement (escape from the aversion of withdrawal) and positive reinforcement approaches to drug addiction, and they found both approaches wanting. Instead, they proposed that incentive salience (the attractiveness of stimuli linked to a drug via conditioning) is the basis of addiction. Of particular importance, they propose that the incentive properties of these stimuli sensitize with continued drug use. That is, they take the thinking about sensitization and extend it from the drug itself to stimuli associated with the drug. Robinson and Berridge conclude that, in the truly addicted individual, the incentive of the drug is maximum, while the actual reward experienced when the drug is consumed may be much lower than upon initial intake.

In a subsequent paper of Berridge's concerning food reward, published in 1996, he posited two processes, which he termed *liking* and *wanting*. Applied to drugs, *liking* means "On a 1 to 10 scale, how much did you like the drug?" and *wanting* means "How much do you want to consume the drug in the future?" Liking is very similar to *reward*, as it is typically thought of, and wanting is very similar to *incentive motivation*. The beauty of these terms, and the reason for their subsequent popularity, lies in the fact that these are everyday terms, not traditional psychological terms, and are thus easily understood.

Robinson and Berridge revisited their theory in 2003 in a paper in which they reviewed their ideas and incorporated intervening developments, including liking and wanting. They explicitly proposed that the core of drug addiction is the sensitization of the "wanting" system, which they had previously identified as being centered on the nucleus accumbens. Finally, they incorporated inhibitory control mechanisms, particularly prefrontal, which may be altered—even at the level of the morphology of single neurons—into their theory.

While not necessarily adopting the theoretical view of Robinson and Berridge, other researchers have presented compelling evidence for the importance of conditioned stimuli in maintaining drug consumption. In particular, work from the laboratories of Barry Everitt and Trevor Robbins, who often publish together, has advanced this knowledge. They have concentrated on using second-order schedules of reinforcement (reviewed in Di Ciano and Everitt, 2005). In this procedure, the drug (most often cocaine) is delivered via IV injection upon a lever-press. However, the press that delivers the drug is only part of a long chain of presses. For instance, in an FR10 (FR10:S) schedule, ten presses result in a brief illumination of a light ("S") that has been previously paired with IV cocaine injection. However, nine such "units" of responding are necessary before the completion of the tenth produces a cocaine injection. In the even more stringent FI15 (FR10:S) schedule (FI meaning "fixed interval"), the first completion of an FR10 sequence, with each completed sequence resulting in the brief presentation of a cocaine-associated light, at least 15 minutes after the previous cocaine infusion, would result in drug infusion. Clearly, incentive motivation must be very important in maintaining responding under these schedules, and the behavior is described as *drug seeking*.

Manipulations of the accumbens shell appear to be ineffective on second-order responding for cocaine. The results of manipulations of other brain regions previously implicated in cocaine reward, particular in regards to conditioned aspects, on responding with second-order schedules are somewhat surprising. Transient deactivation of the basolateral amygdala impaired acquisition of responding for cocaine under a second-order schedule, but it had little effect on previously acquired responding. Based on previously cited work, a large drop in acquired responding would be expected, due to the high degree of incentive motivation required for second-order performance. In addition, the blockade of glutamatergic transmission in the BLA by local injection of an AMPA antagonist also did not affect established responding. However, dopamine receptor blockade in the BLA by the broad-spectrum antagonist flupenthixol did reduce previously acquired responding.

Lesions of the accumbens core had little effect on lever-pressing for cocaine in which each press delivered the drug (FR1), but, like basolateral amygdala inactivation, reduced acquisition of second-order responding. Unlike in the BLA, transient inactivation of the accumbens core also decreased acquired responding on the second-order schedule. Injection of a glutamate antagonist for the AMPA receptor into the accumbens decreased responding for cocaine on a second-order schedule. Surprisingly, the blockade of dopamine receptors in the accumbens core with flupenthixol was ineffective on second-order responding for cocaine. However, this is consistent with a lack of change in dopamine release in the accumbens core during second-order performance.

Broadly stated, the above pattern of effects is consistent with thinking that a glutamate releasing projection from the BLA to the core of the accumbens is important for second-order performance. The major problems with this scheme are the ineffectiveness of transient inactivation and glutamatergic blockade in the BLA on acquired responding. More recently, an experiment from the Everitt laboratory reported that unilateral dopamine blockade in the BLA, coupled with AMPA blockade in the accumbens core of the contralateral hemisphere, reduced acquired second-order responding for cocaine, supporting an amygdalo-accumbens projection system (Di Ciano & Everitt, 2004).

TRANSITION TO THE ADDICTED STATE
Descriptions of drug-addicted humans stress the compulsive nature of the activity. Obtaining the drug comes to dominate most other activities, even in the face of negative consequences. This final stage of addiction has only recently begun to receive attention from investigators using animal models. The major proposals in this area are reviewed below.

Everitt and colleagues, whose work on the role of drug-associated stimuli in maintaining drug taking has been previously surveyed, have proposed an anatomically oriented scheme for the addicted state (Everitt & Robbins, 2005). This concept relies on the knowledge, first developed nearly 40 years ago, of the role of the dorsal striatum in ritualized, stereotyped behaviors. The dorsal striatum consists of the caudate and putamen nuclei in primates, including humans. The two structures are present in the rat but fused into a single structure, often called the caudate-putamen, but nowadays simply called the dorsal striatum. This nomenclature distinguishes it from the ventral striatum, which includes the nucleus accumbens. Whereas the ventral striatum receives glutamatergic afferents—particularly from phylogenetically old "cortical" regions, including the hippocampus and basolateral amygdala (it has been argued the BLA is "cortical")—dorsal striatal glutamatergic afferents come heavily from neocortical regions. In fact, the entire neocortex maps topographically upon the dorsal striatum, with frontal regions projecting to the anterior dorsal striatum, sensorimotor cortex projecting to the midcentral dorsal striatum, and so on.

A burst of work, principally in the 1970s, revealed the importance of the dorsal striatum and of its dopaminergic afferents (which come from the substantia nigra rather than the VTA) in stereotyped behaviors induced by psychostimulants, notably amphetamine. High doses of amphetamine induce rats to repetitively lick and gnaw a limited area of the test chamber. Locomotor activity, which depends upon dopamine transmission in the accumbens, is largely absent as the animal engages in focused stereotypy. Stereotyped behaviors in nonhuman primates include behaviors such as repetitive picking at an area of skin. In humans, such behaviors can be more complex, such as repetitive housecleaning. Stereotyped behaviors are typically seen during IV self-administration of psychostimulants, particularly amphetamine, in rats. These may consist of the licking or gnawing of a particular spot, or there may be a distinct repetitive pattern of moving about in the chamber between lever-presses. Stereotyped behavior directed toward the lever can be lethal. Finally, stereotyped behaviors, like the locomotor behaviors induced by psychostimulants, show sensitization.

Destruction of the dopaminergic projection from substantia nigra to dorsal striatum attenuates or abolishes stereotypy in rats. Focal injection of amphetamine into the dorsal striatum, but not the nucleus accumbens, induces stereotypy in rats. At the neuroanatomical level, the involvement of the dorsal striatum in psychostimulant stereotypy is thought to reflect the inputs and outputs of the region. As previously mentioned, the inputs come particularly from neocortex. A major efferent projection of the nucleus accumbens is to the ventral pallidum, while a major output of the dorsal striatum is to the globus pallidus, which can be considered a "dorsal pallidum."

Everitt and Robbins have proposed that, in the development of addiction, control of drug-taking behaviors moves from the ventral striatum to the dorsal striatum. That is, drug-taking shifts from "instrumental action-outcome" control of behavior—in which the result of a response is compared to the expected result, thought to be mediated by the ventral striatal system—to "habit" control of behavior, thought to be mediated by the dorsal striatal system. Thus, when addiction is completely established, drug seeking and drug-taking are no longer based, as they were initially, on the reward of the drug, but on stereotyped, compulsive behaviors. It is no surprise that current psychiatric work on obsessive-compulsive behavior has focused on systems linking the neocortex to the dorsal striatum, for the final state of addiction can be viewed as a variety of obsessive-compulsive behavior.

Supporting evidence from the laboratories of Everitt and Robbins includes findings that the release of dopamine by drug-paired stimuli does not occur in the nucleus accumbens of rats extensively trained on second-order schedules, but occurs instead in the dorsal striatum; and that dopamine receptor blockade in the dorsal striatum greatly reduces responding on a second-order schedule with cocaine, while (as previously mentioned) having no effect when the blockade is in the nucleus accumbens core.

The noted drug addiction researcher George Koob has proposed a different, although perhaps in the long run not incompatible, view of the "switch to addiction" (Koob & Le Moal, 2000; Koob & Kreek, 2007). When researchers first began using rodent models of drug self-administration, they found it technically difficult to keep the infusion line clear of blood clots and inhibit infection. Their way around these problems was to do the catheter implantation surgery, attach the animal to the infusion line in the test chamber, and let the animal live there for the duration of the experiment. The standard method is for the animal to live in its home cage and be brought to the test chamber for daily sessions lasting only one to two hours. Koob has argued that this method does not model the human addict, who moves from sporadic drug taking to a state where drug taking dominates existence. He suggests that the shorter access sessions model "recreational" drug use. By allowing rats to have much longer (6-hour) test sessions, he has found that the animals progressively increase their drug intake of both cocaine and opiates. This type of escalation does not happen with one-hour test sessions.

Koob and colleagues found that when the rats were infused with a single injection of cocaine, the locomotor response to the drug was diminished 14 days after an 8-day protocol of 6-hour access sessions for cocaine. If this was done after an 8-day protocol of 1-hour access sessions, a sensitized locomotor response was seen. Using these and other data, the Koob group has made the following argument: Sensitization may occur in the periodic "recreational" drug user. However, as the drug use progresses to a more chronic status, the response to the drug actually decreases, and any sensitization also decreases (Ben-Shahar et al., 2004). This is very similar to the more traditional idea of the development of tolerance in the chronic user. Koob and colleagues have shown that the threshold for rewarding brain stimulation (ICSS) of the hypothalamus progressively increases in the long-exposure rats when tested between drug-administration sessions. They believe this reflects a general *anhedonia* (loss of the appreciation of pleasure).

The scheme proposed by Koob and colleagues is similar, but much more advanced, than the traditional idea that a major, if not the major, reason the chronic user continues to take the drug is to stave off withdrawal. In a series of studies over a number of years, the Koob group has shown that during withdrawal from a number of drugs of abuse, the release of corticotropin-releasing hormone (CRH) within the brain in regions such as the amygdala is elevated. Intraventricular administration of CRH in rats evokes behaviors normally seen in conditions of fear and anxiety. (CRH antagonists reduce natural fear and anxiety in rats and are undergoing clinical trials as antidepressants in humans.) The Koob proposal is that, under long-access conditions, drug intake escalates, and this results in anhedonia for nondrug rewarding stimuli and depression or dysphoria. The rat (or human) continues to take the drug to stave off the dysphoric state, not because of the "pleasurable" effect of the drug itself.

SELF-CONTROL AND IMPULSIVITY

Work with human addicts has found increased levels of impulsive behavior in this population. It is not known, however, if the impulsivity predates the drug use or is a consequence of the drug use. In a publication by Belin and colleagues (2008), the Everitt and Robbins group has provided data supporting the idea that impulsive tendencies precede drug use. They screened rats for impulsivity using the five-choice serial reaction time task (5CSRTT). In this task, one of five apertures in a wall of the test chamber was illuminated for 0.5 seconds. The illuminated aperture varied, with a trial presented every 5 seconds. A nose-poke by the rat into the illuminated aperture resulted in a pellet delivery to a central food magazine. Two kinds of errors are possible in this procedure: responses of commission (when a nose-poke is made in any aperture before illumination), and omission (when a nose-poke is not made into an illuminated aperture). After substantial training, accuracy is above 75 percent and omissions are below 20 percent. Data on impulsive responding (errors of commission) were collected during long 60-minute sessions. Other rats were screened for their locomotor response to a novel environment. On both the impulsivity and locomotor tests, rats scoring in the upper and lower quartiles were chosen for IV self-administration of cocaine.

These investigators separated acquisition of self-administration from addiction. Using previous studies, they defined addicted rats using a three-component criterion: (1) motivation to take the drug, (2) inability to refrain from drug seeking, and (3) maintained drug use despite negative consequences. Motivation to take the drug was determined by segmenting the self-administration sessions into three drug-access periods of 40 minutes separated by 15-minute drug-free intervals, and then counting responses during the drug-free intervals. The ability to refrain from drug seeking was determined by a progressive-ratio schedule breakpoint for responding. Intake despite negative consequences was determined by pitting drug intake again with electric footshock. Each rat received a total "addiction score" based on performance in each of the three components.

The results of Belin and colleagues (2008) clearly showed that while the locomotor response to novelty (HR/LR dimension)—in agreement with other work previously discussed—predicted rate of acquisition, it did not predict addiction as measured by the "addiction score." Conversely, premature responding in the impulsivity test did not predict acquisition but it did predict addiction. HR and high-impulsivity rats came from different populations and showed differences in distinct phases of the addictive process.

OVERVIEW OF RODENT RESEARCH ON DRUG ADDICTION

As listed at the beginning of this entry, work on understanding drug addiction using experimental animals suggests the following phases of the development of psychostimulant addiction:

1. Initial exposure to the drug gives a rewarding effect, which appears based on increased dopamine transmission, particularly in the shell of the nucleus accumbens. This is "recreational" drug use. Individuals show considerable differences in their response to the drug during this period: in some, the reward effect dominates; in others, an aversive anxiety effect curtails further drug use. Using the HR-LR (high-responder–low-responder) rat model, the difference between those in whom the reward effect dominates and those in whom the aversive anxiety effect dominates seems related to individual differences in response to stress in general. Although higher cortisol levels in response to stress are seen in HR individuals, their behavioral response is lower than that of LR individuals. The origin of the difference in stress reactivity, while of great interest, has no definitive answer at present. Genetic differences are likely, and environmental influences, particularly stress during early life, are thought to be important in setting the relevant neurobiological systems.

2. Continued exposure to the drug results in a sensitization of the rewarding effect. Again, this happens most readily in the HR-type individual. The sensitization appears to be based on plastic changes (changes in the brain that occur in response to experience) in synaptic transmission utilizing glutamate in the ventral tegmental area. The glutamate is thought to be released either from axons emanating from the prefrontal cortex or from axons of brainstem neurons driven by prefrontal neurons. In addition, the ventral tegmental-accumbens dopamine-using system, and the accumbens itself, appears very involved in incentive motivation for many kinds of rewarding stimuli. Thus, sensitization of incentive motivation, rather than the hedonic reward of the drug itself, has been proposed as the basis for continuing drug use.

3. Because of the initial hedonic reward effect and the subsequent incentive sensitization, drug use continues, resulting in an association of the drug state with external stimuli. These stimuli may be discrete (e.g., needle, sight of the drug) or contextual (e.g., a room). Discrete stimuli are thought to be linked to the nucleus accumbens–based motivational system (particularly the core subarea of the accumbens) via glutamate-using projections from basolateral amygdala. Contextual stimuli are thought

linked to this system via similar projections from the hippocampus. It is thought that the synaptic modifications in the systems are the same as those used elsewhere in the brain for the formation of long-term memories.

4. Relapse to drug use can be triggered by presentation of the drug, presentation of stimuli previously associated with the drug state, or stressful stimuli. The data from rat studies indicate that each of these relapse-inducing events, particularly stress, operate through somewhat unique brain areas and axonal connections.

5. With continued drug use, intake moves from being reward-based to being compulsive. It has been proposed that this entails a shift of the control of drug intake from the reward-based accumbens system to the habit-based dorsal striatum. Another view of the compulsive phase harks back to a more traditional view that physiological mechanisms have been altered by the drug, particularly by heavy drug use, resulting in a new state from which deviation is aversive. These two views are not mutually exclusive.

6. Finally, very recent work with rats suggests that the propensity to traverse all the above stages leading up to addiction only happens in approximately 20 percent of the animals tested, and that it can be predicted by pre-exposure behavioral impulsivity.

Viewed through a historical lens, it is interesting to note that the view of drug addiction, after all the neurobiological work, seems to be returning to the human-based view of decades ago. That is, some are returning to the view that addiction is a kind of compulsion, that aversion to withdrawal plays a major part in maintaining it, and that self-control ("impulsivity") is important in developing and maintaining it.

See also **Addiction: Concepts and Definitions; Antagonist; Brain Structures and Drugs; Conditioned Tolerance; Craving; Dopamine; Dose-Response Relationship; Glutamate; Reinforcement; Relapse; Research: Aims, Description, and Goals; Research: Clinical Research; Research: Measuring Effects of Drugs on Behavior; Reward Pathways and Drugs; Tolerance and Physical Dependence.**

BIBLIOGRAPHY

Bartlett, E., Hallin, A., Chapman, B., & Angrist, B. (1997). Selective sensitization to the psychosis-inducing effects of cocaine: A possible marker for addiction relapse vulnerability? *Neuropsychopharmacology, 16*(1), 77–82.

Belin, D., Mar, A. C., Dalley, J. W., Robbins, T. W., & Everitt, B. J. (2008). High impulsivity predicts the switch to compulsive cocaine-taking. *Science, 320*(5881), 1352–1355.

Ben-Shahar, O., Ahmed, S. H., Koob, G. F., & Ettenberg, A. (2004). The transition from controlled to compulsive drug use is associated with a loss of sensitization. *Brain Research, 995*(1), 46–54.

Berridge, K. C. (1996). Food reward: Brain substrates of wanting and liking. *Neuroscience and Biobehavioral Reviews, 20*(1), 1–25.

Cador, M., Bjijou, Y., Cailhol, S., & Stinus, L. (1999). D-amphetamine-induced behavioral sensitization: implication of a glutamatergic medial prefrontal cortex-ventral tegmental area innervation. *Neuroscience, 94*(3), 705–721.

Covington, H. E., III, & Miczek, K. A. (2001). Repeated social-defeat stress, cocaine or morphine: Effects on behavioral sensitization and intravenous cocaine self-administration "binges." *Psychopharmacology, 158*(4), 388–398.

Crow, T. J. (1972). A map of the rat mesencephalon for electrical self-stimulation. *Brain Research, 36*(2), 265–273.

Di Ciano, P., & Everitt, B. J. (2004). Direct interactions between the basolateral amygdala and nucleus accumbens core underlie cocaine-seeking behavior by rats. *Journal of Neuroscience, 24*(32), 7167–7173.

Di Ciano, P., & Everitt, B. J. (2005). Neuropsychopharmacology of drug seeking: Insights from studies with second-order schedules of drug reinforcement. *European Journal of Pharmacology, 526*(1-3), 186–198.

Erb, S. M., & Parker, L. A. (1994). Individual differences in novelty-induced activity do not predict amphetamine-induced place conditioning. *Pharmacology Biochemistry & Behavior, 48*(3), 581–586.

Everitt, B. J., & Robbins, T. W. (2005). Neural systems of reinforcement for drug addiction: From actions to habits to compulsion. *Nature Neuroscience, 8*(11), 1481–1489.

Everitt, B. J., & Wolf, M. E. (2002). Psychomotor stimulant addiction: A neural systems perspective. *Journal of Neuroscience, 22*(9), 3312–3320.

Goeders, N. E. (2003). The impact of stress on addiction. *European Neuropsychopharmacology, 13*, 435–441.

Gong, W., Neill, D., & Justice, J. B., Jr. (1996a) Conditioned place preference and locomotor activation produced by injection of psychostimulants into ventral pallidum. *Brain Research, 707*(1), 64–74.

Gong, W., Neill, D. B., & Justice, J. B., Jr. (1996b). Locomotor response to novelty does not predict cocaine place preference conditioning. *Pharmacology Biochemistry & Behavior, 53*(1), 191–196.

Grimm, J. W., & See, R. E. (1997). Cocaine self-administration in ovariectomized rats is predicted by response to novelty, attenuated by 17-β estradiol, and associated with abnormal vaginal cytology. *Physiology & Behavior, 61*(5), 755–761.

Guzman, D., & Ettenberg, A. (2007). Runway self-administration of intracerebroventricular cocaine: Evidence of mixed positive and negative drug actions. *Behavioural Pharmacology, 18*(1), 53–60.

Hyman, S. E., Malenka, R. C., & Nestler, E. J. (2006). Neural mechanisms of addiction: The role of reward-related learning and memory. *Annual Review of Neuroscience, 29*, 565–598.

Kabbaj, M., Devine, D. P., Savage, V. R, and Akil, H. (2000). Neurobiological correlates of individual differences in novelty-seeking behavior in the rat: Differential expression of stress-related molecules. *Journal of Neuroscience, 20*(18), 6983–6988.

Kalivas, P. W., & McFarland, K. (2003). Brain circuitry and the reinstatement of cocaine-seeking behavior. *Psychopharmacology, 168*(1-2), 44–56.

Kantak, K. M., Black, Y., Valencia, E., Green-Jordan, K., & Eichenbaum, H. B. (2002). Dissociable effects of lidocaine inactivation of the rostral and caudal basolateral amygdala on the maintenance and reinstatement of cocaine-seeking behavior in rats. *Journal of Neuroscience, 22*(3), 1126–1136.

Kauer, J. A., & Malenka, R. C. (2007). Synaptic plasticity and addiction. *Nature Reviews Neuroscience, 8*, 844–858.

Koob, G., & Kreek, M. J. (2007). Stress, dysregulation of drug reward pathways, and the transition to drug dependence. *American Journal of Psychiatry, 164*(8), 1149–1159.

Koob, G., & Le Moal, M. (2000). Drug addiction, dysregulation of reward, and allostasis. *Neuropsychopharmacology, 24*(2), 97–129.

Marinelli, M. (2005). The many facets of the locomotor response to a novel environment test: Theoretical comment on Mitchell, Cunningham, and Mark (2005). *Behavioral Neuroscience, 119*(4), 1144–1151.

McFarland, K., Davidge, S. B., Lapish, C. C., & Kalivas, P. W. (2004). Limbic and motor circuitry underlying footshock-induced reinstatement of cocaine-seeking behavior. *Journal of Neuroscience, 24*(7), 1551–1560.

McFarland, K., Lapish, C. C., & Kalivas, P. W. (2003). Prefrontal glutamate release into the core of the nucleus accumbens mediates cocaine-induced reinstatement of drug-seeking behavior. *Journal of Neuroscience, 23*(8), 3531–3537.

Mitchell, J. M., Cunningham, C. L., & Mark, G. P. (2005). Locomotor activity predicts acquisition of self-administration behavior but not cocaine intake. *Behavioral Neuroscience, 119*(4), 464–472.

Morgan, D., Liu, Y., & Roberts, D. C. S. (2006). Rapid and persistent sensitization to the reinforcing effects of cocaine. *Neuropsychopharmacology, 31*(1), 121–128.

Mueller, D., & Stewart, J. (2000). Cocaine-induced conditioned place preference: Reinstatement by priming injections of cocaine after extinction. *Behavioural Brain Research, 115*(1), 39–47.

Olds, J., & Milner, P. (1954). Positive reinforcement produced by electrical stimulation of septal area and other regions of rat brain. *Journal of Comparative and Physiological Psychology, 47*(6), 419–427.

Piazza, P. V., & Le Moal, M. (1996) Pathphysiological basis of vulnerability to drug abuse: Role of an interaction between stress, glucocorticoids, and dopaminergic neurons. *Annual Review of Pharmacology & Toxicology, 36*, 359–378.

Piazza, P. V., Deminière, J. M., Le Moal, M., & Simon, H. (1989) Factors that predict individual vulnerability to amphetamine self-administration. *Science, 245*(4925), 1511–1513.

Piazza, P. V., Deroche-Gamonent, V., Rouge-Pont, F., & Le Moal, M. (2000). Vertical shifts in self-administration dose-response functions predict a drug-vulnerable phenotype predisposed to addiction. *Journal of Neuroscience, 20*(11), 4226–4232.

Ray Li, C.-S., Huang, C., Yan, P., Bhagwagar, Z., Milivojevic, V., & Sinha, R. (2008). Neural correlates of impulse control during stop signal inhibition in cocaine-dependent men. *Neuropsychopharmacology, 33*(8), 1798–1806.

Robinson, T. E., & Berridge, K. C. (1993). The neural basis of drug craving: An incentive-sensitization theory of addiction. *Brain Research Reviews, 18*(3), 247–291.

Robinson, T. E., & Berridge, K. C. (2003). Addiction. *Annual Review of Psychology, 54*(1), 25–53.

Schenk, S., & Partridge, B. (2000). Sensitization to cocaine's reinforcing effects produced by various cocaine pretreatment regimens in rats. *Pharmacology Biochemistry & Behavior, 66*(4), 765–770.

Shaham, Y., Shalev, U., Lu, L., De Wit, H., & Stewart, J. (2003) The reinstatement model of drug relapse: History, methodology and major findings. *Psychopharmacology, 168*(1-2), 3–20.

Stein, L. (1964). Self-stimulation of the brain and the central stimulant action of amphetamine. *Federation Proceedings, 23*, 836–850.

Stewart, J., & Vezina, P. (1988). Conditioning and behavioral sensitization. In P. W. Kalivas & C. D. Barnes (Eds.), *Sensitization in the nervous system* (pp. 207–224). New Jersey: Telford Press.

Thorndike, E. L. (1911). *Animal intelligence*. New York: Macmillan.

Wise, R. A. (1982). Neuroleptics and operant behavior: The anhedonia hypothesis. *Behavioral and Brain Sciences, 5,* 39–87.

DARRYL NEILL

REWARD PATHWAYS AND DRUGS.

Two sources of reinforcement can be found in drug-taking behavior associated with the use, abuse, and addiction to drugs: positive and negative reinforcement. Positive reinforcement occurs when presentation of a drug increases the probability of a response to obtain the drug. Animal models of the positive reinforcing or rewarding effects of drugs are extensive and well validated. They include intravenous drug self-administration, conditioned place preference, and brain stimulation reward. Drugs of abuse are readily self-administered by animals that are not dependent; therefore, positive reinforcement and intravenous drug self-administration have been used to predict abuse liability.

Negative reinforcement occurs when presentation of the drug prevents the aversive consequences of removal of the drug, usually in the context of drug dependence. Animal models of the negative reinforcement associated with drug dependence include measures of conditioned place aversion (rather than preference) to precipitated withdrawal or spontaneous withdrawal from chronic administration of a drug, increases in reward thresholds using brain stimulation reward, and dependence-induced increases in drug-taking and drug-seeking behavior. Such increased self-administration in dependent animals has been observed with cocaine, methamphetamine, nicotine, heroin, and alcohol.

BRAIN REWARD PATHWAYS

Electrical brain stimulation reward (or intracranial self-stimulation) has a long history as a measure of activity of the brain reward system and of the acute reinforcing effects of drugs of abuse. Brain stimulation reward involves widespread neurocircuitry in the brain, but the most sensitive sites defined by the lowest thresholds involve the trajectory of the medial forebrain bundle connecting the ventral tegmental area with the basal forebrain (Olds & Milner, 1954). While much emphasis was focused initially on the role of the ascending monoamine systems in the medial forebrain bundle, other non-dopaminergic systems in the medial forebrain bundle clearly have a key role (Hernandez et al., 2006).

EFFECTS OF DRUGS OF ABUSE ON BRAIN REWARD THRESHOLDS

All drugs of abuse, when administered acutely to nondependent animals, decrease brain stimulation reward thresholds (Kornetsky & Esposito, 1979). Measures of brain reward function during acute abstinence from all major drugs with dependence potential have revealed increases in brain reward thresholds measured by direct brain stimulation reward. These increases in reward thresholds may reflect decreases in the activity of reward neurotransmitter systems in the midbrain and forebrain implicated in the positive reinforcing effects of drugs (Koob et al., 2004).

NEUROCIRCUITRY OF POSITIVE REINFORCEMENT ASSOCIATED WITH DRUGS OF ABUSE

The acute reinforcing effects of drugs of abuse are mediated by the activation of dopamine, serotonin, opioid peptides, and gamma-aminobutyric acid (GABA) systems, either by direct actions in the basal forebrain (notably the nucleus accumbens and central nucleus of the amygdala) or by indirect actions in the ventral tegmental area (Koob & Le Moal, 2001). Much evidence exists to support the hypothesis that the mesolimbic dopamine system is dramatically activated by psychostimulant drugs during limited-access self-administration and to some extent by all drugs of abuse. Serotonin systems, particularly those involving serotonin 5-HT$_{1B}$ receptor activation in the nucleus accumbens, also have been implicated in the acute reinforcing effects of psychostimulant drugs. Opioid peptides in the ventral striatum have been hypothesized to mediate the acute reinforcing effects of ethanol self-administration, largely based on the effects of opioid antagonists. Mu opioid receptors in both the nucleus accumbens and ventral tegmental area mediate the reinforcing effects of opioid drugs. GABAergic systems are activated pre- and postsynaptically in the amygdala by ethanol at intoxicating doses, and GABA antagonists block ethanol self-administration (Koob, 2006; Nestler, 2005).

NEUROCIRCUITRY OF NEGATIVE REINFORCEMENT ASSOCIATED WITH DRUGS OF ABUSE

During the development of dependence, the brain systems in the ventral striatum that are important for the acute reinforcing effects of drugs of abuse, such as dopamine and opioid peptides, become compromised and begin to contribute to a negative reinforcement mechanism. Here, the drug is taken to restore the decreased function of the reward systems. However, the extended amygdala, a neuroanatomical entity with neurotransmitter systems that have been implicated in stress, is involved in the negative reinforcement associated with drug taking during dependence. The extended amygdala is composed of the central nucleus of the amygdala, the bed nucleus of the stria terminalis, and a transition zone in the medial (shell) subregion of the nucleus accumbens (Heimer & Alheid, 1991). Several key neurotransmitters localized to the extended amygdala, such as corticotropin-releasing factor (CRF), norepinephrine, and dynorphin, have been shown to be activated during stress, in anxiety-like states, and during drug withdrawal in dependent animals. More importantly, antagonists of these neurochemical systems selectively block drug self-administration in dependent animals, suggesting a key role for these neurotransmitters in the extended amygdala in the negative reinforcement associated with drug dependence.

ROLE OF POSITIVE AND NEGATIVE REINFORCEMENT MECHANISMS IN ADDICTION

The brain reward system is thus implicated in both the positive reinforcement produced by drugs of abuse (ventral striatum) and the negative reinforcement produced by dependence (extended amygdala). Neuropharmacological studies in animal models of addiction have provided evidence for the dysregulation of specific neurochemical systems (dopamine, opioid peptides, GABA) in the ventral striatum associated with positive reinforcement (reward). Recruitment of brain stress systems (CRF, dynorphin, and norepinephrine) in the extended amygdala provides the negative motivational state associated with drug abstinence. The changes in reward and stress systems are hypothesized to contribute to the increased motivation to take drugs in dependence and to remain outside a homeostatic state post-acute dependence,

and as such they contribute to the vulnerability for relapse in addiction.

See also **Research, Animal Model: An Overview.**

BIBLIOGRAPHY

Heimer, L., & Alheid, G. (1991). Piecing together the puzzle of basal forebrain anatomy. In T. C. Napier, P. W. Kalivas, & I. Hanin (Eds.), *The Basal Forebrain: Anatomy to Function: Vol. 295. Advances in Experimental Medicine and Biology* (pp. 1–42). New York: Plenum Press.

Hernandez, G., Hamdani, S., Rajabi, H., Conover, K., Stewart, J., Arvanitogiannis, A., et al. (2006). Prolonged rewarding stimulation of the rat medial forebrain bundle: Neurochemical and behavioral consequences. *Behavioral Neuroscience, 120,* 888–904.

Koob, G. F. (2006). The neurobiology of addiction: A neuroadaptational view relevant for diagnosis. *Addiction, 101* (Suppl. 1), 23–30.

Koob, G. F., Ahmed, S. H., Boutrel, B., Chen, S. A., Kenny, P. J., Markou, A., et al. (2004). Neurobiological mechanisms in the transition from drug use to drug dependence. *Neuroscience and Biobehavioral Reviews, 27,* 739–749.

Koob, G. F., & Le Moal, M. (2001). Drug addiction, dysregulation of reward, and allostasis. *Neuropsychopharmacology, 24,* 97–129.

Kornetsky, C., & Esposito, R. U. (1979). Euphorigenic drugs: Effects on the reward pathways of the brain. *Federation Proceedings, 38,* 2473–2476.

Nestler, E. J. (2005). Is there a common molecular pathway for addiction? *Nature Neuroscience, 8,* 1445–1449.

GEORGE F. KOOB

RHETORIC OF ADDICTION.

Typically drug and alcohol researchers answer the question, "What is addiction?" by identifying a biological or psychological process that takes place within an individual and then determining whether this process is best understood as a disease, a disorder, a syndrome, or a learned behavior. This approach implies that there is a universal truth of addiction underlying the observed diversity of addictive symptoms and experiences. Scientific research is seen as the key to revealing the truth of addiction; in particular, neurological models of reward have become prominent in explaining the ability of alcohol and drugs to produce dependence (Koob et al., 1990).

However, there is a very different approach to understanding addiction that shifts the discussion from the question of what addiction really is. Instead, it focuses on addiction as a particular way of thinking and talking about problems of desire, consumption, and self-control. This rhetorical or discursive approach emphasizes the role of language in shaping beliefs and experiences. It is influenced by the work of post-structuralist philosopher Michel Foucault (1926–1984), who argued that discourses systematically produce the objects and subjects of which they speak. Moreover, discourses determine what can be said about a topic and what can be recognized as true (Foucault, 1971).

The discursive approach examines, therefore, how different institutions and forms of knowledge, including medicine, law, government, education, self-help literature, twelve-step groups, and popular culture construct addiction. While the notion of addiction as a discrete disease or disease-like entity has become dominant, different discourses produce different understandings of addiction, and contradictions and tensions also exist within discourses (Reinarman, 2005). Thus, the identity of addiction and the identity of the addict are mobile and elusive. Depending on the discursive context, the addict may be a sinner requiring redemption, a patient requiring treatment, a tragic victim requiring help, a criminal requiring punishment, or an educator with a unique insight into the dangers of alcohol and drugs.

The proliferation of addictions that took place during the 1980s and 1990s heightened the impact of discursive analyses. As addiction discourse expanded to include objects and activities such as food, sex, work, and exercise, its expression of specific cultural and moral anxieties became increasingly visible. For example, sex addiction emerged at a time when the HIV/AIDS epidemic resonated with the idea of lust and sex as dangerous and uncontrollable forces (Irvine, 1995). More broadly, as literary theorist Eve Sedgwick has argued, addiction discourse is driven by a hierarchical dichotomy in which rationality and freedom of will are constantly threatened by compulsive desire. The more people subject their desires to scrutiny, looking for the perfect space of freedom, the more elusive this freedom becomes as every desire is

revealed to be compromised by compulsion (Sedgwick, 1995).

The expansion of addiction also revealed tensions in medical models. On the one hand, medical discourse stressed the importance of distinguishing between genuine substance addictions and popular notions such as food addiction (Miller, 1995). On the other hand, the emphasis on the subjective experience of compulsion and the presence of harmful consequences in diagnosing addiction, found in the *DSM-IV* criteria for substance dependence, suggests that the disorder can be produced by objects and activities other than psychoactive drugs (American Psychiatric Association, 1994).

One effect of taking a discursive approach to addiction is that the historical and cultural specificity of the concept is highlighted. Rather than being a universal feature of human existence, addiction is a specific way of classifying and regulating certain problems of individual conduct. In his 1978 article "The Discovery of Addiction," Harry Levine describes the pre-modern world as a world without addiction. He argues that while heavy drinking and habitual drunkenness certainly existed in colonial America, this behavior was not viewed as pathological. The notion of alcoholism as a disease of the will only developed in the nineteenth century with the rise of the temperance movement and its vision of the desire for drink as a force that could take over the drinker's life. Social and economic changes that made self-control and discipline crucial traits for success also occurred at this time, enhancing the impact of the addiction concept. Loss of control continues in the twenty-first century to be a central feature of both popular and medical accounts of addiction. As many critics have observed, the threat of losing self-control acquires resonance in individualistic societies in which a person's internal qualities are taken to be the determinants of success and happiness (Room, 2003). Indeed the disorder of addiction makes sense because of a belief in the possibility and importance of self control along with recognition of its fragility.

AA DISCOURSE

Alcoholics Anonymous and other self-help recovery groups have produced an influential and distinctive addiction discourse built around the notion of alcoholism and other addictions as incurable diseases of the self. While the disease entity described in self-help literature is dismissed by some medical experts as vague and unsupported by evidence, its linking of physical and spiritual malaise clearly captures the experience of addiction for many (Keane, 2002). In AA discourse, alcoholism is a biomedical disease with specific symptoms and a predictable course. But more importantly, it is also a moral sickness characterized by self-pity, self-centeredness, and dishonesty; hence recovery requires personal transformation as well as abstinence from alcohol. This hybrid model of disease is central to AA's pragmatic yet demanding approach to recovery. In the *12 Steps of Alcoholics Anonymous*, the inner self is constructed as an object for inspection and rectification. A habit of vigilant self-monitoring is the price of recovery, but lapses are accepted as part of the process (Nowinski & Baker, 1998).

A central feature of AA discourse is the construction of addiction as an identity, rather than a behavior. According to AA, an alcoholic is fundamentally different from a normal drinker, and an alcoholic with twenty years of sobriety is still an alcoholic. To critics, envisioning addiction as an all-encompassing and inescapable master identity that explains everything about a person is restrictive, makes the person pathological, and is not mindful enough of the social factors that encourage harmful forms of consumption (Keane, 2002). But for other commentators, the sense of identity encapsulated in the ritual statement, "I am James and I am an alcoholic," is a powerful expression of community membership and personal transformation. In his sympathetic account of AA discourse, George Jensen argues that this phrase combines both a before and after self; a past self who drank and a present self who does not drink and is trying to live in a new way (2000). The same discourse is open to multiple interpretations, but the autobiographical and confessional mode of self-presentation encouraged by AA is unmistakable (Alasuutari, 1992).

MEDICAL DISCOURSE

In contrast, medical and scientific discourse on addiction presents itself as objective and rational, an antidote to the moral judgment and sensationalism found in popular and public arenas. Neurological accounts of addiction that highlight the effect of drugs on brain chemistry have the authority of a hard science supposedly uncontaminated by cultural and social factors. Their success has depended in part on advances in brain imaging

technologies. Research that uses positron emission tomography (PET) and magnetic resonance imaging (MRI) scans to demonstrate the difference between the addicted and non-addicted brains is rhetorically powerful because these images are seen as revealing the so-called hidden reality of the brain. But these computer-generated images do not provide unmediated access to a hidden object; rather, they translate non-visible phenomena into visual representations. When a cocaine-using subject's neurotransmitter activity is translated into a pattern of color and contrasted with the pattern produced by a brain categorized as normal, a particular conception of addiction as a discrete disorder located within in an individual is made concrete (see Grant et al., 1996). Such images are part of a discourse of addiction, not objective external proof of the validity of that discourse. Their meaning relies on a prior classification of individuals into addicted/not addicted and unhealthy/healthy that is based on an assessment of behavior rather than biological or chemical markers.

The process of diagnosing addiction further demonstrates the limits of objectivity in medical discourse as it relies on judgments about what a so-called normal life looks like, how an apparently healthy body functions, and how personal priorities should be organized. Diagnostic guidelines and screening tests for alcoholism emphasize the subject's feelings and thoughts rather than specifying a level of consumption or physical markers of excessive intake (Valverde, 1998). Is the drinker preoccupied with drinking? Does the drinker feel compelled to drink? Does the drinker feel guilty or worried about habitual drinking? Withdrawal and tolerance are listed in the *DSM-IV* criteria but are not necessary for a diagnosis of substance dependence. What is being identified is not a biological state so much as a pathological relationship to the substance, in which drinking or drug use has assumed too high a priority.

Moreover, the existence of compulsion or impaired control, which is central to the diagnosis of addiction, can only be ascertained through self-reported experiences or behavior observed by others. Binge drinking, staying drunk for days at a time, drinking more than one intended to when one began, and neglecting responsibilities because of drinking are frequently read as signs of compulsion. But the meaning of these experiences is profoundly influenced by social and cultural context, and thus they seem less than robust as the basis for the identification of a disease or disorder (Measham & Brain, 2005). For example, the utility of *neglect of responsibilities* as a measurement of loss of control depends on the salience of those responsibilities to the individual.

A related feature of addiction that is stressed in medical models is continued drug and alcohol use despite harmful consequences such as job loss, relationship conflicts, and health problems. This feature takes for granted a certain level and style of social functioning, assuming that in the absence of drug use, the individual would not be facing issues such as unemployment and poverty. It also assumes middle-class norms of respectability: For a sex worker or bartender, heavy drinking could aid rather than hinder job performance (Valverde, 1998). Drug use can also facilitate as well as impede relationships and time management; for some, it is quitting that brings loneliness and lack of structure. The interpretation of social harms as signs of addiction can lead to a circular logic in which the existence of work and family problems defines addiction and addiction implies the presence of work and family problems. This process can result in the almost automatic attribution of pathology to members of negatively valued groups such as welfare mothers or unemployed youth (Keane, 2005).

DISCOURSE, POWER AND EXPERIENCE

Discursive analyses draw attention to the exercise of power in descriptions and attributions of addiction. Addiction discourses promote the expansion of expert and governmental power over individuals, and while they may have beneficial as well as oppressive effects, their combination of medical and ethical judgment gives them a potent ability to categorize and regulate. Moreover, their classification of bodies and subjects often coincides with existing hierarchies of social value, reproducing inequalities of race, class, sex, and sexuality. For example, while claiming an addict identity may be a useful strategy for a rich white celebrity caught using drugs, poor black mothers identified as addicted are liable to face demonization and punitive intervention (Campbell, 2000). More generally, while conceptualizing addiction as a disease can undermine moralistic accounts of addicts as simply weak-willed, addicts are placed in an infantilized position in which their own views about

their predicament can be dismissed if they contradict expert opinion (Sedgwick, 2005).

Discourse analysis has been criticized for privileging texts, language, and theory at the cost of engaging with the lived and embodied reality of individual experience (Ramazanoglu, 2002). In the case of addiction, the danger of minimizing the terrible impact of compulsive behaviors on many people's lives and the magnitude of their struggles to change their behavior are seen as especially acute. It is the case that discursive scholarship destabilizes the notion of experience by focusing on the way experience is constructed, and it is undeniable that therapeutic outcomes are not its primary concern. However, in critically examining the authoritative and complex forms of knowledge that frame individual experiences of addiction and the range of possible responses to that experience, studies of discourse and rhetoric are an essential component of addiction research.

See also **Addiction: Concepts and Definitions.**

BIBLIOGRAPHY

Alasuutari, P. (1992). *Desire and craving: A cultural theory of alcoholism*. Albany: State University of New York Press.

American Psychiatric Association. (1994). *Diagnostic and statistical manual of mental disorders, fourth edition*. Washington DC: Author.

Campbell, N. (2000). *Using women: Gender, drug policy and social justice*. New York: Routledge.

Foucault, M. (1971). Orders of discourse. *Social Science Information, 10*(2), 7–30.

Grant, S., London, E., Newlin, D., Villemagre, V., Liu, X, Contoreggi, C., et al. (1996). Activation of memory circuits during cue-elicited cocaine craving. *Proceedings of the National Academy of Science, 93*, 12040–12045.

Irvine, J. M. (1995). Reinventing perversion: Sex addiction and cultural anxieties. *Journal of the History of Sexuality, 5*(3), 429–449.

Jensen, G. (2000). *Storytelling in Alcoholics Anonymous: A rhetorical analysis*. Carbondale: Southern Illinois University Press.

Keane, H. (2002). *What's wrong with addiction?* New York: New York University Press.

Keane, H. (2005). Addiction and the bioethics of compulsion and dependency. In M. Shildrick & R. Mykitiuk (Eds.), *Ethics of the body: Postconventional challenges* (pp. 91–112). Cambridge, MA: MIT Press.

Koob, G. F., Barak, C., Hyytia, P., Markou, A., Parsons, L. H., Roberts, A. J., et al. (1999). Neurobiology of drug addiction. In M. D. Glantz & C. R. Hartel (Eds.),

Drug abuse: Origins and interventions (pp. 161–190). Washington, DC: American Psychological Association.

Levine, H. G. (1978). The discovery of addiction: Changing conceptions of habitual drunkenness in America. *Journal of Studies on Alcohol, 39*(1), 143–174.

Measham, F., & Brain, K. (2005). Binge drinking, British alcohol policy and the new culture of intoxication. *Crime, Media, Culture, 1*(3), 262–283.

Miller, N. S. (1995). *Addiction psychiatry: Current diagnosis and treatment.* New York: Wiley-Liss.

Nowinski, J., & Baker, S. (1998). *The twelve-step facilitation handbook: A systematic approach to early recovery.* San Francisco: Jossey-Bass.

Ramazanoglu, C. (with Holland, J.). (2002). Feminist methodology: Challenges and choices. London: Sage.

Reinarman, C. (2005). Addiction as accomplishment: The discursive construction of disease. *Addiction Research and Theory, 13*(4), 307–320.

Room, R. (2003). The cultural framing of addiction. *Janus Head, 6*(2), 221–234.

Sedgwick, E. K. (1992). Epidemics of the will. In J. Crary & S. Kwinter (Eds.), *Incorporations* (pp. 582–595). New York: Zone Books.

Valverde, M. (1998). *Diseases of the will: Alcohol and the dilemmas of freedom.* Cambridge, England: Cambridge University Press.

HELEN KEANE

RISK FACTORS FOR SUBSTANCE USE, ABUSE, AND DEPENDENCE

This entry includes the following essays:

AN OVERVIEW
DRUG EFFECTS AND BIOLOGICAL RESPONSES
GENDER
GENETIC FACTORS
LEARNING
PERSONALITY
PSYCHODYNAMIC PERSPECTIVE
RACE/ETHNICITY
SENSATION SEEKING AND IMPULSIVITY
SEXUAL AND PHYSICAL ABUSE
STRESS

AN OVERVIEW

Risk factors for use, abuse, and dependence on alcohol and drugs are characteristics of individuals or environments that increase risk. Such factors are not absolute determinants of alcohol and drug use or problems but, rather, factors that affect the probability that individuals with these factors will use, abuse, or become dependent on a given substance.

Much individual variation occurs within groups and societies in alcohol and drug use, abuse, and dependence. Some people never use substances although they are readily available in their environments. Others use drugs sporadically or regularly for a short time, or for years, and yet never become dependent. Others become dependent but remit, whereas still others become chronic heavy users who cannot stop despite great costs to themselves and those close to them. The various patterns of use result from a complex combination of environmental and genetic factors.

Risk factors for substance use, abuse, and dependence have been reported at various levels ranging from macro or large-scale societal factors to the molecular level. Large-scale changes in the prevalence of use over time in society indicate shifting macro-level factors. For alcohol, good sources of information on long-term time trends in the U.S. are per capita alcohol consumption statistics (http://pubs.niaaa. nih.gov/). For drugs, a good source of information on time-term time trends is the information from yearly surveys of U.S. high school and college students known as Monitoring the Future (http:// www.monitoringthefuture.org). General articles about sociodemographic risk factors for alcohol abuse and dependence (Hasin et al., 2007a; Compton et al., 2007) in 2001 and 2002 in the United States show that among adult residents of households or group quarters (such as college dormitories), a current or lifetime history of alcohol or drug abuse or dependence was associated with being male, younger, unmarried, of lower socio-economic status, and being white or Native American compared to black, Hispanic, or Asian race/ethnicity.

Macro-level factors affecting use of alcohol and drugs include influences such as laws (local or nationwide) against any use or sales (e.g., drugs) or laws that target certain age groups (e.g., minimum drinking age laws) (Voas et al., 2003; Hingson et al., 1998). An example is the Eighteenth Amendment to the U.S. Constitution, which from 1920 to 1933 outlawed the manufacture, transport, and sale of alcohol. This law was effective in limiting alcohol consumption in the United States. Some scholars believe its unpopularity led to its demise, while others maintain that the amendment was repealed because it was not enforceable and may have actually caused crime to escalate. The strength of law enforcement has also been shown to influence use. Pricing is another macro-level factor that affects alcohol and drug use, as higher prices tend to decrease use (Chaloupka et al., 2002). Availability influences use; for example, the density of alcohol outlets within given geographic areas can affect the proportion of substance users. (LaScala et al., 2001). Advertising and marketing strategies can also influence the use of legal substances, for example, alcohol and cigarettes.

In terms of more local environmental influences, adolescent peer groups have long been shown to influence substance use (Walden et al., 2004; Agrawal et al., 2007). However, while peer groups may provide modeling of substance use and access to substances, recognition has increased that adolescents with certain partially heritable personality traits may seek peer groups that include substance abusers (Kendler et al., 2007). Consequently, the relationship between substance-using peer groups and adolescent substance use is not entirely causal.

External traumatic or stressful experiences can increase the use of substances, as has been shown by both animal and human studies. Childhood abuse is a risk factor for use of substances and for becoming dependent on them (Nelson et al., 2006; Kendler et al., 2000). The role of adult stressors is more difficult to determine because some personality traits associated with substance use (e.g., sensation seeking) may also increase the risk for traumatic experiences such as serious accidents. In such cases, an apparent relationship between accidents and subsequent substance use could actually be due to the common underlying sensation seeking personality trait, and attributing the substance use to the accident would be incorrect. A study that overcomes this difficulty is one that examines adolescent or adult civilian exposure to terrorism, since such exposure to traumatic experiences is independent of any personality or other personal characteristics and thus serves as a type of so-called natural experiment for understanding the relationship of stress exposure and subsequent alcohol or substance use. A series of studies in the United States and Israel have shown that adolescents' exposure to terrorism increases the risk

for use of alcohol and drugs (Schiff et al., 2007; Wu et al., 2006) and adults (Hasin et al., 2007b).

While no single personality trait predicts alcoholism (Sher et al., 2005), traits associated with the development of substance use disorders include novelty seeking (Cloninger et al., 1995) and sensation seeking (Zuckerman & Kuhlman, 2000; Martin et al, 2004). These traits also have their own risk factors, which include environmental and genetic influences.

Cognitive factors that affect the risk for substance use and substance use disorders include expectancies and motivations. *Expectancies* (positive or negative) are beliefs about the expected effects of alcohol or another substance, that is, that use will make the user more social, feel good, or lead to some sort of problem (Goldman & Rather, 1993). A twin study indicated that alcohol expectancies are due to environmental rather than genetic influences (Slutske et al., 2002). Motivations are the reasons that individuals actually use the substances, that is, to socialize, to fit in, because the effects are enjoyable (Cooper et al., 1995). Drinking to cope with negative feelings and emotions has been associated with problem drinking in a number of studies (Mann et al., 1987; Carpenter & Hasin, 1998; Beseler et al., 2008). While expectancies and motives are related, they are not necessarily entirely overlapping.

Neuroscientists investigate aspects of brain functioning and neurotransmission as risk factors or causes of alcohol and drug use, abuse, and dependence. In addition, genetic influences are known to affect the risk for alcohol and drug use and dependence.

See also **Abuse Liability of Therapeutic Drugs: Testing in Animals; Addiction: Concepts and Definitions; Complications: Mental Disorders; Conduct Disorder and Drug Use; Epidemiology of Drug Abuse; Models of Alcoholism and Drug Abuse.**

BIBLIOGRAPHY

Agrawal, A., Lynskey, M. T., Bucholz, K. K., Madden, P. A., & Heath, A. C. (2007). Correlates of cannabis initiation in a longitudinal sample of young women: The importance of peer influences. *American Journal of Preventative Medicine, 45*(1), 31–34.

Beseler, C., Aharonovich, E., Keyes, K., & Hasin, D. (2008). Adult transition from at-risk drinking to alcohol dependence: The relationship of family history and drinking motives. *Alcoholism Clinical and Experimental Research,32*(4), 607–616.

Carpenter, K. M., & Hasin, D. (1998) A prospective evaluation of the relationship between reasons for drinking and *DSM-IV* alcohol use disorders. *Psychology of Addictive Behavior, 23,* 41–46.

Chaloupka, F. J., Grossman, M., & Saffer, H. (2002). The effects of price on alcohol consumption and alcohol-related problems. *Alcohol Research and Health, 26,* 22–34.

Cloninger, C. R., Sigvardsson, S., Przybeck, T. R., & Svrakic, D. M. (1995). Personality antecedents of alcoholism in a national area probability sample. *European Archives of Psychiatry and Clinical Neuroscience, 245,* 239–244.

Compton, W. M., Thomas, Y. F., Stinson, F. S., & Grant, B. F. (2007). Prevalence, correlates, disability, and comorbidity of *DSM-IV* drug abuse and dependence in the United States: Results from the national epidemiologic survey on alcohol and related conditions. *Archives of General Psychiatry, 64*(5), 566–576.

Cooper, M. L., Frone, M. R., Russell, M., & Mudar, P. (1995). Drinking to regulate positive and negative emotions: A motivational model of alcohol use. *Journal of personality and social psychology, 69,* 990–1005.

Goldman, M. S., & Rather, B. C. (1993). Substance use disorders: Cognitive models and architecture. In K. S. Dobson & P. C. Kendall (Eds.), *Psychopathology and cognition* (pp. 245–292). New York: Academic Press.

Hasin, D. S., Stinson, F. S., Ogburn, E., & Grant, B. F. (2007a). Prevalence, correlates, disability, and comorbidity of *DSM-IV* alcohol abuse and dependence in the United States: Results from the National Epidemiologic Survey on Alcohol and Related Conditions. *Archives of General Psychiatry, 64*(7), 830–842.

Hasin, D. S., Keyes, K. M., Hatzenbuehler, M. L., Aharonovich, E. A., & Alderson, D. (2007b). Alcohol consumption and posttraumatic stress after exposure to terrorism: Effects of proximity, loss, and psychiatric history. *American Journal of Public Health, 97*(12), 2268–2275.

Hingson, R., Heeren, T., & Winter, M. (1998). Effects of Maine's 0.05% legal blood alcohol level for drivers with DWI convictions. *Public Health Reports, 113,* 440–446.

Kendler, K. S., Bulik, C. M., Silberg, J., Hettema, J. M., Myers, J., & Prescott, C. A. (2000). Childhood sexual abuse and adult psychiatric and substance use disorders in women: An epidemiological and co-twin control analysis. *Archives of General Psychiatry, 57*(10), 953–959.

Kendler, K. S., Jacobson, K. C., Gardner, C. O., Gillespie, N., Aggen, S. A., & Prescott, C. A. (2007). Creating a social world: A developmental twin study of peer-group deviance. *Archives of General Psychiatry, 64*(8), 958–965.

Lascala, E. A., Johnson, F. W., & Gruenewald, P. J. (2001). Neighborhood characteristics of alcohol-related pedestrian injury collisions: A geostatistical analysis. *Prevention Science, 2,* 123–134.

Mann, L. M., Chassin, L., & Sher, K. J. (1987). Alcohol expectancies and the risk for alcoholism. *Journal of Consulting and Clinical Psychology, 55,* 411–417.

Martin, C. A., Kelly, T. H., Rayens, M. K., Artin, C. A., Brogli, B. R., Himelreich, K., et al. (2004). Sensation seeking and symptoms of disruptive disorder: Association with nicotine, alcohol, and marijuana use in early and mid-adolescence. *Psychological Reports, 94,* 1075–1082.

Nelson, E. C., Heath, A. C., Lynskey, M. T., Bucholz, K. K., Madden, P. A., Statham, D. J., et al. (2006). Childhood sexual abuse and risks for licit and illicit drug-related outcomes: A twin study. *Psychological Medicine, 36*(10), 1473–1483.

Schiff, M., Zweig, H. H., Benbenishty, R., & Hasin, D. S. (2007). Exposure to terrorism and Israeli youths' cigarette, alcohol, and cannabis use. *American Journal of Public Health, 97*(10), 1852–1858.

Sher, K. J., Grekin, E. R., & Williams, N. A. (2005). The development of alcohol use disorders. *Annual Review of Clinical Psychology, 1*(22),1–31.

Slutske, W. S., Cronk, N. J., Sher, K. J., Madden, P. A., Bucholz, K. K., & Heath, C. C. (2002). Genes, environment, and individual differences in alcohol expectancies among female adolescents and young adults. *Psychology of Addictive Behavior, 16,* 308–317.

Voas, R. B., Tippetts, A. S., & Fell, J. C. (2003). Assessing the effectiveness of minimum legal drinking age and zero tolerance laws in the United States. *Accident Analysis and Prevention, 35,* 579–587.

Walden, B., McGue, M., Lacono, W. G., Burt, S. A., & Elkins, I. (2004). Identifying shared environmental contributions to early substance use: The respective roles of peers and parents. *Journal of Abnormal Psychology, 113*(3), 440–450.

Wu, P., Duarte, C. S., Mandell, D. J., Fan, B., Liu, X., Fuller, C. J., et al. (2006). Exposure to the World Trade Center attack and the use of cigarettes and alcohol among New York City public high-school students. *American Journal of Public Health, 96*(5), 804–807.

Zuckerman, M., & Kuhlman, D. (2000). Personality and risk-taking: Common biosocial factors. *Journal of Personality and Social Psychology, 68,* 999–1029.

DEBORAH HASIN

DRUG EFFECTS AND BIOLOGICAL RESPONSES

Although many indirect factors lead to an individual abusing drugs, a person's response to the effects of the drugs themselves contribute both to their use and abuse. These drug effects should be considered in relation to four phases of drug use: (1) initiation-consolidation, (2) maintenance, (3) repeated withdrawal and relapse, and (4) postwithdrawal. During the initiation-consolidation phase, behaviors that lead to the taking of a drug are gradually strengthened through operant and classical conditioning processes and by biochemical changes in the brain. The drug effects include a cascade of discriminative or internally appreciated drug cues (i.e., subjective effects). The presence of these cues often leads to associated autonomic responses and reports of urges in humans. These responses and urges may result in an unfolding of a sequence of behavioral and physiological events leading to continued drug consumption.

After a pattern of chronic drug use is established, individuals may become tolerant to certain effects of a drug. In addition, they may experience withdrawal effects when they stop taking a drug. Withdrawal effects are often opposite to the drug-induced state and usually involve some form of dysphoria—a state of illness and distress. Over time, withdrawal effects become associated with stimuli in the environment, as was the case for the euphoric and other direct effects of the drug. Because of operant and classical conditioning processes, these associated stimuli can then produce conditioned effects that are often characterized as urges or cravings, and that may trigger relapse.

The underlying neurotransmitter systems within the brain, subserving these behavioral features of drug effects, are just beginning to be understood. Early research on the neural substrates of reward in general used electrical brain stimulation as the reward. For example, Olds (1977) found that rats would press a lever to receive a brief electrical pulse to the hypothalamus; rats would press this lever to such an extent that they did not engage in consummatory reward activities such as eating and drinking. Subsequent research indicated that activation of certain systems in the brain, namely the mesolimbic and nigrostriatal dopaminergic systems, were most sensitive to brain stimulation reinforcement. Several theories have been suggested to explain the importance of the brain reward system for the survival of species (Conrad, 1950; Glickman & Schiff, 1967; O'Donahue & Hagmen, 1967; Roberts & Carey, 1965).

Further research demonstrated that most drugs of abuse lower the threshold for this brain stimulation reward, thus suggesting that such drugs may activate the same, or similar, reward pathways (see Koob & Bloom, 1988). As will be seen, furthermore, the reinforcing effects of the drugs themselves—that is, effects that lead individuals to take the drugs—are directly mediated by these reward systems. The fact that many drugs induce activation of these systems may indicate a mechanism underlying the addiction-related effects of drugs of abuse.

COCAINE AND OTHER STIMULANTS

Cocaine is an indirect catecholamine agonist that acts by blocking the reuptake of monoamines, including dopamine (DA), norepinephrine (NE), and serotonin (5-HT). During the process of reuptake, the previously released neurotransmitter is actively transported back from the synaptic cleft into the presynaptic terminal of the neuron where the neurotransmitter was produced and released (Pitts & Marwah, 1987). In contrast to cocaine, amphetamine acts not only by inhibiting uptake, but also by releasing catecholamines from newly synthesized storage pools from the presynaptic terminal of the neuron (e.g., Carlsson & Waldeck, 1966).

Amphetamine and cocaine are both potent psychomotor stimulants. They produce increased alertness and energy and lower anxiety and social inhibitions. The acute reinforcing actions of the stimulants are primarily determined by their augmentation of DA systems. With prolonged consumption: (1) acute tolerance becomes substantial, and (2) the individual starts to regularly consume higher and many more doses if the resources are available. Over time, in high-dose regimens, the behavioral pattern of use becomes stereotyped and restricted. In settings of low availability, the individual focuses on the acquisition and consumption of the drug. These effects of stimulants occur within weeks or months of continued use. The individual may also start "bingeing" during this period. A binge is characterized by the readministration of the drug approximately every ten to twenty minutes, resulting in frequent mood swings (i.e., alternations of highs and lows). Cocaine binges typically last twelve hours, but may last as long as seven days.

It has been proposed that cocaine abstinence consists of a three-phase pattern: crash, withdrawal, and extinction (Gawin & Kleber, 1986; Gawin & Ellinwood, 1988). The crash phase immediately follows the cessation of a binge and is characterized by initial depression, agitation, and anxiety. Over the first few hours, drug craving is replaced by an intense desire for sleep. During this time, the individual may use alcohol, benzodiazepines, or opiates to induce sleep. Following the crash, hypersomnolence (excessive sleep) and hyperphagia (excessive appetite) develop. Following the first few days of hypersomnolence and hyperphagia, other symptoms emerge that are the opposite of the effects of cocaine—withdrawal symptoms. During this withdrawal period, which lasts three to ten days, individuals experience decreased energy, limited interest in their environment, and anhedonia. They are also strongly susceptible to relapse and starting another binge cycle (Gawin & Ellinwood, 1988; Gawin & Kleber, 1986). This phase is followed in time by the extinction phase, in which relapse to cocaine use is prevented. During the extinction phase, brief periods of drug craving also occur. These episodes of craving are thought to be triggered by conditioned stimuli that were previously associated with the drug. If the individual experiences these cues without the associated drug effects—that is, resists relapse—then the ability of these cues to elicit drug cravings should diminish over time, which in turn should lessen the probability of relapse (Gawin & Ellinwood, 1988).

As already noted, acute administration of cocaine produces profound inhibition of dopaminergic uptake (Fuxe, Hamberger, & Malmfors, 1967). The relation between cocaine dose and DA levels is linear; therefore, larger amounts of cocaine result in higher extracellular DA levels. These levels of DA are thought to underlie the reinforcing effects of cocaine (Gawin & Ellinwood, 1988). Because both cocaine and amphetamine result in enhanced dopaminergic neurotransmission, thereby producing elevated extracellular levels of catecholamines, these elevated neurotransmitter levels would presumably have local time-dependent

	Amphetamine		Cocaine	
	Day I	Day 7	Day 1	Day 7
Autoreceptor sensitivity	sub	super	sub	super
Receptors	decreased	decreased	unclear	unchanged
Biosynthesis	reduced	reduced	unchanged	unchanged
Uptake sites	decreased	decreased	unchanged	unchanged

Table 1. Effects of chronic cocaine and amphetamine administration on dopaminergic functioning. ILLUSTRATION BY GGS INFORMATION SERVICES. GALE, CENGAGE LEARNING

inhibitory effects on the enzyme tyrosine hydroxylase, which is responsible for controlling their rate of synthesis. Therefore, this substrate-inhibitory mechanism might compensate for the increased catecholamine levels and activity by decreasing their synthesis. Galloway (1990) found that cocaine, in a way that was consistent with this proposition, decreased DA synthesis in a dose-dependent manner in various brain regions.

Chronic, intermittent stimulant use (e.g., 1–2 injections per 24 hrs) produces other behavioral effects besides euphoria and increased energy: (1) stimulant psychosis, which is characterized by paranoia, anxiety, stereotyped compulsive behaviors, and hallucinations, and (2) sensitization or "reverse tolerance." Sensitization refers to the fact that the effects of cocaine are progressively enhanced. Although sensitization has been demonstrated in animal studies, it is not clear whether it occurs in humans. There are nevertheless several possible explanations for sensitization. First, because cocaine blocks dopaminergic uptake, chronic cocaine use could somehow harm the functioning of the dopamine uptake mechanism; the evidence regarding this possibility is equivocal (Zahniser et al., 1988b). Second, sensitization could also be the result of enhanced dopaminergic release, similar to that found to be chronic after amphetamine administration (Castaneda, Becker, & Robinson, 1988). Akimoto, Hammamura, & Otsuki (1989) found enhanced DA release in the striatum one week following chronic cocaine administration. Similar data has been obtained by others (Kalivas et al., 1988; King et al., 1993a; Pettit et al., 1990). Cocaine levels in blood and cerebrospinal fluid have also been reported to be elevated in chronically treated subjects (Reith, Benuck, & Lajtha, 1987); however, these increases cannot account for most of the change in DA release (Pettit et al., 1990). Furthermore, some researchers report no consistent effects in this regard. Third, there could be changes in autoreceptor sensitivity following chronic cocaine administration. Autoreceptors for particular neurotransmitters are those receptors that reside on the same neuron that releases the neurotransmitter. The autoreceptors on the somatodendritic area of neurons regulate impulse flow along the neuron, whereas autoreceptors on the terminal regions of the neuron regulate the amount of neurotransmitter released per impulse and neurotransmitter synthesis (Cooper, Bloom, & Roth, 1986). Sensitization could, therefore, be the result of decreased autoreceptor sensitivity. Such subsensitivity would result in either increased impulse flow, if somatodendritic autoreceptors were altered, or increased neurotransmission/synthesis, if terminal autoreceptors were altered. The net effect, in either case, would be an increase in dopaminergic neurotransmission. There is some evidence of decreased somatodendritic autoreceptor sensitivity 24 hours after the cessation of chronic cocaine administration (Henry, Greene, & White, 1989). However, seven days after termination of daily cocaine injections, when cocaine-induced sensitization is still fully present, somatodendritic autoreceptors are no longer reduced in sensitivity (Zhang, Lee, & Ellinwood, 1992). Evidence regarding changes in terminal autoreceptor sensitivity is mixed. Dwoskin and colleagues (1988) found that terminal autoreceptors were supersensitive, not subsensitive, to a DA agonist 24 hours following chronic cocaine use. Henry and associates (1989) also found that terminal autoreceptors were supersensitive to DA following chronic daily cocaine injections. Although autoreceptor supersensitivity cannot explain sensitization, it is a possible mechanism underlying the previously described anhedonia and anergy experienced by cocaine abusers during the withdrawal phase. Fourth and last, there could be an increase in the number or sensitivity of postsynaptic DA receptors. The evidence regarding this hypothesis is also mixed (Zahniser et al., 1988a). For example, Peris and colleagues (1990) found an increased number of postsynaptic D2 receptors in the nucleus accumbens one day following cessation of chronic cocaine administration; however, after one

week the number of receptors had returned to normal levels. In contrast, there is some evidence that post-synaptic DA receptors are decreased following chronic cocaine use. Volkow et al. (1990) found lower uptake values for [18 F]n-methylspiroperidol in human cocaine users who had been abstinent for one week, as compared with normal subjects. Uptake values were similar, however, for normal subjects and cocaine users who had been abstinent for one month.

In contrast with these results, Yi and Johnson (1990) have reported that chronic intermittent cocaine use impairs the regulation of synaptosomal 3[H]-DA release by DA autoreceptors, thus suggesting a subsensitivity or down-regulation of release-modulating DA autoreceptors seven days after chronic cocaine administration. The differences in the results of the Yi and Johnson (1990) and the Dwoskin et al. (1988) studies may be due to differences in the administration schedules or in the procedures used to measure autoreceptor sensitivity.

In contrast with the changes induced by intermittent but chronic drug administration, a regimen that involves the chronic administration of steady-state levels of drug results in decreased DA overflow when striatal brain slices are perfused with cocaine. This result may be due to the development of super-sensitive autoreceptors. Autoreceptor supersensitivity would result in decreased dopaminergic activity. There is some support for this hypothesis from research involving the chronic administration of amphetamine. Lee and colleagues (Lee, Ellinwood, & Nishita, 1988; Lee & Ellinwood, 1989) found that 24 hours after withdrawal from a week of continuous administration of amphetamine, all indicators of autoreceptor activity demonstrated a pronounced subsensitivity. Similar results have been found following the continuous infusion of cocaine (Zhang et al., 1992). However, by the seventh day of withdrawal (a period associated with anergia, irritability, and "urges" in human stimulant abusers), nigrostriatal somatodendritic autoreceptors progress from an initial subsensitivity to a supersensitive state, whereas terminal autoreceptors are normosensitive. The changes in sensitivity of receptors clearly depend on the way the drug is administered and which receptors are evaluated. The evidence, moreover, is not always consistent.

There is also evidence that chronic cocaine administration produces neurotoxicity—i.e., actual destruction of neural tissue—although there are conflicting results and the relationship of this neurotoxicity to the addiction process is unclear. For example, Trulson and colleagues (1986) demonstrated decreased tyrosine hydroxylase activity sixty days after chronic cocaine treatment (see also Trulson & Ulissey, 1987), thereby indicating decreased DA synthesis. (Tyrosine hydroxylase is the rate-limiting step in the biosynthesis of DA; Cooper et al., 1986.) Similarly, Taylor and Ho (1978) found that chronic administration of cocaine decreased tyrosine hydroxylase activity in the caudate, but Seiden and Kleven (1988) were unable to replicate the findings of Trulson. As contrasted with the inconclusive results on cocaine, research involving amphetamine is much clearer. First, chronic methamphetamine administration reduces the number of DA uptake sites (Ricaurte, Schuster, & Seiden, 1980; Ricaurte, Seiden, & Schuster, 1984). Second, DA and tyrosine-betahydroxylase levels are reduced for extended periods following chronic amphetamine administration (Ricaurte et al., 1980, 1984). Third, there is evidence of neuronal degeneration, chromatolysis, and decreased catecholamine histofluorescence (Duarte-Escalante & Ellinwood, 1970).

As with cocaine's effects on DA reuptake, cocaine also blocks 5-HT reuptake. Since activation of 5-HT postsynaptic receptors affects neurotransmission in neurons that release DA, this blockade prolongs the inhibitory effects of 5-HT on dopaminergic neurotransmission (Taylor & Ho, 1978). However, cocaine also inhibits the firing rates of dorsal raphe 5-HT neurons (Cunningham & Lakoski, 1988, 1990). Thus, acutely the net effect of cocaine on 5-HT neurotransmission in the nucleus accumbens will depend on the relative contributions of uptake inhibition, which would increase synaptic 5-HT, and inhibition of neuronal firing, which would decrease synaptic 5-HT. Broderick (1991) reported that acute, subcutaneous injections of cocaine resulted in a dose-dependent increase in DA levels, as measured by dialysis of the nucleus accumbens. This suggests a decrease in 5-HT levels that may result from activation of somatodendritic 5-HT autoreceptors located in the dorsal raphe nucleus. Acute cocaine administration

has indeed been reported to almost completely inhibit the basal firing rate of dorsal raphe serotonergic neurons.

As with the effects of chronic amphetamine administration on the functioning of DA systems, chronic methamphetamine administration has been shown to induce pronounced long-term changes in tryptophan hydroxylase activity, as well as in 5-HT content and number of uptake sites (Ricaurte et al., 1980). The effects of chronic cocaine on serotonergic functioning are less well established. For example, Ho and colleagues (1977) found decreased levels of 5-HT following chronic cocaine administration. Seiden and Kleven (1988). however, failed to find any effects of chronic cocaine on the biosynthesis of serotonin.

Some of these discrepancies can be reconciled by the fact that different chronic dosing regimens produce different changes in 5-HT systems. For example, Cunningham and colleagues found that daily injections of cocaine resulted in an increased sensitivity of dorsal raphe somadendritic 5-HT autoreceptors to cocaine's inhibitory effects as measured by electrophysiological techniques (Cunningham & Lakoski, 1988, 1990). These results are consistent with the behavioral data of King and colleagues (1993a), who found that daily cocaine injections produced an enhanced inhibitory effect of NAN-190 on cocaine-induced locomotion and an enhanced excitatory effect of 8-OH-DPAT on locomotion. In contrast with these results, the continuous infusion of cocaine via an osmotic minipump results in a decreased sensitivity of dorsal raphe somadendritic 5HT autoreceptors and a decreased excitatory effect of 8-OH-DPAT on locomotion (King, Joyner, & Ellinwood, 1993b; King et al., 1993a).

Interestingly, the depletion of 5-HT or reduction of 5-HT neurotransmission is associated with impulsive behavior. For example, Linnoila et al. (1983) found that violent offenders with a diagnosis of personality disorder associated with impulsivity had lower levels of 5-hydroxyindoleacetic acid (5-HIAA, the metabolite of 5-HT) than other offenders. After extensively reviewing the literature, Brown and Linnoila (1990) concluded that low levels of CSF 5-HIAA are related to disinhibition of aggressive/impulsive behavior and not to antisocial acts in and of themselves. The transition to high-dose cocaine use might be considered impulsive behavior because the individual is focusing on the immediate, short-term advantages of drug consumption while ignoring the long-term advantages of drug abstinence. Hence, the 5-HT receptor supersensitivity, and resulting inhibition of 5-HT neurotransmission, may be a contributing factor to the development of the high-dose, bingelike pattern of cocaine abuse.

OPIATES

The opiates are derived from the poppy plant and have been used for centuries. A number of types of endogenous opiate receptors have been identified and their locations mapped. There are high concentrations of opiate receptors in the caudate nucleus, nucleus accumbens, periventricular gray region, and the nucleus arcuatus of medobasal hypothalamus (Pert, Kuhar, & Snyder, 1975, 1976). These areas may be differently involved in the reinforcing, aversive, and dependence-producing effects of the opiates. Furthermore, different receptor subtypes may mediate the different effects of the opiates.

The opiates produce analgesia, changes in mood (e.g., euphoria and tranquility), drowsiness, respiratory depression, and nausea (Jaffe & Martin, 1990). These drugs also reduce motivated behavior; there is a decrease in appetite, sexual drive, and aggression. Intravenous administration of opioids results in initial effects of flushing of the skin and sensations in the abdominal regions that have been likened to a sexual orgasm (Jaffe, 1990).

With continuous use of opioids, marked tolerance develops to some, but not all, of the effects of these drugs. Tolerance to opioids is generally characterized by a shorter duration of effect and attenuated analgesia, euphoria, and other CNS-depressant effects; however, there is less tolerance to the lethal effects of opiates. Therefore, if an individual administers ever larger doses to obtain the same effect (e.g., the rush or high), this may increase the probability of a lethal overdose (Jaffe, 1990).

Although the course and severity of withdrawal symptoms following opiate abstinence depend on which opiate was used, the dose and pattern of consumption, the duration of use, and the interdose interval, the opiate withdrawal syndrome follows the same general progression. Approximately 8 to 12 hours after the last dose, individuals experience yawning, lacrimation, and rhinorrhea; 12 to 14 hours after the final dose, they may fall into a fitful, restless sleep and awaken feeling worse than when they went to sleep. With the continuation of opiate withdrawal, they experience increasing dysphoria, anorexia, gooseflesh, irritability, agitation, and tremors. At the peak intensity of the withdrawal symptoms, they may experience exacerbated irritability, insomnia, intense anorexia, weakness, and profound depression. Common symptoms include alternating coldness and intense skin flushing and sweating, vomiting and diarrhea (Jaffe, 1990). This pattern of symptoms indicates that during the initial withdrawal phase there is a generalized CNS hyperexcitability. Thus, the addicted opiate abuser continues to recycle opiate use to both avoid or terminate the wtihdrawal symptoms, and to reexperience the euphoric effects. This powerful combination of euphoria, tolerance, and withdrawal can lead to profound levels of addiction.

Studies have found that rats and monkeys will self-administer opioids, thus indicating that these drugs serve as reinforcers (Koob & Bloom, 1988). Chronic opioid administration results in physical dependence, as demonstrated by the presence of a withdrawal syndrome following drug cessation. Most clinicians hold the classic position that physical dependence (i.e., avoidance of withdrawal symptoms) is a major motivating factor in opiate self-administration, but evidence indicates that reinforcement and withdrawal are separate processes. Bozarth and Wise (1984) demonstrated that rats will self-administer morphine into the ventral tegmental area without the presence or development of any apparent withdrawal symptoms. Chronic administration of morphine into the periaqueductal gray area, however, produces signs of a strong withdrawal syndrome.

Several lines of evidence indicate that dopaminergic neurotransmission may partially mediate the reinforcing effects of opiate administration. First, injection of met-enkephalin into the ventral tegmental area results in increases in DA release in the nucleus accumbens (Di Chiara & Imperato, 1988). Second, although opiates generally produce sedation, low doses of systemic morphine increase locomotor activity (Domino, Vasko, & Wilson, 1976). Third, injections of morphine into the ventral tegmental area produce circling behavior (Holmes, Bozarth, & Wise, 1983); injections of opiates into the ventral tegmental area produce increased locomotion, as with systemic injections of opiates, thereby suggesting increased dopaminergic transmission (Blaesig & Herz, 1980). Fourth, selective lesions of the dopaminergic system decrease opiate self-administration, although not to the extent of affecting cocaine self-administration (Bozarth & Wise, 1985). Fifth, rats learn to self-administer opiates directly into the ventral tegmental area (Bozarth & Wise, 1984), rats also inject opiates into the nucleus accumbens and the lateral hypothalamus (Goeders, Lane, & Smith, 1984). Sixth, administration of the D1 antagonist SCH 23390, but not the D2 antagonists sulpiride and spiperone, block the reinforcing effects of morphine.

Ettenberg and associates (1982) found no effect of alpha flupenthixol, primarily a D2 antagonist, on heroin self-administration, although the same doses decreased cocaine self-administration. Similar results have been reported by others using other dopaminergic antagonists (DeWit & Wise, 1977). Thus, both place preference and self-administration procedures indicate that opiates are not reinforcing through D2 receptors, which are vital to stimulant reinforcement. These results indicate that opiate reinforcement is at least partially independent of the D2 stimulant type of reinforcement, yet they do act through a dopaminergic mechanism to induce a significant part of their effects.

Chronic administration of opiates produces several behavioral and neurochemical effects that may be related to their reinforcing effects. First, chronic administration of morphine results in the augmentation of the behavioral effects of low doses of morphine. In other words, subjects undergoing chronic opiate administration become sensitized to the behavioral effects of morphine (Ahtee, 1973, 1974). Second, chronic morphine administration results in decreased DA turnover in the striatum and limbic system during withdrawal (Ahtee & Attila, 1980, 1987). Third, in mice withdrawn from morphine, the synthesis and release of DA are attenuated (Ahtee et al., 1987); similar results have been obtained with human heroin addicts in which CSF homovanillic acid concentrations were decreased (Bowers, Kleber, & Davis, 1971).

These results indicate that during chronic morphine administration there is a down-regulation of the dopaminergic system and a neuroadaptation to this depletion. During withdrawal from opiate administration there is an augmentation of dopaminergic mechanisms. Indeed, during withdrawal rats are sensitized to the behavioral effects of apomorphine (Ahtee & Atilla, 1987), and small doses of morphine increase striatal homovanillic acid levels more in withdrawn than in control rats, thereby indicating that the dopaminergic system is sensitized at this point (Ahtee, 1973, 1974). Thus, some of the withdrawal symptoms (e.g., irritability and dysphoria) may be mediated by changes in dopaminergic functioning.

Acute administration of opiates increases the synthesis of 5-HT and the formation of 5-HIAA, and these effects are eliminated by the administration of opiate antagonists (Ahtee & Carlsson, 1979), thus suggesting that opiate administration results in increased serotonergic functioning. Indeed, acute administration of dynorphin-(1–13), while it decreases striatal dopamine, actually increases striatal serotonin (Broderick, 1987). This increased serotonergic functioning may contribute to the "post-consummatory calm" produced by opiate drugs: Increasing serotonergic functioning would tend to inhibit incentive-motivated behaviors and produce a calm, tranquil state. Indeed, the atypical anxiolytic drug buspirone exerts its anxiety-reducing effects via serotonergic activation.

During withdrawal from chronic opioid administration, 5-HIAA levels are decreased (Ahtee, 1980; Ahtee et al., 1987). This pattern of serotonin results could well cause increased impulsivity and a higher probability of relapse, similar to that described earlier in relation to the psychomotor stimulants.

In summary, like cocaine, the opiates are consumed because of their reinforcing properties. These reinforcing properties are the result of activation of endogenous opiate receptors; furthermore, activation of the dopaminergic system modulates the reinforcing effects of opiates. During chronic opiate administration, subjects become physically dependent. There is an increase in dynorphin levels that may mediate some of the aversive aspects of the withdrawal syndrome (e.g., decreased dopaminergic functioning). Furthermore, during chronic administration, there is functional down-regulation of both the dopaminergic and serotonergic systems. Upon withdrawal from opiates, there is a subsequent supersensitivity of the dopaminergic system. This dopaminergic supersensitivity may be involved in opiate craving and general irritability during withdrawal.

See also **Addiction: Concepts and Definitions; Brain Structures and Drugs; Opioid Complications and Withdrawal; Research, Animal Model: An Overview; Tolerance and Physical Dependence; Wikler's Conditioning Theory of Drug Addiction.**

BIBLIOGRAPHY

Ahtee, L. (1980). Chronic morphine administration decreases 5-hydroxytryptamine and 5-hydroxyindoleacetic acid content in the brain of rats. *Medical Biology, 58,* 38–44.

Ahtee, L. (1974). Catalepsy and stereotypes in rats treated with methadone: Relation to striatal dopamine. *European Journal of Pharmacology, 27,* 221–230.

Ahtee, L. (1973). Catalepsy and stereotyped behaviour in rats treated chronically with methadone: Relation to brain homovanillic acid content. *Journal of Pharmacy and Pharmacology, 25,* 649–651.

Ahtee, L., & Atilla, L. M. J. (1987). Cerebral monoamine neurotransmitters in opioid withdrawal and dependence. *Medical Biology, 65,* 113–119.

Ahtee, L., & Atilla, L. M. J. (1980). Opioid mechanisms in regulation of cerebral monoamines in vivo. *Advances in Biochemical Psychopharmacology, 25,* 361–365.

Ahtee, L., & Carlsson, A. (1979). Dual action of methadone on 5-HT synthesis and metabolism. *Naunyn-Schmiedeberg's Archives of Pharmacology, 307,* 51–56.

Ahtee, L., et al. (1987). The fall of homovanillic acid and 5-hydroxyindoleacetic acid concentrations in brain of mice withdrawn from repeated morphine treatment and their restoration by acute morphine administration. *Journal of Neural Transmission, 68,* 63–78.

Akimoto, K., Hammamura, T., & Otsuki, S. (1989). Subchronic cocaine treatment enhances cocaine-induced dopamine efflux, studied by in vivo intracerebral dialysis. *Brain Research, 490,* 39–344.

Blaesig, J., & Herz, A. (1980). Interactions of opiates and endorphins with cerebral catecholamines. In L. Szekeres (Ed.), *Handbook of experimental pharmacology: Adrenergic activators and inhibitors* (Vol. 54). Heidelberg: Springer-Verlag.

Bowers, M. B., Kleber, H. D., & Davis, L. (1971). Acid monoamine metabolites in cerebrospinal fluid during methadone maintenance. *Nature, 232,* 581–582.

Brown, G. L. & Linnoila, M. (1990). CSF serotonin metabolite (5-HIAA) studies in depression, impulsivity, and violence. *Journal of Clinical Psychology, 51*(Suppl. 4), 31–41.

Bozarth, M. A., & Wise, R. A. (1984). Anatomically distinct opiate receptor fields mediate reward and physical dependence. *Science, 244,* 516–517.

Bozarth, M. A., & Wise, R. A. (1985). Involvement of the ventral tegmental dopamine system in opioid and psychomotor stimulant reinforcement. In L. S. Harris (Ed.), *Problems of Drug Dependence,* Washington, DC: U.S. Government Printing Office.

Broderick, P. A. (1991). Cocaine: On-line analysis of an accumbens amine neural basis for psychomotor behavior. *Pharmacology, Biochemistry, and Behavior, 40*(4), 959–968.

Broderick, P. A. (1987). Striatal neurochemistry of dynorphin-(1–13): In vivo electrochemical semidifferential analyses. *Neuropeptides, 10,* 369–386.

Carlsson, A., & Waldeck, B. (1966). Effects of amphetamine, tyramine, and protriptyline on reserpine resistant amine-concentrating mechanisms of adrenergic nerves. *Journal of Pharmacy and Pharmacology, 18,* 252–253.

Castaneda, E., Becker, J. B., & Robinson, T. W. (1988). The long-term effects of repeated amphetamine treatment in vivo on amphetamine, KCL and electrical stimulation evoked striatal dopamine release in vitro. *Life Sciences, 42,* 2447–2456.

Conrad, L. (1950). The comparative method of studying innate behavior patterns. In *Symposia of Society for Experimental Biology, 4,* 221–254.

Cooper, J. R., Bloom, F. E., & Roth, R. H. (1986). *The biochemical basis of neuropharmacology,* 5th ed. New York: Oxford University Press. (2002, 8th ed.)

Cunningham, K. A., & Lakoski, J. M. (1990). The interaction of cocaine with serotonin dorsal raphe neurons: Single-unit extracellular recording studies. *Neuropsychopharmacology, 3,* 41–50.

Cunningham, K. A., & Lakoski, J. M. (1988). Electrophysiological effects of cocaine and procaine on dorsal raphe serotonin neurons. *European Journal of Pharmacology, 148,* 457–462.

DeWit, H., & Wise, R. A. (1977). Blockade of cocaine reinforcement in rats with the dopamine receptor blocker pimozide, but not with the noradrenergic blockers phentolamine or phenoxybenzamine. *Canadian Journal of Psychology, 31,* 195–203.

Di Chiara, G., & Imperato, A. (1988). Drugs abused by humans preferentially increase synaptic dopamine concentrations in the mesolimbic system of freely moving rats. *Proceedings of the National Academy of Sciences of the United States of America, 85,* 5274–5278.

Domino, E. F., Vasko, M. R., & Wilson, A. E. (1976). Mixed depressant and stimulant actions of morphine and their relationship to brain acetylcholine. *Life Sciences, 18,* 361–376.

Duarte-Escalante, O., & Ellinwood, E. H., Jr. (1970). Central nervous system cytopathological changes in cat with chronic methedrine intoxication. *Brain Research, 21*, 151–155.

Dwoskin, L. P., et al. (1988). Repeated cocaine administration results in supersensitivity of striatal D-2 DA autoreceptors to pergolide. *Life Sciences, 42*, 255–262.

Ettenberg, A., et al. (1982). Heroin and cocaine intravenous self-administration in rats: Mediation by separate neural systems. *Psychopharmacology, 78*, 204–209.

Fuxe, K. B., Hamberger, B., & Malmfors, T. (1967). The effects of drugs on accumulation of monoamines in tubero-infundibular dopamine neurons. *European Journal of Pharmacology, 1*, 334–341.

Galloway, M. P. (1990). Regulation of dopamine and serotonin synthesis by acute administration of cocaine. *Synapse, 6*, 63–72.

Gawin, F. H., & Ellinwood, E. H., Jr. (1988). Cocaine and other stimulants: Actions, abuse and treatments. *New England Journal of Medicine, 318*, 1173–1182.

Gawin, F. H., & Kleber, H. D. (1986). Abstinence symptomatology and psychiatric diagnosis in cocaine abusers. *Archives of General Psychiatry, 43*, 107–113.

Glickman, S. E., & Schiff, B. V. (1967). A biological theory of reinforcement. *Psychological Review, 74*, 81–109.

Goeders, N. E., Lane, J. D., & Smith, J. E. (1984). Self-administration of methionine enkephalin into the nucleus accumbens. *Pharmacology, Biochemistry and Behavior, 20*, 451–455.

Henry, D. J., Greene, M. A., & White, F. J. (1989). Electrophysiological effects of cocaine in the mesoaccumbens dopamine system: Repeated administration. *Journal of Pharmacology and Experimental Therapeutics, 251*, 833–839.

Ho, B. T., et al. (1977). Behavioral effects of cocaine-metabolic and neurochemical approach. In E. H. Ellinwood, Jr., & M. M. Kilbey (Eds.), *Advances in behavioral biology: Cocaine and other stimulants*. New York: Plenum.

Holmes, L. J., Bozarth, M. A., & Wise, R. A. (1983). Circling from intracranial morphine applied to the ventral tegmental area in rats. *Brain Research Bulletin, 11*, 295–298.

Jaffe, J. H. (1990). Drug addiction and drug abuse. In A. G. Gilman et al. (Eds.), *Goodman and Gilman's the pharmacological basis of therapeutics*, 8th ed. New York: Pergamon. (2005, 11th ed. New York: McGraw-Hill Medical.)

Jaffe, J. H., & Martin, W. R. (1990). Opioid analgesics and antagonists. In A. G. Gilman et al. (Eds.), *Goodman and Gilman's the pharmacological basis of therapeutics*, 8th ed. New York: McGraw-Hill Medical. (2005, 11th ed.)

Kalivas, P. W., et al. (1988). Behavioral and neurochemical effects of acute and daily cocaine administration in rats. *Journal of Pharmacology Experimental Therapeutics, 245*, 485–492.

King, G. R., Joyner, C., & Ellinwood, E. H., Jr. (1993b). Withdrawal from continuous or intermittent cocaine: Behavioral responsivity to 5-HT$_1$ receptor agonists. *Pharmacology, Biochemistry, and Behavior, 45*, 577–587.

King, G. R., Kuhn, C., & Ellinwood, E. H. Jr. (1993c). Dopamine efflux during withdrawal from continuous or intermittent cocaine. *Psychopharmacology, 111*, 179–184.

King, G. R., et al. (1993a). Withdrawal from continuous or intermittent cocaine: Effects of NAN-190 on cocaine-induced locomotion. *Pharmacology, Biochemistry, and Behavior, 44*, 253–262.

Koob, G. F., & Bloom, F. E. (1988). Cellular and molecular mechanisms at drug dependence. *Science, 242*, 715–723.

Lee, T. H., & Ellinwood, E. H. Jr. (1989). Time-dependent changes in the sensitivity of dopamine neurons to low doses of apomorphine following amphetamine infusion: Electrophysiological and biochemical studies. *Brain Research, 483*, 17–29.

Lee, T. H., Ellinwood, E. H., Jr., & Nishita, J. K. (1988). Dopamine receptor sensitivity changes with chronic stimulants. In W. Kalivas & C. B. Nemeroff (Eds.), *The mesocorticolimbic system*. New York: New York Academy of Sciences.

Linnoila, M., et al. (1983). Low cerebrospinal fluid 5-hydroxyindolacetic acid concentrations differentiates impulsive from nonimpulsive violent behavior. *Life Sciences, 33*, 2609–2614.

O'Donahue, N. F., & Hagmen, W. D. (1967). A map of the cat brain for regions producing self-stimulation and unilateral attention. *Brain Research, 5*, 289.

Olds, J. (1977). *Drives and reinforcements: Behavioral studies of hypothalamic functions*. New York: Raven Press.

Peris, J., Boyson, S. J., Cass, W. A., Curella, P., Dwoskin, L. P., Larson, G., et al. (1990). Persistence of neurochemical changes in dopamine systems after repeated cocaine administration. *Journal of Pharmacology and Experimental Therapeutics, 253*, 38–44.

Pert, C., Kuhar, M. J., & Snyder, S. H. (1975). Autoradiographic localization of the opiate receptor in the rat brain. *Life Sciences, 16* 1849–1854.

Pert, C., Kuhar, M. J., & Snyder, S. H. (1976). The opiate receptor: Autoradiographic localization in the rat brain. *Proceedings of the National Academy of Sciences of the United States of America, 73*, 3729–3733.

Pettit, H. O., et al. (1990). Extracellular concentrations of cocaine and dopamine are enhanced during chronic cocaine administration. *Journal of Neurochemistry, 55*, 798–804.

Pitts, D. K., & Marwah J. (1987). Neuropharmacology of cocaine: Role of monoaminergic systems. *Monographs in Neural Science, 13,* 34–54.

Reith, M. E. A., Benuck, M., & Lajtha, A. (1987). Cocaine disposition in the brain after continuous or intermittent treatment and locomotor stimulation in mice. *Journal of Pharmacology and Experimental Therapeutics, 243,* 281–287.

Ricaurte, G. A., Schuster, C. R., & Seiden, L. S. (1980). Long-term effects of repeated methylamphetamine administration on dopamine and serotonin neurons in the rat brain: A regional study. *Brain Research, 193,* 153–163.

Ricaurte, G. A., Seiden, L. S., & Schuster, C. R. (1984). Further evidence that amphetamines produce long-lasting dopamine neurochemical deficits by destroying dopamine nerve fibers. *Brain Research, 303,* 359–364.

Roberts, W. W., & Carey, R. J. (1965). Rewarding affects performance of gnawing aroused by hypothalamic stimulation in the rat. *Journal of Comparative and Physiological Psychology, 59,* 317.

Seiden, L. S., & Kleven, M. S. (1988). Lack of toxic effects of cocaine on dopamine or serotonin neurons in the rat brain. In D. Clouet, K. Asghar, & R. Brown (Eds.), *Mechanisms of cocaine abuse and toxicity* (National Institute on Drug Abuse Research Monograph No. 88). Washington, DC: U.S. Government Printing Office.

Taylor, D., & Ho, B. T. (1978). Comparison of inhibition of monoamine uptake by cocaine and methylphenidate and amphetamine, *Research Communications in Chemical Pathology and Pharmacology, 21,* 67–75.

Trulson, M. E., & Ulissey, J. J. (1987). Chronic cocaine administration decreases dopamine synthesis rate and increases [^{3}H]-spiroperidol binding in rat brain. *Brain Research Bulletin, 19,* 35–38.

Trulson, M. E., et al. (1986). Chronic cocaine administration depletes tyrosine hydroxylase immunoreactivity in the rat brain nigral striatal system: Quantitative light microscopic studies. *Experimental Neurology, 94,* 744–756.

Volkow, N. D., et al. (1990). Effects of chronic cocaine abuse on postsynaptic dopamine receptors. *American Journal of Psychiatry, 147,* 719–724.

Yi, S-J., & Johnson, K. M. (1990). Chronic cocaine treatment impairs the regulation of synaptosomal ^{3}H-DA release by D_2 autoreceptors. *Pharmacology, Biochemistry and Behavior, 36,* 457–461.

Zahniser, N. R., et al. (1988a). Repeated cocaine administration results in supersensitive nigrostriatal D-2 dopamine autoreceptors. In P. M. Beart, G. Woodruff, & D. M. Jackson (Eds.), *Pharmacology and Functional Regulation of Dopaminergic Neurons.* London: Macmillan.

Zahniser, N. R., et al. (1988b). Sensitization to cocaine in the nigrostriatal dopamine system. In D. Clouet, K. Asghar, and R. Brown (Eds.), *National Institute on Drug Abuse Research Monograph.* Washington, DC: U.S. Government Printing Office.

Zhang, H., Lee, T. H., & Ellinwood, E. H. Jr. (1992). The progressive changes of neuronal activities of the nigral dopaminergic neuron upon withdrawal from continuous infusion of cocaine. *Brain Research, 594,* 315–318.

EVERETT H. ELLINWOOD
G. R. KING

GENDER

A consistent finding throughout many epidemiologic investigations in the United States and worldwide is that men are more likely to initiate, use heavily, and become dependent on alcohol and most forms of illicit drugs. Because of the pervasive way in which gender roles affect most aspects of people's lives, it remains a complex task to understand gender differences in patterns of drug and alcohol abuse. This section reviews the evidence for the following factors: 1) a biological basis for sex differences; 2) a social and psychological basis for gender differences; and 3) the narrowing of gender differences over time.

BIOLOGICAL BASIS FOR SEX DIFFERENCES

With regard to alcohol consumption and related problems, epidemiologic data within and across time and culture indicate that women drink less alcohol than men and have a lower overall prevalence of alcohol abuse and dependence than men. Two theories regarding the biologic basis for sex differences are genetic vulnerability and alcohol sensitivity. While early twin and adoption studies suggested greater genetic contribution to alcoholism among men, larger, population based twin samples show no sex difference in heritability. Thus it is commonly accepted that differences in genetic vulnerability do not explain the sex gap in alcohol use disorders. Other biological factors include male-female differences in alcohol metabolism and greater sensitivity to adverse health effects due to heavy drinking among women. Sex differences in the ratio of water to total body weight also cause differential metabolism of alcohol and drugs. This and other biological factors may cause women to have higher blood-alcohol concentrations (BACs) than men at equal dosages. This causes women to feel the ill effects of alcohol after a lower level of consumption, possibly guarding against heavy alcohol consumption that can lead to symptoms of alcohol abuse and dependence.

Similarly, epidemiologic data indicate that men are more likely to be current illicit drug users, and have higher rates of drug abuse and dependence across specific substance. Some data on adolescents show limited gender differences in the rate of drug initiation, with adolescent females more likely to report nonmedical use of prescription drugs such as amphetamines. This pattern could be indicative of decreasing gender differences in drug and alcohol use seen within younger age groups, and the use of amphetamines for weight control that may be desirable for more young women than men. Clinical studies have indicated that women differ from men in the biological response to drug administration. Animal studies show that female rats have a higher behavioral response to cocaine administration compared to male rats but that the difference diminished following ovariectomy (removal of the ovaries). Human studies indicate that women report more anxiety after cocaine administration but less euphoria and dysphoria. Drugs that are deposited in body fat, such as marijuana, may be slower to clear in women than in men because of the higher proportion of body weight that is fat in women.

The path from first use to dependence also differs between men and women, although there is evidence that gender differences in these paths also decrease over time. Women who use alcohol and drugs often start using later than men, have a faster progression from first use to dependence, and enter treatment sooner than men given equal ages of dependence onset, although no such differences have been observed for crack-cocaine users. This phenomenon has been termed *telescoping*, although some evidence indicates that gender differences in the course of alcohol and drug abuse decrease over time. Further, despite drinking less alcohol than men and having a lower overall prevalence of alcohol abuse and dependence than men, women who drink have more alcohol-related problems compared to men who drink.

SOCIAL AND PSYCHOLOGICAL BASIS FOR GENDER DIFFERENCES

Social factors play an important role in the development of substance use disorders across gender, and thus the gender differences in social responses are implicated as the basis for the gender differences seen in substance use disorders.

In the early part of the twentieth century, alcohol researchers theorized that women were less likely to use alcohol and drugs because female sex roles were characterized by "conventionality" and the "acceptance of the dominant 'official' standards of morality and propriety" (Clark, 1967). Women who abstained from drugs and did not drink heavily were hypothetically following the official standards of morality and propriety for women in the time period, and since men were not bound by the same standards with regard to alcohol use, they were more likely to develop chronic alcohol problems. Evidence supporting this theory shows that more women strongly disapprove of a women getting drunk alone or at a party and further anticipate that they would be disapproved of for drinking heavily in public, compared to men. Further, both men and women are more likely to rate a woman who drinks while on a date as sexually aggressive compared to a man who drinks while on a date. Limited data on social stigma toward drug use exist, but existing literature shows similar if not stronger patterns of gender-related stigma. Stigma associated with drug and alcohol use across time and within subgroups of the population remains a rich area for future research.

Other work using gender roles to explain differences in substance use posit that there are distinctive gender styles in expressing pathology. Specifically, the male style features acting-out or externalizing behaviors (including drug and alcohol use), whereas the female style involves the internalization of distress. These distinctions are sometimes labeled "distraction" versus "rumination" (respectively), and have been extensively studied as mechanisms for an abnormal psychological response to stress (Nolen-Hoeksema & Harrell, 2002; Nolen-Hoeksema Larson & Grayson, 1999). However, comorbidity between depression and alcohol use disorders is often greater in women than men, above that which would be expected due to differing base rates of the disorders; additionally, evidence suggests no difference in affective disorder comorbidity between male and female cocaine-dependent patients but females are twice as likely to express an anxiety disorder. Taken together, these data suggest that the presence of psychopathology may obscure traditional gender differences in response styles.

Sociological explanations for gender differences in alcohol and drug use include the hypothesis that stress among women due to the pursuit of both career and family leads to increased alcohol use and misuse. However, since other studies indicate that women with multiple roles are at lower risk for alcohol use disorders, this explanation seems unlikely. An association between the frequency of drinking among women and the number of men in their workplace was interpreted as showing an imitation effect. A study of medical students in the 1980s found that, at the start of medical school, female students had fewer alcohol-related problems than men, but by the start of clinical training, the gender difference had disappeared. Perhaps imitation as well as increased socialization to traditionally male medical roles decreased constraints against drinking shown by the women at the beginning of medical school.

DECREASING GENDER GAP IN SUBSTANCE USE DISORDERS

A wealth of epidemiologic data indicated that the gender gap in the initiation and use of alcohol and drugs was closing between 1998 and 2008 among adolescents and adults, providing support for the validity of sociological theories of the gender difference in alcohol and drug use disorders (as biological differences would not rapidly shift over such a short period).

Studies of adolescent substance use have consistently shown a convergence between males and females in the rates of alcohol and drug use initiation in younger birth cohorts, especially those born after World War II, and many studies of adults across culture indicate convergence in the rates of alcohol consumption. Several genetically informative samples have been studied with respect to sex differences in *DSM-IV* alcohol and drug use disorders over time, unanimously finding support for such a convergence. Similarly, large, representative, cross-sectional studies in the United States support gender convergence in rates of *DSM-IV* alcohol abuse and dependence. Furthermore, evidence indicates that the traditional telescoping phenomenon whereby women exhibit later onset of drug use and disorders but earlier treatment and shorter

course may be diminishing, as women are more closely approximating men in both the onset and course of these disorders.

Many explanations for the gender differences have been proposed, although these theories are difficult to test empirically because they mostly rely on historical analysis. The increases in the proportion of women working outside the home and decreases in the proportion of women having children has been hypothesized to be a cause of the diminishment of many gender-based social norms, possibly including stigma associated with female drinking and drug use. Furthermore, changes in gender-based drinking norms have been documented between 1979 and 1990, indicating that although there was no change in the proportion of respondents who felt that "a man drinking at a bar with friends" was acceptable, there was a significant increase in the proportion that felt "a woman drinking at a bar with friends" was acceptable (Greenfield & Room, 1997). This finding indicates a decrease in the negative perception associated with drinking in women, potentially leading to greater opportunities to experience alcohol problems. Finally, changes in the opportunity to drink and alcohol advertising may have an effect on changing gender differences. For instance, from 2001 to 2002, the proportion of young girls exposed to print advertising of low-alcohol beverages (e.g., wine coolers) increased by 216 percent (Jernigan et al., 2004). These and other time trends in young women's exposure to alcohol advertising may have increased the social acceptability of drinking by women in younger generations.

In conclusion, despite a reduction in the gender gap regarding alcohol and drug use disorders, a robust difference remains. Some large scale epidemiologic data indicate that men are approximately three times more likely to have a current alcohol use disorder and a current drug use disorder (Hasin et al., 2007; Substance Abuse and Mental Health Services Administration, 2005). Regardless of a gender difference, however, alcohol and drug use disorders remain relatively common in both men and women compared to other psychiatric disorders, and drastically under-treated across gender as well. As gender norms continue to shift over time, people could see a further attenuation of the gender gap in the prevalence of disorders and/or new gender differences emerging in the onset, course, and long-term effects of alcohol and drug use disorders. This area is important for continued monitoring and hypothesis testing to better understand the etiology of alcohol and drug dependence, as well as to develop effective treatment strategies for both men and women.

See also **Conduct Disorder and Drug Use; Epidemiology of Alcohol Use Disorders; Epidemiology of Drug Abuse; Gender and Complications of Substance Abuse.**

BIBLIOGRAPHY

Alonso, J., Angermeyer, M. C., Bernert, S., Bruffaerts, R., Brugha, T. S., Bryson, H., et al. (2004). Prevalence of mental disorders in Europe: Results from the European Study of the Epidemiology of Mental Disorders (ESEMeD) project. *Acta Psychiatrica Scandinavica, 420* (Suppl.), 21–27.

Blanco, C., Alderson, D., Ogburn, E., Grant, B. F., Nunes, E.V., Hatzenbuehler, M. L., et al. (2007). Changes in the prevalence of non-medial prescription drug use and drug use disorders in the United States: 1991–1992 and 2001–2002. *Drug and Alcohol Dependence, 90*(2–3), 252–260.

Bloomfield, K., Gmel, G., Neve, R., & Mustonen, H. (2001). Investigating gender convergence in alcohol consumption in Finland, Germany, the Netherlands, and Switzerland: A repeated survey analysis. *Substance Abuse: Official Publication of the Association for Medical Education and Research in Substance Abuse, 22,* 39–53.

Brady, K. T., & Randall, C. L. (1999). Gender differences in substance use disorders. *Psychiatric Clinics of North America, 22*(2), 241–252.

Braude, M. C., & Ludford, J. P. (1984). *Marijuana effects on the endocrine and reproductive systems: ARAUS review report* (NIDA Research Monograph 44). Rockville, MD: National Institute on Drug Abuse.

Clark, W. (1967). *Sex roles and alcoholic beverage use.* (Working Paper Number 16) Berkeley, CA: Mental Research Institute, Drinking Practices Study.

Cloninger, C. R., Bohman, M., & Sigvardsson, S. (1981). Inheritance of alcohol abuse: Cross-fostering analysis of adopted men. *Archives of General Psychiatry, 38,* 861–868.

Compton, W. M., Thomas, Y. F., Stinson, F. S., & Grant, B. F. (2007). Prevalence, correlates, disability, and comorbidity of *DSM-IV* drug abuse and dependence in the United States: Results from the national epidemiologic survey on alcohol and related conditions. *Archives of General Psychiatry, 64*(5), 566–576.

Corcoran, R. J., & Thomas, L. R. (1991). The influence of observed alcohol consumption on perceptions of initiation of sexual activity in a college dating situation. *Journal of Applied Social Psychology, 21,* 500–507.

Corrigan, E. M. (1985). Gender differences in alcohol and other drug use. *Addictive Behaviors, 10,* 313–317.

Denier, C. A., Thevos, A. K., Latham, P. K., & Randall, C. L. (1991). Psychosocial and psychopathology differences in hospitalized male and female cocaine abusers: A retrospective chart review. *Addictive Behaviors, 16,* 489–496.

Dohrenwend, B. P., & Dohrenwend, B. S. (1976). Sex differences in psychiatric disorders. *American Journal of Sociology, 81,* 1447–1454.

Dudish, S. A., & Hatsukami, D. K. (1996). Gender differences in crack users who are research volunteers. *Drug and Alcohol Dependence, 42,* 55–63.

Echols, A. (1989). *Daring to be bad: Radical feminism in America, 1967–1975.* St. Paul: University of Minnesota Press.

Engs, R. C., & Hanson, D. J. (1990). Gender differences in drinking patterns and problems among college students: A review of the literature. *Journal of Alcohol and Drug Education, 35,* 36–47.

Fillmore, K. M. (1984). When angels fall: Women's drinking as cultural preoccupation and as reality. In R. W. Wilsnack & S. C. Wilsnack (Eds.), *Alcohol problems in women: Antecedents, consequences, and intervention* (pp. 7–36). New York: Guilform Press.

Grant, B. F. (1997). Prevalence and correlates of alcohol use and *DSM-IV* alcohol dependence in the United States: Results of the National Longitudinal Alcohol Epidemiologic Survey. *Journal of Studies on Alcohol, 58,* 464–473.

Greenfield, T. K., & Room, R. (1997). Situational norms for drinking and drunkenness: Trends in the U.S. adult population, 1979–1990. *Addiction, 92*(1), 33–47.

Griffin, M. L., Weiss, R. D., Mirin, S. M., & Lange, U. (1989). A comparison of male and female cocaine abusers. *Archives of General Psychiatry, 46*(2), 122–126.

Haavio-Mannila, E. (1991). Impact of co-workers on female alcohol use. *Contemporary Drug Problems, 18,* 597–627.

Hasin, D. S., Stinson, F. S., Ogburn, E., & Grant, B. F. (2007). Prevalence, correlates, disability, and comorbidity of *DSM-IV* alcohol abuse and dependence in the United States: Results from the National Epidemiologic Survey on Alcohol and Related Conditions. *Archives of General Psychiatry, 64,* 830–842.

Heath, A. C., Bucholz, K. K., Madden, P. A., Dinwiddie, S. H., Slutske, W. S., Bierut, L. J., et al. (1997). Genetic and environmental contributions to alcohol dependence risk in a national twin sample: Consistency of findings in women and men. *Psychological Medicine, 27,* 1381–1396.

Hernandez-Avila, C. A., Rounsaville, B. J., & Kranzler, H. R. (2004). Opioid-, cannabis- and alcohol-dependent women show more rapid progression to substance abuse treatment. *Drug and Alcohol Dependence, 74*(3), 265–272.

Holdcraft, L. C., & Iacono, W. G. (2002). Cohort effects on gender differences in alcohol dependence. *Addiction, 97,* 1025–1036.

Holdcraft, L. C., & Iacono, W. G. (2004). Cross-generational effects on gender differences in psychoactive drug abuse and dependence. *Drug and Alcohol Dependence, 74,* 147–158.

Holmila, M., & Raitasalo, K. (2005). Gender differences in drinking: Why do they still exist? *Addiction, 100,* 1763–1769.

Huang, B., Dawson, D. A., Stinson, F. S., Hasin, D. S., Ruan, M. J., Saha, T. D., et al. (2006). Prevalence, correlates and comorbidity of nonmedical prescription drug use and drug use disorders in the United States: Results of the National Epidemiologic Survey on Alcohol and Related Conditions. *Journal of Clinical Psychiatry, 67*(7), 1062–1073.

Jang, K. L., Livesley, W. J., & Vernon, P. A. (1997). Gender-specific etiological differences in alcohol and drug problems: A behavioural genetic analysis. *Addiction, 92,* 1265–1276.

Jernigan, D. H., Ostroff, J., Ross, C., & O'Hara, J. A., III (2004). Sex differences in adolescent exposure to alcohol advertising in magazines. *Archives of Pediatric and Adolescent Medicine, 158,* 629–634.

Johnson, R. A., & Gerstein, D. R. (1998). Initiation of use of alcohol, cigarettes, marijuana, cocaine, and other substances in U.S. birth cohorts since 1919. *American Journal of Public Health, 88,* 27–33.

Johnston, L. D., O'Malley, P. M., Bachman, J. G., & Schulenberg, J. E. (2004*). Monitoring the Future: National survey results on drug use, 1975–2003. Vol. I: Secondary school students* (NIH Publication No. 03-5375). Bethesda, MD: National Institute on Drug Abuse.

Johnston, L. D., O'Malley, P. M., Bachman, J. G., & Schulenberg, J. E. (2005). *Monitoring the Future: National survey results on drug use, 1975–2005. Vol. II: College students and adults ages 19–45* (NIH Publication No. 03-5376). Bethesda, MD: National Institute on Drug Abuse.

Johnston, L. D., O'Malley, P. M., Bachman, J. G., & Schulenberg, J. E. (2007). *Monitoring the Future national survey results on drug use, 1975–2006: Vol. I, Secondary school students* (NIH Publication No. 07-6205). Bethesda, MD: National Institute on Drug Abuse.

Jones, B. M., & Jones, M. K. (1976). Male and female intoxication levels for three alcohol doses or do women really get higher than men? *Alcohol Technical Report, 5,* 11–14.

Kendler, K. S., Heath, A. C., Neale, M. C., Kessler, R. C., & Eaves, L. J. (1993). Alcoholism and major depression in women. A twin study of the causes of comorbidity. *Archives of General Psychiatry, 50*(9), 690–698.

Keyes, K. M., Grant, B. G., & Hasin, D. (2008). Evidence for a closing gender gap in alcohol use, abuse, and dependence in the United States population. *Drug and Alcohol Dependence, 93,* 21–29.

Kohn, R., Dohrenwend, B., & Mirotznik, J. (1998) Epidemiological findings on selected psychiatric disorders in the general population. In B. Dohrenwend (Ed.), *Adversity, stress, and psychopathology* (pp. 235–284). New York: Oxford University Press.

Kosten, T. R., Kosten, T. A., McDougle, C. J., Hameedi, F. A., McCance, E. F., Rosen, M. I., et al. (1996). Gender differences in response to intranasal cocaine administration to humans. *Biological Psychiatry, 39,* 147–148.

Larosa, J. H. (1990). Executive women and health: Perceptions and practices *American Journal of Public Health, 80,* 1450–1454.

Lejeuz, C. W., Bornovalova, M. A., Reynolds, E. K., Daughters, S. B., & Curtin, J. J. (2007). Risk factors in the relationship between gender and crack/cocaine. *Experimental and Clinical Psychopharmacology, 15*(2), 165–175.

Lex, B. W. (1997). Alcohol and other psychoactive substance dependence in women and men. In M. V. Seeman (Ed.), *Gender and psychopathology* (pp. 311–358). Washington, DC: American Psychiatric Press.

Lieber, C. S. (1997). Gender differences in alcohol metabolism and susceptibility. In R. W. Wilsnack & S. C. Wilsnack (Eds.), *Gender and alcohol: Individual and social perspectives* (pp. 77–89). Piscataway, NJ: Rutgers Center of Alcohol Studies.

Light, J. M., Irvine, K. M., & Kjerulf, L. (1996). Estimating genetic and environmental effects of alcohol use and dependence from a national survey: A "quasi-adoption" study. *Journal of Studies on Alcohol, 57,* 507–520.

Lucas, S. E., Sholar, M., Lundahl, L. H., Lamaz, X., Kouri, E., Wines, J. D., et al. (1996). Sex differences in plasma cocaine levels and subjective effects after acute cocaine administration in human volunteers. *Psychopharmacology, 125,* 346–354.

McCrady, B. S. (1988). Alcoholism. In E. A. Blechman & K. O. Brownell (Eds.), *Handbook of behavioral medicine for women* (pp. 356–368). New York: Pergamon.

Mello, N. K., & Mendelson, J. A. (1997). Cocaine's effects on neuroendocrine systems: Clinical and preclinical studies. *Pharmacology, Biochemistry, and Behavior, 57,* 571–599.

Mello, N. K., Mendelson, J. H., & Teoh, S. K. (1989). Neuroendocrine consequences of alcohol abuse in women. *Annals of the New York Academy of Sciences, 562,* 211–240.

Mumenthaler, M. S., Taylor, J. L., O'Hara, R., & Yesavage, J. A. (1999). Gender differences in moderate drinking effects. *Alcohol Research & Health: The Journal of the National Institute on Alcohol Abuse and Alcoholism, 23,* 55–64.

Neve, R. J., Diederiks, J. P., Knibbe, R. A., & Drop, M. J. (1993). Developments in drinking behavior in the Netherlands from 1958 to 1989, a cohort analysis. *Addiction, 88,* 611–621.

Nolen-Hoeksema, S., & Harrell, Z. A. T. (2002). Rumination, depression, and alcohol use: Tests of gender differences. *Journal of Cognitive Psychotherapy: An International Quarterly, 16,* 391–404.

Nolen-Hoeksema, S., Larson, J., & Grayson, C. (1999). Explaining the gender difference in depressive symptoms. *Journal of Personality and Social Psychology, 77*(5), 1061–1072.

Piazza, N. J., Vrbka, J. L., & Yeager, R. D. (1989). Telescoping of alcoholism in women alcoholics. *International Journal of Addiction, 24,* 19–28.

Prescott, C. A., & Kendler, K. S. (2000). Influence of ascertainment strategy on finding sex differences in genetic estimates from twin studies of alcoholism. *American Journal of Medical Genetics, 96,* 754–761.

Prescott, C. A., Aggen, S. H., & Kendler, K. S. (1999). Sex differences in the sources of genetic liability to alcohol abuse and dependence in a population-based sample of U.S. twins. *Alcoholism, Clinical and Experimental Research, 23,* 1136–1144.

Randall, C. L., Roberts, J. S., Del Boca, F. K., Carroll, K. M., Connors, G. J., & Mattson, M. E. (1999). Telescoping of landmark events associated with drinking: A gender comparison. *Journal of Studies on Alcohol, 60*(2), 252–260.

Reed, B. G., & Mowbray, C. T. (1999). Mental illness and substance abuse: Implications for women's health and health care access. *Journal of the American Medical Women's Association, 54,* 71–78.

Reich, T., Cloninger, C. R., Van, E. P., Rice, J. P., & Mullaney, J. (1988). Secular trends in the familial transmission of alcoholism. *Alcoholism, Clinical and Experimental Research, 12,* 458–464.

Rice, J. P., Neuman, R. J., Saccone, N. L., Corbett, J., Rochberg, N., Hesselbrock, V., et al. (2003). Age and birth cohort effects on rates of alcohol dependence. *Alcoholism, Clinical and Experimental Research, 27,* 93–99.

Richman, J. A., & Rospenda, K. M. (1992). Gender roles and alcohol abuse: Costs of noncaring for future physicians. *Journal of Nervous and Mental Disease, 180,* 619–626.

Ridenour, T. A., Cottler, L. B., Compton, W. M., Spitznagel, E. L., & Cunningham-Williams, R. M. (2003). Is there a progression from abuse disorders to dependence disorders? *Addiction, 98*(5), 635–644.

Rosen, R. (2000). *The world split open: How the modern women's movement changed America.* New York: Penguin Books.

Rounsaville, B. J., Anton, S. F., Carroll, K., Budde, D., Prusoff, B. A., & Gawin, F. (1991). Psychiatric diagnoses of treatment-seeking cocaine abusers. *Archives of General Psychiatry, 48*(1), 43–51.

Saelan, H., Moller, L., & Koster, A. (1992). Alcohol consumption in a Danish cohort during 11 years. *Scandinavian Journal of Social Medicine, 20,* 87–93.

Schulenberg, J., Maggs, J. L., Long, S. W., Sher, K. J., Gotham, H. J., Baer, J. S., et al. (2001). The problem of college drinking: Insights from a developmental perspective. *Alcoholism, Clinical and Experimental Research, 25,* 473–47.

Stinson, F. S., Ruan, W. J., Pickering, R., & Grant, B. F. (2006). Cannabis use disorders in the USA: Prevalence, correlates, and co-morbidity. *Psychological Medicine, 36*(10), 1447–1460.

Straus, R. (1984). The need to drink too much. *Journal of Drug Issues, 14,* 125–136.

Substance Abuse and Mental Health Services Administration. (2005). Results from the 2004 National Survey on Drug Use and Health: National Findings (Office of Applied Studies, NSDUH Series H-28, DHHS Publication No. SMA 05-4062). Rockville, MD.

Sutker, P. B., Goist, K. C., Jr., Allain, A. N., & Bugg, F. (1987). Acute alcohol intoxication: Sex comparisons on pharmacokinetic and mood measures. *Alcoholism, Clinical and Experimental Research, 11,* 507–512.

Thomasson, H. R. (1995). Gender differences in alcohol metabolism: Physiological responses to ethanol. In M. Galanter (Ed.), *Recent developments in alcoholism* (pp. 163–179). New York: Plenum, New York.

Thornton, A., & Freedman, D. (1983). The changing American Family. *Population Bulletin 39,* 1–44.

Walker, R. (1992). Substance abuse and B-cluster disorders: I. Understanding the dual diagnosis patient. *Journal of Psychoactive Drugs, 24,* 223–232.

Warner, L. A., Kessler, R. C., Hughes, M., Anthony, J. C., & Nelson, C. B. (1995). Prevalence and correlates of drug use and dependence in the United States. *Archives of General Psychiatry, 52,* 219–229.

Wilsnack, R.W., Kristjanson, A. F., Wilsnack, S. C., & Crosby, R. D. (2006). Are U.S. women drinking less (or more)? Historical and aging trends, 1981–2001. *Journal of Substance Abuse, 67,* 341–348.

Wilsnack, R.W., Vogeltanz, N. D., Wilsnack, S. C., & Harris, T. R. (2000). Gender differences in alcohol consumption and adverse drinking consequences: Cross-cultural patterns. *Addiction, 95*(2), 251–265.

Wilsnack, S. C., & Wilsnack, R. W. (1991). Epidemiology of women's drinking. *Journal of Substance Abuse, 3*, 133–157.

Wilsnack, R. W., Wilsnack, S. C., & Kalssen, A. D. (1996). Antecedents and consequences of drinking and drinking problems in women: Patterns from a U.S. National Survey. *Nebraska Symposium on Motivation, 34*, 85–158.

KATHERINE KEYES
DEBORAH HASIN

GENETIC FACTORS

Substance dependence is strongly influenced by environmental factors, including the availability of the substance. However, substance dependence is also a familial and genetic disorder. Several lines of evidence demonstrate a substantial genetic component for the risk of substance dependence:

1. Alcohol dependence: Compared to the general population, siblings (brothers or sisters) of alcoholic parents have a 3- to 8-fold increased risk of developing alcohol dependence.

2. Drug dependence (including cocaine, opiates, nicotine, cannabis, hallucinogens, sedatives, and/or stimulants): Significant concordance rates between twin pairs shows a familial basis for different forms of drug dependence; the difference in pair wise concordance rates for monozygotic (MZ; i.e., identical) and dizygotic (DZ; i.e., fraternal) twins was significant for the abuse of marijuana, stimulants, cocaine, and all drugs combined. Because MZ twins share 100 percent of their genes and DZ twins share, on average, only 50 percent of their genes, a fully penetrant (expressed) genetic disorder should be twice as common in identical as in fraternal twins. For example, in one study, for stimulant (e.g., cocaine) abuse, the MZ twin correlation coefficient was 0.53 and for DZ twins it was 0.24. For opioid dependence specifically, the MZ twin correlation coefficient was 0.67 and the DZ correlation coefficient was 0.29 (Kendler & Prescott, 1998).

3. In genetics: *Heritability* is the proportion of phenotypic variation in a population that is attributable to genetic variation among individuals, reflecting the relative contributions of genetic

factors to the total risk for a disorder (e.g., substance dependence). The heritability of substance dependence has been estimated from twin studies to be between 0.37 and 0.60, indicating that between 37 percent and 60 percent of the risk of substance dependence is due to genetic factors. For different types of substance dependence, the heritability has been found to be the following, in decreasing order: alcohol dependence (0.60), smoking persistence in males (0.59), smoking initiation in females (0.55), smoking persistence in females (0.46), smoking initiation in males (0.37), stimulant (including cocaine) abuse (0.44) and opioid dependence (0.43).

Findings from family studies show the familial trends in substance dependence, but environmental effects are unaccounted for in these studies. Findings from twin studies have shown a greater weight for the genetic components in these familial trends. Further, findings from adoption studies have decreased estimates of the contribution of environmental components to these familial trends. Together, these three kinds of studies provide evidence that genetic factors constitute a significant cause of substance dependence; in other words, a substantial part of the risk for substance dependence can be attributed to genetic variation.

GENE VARIATION AND DETECTION STUDIES
Gene variation could alter the density or affinity of proteins. Alteration of the functions of proteins may affect risk for diseases including substance dependence. Substance dependence is a genetically complex disorder that is multigenic, meaning that many genes contribute to risk for this disorder, with the effects of each risk gene being minor. These genes may act independently or may interact with each other or with environmental factors to generate additive or multiplicative effects on risk for substance dependence.

To detect risk genes for substance dependence, linkage studies, which detect the gene-disease relationship in families, and association studies, which detect the gene-disease relationship in unrelated cases and controls, are commonly performed. Usually, linkage studies using genome-wide scanning locate one or several chromosomal regions that are 10–20 million nucleotides wide and that may include dozens of genes. Association studies can be used to locate more finely the specific risk variants in those genes. Genome-wide linkage studies have detected multiple risk regions for substance dependence. Risk regions for alcoholism include chromosomes 1, 2, 4, 6, 7, 8, 10, 12, 14, 16, and 17 (in mixed European-American [EA] and African-American [AA] samples). Genome-wide scanning located risk regions for cocaine dependence or cocaine dependence-related traits at chromosomes 10 (in mixed European-American [EA] and African-American [AA] samples); 3 and 12 (in EAs), and 9 and 18 (in AAs); risk regions for opioid dependence at chromosomes 17 (in EAs and AAs) and 2 (in AAs); and eight risk regions for nicotine dependence at chromosomes 2, 4, 9–12, 17, and 18 in EAs, and 9–11 and 13 in AAs. Association studies, which mostly were based on hypothesized effects based on candidate genes (i.e., those involved in processes that have been shown to be important to the development of maintenance of substance dependence), have detected many risk genes for substance dependence (especially alcohol dependence), among which consistent and replicable findings mainly include a dopamine receptor D2 gene (DRD2); kinase-domain-containing gene (ANKK1); alcohol dehydrogenase genes (ADHs); aldehyde dehydrogenase genes (ALDHs); gamma-aminobutyric acid (GABA), type A receptor alpha 2 gene (GABRA2); mu-opioid receptor gene (OPRM1); a cannabinoid receptor gene (CNR1), and a cytochrome P450 gene (CYP2E1). Positive findings have also been obtained for catechol-O-methyltransferase gene (COMT), ð-opioid receptor gene (OPRD1), κ-opioid receptor gene (OPRK1), muscarinic acetylcholine receptor M2 gene (CHRM2) and neuropeptide Y gene (NPY). There are many other genes showing association signals, but these findings are still very preliminary. Researchers are performing genome-wide association studies to search the risk genes for substance dependence, increasing the likelihood that more risk genes will be identified in the near future. By combining the positive predictive values of all risk genes identified to date, the total contribution of genetic factors to risk for substance dependence can be calculated and the risk of substance dependence predicted. Overall, environmental influences account for 42 to 52 percent of the risk for substance dependence, and genetic factors are estimated to contribute 48 to 58 percent of the risk.

GENETIC BASIS FOR THE CO-MORBIDITY IN SUBSTANCE DEPENDENCE

Different types of substance dependence often co-occur. For example, patients with alcoholism are 35 times more likely to have comorbid cocaine dependence than non-alcoholics, and are 13 times more likely to have comorbid opioid dependence than non-alcoholics (Regier et al., 1990). One possible cause of this high rate of co-morbidity is the synergic actions of different substances, such as alcohol, which enhances the effects of many drugs. For example, cocaine and alcohol are metabolized to cocaethylene, which has biological properties similar to cocaine but is longer acting. Many cocaine abusers therefore prefer to use cocaine together with alcohol, contributing to the high rate of co-morbidity of alcohol dependence and cocaine dependence. As another specific example, simultaneous systemic administration of both alcohol and nicotine results in an additive dopamine release in the nucleus accumbens (NAcc). This additive effect of alcohol and nicotine on the mesolimbic *reward pathway* may contribute to the high incidence of smoking in alcoholics. A second possible cause of the high rate of co-occurring substance dependence is a shared mechanism in the development of dependence on various substances. Several types of substance dependence share common features, including symptomatology, neuropsychological impairments, pathogenetic mechanisms, and response to specific treatments (e.g., the effects of disulfiram, an ALDH blocker, which was approved for the treatment of alcohol dependence, has also been shown to be efficacious in the treatment of cocaine dependence). Many studies have also demonstrated that different types of substance dependence may share susceptibility genes; for example, OPRM1 gene variation was found to moderate susceptibility to alcohol dependence and/or drug dependence; in some studies DRD4 gene variation was found to be related to alcohol dependence and/or drug dependence; multiple ADH genes, multiple OPR genes, the CHRM2 gene, and the CNR1 gene were associated with both alcohol dependence and drug dependence; and finally OPRM1 and CHRNA4 have been reported to be associated with both nicotine dependence and alcohol dependence. These common features and shared susceptibility genes suggest that various types of substance dependence have common developmental mechanisms. It is possible that the dopaminergic signaling pathway that plays a role in reward and reinforcement may be the final common pathway in the development of various types of substance dependence. Although various types of substance dependence may have similar mechanisms, these mechanisms probably do not overlap completely. The similarity and specificity of the mechanisms for different subtypes of substance dependence continue to be under investigation.

GENETIC MARKERS: RISK GENES FOR SUBSTANCE DEPENDENCE

Usually, the genotype frequency distribution of a single gene marker displays a balance in the general population; this is known as the Hardy-Weinberg Equilibrium (HWE). This equilibrium in regard to risk markers can be absent in what is known as the Hardy-Weinberg Disequilibrium (HWD), by certain causes, such as disease. Many studies have found that a number of genetic markers were in HWD in the sample with substance dependence, but in HWE in healthy subjects. This suggests that these markers are inherited in a recessive manner. These markers have been found in multiple ADH genes, multiple OPR genes, the CHRM2 gene, and probably in additional genes, suggesting that the mode of inheritance of risk genes for substance dependence may differ substantially from those for other mental illnesses.

Different populations have different generations of ancestry; for example, the African population is much older than the European population. This difference may result in different rates of decay of linkage disequilibrium (LD; correlation between two genetic markers) from the initial generations to the current generations. Although several markers in strong correlation often form an LD block, different rates of decay of LD are one factor that results in different LD block sizes between populations. Some populations could have broader LD blocks (i.e., more markers located in one block) than other populations; this leads to population-specificity of associations between genes and diseases. For example, many associations between ADH genes, ALDH2 genes, and alcohol dependence have been reported in some populations, but not in others. Due to genetic drift or selection, different populations may also have different allele frequencies at the same locus, which also leads to population-specificity of associations between genes and diseases. To generalize the associations, replication studies in different populations is extremely important in research on the genetics of substance dependence.

PERSONALITY TRAITS AND SUBSTANCE DEPENDENCE

Personality traits play an important role in the genetics of substance dependence. There are three hypotheses concerning relationship between genes and personality as risk factors for substance dependence:

1. Genes bridge the association between personality and substance dependence. Common genetic factors may largely underlie the association between personality traits and substance dependence. For example, 70 percent of the association between antisociality and alcohol dependence can be explained by common genetic factors. In addition, alcohol dependence and conduct disorder share many personality traits that may be accounted for by common genetic risk factors. There is also direct evidence that personality traits and substance dependence are linked to polymorphisms in the SLC6A4 gene (which encodes the serotonin transporter), the OPRM1 gene, the ADH4 and ADH7 genes, and the CHRM2 gene. These findings support the theory of a shared genetic basis for personality features and substance dependence; personality traits might have some underlying neurobiological mechanisms that also influence risk for substance dependence.

2. Personality bridges the association between genes and substance dependence. Personality traits may play a central role in the development of substance dependence. Specifically, some pre-morbid personality traits (i.e., those existing before the onset of substance dependence), such as *behavioral undercontrol* (including impulsivity, thrill seeking, rebelliousness, irresponsibility, nonconformity, and aggressiveness), rejection of societal values, antisocial behavior, and hyperactivity, are robust predictors of alcohol dependence. As postulated by many investigators, personality traits could be a substantial heritable component of substance dependence, serving as an intermediate phenotype for substance dependence. In other words,

certain personality traits are inherited and increase the likelihood that subjects who have them will develop substance dependence or substance dependence-related disorders. Thus, personality features may be more clearly genetic in origin than substance dependence *per se*, personality could be a genetically determined risk factor for substance dependence, and the more sensitive gene-personality association study designs could reasonably be used to detect and predict gene-disease associations.

3. Substance dependence bridges the association between personality and gene. It has been argued that personality traits, especially *negative emotionality* (anxiousness, inhibition, moodiness, and unhappiness), may be a consequence (or a secondary phenomenon) rather than a cause of substance dependence. Here, personality serves as an endophenotype (components in the pathway between disease and genotype that are measurable, but not readily apparent) of substance dependence. In short, the association between personality and gene can be attributed to the association between substance dependence and gene.

CURRENT CONTROVERSIES

Substance dependence is multigenic, and thus its etiology is extremely complicated. Researchers have been trying to quantify the relative contributions of genetic and environmental factors to the risk of substance dependence, but the exact ratio of such contributions between these two factors remains under investigation. The genetic effects are population-specific, and the designs vary between different studies, which make many findings difficult to replicate and conclusions controversial. High rates of co-occurrence of different types of substance dependence also complicates these studies because the causes for different types of substance dependence could be shared or independent. Thus, any investigation of a single type of substance dependence needs to be carefully designed. Additionally, the relationships among substance dependence, personality traits, and genes are complicated, and the true associations among them remain unclear. More research is needed in this area. Many hypotheses have been proposed to explain the mechanisms by which genetic variation affects the risk for substance dependence, but much work remains to be done.

Finally, because substance dependence is not influenced by a single gene exerting a large effect (in contrast to, for example, Huntington's Disease), its mode(s) of genetic inheritance (e.g., dominant or recessive) are difficult to derive, a fact that hampers researchers who seek to understand the etiology of substance dependence.

See also **Complications: Mental Disorders; Conduct Disorder and Drug Use; Epidemiology of Drug Abuse; Women and Substance Abuse.**

BIBLIOGRAPHY

Edenberg, H. J., Xuei, X., Chen, H. J., Tian, H., Wetherill, L. F., Dick, D. M. et al. (2006). Association of alcohol dehydrogenase genes with alcohol dependence: A comprehensive analysis. *Human Molecular Genetics, 15,* 1539–1549.

Gelernter, J., Panhuysen, C., Weiss, R., Brady, K., Hesselbrock, V., Rounsaville, B. et al. (2005). Genomewide linkage scan for cocaine dependence and related traits: Significant linkages for a cocaine-related trait and cocaine-induced paranoia. *American Journal of Medical Genetics, Part B Neuropsychiatric Genetics, 136,* 45–52.

Gelernter, J., Panhuysen, C., Weiss, R., Brady, K., Poling J., Krauthammer, M. et al. (2007). Genomewide linkage scan for nicotine dependence: Identification of a chromosome 5 risk locus. *Biological Psychiatry, 61,* 119–126.

Gelernter, J., Panhuysen, C., Wilcox, M., Hesselbrock, V., Rounsaville, B., Poling, J. et al. (2006). Genomewide linkage scan for opioid dependence and related traits. *American Journal of Human Genetics, 78,* 759–769.

Kendler, K. S., Jacobson, K. C., Prescott, C. A., & Neale, M. C. (2003). Specificity of genetic and environmental risk factors for use and abuse/dependence of cannabis, cocaine, hallucinogens, sedatives, stimulants, and opiates in male twins. *American Journal of Psychiatry, 160,* 687–695.

Kendler, K. S., & Prescott, C. A. (1998). Cocaine use, abuse and dependence in a population-based sample of female twins. *British Journal of Psychiatry, 173,* 345–350.

Li, M. D., Ma, J. Z., & Beuten, J. (2004). Progress in searching for susceptibility loci and genes for smoking-related behaviour. *Clinical Genetics, 6,* 382–392.

Long, J. C., Knowler, W. C., Hanson, R. L., Robin, R. W., Urbanek, M., Moore, E. et al. (1998). Evidence for genetic linkage to alcohol dependence on chromosomes 4 and 11 from an autosome-wide scan in an American Indian population. *American Journal of Medical Genetics, 81,* 216–221.

Luo, X., Kranzler, H. R., Zuo, L., Lappalainen, J., Yang, B. Z., & Gelernter, J. (2006). ADH4 gene variation is associated with alcohol dependence and drug dependence in European Americans: Results from HWD tests and case-control association studies. *Neuropsychopharmacology, 31,* 1085–1095.

Luo, X., Kranzler, H. R., Zuo, L., Wang, S., Blumberg, H P., & Gelernter, J. (2005). CHRM2 gene predisposes to alcohol, drug dependence and affective disorder: Results from an extended population structured association study. *Human Molecular Genetics, 14,* 2421–2434.

Luo, X., Kranzler, H. R., Zuo, L., Wang, S., & Gelernter, J. (2007). Personality traits of agreeableness and extraversion are associated with ADH4 variation. *Biological Psychiatry, 61,* 599–608.

Luo, X., Kranzler, H. R., Zuo, L., Wang, S., Schork, N. J., & Gelernter, J. (2006). Diplotype trend regression (DTR) analysis of the ADH gene cluster and ALDH2 gene: Multiple significant associations for alcohol dependence. *American Journal of Human Genetics, 78,* 973–987.

Luo, X., Kranzler, H. R., Zuo, L., Wang, S., Schork, N. J., & Gelernter, J. (2007). Multiple ADH genes modulate risk for drug dependence in both African- and European-Americans. *Human Molecular Genetics, 16,* 380–390.

Luo, X., Kranzler, H. R., Zuo, L., Zhang, H., Wang, S., & Gelernter, J. (2007). CHRM2 variation predisposes to personality traits of agreeableness and conscientiousness. *Human Molecular Genetics, 16,* 1557–1568.

Prescott, C. A., Caldwell, C. B., Carey, G., Vogler, G. P., Trumbetta S. L., & Gottesman, I. I. (2005). The Washington University Twin Study of alcoholism. *American Journal of Medical Genetics, Part B Neuropsychiatric Genetics, 134,* 48–55.

Regier, D. A., Farmer, M. E., Rae, D. S., Locke, B. Z., Keith, S. J., Judd, L. L., et al. (1990). Comorbidity of mental disorders with alcohol and other drug abuse. *Journal of the American Medical Association, 264,* 2511–2518.

Reich, T., Edenberg, H. J., Goate, A., Williams, J. T., Rice, J. P., Van Eerdewegh, P. et al. (1998). Genome-wide search for genes affecting the risk for alcohol dependence. *American Journal of Medical Genetics, 81,* 207–221.

Tsuang, M. T., Lyons, M. J., Eisen, S. A., Goldberg, J., True Lin, N. W., Meyer, J. M. et al. (1996). Genetic influences on *DSM-III-R* drug abuse and dependence: A study of 3,372 twin pairs. *American Journal of Medical Genetics, Part B Neuropsychiatric Genetics, 67,* 473–477.

XINGGUANG LUO

LEARNING

Learning factors in substance abuse have received much attention. Two basic learning mechanisms are involved when an organism repeatedly self-administers a psychoactive substance. First, classical conditioning is engaged when environmental stimuli are associated with, and come to signal, the upcoming effects of the drug. Second, operant conditioning occurs as an organism learns that particular behaviors lead either to a drug reward or to punishment. The effects of these two processes presumably interact and influence repeated drug use and/or relapse to drug use following a period of abstinence.

Classical conditioning occurs when an organism makes an association between two events in the external environment. A typical classical conditioning situation involves learning that a biologically neutral event (the conditioned stimulus [CS], such as a familiar drug dealer) signals the upcoming occurrence of a biologically relevant event (the unconditioned stimulus [US], such as the effects of a drug). As a result of this signaling, the CS produces conditioned responses (CRs), which are related to the US and unconditioned responses (URs). A number of investigators have reported that CRs are elicited in humans by environmental events that signal upcoming drug use or withdrawal (Berger et al., 1996; Payne, McClernon, & Dobbins, 2007; Bordnick et al., 2008). Consistently, CRs to drug-related stimuli play a major role in maintaining drug-taking behavior (Sinha & Li, 2007).

Operant conditioning involves learning about contingencies between behaviors and their outcomes. A typical operant conditioning situation sets up contingencies between three different events: a response (e.g., inhalation of the drug), the outcome of that response (e.g., the reinforcing drug effects), and the stimulus situation in which that response-outcome relationship is established (i.e., the discriminative stimulus). Drugs of abuse function as potent reinforcers for human substance abusers, as evidenced by the fact that a variety of behaviors are directed toward their attainment and use. Consequently, understanding how operant behaviors directed toward drug reinforcers are acquired is critical to understanding human substance abuse and dependence.

Classical and operant conditioning may both be active during drug seeking and self-administration. Events that have consistently signaled drug use may eventually come to evoke CRs in the form of craving—urges to use the drug. In this way, signals of drug use may motivate the drug user to initiate drug-seeking behavior. For example, walking past someone smoking a cigarette might act as a CS for a heavy cigarette smoker, evoking the craving for nicotine. This craving might then increase the likelihood of purchasing and smoking a cigarette (the reward).

OPERANT CONDITIONING WITH DRUG REINFORCERS

A large body of data shows that many drugs abused by humans act as reinforcers for animals in operant-conditioning situations. In typical studies on the reinforcing properties of drugs, rats or monkeys are fitted with venous catheters through which a drug can be administered directly. The animal's response, such as pushing a lever, results in infusions of the drug.

These studies have found that many drugs abused by humans—including cocaine, morphine, heroin, amphetamines, pentobarbital, and alcohol—establish and maintain operant behaviors in animals. Other drugs that are typically not abused by humans—such as aspirin, antidepressants, hallucinogens, and opioid mixed agonists/antagonists—do not cause a response (Gold & Balster, 1991; Hoffmeister & Wuttke, 1975).

The degree to which a drug reinforces behavior depends more on the schedule of reinforcement than on the drug itself. A schedule of reinforcement refers to how often a drug is given. For example, ratio schedules require a certain number of responses before a reinforcer is given. Interval schedules are set up so that reinforcers occur only after a certain amount of time has passed. Reinforcers in ratio schedules depend solely on the number of responses made; therefore, these schedules typically result in higher response rates than interval schedules in which responses made too early are ineffective. Because reinforcement schedules largely determine the response rate in a given situation, the abuse potential of the various drugs cannot be reliably assessed by comparing how quickly participants respond for each substance.

One technique used to compare the reinforcing properties of various substances involves calculating a *breaking point* under a progressive ratio schedule of reinforcement. A progressive ratio schedule requires a participant to make an increasing number of responses (the ratio) for each additional reinforcer. For a given drug dose, the breaking point is reached when the ratio becomes too high to support responding. This breaking point value then shows that drug's reinforcing properties, or *reinforcing efficacy*. Drugs with the highest breaking point are the most reinforcing and, hence, have the highest abuse potential. Of drugs studied using this procedure with animals, cocaine has the highest breaking point (Wang & Woolverton, 2007; Lile et al., 2005). Although there are no published laboratory data comparing the reinforcing efficacy of drugs of abuse in humans, a growing database indicates that several drugs—including cocaine and heroin—are self-administered by humans under progressive ratio schedules of reinforcement (e.g., Haney et al., 1998; Comer et al., 1999).

Choice experiments can also compare the reinforcing properties of different substances. Participants choose between two responses, each leading to different commodities (e.g., drug A vs. drug B, or a drug vs. a non-drug option). A preference for one response indicates a preference for the substance, or commodity, associated with that response. Data collected using choice procedures indicate that the choice to self-administer drugs of abuse is influenced by many factors, including dose, schedules of reinforcement, and magnitude (size or amount) of the other choice. There is a good correspondence between findings obtained for animals and for humans in choice experiments. For example, S. Stevens Negus (2003) found that monkeys self-administered less cocaine when the magnitude of the alternative reinforcer (number of food pellets) increased. Similarly, human cocaine self-administration decreased as the value of the monetary alternative increased (Higgins et al., 1994).

In sum, a body of both animal and human data now exists that documents the way drugs of abuse can act as potent reinforcers. The pattern of drug use exhibited by an individual user, however, appears to depend as much on the schedule of drug availability as on the particular properties of the chosen drug or on the presence or absence of other reinforcers. Therefore, predicting human patterns of drug taking will require a better understanding of drug availability in the real world.

CLASSICAL CONDITIONING OF DRUG-RELATED CUES

A number of investigators have suggested that stimuli previously paired with drug use (e.g., paraphernalia) or that reliably signal drug use (e.g., meeting the drug dealer) become CSs, which elicit CRs. In turn, this relationship (CS-CR) increases the likelihood of further drug use.

Conditioned Withdrawal Model. Abraham Wikler (1973) described unpublished observations supporting this perspective, in which he administered multiple daily doses of morphine, methadone, or heroin to research participants who were previously heroin-dependant and had undergone detoxification, inducing opioid dependence. Subsequently, irregular single doses of the opioid antagonist nalorphine consistently led to withdrawal (i.e., the unpleasant symptoms experienced by drug abusers following the abrupt cessation of drug use). Wikler occasionally substituted saline for nalorphine, evoking less severe withdrawal symptoms. While this supported the role of conditioning factors in opioid withdrawal, a more systematic evaluation in humans is clearly needed.

CONDITIONED TOLERANCE MODEL

A second model using conditioning was put forth by Shepard Siegel (1975; 1979). He proposed that stimuli paired with drug use evoke conditioned compensatory responses, which oppose the direct effects of the drug. As these drug-opposite responses increase over repeated conditioning experiences in the same environment, they increasingly oppose the effects of the drug. Therefore, abusers become tolerant to drug-related effects and find that, over time, they need larger doses to achieve a given effect. Accordingly, tolerance should decrease when drugs are administered in novel environments where CSs are not present. Of course, a plethora of data demonstrates the development and maintenance of drug tolerance in stable drug-taking situations, but the mechanism(s) underlying this phenomenon are multiple and complex. Only additional research can clarify the role conditioning plays in the developing drug tolerance.

Nevertheless, according to Siegel's theory, drug-related cues in the absence of drug-taking produce drug-opposite responses that are not canceled by the direct effects of the drug. These drug-opposite responses represent what the user experiences as withdrawal symptoms. Viewed from this perspective, conditioning can motivate drug use in two ways. First, the withdrawal symptoms following a period of abstinence can lead to drug use aimed at relieving these unpleasant effects. Second, tolerance to the effects of a drug may motivate a user to increase his or her level of use to maintain a fixed level of desired effect.

Siegel's model has not gone unchallenged. The primary objection to it is that CSs do not always produce drug-opposite responses. Instead, CSs sometimes produce responses that resemble the direct effects of the drug (e.g., euphoria), and may motivate drug use as well. Indeed, whether CRs produced by drug-related stimuli are drug-like or drug-opposite has not been determined, and some researchers have asserted that rather than drug-opposite responses, the memory of drug-induced euphoria is the major factor in continual drug use and relapse (e.g., Grant et al., 1996).

CONDITIONED INCENTIVE MODEL

Jane Stewart and colleagues (1984) have proposed that conditioned drug stimuli provide the impetus for further drug use by eliciting CRs that mimic the drug effects, which whet the appetite of the user. Such CRs are positively reinforcing and may lead to drug use by prompting the user to anticipate the pleasurable consequences of drug taking.

Some evidence for this model lies in the observation that many animals show drug-like responses to stimuli paired with drug use. This is particularly evident with stimulant drugs such as cocaine or *d*-amphetamine, as these drugs exhibit high abuse potential. Furthermore, researchers have found that animals that have stopped responding for a drug reinforcer may resume responding following a small unearned dose of the drug (a priming dose) and, importantly, that environmental signals for drug use may act in the same way as these priming doses (de Wit & Stewart, 1981). Some research suggests that CSs, paired with a reinforcing US, release dopamine (DA) in the brain's supposed "reward pathway" (Stewart et al., 1984; Schultz et al., 1998). Other research suggests that the contribution of multiple brain structures (e.g., amygdala, hippocampus, orbitofrontal cortex) and other neurotransmitters, including glutamate and GABA, underlie priming-induced drug seeking.

These three conditioning models similarly propose that events paired with drug use become conditioned stimuli that, upon future presentation, encourage the drug user to initiate drug-seeking behaviors. The models differ only in the characterization of the CRs elicited by the drug-related events.

HUMAN DATA

Since the 1970s investigators have collected data from a number of sources to document that stimuli associated with drug use in humans is conditioned. Evidence for this has come from three primary sources:

- Self-reports by drug abusers about the conditions under which they experience craving and withdrawal.
- Attempts to establish drug conditioning in the laboratory.
- Assessments of responses to cues thought to be drug CSs in the natural environment (in cue-exposure paradigms).

Self-reports of Conditioned Effects. Many drug abusers report drug craving and withdrawal when faced with drug-related stimuli in their home environment or in the laboratory. Several investigators have systematically documented this in response to stimuli associated with a wide range of drugs, including alcohol, cocaine, heroin, and nicotine. It has been more difficult, however, to establish a link between subjective reports of craving and/or withdrawal and drug use. Recently, Rajita Sinha and colleagues (2006) studied outpatient cocaine abusers who had recently completed drug treatment. They found that cocaine craving was predictive of relapse and that stress-induced cocaine craving was a particularly important factor. Similar findings were found for self-reported methamphetamine craving in an outpatient treatment setting (Hartz et al., 2001). Such reports support the idea that events that signal drug self-administration in the home environment can cause conditioned responses of craving, which motivate further drug use.

Laboratory Conditioning Studies. Richard Foltin and Margaret Haney (2000) found that neutral stimuli paired with cocaine administration elicited conditioned physiological (e.g., increased heart rate and blood pressure) and subjective (e.g., cocaine craving) responses. A number of other studies using neutral stimuli paired with alcohol, nicotine, and opioids also reported similar effects brought about by the experimental CSs. Interestingly, Raymond Niaura and colleagues (1989) found that such physiological responses to a laboratory-presented CS predicted relapse to cigarette smoking 90 days later.

Laboratory studies show that such conditioning occurs as a consequence of experienced users taking drugs. However, the connection between potential CSs, drug effects, and CRs in the natural environment is undoubtedly less precise than in the laboratory.

Cue-Assessment Studies. To determine whether events associated with previous drug use in the natural environment acquired conditioned properties, many studies have recreated/presented typical CSs in the laboratory and measured participant responses. In such studies drug-dependent participants are exposed to drug paraphernalia or to audiotapes, videotapes, and photographs with drug-related content (i.e., "drug cues"), while physiological and self-report responses are obtained. Responses to such drug cues are then compared with the responses participants make when they are exposed to comparable stimuli lacking a drug-specific content.

Consistent with conditioning models, exposure to drug cues seems to produce CRs. Specifically, exposure to drug cues produces subjective reports of drug craving as well as other physiological changes (e.g., decreases in skin temperature and increases in heart rate; for review, see Carter & Tiffany, 1999). Data from imaging studies indicate that DA-rich brain structures, including the ventral tegmental area, ventral striatum, and prefrontal cortex, are activated when substance-dependent individuals are presented with drug cues (Volkow et al., 2006; Sinha et al., 2007). This suggests that DA may be involved in establishing conditioned responses to drug cues. In line with this view, S. Paul Berger and colleagues (1996) demonstrated that haloperidol, a DA antagonist, significantly reduced cocaine cue-induced anxiety and craving.

Although drug cues have repeatedly increased drug self-administration in laboratory animals (e.g., de Wit & Stewart, 1981; Epstein et al., 2006), there is a dearth of parallel data collected using humans. In one study Payne and colleagues (1991) exposed tobacco smokers to highly salient smoking cues and found that cue exposure shortened the time participants took to smoke their first cigarette and increased participants' puff duration. Because the assumption that responses to drug-related stimuli motivate actual drug use is central to learning models, more studies using drug taking as a dependent measure are clearly needed.

CLASSICAL/OPERANT CONDITIONING INTERACTION

Although much evidence suggests that psychoactive drugs of abuse have powerful reinforcing properties—and that stimuli associated with those drugs elicit conditioned responses—the question remains as to whether these classically conditioned responses actually motivate drug-seeking behaviors by themselves. Indeed, much of the work on drug conditioning contains the implied notion that classical and operant learning effects combine to motivate drug use (or drug craving, even if no drug use actually occurs). The most common idea is that CSs evoke craving and/or withdrawal states, which motivate subsequent drug-seeking behaviors (via classical conditioning). In cases in which a drug is consumed, the effects of the drug further reinforce the drug-seeking behaviors (via operant conditioning).

TREATMENT IMPLICATIONS

If classical and operant conditioning motivate drug use, then substance-abuse treatments should aim at reducing the impact of these learning effects. The most commonly discussed interventions include aversion training, extinction, and behavioral and cognitive-behavioral alternatives.

Aversion therapy involves teaching drug abusers that those stimuli and responses that once led to positive drug effects will henceforth lead to unpleasant outcomes. The most common technique has been to pair self-administrations of a drug with pharmacologically induced sickness (e.g., the medication disulfiram can cause a variety of unpleasant and uncomfortable effects when followed by the ingestion of alcohol). While disulfiram may prevent alcohol consumption in the short-term, patients are unlikely to continue to self-administer disulfiram outside the treatment setting. Further, since the treatment setting is clearly different from the home environment, drug abusers may simply learn that drug-taking behavior is reinforced at home, but punished in the clinic. In general, disulfiram is ineffective in achieving alcohol abstinence or delaying relapse (Fuller et al., 1986), although it has been useful for patients who are older, highly motivated, and more socially stable (Fuller & Gordis, 2004).

Extinction training consists of repeatedly exposing drug abusers to drug-related stimuli without letting them take drugs. This breaks the association between these stimuli and the effects of drug use. Extinction of classically conditioned stimuli typically requires drug abusers to repeatedly view drug-related scenes, imagine scenarios, and handle paraphernalia without using the abused substance. Such training has the advantage of not subjecting the drug user to punishment. Operant extinction procedures require participants to repeatedly perform drug-use behaviors in the absence of a drug reinforcer. This can be accomplished by having participants administer their drug of abuse in the usual way—while they are maintained on a medication that blocks the effects of the abused drug (e.g., the opioid-blocking drug naltrexone). In this way drug-use behaviors are not reinforced as the drug effects are absent or considerably weakened. Nevertheless, participants might give up the drug in the clinic, but still experience conditioned effects that lead to drug use at home.

Cognitive-behavioral training also reduces the impact of conditioning on behavior. Subjects are taught to identify and avoid drug-related situations and to make different responses in the presence of drug cues (Sholomskas et al., 2005). These new responses compete with drug-seeking behaviors elicited by drug cues. Rather than trying to eliminate the craving produced by drug cues, this treatment gives the patient ways to avoid cues along with alternative behaviors and strategies to replace drug use as well as general coping skills. Behavioral alternatives to drug use range from simple time-outs, to forming images inconsistent with drug use, to acting in ways that reduce the chances of use or cue exposure (e.g., going out to eat with non-drug-using friends). Cognitive strategies include changing expectations about drug use and considering long-term consequences of behavior. Taken as a whole, these approaches are now commonly designated as cognitive therapies or relapse-prevention approaches. The advantage of these procedures over aversion therapy and extinction is that patients use their training in the clinic to deal with high-risk situations in the real world.

Contingency management is another behavioral approach used to treat substance abuse. It has generated increased interest in recent years because it has produced consistent reductions in drug-using behaviors among diverse substance-abusing populations (Higgins et al., 2004). In this approach, individuals receive immediate rewards (e.g., cash or vouchers redeemable for goods or services) for providing drug-free urine samples, and the value of the rewards increases with consecutive drug-free urine samples. However, rewards are withheld if the patient's urine sample tests positive for an illicit drug. In addition to receiving rewards, drug abusers participate in cognitive sessions similar to those described previously, where they learn a variety of skills to help them minimize substance use. One problem with contingency management is that it may be too expensive for less well-funded treatment programs. Whether these particular conditioning interventions provide lasting help to substance abusers remains to be seen, but data suggest that in alcohol-, cocaine-, nicotine-, and opioid-dependent individuals, these cognitive and behavior techniques reduce the probability of relapse.

See also **Addiction: Concepts and Definitions; Conditioned Tolerance; Treatment, Pharmacological Approaches to: Naltrexone; Wikler's Conditioning Theory of Drug Addiction.**

BIBLIOGRAPHY

Berger, S. P., Hall, S., Mickalian, J. D., Reid, M. S., Crawford, C. A., Delucchi, K., et al. (1996). Haloperidol antagonism of cue-elicited cocaine craving. *The Lancet, 347*(9000), 504–508.

Bordnick, P. S., Traylor, A. Copp, H. L., Graap, K. M., Carter, B., Ferrer, M., et al. (2008, June). Assessing reactivity to virtual reality alcohol based cues. *Addictive Behaviors, 33*(6), 743–756.

Carter, B. L. & Tiffany, S. T. (1999). Meta-analysis of cue-reactivity in addiction research. *Addiction, 94*(3), 327–340.

Comer, S. D., Collins, E. D., MacArthur, R. B., & Fischman, M. W. (1999). Comparison of intravenous and intranasal heroin self-administration by morphine-maintained humans. *Psychopharmacology, 143*(4), 327.

de Wit, H. & Stewart, J. (1981). Reinstatement of cocaine-reinforced responding in the rat. *Psychopharmacology, 75*, 134–143.

Epstein, D. H., Preston, K. L., Stewart, J., & Shaham, Y. (2006). Toward a model of drug relapse: An assessment of the validity of the reinstatement procedure. *Psychopharmacology, 189*(1), 1–16.

Foltin, R. W., & Haney, M. (2000). Conditioned effects of environmental stimuli paired with smoked cocaine in humans. *Psychopharmacology, 149*(1), 24–33.

Fuller, R. K., Branchey, L., Brightwell, D. R., Derman, R. M., Emrick, C. D., Iber, F. L., et al. (1986). Disulfiram treatment of alcoholism. A Veterans Administration cooperative study. *JAMA, 256*(11), 1449–1455.

Fuller, R. K., & Gordis, E. (2004). Does disulfiram have a role in alcoholism treatment today? *Addiction, 99*(1), 21–24.

Gold, L. H., & Balster, R. (1991). Evaluation of nefazodone self-administration in rhesus monkeys. *Drug and Alcohol Dependence, 28*(3), 241–247.

Grant, S. E., London, D., Newlin, D. B., Villemagne, V. L., Liu, X., Contoreggi, C., et al. (1996, October 15). Activation of memory circuits during cue-elicited cocaine craving. *The Proceedings of the National Academy of Sciences USA, 93*(21), 12040–12045.

Haney, M., Foltin, R. W., & Fischman, M. W. (1998). Effects of pergolide on intravenous cocaine self-administration in men and women. *Psychopharmacology, 137*(1), 15–24.

Hartz, D. T., Frederick-Osborne, S. L., & Galloway, G. P. (2001). Craving predicts use during treatment for methamphetamine dependence: A prospective, repeated-measures, within-subject analysis. *Drug and Alcohol Dependence, 63*(3), 269–276.

Higgins, S. T., Bickel, W. K., & Hughes, J. R. (1994). Influence of an alternative reinforcer on human cocaine self-administration. *Life Sciences, 55*(3), 179–187.

Higgins, S. T., Heil, S. H., & Lussier, J. P. (2004). Clinical implications of reinforcement as a determinant of substance use disorders. *Annual Review of Psychology, 55*, 431–461.

Hoffmeister, F., & Wuttke, W. (1975). Further studies on self-administration of antipyretic analgesics and combination of antipyretic analgesics with codeine in rhesus monkeys. *Journal Pharmacological and Experimental Therapeutics, 193*(3), 870–875.

Lile, J. A., Ross, J. T., Nader, M. A. (2005, May 9). A comparison of the reinforcing efficacy of 3,4-methyle-nedioxymethamphetamine (MDMA, ecstasy) with cocaine in rhesus monkeys. *Drug and Alcohol Dependence, 78*(2), 135–140.

Ludwig, A. M., Wilker, A., & Stark, L. H. (1974). The first drink: Psychobiological aspects of craving. *Archives of General Psychiatry, 30,* 539–547.

Negus, S. S. (2003). Rapid assessment of choice between cocaine and food in rhesus monkeys: Effects of environmental manipulations and treatment with d-amphetamine and flupenthixol. *Neuropsychopharmacology, 28*(5), 919–931

Niaura, R., Abrams, D., Demuth, B., Pinto, R., & Monti, P. (1989). Responses to smoking-related stimuli and early relapse to smoking. *Addictive Behaviors, 14*(4), 419–428.

Payne, K. B., McClernon, J. F., & Dobbins, I. G. (2007, Aug. 15). Automatic affective responses to smoking cues. *Experimental and Clinical Psychopharmacology, 15*(4), 400–409.

Payne, T. J., Schare, M. L., Levis, D. J., & Colletti, G. (1991). Exposure to smoking-relevant cues: Effects on desire to smoke and topographical components of smoking behavior. *Addictive Behaviors, 16,* 467–479.

Schultz, W., Tremblay, L. & Hollerman, J. R. (1998, April–May). Reward prediction in primate basal ganglia and frontal cortex. *Neuropharmacology, 37*(4–5), 421–429.

Sholomskas, D. E., Syracuse-Siewert, G., Rounsaville, B. J., Ball, S. A., Nuro, K. F., & Carroll, K. M. (2005). We don't train in vain: A dissemination trial of three strategies of training clinicians in cognitive-behavioral therapy. *Journal of Consulting and Clinical Psychology, 73*(1), 106–115.

Siegel, S. (1975). Evidence from rats that morphine tolerance is a learned response. *Journal of Comparative and Physiological Psychology, 89*(5), 498–506.

Siegel, S. (1979). The role of conditioning in drug tolerance and addiction. In J. D. Keehn (Ed.), *Psychopathology in animals: Research and treatment implications* (pp. 143–168). New York: Academic Press.

Sinha, R., Garcia, M., Paliwal, P., Kreek, M. J., & Rounsaville, B. J. (2006). Stress-induced cocaine craving and hypothalamic-pituitary-adrenal responses are predictive of cocaine relapse outcomes. *Archives of General Psychiatry, 63*(3), 324–331.

Sinha, R., & Li, C.-S. R. (2007). Imaging stress- and cue-induced drug and alcohol craving: Association with relapse and clinical implications. *Drug and Alcohol Review, 26*(1), 25–31.

Stewart, J., de Wit, H., & Eikelboom, R. (1984). Role of unconditioned and conditioned drug effects in the self-administration of opiates and stimulants. *Psychological Review, 91*(2), 251–268.

Volkow, N. D., Wang, G. J., Telang, F., Fowler, J. S., Logan, J., & Childress, A. R., et al. (2006, June 14). Cocaine cues and dopamine in dorsal striatum: Mechanism of craving in cocaine addiction. *The Journal of Neuroscience, 26*(24), 6583–6588.

Wang, Z. & Woolverton, W. L. (2007). Estimating the relative reinforcing strength of (+−)-3,4-methylene-dioxymethamphetamine (MDMA) and its isomers in rhesus monkeys: Comparison to (+)−methamphetamine. *Psychopharmacology, 189*(4), 483–488.

Wikler, A. (1973). Dynamics of drug dependence. Implications of a conditioning theory for research and treatment. *Archives of General Psychiatry, 28*(5), 611–616.

STEVEN J. ROBBINS
REVISED BY HEDY KOBER (2009)
ALLISON C. TURZA (2009)
CARL L. HART (2009)

PERSONALITY

Clinicians and researchers alike have long posited that personality plays an important role in the etiology of substance use disorders (SUDs). Although empirical research has failed to identify a unique constellation of traits equivalent to a so-called addictive personality, a substantial body of research points to a few important traits that appear to put one at risk for developing SUDs, in particular, traits related to the tendency to experience negative emotions—e.g., neuroticism or negative emotionality—and traits related to self-control—e.g., impulsivity, sensation seeking, behavioral undercontrol (see Sher et al., 1999, for a review). Observing a statistical association between these traits and SUDs is not the end point of research on personality and SUDs but, rather, a starting point that helps to identify distinct etiological processes which contribute to the development of SUDs. Accumulating research suggests that personality is associated with multiple, distinct etiological pathways and indexes, core dimensions of individual vulnerability to SUDs that are heritable. Most, though certainly not all, research suggests that some traits represent vulnerability to a range of SUDs. However, even in the context of a general vulnerability to SUDs, it appears that some traits may differentially predispose an individual more to one type of SUD (e.g., alcohol dependence) than another (e.g., tobacco dependence).

DEFINING PERSONALITY AND IDENTIFYING ITS DIMENSIONS

Although various definitions of personality exist, most formal definitions state that personality is, as suggested by Watson and colleagues, "internal, organized, and characteristic of an individual over time and situations...[and has] motivational and adaptive significance" (1994, p. 18). Of particular relevance to research on addiction are *general factor models* that attempt to comprehensively map the major dimensions of adult personality (Watson, Clark, & Harkness, 1994). Typically, these models focus on either three major dimensions (known as the Big Three) or five (the Big Five).

Big Three models of personality reduce it to three dimensions, often labeled as neuroticism/negative emotionality, impulsivity/disinhibition, and extraversion/sociability. Neuroticism/negative emotionality includes facets such as anxiety, depression, guilt, stress reactivity, and emotionality. Extraversion/sociability includes liveliness, surgency, and social closeness. Impulsivity/disinhibition (often called behavioral undercontrol in the substance use literature) includes nontraditionalism, embracing risk, and impulsivity. More generally, behavioral undercontrol describes a broad range of behaviors that collectively reflect difficulty in inhibiting behavioral impulses (Elkins et al., 2006). It is important to note that some early-twenty-first-century work (Smith et al., 2007; Whiteside & Lynam, 2003) has utilized factor analyses to identify four distinct personality facets associated with impulsive-like behavior: sensation seeking, lack of planning, lack of persistence, and urgency (acting rashly when distressed).

Big Five models of personality include neuroticism (N), extraversion (E), openness to experience (O), agreeableness (A), and conscientiousness (C). In Big Five models, neuroticism and extraversion correspond to the similarly named traits in most Big Three systems. Agreeableness includes altruism, compliance, and modesty. Conscientiousness includes competence, achievement striving, and deliberation (and is closely related to, but not isomorphic with, impulsivity/disinhibition in Big Three systems). Depending on the specific form of the Big Five model being considered, the fifth dimension is sometimes referred to as either openness to experiences (Costa & McCrae, 1992) or intellect (Goldberg, 1990). The Big Three and Big Five models of personality appear to represent replicable structures of personality across diverse cultures, can serve as useful structures to examine the relationship of personality with SUDs (Sher et al., 1999), and may be integrated with some success (Watson et al., 1994).

PERSONALITY TRAITS AND SUDS

A number of personality traits have been associated with SUDs. As noted previously, it remains unclear if different personality traits predict different types of substance dependence. Some research suggests that personality traits, such as neuroticism/negative emotionality and disinhibition/impulsivity, correspond to the increased use and misuse of a number of substances, such as alcohol, tobacco, and illicit drugs (e.g., Sher et al., 1995). However, other research suggests that different personality traits predict different types of SUDs (e.g., Sher, Bartholow, & Wood, 2000).

To determine which personality traits predict alcohol, drug, and tobacco dependence symptoms and whether the strength of personality and SUD relationships differ by substance, Grekin, Sher, and Wood (2006) conducted a study in a large, longitudinal college student sample using well-validated factor models of personality. These researchers found that novelty seeking (a trait similar to behavioral undercontrol) and neuroticism predicted alcohol, drug, and tobacco dependence symptoms. These findings are consistent with previous research showing associations with SUDs and both disinhibition/impulsivity and neuroticism/negative affectivity.

However, these researchers also found that several personality traits were differentially related to alcohol, drug, and tobacco dependence symptoms. Specifically, alcohol symptomatology was predicted by low openness to experience and extraversion. Drug symptomatology was predicted by low conscientiousness, and tobacco symptomatology was predicted by low conscientiousness and openness to experience. These findings suggest that drug- and tobacco-dependent individuals have a less socially oriented, undependable personality profile than alcohol-dependent individuals.

In a similar study, Elkins and co-workers (2006) examined the association of personality at age 17 with the timing of onset and with the prospective prediction of nicotine, alcohol, and illicit drug disorders 3 years later in a twin sample. The earlier onset of alcohol and drug disorders (i.e., onset by age 17) was related to low constraint (lack of behavioral inhibition and conventionality) compared to later onsets (i.e., onsets by age 20). High negative emotionality (the tendency to experience distress or anger) was related to the onset of either alcohol or drug disorders. Furthermore, the researchers found that low constraint and negative emotionality contribute uniquely (i.e., when adjusting for the other's contribution) and prospectively to the new onset of nicotine, alcohol, and illicit drug disorders, even when taking a past history of substance use into account. The authors conclude that the personality traits of low constraint and high negative emotionality represent a generalized risk for substance disorders during the peaks ages of onset during late adolescence and early adulthood.

In sum, nicotine, alcohol, and drug symptomatology appears to be related to impulsivity/low constraint and neuroticism/negative emotionality. Furthermore, alcohol-dependent individuals may have more socially oriented, dependent personality profiles than drug- and tobacco-dependent individuals. These findings suggest that core personality traits such as impulsivity/low constraint and neuroticism/negative emotionality increase the risk for developing any substance disorder, but some personality traits are more strongly linked with some substance disorders than with others.

MODELS OF THE RELATIONSHIP BETWEEN PERSONALITY AND SUDS

Observed associations between personality traits and SUDs suggest that personality variation is relevant to understanding substance abuse and dependence but does not necessarily inform us as to how or why personality contributes to the development and maintenance of SUDs. Existing literature suggests at least three etiological processes linking personality and SUDs (e.g., Sher et al., 1999; Sher & Grekin, 2007): (1) pharmacological vulnerability, (2) affect regulation, and (3) deviance proneness.

Pharmacological Vulnerability. The pharmacological vulnerability model posits that some individuals are pharmacologically predisposed to experience the effects of a substance in a way that increases their risk to engage in excessive consumption of the substance and/or to experience pronounced difficulties from the substance. Seemingly opposing predictions can be made from this model. For instance, it is hypothesized that individuals

with *increased* sensitivity to positive or negative reinforcement from a substance are at an increased risk for a SUD because they receive a greater effect from the substance. However, it is also possible that individuals with *decreased* sensitivity to reinforcement use substances at larger amounts in order to achieve a desired effect, thus increasing their risk of physiological dependence.

Over the better part of the last century, there has been continual interest in the idea of personality traits influencing sensitivity to the effects of drugs. Several researchers (e.g., Claridge, 1967) have examined the effects of different drugs on behavioral performance and sedation thresholds (e.g., determining the dose of an intravenously administered barbiturate required to bring an individual to a predefined level of drowsiness) to test hypotheses of the relationship of drug effects to personality. These studies indicated that sensitivity to drug effects varied as a function of neuroticism and extraversion.

The rationales for these types of studies rely, in part, on neurobiological theories of personality positing that personality variation is a function of individual differences in the activity of major neurotransmitter and hormonal systems. Thus, drugs acting on these systems would be expected to have differential effects as a function of underlying (i.e., typical) variability in the activity of these motivationally important neurobiological systems. Alternatively, personality dimensions represent basic patterns of reacting to biologically meaningful stimuli, and thus individual differences in personality lead to characteristic responses to substances, such as alcohol, tobacco, and drugs. Research has indicated that individuals high in impulsivity/disinhibition appear to be more sensitive to the stress-reducing properties of alcohol, which is thought to make the effects of alcohol more reinforcing (e.g., Sher & Levenson, 1982).

Affect Regulation. It has long been recognized that individuals are motivated to use substances for a variety of reasons. Motivational theorists regard motivations as a gateway to substance use through which more distal influences, such as personality, are mediated (Cooper et al., 1995). Cooper developed and validated a four-factor model for drinking motivations among adolescents. Drinking motives were characterized along two underlying dimensions reflecting the valence (positive or negative) and source (internal or external) of the outcomes an individual hopes to achieve by drinking. Crossing these two dimensions produces four classes of motives: (1) intrinsic positive reinforcement or enhancement (e.g., "How often do you drink to get high?"), (2) extrinsic, positive reinforcement for social rewards (e.g., "How often would you say you drink to be sociable?"), (3) intrinsic, negative reinforcement or coping (e.g., "How often do you drink because it helps you when you feel depressed or nervous?"), and (4) extrinsic, negative reinforcement to avoid social censure or conformity (e.g., "How often would you say you drink to fit in with a group you like?"). These motives have been extended to include motives for cigarette smoking, marijuana use, and other drugs.

Drinking for *positive reinforcement* or enhancement is strongly associated with personality traits related to reward seeking, and these motives have been shown to mediate the influence of personality on alcohol outcomes (Cooper et al., 1995). Theorists suggest that motivations for positive reinforcement from alcohol and other drugs of abuse are based on these substances' neuropharmacological effects on the brain centers involved in basic reward mechanisms.

On the other hand, *negative reinforcement* motives to drink are based on the hypothesis that alcohol and other drugs of abuse relieve negative affect. This self-medication or tension-reduction hypothesis has garnered considerable empirical support. Many people report that they drink to cope with negative affect, and these coping motives appear to mediate the effects of neuroticism/negative emotionality on drinking outcomes (Cooper et al., 1995). However, it is clear that not all individuals who have SUDs use substances to regulate affect, and there is considerable inter-individual variation in how effective various substances are in reducing negative affect.

Several things should be noted about the relationship between motives and personality. First, personality traits do not account for a high proportion of variance in substance use motives. Second, in several studies, the influence of personality on substance use outcomes still remains when controlling for motives, implying that mechanisms other than self-reported motivations are important in mediating personality effects on substance use.

Consequently, although evidence exists that motivations act as a gateway to substance use through which more distal influences, such as personality, exert their effects, it is clear that additional mechanisms relate personality to substance use.

In addition, both correlational and experimental data support the mediating role of affect regulation on personality-substance use relations. The self-awareness model of alcohol (Hull, 1987) suggests that painful affective states, such as depression from a failure experience, are mediated by a state of self-awareness. Alcohol and other sedative/hypnotic drugs of abuse are thought to reduce this distress by disrupting the psychological mechanisms underlying self-awareness. Individuals with certain personality traits, such as high private self-consciousness (i.e., the trait counterpart of the state of self-awareness), are thought to be especially vulnerable to experiencing negative affect when presented with negative information about the self. Thus, these individuals are more likely to obtain relief from substances that reduce self-awareness when experiencing negative affect caused by self-awareness processes. Also, indirect evidence for the affect regulation model is based on the high comorbidity between SUDs and anxiety and mood disorders (Compton et al., 2007; Grant et al., 2004; Kessler et al., 1997; Hasin et al., 2007). Personality traits, such as neuroticism/negative emotionality, have been linked to both anxiety and mood disorders, and low extraversion/sociability appears to increase the vulnerability for depression (Clark, Watson, & Mineka, 1994). However, as noted above, not all individuals are likely to increase their substance use when anxious or depressed.

Deviance Proneness. The deviance proneness model posits that excessive substance use is not necessarily the result of physiological or psychological vulnerabilities to substances or the result of affective states. Rather, this model suggests that substance use is just one facet of a more general, deviant pattern of behaviors that originates in childhood and is the result of deficient socialization. These deficits are associated with a range of problem behaviors, such as a history of delinquent behaviors, childhood achievement problems, association with deviant peers, and substance use and abuse. Although a variety of theories exists on the relationship of these various problem behaviors to substance use, most view personality as an extremely distal influence, such that personality is thought to influence long-term socialization processes created by parents and institutions in the community, such as schools. Other theories suggest that *risky* personality styles are associated with decision-making styles which are proximal to substance use (i.e., impulsive decisions surrounding substance use). It is important to note that these two models are not necessarily incompatible. For example, it is possible that personality affects substance use by influencing both peer group affiliations and risky decision making regarding substance use.

These three classes of models (pharmacological vulnerability, affect regulation, and deviance proneness) should not be viewed as exhaustive or mutually exclusive. Personality influences substance use through multiple pathways, although these pathways are largely theorized to be indirect and mediated by more proximal variables. However, the traitlike nature of personality makes it an important variable in the identification of individuals at future risk to develop SUDs.

PERSONALITY AND THE GENETIC RISK FOR SUDS
Some theories suggest that the genetic risk for SUDs is, in part, mediated by personality. It is believed that genetic factors account for individual differences in personality, with approximately one-third to one-half of the variation in personality attributed to genetics (e.g., Loehlin, 1992). Slutske et al. (2002) examined the extent to which the genetic risk for alcohol dependence and conduct disorder and their common genetic risk overlap with genetic factors contributing to a variation in dimensions of personality. These researchers found that genetic influences on personality dimensions accounted for a substantial proportion of the genetic risk for alcohol dependence. Specifically, behavioral undercontrol accounted for about 40 percent of the genetic variation in alcohol dependence risk, whereas negative emotionality accounted for a modest, yet significant, 4 percent of the genetic variation in alcohol dependence risk in men (but not women). Furthermore, the genetic influences contributing to variation in behavioral undercontrol accounted for about 90 percent of the common genetic risk for alcohol dependence and conduct disorder.

These findings suggest that genetic factors contribute to variation in dimensions of personality, which contribute to the risk for SUDs. In particular, behavioral undercontrol appears to be the personality dimension most strongly associated with alcohol dependence and explained the most genetic variation in alcohol dependence risk. Several theoretical models have been proffered to explain the causal link between genetically influenced variation in behavioral undercontrol and alcohol dependence (see above). Consistent with the deviance proneness model, higher levels of behavioral undercontrol may indirectly influence alcohol dependence risk (e.g., by leading to association with deviant, heavy-drinking peers), because it is associated with enhanced reinforcement from alcohol, or because of impaired decision making about drinking surrounding drug use.

PERSONALITY DISORDERS AND SUDS
Although traditionally there has been an interest in the role of personality in the development of SUDs, recent interest has turned to the comorbidity of SUDs and personality disorders (Compton et al., 2007; Grant et al., 2004; Hasin et al., 2007; Trull, Waudby, & Sher, 2004). *DSM-IV* personality disorders are composed of maladaptive personality traits. Thus, an interesting possibility raised by substance use and personality disorder comorbidity is whether this comorbidity is a function of the personality traits shared by both groups of disorders.

Trull and colleagues (2004) examined the relationships between major personality traits, *DSM-IV* personality disorder symptoms, and alcohol, tobacco, and drug use disorders. This study yielded two major findings. First, the relations between personality disorder symptoms (PDs) and SUDs were not completely explained by the covariation between PDs and SUDs and scores on major personality traits. Personality disorder symptoms predicted alcohol, tobacco, and drug use disorder diagnoses over and above the influence of major personality traits, including both Big Three and Big Five dimensions of personality. Second, the researchers found differential relations between personality disorder symptoms and substance use diagnoses. Symptoms of Cluster B personality disorders, which include antisocial, borderline, histrionic, and narcissistic personality disorders, were significant and unique predictors of alcohol and drug use diagnoses. Symptoms of Cluster A personality disorders, which include paranoid, schizoid, and schizotypal personality disorders, were unique predictors of tobacco dependence. Differential relations among personality disorder symptoms suggest that different maladaptive personality traits are relevant to different forms of SUDs.

EFFECTS OF SUDS ON PERSONALITY

Although personality is typically viewed as a fixed trait that antedates the development of SUDs, for at least three decades it has been known that the development of SUDs can alter aspects of personality and the concept of pre-alcoholic or predependent personality characteristics is distinct from clinical alcoholic or dependent personality characteristics (Sher et al., 1999). This observation is based on the finding that several personality traits, especially those related to negative affectivity, tend to become less extreme over a period of abstinence in alcohol-dependent individuals. Neurobiological theories posit that adaptive strain imposed by heavy substance use on brain motivational systems (e.g., Koob & Le Moal, 1997) disrupts hedonic tone and contributes to a "downward cycle of addiction." In addition, over the course of development, a systematic change in personality occurs (Roberts, Walton, & Viechtbauer, 2006). Consequently, personality is probably less fixed than is typically assumed, changing systematically as a normal feature of development and, possibly, as a consequence of the dependence process itself (at least when the level of dependence is severe).

IN SUMMARY

Personality traits can be viewed as abiding, individual difference variables that play crucial roles in the development of SUDs. Existing research suggests that much of the genetic liability for SUDs is associated with a heritable variation in personality traits, and these traits may be etiologically important for multiple, and conceptually and empirically distinct reasons. For example, someone who is high on the broad trait of disinhibition may be vulnerable to substance dependence because he or she is more venturesome and likely to be exposed to substance use, may experience a bigger "kick" from a drug or simply enjoy altered states of consciousness more than average, and may have trouble inhibiting substance-using impulses (especially as dependence processes develop). Moreover, individuals who have

SUDs are likely to have not only multiple SUDs but also a range of other psychological disorders (e.g., anxiety and mood disorders, or personality disorders) and these comorbid conditions can reflect, in part, the influence of personality. As dependence progresses, substance-induced disorders (i.e., transitory syndromes that are present only during and for a time after a period of active use) can develop and, presumably, reflect intra-individual personality change. Thus, the picture emerging from contemporary research is that personality is intimately linked not only with vulnerability to the development of SUDs but also with their course and in myriad ways. Although some differences clearly exist in the mean personality profiles of individuals with different forms of SUDs, in general, there are more similarities than differences in the personality risk for different SUDs. Indeed, certain constellations of personality traits (e.g., high neuroticism, low extraversion, low agreeableness, and low conscientiousness) appear to be risk factors for SUDs as well as psychopathology more generally (Trull & Sher, 1994).

See also **Conduct Disorder and Drug Use; Coping and Drug Use; Families and Drug Use; Risk Factors for Substance Use, Abuse, and Dependence: An Overview.**

BIBLIOGRAPHY

American Psychiatric Association. (1994). *Diagnostic and statistical manual of mental disorders* (4th ed.). Washington, DC: American Psychiatric Publishing.

Claridge, G. (1967). *Personality and arousal.* Oxford, UK: Pergamon.

Clark, L. A., Watson, D., & Mineka, S. (1994). Temperament, personality, and the mood and anxiety disorders. *Journal of Abnormal Psychology, 103,* 103–116.

Compton, W., Thomas, Y. F., Stinson, F. S., & Grant, B. F. (2007). Prevalence, correlates, disability, and comorbidity of DSM-IV drug abuse and dependence in the United States: Results from the National Epidemiologic Survey on Alcohol and Related Conditions. *Archives of General Psychiatry, 64,* 566–576.

Cooper, M. L., Frone, M. R., Russell, M., & Mudar, P. (1995). Drinking to regulate positive and negative emotions: A motivational model of alcohol use. *Journal of Personality and Social Psychology, 69,* 990–1005.

Costa, P. T., Jr., & McCrae, R. R. (1992). *NEO Personality Inventory (NEO-PI-R) and NEO Five-Factor Inventory (NEO-FFI) professional manual* (Rev. ed.). Odessa, FL: Psychological Assessment Resources.

Elkins, I. J., King, S. M., McGue, M., & Iacono, W. G. (2006). Personality traits and the development of nicotine, alcohol, and illicit drug disorders: Prospective links from adolescence to young adulthood. *Journal of Abnormal Psychology, 115*, 26–39.

Goldbeg, L. R. (1990). An alternative "description of personality": The Big-Five factor structure. *Journal of Personality and Social Psychology, 59*, 1216–1229.

Grant, B. F., Hasin, D., Chou, S. P., Stinson, F. S., & Dawson, D. A. (2004). Nicotine dependence and psychiatric disorders in the US: Results from the National Epidemiologic Survey on Alcohol and Related Conditions. *Archives of General Psychiatry, 61*, 1107–1115.

Grekin, E. R., Sher, K. J., & Wood, P. K. (2006). Personality and substance dependence symptoms: Modeling substance-specific traits. *Psychology of Addictive Behavior, 20*, 415–424.

Hasin, D. S., Stinson, F. S., Ogburn, E. O., & Grant, B. F. (2007). Prevalence, correlates, disability, and comorbidity of DSM-IV alcohol abuse and dependence in the United States: Results from the National Epidemiologic Survey on Alcohol and Related Conditions. *Archives of General Psychiatry, 64*, 830–842.

Hull, J. (1987). Self-awareness model. In H. T. Blane & K. E. Leonard (Eds.), *Psychological theories of drinking and alcoholism* (pp. 272–304). New York: Guilford.

Kessler, R. C., Crum, R. M., Warner, L. A., & Nelson, C. B. (1997). Lifetime co-occurrence of DSM-III-R alcohol abuse and dependence with other psychiatric disorders in the National Comorbidity Survey. *Archives of General Psychiatry, 54*, 313–321.

Koob, G. F., & Le Moal, M. (1997). Drug abuse: Hedonic homeostatic dysregulation. *Science, 278*, 52–58.

Loehlin, J. C. (1992). *Genes and the environment in personality development.* Newbury Park, CA: Sage.

Roberts, B. W., Walton, K. E., & Viechtbauer, W. (2006). Patterns of mean-level change in personality traits across the life course: A meta-analysis of longitudinal studies. *Psychological Bulletin, 132*, 1–25.

Sher, K. J. (1991). *Children of alcoholics: A critical appraisal of theory and research.* Chicago: University of Chicago Press.

Sher, K. J., Bartholow, B. D., & Wood, M. D. (2000). Personality and substance use disorders: A prospective study. *Journal of Consulting and Clinical Psychology, 68*, 818–829.

Sher, K. J., & Grekin, E. R. (2007). Alcohol and affect regulation. In J. Gross (Ed.), *Handbook of emotion regulation* (pp. 560–580). New York: Guilford.

Sher, K. J., & Levenson, R. W. (1982). Risk for alcoholism and individual differences in the stress-response-dampening effect of alcohol. *Journal of Abnormal Psychology, 91*, 350–367.

Sher, K. J., Trull, T. J., Bartholow, B. D., & Vieth, A. (1999). Personality and alcoholism: Issues, methods, and etiological processes. In Kenneth E. Leonard & Howard T. Blane (Eds.), *Psychological theories of drinking and alcoholism* (2nd ed., pp. 54–105). New York: Guilford.

Sher, K. J., Wood, M. D., Crews, T. M., & Vandiver, P. A. (1995). The tridimensional personality questionnaire: Reliability and validity studies and derivation of a short form. *Psychological Assessment, 7*, 195–208.

Slutske, W. S., Cronk, N. J., Sher, K. J., Madden, P. A. F., Bucholz, K. K., & Heath, A. C. (2002). Genes, environment, and individual differences in alcohol expectancies among female adolescents and young adults. *Psychology of Addictive Behaviors, 16*, 308–317.

Smith, G. T., Fischer, S., Cyders, M. A., Annus, A. M., Spillane, N. S., & McCarthy, D. M. (2007). On the validity and utility of discriminating among impulsivity-like traits. *Assessment, 14*, 155–170.

Trull, T. J., & Sher, K. J. (1994). Relationship between the five-factor model of personality and Axis I disorders in a nonclinical sample. *Journal of Abnormal Psychology, 103*, 350–360.

Trull, T. J., Waudby, C. J., & Sher, K. J. (2004). Alcohol, tobacco, and drug use disorders and personality disorder symptoms. *Experimental and Clinical Neuropsychopharmacology, 12*(1), 65–75.

Watson, D., Clark, L. A., & Harkness, A. R. (1994). Structures of personality and their relevance to psychopathology. *Journal of Abnormal Psychology, 103*, 18–31.

Whiteside, S. P., & Lynam, D. R. (2003). Understanding the role of impulsivity and externalizing psychopathology in alcohol abuse: Application of the UPPS Impulsive Behavior Scale. *Experimental and Clinical Psychopharmacology, 11*, 210–217.

KENNETH J. SHER
ANDREW K. LITTLEFIELD

PSYCHODYNAMIC PERSPECTIVE

The psychological study and understanding of substance abusers has tended to be difficult, controversial, and complicated. Part of this contention derives from the nature of addictive illness; the acute (short-term) and the chronic (long-term) use of drugs and alcohol cause individuals to seem pleasure oriented, self-centered, and/or destructive to self and others, thus making them difficult to approach, understand, or treat. In other respects, the controversy or lack of understanding derives from competing ideas or schools of thought that debate (if not hotly contend) whether substance abuse is a disease or a symptom, whether biological and genetic factors are more important than environmental or psychological ones, and/or whether substance abuse causes or is the result of human psychological suffering. Furthermore, during the final third of the twentieth century, psychological factors were minimized as researchers entered an era of biological psychiatry/psychology, in which empirical interest in brain structure and function (down to the microscopic and molecular level) predominated over interest in the person, the person's mind, and subjective aspects of human psychological life that govern both emotions and behavior. Although one cannot ignore that substances of abuse are psychoactive (powerful chemicals that act on the brain), there is a tendency to lose sight of the total person whose ways of thinking, feeling, and behaving (including subjective feelings about self and others) are equally and profoundly affected both by that chemistry and by the subjective effects produced by those psychoactive substances.

Clearly, biological, genetic (i.e., hereditary), and sociological factors are important in the development of drug abuse and dependence. Such factors, best studied by empirical methods, and modern technology have yielded new and valuable data since the late 1960s to explain aspects of addictive behavior. It is also noteworthy that during this period, clinical work with substance abusers has yielded data and findings of equal importance and validity, and this work has focused on some of the important subjective psychological factors that also explain aspects of addictive behavior, some of which empirical methods alone do not adequately explain.

This entry presents a psychological understanding of drug abuse and dependence based on the perspective gained from clinical work with alcoholic and drug-dependent individuals. In psychology and clinical psychiatry, it is referred to as the *case method* of study of human psychological problems. Guided by psychodynamic principles, this entry reviews what four decades of clinical work and case study with substance abusers has yielded on some of the main psychological influences that make likely or compelling the dependence on, and continued use and relapse to, drugs and alcohol.

ASSUMPTIONS

A psychodynamic perspective of human psychological life problems rests on the principle that people are all more or less susceptible to various forms of human psychological vulnerabilities; at the same time, they

are also more or less endowed with human psychological strengths or capacities to protect against these vulnerabilities. Without ignoring hereditary factors, especially those that affect temperament, a psychological, and in this case psychodynamic perspective attempts to understand psychological forces at work (for example, drives and feelings) that operate within the individual at the same time that there is a corresponding interest in the psychological structures, functions, and defenses that observably (and just as often, less obviously) operate to regulate or control human drives, feelings, and behavior.

A psychodynamic approach to human psychology greatly depends on a developmental perspective or an appreciation of the psychological forces, structures, and functions as they develop and change over one's lifetime. Psychodynamic clinicians are especially interested in the way individuals are influenced in the earliest phases of development by parents (and other caregivers), and then in the development of relationships with other children and peers, and later in the life cycle in relationships with adults and small and large groups, all of which shape their life views and experiences, as well as their attitudes, values, and characteristic ways of reacting and behaving.

Based on these assumptions, clinicians have the opportunity, most usually in the context of treating patients, to study and understand how the degree of developmental impairments (or strengths) has predisposed toward (or protected against) psychological and psychiatric dysfunction, including addictive vulnerability. According to some clinicians modern psychodynamic-clinical approaches are as relevant and useful for studying and treating substance-dependent individuals as they are for the many other patients who benefit from them.

The psychological study and understanding of addictive illness necessarily requires the condition of abstinence (being free of drug/alcohol use). There is considerable debate about the duration of abstinence required before meaningful or valid psychological inferences can be made about individuals with addictive disorders. The confounding effects of acute and chronic drug/alcohol use are variable, and it is often surprising that within days or weeks—but certainly within several months of abstinence—how much can be learned about individuals' makeup and psychology that predisposed them to use and become dependent on substances. This point about the requirement for a period of abstinence from drugs and alcohol is important to emphasize; otherwise, it can be and is rightfully argued that what appear to be the psychological causes of dependence on psychoactive substances are actually the result of such a dependence. Fortunately, in recent years, the combination of modern detoxification approaches, psychoeducational/rehabilitation/relapse prevention programs, twelve-step groups, and individual and group psychotherapeutic approaches, have been increasingly successful in establishing and maintaining abstinence. This result, in turn, has made psychological treatments and understanding increasingly possible.

PSYCHOLOGICAL SUFFERING AND SELF-CONTROL

A clinical-psychodynamic perspective suggests that human psychological suffering and problems with self-control are at the heart of addictive disorders. In fact, it is probably safe to say that to understand the psychology of addictive behavior is to understand a great deal about human psychological problems of suffering and control in general. The suffering that influences addictive behavior occurs at many levels, but it principally evolves out of susceptibilities involving individuals' self-esteem, relationships, emotions, and capacities to take care of themselves. Individuals who find various or particular drugs appealing (including alcohol) or who become dependent on them discover that, short-term, the drug action or effect relieves or controls their distress; that is, such drugs are used to self-medicate distress. Although problems with self-esteem and relationships are important parts in the equation of addictive behavior, it is mainly the problems with how substance-dependent individuals experience, tolerate, and express their feelings and their problems with self-care that makes addictive behavior so malignantly likely and compelling.

Problems with emotions and self-care painfully and repetitiously become involved with attempts to control suffering and behavior. This process includes such self-defeating coping patterns as impulsive actions and behaviors, psychological defensiveness (e.g., denial, boastful or arrogant postures, attitudes of invulnerability and toughness), and, ultimately, the use of drugs and alcohol. What originally is a solution for suffering and self-regulation—in which substances are used for relief or control—turns into a problem in which there is a progressive loss of control of one's self, the drugs or alcohol employed to combat one's difficulties, and possibly life itself.

THE SELF-MEDICATION HYPOTHESIS

The *self-medication hypothesis* specifically applies to some individuals who, by dint of temperament or developmental factors, experience and find that certain painful feelings (or affects) are intense and unbearable and that the specific action or effect of one of the various classes of abused drugs (e.g., analgesics, depressants, or stimulants) relieves their psychological pain and suffering. The self-medication hypothesis also implies that the particular drug or class of drugs preferred is not random. Rather, it is determined by how that class of drugs with its specific actions interacts with emotional states or particular painful feelings unique to the individuals who use or select their so-called drug-of-choice.

This is only one aspect of addictive suffering: Namely, emotions are experienced in the extreme, and addictive-prone individuals feel too much pain, so they resort to particular drugs to relieve their suffering. Another aspect of addictive suffering is that emotions are just as often absent, nameless, and confusing and that such individuals experience pain of a different type: They consciously feel too little of their distress and do not know when or why they are bothered (e.g., feeling empty, void, or cut off from emotions), and drugs or alcohol in these instances are used to change or control their emotions or suffering. In the first instance the operative motive is the relief of suffering; in the second, it is the control of suffering.

The self-medication hypothesis rests on the observation that patients, if asked, will indicate that they prefer or discover that one class of drugs has more appeal than another. Still, the drugs preferred by an individual are not the ones that are always used. Drugs that are actually used are just as often the result of other factors, such as cost and availability.

The three main classes of drugs that have been studied are the opioid analgesics (pain relievers), depressants or sedative-hypnotics (soothing, relaxing, or sleep-inducing drugs), and stimulants (activating or energizing drugs). The main appeal of opioids (e.g., heroin, morphine, oxycodone) is that they are powerful subduing or calming agents. Besides calming or subduing physical pain for which they were originally intended, opioids are also effective in reducing or alleviating distressing or disruptive emotions. Beyond its calming influence on physical and emotional pain in general, however, the main and specific action of opioids, namely as an anti-rage or anti-aggression drug, may make them especially appealing and compelling for those who struggle within, and with others, with feelings of intense anger, aggression, and hostility. Such a state of affairs is not uncommon for people who, in their early life development or in later life experiences, have suffered major trauma, neglect, or abuse. Such individuals, when they first use opioids, discover the extraordinary calming and soothing effects of these drugs on their intense anger and rage, and thus they become powerfully drawn or attached to them.

Whereas opioid-dependent people have much difficulty controlling their feelings, especially anger and rage, those who prefer or who are dependent on depressants generally have the opposite problem: Namely they are too controlled or too tightly wrapped around their feelings. As is the case with other substance abusers, developmental life experiences, in this case often involving distrust and traumatic disappointment, have had a special influence on their experience of emotions. People who prefer depressants have special difficulties experiencing emotions involving loving or caring feelings, interpersonal dependency, and closeness; in psychological terms, they are defensive and repressed around these emotions and have difficulty in experiencing or expressing them. Depressants (e.g., alcohol, Seconal, Xanax) have appeal for these people because such drugs help them to relax their defenses and release them from their repressions. Mainly, such drugs briefly (the short- or quick-acting depressants) produce a sense of safety and an inner sense of warmth, affection, or closeness that otherwise these people cannot experience or allow.

Finally, stimulants (i.e., amphetamines and cocaine are the most popular and widely used) have appeal for those who suffer with overt and/or subtle states of depression, mania, and hyperactivity, in which problems with activation, activity, and energy are common. For example, ambitious driven types, for whom performance, prowess, and achievement are essential, find

such drugs especially appealing on two counts: (1) stimulants are uplifting when individuals become depressed as their goals and ambitions, often unrealistic, fail them; (2) stimulants are facilitating and make action and activity easier when such people are on the upswing, making it easier for them to be the way they like to be when they are performing at their best. Stimulants cast a wide net of appeal because they also counter feelings of low energy, low activity, and low self-esteem in those suffering with overt or less overt (unrecognized or atypical) depression. Finally, those individuals suffering with attention deficit-hyperactivity disorder (ADHD), often sub-clinical or not recognized, are also drawn to and become dependent on stimulants because of the paradoxically opposite calming effect that stimulants have for people with this disorder—much like hyperactive children who are calmed by the prescribed stimulant Ritalin.

SELF-REGULATION VULNERABILITIES

To explain why people become addicted, early psychodynamic theory places great emphasis on subconscious and unconscious factors, pleasure and aggressive instincts or drives, and the symbolic meaning of drugs. To some extent, the stereotype of substance abusers as pleasure-seeking destructive characters (to self and others), in part, persists and derives from these early formulations. Albeit useful and innovative at the time, much of this early perspective is perceived in the early twenty-first century as outdated, counterempathic, and a disservice to understanding the motives of addicted and alcoholic individuals.

In contrast, the self-medication hypothesis has evolved from contemporary psychodynamic theory, which has placed the centrality of feelings (or affects) ahead of drives or instincts and has emphasized the importance of self-regulation, involving self-development or self-esteem (i.e., self-psychology), relationship with others (i.e., object-relations theory), and self-care (i.e., ego or structural psychology/ theory). These contemporary psychodynamic findings have evolved since the 1950s, based on the works of investigators such as Weider and Kaplan; Milkman and Frosch; Wurmser, Krystal, Woody and associates; Blatt and associates; and Wilson, Dodes, Burton, Director, and Khantzian.

Although the self-medication hypothesis has gained acceptance as an explanation for drug/

alcohol dependency, it is not without its critics and it fails to deal with at least two fundamental problems or observations. First, many individuals suffer with the painful feelings and emotions that substance abusers experience, but they do not become addicted or alcoholic. Second, the self-medication hypothesis fails to take into account that addicted and alcoholic individuals suffer as much if not more as a result of their drug/alcohol use, and this point might appear to contradict the hypothesis that substances are used to relieve suffering.

Many of these criticisms, inconsistencies, and apparent contradictions are better understood or resolved when addictive problems are considered more broadly, in terms of self-regulation vulnerabilities or as a self-regulation disorder. For humans, life is the constant challenge of self-regulation, as opposed to the release, relief, or control of instincts and drives as early theory suggested. What is in need of regulation involves feelings, the sense of self (or self-esteem), relationships with others, and behavior. Those prone to addictive problems are predisposed to be so because they suffer with a range of self-regulation vulnerabilities. Their sense of self, including self-regard, is often shaky or defective from the outset of their lives. A basic sense of well-being and a capacity for self-comfort and self-soothing is very often lacking or underdeveloped from the earliest phases of development. Subsequent development of self-esteem and self-love, if it develops at all, remains shaky and inconsistent, given the compromised sense of self from which self-regard evolves. Needless to say, a poor sense of self or low self-esteem (which usually originates in a compromised or deficient self-other parenting relationship), ultimately affects subsequent self-other relationships and profoundly affects one's capacity to trust or to be dependent upon or to become involved with others. Psychodynamic formulations suggest that the self-regulation problems of addicted individuals are experienced as feelings of helplessness and powerlessness and play out in omnipotent posturing and dissociation.

It should not be surprising, then, that for some the energizing and activating properties of stimulants help self-doubting reticent individuals to overcome their depressive slumps and withdrawal, or that the soothing, relaxing effects of depressants help individuals who are restricted and cut off from others to break through their inhibitions and briefly experience the warmth and comfort of human contact that they otherwise do not allow or trust or that those whose lives are racked by anger and related agitation would find a drug such as heroin (an opioid analgesic) to be a powerful containing, calming antidote to their intense and threatening emotions, which disrupt them from within and threaten most of their relationships with others. These examples, and those previously covered in relation to self-medication motives that govern drug use and dependency, help demonstrate the how and why of specific drug effects, which often become so compelling that they may consume the lives of some users.

The regulation of feelings (or affects) and self-care are among the most compelling self-regulatory problems; they combine to make dependence on substances more likely than any other self-regulation factors. Focus on these two factors explains clearly why most people who suffer subjective painful emotions do not necessarily become addicted as well as why so many substance abusers persist in using debilitating substances despite the great suffering that ensues from their abuse.

The psychoanalytic perspective assumes that substance abusers suffer in the extreme with their emotions: They feel too much or they feel too little. When there is too much, drugs can relieve the intense unbearable feelings that addicts and others experience. Where there is too little and people are (or seem to be) devoid of, cut off from, or confused by their feelings (e.g., alexithymia, disaffected, or affect deficits), addicts prefer to counter the helplessness and loss of control caused by their lack of feelings. They choose to use drugs to change and control their feelings, even if doing so causes them more distress. They exchange feelings that are vague, confusing, and out-of-control, for drug-induced feelings that they recognize, understand, and control, even if such are painful and uncomfortable. Therefore, the factors of relief and control dominate people's motives for depending on drugs, even if these people have to endure the pain that their dependence on drugs also entails.

Finally, deficits in self-care (again deriving from early-life developmental problems) make it likely that certain individuals will become involved with hazardous activities and relationships that lead to drug experimentation, use, and dependence. Self-care deficits refer to a major self-regulation problem, wherein individuals feel and think differently in potential or actually dangerous situations and activities, including those that involve drug/alcohol experimentation and use. Where most people would be apprehensive or frightened or would anticipate some guilt and shame, addictive and alcoholic-prone individuals show little or no such worry. Studying these patients' pre- and post-addictive behavior patterns often reveals similar unfeeling, unthinking, fearless behavior in conducting other aspects of their lives; for example, preventable accidents, health-care problems, and financial difficulties seem evident and common. Being out of touch with, or not feeling, their feelings (that is, their affect deficits or disaffected state) contributes to their self-care problems and thus makes it more likely that they would engage in the dangerous pursuit of drug/alcohol abuse, whereas others with better self-care functions would not (even in those instances in which the unbearable psychological suffering and states of distress are like those experienced by addicts). In this respect, painful or unbearable feelings, alone, are not sufficient to cause substance abuse or dependence. Rather, it is when individuals lack adequate self-care capacities and experience intense suffering that conditions exist for addictive behavior to develop or be likely.

See also **Conduct Disorder and Drug Use; Families and Drug Use; Religion and Drug Use.**

BIBLIOGRAPHY

Blatt, S. J., Berman, W. H., Bloom-Feshbach, S., Sugarman, A., Wilber, C. H., & Kleber, H. D. (1984). Psychological assessment of psychotherapy in opiate addicts. *Journal of Nervous and Mental Disease, 172,* 156–165.

Burton, N. (2005). Finding the lost girls: Multiplicity and dissociation in the treatment of addictions. *Psychoanalytic Dialogues 15*(4), 587–612.

Director, L. (2005). Encounters with omnipotence in the psychoanalysis of substance users. *Psychoanalytic Dialogues 15*(4), 567–586.

Dodes, L. M. (1990). Addiction, helplessness, and narcissistic rage. *Psychoanalytic Quarterly, 59,* 398–419.

Khantzian, E. J. (1985). The self-medication hypothesis of addictive disorders. *American Journal of Psychiatry, 142,* 1259–1264.

Khantzian E. J. (1995). Self-regulation vulnerabilities in substance abusers: Treatment implications. In S. Dowling (Ed.), *The psychology and treatment of addictive behavior* (pp. 17–41). New York: International University Press.

Khantzian, E. J. (1997). The self-medication hypothesis of substance use disorders: A reconsideration and recent applications. *Harvard Review of Psychiatry, 4,* 231–244.

Khantzian, E. J. (1999). *Treating addiction as a human process.* Northvale NJ: Jason Aronson.

Khantzian, E. J., & Mack, J. E. (1983). Self-preservation and the care of the self-ego instincts reconsidered. *Psychoanalytical Study of Childhood, 38,* 209–232.

Krystal, H. (1982). Alexithymia and the effectiveness of psychoanalytic treatment. *International Journal of Psychoanalysis and Psychotherapy, 9,* 353–378.

Milkman, H., & Frosch, W. A. (1973). On the preferential abuse of heroin and amphetamine. *Journal of Nervous and Mental Disease, 56,* 242–248.

Weider, H., & Kaplan, E. (1969). Drug use in adolescents. *Psychoanalytical Study of Childhood, 24,* 399–431.

Wilson, A., Passik, S. D., Faude, J., Abrams, J. & Gordon, E. (1989). A hierarchical model of opiate addiction: Failures of self-regulation as a central aspect of substance abuse. *Journal of Nervous and Mental Disease, 177,* 390–399.

Woody, G. E., Luborsky, L., McLellan, A. T., & O'Brien, C. P. (1986). Psychotherapy for substance abuse. *Psychiatric Clinics of North America, 9,* 547–562.

Wurmser, L. (1974). Psychoanalytic considerations of the etiology of compulsive drug use. *Journal of the American Psychoanalytical Association, 22,* 820–843.

E. J. KHANTZIAN

RACE/ETHNICITY

There is a common perception that minority groups in the United States, particularly African Americans and Hispanics, use drugs more than Caucasians, even though population epidemiologic data show little difference in drug use among these groups. In fact, minority groups are, overall, less likely to use licit or illicit drugs. However, according to a 2003 report by the National Institute on Drug Abuse, the adverse consequences of substance abuse tend to be greater for minorities than for Caucasians.

The percentage of minority groups in the U.S. population is projected to increase rapidly over the early decades of the twenty-first century. Therefore, it is important to monitor trends and reduce substance abuse–related disparities that adversely affect minority populations. Different patterns of use and addiction across races and ethnicities provide insights into how underlying risk and protective factors affect substance use, addiction, and adverse consequences because race and ethnicity are markers of differences in these underlying factors. In addition, new knowledge regarding human genomic and neurobiological differences may help reduce disparities in substance use and addiction. Because racial and ethnic disparities widen with the consequences of substance use and addiction, research is needed to understand societal and interpersonal mechanisms that exacerbate such disparities.

RACE DIFFERENCES IN THE GENERAL POPULATION

Recent reports of the annual National Survey on Drug Use and Health (NSDUH; formally the National Household Survey on Drug Abuse [NHSDA]) support previous research in suggesting that Native Americans and Alaska Natives (NA/AN) suffer disproportionately from substance use and addiction compared with other racial groups in the United States. The 2002–2005 surveys show that NA/AN were significantly more likely to have past-year alcohol or illicit drug use disorders. In addition, the use of a variety of illicit drugs and cigarette smoking are considerably higher in this group compared to other racial groups. In contrast, the prevalence of substance use disorders among Asians and Pacific Islanders (APIs), as a whole, has generally been lower than in other racial/ethnic groups. Non-Hispanic African Americans tended to report lower rates of both alcohol and tobacco use than non-Hispanic Caucasians, although the prevalence of licit and illicit substance use disorders has become somewhat higher than in non-Hispanic Caucasians.

ETHNIC DIFFERENCES IN THE GENERAL POPULATION

Prevalence rates of substance use and addiction vary markedly across Hispanic subgroups. Compared to the general U.S. population, Puerto Ricans and Mexicans tend to have higher rates of licit and illicit substance use, problem alcohol use, and alcohol use disorders. In comparison, Cubans and Central Americans tend to have lower prevalence rates of these behaviors and disorders. Although prevalences of both licit and illicit substance use for APIs combined are generally lower than for any other racial groups, Native Hawaiians report higher levels of such substance use (both recent and lifetime). Their patterns of substance use

and abuse are closer to Native Americans than Asian subgroups. As in Hispanic subgroups, prevalence rates of substance use and abuse are considerably different across Asian subgroups and appear to be changing over time. In the 1990s, rates among Japanese were highest. In the early 2000s, however, other subgroups, such as Koreans and Filipinos (and sometimes Vietnamese), appear to have higher use and abuse rates across several illicit drugs, alcohol, and tobacco. The immigration history of the ethnic groups and individuals are correlated with a variety of substance use and abuse indicators.

YOUTH PATTERNS

Data from the Monitoring the Future Study (MTF) and the Youth Risk Behavior Surveillance System (YRBSS) show remarkably consistent patterns indicating that African-American adolescents are less likely to use most illicit drugs, alcohol, and tobacco than their non-Hispanic Caucasian and Hispanic counterparts. Furthermore, the proportion of early-onset users is lower among African Americans than among non-Hispanic Caucasians and Hispanics. These patterns have been persistent over many years. Other school-based studies also support the finding that being African American is protective for a variety of substance use and abuse indicators during adolescence. However, data from adult populations show that the prevalence differences are smaller. In some instances, as in the 2002 NSDUH, rates of some illicit drugs, heavy alcohol use, and recent cigarette use among African Americans surpass those of Caucasians in the same age group. Longitudinal studies suggest that this narrowing of differences between African Americans and Caucasians reflect higher ratios of African American than Caucasian youth who continue to use substances once initiated, rather than reflecting cohort differences.

PATTERNS AMONG MIXED-RACE ADULTS AND YOUTH

With the 2000 Census's introduction of multiple race/ethnicity reporting, more information is available to document substance use and addiction patterns of people who self-identify with two or more races or ethnicities. The 2000-2003 NSDUH data show that the prevalence rates of past-month nicotine dependence, past-year alcohol dependence, and past-year illicit drug dependence were all highest among those who reported more than one racial heritage, compared to any monoracial groups.

Within each racial group, higher rates of use and abuse of most substances were documented among those who reported mixed heritage compared to those reporting only one race or ethnicity. This trend is most striking among adolescents. Being a mixed heritage adolescent was found to be a predictor of substance use and misuse independent of other sociodemographic and acculturation measures among Hispanics, African Americans, and APIs.

PSYCHIATRIC COMORBIDITY

Psychiatric disorders have long been known to co-occur with substance use problems and disorders. Very large surveys using diagnostic instruments have made it easier to examine a variety of psychiatric disorders at racial group, and sometimes ethnic group, levels. The National Epidemiologic Survey on Alcohol and Related Conditions (NESARC) allowed detailed examination of both Axis I and II (personality) disorders, including those diagnoses with low prevalence estimates. Having a psychiatric disorder most frequently increases the odds of having a substance use disorder by a minimum of 50 percent, regardless of racial/ethnic category. However, the odds ratios exceeded 5.0 (reflecting a five-fold risk) for some racial groups for certain psychiatric conditions, even when adjusting for sex, age, income, marital status, education, religion, and urbanicity. A study using the NESARC data reported odds ratios of 7.7 and 5.6 for any past-year drug use disorder with any mood disorder and personality disorder, respectively, among Native Americans; 6.3 for any drug use disorder with any personality disorder among Hispanics; and 5.0 for any past-year alcohol use disorder with any personality disorder among Asians. Higher risk for comorbidity, therefore, is not necessarily a function of how pervasive a substance use disorder is within a specific racial or ethnic group. Future studies are needed to uncover the underlying mechanisms of excess comorbidity in different racial/ethnic groups.

TREATMENT AND EMERGENCY ROOM USE

The Treatment Episode Data Set (TEDS) provides information on the demographic and substance abuse characteristics of people admitted to substance abuse treatment. In 2005, TEDS reported approximately 1.8 million admissions to treatment for abuse of alcohol and drugs in facilities that report to individual state administrative data systems. Five substances accounted for 95 percent of all TEDS admissions in 2004: alcohol (39%), opiates (17%), marijuana/hashish (16%), cocaine (14%), and stimulants (9%). Among all racial/ethnic groups except Hispanics of Puerto Rican origin, primary alcohol use was the most frequently reported substance at treatment admission. However, the proportion reporting use of the next four most common substances (opiates, marijuana, cocaine, and stimulants) varied considerably by racial/ethnic group. Compared to the demographic distributions of all admissions, African Americans were more than twice as likely to be admitted for smoked cocaine abuse (52%) as all groups were (22%). Mexicans and APIs were over two times more likely to be admitted for methamphetamine abuse than was true for all groups.

Racial and ethnic variations are also shown in the Drug Abuse Warning Network (DAWN), which reports trends in drug-related emergency department visits and deaths. There are, however, missing race and ethnicity data in DAWN (i.e., the data were not tabulated or are unknown for about 15%). Nonetheless, some observed trends are consistent with TEDS data: reports of cocaine-related episodes are disproportionately higher in African Americans, and heroin-related episodes are higher in Hispanics.

General population surveys make it possible to assess undermet needs, assuming diagnostic criteria accurately capture treatment needs. For example, only about 15 percent of individuals who meet lifetime criteria for an alcohol use disorder report ever having received alcohol treatment. In addition, considerable racial differences exist in the receipt of treatment, among individuals meeting criteria for a substance use disorder. In the 2000–2002 NHSDA/NSDUH surveys, 7.2 percent of Asians, 11.0 percent of African Americans, and 10.1 percent of Hispanics who met past-year *DSM-IV* alcohol dependence criteria reported treatment in the past year. These rates are lower than the 14.7 percent of Caucasians who met the same criteria. Similar trends are observed for drug abuse treatment, except that 23.8 percent of African Americans who met *DSM-IV* drug dependence criteria reported treatment compared to 18.3 percent of Caucasians who met the same criteria. Overall, these surveys found that although African

Americans were more visible in treatment and emergency room facilities, Asian substance abusers represented a less visible segment of racial minority abusers.

OTHER ADVERSE CONSEQUENCES OF SUBSTANCE USE AND ADDICTION

Greater disparities for adverse consequences of substance abuse are evident in racial and ethnic minority communities. For example, disparities exist in reported rates of arrest, sentencing, and incarceration (in particular among African Americans); victimization; school dropout; and HIV/AIDS infection. Given the magnitude of these disparities, there is an urgent need to better understand the factors—such as socioeconomic status, discrimination, culture, neighborhood and environmental conditions, access to health care, and employment status—that place minorities at risk (or that may be protective) for substance use and its adverse consequences.

See also **African Americans, Ethnic and Cultural Factors Relevant to Treatment for; Chinese Americans, Alcohol and Drug Use among; Drug Abuse Warning Network (DAWN); Hispanic Americans, Alcohol and Drug Use among; Jews and Alcohol; National Survey on Drug Use and Health (NSDUH); Structured Clinical Interview for DSM-IV (SCID).**

BIBLIOGRAPHY

Chae, D. H., Gavin, A. R., & Takeuchi, D. T. (2006). Smoking prevalence among Asian Americans: Findings from the National Latino and Asian American Study (NLAAS). *Public Health Reports, 121*(6), 755–763.

Cohen, E., Feinn, R., Arias, A., & Kranzler, H. R. (2007). Alcohol treatment utilization: Findings from the National Epidemiologic Survey on Alcohol and Related Conditions. *Drug and Alcohol Dependence, 86*(2–3), 214–221.

Eaton, D. K., Kann, L., Kinchen, S., Ross, J., Hawkins, J., Harris, W.A., et al. (2006). Youth risk behavior surveillance—United States, 2005. *Morbidity and Mortality Weekly Report, Surveillance Summaries, 55*(SS05), 1–108.

Grant, B. F., Stinson, F. S., Hasin, D. S., Dawson, D. A., Chou, S. P., & Anderson, K. (2004). Immigration and lifetime prevalence of DSM-IV psychiatric disorders among Mexican Americans and non-Hispanic whites in the United States: Results from the National Epidemiologic Survey on Alcohol and Related Conditions. *Archives of General Psychiatry, 61*(12), 1226–1233.

Hallfors, D. D., Iritani, B. J., Miller, W. C., & Bauer, D. J. (2007). Sexual and drug behavior patterns and HIV and STD racial disparities: The need for new directions. *American Journal of Public Health, 97*(1), 125–132.

Harris, K. M., Gordon-Larsen, P., Chantala, K., & Udry, J. R. (2006). Longitudinal trends in race/ethnic disparities in leading health indicators from adolescence to young adulthood. *Archives of Pediatrics & Adolescent Medicine, 160*(1), 74–81.

Huang, B., Grant, B. F., Dawson, D. A., Stinson, F. S., Chou, S. P., Saha, T. D., et al. (2006). Race-ethnicity and the prevalence and co-occurrence of *Diagnostic and Statistical Manual of Mental Disorders*, Fourth Edition, alcohol and drug use disorders: United States, 2001 to 2002. *Comprehensive Psychiatry, 47*(4), 252–257.

Iguchi, M. Y., Bell, J., Ramchand, R. N., & Fain, T. (2005). How criminal system racial disparities may translate into health disparities. *Journal of Health Care for the Poor and Underserved, 16*(4 Suppl. B), 48–56.

Johnston, L. D., O'Malley, P. M., Bachman, J. G., & Schulenberg, J. E. (2008). *Monitoring the future national results on adolescent drug use: Overview of key findings, 2007.* NIH Publication No. 08-6418. Bethesda, MD: National Institute on Drug Abuse.

National Institute on Drug Abuse. (2003). *Drug use among racial/ethnic minorities.* NIH Publication No. 03-3888. Rockville, MD: Author.

National Institute on Drug Abuse. (2004). Strategic Plan on Reducing Health Disparities: NIH Health Disparities Strategic Plan, Fiscal Year 2004–2008. Available from http://www.drugabuse.gov/.

Price, R. K., Risk, N. K., Wong, M. M., & Klingle, R. S. (2002). Substance use and abuse by Asian Americans and Pacific Islanders: Preliminary results from four national epidemiologic studies. *Public Health Reports, 117*, S39–S50.

Sakai, J. T., Ho, P. M., Shore, J. H., Risk, N. K., & Price, R. K. (2005). Asians in the United States: Substance dependence and use of substance-dependence treatment. *Journal of Substance Abuse Treatment, 29*(2), 75–84.

Substance Abuse and Mental Health Services Administration, Office of Applied Studies. (2006). *Treatment episode data set (TEDS), Highlights 2005: National admissions to substance abuse treatment services* (DASIS series: S-36; DHHS Publication No. [SMA] 07-4229). Rockville, MD: Author.

Substance Abuse and Mental Health Services Administration, Office of Applied Studies. (2007). *Drug Abuse*

Warning Network, 2005: National estimates of drug-related emergency department visits (DAWN Series D-29; DHHS Publication No. [SMA] 07-4256). Rockville, MD: Author.

Substance Abuse and Mental Health Services Administration, Office of Applied Studies. *National Survey on Drug Use and Health: Race and ethnic groups, reports and data.* (n.d.). Rockville, MD: Author. Available from http://oas.samhsa.gov/.

Wong, M. M., Klingle, R. S., & Price, R. K. (2004). Alcohol, tobacco and other drug use among Asian American and Pacific Islander adolescents in California and Hawaii. *Addictive Behaviors, 29*(1), 127–141.

RUMI KATO PRICE

SENSATION SEEKING AND IMPULSIVITY

Sensation seeking is a multidimensional personality construct characterized as "the seeking of varied, novel, complex, and intense sensations and experiences, and the willingness to take physical, social, legal, and financial risks for the sake of such experience" (Zuckerman, 1979). Sensation seeking is often assessed using the Sensation Seeking Scale, containing 40 items divided into four subscales: Thrill and Adventure Seeking, Experience Seeking, Disinhibition, and Boredom Susceptibility. The four subscales are summed to produce an overall score. Drug users rate higher in sensation seeking than users of alcohol, revealing their willingness to take the extra risks associated with the use of illegal substances. Impulsive Sensation Seeking is a scale that combines sensation-seeking items with those of a closely related trait, impulsiveness (Zuckerman, 1993). Although distinct, these components overlap because they are inherently related to achieving an optimal level of stimulation and arousal. They may involve risk-taking behaviors such as driving while intoxicated, unsafe sexual behaviors, and criminal activities, all of which have elements of disinhibitory behavior, as well as thrill seeking. Novelty seeking is a highly correlated component of sensation seeking (Cloninger et al., 1993; Zuckerman & Cloninger, 1996).

Sensation seeking has been used as a criterion to classify alcoholics. Type II (Cloninger et al., 1981) and Type B (Babor et al., 1992) alcoholics are characterized by early age of onset of alcoholism, a positive family history of alcoholism, high sensation seeking, impulsive temperament, and greater severity of alcohol dependence. This paradigm has been extended to illicit substance use as well (Feingold et al., 1996; Ball et al., 1995). Type II/B alcoholism is found predominantly in men (Cloninger, 1987) and, in part, that may be because men score higher on sensation seeking scales than woman and they endorse its subscales differently than women (Zuckerman et al., 1978; Scourfield et al., 1996; Ball et al., 1984). However, sensation seeking has shown stronger associations with substance abuse in females than in men and can distinguish women who are pure substance abusers from those with comorbid anxiety (Scourfield et al., 1996).

Younger individuals score higher on sensation seeking than older individuals and have a concomitant tendency to discount the risks involved in drug use (Romer & Hennessy, 2007; Wills et al., 1998). Age, sensation seeking, and negative affectivity predict frequent risk-taking and substance use in young people (Desrichard & Denarie, 2005). Both sensation seeking and impulsivity are strongly associated with early age of onset of drinking (Dom et al., 2006) and with greater quantity and frequency of alcohol consumption and greater illicit drug use (Zuckerman, 1994). Adults in treatment who score high on sensation seeking generally have an earlier age of onset of both alcohol consumption and alcohol abuse (Ball et al., 1994). High sensation seeking was significantly associated with methamphetamine and stimulant use in 17,000 young adults participating in the 2002 National Survey on Drug Use and Health (NSDUH) (Herman-Stahl et al., 2007). Sensation seeking has been associated with the use of club drugs (Low & Gendaszek, 2002), but possibly with frequency of use rather than initiation of use (Simons et al., 2005).

The biological basis for the association between sensation seeking and a vulnerability to substance abuse has been sought for many years. Low platelet monoamine oxidase (MAO) has long been associated with risk-taking behaviors (Buchsbaum et al., 1976; Fowler et al., 1980). Decreased MAO activity results in an increase in dopamine (as well as other monoamine neurotransmitters, including norepinephrine and serotonin). The increased dopamine drives reward-seeking structures in the striatum and nucleus accumbens in the brain resulting in an increased use of alcohol and drugs. A positive feedback loop results because alcohol and drugs cause a further increase in the release of dopamine in the ventral striatum and nucleus accumbens. However, the relationship of low platelet MAO to personality factors such as sensation seeking is not understood as of 2008. Platelet MAO might be correlated with brain MAO-B and affect the rate of monoamine degradation: It may influence the level of a trace amine that itself is related to behavior; it might be correlated with other mitochondrial enzymes and reduce the functioning of an entire neurotransmitter system; or it might be a marker of expression of a set of monoamine neurotransmitter genes (Oreland et al., 2004). The evidence suggests that platelet MAO is a genetic marker of alterations in several neurotransmitter systems. This evidence stems from the fact that no genetic polymorphisms have been identified in MAO-B (Pivac et al., 2006) and complete inhibition of MAO-B does not change behavior in knock-out mice (Holschneider et al., 2001), or in humans after administration of MAO-B inhibitors in Parkinson's patients (Oreland et al., 2004). Platelet MAO levels correlate to CSF 5-HIAA levels, which have also been found to be higher in type II alcoholics (Virkkunen & Linnoila, 1993), suggesting involvement of the serotonergic system. If sensation seeking is linked to the reward centers in the brain, then norepinephrine levels should differ by sensation seeking level. Sensation seeking was strongly associated with both testosterone and norepinephrine in 74 healthy male adults (Gerra et al., 1999). In summary, neurobiological evidence shows that monoaminergic (dopaminergic, noradrenergic, and serotonergic) neurotransmitter systems play an important role in impulsivity.

Sensation seeking is estimated to be 48 percent to 63 percent heritable (Koopmans et al., 1995; Benjamin et al., 1996). Alleles of genes encoding the D1, D2, and D4 dopamine receptors and the dopamine transporter have been associated with sensation seeking.

See also **Adolescents and Drug Use; Conduct Disorder and Drug Use; Impulsivity and Addiction; Prevention.**

BIBLIOGRAPHY

Babor, T. F., De Hofmann, M. I., Boca, F. K., Hesselbrock, V., Meyer, R. E., Dolinsky, Z. S., et al. (1992). Types of alcoholics: I. Evidence for an empirically derived typology based on indicator of vulnerability and severity. *Archives of General Psychiatry, 49,* 599–608.

Ball, I. L., Farnill, D., & Wangeman, J. F. (1984) Sex and age differences in sensation seeking: Some national comparisons. *British Journal of Psychology, 75,* 257–265 .

Ball, S. A., Carroll, K. M., Babor, T. F., & Rounsaville, B. J. (1995). Subtypes of cocaine abusers: Support for a type A-type B distinction. *Journal of Consulting and Clinical Psychology, 63,* 115–125.

Ball, S. A., Carroll, K. M., & Rounsaville, B, J. (1994). Sensation seeking, substance abuse, and psychopathology in treatment-seeking and community cocaine abusers. *Journal of Consulting and Clinical Psychology, 62,* 1053–1057.

Benjamin, J., Li, L., Patterson, C., Greenberg, B. D., Murphy, D. L., & Hammer, D. H. (1996). Population and familial association between the D4 dopamine receptor gene and measures of novelty seeking. *Nature Genetics, 12,* 81–84.

Buchsbaum, M. S., Coursey, R. D., & Murphy, D. L. (1976). The biochemical high-risk paradigm: Behavioral and familial correlates of low platelet monoamine oxidase activity. *Science, 194,* 339–341.

Cloninger, C. R. (1987). A systematic method for clinical description and classification of personality variants. *Archives of General Psychiatry, 44,* 573–588.

Cloninger, C. R., Bohman, M., & Sigvardsson, S. (1981). Inheritance of alcohol abuse: Cross-fostering analysis of adopted men. *Archives of General Psychiatry, 38,* 861–868.

Cloninger, C. R., Svrakic, D. M., & Przybeck, T. R. (1993). A psychobiological model of temperament and character. *Archives of General Psychiatry, 50,* 975–990.

Connor, J. P., Young, R. M., Lawford, B. R., Ritchie, T. L., & Noble, E. P. (2002). D2 dopamine receptor (DRD2) polymorphism is associated with severity of alcohol dependence. *European Psychiatry, 17,* 17–23.

Damberg, M., Garpenstrand, H., Alfredsson, J., Ekblom, J., Forslund, K., Rylander, G., et al. (2000). A polymorphic region in the human transcription factor AP-2beta gene is associated with specific personality traits. *Molecular Psychiatry, 5*: 220–224.

Damberg, M., Garpenstrand, H., Berggard, C., Asberg, M., Hallman, J., & Oreland, L. (2000). The genotype of human transcription factor AP-2beta is associated with platelet monoamine oxidase B activity. *Neuroscience Letters, 291,* 204–206.

Desrichard, O., & Denarie, V. (2005). Sensation seeking and negative affectivity as predictors of risky behaviors: A distinction between occasional versus frequent risk-taking. *Addictive Behavior, 30,* 1449–1453.

Dom, G., Hulstijn, W., & Sabbe, B. (2006). Differences in impulsivity and sensation seeking between early- and late-onset alcoholics. *Addictive Behaviors, 31,* 298–308.

Ebstein, R. P., Novick, O., Umansky, R., Priel, B., Osher, Y., Blaine, D., et al. (1996). Dopamine D4 (D4DR) exon III polymorphism associated with the human personality trait of novelty seeking. *Nature Genetics, 12*, 78–80.

Feingold, A., Ball, S. A., Kranzler, H. R., & Rounsaville, B. J. (1996). Generalizability of the type A/type B distinction across different psychoactive substances. *American Journal of Drug and Alcohol Abuse, 22*, 449–462.

Fowler, C. J., von Knorring, L., & Oreland, L. (1980). Platelet monoamine oxidase activity in sensation seekers. *Psychiatry Research, 3*, 273–279.

Gerra, G., Avanzani, P., Zaimovic, A., Sartori, R., Bocchi, C., Timpano, M., et al. (1999). Neurotransmitters, neuroendocrine correlates of sensation-seeking temperament in normal humans. *Neuropsychobiology, 39*, 207–213.

Herman-Stahl, M. A., Krebs, C. P., Kroutil, L. A., & Heller, D. C. (2007). Risk and protective factors for methamphetamine use and nonmedical use of prescription stimulants among young adults aged 18 to 25 years. *Addictive Behaviors, 32*, 1003–1015.

Holschneider, D. P., Chen, K., Seif, I., & Shih, J. C. (2001). Biochemical, behavioral, physiologic, and neurodevelopmental changes in mice deficient in monoamine oxidase A or B. *Brain Research Bulletin, 56*, 453–462.

Koopmans, J. R., Boomsma, D. I., Heath, A. C., & van Doornen, L. J. (1995). A multivariate analysis of sensation seeking. *Behavior Genetics, 25*, 349–356.

Limosin, F., Loze, J.-Y., Rouillon, F., Ades, J., & Gorwood, P. (2003). Association between dopamine receptor D1 gene DdeI polymorphism and sensation seeking in alcohol-dependent men. *Alcoholism: Clinical and Experimental Research, 27*, 1226–1228.

Low, K. G., & Gendaszek, A. E. (2002). Illicit use of psychostimulants among college students: A preliminary study. *Psychology, Health and Medicine, 7*, 283–287.

Oreland, L., Hallman, J., & Damberg, M. (2004). Platelet MAO and personality—function and dysfunction. *Current Medicine Chemistry, 11*, 2007–2016.

Pivac, N., Knezevic, J., Mustapic, M., Dezeljin, M., Muck-Seler, D., Kozaric-Kovacic, D., et al. (2006). The lack of association between monoamine oxidase (MAO) intron 13 polymorphism and platelet MAO-B activity among men. *Life Sciences, 30*, 45–49.

Romer, D., & Hennessy, M. (2007). A biosocial-affect model of adolescent sensation seeking: The role of affect evaluation and peer-group influence in adolescent drug use. *Prevention Science, 8*, 89–101.

Scourfield, J., Stevens, D. E., & Merikangas, K. R. (1996). Substance abuse, comorbidity, and sensation seeking: Gender differences. *Comprehensive Psychiatry, 37*, 384–392.

Simons, J. S., Gaher, R. M., Correia, C. J., & Bush, J. A. (2005). Club drug use among college students. *Addictive Behaviors, 30*, 1619–1624.

Virkkunen, M., & Linnoila, M. (1993). Brain serotonin, type II alcoholism and impulsive violence. *Journal of Studies on Alcoholism Supplement, 11*, 163–169.

Wills, T. A., Windle, M., & Cleary, S. D. (1998). Temperament and novelty seeking in adolescent substance use: Convergence of dimensions of temperament with constructs from Cloninger's theory. *Journal of Personality and Social Psychology, 74*, 387–406.

Zuckerman, M. (1979). *Sensation seeking: Beyond the optimal level of arousal*. Hillsdale NJ: Erlbaum.

Zuckerman, M. (1993). P-impulsive sensation seeking and its behavioral, psychophysiological and biochemical correlates. *Neuropsychobiology, 28*, 30–36.

Zuckerman, M. (1994). *Behavioral expression and biosocial bases of sensation seeking*. New York: Cambridge University Press.

Zuckerman, M., & Cloninger, C. R. (1996). Relationships between Cloninger's, Zuckerman's, and Eysenck's dimensions of personality. *Personality and Individual Differences, 21*, 283–285.

Zuckerman, M., Eysenck, S., & Eysenck, H. J. (1978). Sensation seeking in England and America: Cross-cultural, age, and sex comparisons. *Journal of Consulting and Clinical Psychology, 46*, 139–149.

CHERYL BESELER

SEXUAL AND PHYSICAL ABUSE

There has been considerable variation in the estimated prevalence of childhood sexual abuse (CSA), with estimates from early studies ranging from 6 to 60 percent in females and from 3 to 30 percent in males (Fergusson & Mullen, 1999). At least some of this variation may be attributed to variations in the definition of CSA itself, with some studies confining the definition to incidents involving rape or attempted rape and others utilizing broader definitions, including noncontact forms of sexual abuse. Child maltreatment or physical abuse is also relatively common: A recent study of 15,197 young adults in the United States estimated that 28.4 percent of the population experienced physical assault as a child, 11.8 percent experienced physical neglect, and 41.5 percent reported being left at home as a child, which was interpreted as being indicative of supervisory neglect (Hussey, Chang, & Kotch, 2006). Nevertheless, considerable controversy remains concerning the definition of child maltreatment and the extent to which retrospective reports of these events are reliable and valid.

In general, there have been two principal approaches to studying factors associated with child maltreatment. The first of these relies on an examination of individuals identified through official records (e.g., police or treatment agency records) as having a known history of exposure to child maltreatment. Although this approach provides valuable insights, it is limited in its ability to provide an accurate appraisal of the consequences of child maltreatment, as those identified through official records may be unrepresentative of all individuals exposed to child maltreatment (typical estimates suggest that only a fraction of individuals who experience child maltreatment ever come to official attention). A second approach relies on retrospective assessments of childhood experiences in general population samples of adults. Although this approach has the potential advantage of identifying a representative sample of individuals exposed to childhood maltreatment, increasing concerns exist about the reliability and validity of retrospective reports of childhood abuse because individuals may either forget, decline to report, or, more controversially, repress memories of abuse. Indeed, follow-up studies have suggested that a substantial proportion of individuals with known histories of childhood maltreatment may not report such histories during an interview (Widom & Morris, 1997; Widom & Shepard, 1996).

Fergusson and colleagues (2000) examined the reliability of retrospective reports of child maltreatment within the context of a repeated measures design, in which individuals were evaluated twice. They reported relatively low consistency in reports of CSA and regular physical punishment: Approximately half of those reporting such behaviors at age 18 did not report them at the other assessment. These inconsistencies in reports lead to an underestimation of the prevalence of abuse. For example, the application of latent class analysis estimated the prevalence of CSA as 30.4 percent in females and 6.1 percent in males (relative to estimates based on single reports of between 13.9–17.3% among females and 2.7% among males). However, although there was considerable instability in abuse reports, further analyses indicated that errors in reporting were largely unrelated to outcome risks and did not influence estimated associations between childhood abuse and adult psychopathology (including alcohol and illicit drug abuse or dependence).

EXPOSURE TO CHILDHOOD SEXUAL ABUSE AND LATER ADJUSTMENT

Although both childhood sexual and physical abuse are remarkably common, considerable controversy surrounds the extent to which exposure to child abuse may have deleterious effects on subsequent well-being, including possibly increasing risks for alcohol and other drug use, abuse, and dependence. In addition to concerns about the representativeness of samples identified through official records and the reliability and validity of retrospective reports described above, early work in this area was plagued by a number of further methodological weaknesses, including small and nonrepresentative samples, and inadequate control for potentially confounding covariates that could act to increase both the risks of experiencing abuse and, independently of this, the risks for subsequent psychopathology.

One early study that addressed many of these methodological weaknesses was reported by Fergusson and colleagues (1996), who examined associations between the extent of exposure to CSA (no abuse, noncontact, contact, rape or attempted rape) and a range of psychiatric and substance use outcomes after control for a range of factors, including socioeconomic status, family disruption, childhood adversity, parenting practices, and parental criminal offenses and illicit drug use, which were associated with increased risks of CSA. Sample members had been studied from birth and thus prospective assessments of these risk factors were available, although self-reports of CSA were not assessed until age 18. Results indicated that CSA involving intercourse or attempted intercourse was associated with a 2.7-fold increase in the odds of alcohol abuse and a 6.6-fold increase in the odds of other substance abuse or dependence. Importantly, evidence of a strong dose-response relationship between the extent of CSA and risks of alcohol and drug abuse or dependence existed.

Although research on the longer-term sequelae of other forms of child maltreatment is plagued by many of the same methodological issues as research on CSA, an emerging consensus is that childhood physical abuse increases the risk for subsequent alcohol and other drug use disorders, that a dose-response association exists between the extent of physical abuse and later outcomes, and that these associations are independent from the effects of social, family, and contextual factors which may be associated with increased risks for experiencing physical abuse during childhood. For example, Hamburger and coworkers (2008) reported that school students who reported experiencing physical abuse were over twice as likely to report early onset alcohol use, whereas Fergusson and Lynskey (1997) found that severe physical punishment or maltreatment was associated with elevated rates of alcohol abuse or dependence in young adulthood.

In addition to studies employing general population samples and attempting to control for background differences between individuals exposed and not exposed to maltreatment, there is also an emerging literature based on genetically informative research designs that have attempted to address the issue of whether maltreatment, and specifically CSA, make independent contributions to the risks for substance use disorders in adulthood. For example, in a sample of female twins discordant for CSA, Kendler and colleagues (2000) reported that CSA was associated with a 2.83-fold increase in the odds of alcohol dependence. Although an elevated risk of other drug dependence is present in those exposed to CSA, relative to their nonexposed co-twin, this association did not reach statistical significance, likely due to the relatively low number of discordant twin pairs and the low base rate of other drug dependence in this general population sample. Dinwiddie et al. (2000) reported that CSA was associated with a marginally significant elevation in the odds of alcohol dependence in women (OR = 2.50, 95% CI = 0.97–6.44) but not in men, although the nonsignificant association in males may partly be a function of reduced statistical power, as Dinwiddie and coworkers were able to identify only 25 male twin pairs who were discordant for exposure to CSA. Similarly, Nelson et al. (2002) identified twin pairs discordant for CSA from a larger sample of Australian twins and reported that those individuals who reported

experiencing CSA had significantly elevated rates of both alcohol and nicotine dependence compared to their own co-twin who had not experienced CSA. In a follow-up to this study using the same sample of twins discordant for CSA, Nelson and colleagues (2006) reported that CSA was also associated with elevated rates of cannabis and other illicit drug abuse or dependence.

GENE BY ENVIRONMENT INTERACTIONS

Given the emerging consensus that childhood maltreatment is strongly associated with alcohol- and other drug-related problems (as well as with a range of other psychiatric and related conditions), increasing attention is focusing on the mechanisms underlying these putatively causal associations. There is increasing interest in—and evidence for—the role of gene by environment (GxE) interactions in the development of psychopathology (Rutter, Moffitt, & Caspi, 2006). Jaffee and colleagues (2005) found that childhood physical maltreatment was associated with dramatically elevated risks for the development of conduct disorder in those with a genetic vulnerability to this disorder, whereas in those without such a genetic predisposition, physical maltreatment was associated with only a very modest increase in risks of conduct disorder. Similarly, Caspi and his colleagues demonstrated significant interactions between childhood abuse—and other measures of childhood disadvantage or stress—and functional polymorphisms in two different genes (one that encodes the enzyme monoamine oxidase A [MAO-A], and the other that encodes the serotonin transporter protein) on outcomes frequently correlated or comorbid with alcohol and drug dependence, including antisocial behavior (Caspi et al., 2002) and depression (Caspi et al., 2003). Kaufman and coworkers (2007) found interactive effects of childhood maltreatment and the functional genetic polymorphism in the serotonin transporter gene on the onset of drinking and heavy drinking in childhood. A GxE interaction was also seen among sexual abuse survivors involving the MAO-A gene, alcoholism, and antisocial personality disorder (Ducci et al., 2008).

IMPLICATIONS FOR PREVENTION

Although childhood abuse is associated with increased risks for the development of alcohol- and other drug-abuse dependence (as well as other psychiatric disorders), it is not the case that maltreatment inevitably leads to maladjustment, with some studies suggesting that approximately 30 to 40 percent of individuals who experience child maltreatment will not meet diagnostic criteria for any psychiatric disorder. For example, in a follow-up to the Isle of Wight studies, Collishaw and colleagues (2007) reported that 44.5 percent of those reporting childhood abuse did not meet criteria for any Axis I psychiatric disorder. Factors associated with resilience included perceived parental care, adolescent peer relationships, adult relationships, and personality.

Consideration of official reports of child victimization suggests that rates of physical and sexual abuse of children may have declined in the United States in the early twenty-first century: Specifically, Jones and colleagues (2006) reported that substantiated cases of physical abuse declined by 36 percent and substantiated case of CSA by 47 percent during the 1990s. While acknowledging potential limitations in official reports of child maltreatment, Jones and colleagues argue that at least some component of this observed change may reflect a real decline in cases of child maltreatment which they attribute to a number of possible causes, including direct prevention efforts, economic improvements, more aggressive criminal justice efforts, improved and increased use of psychiatric medications, and generational changes. There appeared, however, to be no corresponding decline in cases of child neglect. Nonetheless, the analysis by Jones and colleagues (2006) suggests promise for a reduction in—or even elimination of—child maltreatment. Given convincing evidence of long-term adverse consequences associated with exposure to child maltreatment, it is clear that a promising avenue for the reduction of alcohol and other drug problems (as well as other psychopathology) would involve efforts to reduce further the occurrence of childhood sexual and physical abuse. This effort could be coupled with treatment and interventions that have increasingly been shown to be effective in ameliorating the adverse effects of exposure to childhood maltreatment (Cohen, 2005; MacDonald et al., 2006).

See also **Child Abuse and Drugs; Childhood Behavior and Later Substance Use; Families and Drug Use; Intimate Partner Violence and Alcohol/Substance Use.**

BIBLIOGRAPHY

Caspi, A., McClay, J., Moffitt, T. E., Mill, J., Martin, J., Craig, I. W., et al. (2002). Role of genotype in the cycle of violence in maltreated children. *Science, 297,* 851–854.

Caspi, A., Sugden, K., Moffitt, T. E., Taylor, A., Craig, I. W., Harrington, H., et al. (2003). Influence of life stress on depression: Moderation by a polymorphism in the 5-HTT gene. *Science, 301,* 386–389.

Cohen, J. A. (2005). Treating traumatized children: Current status and future directions. *Journal of Trauma and Dissociation, 6,* 109–121.

Collishaw, S., Pickles, A., Messer, J., Rutter, M., Shearer, C., & Maughan, B. (2007). Resilience to adult psychopathology following childhood maltreatment: Evidence from a community sample. *Child Abuse & Neglect, 31,* 205–209.

Dinwiddie, S., Heath, A. C., Dunne, M. P., Bucholz, K. K., Madden, P. A. F., Slutske, W. S., et al. (2000). Early sexual abuse and lifetime psychopathology: A co-twin control study. *Psychological Medicine, 30,* 41–52.

Ducci, F., Enoch, M.-A., Hodgkinson, C., Xu, K., Catena, M., Robin, R. W., et al. (2008). Interaction between a functional MAOA locus and childhood sexual abuse predicts alcoholism and antisocial personality disorder in adult women. *Molecular Psychiatry, 13*(3), 334–347.

Fergusson, D. M., Horwood, L. J., & Lynskey, M. T. (1996). Childhood sexual abuse and psychiatric disorder in young adulthood: II. Psychiatric outcomes of childhood sexual abuse. *Journal of the American Academy of Child and Adolescent Psychiatry, 35,* 1365–1374.

Fergusson, D. M., Horwood, L. J., & Woodward, L. J. (2000). The stability of child abuse reports: A longitudinal study of the reporting behavior of young adults. *Psychological Medicine, 30,* 529–544.

Fergusson, D. M., & Lynskey, M. T. (1997). Physical punishment/maltreatment during childhood and adjustment in young adulthood. *Child Abuse & Neglect, 21,* 617–630.

Fergusson, D. M., & Mullen, P. E. (1999). *Childhood sexual abuse: An evidence based perspective.* Thousand Oaks, CA: Sage Publications.

Hamburger, M. E., Leeb, R. T., & Swahn, M. H. (2008). Childhood maltreatment and early alcohol use among high risk adolescents. *Journal of Studies on Alcohol and Drugs, 69,* 291–295.

Hussey, J. M., Chang, J., & Kotch, J. B. (2006). Child maltreatment in the United States: Prevalence, risk factors, and adolescent health consequences. *Pediatrics, 118,* 933–942.

Jaffee, S. R., Caspi, A., Moffitt, T. E., Dodge, K. A., Rutter, M., Taylor, A., et al. (2005). Nature X nurture: Genetic vulnerabilities interact with physical maltreatment to promote conduct problems. *Development and Psychopathology, 17*, 67–84.

Jones, L. M., Finkelhor, D., & Halter, S. (2006). Child maltreatment in the 1990s: Why does neglect differ from sexual and physical abuse? *Child Maltreatment, 11*, 107–120.

Kaufman, J., Yang, B. Z., Douglas-Palumberi, H., Crouse-Artus, M., Lipschitz, D., Krystal, J. H., et al. (2007). Genetic and environmental predictors of early alcohol use. *Biological Psychiatry, 61*(11), 1228–1234.

Kendler, K. S., Bulik, C. M., Silberg, J., Hettema, J. M., Myers, J., & Prescott, C. A. (2000). Childhood sexual abuse and adult psychiatric and substance use disorders in women: An epidemiological and co-twin control analysis. *Archives of General Psychiatry, 57*, 953–959.

MacDonald, G. M., Higgins, J. P. T., & Ramchandani, P. (2006). Cognitive-behavioral interventions for children who have been sexually abused. *Cochrane Database of Systematic Reviews, 4*, CD001930.

Nelson, E. C., Heath, A. C., Lynskey, M. T., Bucholz, K. K., Madden, P. A. F., Statham, D. J., et al. (2006). Childhood sexual abuse and risks for licit and illicit drug-related outcomes: A twin study. *Psychological Medicine, 36*, 1473–1483.

Nelson, E. C., Heath, A. C., Madden, P. A. F., Cooper, M. L., Dinwiddie, S. H., Bucholz, K. K., et al. (2002). Association between self-reported childhood sexual abuse and adverse psychosocial outcomes: Results from a twin study. *Archives of General Psychiatry, 59*, 139–145.

Rutter, M., Moffitt, T. E., & Caspi, A. (2006). Gene-environment interplay and psychopathology: Multiple varieties but real effects. *Journal of Child Psychology and Psychiatry, 47*, 226–261.

Widom, C. S., & Morris, S. (1997). Accuracy of adult recollections of childhood victimization. Part 2: Childhood sexual abuse. *Psychological Assessment, 9*, 34–46.

Widom, C. S., & Shepard, R. L. (1996). Accuracy of adult recollections of childhood victimization. Part 1: Childhood physical abuse. *Psychological Assessment, 8*, 412–421.

Michael T. Lynskey

STRESS

The term *stress* refers to processes involving perception, appraisal, and response to harmful, threatening, or challenging events or stimuli (Levine, 2005; Sinha, 2005). Stressful experiences can be emotionally or physiologically challenging and can activate stress responses and adaptive processes to regain homeostasis (Charmandari et al., 2005; McEwen, 2007). Examples of emotional stressors include interpersonal conflict, loss of relationship, and death of a close family member or loss of a child. Common physiological stressors are hunger or food deprivation, sleep deprivation or insomnia, psychoactive drug use, and extreme increases or decreases in body temperature. The differences between emotional and physiological stressors allow for separate consideration of (1) internal and external events or stimuli that exert demands or load on the organism; (2) the neural processes that evaluate the demands and assess availability of adaptive resources to cope with the demands (appraisal); (3) the subjective, behavioral, and physiological activity that signal stress to the organism; and (4) behavioral, cognitive, and physiological adaptation to the stressful event.

While stress is associated with negative affect and distress, it has been linked with positive effects too. For example, "good" stress includes external and internal stimuli that are challenging and increase arousal, but limited in duration, resulting in cognitive and behavioral responses that generate a sense of mastery and accomplishment, and can be perceived as pleasant and exciting (Levine, 2005; McEwen, 2007). Such situations rely on adequate motivational and executive functioning to achieve goal-directed outcomes and homeostasis (Levine, 2005; Paulus, 2007; McEwen, 2007). However, the more prolonged, repeated, or chronic the stress—that is, states associated with increased intensity or persistence of distress—the greater the uncontrollability and unpredictability of the stressful situation, the less the sense of mastery or adaptability that results and the greater the magnitude of the stress response and risk for persistent homeostatic dysregulation (Meaney et al., 2002; McEwen, 2007). Thus, the dimensions of intensity, controllability, predictability, mastery, and adaptability are important in understanding the role of stress in increasing the risk of maladaptive behaviors such as addiction.

The perception and appraisal of stress rely on specific aspects of the presenting external or internal stimuli, personality traits, availability of internal resources, and prior emotional state, including beliefs and expectancies. Specific brain regions mediate the appraisal of stimuli as distressing and the resulting physiological, behavioral and emotional experiences and adaptive responses. Brain regions such as the amygdala, hippocampus, insula, orbitofrontal cortex, and medial prefrontal and cingulate cortices are involved in the perception and appraisal of emotional and stressful stimuli; the brainstem (locus ceruleus and related arousal regions), hypothalamus, thalamus, and striatal and limbic regions are involved in the physiological and emotional responses to stress. Together these regions contribute to the experience of distress. The physiological responses are manifested through the two major stress pathways: (1) the hypothalamic-pituitary-adrenal (HPA) axis, in which corticotrophin releasing factor (CRF) is released from the paraventricular neucleus (PVN) of the hypothalamus, which stimulates adrenocorticotrophin hormone release from the anterior pituitary and subsequently stimulates the secretion of cortisol/corticosterone from the adrenal glands, and (2) the autonomic nervous system, which is coordinated via the sympathoadrenal medullary (SAM) systems (Phan et al., 2005; Charmandari et al., 2005).

In addition, extrahypothalamic CRF in the corticostriatal limbic pathways has an extensive influence in modulating subjective and behavioral stress responses (Heinrichs, 2005). Central catecholamines, particularly noradrenaline and dopamine, are involved in modulating brain motivational pathways (including the ventral tegmental area (VTA), nucleus accumbens (NAcc), and the medial prefrontal (mPFC) regions) that are important in regulating distress, exerting cognitive and behavioral control and negotiating behavioral and cognitive responses critical for adaptation and homeostasis (Phan et al., 2005). The hypothalamic and extrahypothalamic CRF pathways and central catecholamines target brain motivational pathways to critically affect adaptive and homeostatic processes. For example, different parts of the medial prefrontal cortex are involved in higher cognitive or executive control functions, such as controlling and inhibiting impulses, regulating distress, focusing and shifting attention, monitoring behavior, linking behaviors and consequences over time, and considering alternatives before acting and decision-making responses (Roberts et al., 1998). Psychosocial and behavioral scientists have elegantly shown that with increasing levels of emotional and physiological stress or negative affect, there is a decrease in behavioral control and an increase in impulsivity, such that increasing levels of distress and persistence of stress increase the risk of maladaptive behaviors (Mischel, 1996; Tice et al., 2001; Hayaki et al., 2005; Greco & Carli, 2006; Fishbein et al., 2006; Verdejo-García

et al., 2007; Anestis et al., 2007; Hatzinger et al., 2007). From neurobiological studies, increasing stress has been shown to decrease prefrontal functioning and increased limbic-striatal level responding, which perpetuates low behavioral and cognitive control (Sinha, 2005; Li & Sinha, 2008). Thus, the motivational brain pathways are key targets of brain stress chemicals and provide a potential mechanism by which stress affects addiction vulnerability and relapse risk.

STRESS AND INCREASED RISK OF ADDICTION

Considerable evidence from population-based and clinical studies supports a positive association between psychosocial adversity, negative affect and chronic distress, and addiction vulnerability. Adolescents facing high recent negative life events show increased levels of drug use and abuse (Sinha, 2005). Longitudinal studies support the effects of stress on drug use initiation and escalation in adolescents and young adults (see review in Sinha, 2005; Wills et al., 2006).

Overwhelming evidence exists for an increased association between childhood sexual and physical abuse and victimization and increased drug use and abuse (Sinha, 2005). In addition to sexual and physical abuse, negative affect and chronic distress states—such as mood and anxiety disorders, including post-traumatic stress disorder (PTSD)—and behavioral conduct problems are predictive of addiction vulnerability (Brady & Sinha, 2005; Cichetti & Toth, 2005). Findings indicate that negative affect, including temperamental negative emotionality, are associated with substance abuse risk (Measelle et al., 2006). Furthermore, there are sex differences in the effects of early trauma and maltreatment on the increased risk of addiction (MacMillan et al., 2001; Simpson & Miller, 2002; Hyman et al., 2006).

Evidence also indicates that lifetime exposure to stressors and cumulative adversity has a significant impact on addiction vulnerability after accounting for a number of control factors such as race/ethnicity, gender, socioeconomic status, prior drug abuse, prevalence of psychiatric disorders, family history of substance use, and behavioral and conduct problems (Turner & Lloyd, 2003; Lloyd & Turner, 2008). Findings indicate that cumulative instances of stressful events are predictive of alcohol and drug dependence in a dose-dependent manner, after accounting for control factors. The dose-dependent effects of cumulative stressors on risk for addiction exist for both genders and for Caucasian, African American and Hispanic race/ethnic groups. The types of adverse events significantly associated with addiction vulnerability are parental divorce or conflict; abandonment; being forced to live apart from one's parents; loss of a child by death or removal; unfaithfulness of a significant other; loss of one's home to natural disaster; death of a loved one; emotional abuse or neglect; sexual abuse; rape; physical abuse by a parent, caretaker, family member, spouse or significant other; being a victim of a shooting or other violent act; and observing violent victimization. These represent highly stressful and emotionally distressing events, with uncontrollable and unpredictable stress characteristics.

All of the above findings indicate the need to examine evidence supporting the possible mechanisms that explain how stress increases addiction vulnerability. Animal and human studies indicate that the reinforcing properties of drugs of abuse are mediated by the mesolimbic dopaminergic (DA) pathways, which include dopamine neurons originating in the ventral tegmental area and extending to the ventral striatum (nucleus accumbens) and the prefrontal cortex (Pierce & Kumaresan, 2006; Volkow et al., 2007 Oswald et al., 2005). This pathway is also involved in assigning salience to stimuli, in reward processing, and in learning and adaptation (Kauer & Malenka, 2007).

Furthermore, stress exposure and increased levels of glucocorticoids (GC) also enhance dopamine release in the NAcc (Sinha, 2005; Pruessner et al., 2004; Oswald et al., 2005), and drug-induced increases in cortisol are associated with both dopamine binding in the ventral striatum and with ratings of amphetamine-induced euphoria (Wand et al., 2007). Suppression of GC by adrenalectomy reduces extracellular levels of dopamine under basal conditions and in responses to stress and psychostimulants, and chronic GC inhibits DA synthesis and turnover in the NAcc (Pacak et al., 2002; Sinha, 2005). These data suggest that DA transmission is highly sensitive to alterations in the HPA axis and glucocorticoid secretion. Furthermore, drugs of abuse, stress, and concomitant increases in CRF and glucocorticoids are known to enhance glutamate activity in the VTA, which in turn enhances activity of dopaminergic neurons (Saal et al., 2003; Wang et al., 2005).

Finally, stress-related alterations in the mesolimbic DA pathways could impact additional regions connected to DA pathways, such as the amygdala, hippocampus, insula, and related corticolimbic regions, which are involved in reward, learning, and adaptive and goal-directed behaviors (Everitt & Robbins, 2005; Kauer & Malenka, 2007). These regions, along with the mesolimbic DA pathways, play an important role in interoception, emotion and stress processing, impulse control and decision making, processes that promote loss of control, compulsions, and addictive processes that increase the risk of developing addiction (Baler & Volkow, 2006; Li & Sinha, 2008).

CHRONIC DRUG USE AND VULNERABILITY TO STRESS

Acute, regular, and chronic use of the most commonly abused drugs such as alcohol, nicotine, cocaine, amphetamines, and marijuana that activate brain reward pathways (mesocorticolimbic dopaminergic systems) have direct effects on brain stress pathways (Koob & Kreek, 2007; Chen et al., 2008). Chronic use of drugs also alters stress responses in addicted individuals compared to healthy volunteers, with addicted individuals showing greater emotional and behavioral distress and stress and cue-induced craving and blunted stress hormone responses compared to healthy volunteers (Al'Absi et al., 2005; Fox et al., 2007; Sinha et al., 2008). Regular and chronic use of drugs of abuse and acute withdrawal states are also associated with a downregulation of the mesolimbic dopamine pathways, and decreases in basal and stimulated dopamine have been reported in several preclinical studies (Nader et al., 2006; Koob et al., 2004; Mateo et al., 2005) and in human brain imaging studies (see review by Volkow et al., 2007). Chronic cocaine use also dramatically alters central noradrenergic pathways in the ventral and dorsal striatum, other areas of the forebrain, and the ventromedial prefrontal cortex (Beveridge et al., 2005; Porrino et al., 2007). Thus, there are significant physiological, neurochemical, and behavioral alterations in stress and dopaminergic pathways associated with chronic drug use, and these changes are accompanied by enhanced sensitivity to distress and drug craving when addicts are faced with environmental stress or drug-related stimuli known to increase drug craving and drug use.

Although there are efficacious treatments to address alcoholism and drug abuse, rates of relapse remain high for these disorders (Sinha, 2007). Research in humans has also begun to assess whether early life and/or chronic stress and psychobiological markers of stress and craving states contribute to the high rate of relapse outcomes in alcohol and drug use disorders. Childhood trauma and psychiatric distress have been associated with treatment outcome and relapse rates, with some evidence of sex differences in the extent of the association (Brady & Sinha, 2005; Hyman et al., 2008). Among cocaine dependent individuals, stress-induced cocaine craving in the laboratory significantly predicted time to cocaine relapse. While stress-induced ACTH and cortisol responses were not associated with time to relapse, these responses were predictive of the amount of cocaine consumed during follow-up (Sinha et al., 2006). Although in this study drug cue-induced craving was not predictive of relapse, there was a high correlation between stress and cue-induced drug craving and in stress and cue-induced HPA responses.

There is also evidence that stress responsivity has an impact on relapse outcomes in alcohol and nicotine dependence. Negative mood and stress-induced alcohol craving and blunted stress and cue-induced cortisol responses have been associated with alcohol relapse outcomes (see Sinha, 2007 for review). Nicotine-deprived smokers exposed to a series of stressors show blunted ACTH, cortisol and blood pressure responses to stress but increased nicotine withdrawal and craving scores, and these responses were predictive of nicotine relapse outcomes (Al'Absi et al., 2005). Thus, for alcoholic and smoking samples, as in those with cocaine dependence, it appears that the drug craving state marked by increasing distress and compulsive motivation for the drug (craving), along with poor stress regulatory responses, results in an enhanced susceptibility to addiction relapse. These data support the need for addressing stress-related changes in the treatment of addiction in order to decrease the high rates of relapse observed in substance abuse.

Clearly, stress and adaptation are related to addictive behavior. Facing stress is basic to all organisms, but how people adapt to stress can differ significantly across individuals. The close interaction between stress neurobiology and susceptibility to drug use, abuse, and relapse are important areas of research. Acute and chronic stress and life adversity may increase the risk of developing substance abuse. Drugs of abuse affect the stress pathways, and the interaction between stress and reward/motivational circuits are vital for participating in adaptive, goal directed behaviors. Growing evidence suggests that the effects of chronic stress and drug abuse interact to increase both the risk of developing and of perpetuating substance abuse. Future advances in the understanding of these interactions is expected to lead to specific prevention and treatment efforts to decrease the stress-related vulnerability to risk of substance abuse.

See also **Addiction: Concepts and Definitions; Endorphins; Epidemiology of Drug Abuse; Families and Drug Use; Intimate Partner Violence and Alcohol/ Substance Use.**

BIBLIOGRAPHY

Al'Absi, M., Hatsukami, D. K., & Davis, G. (2005). Attenuated adrenocorticotropic responses to psychological stress are associated with early smoking relapse. *Psychopharmacology (Berlin), 181*(1), 107–117.

Anestis, M. D., Selby, E. A., & Joiner, T. E. (2007). The role of urgency in maladaptive behaviors. *Behavioral Research and Therapy, 45*(12), 3018–3029.

Baler, R. D., & Volkow, N. D. (2006). Drug addiction: The neurobiology of disrupted self-control. *Trends in Molecular Medicine, 12*(12), 559–566.

Beveridge, T., Smith, H., Nader, M., & Porrino, L. (2005). Effects of chronic cocaine self-administration on norepinephrine transporters in the nonhuman primate brain. *Psychopharmacology, 180,* 781–788.

Brady, K. T., & Sinha, R. (2005). Co-occurring mental and substance use disorders: The neurobiological effects of chronic stress. *American Journal of Psychiatry, 162*(8), 1483–1493.

Charmandari, E., Tsigos, C., & Chrousos, G. (2005). Endocrinology of the stress response. *Annual Review of Physiology, 67,* 259–284.

Chen, H., Fu, Y., & Sharp, B. M. (2008). Chronic nicotine self-administration augments hypothalamic-pituitary-adrenal responses to mild acute stress. *Neuropsychopharmacology, 33*(4), 721–730.

Cicchetti, D., & Toth, S. L. (2005). Child maltreatment. *Annual Review of Clinical Psychology, 1,* 409–438.

Everitt, B. J., & Robbins, T. W. (2005). Neural systems of reinforcement for drug addiction: From actions to habits to compulsion. *Nature Neuroscience, 8*(11), 1481–1489.

Fishbein, D. H., Herman-Stahl, M., Eldreth, D., Paschall, M. J., Hyde, C., Hubal, R., et al. (2006). Mediators of the stress-substance-use relationship in urban male adolescents. *Prevention Science, 7*(2), 113–126.

Fox, H. C., Bergquist, K. L., Hong, K. I., & Sinha, R. (2007). Stress-induced and alcohol cue-induced craving in recently abstinent alcohol dependent individuals. *Alcoholism: Clinical and Experimental Research, 31*(3), 395–403.

Greco, B., & Carli, M. (2006). Reduced attention and increased impulsivity in mice lacking NPY Y2 receptors: Relation to anxiolytic-like phenotype. *Behavioural Brain Research, 169*(2), 325–334.

Hatzinger, M., Brand, S., Perren, S., von Wyl, A., von Klitzing, K., & Holsboer-Trachsler, E. (2007). Hypothalamic-pituitary-adrenocortical (hpa) activity in kindergarten children: Importance of gender and associations with behavioral/emotional difficulties. *Journal of Psychiatric Research, 41*(10), 861-870.

Hayaki, J., Stein, M. D., Lassor, J. A., Herman, D. S., & Anderson, B. J. (2005). Adversity among drug users: Relationship to impulsivity. *Drug and Alcohol Dependence, 78*(1), 65–71.

Hayatbakhsh, M. R., Najman, J. M., Jamrozik, K., Mamun, A. A., & Alati, R. (2006). Do parents' marital circumstances predict young adults' DSM-IV cannabis use disorders? A prospective study. *Addiction, 101*(12), 1778–1786.

Heinrichs, S. (2005). Behavioral consequences of altered corticotropin-releasing factor activation in brain: A functionalist view of affective neuroscience. In T. Steckler, N. H. Kalin, & J. M. H. M. Reul (Eds.), *Handbook of stress and the brain. Part 1: The neurobiology of stress* (Vol. 15, pp. 155–177). Amsterdam: Elsevier.

Hyman, S. M., Garcia, M., & Sinha, R. (2006). Gender specific associations between types of childhood maltreatment and the onset, escalation and severity of substance use in cocaine dependent adults. *American Journal of Drug and Alcohol Abuse, 32*(4), 655–664.

Hyman, S. M., Paliwal, P., Chaplin, T. M., Mazure, C. M., Rounsaville, B., & Sinha, R. (2008). Severity of childhood trauma is predictive of cocaine relapse outcomes in women but not men. *Drug and Alcohol Dependence, 92*, 208–216.

Kauer, J. A., & Malenka, R. C. (2007). Synaptic plasticity and addiction. *Natural Review of Neuroscience, 8*(11), 844–858.

Koob, G. F., Ahmed, S. H., Boutrel, B., Chen, S. A., Kenny, P. J., Markou, A., et al. (2004). Neurobiological mechanisms in the transition from drug use to drug dependence. *Neuroscience and Biobehavioral Reviews, 27, 739–749*.

Koob, G., & Kreek, M. J. (2007). Stress, dysregulation of drug reward pathways, and the transition to drug dependence. *American Journal of Psychiatry, 164*(8), 1149–1159.

Levine, S. (2005). Developmental determinants of sensitivity and resistance to stress. *Psychoneuroendocrinology, 30*, 939–946.

Li, C.-S. R., & Sinha, R. (2008). Inhibitory control and emotional stress regulation: Neuroimaging evidence for frontal-limbic dysfunction in psycho-stimulant addiction. *Neuroscience and Biobehavioral Reviews, 32*(3), 581–597.

Lloyd, D. A., & Turner, R. J. (2008). Cumulative lifetime adversities and alcohol dependence in adolescence and young adulthood. *Drug and Alcohol Dependence, 93*(3), 217–226.

MacMillan, H. L., Fleming, J. E., Streiner, D. L., Lin, E., Boyle, M. H., Jamieson, E., et al. (2001). Childhood abuse and lifetime psychopathology in a community sample. *American Journal of Psychiatry, 158*(11), 1878–1883.

Martinez, D., Gil, R., Slifstein, M., Hwang, D. R., Huang, Y., Perez, A., et al. (2005). Alcohol dependence is associated with blunted dopamine transmission in the ventral striatum. *Biological Psychiatry, 58*(10), 779–786.

Martinez, D., Narendran, R., Foltin, R. W., Slifstein, M., Hwang, D. R., Broft, A., et al. (2007b). Amphetamine-induced dopamine release: Markedly blunted in cocaine dependence and predictive of the choice to self-administer cocaine. *American Journal of Psychiatry, 164*(4), 622–629.

Mateo, Y., Lack, C. M., Morgan, D., Roberts, D. C., & Jones, S. R. (2005). Reduced dopamine terminal function and insensitivity to cocaine following cocaine binge self-administration and deprivation. *Neuropsychopharmacology, 30*(8), 1455–1463.

McEwen, B. S. (2007). Physiology and neurobiology of stress and adaptation: Central role of the brain. *Physiology Review, 87*(3), 873–904.

Meaney, M. J., Brake, W., & Gratton, A. (2002). Environment regulation of the development of mesolimbic dopamine systems: A neurobiological mechanism for vulnerability to drug abuse? *Psychoneuroendocrinology, 27*(1–2), 127–138.

Measelle, J. R., Stice, E., & Springer, D. W. (2006). A prospective test of the negative affect model of substance abuse: Moderating effects of social support. *Psychology of Addictive Behavior, 20*(3), 225–233.

Mendelson, J. H., Sholar, M. B., Goletiani, N., Siegel, A. J., & Mello, N. K. (2005). Effects of low- and high-nicotine cigarette smoking on mood states and the hpa axis in men. *Neuropsychopharmacology, 30*(9), 1751–1763.

Mischel, W. (Ed.). (1996). *From good intentions to will-power.* New York: Guildford Press.

Nader, M. A., Morgan, D., Gage, H. D., Nader, S. H., Calhoun, T. L., Buchheimer, N., et al. (2006). PET imaging of dopamine d2 receptors during chronic cocaine self-administration in monkeys. *Natural Neuroscience, 9*(8), 1050–1105.

Oswald, L. M., Wong, D. F., McCaul, M., Zhou, Y., Kuwabara, H., Choi, L., et al. (2005). Relationships among ventral striatal dopamine release, cortisol secretion, and subjective responses to amphetamine. *Neuropsychopharmacology, 30*(4), 821–832.

Pacak, K., Tjurmina, O., Palkovits, M., Goldstein, D. S., Koch, C. A., Hoff, T., et al. (2002). Chronic hypercortisolemia inhibits dopamine synthesis and turnover in the nucleus accumbens: An in vivo microdialysis study. *Neuroendocrinology, 76*(3), 148–157.

Paulus, M. P. (2007). Decision-making dysfunctions in psychiatry—altered homeostatic processing? *Science, 318*(5850), 602–606.

Phan, K. L., Fitzgerald, D. A., Nathan, P., Moore, G., Uhde, T., & Tancer, M. (2005). Neural substrates for voluntary suppression of negative affect: A functional magnetic resonance imaging study. *Biological Psychiatry, 57,* 210–219.

Pierce, R. C., & Kumaresan, V. (2006). The mesolimbic dopamine system: the final common pathway for the reinforcing effect of drugs of abuse? *Neuroscience and Biobehavioral Reviews, 30*(2), 215–238.

Porrino, L. J., Smith, H. R., Nader, M. A., & Beveridge, T. J. (2007). The effects of cocaine: A shifting target over the course of addiction. *Progress in Neuro-Psychopharmacology & Biological Psychiatry 31*(8), 1593–1600.

Pruessner, J. C., Champagne, F., Meaney, M. J., & Dagher, A. (2004). Dopamine release in response to a psychological stress in humans and its relationship to early life maternal care: A positron emission tomography study using [11c]raclopride. *Journal of Neuroscience, 24*(11), 2825–2831.

Roberts, A., Robbins, T., & Weiskrantz, L. (Eds.). (1998). *The prefrontal cortex: Executive and cognitive functions.* Oxford: Oxford University Press.

Saal, D., Dong, Y., Bonci, A., & Malenka, R. C. (2003). Drugs of abuse and stress trigger a common synaptic adaptation in dopamine neurons. *Neuron, 37*(4), 577–582.

Simpson, T., & Miller, W. (2002). Concomitance between childhood sexual and physical abuse and substance use problems: A review. *Clinical Psychology Review, 22,* 27–77.

Sinha, R. (2005). Stress and drug abuse. In N. H. K. T. Steckler, & J. M. H. M. Reul (Ed.), *Handbook of stress and the brain. Part 2 stress: Integrative and clinical aspects* (Vol. 15, pp. 333–356). Amsterdam: Elsevier.

Sinha, R. (2007) The role of stress in addiction relapse. *Current Psychiatry Reports,* Vol 9(5), 388–395.

Sinha, R., Fox, H. C., Hong, K. A., Bergquist, K., Bhagwagar, Z., & Siedlarz, K. (2008). Enhanced negative emotion and alcohol craving and altered physiological responses to stress and alcohol cues in abstinent alcohol dependent individuals. *Neuropsychopharmacology.*

Sinha, R., Garcia, M., Paliwal, P., Kreek, M. J., & Rounsaville, B. J. (2006). Stress-induced cocaine craving and hypothalamic-pituitary-adrenal responses are predictive of cocaine relapse outcomes. *Archives of General Psychiatry, 63*(3), 324–331.

Tice, D., Bratslavsky, E., & Baumeister, R. (2001). Emotional distress regulation takes precedence over impulse control: If you feel bad, do it! *Journal of Personality and Social Psychology, 80*(1), 53–67.

Turner, R. J., & Lloyd, D. A. (2003). Cumulative adversity and drug dependence in young adults: Racial/ethnic contrasts. *Addiction, 98*(3), 305–315.

Verdejo-García, A., Bechara, A., Recknor, E. C., & Pé'rez-García. M. (2007). Negative emotion-driven impulsivity predicts substance dependence problems. *Drug and Alcohol Dependence, 91*(2–3), 213–219.

Volkow, N. D., Fowler, J. S., Wang, G. J., Swanson, J. M., & Telang, F. (2007). Dopamine in drug abuse and addiction: Results of imaging studies and treatment implications. *Archives of Neurology, 64*(11), 1575–1579.

Wand, G. S., Oswald, L. M., McCaul, M. E., Wong, D. F., Johnson, E., Zhou, Y., et al. (2007). Association of amphetamine-induced striatal dopamine release and cortisol responses to psychological stress. *Neuropsychopharmacology, 32*(11): 2310–2320.

Wang, B., Shaham, Y., Zitzman, D., Azari, S., Wise, R. A., & You, Z. B. (2005). Cocaine experience establishes control of midbrain glutamate and dopamine by corticotropin-releasing factor: A role in stress-induced relapse to drug seeking. *Journal of Neuroscience, 25*(22), 5389–5396.

Wills, T. A., Walker, C., Mendoza, D., & Ainette, M. G. (2006). Behavioral and emotional self-control: Relations to substance use in samples of middle and high school students. *Psychology of Addictive Behavior, 20*(3), 265–278.

LORENZO COHEN
ANDREW BAUN
REVISED BY RAJITA SINHA (2009)

ROCKEFELLER DRUG LAWS. The
Rockefeller drug laws are a set of New York mandatory sentencing statutes for drug crimes. They were proposed by New York's Governor Nelson A. Rockefeller in reaction to a heroin epidemic in his state. These laws, which took effect on September 1, 1973, require that judges impose lengthy prison sentences on drug traffickers, with a large category of drug offenders receiving life imprisonment. The goal was to deter people from both drug use and trafficking by imposing tough and certain punishments. Although the law was immediately challenged as violating the Cruel and Unusual Punishment clause of the U.S. and New York constitutions, the New York Court of Appeals unanimously upheld the law

Within a few years, however, the state's prison population began to swell as increasing numbers of defendants were subjected to the provisions of the Rockefeller laws. From 1969 to 1979, the prison population doubled from 12,000 to 24,000. In the same time period, the percentage of incarcerated nonviolent drug offenders increased from 10 percent to over 30 percent. In spite of these laws, the crime rate continued to grow. A major evaluation concluded that neither drug use nor drug trafficking was reduced after the law was passed. The likelihood that a defendant, once arrested, would be incarcerated did not increase—although the likelihood that a defendant, once convicted, would be imprisoned did increase (Joint Committee on New York Drug Law Evaluation, 1977).

The processing of cases became much more expensive for New York. For every crime affected by the law, the percentage of defendants pleading guilty fell and the proportion of trials increased. The evaluators concluded that it "took between ten and fifteen times as much court time to dispose of a case by trial as by plea." The average time to handle a drug prosecution in New York City, for example, doubled, rising from 172 days in 1973 to 351 days in 1976.

Although the legislature realized the ineffectiveness of the stated purposes of the laws, neither it nor a succession of governors has proposed repealing the laws. Instead, the legislature has sought to amend the laws in ways that reduce their scope. In 1977, the legislature removed marijuana from the definition of crimes dealing with controlled substances and created a new sentencing law for marijuana sale and possession. The possibility of life imprisonment for marijuana offenses was eliminated.

The legislature tinkered with the laws again in 1979. This time it increased the amount of weight of the drug necessary to trigger higher-level felonies. It also reduced the minimum sentence range for certain drug convictions and eliminated a classification from the statute. The 1979 amendments also gave the courts the ability to retroactively resentence defendants who had been convicted based on the original weight and classification schemes.

Despite these changes, they have done little to reduce the harshness of the sentencing practices or reduce the prison population. In 2007, the state prisons held over 63,000 inmates. Twenty-two percent of the prison population is comprised of nonviolent drug offenders.

By the late 1990s, many in the legal community argued for repeal of the Rockefeller laws, believing that they imposed disproportionate punishment on nonviolent drug offenders and ignored drug treatment options. However, Governor George Pataki responded in 1999 with only a minor change in the laws. Pataki proposed legislation that would slightly alter the laws by offering first-time drug couriers a chance to cut their sentences by five years. Under this proposal, the appellate courts would be allowed to review and reduce sentences by five years for first-time felony offenders under the harshest provision of the laws, which now calls for a maximum of fifteen years to life. This proposal was similar to one proposed by Chief Judge Judith S. Kaye, who also called for allowing trial judges to defer the prosecution of nonviolent drug offenders for up to two years and to divert them to drug treatment programs. However, the legislature did not act on these reform efforts.

In 2004 the New York State legislature passed the Drug Law Reform Act (DLRA). Some of these reforms include lowered drug sentences, expanded eligibility for prison-based drug treatment, and the ability to apply for re-sentencing.

See also **Drug Laws, Prosecution of.**

BIBLIOGRAPHY

Joint Committee on New York Drug Law Evaluation (1977). *The nation's toughest drug law: Evaluating the New York experience.* Washington, D.C.: U.S. Government Printing Office.

Piana, L. D. (2005). David Soares' election as District Attorney marks a turning tide against New York's Rockefeller Drug Laws. *Colorlines Magazine, 8*, 1.

Tsimbinos, S. A. (1999). Is it time to change the Rockefeller drug laws? *St. John's Journal of Legal Commentary, 13*, 613.

MICHAEL TONRY
REVISED BY FREDERICK K. GRITTNER (2001)

ROHYPNOL. Known by a variety of street names such as roofies, roach, R-2, trip and fall, and rope or "the date-rape drug," Rohypnol is the trade name for benzodiazepine flunitrazepam, a sedative-hypnotic drug used medically in a number of countries. Rohypnol has recently become a widely abused drug in Sweden, Mexico, Italy, the United Kingdom, the United States, and South Africa, a trend made more troubling by the fact that many users regard it as relatively safe. Rohypnol, in fact, has many dangerous and undesirable effects for the illicit user. It has been associated with an increased risk of violence and accidents as well as stupor, coma, memory loss, and death. Its ability to induce unconsciousness and amnesia has led to its use in sexual assaults in the United States (hence, its reputation as a date-rape drug) as well as robberies.

Although never approved for use in the United States (where it is illegal) Rohypnol is a commonly prescribed benzodiazepine in Europe and elsewhere. Like other benzodiazepines, such as Valium (Diazepam) or Xanax (Alprazolam), it is useful in the medical treatment of sleep disorders and anxiety, though only under supervision by a doctor. Benzodiazepines act at brain receptors for the inhibitory neurotransmitter GABA, which is also the site of action for another, older class of sedative-hypnotic drugs and barbiturates. Although generally safer than barbiturates, benzodiazepines like Rohypnol share some of the same dangers, especially when mixed with ethanol, a common practice among

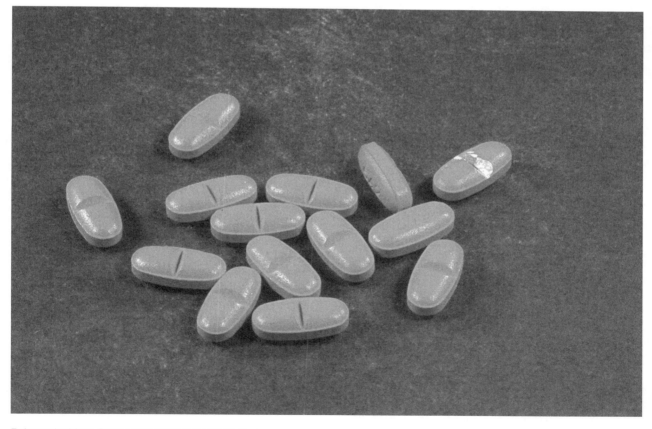

Rohypnol tablets. DAVID HOFFMAN PHOTO LIBRARY/ALAMY.

illicit drug users. These dangerous effects range from incontinence, behavioral disinhibition, violence, delirium, and blackouts to stupor, respiratory depression, and death. These effects all stem from the ability of rohypnol to depress brain function.

At lower doses, benzodiazepines can reduce anxiety and cause relaxation and a loosening of inhibitions somewhat similar to the effects of alcohol, another drug that acts as a depressant on the central nervous system. As with many abused drugs, the continued use of Rohypnol results in increased tolerance, requiring larger doses to produce the same effects. Larger doses mean narrower margins of safety and the increased incidence of side effects, especially memory loss and deficits in learning. Drinking alcohol in combination with Rohypnol makes serious consequences all the more likely. Of still greater concern for the illicit user is that chronic use of sedative-hypnotic drugs like Rohypnol can produce a level of physiologic dependence greater than that resulting from opiate drugs like heroin or morphine. Abrupt withdrawal from regular use can produce complications ranging from the relatively mild, such as restlessness and anxiety, to more severe effects like tremor, hallucinations and convulsions similar to those experienced during severe alcohol withdrawal. These complications can be best avoided through a medically supervised withdrawal.

Rohypnol has received much media attention in the United States for its apparent involvement in a number of sexual assaults or rapes. Because it can quickly render an unsuspecting victim unconscious, Rohypnol lends itself to this kind of crime. As Rohypnol is odorless and tasteless and easily dissolved in drinks, it can be offered to a victim without arousing suspicion. Although media attention has focused on particular drugs like Rohypnol and GHB, it should be noted that a variety of drugs can and are being used in this manner, including barbiturates, opiates, other benzodiazepines, and ethanol. Ethanol remains several times more likely to be associated with sexual assault than any other drug, including Rohypnol, even though Rohypnol and drugs like it are more effective in rapidly producing the stupor and memory loss desired by this type of criminal.

See also **Benzodiazepines; Gamma-Aminobutyric Acid (GABA); Neurotransmitters.**

BIBLIOGRAPHY

Brunton, L. L., et al., Ed. (2005). Hypnotics and sedatives. In *The pharmacological basis of therapeutics*, 11th ed. New York: McGraw-Hill Medical.

Gahlinger, P. M. (2004). Club drugs: MDMA, gamma-hydroxybutyrate (GHB), Rohypnol, and ketamine. *American Family Physician, 69*, 11, 2619–2626.

Karch, S. B. (2006). *Drug abuse handbook*, 2nd ed. Boca Raton, FL: CRC Press.

Trimble, M. (2001). *Benzodiazepines*. New York: Routledge.

RICHARD G. HUNTER

RUBBING ALCOHOL. Rubbing alcohol is known as isopropyl alcohol (C_3H_8O); it is one of the more useful of the commercial alcohols, included in hand lotions and many cosmetic items as well as in antifreeze or deicer products. A 70 percent solution of isopropyl alcohol has more germicidal properties than does ethanol (drinking alcohol), so it is used in many healthcare situations, both in households and in medical facilities. It is also used for massages and by athletic trainers to treat skin and muscle groups, hence the term *rubbing*. It has a drying effect on the skin and causes blood vessels to dilate; its distinctive odor is associated with doctor's offices, since it is used to clean the skin being prepared for an injection.

When rubbing alcohol is ingested either pure or added to beverages, the result is toxic—with symptoms lasting longer than those seen after drinking ethanol (alcoholic beverages), because isopropyl alcohol is slowly metabolized to acetone, another toxic substance.

See also **Inhalants.**

BIBLIOGRAPHY

Csaky, T. Z., & Barnes, B. A. (1984). *Cutting's handbook of pharmacology*, 7th ed. Norwalk, CT: Appleton-Century-Crofts.

O'Neil, M. J. (Ed.) (2006). *The Merck index: An encyclopedia of chemicals, drugs, and biologicals*, 14th ed. Whitehouse Station, NJ: Merck.

SCOTT E. LUKAS